PROVIDENCE IN
EARLY MODERN ENGLAND

Providence in
Early Modern England

ALEXANDRA WALSHAM

OXFORD
UNIVERSITY PRESS

OXFORD
UNIVERSITY PRESS

Great Clarendon Street, Oxford OX2 6DP

Oxford University Press is a department of the University of Oxford.
It furthers the University's objective of excellence in research, scholarship,
and education by publishing worldwide in

Oxford New York

Athens Auckland Bangkok Bogotá Buenos Aires Calcutta
Cape Town Chennai Dar es Salaam Delhi Florence Hong Kong Istanbul
Karachi Kuala Lumpur Madrid Melbourne Mexico City Mumbai
Nairobi Paris São Paulo Shanghai Singapore Taipei Tokyo Toronto Warsaw

with associated companies in Berlin Ibadan

Oxford is a registered trade mark of Oxford University Press
in the UK and in certain other countries

Published in the United States
by Oxford University Press Inc., New York

British Library Cataloguing in Publication Data

Data available

Library of Congress Cataloging in Publication Data

Data available

ISBN 0-19-820655-0 (hbk)
ISBN 0-19-820887-1 (pbk)

1 3 5 7 9 10 8 6 4 2

Typeset in Ehrhardt
by Best-set Typesetter Ltd., Hong Kong
Printed in Great Britain
on acid-free paper by
Biddles Ltd., Guildford and King's Lynn

For my mother, with love

ACKNOWLEDGEMENTS

Researching and writing a book always represents a voyage of discovery. Begun in Melbourne and completed in Exeter, this one has been a long and very gruelling, but immensely rewarding journey. Many institutions and individuals have offered assistance and shelter, support and reassurance along the way.

I am grateful to the following for permission to reproduce copyright material: The Ashmolean Museum, Oxford; The British Library, London; The Trustees of the British Museum; The Bodleian Library, University of Oxford; The Syndics of Cambridge University Library; The Guildhall Library, Corporation of London; The Huntington Library, San Marino, California; Manchester Central Library; The Board of Trustees of the National Museums and Galleries on Merseyside (Lady Lever Art Gallery, Port Sunlight); The Pepys Library, Magdalene College, Cambridge; The Society of Antiquaries of London; The Board of Trinity College Dublin.

In addition to those mentioned above, I should like to thank the large number of libraries, archives, and organizations which have allowed me to inspect material in their collections, answered enquiries, and supplied copies of unique and rare items: Aberdeen University Library; Archbishop Marsh's Library, Dublin; Bibliotheca Thysiana, Leiden; Dr Williams's Library, London; Emmanuel College Library, Cambridge; The Folger Shakespeare Library, Washington DC; The Library of Jesus College, Cambridge; The Centre for Kentish Studies, Maidstone; Lambeth Palace Library, London; Lancashire Record Office, Preston; The Marquess of Bath, Longleat; The National Library of Scotland, Edinburgh; The National Library of Wales, Aberystwyth; New College, Oxford; The Newberry Library, Chicago; The Royal Commission on the Historical Monuments of England; St Paul's Cathedral Library, London; The Library of Shrewsbury School; Lord Coutanche Library, Société Jersaise, St Helier, Jersey; Stonyhurst College, Lancashire; Suffolk Record Office, Bury St Edmunds and Lowestoft; The University of London Library; The Victoria and Albert Museum, London; and The Wren Library, Trinity College, Cambridge. The Rare Books Room in Cambridge University Library has been a place of solace and pleasure as well as fruitful endeavour and I am especially grateful to the staff for the patience, kindness, and efficiency with which they have responded to countless requests for books and microfilm over the years in which I have been so preoccupied with matters relating to providence.

Parts of Chapter 5 have been anticipated in essays published in *Past and Present* and Studies in Church History, vol. 33, *The Church Retrospective*, and I acknowledge the Past and Present Society and the Ecclesiastical History Society for permitting me to use copyright material in an abbreviated and revised form here.

Without generous grants from the British Academy and Emmanuel College, Cambridge, it would not have been possible to include the illustrations. I wish to record my deep gratitude to both institutions for assisting with the considerable costs.

This book grew out of a PhD dissertation submitted to the Faculty of History at the University of Cambridge in December 1994. As a research student at Trinity College between 1990 and 1993 I was supported by a Commonwealth Scholarship and I am greatly indebted to the Commission for affording me the opportunity to pursue postgraduate study in the United Kingdom. I am equally grateful to the Master and Fellows of Emmanuel College for electing me to a Research Fellowship in 1993 and providing me with such a peaceful and congenial setting in which to work during the following three years. I must also thank my colleagues in the Department of History and Archaeology at the University of Exeter for welcoming me so warmly into their midst in September 1996, for arranging my teaching to facilitate the completion of the manuscript, for offering encouragement and advice at critical points, and for keeping me cheerful with cups of tea and plenty of laughter in the Senior Common Room in Queen's. Together with friends too numerous to mention by name, they have helped me weather many vicissitudes and made this enterprise a little less arduous than it might otherwise have been.

In attempting to grapple with a large and slippery subject, I have benefited from discussions with many scholars. Among those who provided invaluable suggestions and references, saved me from embarrassing mistakes, spared time for stimulating discussions, shared their expertise, read chapters, and acted as a human sounding board, I would particularly like to acknowledge Margaret Aston, Jonathan Barry, John Bossy, Patrick Carter, Eamon Duffy, Thomas Freeman, Eileen Groth, Steve Hindle, Arnold Hunt, Peter Lake, Anthony Milton, Alison Shell, Susan Wabuda, Helen Weinstein, and the late Bob Scribner. The generosity of other researchers is recorded in the footnotes.

This book has been shaped and improved by the judicious criticisms and comments of my PhD examiners, Professor John Morrill and Sir Keith Thomas, and to both of them I convey my sincere appreciation. My greatest intellectual debt, however, is to my supervisor, Professor Patrick Collinson. The mark he has left on my work will be apparent on every page; the many practical and personal ways in which he and his wife Liz have helped me are acknowledged fondly here. From my very first meeting with him—shy, tongue-tied, and newly arrived from Australia—Pat has been an infinite treasury and unfailing source of inspiration, guidance, and, above all, reassurance. His door has always been open, and he has never been too busy to write a cheering note, offer a word of encouragement, or dispel my worries with a smile. For all this, I thank him with great affection and deepest respect.

Members of my immediate family have shared both the strain and the joy of bringing this book into the world. Without their patience, understanding, and constant support it would have been very much longer in the making.

A. W.

Exeter
Whitsunday 1998

CONTENTS

NOTE FOR THE READER

All quotations from contemporary manuscript and printed works retain original punctuation, capitalization, and spelling, except in rare cases where confusion would otherwise arise. The use of i and j, u and v, however, has been modernized. Greek letters have been transliterated. In citations from manuscript sources, standard abbreviations and contractions have been silently expanded. Mispagination and irregular repeated pagination are indicated by *vere* and *sic* respectively. For the sake of clarity and consistency, signature numbers are cited in arabic numerals throughout. Long titles have been curtailed. For ease of reference, *STC* and Wing numbers have been included in the bibliography. The place of publication is London, unless otherwise stated. Dates are given in Old Style, except that the year is reckoned to begin on 1 January. Except where indicated, biblical references are to the Authorized Version of 1611.

ABBREVIATIONS

Add. MS	Additional Manuscript
APC	*Acts of the Privy Council of England.* NS *1542–1631*, ed. John Roche Dasent *et al.*, 46 vols. (1890–1964)
BIHR	*Bulletin of the Institute of Historical Research*
BL	British Library, London
BM DP&D	British Museum, Department of Prints and Drawings
BM *Satires*	F. G. Stephens and M. D. George, *Catalogue of Prints and Drawings in the British Museum. Division I. Political and Personal Satires (1320–1832)*, 11 vols. (1870–1954)
CRS	Catholic Record Society
CS	Camden Society
CSPD	*Calendar of State Papers, Domestic Series, of the Reigns of Edward VI, Mary, Elizabeth and James I, 1547–1625*, ed. R. Lemon and M. A. E. Green, 12 vols. (1856–72); *Calendar of State Papers, Domestic Series, of the Reign of Charles I, 1625–1649*, ed. J. Bruce *et al.*, 23 vols. (1858–97)
CSP Venetian	*Calendar of State Papers and Manuscripts, Relating to English Affairs, Existing in the Archives and Collections of Venice, and in other Libraries of Northern Italy*, ed. R. Brown *et al.*, 38 vols. (1864–1947)
CUL	Cambridge University Library
DNB	*The Dictionary of National Biography*, 63 vols., ed. Leslie Stephen and Sidney Lee (1885–1900); *Supplements* (1901–13)
EETS	Early English Text Society
EHR	*English Historical Review*
FSL	Folger Shakespeare Library, Washington DC
Foster	Joseph Foster, *Alumni Oxonienses. The Members of the University of Oxford, 1500–1714*, 4 vols. (Oxford, 1891–2)
HJ	*Historical Journal*
HMC	Historical Manuscripts Commission
JBS	*Journal of British Studies*
JEH	*Journal of Ecclesiastical History*
LRO	Lancashire Record Office, Preston
NS	New Series
OS	Original Series
P&P	*Past and Present*
PRO	Public Record Office, Chancery Lane, London
RO	Record Office

SCH	Studies in Church History
SCJ	*Sixteenth Century Journal*
ser.	series
soc.	society
SP	State Papers Domestic
SR	Edward Arber (ed.), *A Transcript of the Registers of the Company of Stationers of London 1554–1640 A.D.*, 5 vols. (1875–94)
STC	A. W. Pollard and G. R. Redgrave, *A Short-Title Catalogue of Books Printed in England, Scotland, and Ireland and of English Books Printed Abroad 1475–1640*, 2nd edn., revised and enlarged by W. A. Jackson, F. S. Ferguson, and Katharine F. Pantzer, 3 vols. (1976–91)
TRHS	*Transactions of the Royal Historical Society*
VCH	*Victoria County History*
Venn	John Venn and J. A. Venn, *Alumni Cantabrigienses: A Biographical List of All Known Students, Graduates and Holders of Office at the University of Cambridge. Part I: From the Earliest Times to 1751*, 4 vols. (Cambridge, 1922–7)
Wing	Donald Wing, *Short-title Catalogue of Books Printed in England, Scotland, Ireland, Wales and British America and of English Books Printed in Other Countries 1641–1700*, 2nd edn., revised and enlarged by the Index Committee of the Modern Language Association of America, 3 vols. (New York, 1972–88)

LIST OF ILLUSTRATIONS

'Let us look into providences; surely they mean somewhat'
Oliver Cromwell to Colonel Robert Hammond, 25 November 1648

Introduction

In 1595, 'to the amasement of many hearers', an ancient oak in the grounds of Herongate Park near Brentwood in Essex 'was hard to grone for three days space most grevously . . . lycke as a man had been at the poynt of deathe'. Felled by order of the local bailiffs and its massive trunk 'cut in twayne', the 'myghty' tree gave one last mortal moan before shuddering into silence for ever. This strange prodigy was recorded in an anonymous town chronicle containing summaries of hundreds of inexpensive news pamphlets which reached the Shropshire market town of Shrewsbury in the course of the reign of Elizabeth I. The author, together with at least some of those who flocked to see the botanical wonder, 'geatherid therby a just ensample of god to call us all to repentance to leave our excessive pride and umble oure wickid and stony hartes . . . sleepinge in this worldly cradle of securitie beringe of a careles mynde, hasting godes judgement and singnifienge the latter daye cannot be farr of'. 'God gyve us grace to repent in tyme', he concluded fervently, 'Amen Amen for his mercye sacke'.[1]

Two years later the Huntingdon schoolmaster Dr Thomas Beard published *The theatre of Gods judgements*, a famous anthology of anecdotes of heavenly vengeance visited upon evildoers from Hebrew times to the present. In it he solemnly described the extraordinary fate of a sabbath-breaking nobleman who habitually rode 'a hunting' with his hounds 'in the Sermon while': 'which impietie the Lord punished' all too appropriately, causing 'his wife to bring forth a child with a head like a dog, that seeing hee preferred his dogges before the service of God, he might have one of his owne getting to make much of'. Retold by moralizing preachers from their pulpits and read aloud by godly heads of households, the cautionary tale of the canine-faced baby is entirely typical of the countless edifying cases of divine justice collected and circulated by contemporaries in the late Tudor and Stuart period.[2]

No less characteristic of the age was the conviction of the young Wiltshire vicar George Webbe that God had a 'controversie' with England—an old score to settle with a nation as stubbornly iniquitous as Old Testament Israel. Addressing the congregation which had assembled to hear him preach at Paul's Cross on Trinity Sunday 1609, he earnestly prosecuted his case concerning the 'fearefull and lamentable estate' in which his native country currently stood. Echoing Hosea and Amos, Webbe declared that since sin was so rife and irrepressible, since none

---

[1] Shrewsbury School, Shrewsbury, MS Mus X. 31 ('Dr Taylor's Book'), fos. 206^{r-v}. The groaning oak is also alluded to in *Strange newes out of Kent, of a monstrous and misshapen child borne in Olde Sandwitch* (1609), sig. B4^v.

[2] Thomas Beard, *The theatre of Gods judgements: revised, and augmented* (1631 edn.), 210. All subsequent references are to this edn., unless otherwise stated.

seemed to heed the Lord's repeated warnings of His swelling displeasure, 'I dare assure you . . . he hath a judgement now comming, which will pay home for all'. The land would mourn when the consuming wrath of the Almighty was eventually unleashed: 'Behold he will bring a plague upon this place, the which whosoever heareth, his eares shall tingle.'[3]

These stories and statements are compelling testimonies to the belief that God was no idle, inactive spectator upon the mechanical workings of the created world, but an assiduous, energetic deity who constantly intervened in human affairs. His finger could be discerned behind every inexplicable occurrence; He regularly stepped in to discipline sinners and bestow blessings upon the righteous and good. History was the canvas on which the Lord etched His purposes and intentions; nature a textbook and a laboratory in which He taught, demonstrated, and tested His providence.

'Providence' is a word and a concept which many readers of this monograph may associate instinctively with zealous Protestantism. This is not surprising: the bulk of specialized research on early modern providentialism has focused upon the mentality of those 'godly people' whom hostile contemporaries labelled puritans.[4] Even Sir Keith Thomas—in whose shadow and upon whose shoulders all subsequent commentators stand—has fed the impression that this was an outlook on life largely confined to an intensely and rather pretentiously pious minority.[5] Certainly 'providence' is an all too familiar ingredient of the daily vocabulary of that select and cliquish company of sixteenth- and seventeenth-century Englishmen and women who called themselves the 'saints'. It was a learned technical term for an elaborate theological doctrine which they used as an evocative shorthand for the powerful spiritual presence they detected within and around them.

This book, however, rests on the premiss that puritans were simply the 'hotter sort' of providentialists. To adapt one of Patrick Collinson's most classic formulations, the difference between their beliefs about divine activity and those of their neighbours and peers was essentially one of temperature rather than substance.[6] Providentialism was not a marginal feature of the religious culture of early modern England, but part of the mainstream, a cluster of presuppositions which enjoyed near universal acceptance.[7] It was a set of ideological spectacles through which individuals of all social levels and from all positions on the confessional spectrum

---

[3] George Webbe, *Gods controversie with England. Or a description of the fearefull and lamentable estate which this land at this present is in* (1609), 129–30.

[4] See the works cited in Ch. 1 nn. 55–8, below.

[5] Keith Thomas, *Religion and the Decline of Magic: Studies in Popular Beliefs in Sixteenth- and Seventeenth-Century England* (Harmondsworth, 1971), ch. 4.

[6] Patrick Collinson, *The Elizabethan Puritan Movement* (1967), 26–7.

[7] As recent studies of providentialism in early modern Ireland and New England have stressed: Raymond Gillespie, *Devoted People: Belief and Religion in Early Modern Ireland* (Manchester, 1997), esp. chs. 3, 6; David D. Hall, *Worlds of Wonder, Days of Judgment: Popular Religious Belief in Early New England* (Cambridge, Mass., 1990), ch. 2; Michael P. Winship, 'A Theater of God's Judgments: Providentialism and Intellectual Change in Early Massachusetts Orthodoxy', PhD thesis (Cornell, 1992).

were apt to view their universe, an invisible prism which helped them to focus the refractory meanings of both petty and perplexing events. Central to the political, medical, and philosophical thought and the literary and historical discourse of the period, it was also an ingrained parochial response to chaos and crisis, a practical source of consolation in a hazardous and inhospitable environment, and an idea which exercised practical, emotional, and imaginative influence upon those who subscribed to it.

But to insist upon the ubiquity of such convictions is not to ignore their polymorphous and protean qualities. This was a fluid and diffuse body of opinions, individual components of which could assume varying colours and forms according to the social context and cultural arena in which they were invoked and employed. It was one element of a matrix of explanatory frameworks upon which contemporaries drew eclectically and with little sense of latent contradiction. Nor was it static or impermeable to wider intellectual and epistemological developments.

It is the contention of the six chapters which follow that this bundle of assumptions about the intrusion of the supernatural in the secular sphere sheds considerable light on the way in which Protestantism gradually implanted itself in the hearts and minds of the Elizabethan and early Stuart populace. This study is constructed above all as a contribution to the ongoing debate about the impact, character, and broader cultural repercussions of the English Reformation. It is an attempt to add subtlety and complexity to the rather pessimistic picture painted by a significant strand of the recent historiography of the subject. Revisionist historians have persuaded us that the majority of Englishmen and women responded to this theological and liturgical *coup d'état* with a mixture of bewilderment, indifference, and outright hostility. Meticulous research in local archives has revealed that the Reformation was not merely a painfully slow and protracted process at the parochial level, but that it was actively or passively resisted by large sections of the laity. In most parts of the country it was the very opposite of a walkover, an uphill struggle all the way. Far from being spontaneously generated and embraced by underground, grass-roots movements from 'below', this was a supremely unwelcome official act, a succession of unwanted innovations coercively imposed from 'above'. The advent of Protestantism, Eamon Duffy has argued, represented a radical disjuncture with the Roman Catholic past, a violent disruption of the settled patterns of a late medieval piety which betrayed no signs of decline or decay, and, on the contrary, every indication of continuing vitality and vigour. Intent on eradicating 'superstition' and removing 'magic' from 'religion', the reformers relegated saints and their cults to the dustbin, destroyed images, stripped altars, and did away with comforting and satisfying rituals. The formidable doctrinal content of the Calvinist creed, combined with its insistence on reading as the chief engine of spiritual enlightenment, ensured that it never made much headway among the humble and subliterate—at least in the eyes of Christopher Haigh. Its association in its second generation with an aggressive campaign to impose a 'culture of discipline' and practise a form of moral espionage only exacerbated its socially polarizing potential, widening the rift between the 'better' and 'middling' and the 'meaner' or 'common sorts' of people, and superimposing it upon the perennial antagonism between the profane and the pious. The result was widespread disaffection from the Reformed Church of England and the survival of a sizeable constituency which clung tenaciously to 'popish' ways of thinking and living.[8]

Over the last few years, however, we have begun to witness a discernible retreat from the high watermark of negative assessments of the reception of Protestant teaching, a backlash against the tendency to whittle away the cultural significance of the Reformation completely, to write it off as a brave but abortive missionary enterprise which made barely any perceptible alteration to the assumptions of the average parishioner. Scholars are starting to reject the starkly dichotomous model of religious change put forward by the revisionists and emphasize the existence of a broad continuum and spectrum of degrees and types of Christian profession.[9] Fresh attention is being paid to the 'unspectacular orthodoxy' of the silent conforming majority, to the piety of 'prayer book Protestants', and to the significant inroads which the Calvinist gospel made among the poorest and most educationally deprived members of English society.[10] England's Reformation was long and partial and it left many trapped for some time in a kind of confessional limbo. It did meet with fierce opposition in its earliest phase, but as Diarmaid MacCulloch has remarked, in the long run it was nothing less than a 'howling success'. By the end of the 1570s, as Eamon Duffy admits on the very last page of his now famous book, a generation was growing up 'which believed the Pope to be Antichrist' and 'the Mass a mummery', and which looked back to the Catholic past as a profoundly foreign country.[11]

---

[8] See esp. the views espoused by Haigh in 'Puritan Evangelism in the Reign of Elizabeth I', *EHR* 92 (1977), 30–58; 'The Recent Historiography of the English Reformation', *HJ* 25 (1982), 998–1007; 'The Church of England, the Catholics and the People', in id. (ed.), *The Reign of Elizabeth I* (Basingstoke, 1984), 195–219; id. (ed.), *The English Reformation Revised* (Cambridge, 1987); and id., 'The English Reformation: A Premature Birth, a Difficult Labour and a Sickly Child', *HJ* 33 (1990), 449–59. Note, however, the change of tone and emphasis in his *English Reformations: Religion, Politics, and Society under the Tudors* (Oxford, 1993). This argument is also implicit in J. J. Scarisbrick, *The Reformation and the English People* (Oxford, 1984). On the vitality of late medieval piety, see Eamon Duffy, *The Stripping of the Altars: Traditional Religion in England 1400–1580* (New Haven, 1992), 4 and *passim*. On zealous Protestantism and moral discipline, see Keith Wrightson and David Levine, *Poverty and Piety in an English Village: Terling 1525–1700* (Oxford, 1995 edn.; 1st pub. 1979), esp. chs. 5–7; William Hunt, *The Puritan Moment: The Coming of Revolution in an English County* (Cambridge, Mass., 1983), esp. ch. 5.

[9] Eamon Duffy, 'The Godly and the Multitude in Stuart England', *The Seventeenth Century*, 1 (1986), 31–55.

[10] See Martin Ingram, *Church Courts, Sex and Marriage in England, 1570–1640* (Cambridge, 1987), ch. 3; Judith Maltby, ' "By this Book": Parishioners, the Prayer Book and the Established Church', in Kenneth Fincham (ed.), *The Early Stuart Church, 1603–1642* (Basingstoke, 1993), 115–37 and ead., *Prayer Book and People in Elizabethan and Early Stuart England* (Cambridge, 1998); Margaret Spufford (ed.), *The World of Rural Dissenters, 1520–1725* (Cambridge, 1995), 1–102.

[11] See Diarmaid MacCulloch, 'The Impact of the English Reformation', *HJ* 38 (1995), 152; Duffy, *Stripping of the Altars*, 593. See also Peter Marshall, 'Introduction', in id. (ed.), *The Impact of the English*

The debate about the English Reformation is thus in the process of being refocused. Interest is shifting from why and when to how England became a Protestant nation. There is a growing conviction that too much ink has been spilt arguing about the pace, geography, and social distribution of conversion and change and too little charting the ways in which the populace adjusted to the doctrinal and ecclesiastical revolution as a permanent fact. Tessa Watt has diverted our gaze away from the iconoclastic effects of Protestant ideology and traced the manner and the mechanisms through and by which traditional piety was modified and Reformed ideas and concepts put down lasting roots. Ronald Hutton has highlighted some of the creative strategies which helped people adapt to the loss of much loved elements of the 'old religion' and, together with David Cressy, analysed the new festive calendar and customs which evolved to fill the resulting vacuum and void. We are beginning to see the outlines of a religious culture which, if not thoroughly Protestant by exacting clerical standards, was distinctively post-Reformation: a culture consisting of 'a patchwork of beliefs' and practices which displays as many points of overlap with, as departures from, the moral and devotional emphases of medieval Catholicism—a culture, furthermore, which cut across the barriers erected by status and class, education and wealth.[12]

My own study likewise seeks to deflect attention towards the undercurrents of continuity which eased, alleviated, and even transcended the upheavals of the mid-sixteenth century and to explore the ideas and observances that emerged in their wake. It also reveals the indelible mark which the Reformation left upon English society and suggests that providentialism played a pivotal role in forging a collective Protestant consciousness, a sense of confessional identity which fused anti-Catholicism and patriotic feeling and which united the elite with their social inferiors.

In seeking to expose areas of homogeneity and consensus and in stressing the extent to which convictions about providence functioned as a kind of cultural cement, this book nevertheless remains fully alive to the splits, tensions, and frictions this complex web of assumptions served to exacerbate in the eighty-year period between 1560 and 1640. Providentialism became a dangerously politicized discourse in the decades preceding the outbreak of the Civil War, not in the sense that it became the exclusive property of one party or faction, but because it

Reformation 1500–1640 (1997), 1–11; Nicholas Tyacke (ed.), *England's Long Reformation 1500–1800* (1998), esp. Eamon Duffy, 'The Long Reformation: Catholicism, Protestantism and the Multitude', 36, and Patrick Collinson's 'Comment', 71–84. Patrick Collinson, of course, has always insisted that the Reformation had a profound effect on English society and culture. See esp. his *The Religion of Protestants: The Church in English Society 1559–1625* (Oxford, 1982) and *The Birthpangs of Protestant England: Religious and Cultural Change in the Sixteenth and Seventeenth Centuries* (1988).

[12] Tessa Watt, *Cheap Print and Popular Piety, 1550–1640* (Cambridge, 1991), esp. 72–3, 324–8; Ronald Hutton, 'The English Reformation and the Evidence of Folklore', *P&P* 148 (1995), 89–116; id., *The Rise and Fall of Merry England: The Ritual Year 1400–1700* (Oxford, 1994); David Cressy, *Bonfires and Bells: National Memory and the Protestant Calendar in Elizabethan and Stuart England* (1989). See also Mark Byford, 'The Price of Protestantism: Assessing the Impact of Religious Change in Elizabethan Essex: The Cases of Heydon and Colchester, 1558–1594', DPhil thesis (Oxford, 1988).

operated as a catalyst for criticism and as a weapon and tool wielded with increasing aggression and crudity. It not only helped to destabilize a situation which was swiftly unravelling and to propel the nation into a military conflict which culminated in the execution of that 'man of blood' Charles I and the proclamation of a godly republic; it also supplied a conceptual framework within which these cataclysmic events were explicable and, moreover, predictable.

These two overarching themes intersect and converge with a third: the slow transition from a society reliant on oral and pictorial modes of communication to one deeply penetrated by and dependent upon the medium of print. This book examines not merely beliefs about providence but the media by which they were diffused, and it argues that the two are inextricably linked. Based on an integrated analysis of sermons and tracts by Protestant ministers and ballads and pamphlets reporting 'strange and wonderful newes', it locates itself within a chronological context in which the cultures of orality and literacy were tightly interwoven. For at least the first century and a half after its introduction, the technology of print did not so much displace the spoken word as supplement and complement it; it led not to the annihilation of the rich vernacular traditions for which speech provided a vehicle but to their efflorescence. Likewise visual and verbal, image and text continued to hybridize. And although the adolescent publishing industry was rapidly maturing, it was as yet the understudy and apprentice of the pulpit, a subordinate agency of instruction, persuasion, and propaganda. Cheap print competed keenly with preaching, but it was also parasitical upon it. Only slowly did the clerical monopoly on religious discourse dissolve and the locus of authority modulate and shift.[13] Yet, lest we forget Elizabeth Eisenstein, typography was also an agent of change.[14] Print, it will be suggested, presented providential ideas in a way which at once intensified and subtly transfigured them: it gave them a fixity and a familiarity which both contributed to their potency and prevalence and began to sow tiny seeds of suspicion and scepticism in at least some hearers and readers.

This book focuses upon critical moments at which God's hand was widely perceived to be directly at work in the world. Its subject is not the deeply internalized brand of providentialism displayed in the private writings of the Oliver Cromwells and Nehemiah Wallingtons who inhabited early modern England,[15] but

---

[13] See esp. Keith Thomas, 'The Meaning of Literacy in Early Modern England', in Gerd Baumann (ed.), *The Written Word: Literacy in Transition*, Wolfson College Lectures, 1985 (Oxford, 1986), 97–131; Watt, *Cheap Print, passim*, esp. 324–5, 328–31; Adam Fox, 'Aspects of Oral Culture and its Development in Early Modern England', PhD thesis (Cambridge, 1992), esp. chs. 1, 6; Dagmar Freist, *Governed by Opinion: Politics, Religion, and the Dynamics of Communication in Stuart London 1637–1645* (1997). On preaching and cheap print, see Lawrence Manley, *Literature and Culture in Early Modern London* (Cambridge, 1995).

[14] Elizabeth Eisenstein, *The Printing Press as an Agent of Change: Communications and Cultural Transformations in Early Modern Europe*, 2 vols. (Cambridge, 1979).

[15] As explored by, among others, Blair Worden, 'Providence and Politics in Cromwellian England', *P&P* 109 (1985), 55–99; Paul Seaver, *Wallington's World: A Puritan Artisan in Seventeenth Century London* (Stanford, Calif., 1985); and Kaspar Von Greyerz, *Vorsehungsglaube und Kosmologie: Studien zu Englischen Selbstzeugnissen des 17. Jahrhunderts*, Publications of the German Historical Institute, London, 25 (Göttingen, 1990).

the more collective and public manifestations of contemporary belief in an omnipotent deity. Chapter 2 explores stories of the spectacular punishments meted out to notorious sinners and the compilation of such anecdotes into encyclopedic anthologies. Chapter 3 considers interpretations of and reactions to natural disasters, public calamities, and outbreaks of epidemic disease. Chapter 4 investigates attitudes towards portents, prodigies, and the appearance of prophets preaching repentance and foretelling the future. Chapter 5 examines the way in which providence became engulfed in the bitter confessional war between the Churches of England and Rome and the emergence of a powerful myth of Protestant nationhood. Chapter 6 is a detailed study of the English jeremiad, particularly as manifested in the tradition of preaching in the mould of the Old Testament prophets at Paul's Cross in the shadow of London's massive cathedral. And Chapter 1 erects the broad theological and cultural backdrop against which these five thematic essays are set.

I

Providence, Print,
and the Religion of Protestants

PROTESTANT THEOLOGY AND PURITAN PIETY

The Doctrine of Providence

There can be no doubt that the magisterial reformers placed fresh and even novel emphasis on the sovereignty of God and His unceasing supervision of and intervention in the earthly realm. For John Calvin, who devoted a whole treatise, as well as several crucial chapters of his influential *Institutes* to the doctrine of providence, this was the very kernel and keystone of Christian life and thought. All piety and godliness, declared the author of the Heidelberg Catechism, Zacharias Ursinus, would be 'pulled asunder' and 'shaken in peeces' if this precept was denied and undermined. A true understanding and 'an holy acknowledging' of providence was the foundation and essence of faith, asserted the famous preacher and fellow of Magdalen Hall, Oxford, William Pemble. 'I dare say without it cannot stand firme, so much as the first principles of Religion.'[1]

Belief in the ultimate ordering of the universe by a supreme supernatural being or sublime overriding force was, of course, firmly entrenched in traditional Judaeo-Christian thinking. It can also be found in ancient Greek and Roman philosophy. Indeed, the teachings of Plato, Aristotle, and the Stoics were of considerable influence in shaping the monotheistic theology of the primitive and medieval Church. The pagan idea of nemesis, the goddess of divine vengeance who embodied the principle of retribution for wickedness and vice, readily fused with the jealous and righteous Jehovah delineated by Moses and the Old Testament prophets. Both were refined by the Gospel writers and Apostles, who stressed the intensely personal and loving care exercised by God the Father through His Son. In the first few centuries after Christ's death, a powerful synthesis of heathen and biblical precepts prevailed. Early Church Fathers, including St John Chrysostom and Bishop Theodoret of Cyrus, systematically expounded the notion of an omniscient and all-controlling deity, but it took a particularly sophisticated and enduringly persuasive form in the fifth century in St Augustine's *De civitate dei*. Scholasticism did much to further elaborate and formulate the doctrine—a process which culminated in St Thomas Aquinas's *Summa theologica*, which became the

---

[1] John Calvin, *Institutes of the Christian Religion*, trans. John Allen, 2 vols. (Philadelphia, 1936), bk. I, chs. 16–17; id., *A Defense of the Secret Providence of God 1558*, trans. Henry Cole (1857); Zacharius Ursinus, *The summe of Christian religion*, trans. H. Parrie (1611 edn.), 368; William Pemble, *A treatise of the providence of God*, in *The workes . . .* (1635 edn.), 261.

basis for Tridentine dogma on the topic. Acknowledgement of an omnipotent providence which preordained and governed all events, from quotidian happenings to the watersheds of world history, thus transcended the confessional divisions ushered in by the Lutheran schism.[2]

The particular preoccupation which Protestants displayed with the workings of providence stemmed in large part from their expulsion of all intermediaries between God and the individual soul, from their uncompromising insistence upon mankind's utter impotence and depravity and complete dependence upon the mercy of its Maker and Redeemer. Heightened awareness of the awesome and irresistible power of the Almighty was a logical corollary of elevating divine grace above strenuous human effort and making it the sole criterion for salvation.[3] Like their Continental counterparts, English Protestant divines discussed the doctrine in exhaustive detail and with wearisome frequency; it was a prominent theme of sixteenth- and seventeenth-century academic theology and practical divinity.

Technically, providence had a dual definition: it comprised both knowledge and power. It referred firstly to the immutability of the Lord's eternal and unchangeable decree; it was 'an order thoughte upon from everlasting', insisted Dr Edward Cradocke, Lady Margaret Professor of Divinity at Oxford, 'without any alteration to be looked for'.[4] This was the single teleological thread which wove together past, present, and future, the blueprint for human history drawn up in the beginning. In His infinite wisdom God had foreseen every eventuality and all that came to pass accomplished predetermined ends. According to Dr Thomas Gataker, rector

---

[2] A number of classical and medieval writings on the subject were published in the early modern period: Lucius Annaeus Seneca, 'Discourse of Providence', in *The workes . . . both morrall and naturall*, trans. T. Lodge (1614), 497–509; Anicius M. T. S. Boethius, *De consolationae philosophiae. The boke called the comforte of philosophye* (1556 edn.), esp. bks. IV–V; St John Chrysostom, *De providentia dei, ac fato, orationes sex* (1545); Bishop Theodoret, *The mirror of divine providence . . .* , ed. J. C. (1602); *Saint Augustine, of the citie of God*, trans. J. H[ealey] (1620 edn.), esp. bk. v, chs. 8–9. See also *The 'Summa Theologica' of St Thomas Aquinas*, trans. the Fathers of the English Dominican Province, 27 vols. (1911–35), i. 303–13. For concise discussions of pre-Reformation developments in the theology of providence, see Michael J. Langford, *Providence* (1981), ch. 2; T. J. Gorringe, *God's Theatre: A Theology of Providence* (1991), 8–11.

[3] On the centrality of the concept of divine sovereignty in Protestant thought, see Alister E. McGrath, *Reformation Thought: An Introduction* (Oxford, 1988), 86–93; Ronald J. Vander Molen, 'Providence as Mystery, Providence as Revelation: Puritan and Anglican Modifications of John Calvin's Doctrine of Providence', *Church History*, 47 (1978), 29–33; W. P. Stephens, *The Theology of Huldrych Zwingli* (Oxford, 1986), 86–98; Richard Kyle, 'John Knox's Concept of Divine Providence and its Influence on his Thought', *Albion*, 18 (1986), 395–410. For key discussions of the doctrine by Continental reformers other than Calvin, see Martin Luther, *The Bondage of the Will* (1526), repr. in *Luther's Works*, ed. Jaroslav Pelikan and Helmut Lehmann, 56 vols. (St Louis, 1955–75), xxxiii; Ulrich Zwingli, *Zwingli on Providence and Other Essays*, ed. W. J. Hinke (Durham, NC, 1983); Theodore Beza, *Propositions and principles of divinitie*, trans. [J. Penry] (Edinburgh, 1591), 17–19; *The Decades of Henry Bullinger Minister of the Church of Zurich*, trans. H. I., ed. Thomas Harding, 5 vols., Parker Soc. (Cambridge, 1849–51), iv. 173–94; [Andreas Gerardus (*Hyperius*)], *A speciall treatise of Gods providence, and of comforts against all kinde of crosses & calamities to be fetched from the same*, trans. J. L[udham] ([1588?]); Ursinus, *Summe*, 329–68; Peter Martyr Vermigli, *The common places . . .* trans. A. Marten ([1583]), pt. i, ch. 16.

[4] Edward Cradocke, *The shippe of assured safetie . . . conteyning . . . a discourse of Gods providence* (1572), 273.

of Rotherhithe, He stood outside time, like 'one standing aloft on a sentinell, that seeth all both before and behind under one view at one instant'.[5]

Yet providence was not confined to divine clairvoyance. It pertained to the Lord's 'operating hands' no less than His 'observing eyes'. Foreknowledge was linked with perpetual, purposeful action, with direct and dynamic government of the terrestrial realm. It was 'ignorant trifling to talk of mere prescience', wrote Calvin reprovingly.[6] Christians should not conceive of their Creator as a watchmaker deity who had set the machine of the world in motion and then left it to whirr away on its own, a shipwright who committed his finished vessel to the waves to be 'tossed to and fro' like 'a boat destitute of a steersman'. 'God doth not put things into a frame', said Richard Sibbes, preacher at London's Gray's Inn, 'as we do clocks'; He always held 'the helm of the universe' and expertly piloted its course.[7] Providence did not describe a divine being 'idly beholding from heaven the transactions' which happened below: an indolent, unconcerned spectator who 'setteth at six and seven' and frequently slumbered in 'a profound sleepe'.[8] The Lord was never unoccupied, stressed the German reformer Andreas Gerardus, nor did he work erratically or haphazardly, 'by turnes or fittes'.[9] He was the final cause of every occurrence without exception, earth-shattering or inconsequential. It was an incontestable truth that 'not a drop of rain falls but at the express command of God'.[10] Nothing escaped His 'broade eye' and 'eare that heareth everyman'; no one evaded His restless, penetrating gaze and 'dredful presence'. All was detected and regulated by what the Suffolk parson Elnathan Parr called an 'Ocular Providence'. In the sight of the Almighty, remarked the Oxford divine Edward Corbett, men and women were morally and physically naked: 'we are as it were divided and bowelled, without our clothes, without our skin'.[11]

God's sovereignty extended from the most contemptible of His creatures to the celestial, from the basest creeping worm, tiniest gnat, and fly to the noblest angels in heaven. Few ministers failed to allude to the text of Matthew x. 29–30: not one 'poore sillie sparrow' worth less than half a farthing fell to the ground, nor a single hair from one's head perished without His permission. It was by no means 'unsemely' for the Lord to be 'busied' with small insignificances. Far from derogating from divine majesty, such meticulous attention to 'tittles' and trivialities

---

[5] Thomas Gataker, *Of the nature and use of lots* (1627 edn.), 44. See also [Gerardus], *Speciall treatise*, sig. C3ʳ.

[6] Calvin, *Defense*, 4; id., *Institutes*, bk. I, ch. 16, §4. See also [Gerardus], *Speciall treatise*, sig. A8ʳ; Pemble, *Workes*, 271.

[7] Bullinger, *Decades*, iv. 178; Richard Sibbes, 'Of the Providence of God', repr. in *The Works . . . ,* ed. Alexander B. Grosart, 7 vols. (Edinburgh, 1862–4), i. 204; Calvin, *Institutes*, bk. I, ch. 16, §4.

[8] Calvin, *Institutes*, bk. I, ch. 16, §4; Thomas Rogers, *The general session, conteining an apologie concerning the ende of this world* (1581), 68; Vermigli, *Common places*, 200.

[9] [Gerardus], *Speciall treatise*, sigs. A8ᵛ, B1ᵛ. Cf. Calvin, *Institutes*, bk. I, ch. 16, §3.

[10] Calvin, *Institutes*, bk. I, ch. 16, §5.

[11] Cradocke, *Shippe of assured safetie*, 465; Elnathaw Parr, *The grounds of divinitie, plainely discovering the mysteries of Christian religion* (1614), 124; Edward Corbett, *Gods providence, a sermon preached before the honourable House of Commons* (1642), 6; [Walter Ralegh], *The history of the world* (1614), 18.

PLATE 1 Walter Ralegh, *The history of the world* (London, 1614), title-page. By permission of the Syndics of Cambridge University Library. Shelfmark: M. 3. 14. Ralegh referred to Providence as '*oculus infinitus*, an infinite eye'.

actually enhanced it.[12] Nor did He defile Himself by deigning 'to entermeddle in filthy, and uncleane matters' alleged Arthur Dent, vicar of South Shoebury in Essex. If the sun was not polluted by shining on a dunghill, much less could God be stained and infected by the corrupt universe He providentially upheld.[13] If

[12] Bartholomew Traheron, *An exposition of the .4. chap. of S. Joans Revelation . . . wherein the providence of God is treated* ([Wesel?], 1557), sigs. C3^v–4^r; Sebastian Benefield, *A commentary or exposition upon the three first chapters of the prophecie of Amos* (1629), first pagination, 10.

[13] Arthur Dent, *A platforme, made for proofe of Gods providence* (1608), 26–8, quotation at 26. Cf. Vermigli, *Common places*, 168; [Gerardus], *Speciall treatise*, sig. B4^v.

contemporaries surveyed the wonders of nature surrounding them, insisted the Scottish clergyman Alexander Hume, they would be compelled to acknowledge Him to be a 'singular artificer'. In silkworms and bees, in oxen, crocodiles, and elephants, they were presented with exquisite emblems of His benevolence and omniscience.[14]

Most writers differentiated between 'general' and 'special', or 'universal' and 'particular' providence, though they defined these terms rather diversely.[15] The former almost invariably meant the Lord's all-encompassing programme for the evolution of the macrocosm, His preservation and continuation of the world according to the laws He had established at the Creation. The latter generally denoted either His dealings with humanity at large, or His special care of His Church and chosen people. Sometimes it referred to the vigilant manner in which God sustained life on a microscopic scale: every organism and process, asserted Calvin, Ames, and others, was actuated by a 'secret instinct' and 'peculiar stirring' without which it would collapse, disintegrate, or die.[16] Others used 'special' and 'particular providence' to identify His spontaneous interruptions of the normal sequence, the individual dispensations He dealt out as occasion demanded, to uphold the moral order and to admonish, chastise, and reward man and womankind.

A related issue was the varying methods and mechanisms by which the Almighty conducted His providential operations. Most divines insisted that God usually worked mediately, employing inferior instruments and forces, though they stressed that He was not 'so tied to second causes, as when they faile, his Providence ceaseth unto us'. The Lord was quite capable of bringing about His objectives immediately, maintained the Essex vicar Ralph Walker, without the assistance of any such agents or tools. He could, and very occasionally did, cross the established course and stream of nature and perform extraordinary acts outside and against it—in other words miracles. In some polemical contexts Protestants can be found insisting that this kind of occurrence had ceased after biblical times, but it is important to note that in the technical treatises and sermons analysed here they emphatically upheld the prerogative of the deity to overrule and suspend the natural order. Miracles were held to be necessary to convince the disbelieving and humble the arrogant and overweening. As Sibbes explained, God used them 'to shew his own sovereignty and to exercise our dependence'.[17] For the most part, however,

---

[14] [A]lexander H[ume], *Foure discourses of praise unto God* (Edinburgh, 1594), 46; Theodoret, *Mirror*, 43–4, 62 [*vere* 46]–48, 49–52.

[15] See e.g. Richard Greenham, *The works . . .*, ed. H. H[olland] (1599), 112–13; Parr, *Grounds of divinitie*, 118; Pemble, *Workes*, 278; William Perkins, *An exposition of the symbole or creede of the apostles*, in *The workes . . .*, 3 vols. (Cambridge, 1608–9 edn.), i. 160; Ursinus, *Summe*, 332; Ralph Walker, *A learned and profitable treatise of Gods providence* (1608), 4–7.

[16] Calvin, *Institutes*, bk. 1, ch. 16, §4; William Ames, *The marrow of sacred divinity* (1642), 43.

[17] Walker, *Learned and profitable treatise*, 52–4; Sibbes, *Works*, i. 205. On God working mediately and immediately, see also Robert Hill, *Life everlasting* (Cambridge, 1601), 481–5; John Pelling, *A sermon of the providence of God* (1607), 10–13; Pemble, *Workes*, 278; Ursinus, *Summe*, 332–3. For assertions that 'miracles have ceased', see Ch. 5 below, pp. 226–32.

God chose to veil His providence behind 'mediums' and 'curtains'. This too he did for the benefit and edification of human beings, to encourage due and grateful recognition of His wise provision for every contingency and to teach people to honour rather than despise lower forms of life. He did so, declared William Ames, that 'he might communicate a certaine dignity of working to his Creatures also, and in them might make his efficiency more perceivable'.[18] But in transferring His executive power to deputies the Lord did not thereby invest them with mystical divinity. He did not make 'petty', 'halfe', or 'lieftenant Gods'—this was where 'blind gentilisme' had stumbled. Nor, stressed Theodore Beza, did He bestow a 'subalternall or second providence' upon the saints, as the papists so sacrilegiously assumed.[19]

Many authors admitted that the Lord's propensity to intervene unpredictably appeared to contradict the axiom that He adhered strictly to a prearranged scheme. They solved this problem by declaring that special providences and miracles were not hasty improvisations but events which fitted perfectly into the programme for history framed and fixed before time began. Strange alterations in nature, emphasized John Pelling, rector of Trowbridge in Wiltshire, did not prove that God had a mercurial and changeable will, *'mutatio voluntatis'*; on the contrary, He willed changes in His creatures without deviating a whisker from His original intentions. There was no 'mutabilitie' in the Almighty, only 'multiplicitie of power', and an accurate anticipation at the outset of all that the diversity of subsequent ages would require.[20] In struggling to reconcile the inconsistencies within this twin-stranded definition, Protestant theorists distinguished between God's 'secret' or 'effectual' will and His 'revealed' or 'signified' will, as disclosed to Christians in Scripture. Occurrences which ostensibly controverted biblical edicts undoubtedly agreed wholly with His hidden and steadfast intentions.[21] Only in the defective judgement of fallen man, who foolishly measured divine matters by his own narrow 'scantling', did such discrepancies smell distinctly of duplicity.[22]

Another testing question was how anarchy and disorder could be squared with the claim that God was intrinsically good. How could the concept of a benign providence coexist with the harsh reality of widespread suffering and misery? Why, asked a host of imaginary 'cavillers', did the Lord allow horrific things to happen if He was easily able to prevent them? All, retorted the clergy, had an appointed

---

[18] Calvin, *Defense*, 11; Ames, *Marrow of sacred divinity*, 40. See also Walker, *Learned and profitable treatise*, 57–9; [Gerardus], *Speciall treatise*, sigs. F7ʳ–8ʳ.

[19] Beza, *Propositions and principles of divinitie*, 18–19; Dent, *Platforme*, 8.

[20] Pelling, *Sermon*, 15–16. Cf. [Gerardus], *Speciall treatise*, sig. K2ʳ; Vermigli, *Common places*, 168, 173; Walker, *Learned and profitable treatise*, pt. III.

[21] On the distinction of wills, see Calvin, *Defense*, 86–8; Pelling, *Sermon*, 24–5; Ursinus, *Summe*, 356–7; Vermigli, *Common places*, 201; Walker, *Learned and profitable treatise*, 241–4. A number of writers paid particular attention to the sense in which God could be said to 'change' His mind or 'repent'. See Calvin, *Institutes*, bk. I, ch. 17, §12–14; [Gerardus], *Speciall treatise*, sigs. K1ᵛ–2ʳ; Jean Veron, *A fruteful treatise of predestination and of the divine providence of God* ([1561]), fos. 102ʳ–105ʳ.

[22] Dent, *Platforme*, 30–1; Pemble, *Workes*, 270; Calvin, *Defense*, 35.

role in His grand and labyrinthine design for the universe.[23] Pursued to its logical conclusions, the doctrine of divine omnipotence also implied that the Almighty Himself was the author of sin. Calvin gave this kind of syllogistic reasoning very short shrift: nothing, he expostulated, was more 'impious and preposterous' than to drag the deity into humanity's guilt.[24] But it demanded some elaborate theological gymnastics to absolve Him from blame. A God who had proclaimed Himself to be the first revenger of evil, it was contended, could hardly be the initial stimulus for it; at the same time, to suggest that sin occurred in spite of His providence was effectively to defraud Him of His glory. Academics like Peter Martyr Vermigli were thus obliged to confess that the Lord could, 'after some sort', be called 'the cause of those things which afterward be naughtilie doone', for 'even that which is doone against his will, is not doone without his will'.[25] Men and women, affirmed Calvin and his disciples sternly, acted perversely by the 'ordaining purpose' of the deity. '[T]o flee to the common refuge' of His bare permission for wickedness was a 'flimsy defence of the Divine justice', 'a mere way of escape from the truth, utterly frivolous and vain'.[26] God did not carelessly connive and 'idly winck' at sin, He authoritatively and righteously decreed it. He did not actively infuse iniquity into individuals, but rather withdrew his protection and grace, 'delivering . . . them most justly to Satan, and to the lusts of their owne hearts'.[27] Nevertheless the Lord did use the devil and his minions to execute His judgements on earth. The turpitude of His chosen instruments neither blemished His integrity nor diminished human culpability.[28] He was no more responsible for their crimes and transgressions than the rider of a lame horse was for its halting progress or 'a cunning musician' for the discordant notes produced by a poorly tuned lute.[29] Men and women might be seduced by Lucifer (who was himself licensed and bridled by the Almighty), but, because they had been endowed with the capacity to resist such temptations, they remained entirely at fault. There were dangerously antinomian implications in any assertion to the contrary: it was all too easy to justify libertinism if one argued that by their heinous acts sinners were indirectly doing God's work.[30]

[23] This objection is raised and answered by Cradocke, *Shippe of assured safetie*, bk. II, ch. 15; Dent, *Platforme*, 35–6; Pemble, *Workes*, 270; Vermigli, *Common places*, 169.

[24] Calvin, *Defense*, 85–6, cf. 25–6, 104–18. On this theme, see also Cradocke, *Shippe of assured safetie*, bk. II, chs. 3–4; Robert Crowley, *An apologie, or defence, of those Englishe writers & preachers which Cereberus . . . chargeth wyth false doctrine, under the name of predestination* (1566), fos. 57ᵛ–58ᵛ; [Gerardus], *Speciall treatise*, sig. E3ʳ; Pelling, *Sermon*, 23–6; Traheron, *Exposition*, sigs. A3ᵛ–4ᵛ, B6ʳ⁻ᵛ; Walker, *Learned and profitable treatise*, pt. IV.

[25] Vermigli, *Common places*, 181, 186.

[26] Calvin, *Defense*, 21–2, 24, and 64–78; Perkins, *Workes*, i. 158–9.

[27] Parr, *Grounds of divinitie*, 120. See also Ursinus, *Summe*, 336–7.

[28] See esp. Calvin, *Institutes*, bk. I, ch. 17, §5, 18; Perkins, *Workes*, i. 159–60.

[29] For the lame horse, see Cradocke, *Shippe of assured safetie*, 132; Pelling, *Sermon*, 23; Ursinus, *Summe*, 352; Walker, *Learned and profitable treatise*, 169. For the simile of the lute, see John Manningham's notes of a sermon preached by Mr Moore of Balliol College, Oxford, on 13 May 1602: *The Diary of John Manningham of the Middle Temple, and of Bradbourne, Kent, Barrister-at-law, 1602–1603*, ed. John Bruce, CS, 1st ser. 99 (1868), 27.

[30] See Calvin, *Defense*, 110–11; Walker, *Learned and profitable treatise*, 97.

Paradoxically, then, an all-compelling providence was not incompatible with free will. Divine sovereignty, 'rightly considered', did not rule out or frustrate moral autonomy.[31] In fact, far from tying man's hands, it actually freed them.[32] Although their choices and actions had been foreseen from eternity, stressed Andreas Gerardus, people were not the mere pawns and puppets of a higher power, 'sencelesse blocks' who simply acted out parts scripted long before. Liberty and volition were no illusion, yet in pursuing their independent preferences individuals unwittingly contrived to bring about their Maker's own objectives.[33]

Experimental Providentialism

The real hallmark of Calvinist teaching on this subject, however, was an anthropomorphic emphasis on the intimate link between the dispensations of providence and the enigma of predestination—God's mysterious double decree of salvation and damnation. According to learned divines, the Lord supplied the basic material needs of all human beings, but bestowed regenerative grace solely upon the elect, whose redemption took pride of place in the divine master plan. The invisible Church of true believers, observed Calvin, was the 'great *work-room* of God', where 'in a more especial manner' He displayed His dominion; it was 'the more immediate theatre of his glorious Providence'.[34] Predestination thus defined the interpenetration of His sovereignty into the self.

As John Pelling told an audience at Paul's Cross in the autumn of 1607, these theological precepts were 'not a matter of speculation, but of practice'.[35] Providentialism lay at the heart of that peculiarly intense and strenuous brand of Protestant piety which godly preachers maintained that every Christian ought to embrace. Every happening, catastrophic or trivial, was held to be relevant to the quest for assurance that one numbered among the 'saints', a signpost concerning the Lord's soteriological intentions.

Such 'particular providences' were the Lord's chosen method of communicating with the predestinate elite. They comprised a sort of Morse code or semaphore between the soul and its Saviour; a cryptic language, said Richard Sibbes, which was readily comprehensible to those that had 'a familiar acquaintance with God's dealing'.[36] It was the duty of the pious to decipher and register, 'sanctify' and 'improve' these divine tokens. Slowly, the jumbled pieces of the jigsaw puzzle would fit together to form a complete picture. Calamities as well as mercies were to be scrutinized in the same way, because whereas the temporal miseries which befell the wicked were a foretaste of their future ordeals in the inferno below—'a kind of antechamber of hell, whence they already have a distant prospect of their

---

[31] Calvin, *Defense*, 16.   [32] Ursinus, *Summe*, 358.

[33] [Gerardus], *Speciall treatise*, sig. D6ʳ, and see sigs. E2ʳ–3ᵛ. On providence and free will, see also Cradocke, *Shippe of assured safetie*, bk. ɪɪ, ch. 2; Walker, *Learned and profitable treatise*, 94, 239–41. This seems to have been the main theme of a tract by A[rthur] G[urney] of which only the title-page has survived: *A fruitfull dialogue touching the doctrine of Gods providence, and mans free will* ([*c*.1580?]).

[34] Calvin, *Defense*, 6–7. In the *Institutes* providence and predestination are discussed in separate books: bk. ɪ, chs. 16–18 and bk. ɪɪɪ, chs. 21–4 respectively. This important connection was also present in Zwingli's thought: *Zwingli on Providence*, ed. Hinke, *passim*.

[35] Pelling, *Sermon*, 32.   [36] Sibbes, *Works*, i. 211.

eternal damnation'[37]—the tribulations of the saints were merely fatherly chastisements. By such 'crosses' and 'stripes' the Lord tenderly nurtured and disciplined His dearest children, 'least . . . by overmuch cockering' they became too complacent, weaning them like a wise parent from their inordinate love of worldly pleasure and sensual delight. 'Yea he useth us much like a mother frayeth hir chylde with Hodge Goblin', noted Edward Cradocke, 'to the intente he mighte runne into hir lappe'; like a mother who threatened to throw her infant to 'the Woolfe, or scarreth it with some pokar, or bull-beggar', echoed Arthur Dent, 'that they perish not with the wicked'.[38] Remembering the insights of the innocent sufferer Job, the righteous would recognize that 'Afflictions are their scoolings, and Adversitie, their best Universitie'.[39] These were 'Gods potions to cure our spirituall maladies', 'heavenly physicke' sent to exercise and strengthen one's patience and faith. 'Even as the skilfull Apothecary', observed Elnathan Parr, the Almighty knew 'how to use poyson well, and to the good of the patient'.[40] Hardship and disaster could also be compared with the furnace in which a potter tested his clay vessel, the crucible in which a goldsmith refined and 'skoured' precious metals. They were a form of trial by fire by which the Lord purged and proved His own.[41]

God afflicted the elect in this world that they might escape perdition in the next. They had a considerably better 'bargaine' than the reprobate, alleged John 'Decalogue' Dod, for who would not endure temporary sorrows and vicissitudes in exchange for everlasting felicity and joy? Who would settle for happiness 'for a season' if it meant excruciating torment without end after death? Such preachers came dangerously close to suggesting that temporal castigations expiated the minor moral lapses of the saints.[42] Retributive providences began to look remarkably like a Protestant replacement for purgatory.[43] Postulating an inverse relationship

---

[37] Calvin, *Institutes*, bk. III, ch. 4, §32 and see §34.

[38] [Gerardus], *Speciall treatise*, 266; Cradocke, *Shippe of assured safetie*, 258, 276; Arthur Dent, *The plaine mans path-way to heaven* (1601), 123.

[39] Dent, *Plaine mans path-way*, 124. Calvin, *Defense*, 12, called them 'the very wrestling-school, in which God exercises and tries our faith'.

[40] Walker, *Learned and profitable treatise*, 193; Parr, *Grounds of divinitie*, 120–1. For the pervasiveness of the metaphor of physic, see David Harley, 'Spiritual Physic, Providence and English Medicine, 1560–1640', in Ole Peter Grell and Andrew Cunningham (eds.), *Medicine and the Reformation* (1993), 101–17.

[41] Eccles. xxvii. 5; Prov. xvii. 3; Ps. lxvi. 10. See e.g. Thomas Cooper, *Certaine sermons wherein is contained the defense of the gospell nowe preached* (1580), 174; Dent, *Plaine mans path-way*, 123; Perkins, *Workes*, i. 158; Willem Teellinck, *The resting place of the minde. That is, a propounding of the wonderfull providence of God*, trans. T. Gataker (1622), 42. An extended discussion of this 'rhetoric of suffering' can be found in J. Sears McGee, *The Godly Man in Stuart England: Anglicans, Puritans, and the Two Tables, 1620–1670* (New Haven, 1976), ch. 2.

[42] John Dod and Robert Cleaver, *Ten sermons tending chiefely to the fitting of men for the worthy receiving of the Lords Supper* (1610 edn.), 170. See also Jeremy Corderoy, *A warning for worldlings, or a comfort to the godly, and a terror to the wicked* (1608), 228–9; Dent, *Platforme*, 43; [Gerardus], *Speciall treatise*, sig. B5ᵛ and p. 276; Rogers, *General session*, chs. 12, 14, esp. pp. 102–3; Griffith Williams, *The best religion* (1636), 719.

[43] It is interesting to note that the Henrician reformer John Frith rejected the Catholic concept of purgatory but polemically appropriated the term, speaking of two 'purgatories' in this life, the word

between prosperity and piety, ministers went on to remind their flocks that 'those whom the Lord loveth he chasteneth, and scourgeth', those who tasted not of the cup of His wrath were in all likelihood 'bastards, and not sons'.[44] By this circular logic, judgements began to acquire the character of blessings, infallible marks and 'special notes' of celestial patronage and favour. While adversity merely hardened the hearts of the wicked, rendering them all the more inexcusable, the godly rejoiced in their 'smitings' as 'a signe we are espoused to Christ' and 'graffed into his house and family'.[45]

Providentialism of this ilk was both suspiciously self-confirming and potentially egotistical in the extreme. It was a set of rose-coloured spectacles through which the setbacks, no less than the successes, of 'professors of the faith' were transformed into emblems of divine approbation. Evildoers, on the other hand, were ensnared within a catch-22. Whenever disaster overtook them, this was unambiguous evidence of God's unappeasable ire, but so was a life of freedom and ease—it suggested the Almighty had completely abandoned them to their own sinful impulses and lost all interest in their spiritual welfare and health. According to the rector of Horningsheath, Thomas Rogers, it was 'an undoubted argument of their destruction at hande'.[46] It was the adeptness with which the hotter sort of Protestants exploited the elastic and ambidextrous strands of this doctrine which gave them their unsavoury reputation for hypocrisy.

Yet it was equally capable of precipitating self-loathing, melancholy, and debilitating despair. The struggle to discern some pattern behind one's violently swinging fortunes could induce an obsession, not to say neurosis, revolving around the unintelligibility of God's predestinarian scheme. Predicated upon a causal connection between affliction and guilt, this was a philosophy with a distinct tendency to deflate the self-esteem of the sufferer and foster a masochistic internalization of blame. When combined with ingrained convictions about human depravity, a paranoid reading of providential events was liable to intensify mental stress and lead to suicidal anxiety that the Lord had secretly delivered one over to a 'reprobate sense'. Direful apprehensions of divine victimization, whether in the guise of objectively verifiable experience or inner anguish and torment, encouraged an unhealthy degree of introspection.[47]

Ironically, then, acknowledging that the entire course of human history had been predetermined from eternity did not give grounds for spiritual inertia or moral

---

of God and the 'cross of Christ', which he defined as the adversities and tribulations of the elect. See Carl R. Trueman, *Luthers's Legacy: Salvation and the English Reformers, 1525–1556* (Oxford, 1994), 131.

[44] Heb. xii. 6–8 and see 1 Cor. xi. 32. Another favourite text was 1 Pet. iv. 17 ('Judgement must begin at the house of God'). See e.g. Cooper, *Certaine sermons*, 175; Dent, *Platforme*, 42; [Gerardus], *Speciall treatise*, sig. B5ᵛ; Rogers, *General session*, 103.

[45] Corderoy, *Warning for worldlings*, 156 and see 127, 145–6; [Gerardus], *Speciall treatise*, 275, cf. sig. B5ᵛ; Walker, *Learned and profitable treatise*, 196–7.

[46] Rogers, *General session*, 88.

[47] For this theme, see John Stachniewski, *The Persecutory Imagination: English Puritanism and the Literature of Religious Despair* (Oxford, 1991), esp. ch. 1.

passivity. On the contrary, framing one's conduct in accordance with divine will was emotionally demanding and psychologically taxing. No less delicate and difficult was negotiating the fine line between fully relying upon providence and presumptuously tempting it. Providence was the 'shippe of assured safetie' in which total trust ought to be placed: without God's helping hand, declared Edward Cradocke, 'oure surest buckler of defence [is] noughte else but a ruinouse and rotten piller'. Nevertheless, one should not wholly neglect or reject lawful secondary means, feebly surrendering oneself to whatever destiny held in store. It was wrong to take unnecessary risks: to refuse the remedies prescribed by licensed medical practitioners on the grounds that repentance alone cured diseases and fever, or recklessly to imperil one's life in confident expectation of being miraculously delivered from danger. This was 'to looke for that, as of duetie, which is done of an especiall priviledge'. Subsidiary helps and 'stays' prevailed only if the Lord so wished, but it was still obligatory to make all possible use of them.[48]

To the outsider, this paradoxical system of thinking and living could seem both a perverse refusal to face the facts, and an unwarrantable twisting of them. To speak of the inscrutability of divine justice in circumstances where a highly scrutable form of injustice appeared to be in operation might well be discounted as sophistical quibbling. Who would not be forgiven for finding Ralph Walker's assertion that 'it agrees excellentlie wel with Gods Providence, that the godly should live in want, and the wicked in abundance' indigestible? Perceptive pastors conceded that it 'astonied' and discouraged even the Lord's 'dearest and wisest children' that they were 'often as the sheepe feeding on bare commons, whilst the wicked are as fat bulls of Bashan grasing to the full in goodly greene medowes'. This was a great stumbling block, a sore point that 'toucheth the quicke'.[49]

Divine goodness, then, was a matter of credal definition rather than empirical observation. '[M]en are not to imagine that a thing must first be just', said William Perkins sternly, 'and then afterward that God doth will it: but contrariwise, first God wils a thing, and thereupon it becomes just'.[50] Even if one seemed to be participating in a jesuitical defence of double standards, one was bound to acknowledge that the Almighty was not answerable to the moral laws He had ordained for mankind.[51] Predestination, Calvin had to admit, was an 'awful' decree. It delineated a deity who resembled nothing so much as a cruel, inhuman, and deceitful tyrant: a deity who had condemned most human beings to reprobation before they even had the chance to offend, and then proceeded to insist upon their absolute obedience to biblical commandments they were doomed to be unable to obey, and

---

[48] Cradocke, *Shippe of assured safetie*, 173–4, and bk. II, ch. 5. See also Bullinger, *Decades*, iv. 181–2; [Gerardus], *Speciall treatise*, sig. G4ᵛ; Parr, *Grounds of divinitie*, 125; Pelling, *Sermon*, 42; Pemble, *Workes*, 278; Sibbes, *Works*, i. 209; Ursinus, *Summe*, 364; Veron, *Fruteful treatise*, fos. 90ʳ–91ʳ; Walker, *Learned and profitable treatise*, 55.

[49] Walker, *Learned and profitable treatise*, 202, 17–18; Cradocke, *Shippe of assured safetie*, 254. See also John Carpenter, *A preparative to contentation* (1597), 279; Perkins, *Workes*, i. 158; Traheron, *Exposition*, sig. B2ᵛ.

[50] Perkins, *Workes*, i. 415.   [51] See e.g. Pelling, *Sermon*, 25.

to reveal to them through the preaching of the Gospel a mere mirage of salvation—a vision of the paradise from which they had already been banned. 'Flesh' solicited many to 'murmur' against God, as if He 'amused himself with tossing men about like tennis-balls', but it was 'insolent curiosity', 'monstrous madness', and 'nefarious temerity' to try to unravel His riddles.[52] The Lord's judgements were unfathomable: He 'oft wraps himself in a cloud and will not be seen till afterward', stressed Richard Sibbes.[53] His concealed will was 'not alto-gither to be compassed with mans wit'.[54] As arbitrary, baffling, and even sadistic as His earthly dealings sometimes appeared, they were to be accepted without ques-tion nonetheless.

Notwithstanding its manifold complexities, the Calvinist doctrine of providence exerted a powerfully formative influence on puritan piety. Breeding self-scrutiny, even morbid self-absorption, providentialism became a major element in the sub-jective experience of the godly, a critical feature of what R. T. Kendall has called 'experimental predestinarianism'.[55] It was the at once arrogant and humbling assumption that one was the personal preoccupation of an officious and omnipo-tent deity, alternately the apple of His affectionate eye and the focus of His irate and glowering gaze, which helped to mark out 'puritans' from those they con-demned as the unholy multitude. As distinguished historians on both sides of the Atlantic, from Perry Miller and Paul Seaver to Barbara Donagan and Peter Lake, have shown, this was the matrix within which the self-styled 'saints' conducted the most intimate details of their everyday lives. Meticulous analysis of minutiae stood at the centre of that all-consuming search for certainty about one's eschatological status which came to characterize second-generation Calvinism.[56] Providence played a key role in domestic decision-making, in household divinity, and in the private management of crisis and calamity;[57] it shaped political argument, tactics, and action in the heady atmosphere of the Civil War and Cromwellian Interregnum.[58] It provided puritans with consolation when their children, friends,

---

[52] Calvin, *Institutes*, bk. i, ch. 17, §1–2; bk. iii, ch. 23, §7, 12; id., *Defense*, 8, 34–5, 75, 78–9, 109, and esp. 118 (Calvin's 'Calumniator's Description of the False God').

[53] Sibbes, *Works*, i. 207.   [54] Cradocke, *Shippe of assured safetie*, 375.

[55] R. T. Kendall, *Calvin and English Calvinism to 1649* (Oxford, 1979), esp. pt. iii.

[56] See Perry Miller, *The New England Mind: The Seventeenth Century* (Cambridge, Mass., 1954), esp. 14–17, 32–4, 224–6, 228–31, 463–6; Peter Lake, *Moderate Puritans and the Elizabethan Church* (Cambridge, 1982), ch. 7; Seaver, *Wallington's World*, esp. 8, 47–66, 152–6, 204; Barbara Donagan, 'Providence, Chance and Explanation: Some Paradoxical Aspects of Puritan Views of Causation', *Journal of Religious History*, 11 (1981), 385–403. See also Dewey D. Wallace, *Puritans and Predestination: Grace in English Protestant Theology 1525–1695* (Chapel Hill, NC, 1982), 58–9 and *passim*; Von Greyerz, *Vorsehungsglaube und Kosmologie*, ch. 4.

[57] Barbara Donagan, 'Godly Choice: Puritan Decision-Making in Seventeenth Century England', *Harvard Theological Review*, 76 (1983), 307–34; ead., 'Understanding Providence: The Difficulties of Sir William and Lady Waller', *JEH* 39 (1988), 433–44.

[58] Worden, 'Providence and Politics'. See also Karl H. Metz, '"Providence" und Politisches Handeln in der Englischen Revolution (1640–1660): Eine Studie zu einer Wurzel Moderner Politik, Dargestellt am Politischen Denken Oliver Cromwells', *Zeitschrift für Historische Forschung*, 12 (1985), 43–84. On Cromwell's providentialism, see also R. S. Paul, *The Lord Protector: Religion and Politics in the Life of*

and relatives died, and with stoical courage and patience in the face of chronic illness, financial misfortune, and military defeat. Resigning themselves serenely to whatever the Lord laid upon their shoulders and turning to earnest repentance and prayer, men and women from all sections of the social spectrum—from artisans like Nehemiah Wallington to wealthy gentry such as Sir William and Lady Waller—found themselves able to bear up during difficult times.

Nowhere is the puritan propensity for detecting the finger of God in the most mundane events more vividly exhibited than in their journals and diaries, letters, autobiographies, and private memorabilia. Ralph Josselin, for instance, saw divine providence at work in a simple bee-sting he suffered on 5 September 1644 and in the white pus which seeped from his navel one November day in 1649; John Winthrop, the first governor of the colony of Massachusetts, acknowledged it in the timely discovery of a spider in the family porridge bowl on 15 December 1610; and just one of the 'remarkabell provedenses' vouchsafed to the Ipswich apprentice and New England immigrant John Dane was his narrow escape from the clutches of a buxom prostitute who thrust herself upon him in an inn where he lodged around 1629. 'O, wonderfull, unspekable, unsarchabl marseys of a god that taketh care of use when we take no Care of ourselvese', he wrote in a little notebook destined to become a precious family heirloom.[59] Saturated with references to the special blessings and judgements which the Lord had graciously bestowed upon the writer such texts record the perennial inner struggle of the godly for assurance of their elect status on paper.[60]

Rival Ideologies

Providentialism, then, was a central strand in the religiosity of evangelical Protestants. But, according to the Elizabethan and early Stuart clergy, the bulk of the populace had no understanding of, if not outright contempt for, this crucial doctrine. Nothwithstanding the fact that the whole world was 'a schoole of the same', observed Ralph Walker, 'lamentable experience doth teach' that 'most men, if not in all, yet in some points are whollie ignorant of the same'.[61] Too many, in their view, adhered tenaciously and stubbornly to convictions and practices sharply at odds with Calvinist, not to say Christian, theology.

Protestant divines confronted a context in which 'heathenish' concepts of fate and fortune seemed to be disturbingly prevalent. There was a general consensus

Oliver Cromwell (1955); Christopher Hill, *God's Englishman: Oliver Cromwell and the English Revolution* (1970), ch. 9; J. C. Davis, 'Cromwell's Religion', in John Morrill (ed.), *Oliver Cromwell and the English Revolution* (1990), 181–208.

[59] *The Diary of Ralph Josselin 1616–1683*, ed. Alan Macfarlane, Records of Social and Economic History, NS 3 (Oxford, 1976), 19, 184; *The Winthrop Papers*, ed. W. C. Ford *et al.*, 6 vols., Massachusetts Historical Soc. (Boston, 1929–92), i. 165; Dane, 'John Dane's Narrative, 1682', *New England Historical and Genealogical Register*, 8 (1854), 151.

[60] See Neil Keeble, *Richard Baxter: Puritan Man of Letters* (Oxford, 1982), esp. 139–45; Von Greyerz, *Vorsehungsglaube und Kosmologie*; id., 'Der Altägliche Gott im 17. Jahrhundert: Zur Religiös-Konfessionellen Identät der Englischen Puritaner', *Pietismus und Neuzeit*, 16 (1990), 11–30.

[61] Walker, *Learned and profitable treatise*, unpaginated epistle 'To the Reader'.

that the greater part of the laity, learned as well as ignorant and poor, had yet to abandon a vestigial belief in chance, 'haphazard', and luck. It was the 'common persuasion' and 'almost universal opinion' of the age, complained Calvin and his English apostles, that all things happened at random.[62] 'How frequent in mens mouths', bewailed William Gouge, rector of St Anne, Blackfriars, 'are these phrases, good luck, ill luck . . . good fortune . . . ill fortune'. According to the preacher John Northbrooke the inhabitants of Elizabethan Bristol also had the 'very evill custome' of substituting these profane terms for 'providence'.[63] This endemic practice, declared Ralph Walker, grew out of 'ignorance, the mother of superstition'.[64] Dozens of ministers quoted St Basil to the effect that such words were part of the vocabulary of 'paynims' and therefore utterly 'unworthie of Christian eares'.[65]

Even more intolerable was the widespread tendency to personify earthly instability and attribute the vicissitudes of one's existence to the fickle goddess Fortuna. This legendary figure, insisted Thomas Gataker and others, was no more than 'a poeticall figment', 'a meere fiction', a 'vaine conceit, or rather a plaine deceit of mans idle braine'. Yet it was patently clear to the clergy that traditional depictions of this capricious lady—blindfolded and balanced precariously on a slippery ball or turning her wheel and indiscriminately dispensing her gifts—maintained a retentive grip on sixteenth- and seventeenth-century minds.[66] Contemporaries who clung to this competing theory of causation were unconsciously committing the grave spiritual crime of idolatry.

The fact that so much seemed chaotic and contingent merely exposed the feeble insight of humanity into the mysterious purposes of the Almighty; it was only in the 'carnal judgement', 'the dull and weak cogitation' of inferior beings that events lacked any discernible arrangement or authorship.[67] What 'we call chaunce', emphasized Andreas Gerardus, was 'nothing els, then that whose course and cause is hidden from our eyes'. 'Fortune', noted Gataker, was 'no other then but God nicknamed'.[68] There was, in short, no such thing as an accident or a coincidence. Even the most brutally casual of mishaps had to be ascribed unflinchingly to divine intervention. The Lord could be said to have killed a man slain by the fall of an

---

[62] Calvin, *Institutes*, bk. i, ch. 16, §2; Carpenter, *Preparative*, 279; Bezaleel Carter, *A sermon of Gods omnipotencie and providence* (1615), 13; [Gerardus]. *Speciall treatise*, sig. H7ᵛ.

[63] William Gouge, *The extent of Gods providence*, bound with *Gods three arrowes: plague, famine, sword, in three treatises* (1631), 380; John Northbrooke, *Spiritus est vicarius Christi in terra. The poore mans garden* (1600 edn.), fo. 24ʳ.

[64] Walker, *Learned and profitable treatise*, 261–2.

[65] e.g. Hill, *Life everlasting*, 509; John Knox, *The Works . . .* , ed. David Laing, 6 vols. (Edinburgh, 1846–64), v. 32; Northbrooke, *Poore mans garden*, fo. 24ᵛ; Calvin, *Institutes*, bk. i, ch. 16, §8.

[66] Gataker, *Of the nature and use of lots*, 27; Gouge, *Extent of Gods providence*, in *Gods three arrowes*, 379, cf. 381. See also [Gerardus], *Speciall treatise*, sigs. H4ᵛ–5ʳ; George More, *A demonstration of God in his workes* (1597), 122–4; Walker, *Learned and profitable treatise*, 262.

[67] Pemble, *Workes*, 270; Vermigli, *Common places*, 168–9.

[68] [Gerardus], *Speciall treatise*, sigs. H8ᵛ and H4ᵛ–8ᵛ passim; Gataker, *Of the nature and use of lots*, 27.

axe or sword, declared Sibbes, alluding to Deuteronomy xix. 5.[69] This might be distasteful, but it was unequivocally true. In their recurrent struggle against 'ethnick fortune',[70] Protestants were attempting to outlaw, if only nominally, an idea that could, and indeed in the pre-Reformation period had, comfortably coexisted with the notion of providence. Medieval thinkers from Boethius to Dante had reconciled the two by placing fortune in complete subservience to God, but to ardent Calvinists this kind of philosophical compromise was nothing less than anathema.[71]

Equally detrimental to providential doctrine was the opinion that adversity and prosperity were the consequence of 'a fatall kind of necessity', a remorseless, inexorable force which men and women could do nothing to evade.[72] According to the post-Reformation ministry, an unhealthy confusion between divine determinism and pagan fatalism persisted throughout English society. Those who truly understood Protestant tenets, wrote Philip Stubbes in the second part of his *Anatomie of abuses*, 'wold leave of' saying complacently 'Oh, I was borne to it, it was my destonie' whenever they came to any 'shamefull end'.[73] What they irreligiously described as their 'fate' or 'lot' was really the result of a divine decree, a just punishment for their immoral and profligate conduct. 'Stoicall destinie', declared the clergy, created an impersonal causal nexus which knitted events together with 'an indissoluble knot' and in a crippling, 'false lincked chaine'.[74] By tying the Almighty to secondary causes and putting him at the beck and call of His creatures, it 'pinioned' both His actions and His arms, wresting His 'scepter' right 'oute of hys handes'.[75] This was a scheme, said Calvin, insolently 'calculated to call God himself to order' and 'set Him laws whereby to work'.[76] In theory, then, these rival ideologies could not stand side by side, but it was very difficult to ignore the fact that in practice there was considerable overlap. The cynical objection of 'calumniators' that providence was merely a Calvinist rehash of classic Senecan thinking had all too convincing a ring.[77]

Dame Nature was another notable focus of clerical hostility. George Herbert

---

[69] Sibbes, *Works*, i. 205. Cf. Veron, *Fruteful treatise*, fo. 87ʳ; Walker, *Learned and profitable treatise*, 48.

[70] Bullinger, *Decades*, iv. 181.

[71] On fortune's medieval heritage, see Vincenzo Cioffari, *Fortune and Fate from Democritus to St Thomas Aquinas* (New York, 1935); Howard R. Patch, *The Goddess Fortuna in Mediaeval Literature* (1967 edn.).

[72] George Hakewill, *An apologie or declaration of the power and providence of God in the government of the world* (Oxford, 1627), 12 [*vere* 16].

[73] *Phillip Stubbes's Anatomy of Abuses in England in Shakspere's Youth. A.D. 1583*, pt. 2. *The Display of Corruptions Requiring Reformation*, ed. Frederick J. Furnivall (1882), 63.

[74] Walker, *Learned and profitable treatise*, 232; Hill, *Life everlasting*, 459; Cradocke, *Shippe of assured safetie*, 14, 272–3.

[75] Stephen Gosson, *The trumpet of warre* ([1598]), sig. D7ᵛ; Cradocke, *Shippe of assured safetie*, 14.

[76] Calvin, *Defense*, 42.

[77] See e.g. Crowley, *Apologie*, fo. 60ʳ⁻ᵛ; [Gerardus], *Speciall treatise*, sigs. G5ᵛ, G8ᵛ; Ursinus, *Summe*, 359–62; and the marginal glosses to Thomas Lodge's trans. of Seneca's 'Discourse of Providence', in *Workes*, 497–509.

deplored 'the great aptnesse countrey people have to think that all things come by a kind of naturall course; and that if they sow and soyle their grounds, they must have corne; if they keep and fodder well their cattel, they must have milk, and Calves'. The average rural vicar had to labour hard to replace his parishioners' materialistic, almost animistic trust in a self-evolving universe with due and grateful respect for the dispensations of providence. 'That wee call and esteeme nature', admonished Bishop Thomas Cooper of Lincoln, 'is nothing but the very finger of God working in his creatures'.[78] When George Hakewill, Archdeacon of Surrey, wrote his extended *Apologie of the power and providence of God* (1627), his aim was to correct the 'common errour' touching cosmological decay, by which most men and women flattered themselves that disasters were not divine scourges for their sins, but merely symptoms of the world's advancing infirmity and age. This fallacy ran rife among the vulgar, but many of the learned had likewise 'sucked' it in 'with their milke' (Plate 2).[79] Men with an advanced knowledge of natural philosophy who laid too much emphasis on secondary causes and were wary of admitting the continuance of special providences and miracles were also liable to be accused of detracting from divine omnipotence and of outrageous 'impietie'.[80]

Even more alarming to Protestant ministers was the growing interest of contemporaries in judicial astrology, the science of determining the occult influence of the stars, sun, moon, and other celestial bodies on human affairs. Rooted in Babylonian learning and augmented by the Arabs and Greeks, by the late Middle Ages a loosely Christianized version of this ancient system of thought enjoyed extensive appeal and prestige: heavenly bodies were declared to be delegated agents and instruments of the deity.[81] Protestants like Williams Perkins and Fulke, however, vociferously rejected this ideological marriage of convenience. They loudly condemned amateur and professional astrologers who predicted the fortunes of their clients by casting personal horoscopes, mathematically analysing the positions, movements, and conjunctions of the major constellations and signs of

[78] George Herbert, *A priest to the temple. Or, the country parson*, repr. in *The Works . . .*, ed. F. E. Hutchinson (Oxford, 1941), 270–1; Cooper, *Certaine sermons*, 163, and 176, 192. See also [Ralegh], *History of the world*, sig. E2ᵛ.

[79] Hakewill, *Apologie*, title-page, sigs. B4ʳ, C2ʳ, pp. 19–20. The last quotation is taken from the expanded 3rd edn. (1635), bk. VI, pp. 272–3. This edn., esp. bk. V, was intended to confute the arguments of Godfrey Goodman, *The Fall of Man, or the Corruption of Nature* (1616). For this debate, see Victor Harris, *All Coherence Gone: A Study of the Seventeenth Century Controversy over Disorder and Decay in the Universe* (1966).

[80] As anticipated by Walter Bailey, *A briefe discours of certain bathes or medicinall waters in the countie of Warwicke neere unto a village called Newnam Regis* (1587), 5. See the discussion in Paul H. Kocher, *Science and Religion in Elizabethan England* (New York, 1969), ch. 5.

[81] On astrology in the Middle Ages, see Richard Kieckhefer, *Magic in the Middle Ages* (Cambridge, 1989), 86–8, 120–31; Valerie I. J. Flint, *The Rise of Magic in Early Medieval Europe* (Oxford, 1991), 92–101, 128–46. For the early modern period, Thomas, *Religion and the Decline of Magic*, ch. 12. For its gradual decline as part of the intellectual mainstream, see Patrick Curry, *Prophecy and Power: Astrology in Early Modern England* (Cambridge, 1989) and 'Astrology in Early Modern England: The Making of a Vulgar Knowledge', in Stephen Pumfrey, Paolo L. Rossi, and Maurice Slawiniski (eds.), *Science, Culture and Popular Belief in Renaissance Europe* (Manchester, 1991), 274–91.

PLATE 2 George
Hakewill, *An apologie or
declaration of the power
and providence of God in
the government of the
world* (Oxford, 1630),
title-page. By
permission of the
Syndics of Cambridge
University Library.
Shelfmark: Hunter b.
62.1.

the zodiac, and determining nativities, elections, and inceptions. To seek and follow
their advice about the most propitious times to plant crops, castrate animals, undertake a journey, and even cut one's hair or toenails was 'a superstitious conceit and
diabolicall confidence'. In the eyes of its assailants, the 'forged skill' and 'unchristian art' of astrology turned all 'topsie turvie' by allowing the stars to supplant God
as the controlling factor in temporal affairs.[82] By distracting mankind from sober

    [82] William Perkins, *A discourse of the damned art of witchcraft* (Cambridge, 1610 edn.), 78, 92; Stubbes,
Anatomy, pt. 2, ed. Furnivall, 59. See also William Fulke, *Antiprognosticon . . . an invective agaynst the
vayne and unprofitable predictions of the astrologians as Nostradame. &c.* (1560); John Calvin, *An admonicion against astrology judiciall and other curiosities . . .* , trans. G. G[ylby] ([1561]); Andreas Gerardus

contemplation of divine mercies and judgements, it seriously reduced moral responsibility: murderers and adulterers could excuse their vicious crimes by protesting 'it was not I, it was *Planetarum injuria*', the mesmeric influence of the planets, 'that compelled me to sinne'.[83]

The clergy also denounced the authors of the printed prognostications and almanacs flooding from early modern presses as swindlers and 'lyers' who undermined the dogma of providence by presuming to be able to unravel the secrets of the future. It was 'utterly unlawfull to buye or use' the precise forecasts they issued about imminent political and religious upheavals, together with the state of the harvest and weather.[84] Presaging as confidently 'as though they sate in Gods lap', these impious 'figure-flingers' and 'vaineglorious fellowes' effectively pulled Him from His throne on high and made Him 'a jacke out of office'. 'For if all our actions depend of the starres', John Chamber, canon of Windsor, concluded scoffingly, 'then may God have an everlasting playing day, and let the world wag.'[85] Sound instruction in Calvinist precepts would discredit the absurd predictions and 'fond dreames of destinie Setters' and dispel the idiotic fears of those paralysed by 'the aspecte of any inferioure starre'.[86]

When it came to accounting for personal calamities, as opposed to communal or national catastrophes, too many parishioners apparently preferred to attribute them to the 'subtill' magical practices of witches rather than meekly accept them as spiritual trials and penalties sent by their heavenly Father.[87] As Stuart Clark has demonstrated, European witchcraft tracts in this period were overwhelmingly the work of 'pastor-demonologists': they embodied an evangelical effort to combat plebeian misapprehensions about the origin and nature of unpleasant events.[88]

(Hyperius), *Two common places . . . whereof . . . he sheweth the force that the sonne, moone and starres have over men*, trans. R. Y. (1581); Henry Howard, *A defensative against the poyson of supposed prophesies* (1583); John Chamber, *A treatise against judicial astrologie* (1601).

[83] Walker, *Learned and profitable treatise*, 233; Stubbes, *Anatomy*, pt. 2, ed. Furnivall, 61, and see 55–66 passim.

[84] See esp. William Perkins, *Four great lyers, striving who shall win the silver whetstone. Also, a resolution to the countri-man, proving it utterly unlawfull to buye or use our yeerly prognostications* ([1585]). On almanacs, see Bernard Capp, *English Almanacs 1500–1800: Astrology and the Popular Press* (Ithaca, NY, 1979), ch. 5; id., 'The Status and Role of Astrology in Seventeenth-Century England: The Evidence of the Almanac', in *Scienze credenze occulte livelli di cultura: Convegno internazionale di studi* (Florence, 1982), 279–90.

[85] Quotations from Stubbes, *Anatomy*, pt. 2, ed. Furnivall, 56, 60; Chamber, *Treatise*, 2, 4.

[86] Walker, *Learned and profitable treatise*, 66; Cradocke, *Shippe of assured safetie*, 14.

[87] Quotation from the title of George Gifford, *A discourse of the subtill practises of devilles by witches and sorcerers* (1587).

[88] Stuart Clark, 'Protestant Demonology: Sin, Superstition, and Society (c.1520–c.1630)', in Bengt Ankarloo and Gustav Henningsen (eds.), *Early Modern European Witchcraft: Centres and Peripheries* (Oxford, 1990), esp. 59, 69–70; id., *Thinking with Demons: The Idea of Witchcraft in Early Modern Europe* (Oxford, 1997), chs. 29–30 and pt. IV passim. This reinforces the work of John L. Teall, 'Witchcraft and Calvinism in Elizabethan England: Divine Power and Human Agency', *Journal of the History of Ideas*, 23 (1962), 21–36; James Hitchcock, 'George Gifford and Puritan Witch Beliefs', *Archiv für Reformationsgeschichte*, 58 (1967), 90–9; Alan Macfarlane, *Witchcraft in Tudor and Stuart England: A Regional and Comparative Study* (1970), ch. 15; id., 'A Tudor Anthropologist: George Gifford's *Discourse*

It was all too typical of the 'superstitious' and 'popishly-affected', of carnal and cold statute Protestants, remarked the West Country parson Richard Bernard, 'to thinke presently, when any evill betideth them, that they . . . are bewitched'. The poorer sort jumped to this conclusion when they saw anyone 'strangely visited', agreed William Perkins, recording it among the rural sayings he regarded as symptomatic of the 'grosse ignorance' and 'damnable case' in which the majority of the English populace still stood.[89] Whenever they fell ill, their crops failed, their barn burnt down, their livestock died, or their butter and cheese spoiled, 'by and by' they blamed it upon a villager who had built up a bad reputation among her neighbours and made the mistake of wishing a pox or plague upon them in a fit of pique.[90]

   To Ralph Walker and George Gifford, both vicars in Essex, such accusations were proof of just how few fully comprehended the fact that the Lord was the 'sole inflicter' of their sufferings and that suffering was the fruit of His anger and indignation against human iniquity.[91] The 'blockish' and besotted 'multitude', deplored the London preacher Henry Holland, were possessed by the opinion 'that witches have power to turne the world upside down at their pleasure', whereas the truth was these wicked women could only effect their *maleficia* through the agency of Satan, who in turn was acting in complete accordance with divine will and natural law.[92] The common people, grumbled Daniel, the godly interlocutor in Gifford's homespun *Dialogue* on this subject, were 'carried along so hedlong withall', that they could 'by no means see, that God is provoked by their sinnes to give the devil such instruments to work withall, but rage against the witch even as if she could do all'.[93] If individuals who suspected they were the victims of curses and spells conducted a 'diligent enquirie' and engaged in some rigorous soul-searching, declared Perkins, they would soon find that their own moral frailty, not sorcery, was the real cause of their hardships. Instead of furiously seeking revenge, they

---

and *Dialogue*', in Sydney Anglo (ed.), *The Damned Art: Essays in the Literature of Witchcraft* (1977), 140–55; Stuart Clark and P. T. J. Morgan, 'Religion and Magic in Elizabethan Wales: Robert Holland's Dialogue on Witchcraft', *JEH* 27 (1976), 31–46. See also Alison Rowlands, 'Witchcraft and Popular Religion in Early Modern Rothenburg ob der Tauber', in Bob Scribner and Trevor Johnson (eds.), *Popular Religion in Germany and Central Europe, 1400–1800* (Basingstoke, 1996), 101–18.

   [89] Richard Bernard, *A guide to grand-jury men . . .* (1629 edn.), 75 [sic], and bk. 1, ch. 1 *passim*; William Perkins, *The foundation of Christian religion . . .* (1595 edn.), sig. A2^{r-v}. Cf. John Cotta, *A short discoverie of the unobserved dangers of severall sorts of ignorant and unconsiderate practisers of physicke in England* (1612), 58.

   [90] Reginald Scot, *The discoverie of witchcraft* (1584), bk. 1, ch. 1. See also Thomas Ady, *A candle in the dark* (1655), 114.

   [91] Walker, *Learned and profitable treatise*, 331–5, cf. 238; George Gifford, *A dialogue concerning witches and witchcraftes* (1593), sig. D1^r; id., *Discourse*, sigs. H2^v–3^r.

   [92] Henry Holland, *A treatise against witchcraft* (Cambridge, 1590), sigs. B1^r, G3^r. See also Bernard, *Guide to grand-jury men*, 3–4; Gifford, *Discourse*, sigs. D2^{r-v}, H2^v–3^r; id., *Dialogue*, sigs. D1^v–2^v. On the devil as a natural magician, see Stuart Clark, 'The Rational Witchfinder: Conscience, Demonological Naturalism and Popular Superstitions', in Stephen Pumfrey, Paolo L. Rossi, and Maurice Slawinksi (eds.), *Science, Culture and Popular Belief in Renaissance Europe* (Manchester, 1991), 222–7 and *passim*; id., *Thinking with Demons*, pt. II, esp. ch. 11.

   [93] Gifford, *Dialogue*, sig. D2^v, cf. sig. D2^r. See also id., *Discourse*, sig. D2^{r-v}.

should do their utmost to placate their Maker: it was repentance and amendment of life, rather than witch-hunting, that would ultimately cure one's miseries and ills.[94]

In his famously sceptical *Discoverie of witchcraft* (1584), the Kentish gentleman Reginald Scot echoed some of these clerical sentiments. It was insufferable, he said, that the Lord's own handiwork 'should be referred to a baggage old womans nod or wish' and that ill-tempered but, in his opinion, innocent old crones should be made the first cause of all mischiefs and plagues. These 'fables' had 'taken so fast hold and deepe root in the heart of man', he observed, 'that fewe or none can (nowadaies) with patience indure the hand and correction of God'. According to Scot, witch-hunting was thus pointless and futile: 'if all the divels in hell were dead, and all the witches in England burnt or hanged; I warrant you we should not faile to have raine, haile and tempests, as now we have: according to the appointment and will' of the Lord.[95] Following providentialism through to its logical conclusions, he implied that the rash of allegations against melancholic elderly females sweeping the land would soon cease if the wrong-headed assumptions of the rural laity were thoroughly reformed.[96] To this extent Protestant demonology held within it the seeds of a kind of scepticism: it could justify the conclusion that persecution was not merely misguided but downright impious. On the other hand, however, most divines sternly repeated the judicial sentence in Exodus xxii. 18 that witches should not be suffered to live. They deserved death not because of any actual bodily harm they inflicted upon their victims, but because they had entered into a pact with Satan and thereby revealed themselves to be enemies of God.[97]

This also explains why Reformed ministers regarded black and white, 'binding' and 'unbinding', witches with equal abhorrence. Both were vassals of the Archfiend and of the two the latter was without doubt 'the more horrible & detestable Monster'. Indeed, as Perkins explained, the good magician was 'the most pernicious enemie of our salvation, the most effectuall instrument of destroying our soules, and of building up the devills kingdome'. By flying to cunning men and wise women to cure their aches and pains, to recover lost and stolen objects, and to counteract malevolent witchcraft, 'thousands are carried away to their finall confusion'. To make use of the services of such 'superstitious and unlawfull helpers', stressed Alexander Roberts, preacher at King's Lynn, not only showed

---

[94] Perkins, *Damned art of witchcraft*, 230. See also Bernard, *Guide to grand-jury men*, 6–10; Thomas Cooper, *The mystery of witch-craft* (1617), ch. 16; Gifford, *Discourse*, sigs. H3ʳ, I2ʳ⁻ᵛ; id., *Dialogue*, sig. H3ᵛ; Holland, *Treatise against witchcraft*, sigs. H1ᵛ–4ʳ.

[95] Scot, *Discoverie of witchcraft*, unpaginated dedicatory epistle and bk. I, ch. 1.

[96] Ibid. esp. bk. I, chs. 1, 3, 9; bk. III, ch. 7, 9–14, 18–19. Note also Gifford's remark that witch-hunting too often proceeded from 'furious rage' rather than 'godly zeale': *Discourse*, sigs. H4ʳ–E1ᵛ.

[97] See e.g. Perkins, *Damned art of witchcraft*, ch. 6. On the double-edged character of Protestant theology with regard to witch hunting, see Richard Godbeer, *The Devil's Dominion: Magic and Religion in Early New England* (Cambridge, 1992), esp. 225–6; Robin Briggs, *Witches and Neighbours: The Social and Cultural Context of European Witchcraft* (1996), 199–201; James Sharpe, *Instruments of Darkness: Witchcraft in England 1550–1750* (1996), esp. 54–7, 240–1.

insufficient trust in God's care and the efficacy of heartful contrition and prayer, but implied that human beings had the ability to manipulate and channel super-natural power. The charms and coercive rituals employed by wizards, healers, and 'the whole rabble of sorcerers' were the 'sacraments' of Lucifer and a serious hazard to one's spiritual health.[98] Clerical attempts to uproot such opinions and practices were part of an all-out assault on what were perceived as fundamentally non-Protestant ways of explaining and alleviating misfortune.

So too was their antagonism towards an allied body of beliefs about the exis-tence and activities of ghosts, fairies, hobgoblins, elves, and other ethereal spirits. The Reformers poured scorn on the notion that the souls of the dead returned to avenge crimes and to punish relatives who failed to carry out their last wishes or dishonoured them: such spectres were either 'counterfeit apparitions' manufac-tured by Satan acting as God's lieutenant, or monkish fables and 'lewd inven-tions'.[99] Fairies and elves were likewise defined as devils or devilish illusions, figments devised by Catholic priests to cover up their trickery, 'conceits', as Thomas Cooper claimed, 'whereby the Papists kept the ignorant in awe'.[100] These little people sometimes performed domestic chores for mortals in return for food, but they could also be rather spiteful and predatory creatures who mercilessly tor-mented housewives and servants who did not share their penchant for meticulous tidiness. They were supposed to have a particular predilection for kidnapping the infants of negligent parents and substituting weak and sickly changelings who died prematurely. This too might be seen as a way of explaining disappointments and tragedies without accepting the burden of moral responsibility; it could be mobi-lized to justify resentment towards a retarded child and release the mother and father from oppressive feelings of guilt. By the early modern period, fairy-lore may well have been 'a store of mythology rather than a corpus of living beliefs', but Protestants were not prepared to brook any trace of popery and paganism which involved sidestepping the full implications of providential theology.[101]

Seen through a professional lens, adherence to these alternative explanatory systems was a tell-tale sign of the rising tide of religious indifference the clergy were convinced was engulfing both England and Continental Europe as a whole. When divines like William Perkins addressed the question 'is there any pro-vidence?' it was in response to a strong suspicion that 'the minds of men are troubled with many doubtings thereof'; Jean Veron's *Fruteful treatise* on the

---

[98] Perkins, *Damned art of witchcraft*, 174, 175, 177, 256; Alexander Roberts, *A treatise of witchcraft* (1616), 72–3. See also Gifford, *Dialogue*, sigs. E2ᵛ–F1ʳ, F2ʳ⁻ᵛ.

[99] Perkins, *Damned art of witchcraft*, 115–16; Scot, *Discoverie of witchcraft*, bk. VII, ch. 15; bk. XV, ch. 39.

[100] Cooper, *Mystery of witch-craft*, 123.

[101] Thomas, *Religion and the Decline of Magic*, 726 and 724–35 *passim*. On fairies, see also K. M. Briggs, *The Anatomy of Puck: An Examination of Fairy Beliefs among Shakespeare's Contemporaries and Successors* (1959), esp. chs. 2–3; M. W. Latham, *The Elizabethan Fairies* (New York, 1930), esp. chs. 2–4. I am grateful to Dr Alison Shell for allowing me to read a section on Protestant condemnations of fairy-lore as Catholic 'superstition' in her forthcoming book.

subject was similarly provoked by widespread 'swynyshe gruntinge' against it.[102] Providence appeared to be challenged and menaced by latent distrust, even overt ridicule of the proposition that God regularly descended from the clouds to dabble in human affairs. Most people were willing to admit that the Lord sustained the natural order by remote control, but many disputed both His ability and His inclination constantly to tinker with and interrupt the process He had initiated as Creator. Like the ancient Peripatetics and later seventeenth-century Deists this 'impious rabble' accepted that the principle of motion originated with the Almighty, but assumed that He left the rest to the disposition of nature, fortune, and free will. They believed God confined Himself to walking 'aboute the coastes of the heavens' and that He had 'noo stroke' in 'inferiour thynges' 'below the Moone', which proceeded erratically 'by chaunce and at adventure'.[103] 'Tush,' they were apt to retort, 'God neither knoweth, nor doth greatly trouble himself about these toys.'[104] This, said the clergy, was to reduce the deity to an absentee landlord. It pointed to an alarming revival of the scheme of ethics devised by the Greek thinker Epicurus: a 'daintie', ineffectual God, absorbed in sloth and impervious to human concerns, was a precondition for hedonism. Libertines, asserted Edward Cradocke, did their best to extinguish and blot out providence so that they might immerse themselves in fleshly pleasures and go forward in wickedness without remorse or terror of conscience.[105] These 'godlesse miscreants' sniggered at the possibility of spontaneous retribution for their sins, deluding themselves they would escape scot-free. Nothing was 'more odious' than this kind of 'incredulitie'.[106] 'Let us eat and drink', they scoffed, 'for to morrow we shall die.' Such speeches, said the Suffolk minister Thomas Rogers, identified 'the reprobat Epicures of this world'.[107]

But a divine being dreamt and babbled of in these terms was 'fantasticall'—'an impotent God, and therefore no God', concluded Bishop Cooper reprovingly. A God without providence, echoed Ralph Walker, was a mere cardboard cut-out, a lifeless idol.[108] Those who conceived of Him thus were little better than gentiles or infidels. It was a clerical commonplace to conflate failure to acknowledge divine sovereignty and a preference for natural over supernatural causation with overt and

---

[102] Perkins, *Workes*, i. 157; Veron, *Fruteful treatise*, title-page.

[103] Quotations from Benefield, *Commentary . . . upon . . . Amos*, 1st pagination, 10; *Certaine sermons appoynted by the quenes majesty, to be declared and read* (1563), fo. 240ʳ. See also Calvin, *Institutes*, bk. I, ch. 16, §4. Dent's *Platforme* was chiefly concerned to examine 'the truth of this doctrine, whether God by his providence rule all things generally, and every creature and action particularly'; see esp. 7–9.

[104] Bullinger, *Decades*, iv. 179.

[105] Beza, *Propositions and principles of divinitie*, 18; Cradocke, *Shippe of assured safetie*, 8. See also Richard Crakanthorp, *A sermon of predestination, preached at Saint Maries in Oxford* (1620), 14. Crakanthorp also published *De providentia dei tractatus* (Cambridge, 1623).

[106] Carpenter, *Preparative*, 326; Sheltco à Geveren, *Of the ende of this worlde, and seconde comming of Christ*, trans. Thomas Rogers (1578 edn.), fo. 6ᵛ.

[107] Rogers, *General session*, sig. ¶3ʳ⁻ᵛ. The scriptural allusion is to Isa. xxii. 13.

[108] [Gerardus], *Speciall treatise*, sig. C5ʳ; Cooper, *Certaine sermons*, 191; Walker, *Learned and profitable treatise*, 36. Cf. Calvin, *Defense*, 115; Dent, *Platforme*, 12.

articulate hostility towards orthodox Christianity. Anti-providentialism figured prominently in the stereotyped profile of the 'atheist' outlined in Elizabethan and early Stuart tracts like Jeremy Corderoy's well-known *Warning for worldlings* (1608).[109] The Catholic priest Thomas Fitzherbert likewise included in this category those who repudiated 'particuler providence' no less than those who disputed the existence of the deity per se.[110] The scattering of legally documented cases of real religious cynicism of which this was a feature reinforced fears that explicit misgivings about divine intervention were both a positive step towards and a central component of a coherent intellectual discourse of unbelief.[111]

'Atheism', however, was a label contemporaries applied liberally and with a high level of imprecision. As Michael Hunter has demonstrated, it was a blanket term of abuse covering a broad spectrum of phenomena, an inclusive concept encapsulating a wide range of clerical anxieties.[112] Genuine philosophical doubt was repeatedly confounded with practical godlessness and inveterate impiety—rejection of God through dissolute deeds rather than the vocal declaration of a secular creed. As John Carpenter, rector of Northleigh in Devon, remarked, many protested when they were condemned as atheists but their base and debauched behaviour plainly proved the justice of the charge—'their lives and conversations, theyr wordes and manner of languages decipher the same'.[113] Denying providence was equivalent to denying God, concluded Elnathan Parr, 'and this indeede is a maine cause of the prophaneness of vile men'.[114] The very fact that the vast majority lived as licentiously as 'brute beasts' and made 'a sport of sinne' persuaded experienced pastors like Richard Greenham and John Northbrooke that they dismissed heavenly threatenings lightly and passed over 'Gods heavie indignation as over burning coales'. They shrugged off divine justice as 'a jesting stocke', a paper tiger, and a 'fayned thing'. Supernatural punishments, like other matters mentioned in Scripture, were disparaged as 'Poeticall fables, or (at the least) Bugges, by policie devised to feare Babes'.[115] They and their colleagues regarded the current epidemic of immorality as evidence that this 'il brood' was proliferating at a frightening rate.[116]

[109] Corderoy, *Warning for worldlings*, 30, 112–17.

[110] Thomas Fitzherbert, *The second part of a treatise concerning policy, and religion* ([Douai], 1610), 69–70. Cf. Philippe Du Plessis Mornay, *A woorke concerning the trewnesse of the Christian religion* (1587), 171–2; Pelling, *Sermon*, 28.

[111] For some examples see Thomas, *Religion and the Decline of Magic*, 201.

[112] Michael Hunter, 'The Problem of "Atheism" in Early Modern England', *TRHS* 35 (1985), esp. 141, 143. David Wootton, 'Unbelief in Early Modern Europe', *History Workshop*, 20 (1985), esp. 86–7. G. E. Aylmer, by contrast, is concerned only with actual scepticism: 'Unbelief in Seventeenth Century England', in Donald Pennington and Keith Thomas (eds.), *Puritans and Revolutionaries: Essays in Seventeenth Century History Presented to Christopher Hill* (Oxford, 1978), 22–46.

[113] Carpenter, *Preparative*, 234. See also Corderoy, *Warning for worldlings*, sig. A4^{r-v}.

[114] Parr, *Grounds of divinitie*, 124.

[115] Northbrooke, *Spiritus est vicarius Christi in terra. A treatise wherein dicing, dauncing, vaine playes or enterludes with other idle pastimes . . . are reproved* ([1577]), sig. A3^v; Greenham, *Works*, 267; Cooper, *Certaine sermons*, 189.

[116] Corderoy, *Warning for worldlings*, unpaginated epistle to the reader.

Of course, clerical apprehensions about the anti-providential bias of 'countrie divinitie' are merely a caricature of the actual situation. The pessimism of preachers and ministers was at least in part a function of the unrealistically high standards by which they judged 'sincere' profession of the Protestant faith. In their view, only a small minority, a tiny remnant truly understood the doctrine of providence and applied it to their lives. The rest preferred causal theories which allowed them to save face by finding an external scapegoat for their misfortunes, such as the stars, a local sorceress, or the pagan goddess Fortuna. And rather than submit patiently to the trials which God had predestined them to undergo, they turned to concrete and tangible sources of consolation and relief like white magic and astrology, which were incompatible with Calvinist belief. These tendencies and attitudes were symptoms of residual Catholicism and 'superstition', relics of a religious culture which the reformers regarded it as their foremost duty to remould and eradicate.

Modern historians have tended to echo and endorse the verdict of sixteenth- and seventeenth-century ministers that providentialism was essentially a monopoly of the godly elite, a method of interpreting and coping with events which clashed with traditional convictions and instincts and consequently never won widespread assent. According to Keith Thomas, Protestant divines endeavoured to impose the ideology of divine omnipotence on a populace which had long been accustomed to accounting for adversity and prosperity in ways which were not quite as corrosive of a collective and individual sense of self-worth. As a system of diagnosing and alleviating distress it was faulty and flawed, a particularly inadequate placebo and surrogate for technological mastery and medical advance. In both its guises, as a dogma which equated success with virtue and as a 'gloomy philosophy, teaching men how to suffer, and stressing the impenetrability of God's will', it may have been a 'comfortable doctrine for the well-to-do'—one they could literally afford to adhere to—but it offered cold comfort to their social inferiors. It could 'hardly' have been attractive to that sizeable fraction of society which 'never had any hope of dragging itself above subsistence level'. It is hardly surprising, he argues, that many gravitated away from Protestantism towards non-religious modes of thought and practice which offered more direct prospects of redress and more effective techniques for counteracting the hazards of an insecure environment.[117] Keith Wrightson has been no less sceptical about the compatibility of 'providential theodicy' with the stubborn utilitarianism of the poor: 'it is in the nature of their approach to the explanation and relief of human misfortune', he says, 'that the beliefs and attitudes of the mass of the common people can be most sharply distinguished from those of their religious teachers'. Anthony Fletcher and John Stevenson also concur with the clergy in thinking that most individuals 'were never persuaded to see life's travails in terms of the workings of God's providence' or to accept the link between sin and adversity which was the crux of Calvinist

---

[117] Thomas, *Religion and the Decline of Magic*, ch. 4, esp. 130–2.

divinity.[118] On both a practical and psychological level, providentialism was a doctrine which failed to make much headway outside puritan circles.

This line of thinking reflects an interpretation of the cultural impact and socially stratifying effects of the English Reformation which, as we have seen, is swiftly receding. It embodies the view that the advent of Protestantism represented a drastic and unwelcome break with the patterns and structures of late medieval piety—a view over which current research is casting more than a shadow of doubt. The rest of this book aims to place a further large question mark beside the sharp polarities inherent in contemporary ecclesiastical and recent historiographical assessments. The chapters which follow contest the claim that providentialism played no part in the 'plaine mans religion' and suggest that the relationship between evangelical Calvinism and the eclectic culture it sought to efface and replace was far more intimate and intricate than is still widely assumed. They do so by confronting and discarding another false but enduring dichotomy: the polemical commonplace that cheap print and Protestant preaching should be situated in stark opposition.

CHEAP PRINT AND GODLY PREACHING

Elizabethan and early Stuart ministers recurrently complained that the messages emanating from the pulpit and popular press were as incongruous as chalk and cheese: they presented them as embodying rival poles of spiritual 'edification' and idle 'recreation'. In the preface to a sermon printed in 1578, Thomas White, rector of St Gregory's under St Paul's, inveighed against 'the thousands of Pamphlets & Toyes' which issued from metropolitan printing houses and profaned London bookstalls: 'caught up quickly, & devoured in hast,' he said, 'they shal never be digested unto any good substaunce . . . they are so full fraught with poyson'. It was his earnest wish that they might all be 'buried in darknes, or burned in the light, which minister matter to Fansies Schole, or Pleasures pallace', since it was this which induced such a large proportion of the English populace to 'let all Sermons slip'. William Perkins likewise condemned ballads, along with 'idle discourses and histories', as 'enticements and baits' unto sin, 'fitter for Sodome and Gomorrah then for Gods Church'. They were 'good for nothing but an Ephesian Bonefire', echoed the Kentish preacher Thomas Jackson in 1609, one of the 'manifolde discouragements' from religious publishing.[119]

Notwithstanding the tirades of the clergy, sermons and ephemeral literature did not always strike a discordant and contradictory note. At the very simplest level,

[118] Keith Wrightson, *English Society 1580–1680* (1982), 201–2; Anthony Fletcher and John Stevenson, 'Introduction', in eid. (eds.), *Order and Disorder in Early Modern England* (Cambridge, 1985), 23.

[119] T[homas] W[hite], *A sermon preached at Pawles Crosse on Sunday the ninth of December. 1576* (1578), sig. A3^{r-v}; William Perkins, *A direction for the government of the tongue according to Gods worde* (Cambridge, 1595 edn.), 30; Thomas Jackson, *Londons new-yeeres gift. Or the uncouching of the foxe* (1609), sig. A2^{r-v}. See also Edward Dering, *A briefe and necessarie catachisme or instrucion*, in *Maister Derings workes* (1590), sigs. A1^{v}–2^{r}.

both were saturated with references to divine providence; both shared a preoccupation with the blessings and punishments God showered down upon mankind to reward virtue and correct vice; both cried in unison for repentance and amendment. These parallel modes of public discourse must now be introduced.

Strange Newes

The early modern period witnessed an explosion of cheaply priced printed texts designed to entertain, edify, and satisfy the thirst of a rapidly expanding reading public for information. 'Strange and wonderful newes' of terrible disasters, sudden accidents, and bizarre prodigies was a major theme of the blackletter broadside ballads and catchpenny quarto and octavo pamphlets which flowed from city publishers in growing profusion between 1560 and 1640. Both predating and overlapping with the fitful beginnings of serial newsbooks in the 1620s, these sheets and tracts found a receptive audience in the constantly changing urban milieu that was late Tudor and early Stuart London. Hawked and chanted at the doors of theatres, alehouses, and other habitual meeting spots, and displayed for sale in shops in the vicinity of St Paul's churchyard, they also penetrated the provinces and countryside to a degree which is only gradually coming to light. Itinerant minstrels recited them at markets and fairs; petty chapmen peddled them together with pins, needles, and handkerchiefs in remote rural areas; carriers, travellers, and tradesmen conveyed them with rumour, mail, and merchandise of all kinds along an established network of trade and transport routes.[120]

Like relations of the 'last dying speeches' of executed criminals and traitors, gruesomely circumstantial accounts of shocking murders, and bulletins of military campaigns on the Continent,[121] a sizeable sample of providential ballads and pamphlets survives—albeit only a fraction of the original output of perishable items of this type.[122] It may well be that these printed artefacts had a higher mortality rate than comparable classes of text: stale and obsolete news seems less likely to have been treasured than romantic tales of courtship and unrequited love, the legends of Robin Hood, or favourite stories from Scripture such as David and

---

[120] Essential groundwork on the subject of distribution and circulation has been done by Margaret Spufford, *Small Books and Pleasant Histories: Popular Fiction and its Readership in Seventeenth-Century England* (Cambridge, 1981), ch. 5; ead., *The Great Reclothing of Rural England: Petty Chapmen and their Wares in the Seventeenth Century* (1984); Robin Myers and Michael Harris (eds.), *Spreading the Word: The Distribution Networks of Print 1550–1850* (Winchester, 1990); Watt, *Cheap Print*, 14–33; Michael Frearson, 'The English Corantos of the 1620s', PhD thesis (Cambridge, 1993), ch. 1.

[121] For a survey, see Bernard Capp, 'Popular Literature', in Barry Reay (ed.), *Popular Culture in Seventeenth Century England* (1988), 198–243.

[122] I have identified around 250 extant items from the period *c.*1560–1640 by a systematic search of the revised *STC*. Those licensed but now lost have been traced through Edward Arber (ed.), *A Transcript of the Registers of the Company of Stationers of London 1554–1640 A.D.*, 5 vols. (1875–94) and with the help of Hyder E. Rollins, *An Analytical Index to the Ballad-entries (1557–1709) in the Registers of the Company of Stationers' of London*, introd. Leslie Shepard (Hatboro, Penn., 1967 edn.). For estimates of the magnitude of the original output and the enormous attrition rate of 16th- and 17th-cent. ephemera, as well as the percentage licensed, see Watt, *Cheap Print*, 42–50. See also Franklin B. Williams, 'Lost Books of Tudor England', *The Library*, 5th ser. 33 (1978), 1–14.

Bathsheba and Susannah and Tobias. It was more liable to be recycled by econo-
mizing printers and reused by its purchasers for wrapping soap and spices, lining
pie-dishes, or stopping the proverbial mustard pot. And, as the Oxford vicar Robert
Burton remarked, 'not only Libraries and shoppes, are full of our putid papers,
but every close-stoole and jakes'. These 'chimeras', observed the character writer
Richard Brathwait, had little hope of living long; they were apt to 'melt like butter,
or match a pipe and so burne'.[123]

Such literature was not prohibitively expensive. Folio sheets typically sold for
1d. or less and before the Civil War pamphlets were widely referred to as 'three
halfpeny ware'.[124] They were certainly luxury items which would stretch the
average wage earner's weekly budget, but not necessarily somersault him or her
into debt. They competed with other leisure attractions—the stage and bowling
alley, alehouse and bear-baiting pit—for the spare funds of impecunious artisans,
servants, and apprentices. Furthermore, even if these publications were beyond
the means of many would-be consumers, it should be remembered that the buying
public was only a small subset of the reading public. Newsbooks and broadsides
need to be seen less as jealously guarded personal possessions than forms of
common property which were constantly being borrowed, exchanged, shared, and
passed on. Some people seem to have clubbed together to purchase cheap print;
others, by all accounts, browsed already grubby copies displayed on booksellers'
booths.[125] 'Pestering' and 'besmearing' many suburban signposts and plastered on
walls for 'every dull-Mechanicke to beholde', ballads and the verbose title-pages
of pamphlets were also erected as 'lasting-pasted monuments' inside rural taverns
where, as more than one social commentator observed, all and sundry could
'sojourne without expence of a farthing'.[126]

Increasingly aware that the ability to read was far more widely diffused than
knowledge of how to write, historians are now emphasizing the extent rather
than the limits of literacy in early modern England. Statistics based on the capacity to sign one's name, such as those compiled by David Cressy, must be regarded

[123] Robert Burton, *The anatomy of melancholy* (Oxford, 1621), 8; Richard Brathwait, *Whimzies: or,
a new cast of characters* (1631), 21–2.

[124] *The Letters of John Chamberlain*, ed. Norman Egbert McClure, 2 vols. (Philadelphia, 1939), i. 55.
Martin Cromer's octavo pamphlet *A notable example of Gods vengeance, uppon a murdering king* ([1560?])
was 'to be solde ready stitched for a penny', according to the title-page. Cf. Francis R. Johnson who
argues that the minimum price for multiple-page printed works was 2d.: 'Notes on English Retail Book-
Prices, 1550–1640', *The Library*, 5th ser. 5 (1950), 93. Ballads could be as cheap as a halfpenny: Watt,
Cheap Print, 12. In the 1640s, in nominal terms pamphlet prices may have dropped: Henry Peacham,
The worth of a penny, or, a caution to keep money (1669 edn.; 1st pub. 1641), 21.

[125] For references to this practice, see B. V., *The run-awyaes [sic] answer, to a booke called, A rodde for
runne-awayes* (1625), sig. A3ʳ; Thomas Churchyard, *The mirror of man, and manners of men* (1594),
unpaginated epistle 'To the generall Readers'.

[126] J[ohn] D[avies], *A scourge for paper-persecutors, or papers complaint, compil'd in ruthfull rimes against
the paper-spoylers of these times . . .* (1625), sig. B1ʳ; A[braham] H[olland], *A continu'd just inquisition of
the same subject, fit for this season. Against paper-persecutors* (printed as part of the previous item), 7;
H[enry] P[arrot], *The mastive or young-whelpe of the olde-dogge. Epigrams and satyrs* (1615), sig. A4ᵛ;
Brathwait, *Whimzies*, 9.

as pessimistic, minimum figures. Margaret Spufford's insight that reading was taught before writing—an advanced skill learnt later, if at all—suggests they amount to spectacular underestimates of the size of the potential audience for small 'ready stitched' books and single sheets. Tudor and Stuart London was a prodigiously literate context, but even outside the sprawling capital, the spread of dame schools was ensuring that many children could make at least some sense of printed texts.[127]

The impact of such publications, moreover, extended beyond the hazy and shifting frontier between literacy and illiteracy in a variety of ways. As Tessa Watt's pioneering research has revealed, these were mixed media which adeptly exploited the continuing vitality of audio-visual modes of communication and in which typography struggled to establish a modus vivendi with the still thriving oral and pictorial traditions. Invariably illustrated with crude but vivid woodcuts, ballads and pamphlets filled with unintelligible symbols for spoken words could still be meaningful—despite the often glaring incongruity between the story told in the text and plates made from a narrow repertoire of worn and worm-eaten blocks, many of which had been inherited from pre-Reformation printers.[128] Pictures allowed readers to be vicarious witnesses of morally improving spectacles and events. They served as a substitute for the assumed spiritual efficacy of seeing, but they did not supersede it.[129] Indeed, one function of broadsheets and books was to direct people to locations where they could inspect the providential sights and wonders described for themselves: 'at the red Lyon, in Fletestreete', Covent Garden, or St Bartholomew's Hospital in Smithfield.[130]

Ballads were above all vocal performances, songs sung with spontaneous

[127] R. S. Schofield, 'The Measurement of Literacy in Pre-Industrial England', in Jack Goody (ed.), *Literacy in Traditional Societies* (Cambridge, 1968), 311–25; David Cressy, 'Levels of Illiteracy in England, 1530–1730', *HJ* 20 (1977), 1–23; id., *Literacy and the Social Order: Reading and Writing in Tudor and Stuart England* (Cambridge, 1980). Margaret Spufford, 'First Steps in Literacy: The Reading and Writing Experiences of the Humblest Seventeenth-Century Spiritual Autobiographers', *Social History*, 4 (1979), 407–35. See also Thomas Laqueur, 'The Cultural Origins of Popular Literacy in England 1500–1850', *Oxford Review of Education*, 2 (1976), 255–75; Thomas, 'Meaning of Literacy'; Jonathan Barry, 'Literacy and Literature in Popular Culture: Reading and Writing in Historical Perspective', in Tim Harris (ed.), *Popular Culture in England, c.1500–1850* (Basingstoke, 1995), 69–94.
[128] For the visual context, see Marie-Hélène Davies, *Reflections of Renaissance England: Life, Thought and Religion Mirrored in Illustrated Pamphlets 1535–1640*, Princeton Theological Monographs ser. 1 (Allison Park, Penn., 1986); Watt, *Cheap Print*, pt. II, esp. ch. 4; and R. W. Scribner, *For the Sake of Simple Folk: Popular Propaganda for the German Reformation* (Cambridge, 1981).
[129] See the comments in *A myraculous, and monstrous, but yet, most true, and certayne discourse of a woman . . . in the midst of whose fore-head . . . there groweth out a crooked horne* (1588), sig. A1[r]; *The Protestants and Jesuites up in armes in Gulicke-land. Also, a true and wonderfull relation of a Dutch maiden . . . who . . . hath fasted for the space of 14 yeares* (1611), 2–3; V. Rejaule, *Newes from Spain. A true relation of the lamentable accidents, caused by the inundation and rising of Ebro, Lobsegat, Cinca and Segre, rivers of Spaine* (1618), sig. A3[v].
[130] See C. R., *The true discripcion of this marveilous straunge fishe* ([1569]); L[awrence] P[rice], *A monstrous shape. Or a shapelesse monster* ([1639]); *A certaine relation of the hog-faced gentlewoman called Mistris Tannakin Skinker* (1640), sig. B4[v]; H. I., *An example for all those that make no conscience of swearing and forswearing* ([c.1625]); *A true relation of Gods wonderfull mercies, in preserving one alive, which hanged five dayes, who was falsely accused* ([c.1613]), sig. B4[r].

improvisations in the market place and street, 'to a vile tune', quipped John Earle in his *Micro-cosmographie*, 'and a worse throat'.[131] In the case of 'doleful ditties' of divine judgement, the melody in question was often (somewhat ironically) 'Fortune my Foe'—better known to contemporaries as the 'preaching' or 'hanging tune'.[132] The printed text may have been envisaged primarily as a souvenir of the aural and musical experience, a mnemonic device to aid private imitation of the professional rendition. Artificially fixed on a two-dimensional page, such songs could still pass into the consciousness of the unlearned and thereby re-enter the oral sphere. When a ballad first reached the country it was admired as much as 'a Gyant in a pageant', observed Brathwait, but it soon grew so common that 'every poore Milke maid' could 'chant and chirpe it under her Cow'.[133]

Furthermore, despite the emergence of 'an increasingly introspective relation-ship with the written word', in early modern Europe reading was not usually a silent, reclusive activity. First-generation literates might share and show off their mastery of this esoteric art by reading aloud to friends, family, and neighbours at home or in local centres of sociability.[134] Second-hand literacy mediated the message of printed works far beyond the cultural barrier erected by a rudimentary education. '[A]t length', noted Thomas Nashe, 'they become the Alehouse talke of every Carter'.[135]

The popularity of providential news was notorious, a perpetual target of the stinging satire, acid comment, and lofty contempt of city wits. The Elizabethan and early Stuart public apparently had an insatiable appetite for metrical misery and gloom, an infatuation with what Henry Fitzgeffrey and others spurned as 'carelesse scarelesse Pamphlets' and 'waste paper . . . fraught with nought els save dogge daies effects'.[136] The 'simpler sorte' in particular greedily devoured these penny and three-halfpenny jeremiads and diatribes inspired by recent omens, portents, and catastrophes. According to Abraham Holland, the world 'hugged' ephemera about 'Monsters and deformed things' more fervently than the finely

---

[131] John Earle, *Micro-cosmographie. Or, a peece of the world discovered; in essayes and characters* (1628), ed. Edward Arber (1868), 46. On the musical background, see Watt, *Cheap Print*, pt. I, chs. 1, 2. Useful points on performance and its relationship with the printed text are also made by Natascha Würzbach, *The Rise of the English Street Ballad, 1550–1650* (Cambridge, 1990), 13–17, 20.

[132] On 'Fortune my Foe', also known as 'Aim not too high' and 'Dr Faustus', see W. Chappell, *Popular Music of the Olden Time: A Collection of Ancient Songs, Ballads, and Dance Tunes, Illustrative of the National Music of England*, 2 vols. ([n.d.]), i. 162–4; Claude M. Simpson, *The British Broadside Ballad and its Music* (New Brunswick, NJ, 1966), 225–31.

[133] Brathwait, *Whimzies*, 12.

[134] Thomas, 'Meaning of Literacy', 116. On communal reading practices, see Roger Chartier, 'Leisure and Sociability: Reading Aloud in Early Modern Europe', in Susan Zimmerman and Ronald F. E. Weissman (eds.), *Urban Life in the Renaissance* (Newark, NJ, 1989), 103–20; R. W. Scribner, 'Oral Culture and the Diffusion of Reformation Ideas', in id., *Popular Culture and Popular Movements in Reformation Germany* (1987), 54–60.

[135] Thomas Nashe, *The Works . . .* , ed. Ronald B. McKerrow, 5 vols. (1904–10), i. 23.

[136] Henry Fitzgeffrey, *Satyres and satyricall epigrams: with certaine observations at Black-Fryers?* (1617), satyra prima Lib. I; Nashe, *Works*, ed. McKerrow, i. 20.

wrought compositions of real poets—among which he naturally numbered himself.[137]

Is cheap print of this kind a transparent window into the psychology of its consumers, a mirror of the tapestry of habits, attitudes, and beliefs which make up collective mentalities? To what extent did these news ballads and books shape and fashion readers' reactions? While Victorian folklorists and antiquarians blithely assumed that they epitomized the 'vulgar' sensibilities and 'superstitious' fears of the ignorant and poor,[138] later commentators, including Louis B. Wright and Sandra Clark, have interpreted them as the embodiment of nascent 'bourgeois' values—the 'middle class culture' of artisans, shopkeepers, yeomen, and their wives.[139] But this kind of vernacular literature does not seem to have been expressly aimed at and written down to the understanding of the lower grades of the literate populace, and in any case it would be a grave mistake to suppose that they were read solely at these levels.[140] The very fact that we owe the preservation of most sixteenth- and seventeenth-century ephemera to noble and gentlemen bibliophiles like John Selden, Anthony Wood, Samuel Pepys, and Robert Harley testifies to the existence of an avid, or at least casual, audience among the affluent and educated.[141] So too do the countless transcriptions and references to be found in the journals, commonplace books, and correspondence of country squires, merchants, burgesses, and other professionals.[142] Such printed wares clearly reached a

---

[137] Nashe, *Works*, ed. McKerrow, i. 22; Holland, *Continu'd just inquisition of . . . paper-persecutors* (printed as part of D[avies], *Scourge for paper-persecutors*), 4. See also Ben Jonson's address 'To the Readers' before Act III in *The staple of newes. A comedie acted in the yeare, 1625* (1631), repr. in *Ben Jonson*, ed. C. H. Herford and Percy Simpson, 11 vols. (Oxford, 1925–52), vi. 325.

[138] This is implicit e.g. in John Ashton (ed.), *A Century of Ballads* (1867), pp. xx, 75; Joseph Lilly (ed.), *A Collection of Seventy-Nine Black-Letter Ballads and Broadsides* (1867), pp. v, xvi; Joseph Woodfall Ebsworth (ed.), *The Bagford Ballads . . .* (Hertford, 1876–80), p. xv; William Chappell and J. Woodfall Ebsworth (eds.), *The Roxburghe Ballads*, 9 vols. in 14 (1869–97), vol. i, p. viii; John Payne Collier (ed.), *A Book of Roxburghe Ballads* (1847), p. vii. See also Leslie Shepard, *The History of Street Literature* (Newton Abbot, 1973), esp. 9; Victor E. Neuberg, *Popular Literature: A History and Guide* (Harmondsworth, 1977), esp. 11–17.

[139] Louis B. Wright, *Middle Class Culture in Elizabethan England* (Chapel Hill, NC, 1935), ch. 12; Sandra Clark, *The Elizabethan Pamphleteers: Popular Moralistic Pamphlets 1580–1640* (1983), esp. 18–19, 22–3.

[140] Even vernacular literature which professes to be aimed at the poor belies this alleged intent: see Paul Slack, 'Mirrors of Health and Treasures of Poor Men: The Uses of the Vernacular Medical Literature of Tudor England', in Charles Webster (ed.), *Health, Medicine and Mortality in the Sixteenth Century* (Cambridge, 1979), esp. 258–61, and Natalie Zemon Davis, 'Printing and the People', in *Society and Culture in Early Modern France* (Stanford, Calif., 1975), 197–9, 208.

[141] Pepys's collection, now preserved in the library of Magdalene College, Cambridge, was begun by Selden: W. G. Day (ed.), *The Pepys Ballads*, 5 vols. (Cambridge, 1987). Harley's ballads and news pamphlets are now held by the British Library: Chappell and Ebsworth (eds.), *Roxburghe Ballads* and *The Harleian miscellany: or, a collection of scarce, curious, and entertaining pamphlets and tracts*, 8 vols. (1744–53). Wood's collection is in the Bodleian.

[142] For only a few examples, see BL Add. MS 38599 (Commonplace book of the Shanne family of Methley, Yorkshire); CUL MS Oo. 6. 115 (Miscellaneous notes and extracts of William Jackson, fl. 1675–95); BL Cotton MS Vespasian A. XXV (Collection of ballads, songs, and other miscellaneous transcriptions made by Henry Savile of Banke, *c*.1576). Notable MS collections of ballads include Andrew

heterogeneous cross-section of English society, a society upon which it may be premature to superimpose any rigid class divide and in which cultural fissures and splits ran along vertical as well as horizontal fault-lines.

Historians, moreover, are questioning and shedding the supposition that these pamphlets and broadsides unambiguously reflected and conditioned the opinions of the social groups who used and perused them, and recognizing that the evidence they yield is at best speculative and conjectural. We see the religious outlook of their readers through a glass darkly—no less darkly than through the opaque and distorting prism of clerical polemic. Some scholars are extremely sceptical about using such material in the quest to recover that slippery and contentious historical construct 'popular culture', especially when it is defined as a fluid relationship and ongoing process, rather than an immobile entity or 'cultural fossil'.[143] Growing emphasis on the existence of multiple subcultures has made this enterprise more problematical still. The late Bob Scribner played the devil's advocate in this regard and asked whether such artefacts amount to anything more than 'forms of downward mediation by educational and literate elites', insidious instruments of ideological hegemony and social control.[144] Others, notably Tessa Watt, have fewer reservations about their value, but are nevertheless approaching them with growing caution, sophistication, and subtlety, and endeavouring to relocate them within the constantly modifying contexts in which they were produced and consumed. However, the point holds that we may in the end learn more about the nature and agencies of cultural midwifery than about that elusive quarry 'culture' itself, and it is these processes of interaction and negotiation which this study seeks to highlight and to foreground.[145]

Furthermore, as Roger Chartier has stressed, it is less the texts themselves that deserve scrutiny than the varying manner in which they were decoded and comprehended, appropriated and employed. Reading is not a passive process in which authorially intended messages are mechanically inscribed on the palimpsest of the reader's mind, but rather an inventive, selective, and even subversive practice, a hermeneutic struggle and 'an act of poaching'.[146] And having lost the tone, gesture,

---

Clark (ed.), *The Shirburn Ballads 1585–1616* (Oxford, 1907) (from a MS in Shirburn Castle, Oxfordshire); BL Add. MS 15225 (Poems and songs compiled *c.*1616). Shrewsbury School, MS Mus X. 31 is a semi-official town chronicle containing summaries of hundreds of Elizabethan news pamphlets.

[143] Bob Scribner, 'Is a History of Popular Culture Possible?', *History of European Ideas*, 10 (1989), 180.

[144] Ibid. 177. Cf. J. A. Sharpe, ' "Last Dying Speeches": Religion, Ideology and Public Execution in Seventeenth Century England', *P&P* 107 (1985), 148, 166. Note also the reservations expressed by Barry Reay in 'Popular Literature in Seventeenth Century England', *Journal of Peasant Studies*, 10 (1983), 243–9; Keith Thomas, 'From Edification to Entertainment: Oral Tradition and the Printed Word in Early Modern England', *Times Literary Supplement*, 4612 (23 Aug. 1991), 5–6.

[145] Watt, *Cheap Print*, passim, esp. 4. See also the remarks of Tim Harris, 'Problematising Popular Culture', in id. (ed.), *Popular Culture in England, c.1500–1850* (Basingstoke, 1995), 7–9.

[146] Roger Chartier, 'Texts, Printing, Readings', in Lynn Hunt (ed.), *The New Cultural History* (Berkeley and Los Angeles, 1989), 156. Cf. his 'Culture as Appropriation: Popular Cultural Uses in Early Modern France', in Steven L. Kaplan (ed.), *Understanding Popular Culture: Europe from the*

and facial expressions of the minstrel, we can only hypothesize how the staging must have altered, qualified, and even violated the script. Did people 'Reade and Tremble', as the title-pages of John Trundle's pamphlets advised?[147] Or did they cheerfully laugh off the sins ballad-mongers deduced to be the cause of recent disasters? How these songs and books were received is rarely retrievable, but we must nevertheless be sensitive to the plural and potentially contradictory meanings they contain.

This point takes on particular importance when one considers the curious blend of luridly realistic reportage with platitudinous, sermonizing editorial which is such a salient feature of the genre. Earlier commentators gagged at this awkward mixture, taking exception to news encrusted with 'superfluous verses' of 'jejune' piety and 'sicklied o'er with didacticism'; to the intrusion of 'pharisaical preaching' and 'tedious' evangelical 'impertinences' into factual narrations of topical events; and to the inveterate habit of intermingling 'liberal doses of smug moralizing' with vivid description.[148] Sometimes the homiletic reflection was confined to an introductory formality or a final afterthought; sometimes, as one writer admitted, it waxed 'larger than the Relation itselfe', drowning the enticing titbit promised on the title-page in a torrent of violent, tub-thumping, religious tirade.[149] Louis Wright and Matthias Shaaber thought this pious varnish was a token concession to the utilitarian conscience of the urban middle class, providing them with a pretext for reading publications of an otherwise rather frivolous kind. But it is equally possible that providential admonition was their principal intention and aim.[150] Nor can we be sure how Elizabethan and early Stuart people reacted to the rather banal moral commentary which permeated supernatural pamphlets and ballads. It will never be clear whether they skipped over or lapped it up; whether they derived ghoulish pleasure or a sober warning from stories of God's terrible vengeance; whether they sought spiritual edification or cheap thrills from these tales—or, perhaps, a measure of both.

These ambiguities suggest that it is misguided to attempt to disentangle 'news' from the 'extraneous matter' with which it was published. Although these sheets and tracts have been heralded as 'forerunners' of the tabloid newspaper and precursors of the yellow sensational press, it is anachronistic to speak of 'journalism'

Middle Ages to the Nineteenth Century (Berlin, 1984), esp. 234–5; *The Cultural Uses of Print in Early Modern France*, trans. Lydia G. Cochrane (Princeton, 1987), 6–8; *Cultural History: Between Practices and Representations*, trans. Lydia G. Cochrane (Cambridge, 1988), esp. 12–14.

[147] See e.g. John Hilliard, *Fire from heaven. Burning the body of one John Hitchell of Holne-hurst* (1613) and *Anthony Painter. The blaspheming caryar* (1614).

[148] Hyder E. Rollins (ed.), *Old English Ballads 1553–1625 Chiefly from Manuscripts* (Cambridge, 1920), p. xxv; Clark (ed.), *Shirburn Ballads*, 8; H. E. Rollins, 'The Black-Letter Broadside Ballad', *Publications of the Modern Language Association of America*, 34 (1919), 268, 331; Matthias A. Shaaber, *Some Forerunners of the Newspaper in England 1476–1622* (Philadelphia, 1929), 6, 210–11, and ch. 9 *passim*.

[149] As admitted by [Henry Holland], *Motus Medi-terraneus. Or, a true relation of a fearefull and prodigious earthquake, which lately happened in the ancient citie of Coventrie* (1626), sig. A4ᵛ.

[150] Wright, *Middle Class Culture*, 433, 462; Shaaber, *Forerunners*, 7–8.

as such in early modern England.[151] The notion of supplying raw and undigested information for its own sake was embryonic, but still ethically suspect. Like the discourse of history, the writing of 'newes' was unashamedly subservient to the ends of religious indoctrination and political propaganda. Bias was not only expected but inbuilt. That said, this literature is marked by increasingly self-conscious claims to empirical fidelity. Filling their reports with plausible statistics and precise names, locations, and dates, the authors of such ballads and booklets invariably insisted that though 'strange' and 'wonderfull' they were indisputably 'true'[152]—not grounded on hearsay and 'taken up at second hand', but based on the depositions of honest, 'worshipfull', and reliable witnesses prepared to testify to the authenticity of their stories under oath. Some supplied certificates signed by local magistrates or appended the 'censure of a learned Preacher'; others went so far as to list the addresses of their informers, just in case any reader wished to interrogate the reporter.[153] However, the drift towards impartial reportage and 'unadulterated' news must not be exaggerated. Often claims to candour and veracity call those very qualities into question themselves: this was a trope which some contemporaries regarded as tantamount to denial, a disclaimer rather than a warranty. Shakespeare poked fun at this prevalent and sometimes fraudulent practice in *The winter's tale*, where the rogue ballad-seller Autolycus protests to his fastidious customers that one of the more fanciful pieces he peddles has 'Five justices' hands at it, and witnesses more than my pack will hold', while another is subscribed by a trustworthy midwife, one 'Mistress Taleporter'.[154] Many pamphleteers recognized this undercurrent of distrust and vigorously resisted the imputation that they forged and manufactured 'fabulous lyes'.[155] But this too was sales talk—a form of bait regularly dangled before the eyes of addicted buyers.

---

[151] This is the main flaw of Shaaber, *Forerunners*, quotation at 8, though cf. 210–11. See also Arundell Esdaile, 'Autolycus' Pack: The Ballad Journalism of the Sixteenth Century', *Quarterly Review*, 218 (1913), 372–91. For subtler accounts, see Würzbach, *Rise of the English Street Ballad*, 146–62; Clark, *Elizabethan Pamphleteers*, 89, 104, and ch. 2 *passim*.

[152] e.g. *A most miraculous, strange, and trewe ballad, of a younge man of the age of 19 yeares, who was wrongfully hangd at a town called Bon* ([*c*.1612]), printed in Clark (ed.), *Shirburn Ballads*, 159–63; John Chapman, *A most true report of the myraculous moving and sinking of a plot of ground, about nine acres, at Westram in Kent* (1596); I. R., *A most straunge, and true discourse, of the wonderfull judgement of God* (1600).

[153] Quotations from *A second and most exact relation of those sad and lamentable accidents, which happened in and about the parish church of Wydecombe* (1638), sig. A3ʳ; *Strange newes of a prodigious monster, borne in the towneship of Adlington in the parish of Standish* (1613). See also Alexander Gurth, *Most true and more admirable newes, expressing the miraculous preservation of a young maiden of the towne of Glabbich* (1597), sig. A3ʳ⁻ᵛ; *Myraculous, and monstrous, but yet, most true, and certayne discourse of a woman*, sig. A1ᵛ; *A true discourse. Declaring the damnable life and death of one Stubbe Peeter, a most wicked sorcerer* ([1590]), 14.

[154] *The Winter's Tale*, IV. iv. 263–4, 277–8, in *The Complete Works of William Shakespeare*, ed. Peter Alexander (1978), 399–400.

[155] Gurth, *Most true and more admirable newes*, sig. A3ʳ. See also *A true and most dreadfull discourse of a woman possessed with the devill . . . At Dichet in Sommersetshire* ([1584]), sig. A3ʳ; Chapman, *Most true report*, sig. B3ᵛ; *A wonder woorth the reading, or a true and faithfull relation of a woman . . . who . . . was*

The boundary between fiction and fact in these texts thus remains very vague and blurred. Literary critics have stressed their generic ambivalence, suggesting that it is in the 'undifferentiated matrix' of providential 'newes' that we must seek the origins and 'threshold' of the English novel. According to Lennard Davis and Michael McKeon, only in the late seventeenth century did this transitional discourse begin to split, permanently dividing journalism/history from the prose story with an invented plot. Prior to this 'early modern revolution in narrative epistemology', circumstantial accuracy mattered less than 'moral verisimilitude'.[156] Mere tattle and chat, even bogus and make-believe could serve this purpose as effectively as carefully corroborated evidence: as Sir Philip Sidney maintained in his *Defense of poesie* (1595), 'a feigned example hath as much force to teach as a true example'. Judged by these standards, it was quite legitimate to doctor and 'improve' the details of actual events.[157] The translator of an Italian pamphlet about a series of Turkish apparitions thought that there was a fair chance that this particular 'bulrush of noveltie' and Arabian fairy tale was '*trouata* or *bugiarda*', a trick or a fake, but advised his 'good reader' not to be too pedantic about the 'infallibilitie of the matter': 'if you cannot beleeve it as truth, yet . . . make that use of it, as if it were true'.[158]

Who, then, lay behind the publication of 'strange newes'? What were the motives of the middlemen who collaborated in its production and sale: profit, piety, or a fragile alliance of the two? Was this ephemera churned out in response to market demand; or did it embody an imaginative evangelizing strategy masterminded by ardent lay and clerical elites?

We know frustratingly little about the authors of these flimsy leaflets and sheets. The overwhelming majority are either anonymous or identified only by cryptic initials. Many appear to have been written by members of an emerging class of semi-professional rhymsters and pamphleteers. Most of the aspiring writers who flocked to the metropolis in the Elizabethan period ended up as unknown hacks, freelance journalists, and Englishers of foreign books and tracts, but some won popular acclaim and became public celebrities, among them the celebrated comedian Richard Tarlton; Thomas Churchyard, ex-soldier, impoverished gentleman, and

delivered of a prodigious and monstrous child (1617), sig. A1ᵛ, p. 5; *The wonderfull battell of starelings: fought at the citie of Corke in Ireland* (1622), sig. A3ʳ⁻ᵛ. Cf. the comments of Würzbach, *Rise of the English Street Ballad*, 47–9.

[156] Michael McKeon, *The Origins of the English Novel 1600–1740* (Baltimore, 1987), esp. ch. 1, quotation at p. 48; Lennard J. Davis, *Factual Fictions: The Origins of the English Novel* (New York, 1983), esp. chs. 3, 4, quotation at pp. 32–3. See also William Nelson, *Fact or Fiction: The Dilemma of the Renaissance Storyteller* (Cambridge, Mass., 1973), esp. chs. 1, 2, 5; Leopold Damrosch, *God's Plot and Man's Stories: Studies in the Fictional Imagination from Milton to Fielding* (Chicago, 1985). On the 'fictional' aspects of 'factual' documents, see Natalie Zemon Davis, *Fiction in the Archives: Pardon Tales and their Tellers in Sixteenth Century France* (Cambridge, 1987), esp. 3–4.

[157] Philip Sidney, *A Defence of Poetry*, ed. Jan Van Dorsten (Oxford, 1966), 36. Cf. Francis Bacon, *The Works . . .*, ed. James Spedding *et al.*, 7 vols. (1857–9), iii. 343.

[158] Ludovico Cortano, *Good newes to Christendome . . .* (1620), sigs. A3ʳ, A4ʳ, p. 39.

wit; John Taylor, the Gloucestershire-born 'water poet'; and Anthony Munday, draper, playwright, and jack-of-all-literary-trades.[159] No less deserving of note are those three successive ringleaders of London's 'scribbling crew' and ballad-mongering brigade—William Elderton, the actor with the notorious 'ale-crammed nose'; Thomas Deloney, the silkweaver of Huguenot ancestry; and Martin Parker, the acknowledged king of Grub Street before the Civil War.[160] These prolific and versatile figures wrote to suit—and exploit—the unadventurous palates of the reading public: they could as readily compose lugubrious 'goodnights' and senti-mental lyrics of thwarted lovers as grimly decipher the divine warning encoded in the anatomy of a misshapen sow, or sound the trumpet to fall to sackcloth and ashes following a devastating storm or flood. The speed and ease with which this 'rablement of botchers' could squeeze moral import from the most mundane and domestic of mishaps was notorious:

> Let but a Chapell fall, or a street be fir'd,
> A foolish lover hange himselfe for pure love,
> Or an such like accident, and before
> They are cold in their graves, some damn'd Dittie's made . . .

There are 'ten-grot-Rimers | About the Towne growne fat on these occasions', observed a character in one of Philip Massinger's plays.[161] If so much as 'a Brick-bat from a Chimney fall | When puffing Boreas nere so little bralls', complained John Davies, then 'Paper-Persecutors' promptly 'clapped' it in print 'like Butterflees' in jars. '[S]carce a cat can looke out of a gutter', objected another, 'but out starts a halfpenny Chronicler, and presently *A propper new ballet of a strange sight* is entited'.[162] These paltry, stylistically predictable pieces required little inge-nuity or literary skill, scoffed Thomas Nashe—a quart of cheap alcohol would

[159] On professional writers, see Phoebe Sheavyn, *The Literary Profession in the Elizabethan Age*, rev. J. W. Saunders (Manchester, 1967); Edwin Haviland Miller, *The Professional Writer in Elizabethan England: A Study of Nondramatic Literature* (Cambridge, Mass., 1959); and Manley, *Literature and Culture*, ch. 6. L. B. Campbell, 'Richard Tarlton and the Earthquake of 1580', *Huntington Library Quarterly*, 4 (1940–1), 293–301. Henry W. Adnitt, 'Thomas Churchyard', *Transactions of the Shropshire Archaeological and Natural History Soc.* 3 (1880), 1–68; Merrill Harvey Goldwyn, 'Notes on the Biography of Thomas Churchyard', *Review of English Studies*, NS 17 (1966), 1–15. Wallace Notestein, *Four Worthies: John Chamberlain, Anne Clifford, John Taylor, Oliver Heywood* (1956), 169–208; Bernard Capp, 'John Taylor "The Water Poet": A Cultural Amphibian in 17th-Century England', *History of European Ideas*, 11 (1989), 537–44; id., *The World of John Taylor the Water-Poet 1578–1653* (Oxford, 1994). Celeste Turner, *Anthony Mundy: An Elizabethan Man of Letters* (Berkeley and Los Angeles, 1928).

[160] See Hyder E. Rollins, 'William Elderton: Elizabethan Actor and Ballad Writer', *Studies in Philology*, 17 (1920), 199–245; id., 'Martin Parker, Ballad Monger', *Modern Philology*, 16, (1919), 113–38; and *The Works of Thomas Deloney*, ed. Francis Oscar Mann (Oxford, 1912), pp. vii–xlviii. Quotations from Gabriel Harvey, *Three Letters, and Certaine Sonnets* (1592), repr. in *The Works . . .* , ed. Alexander B. Grosart, 3 vols. (1884–5), i. 164.

[161] Gabriel Harvey, *Pierces supererogation or a new prayse of the old asse* (1593), repr. in *Works*, ed. Grosart, ii. 280; Philip Massinger, *The bond-man: an antient storie* (1624), v. iii, repr. in *The Plays and Poems . . .* , ed. Philip Edwards and Colin Gibson, 5 vols. (Oxford, 1976), i. 394–5.

[162] D[avies], *Scourge for paper-persecutors*, sig. B4ʳ; R. W., *Martin Mar-sixtus* (1591), sig. A3ᵛ.

do.[163] Experienced wordsmiths could evidently compose items to fit this conventional mould in under two hours.[164]

According to crusading clerics and men of letters who flattered themselves they had more artistic talent, this 'company of silly beetleheaded Asses' had an at best ambivalent relationship with respectable society and godly Protestantism.[165] John Earle's pen portrait of the 'pot poet' depicted a drunken sonneteer sitting in a 'Baudy-house' concocting tales of God's terrible judgements on sinners inflamed by 'a cup of Sacke'. Abraham Holland was equally contemptuous of mercenary journalists who hypocritically whipped together providential ephemera at the drop of a hat—'rooks | Whose hungry braines compile prodigious books'. Their works were among the 'fopperie' displayed on stalls in the cathedral churchyard which kindled supernatural wrath. It was 'no wonder'

> That Pauls so often hath beene strucke with Thunder:
> T'was aimed at these Shops, in which there lie
> Such a confused World of Trumpery.[166]

Nashe also suspected that most writers put on a 'cloake of zeale', 'pretence of puritie', and 'glose of godlines', 'the sum of their divinitie' consisting merely in 'twopennie Catichismes'.[167] Ministers like William Cupper made similar complaints about the presumption of lay pamphleteers who dared to assume the mantle of preachers. In his view, too 'manie private persons, tickeled with vaine-glorie, blinded with self-love, bewitched with gaine, or such lyke carnall affections . . . bolde in the pride of their wittes upon the reading of a fewe bookes, or the hearing of a fewe bookes, or the hearing of a fewe Sermons . . . thrust foorth a Pamphlette unto the worlde, never reverencing the grave censure of learned men'.[168] Such writers were shameless parasites on the ecclesiastical establishment. The Welsh magistrate William Vaughan no less vehemently condemned the 'apish spleene' of London hacks who turned out scores of 'bastard Bookes' 'to gaine themselves windy applauses and popular praises among Sathans posteritie', publishing 'the puffed leaven of their phantasies' to the dishonour of the Gospel and God.[169]

No less indignation was directed against the average printer, whose reputation was almost as unsavoury as that of the ink-slingers he employed. To George Wither, who claimed to have suffered much at the hands of these 'neede lesse

---

[163] Thomas Nashe, *Have with you to Saffron-Walden. Or Gabriell Harveys hunt is up* (1596), repr. in *Works*, ed. McKerrow, iii. 84.

[164] The author of the pamphlet *Wonder woorth the reading*, 10, claimed that 'in two houres, this had both birth, and end'.

[165] Edmund Spenser and Gabriel Harvey, *Three proper, and wittie, familiar letters* (1580), repr. in Harvey, *Works*, ed. Grosart, i. 67.

[166] Earle, *Micro-cosmographie*, 46; Holland, *Continu'd just inquisition . . . of paper-persecutors* (printed as part of D[avies], *Scourge for paper-persecutors*, 1, 7.

[167] Nashe, *Works*, ed. McKerrow, i. 21–2.

[168] William Cupper, *Certaine sermons concerning Gods late visitation in the citie of London and other parts of the land* (1592), sig. A4ᵛ.

[169] William Vaughan, *The spirit of detraction, conjured and convicted in seven circles* (1611), 105–9.

excrements' and 'vermine', the 'stationers common-wealth' was not only the 'schollers purgatory', but the bane of a Christian state.[170] News ballads and pamphlets were produced by a wide spectrum of commercially minded publishers with a sharp nose for sniffing out lucrative lines—publishers no less willing to set their presses to work reeling off moralistic tracts about recent marvels than salacious broadsides about sexual impropriety, if they stood the stiff test of market whims.[171] Providential journalism seems to have been a fiercely competitive branch of the monopolistic and increasingly specialized London book trade, nothing less than a recipe for professional success. Within twenty-four hours of any strange accident or awful catastrophe, 'doleful ditties' and 'true and wonderful' reports would be rolling off the production line.[172] Some appear to have run small factories to supply consumer demand: John Danter was only one of those who hired teams of ghost-writers to turn edifying verses on disastrous events, and to edit, translate, and patch together miscellaneous items to fill one or two signatures. Such publishers also paid freelances to rewrite accounts of outlandish occurrences acquired from correspondents in the country or abroad, draw them into 'a plain method according to the written copye', and 'bestow' a suitable exhortation upon them.[173] Others, including William Barley, evidently undertook the task of editing and revising themselves.[174] And it was normally the printer who drafted the often deceptive title-page blurb, and selected an eye-catching if somewhat irrelevant woodcut to slap on the front—this was an essential ingredient of the ephemeral publications which regular customers quickly snapped up.

Aggressive individuals devised crafty schemes for scooping their rivals, like importing and translating reports of Continental prodigies during periods when home-bred providences were in short supply,[175] and resurrecting and repackaging

---

[170] George Wither, *The schollers purgatory, discovered in the stationers common-wealth* ([1624]), 9, title-page.

[171] See Watt, *Cheap Print*, 264–5; Shaaber, *Forerunners*, ch. 11.

[172] Note the number of items registered within two days of the 'great earthquake' on 6 Apr. 1580 and the publications generated by the floods in Feb. 1607: *SR* i. 367–73, iii. 339–41. In the 1620s news books were 'set out every Saturday': Ben Jonson, *The staple of newes*, in *Ben Jonson*, ed. Herford and Simpson, vi. 325.

[173] See Miller, *Professional Writer*, 166; Shaaber, *Forerunners*, 225–35. John Wolfe is another case in point: Harry R. Hoppe, 'John Wolfe, Printer and Publisher, 1579–1601', *The Library*, 4th ser. 14 (1933), 241–88. Quotations from *1607. Lamentable newes out of Monmouthshire in Wales* ([1607]), sig. A3ʳ; Abraham Fleming, *A straunge and terrible wunder wrought very late in the parish church of Bongay* ([1577]). A good example of a 'patchwork' pamphlet is *True newes from [Mecare:] and also out of Worcestershire* ([1598]).

[174] John L. Lievsay, 'William Barley, Elizabethan Printer and Bookseller', *Studies in Bibliography*, 8 (1956), 223. See also Gerald D. Johnson, 'William Barley, "Publisher and Seller of Books", 1591–1614', *The Library*, 6th ser. 11 (1989), 10–46. See also Shaaber, *Forerunners*, 228–9.

[175] e.g. Eyriak Schlichtenberger, *A prophesie uttered by the daughter of an honest countrey man, called Adam Krause* (John Charlewood, for William Wright, 1580), a European best-seller which had already been published in Gdansk, Lübeck, Hamburg, and elsewhere. Both Edward White and John Allde soon published ballads on the subject: *SR* ii. 375, 383. John Trundle's *Anthony Painter. The blaspheming caryar*, was based on a French *canard*, which was itself derived from an Italian pamphlet. Traffic also

earlier successes to lure unwary purchasers to part with their pennies twice for a nearly identical product.[176] In a period before copyright laws, the original author was liable to find himself unceremoniously displaced: 'if one name will not make an idle booke sel,' complained the Jacobean clergyman Oliver Ormerod, 'the Stacioners will bee Godfathers to it, and . . . father it on an other man'.[177] Some tried to corner the market by securing exclusive rights to all publications on a particular topic and concurrently issuing ballads and pamphlets, with the doggerel verse often advertising the pedestrian prose.[178] Pirating was likewise far from rare[179] and shrewd budding capitalists like John Wolfe engaged in surreptitious printing in foreign vernaculars under fictitious imprints in order to evade the tight controls on the English press, defy the restrictive privileges confined to full members of the Stationers' Company, and attract interest at European book fairs.[180] These were standard tricks of the trade. Ben Jonson exposed yet more unethical practices in *The staple of newes*, where reference was made to printers who impudently 'cheat upon the Time' by 'buttering over againe' 'antiquated Pamphlets, with new dates', as 'the age doates' and 'growes forgetfull o'them'.[181] He was alluding to Nathaniel Butter, but this expense-saving ploy was particularly associated with John Trundle, arguably the most enterprising—and unprincipled—publisher of the early Stuart age. Trundle's most outrageous offence was to avail himself of the inability of his unseen London audience to check distant facts and publish an entirely apocryphal

went in the other direction: see e.g. *Discours veritable et tres-piteux, de l'inondation et debordement de mer, survenu en six diverses provinces d'Angleterre* (Paris, 1607), a trans. of *1607. A true report of certaine wonderfull overflowings of waters* ([1607]). For French *canards*, see Jean-Pierre Seguin, *L'Information en France avant le périodique: 517 canards imprimés entre 1529 et 1631* (Paris, 1964).

[176] A good example is *Gods warning to his people of England. By the great overflowing of the waters or floudes lately happened in South-Wales and many other places* (1607) (*STC* 10011), reissued and repackaged twice in the same year (*STC* 10011.2, 10011.4). All three were printed by Ralph Blower for William Barley and John Bailey.

[177] Oliver Ormerod, *A picture of a papist* (1606), sig. A4ᵛ. See also Wither, *Schollers purgatory*, 121: the average stationer made 'no scruple . . . when the impression of some pamphlet lyes upon his hands, to imprint new Titles for yt, (and so takes mens moneyes twice or thrice, for the same matter under diverse names)'.

[178] See e.g. Edward Allde's ballad *The lamentable burning of the citty of Corke (in the province of Munster in Ireland) by lightning* ([1622]) and the pamphlet printed by John Dawson for Nicholas Bourne and Thomas Archer, *A relation of the most lamentable burning of the cittie of Corke* (1622); *A most miraculous, strange, and trewe ballad, of a younge man of the age of 19 yeares, who was wrongfully hangd at a town called Bon*, printed in Clark (ed.), *Shirburn Ballads*, 159–63, and Allde's pamphlet *A true relation of Gods wonderfull mercies, in preserving one alive, which hanged five dayes*. For examples of publishers entering books and ballads simultaneously, see *SR* ii. 570; iii. 341, 492.

[179] In 1583 e.g. Richard Jones published 'a thinge beinge *A monster*' at 'his own perill' and in 1597 George Shaw infringed John Oxenbridge's rights to *Trewe and dreadfull newe tydinges of bloode and brymstone . . . with a wonderfull apparition*: *SR* ii. 428; iii. 91.

[180] Denis B. Woodfield, *Surreptitious Printing in England 1550–1640* (New York, 1973), esp. chs. 2, 4. See Wolfe's broadside about a worm found in a horse's heart, *Le vray purtrait d'un ver monstrueux qui a esté trouvé dans le coeur d'un cheval qui est mort en la ville de Londres le 17. de Mars. 1586* ([1586]). A ballad on the subject was licensed to Edward White on 1 Aug. 1586: *SR* ii. 451.

[181] Jonson, *The staple of newes*, i. v. 58–61, repr. in *Ben Jonson*, ed. Herford and Simpson, vi. 295. Cf. *Newes from the new world*, ll. 65–7 (vol. vii, p. 515). See also Shaaber, *Forerunners*, 290–2.

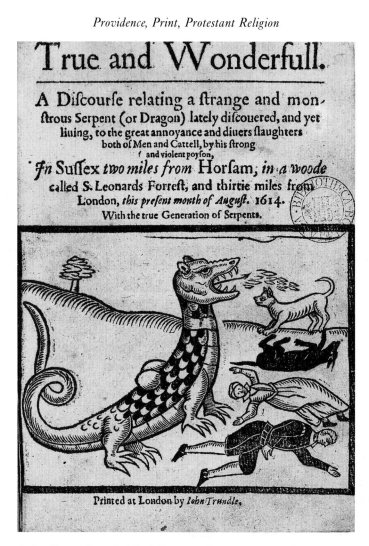

PLATE 3 A. R., *True and wonderfull. A discourse relating a strange and monstrous serpent (or dragon) lately discovered . . . in Sussex* (London, 1614), title-page. By permission of the Bodleian Library, University of Oxford. Shelfmark: 4° R 21 Art. Seld. (5).

account of a serpent 'lately discovered, and yet living' in Sussex, which he went so far as to embellish with a list of mythical eyewitnesses (Plate 3).[182] *True and wonderfull* earned him countless clever slurs and puns from his peers: one writer warned against the 'Spuriall Pamphlets', 'Broods of Barbican, Smithfield, and the

---

[182] A. R., *True and wonderfull. A discourse relating a strange and monstrous serpent (or dragon) lately discovered . . . in Sussex two miles from Horsam . . .* (1614). *Three bloudie murders* (1613) contained two recent homicidal crimes and an earlier runaway favourite, *The manner of the cruell outragious murther of*

Bridge' which were constantly 'spewed out . . . and Trundled, trolled and marshalled up and downe . . . the Streets'.[183]

There was generally a third party implicated in the production of providential news. Early modern England was a context in which news-gathering and broadcasting were still supremely oral and chirographic modes: rumour, gossip, and verbal and handwritten report remained the dominant mode of disseminating information at all social levels.[184] Many stories about inauspicious accidents and strange phenomena seem to have originated in the very spheres in which they subsequently recirculated as printed commodities. Sometimes it was a case of the local squire, vicar, or some other village worthy scrawling an account of a strange happening which had occurred in the vicinity and forwarding it to a publishing house in the City.[185] On occasion it was allegedly an executive decision on the part of 'the chiefest in the Parish', churchwardens, bailiffs, and members of the vestry.[186] Pamphlets were not uncommonly the consequence of the interception of private post—casual correspondence between relatives, business acquaintances, and friends which found its way into the public domain. Not every tract which purported to be *A copy of a letter* was actually that, but this literary contrivance did have a sound basis in historical fact.[187] Much news simply spread by word of mouth. Elizabethan and Jacobean journalists apparently crowded into alehouses,

---

W. Storre Mast. of Art, at Market Raisin committed by F. Cartwright (Oxford: Joseph Barnes, 1603). Trundle's T. I., *A miracle, of miracles* (1614) reprints Schlichtenberger, *Prophesie* (1580) and *True and most dreadfull discourse of a woman possessed with the devill* ([1584]) (see above nn. 175 and 155 respectively) with altered dates.

[183] *Lachrymae Londinenses. Or, Londons teares and lamentations, for Gods heavie visitation of the plague of pestilence* (1626), sig. B2ʳ. See also *A true report and exact description of a mighty sea-monster, or whale, cast upon Langar-shore over against Harwich in Essex* (1617), 7; Brathwait, *Whimzies*, 9; Jonson, *Newes from the new world*, ll. 49–51, repr. in *Ben Jonson*, ed. Herford and Simpson, vii. 515. See also Gerald D. Johnson, 'John Trundle and the Book-Trade 1603–1626', *Studies in Bibliography*, 39 (1986), 177–99. *True and wonderfull* was nevertheless a success: less than two weeks later Henry Gosson brought out 'a ballett of the manner' of the viper's capture and killing: *SR* iii. 553.

[184] See F. J. Levy, 'How Information Spread among the Gentry, 1550–1640', *JBS* 21 (1982), 11–34; Richard Cust, 'News and Politics in Early Seventeenth Century England', *P&P* 112 (1986), 60–90; Adam Fox, 'Aspects of Oral Culture', ch. 5, pt. 2; id., 'Rumour, News and Popular Political Opinion in Elizabethan and Early Stuart England', *HJ* 40 (1997), 597–620.

[185] *A warning-peice for ingroossers of corne; being a true relation how the divell met with one Goodman Inglebred of Bowton* ([1643]) was 'Sent in a letter to be Printed' to the bookseller William Gilbertson. The story of the appearance of the devil in Ditcheat, Somerset, was also allegedly 'sent by divers credible witnesses to be published in London': T. I., *Miracle, of miracles*. See also Shaaber, *Forerunners*, 245–50, 253–6.

[186] e.g. *Strange and true news from Westmoreland* ([1642?]); *A true relation of the birth of three monsters in the city of Namen in Flanders* (1609), sig. B1ᵛ; *A notable and prodigious historie of a mayden, who for sundry yeeres neither eateth, drinketh, nor sleepeth* (1589).

[187] Examples include P. G., *A most strange and true report of a monsterous fish, who appeared in the forme of a woman, from her waste upwards* ([1604]), a letter by P. G. from Carmarthen to 'his loving Kinsman' and 'Coosen' 'M. H. P. at his lodging in London'; *A most certaine report of a monster borne at Oteringham in Holdernesse* ([1595]), one Mr Duncalfe's reply to a written request from his neighbour M. S. in Ross 'to be certified of the truth of the shape' of the unfortunate child; John Fisher, *T[he copy of a letter]* descr[ibing the wonderful] woorke of G[od in delivering a] mayden withi[n the city of Che]ster, from an [horrible kind] of torment (1564).

anxious to glean the latest 'country intelligence', 'flienge tale', 'buzzing speech', and 'running report' from loquacious travellers, soldiers, sailors, carriers, and ferrymen.[188] They made regular expeditions to the Royal Exchange and Paul's Walk, which John Earle described as 'the eares Brothell' and the 'generall Mint of all famous lies', where 'all turne Merchants . . . and trafficke for Newes'.[189] Frantically scribbling down hearsay inevitably led to inaccuracy and there was ample room for error when it came to unravelling garbled statements made by illiterate country folk who spoke with a thick rural accent. Reporters were at pains to stress that their pamphlets derived from an impeccable source rather than irresponsible prattle and 'improbable talk', but it is clear that they made as much use of malicious innuendo as irrefutable truth.[190] There are, then, some respects in which this literature can be said to have been created as well as consumed by its readers.[191]

But it would be a mistake to suggest that the production of this type of cheap print lay exclusively in the hands of hard-nosed businessmen. Not all publishers of sensational news can be relegated to the margins of moral respectability; not all changed their religion with the prevailing wind. Robert Waldegrave and William Jones, for instance, were men of dogmatically puritan views who attached themselves to the political left wing of the presbyterian movement. Waldegrave was responsible for printing most of the scurrilous Marprelate tracts in the late 1580s and early 1590s and in the wake of the Hampton Court Conference in 1604 Jones's press illegally produced some sixteen works attacking the bishops which the Star Chamber judged to be 'scandalous', 'factious', and begetters of schism. But both also ran off ostensibly harmless ephemera about monstrous births and prophetic children as a sideline, probably in order to scrape together a living.[192]

---

[188] These are typical of the phrases used by Joseph Mede and John Chamberlain in their correspondence and by John Rous, Walter Yonge, and William Whiteway in their journals: BL Harleian MSS 389–90; *Letters of John Chamberlain*, ed. McClure; *The Diary of John Rous, Incumbent of Santon Downham, Suffolk, from 1625 to 1642*, ed. Mary Anne Everett Green, CS, 1st ser. 66 (1856); *The Diary of Walter Yonge, Esq. . . . from 1604 to 1628*, ed. George Roberts, CS, 1st ser. 41 (1848); BL Egerton MS 784 (Diary of William Whiteway 1618–34). *The last terrible tempestious windes and weather* (1613) was derived from the accounts of 'Certaine Saylers and Countrey people', sig. D1ʳ.

[189] Earle, *Micro-cosmographie*, 73.

[190] e.g. *1607. Lamentable newes out of Monmouthshire*, sigs. A3ʳ, B4ᵛ; *Second and most exact relation*, sig. A3ʳ. It was the 'manifolde untruthes' in 'sundrie written Copies' which provoked the publication of *Newes from Scotland, declaring the damnable life and death of Doctor Fian, a notable sorcerer* ([1592?]), sig. A3ʳ⁻ᵛ.

[191] See Chartier, *Cultural History*, 40; Scribner, 'Is a History of Popular Culture Possible?', 184; Watt, *Cheap Print*, 4.

[192] Waldegrave printed John Phillip's *The wonderfull worke of God shewed upon chylde, whose name is William Withers* (1581). *Wonder worth the reading* (cited in n. 155, above) came from Jones's press in 1617. He may also have been responsible for *A brief and true report of an extraordinary and memorable judgement from heaven upon one Isabell Goldinge*, entered 2 Apr. 1604: *SR* iii. 259. See the relevant entries in R. B. McKerrow (ed.), *A Dictionary of Printers and Booksellers in England, Scotland, and Ireland, and of Foreign Printers of English Books 1557–1640* (1910) and Mark H. Curtis, 'William Jones: Puritan Printer and Propagandist', *The Library*, 5th ser. 19 (1964), 38–66. The output of their presses can be traced through the printers' index in *STC*, vol. iii.

Nor should we dismiss every author as a licentious tippler. Some seem to have been devout laymen who fulfilled their religious vocation and found an outlet for their moral zeal in the press rather than the pulpit: obscure, quasi-clerical figures like John Phillip, who composed journalistic pamphlets and ballads alongside tiny devotional books in which he was styled 'student of divinitie' and even 'preacher of God's word'.[193] John Andrewes, who was described on the title-pages of his best-selling penny godlies as 'Minister and Preacher of the word at Barwicke Basset in the County of Wilts', also appears to have hovered on the edges of the ecclesiastical mainstream and may not in fact have been in holy orders: one contemporary dismissed him scornfully as a 'marketplace Theologian'.[194] William Averell, a London schoolmaster hopeful of entering the Church who wrote didactic novelettes for adolescents as well as moralizing 'newes', may be another example of this hitherto neglected species.[195]

Rather better known is Philip Stubbes, whose intemperate attack on contemporary vice in *The anatomie of abuses* (1583) has earned him an enduring reputation as a 'Puritan'. Stubbes vocally dissociated himself from the 'drunken sockets and bawdye parasits' who produced and peddled frivolous ephemera and signed himself 'Thine in the Lord'. However, Gabriel Harvey did not bracket him with 'the common pamfletters of London' merely out of spite. His output consists of an eclectic assortment of patriotic anti-popery, miniature compilations of meditations and prayers, appalling poems about divine punishments visited on blasphemers and unforgiving widows, and an immensely successful biography of his godly teenage bride. A vehement critic of presbyterian principles and staunch defender of episcopacy, Stubbes was earnest, pious, but also a man who inhabited the fringes of a burgeoning and rather disreputable literary underworld.[196] Pot-poets, popular moralists, and hot Protestant preachers cannot always be confidently distinguished.

[193] See W. W. Greg, 'John Phillip—Notes for a Bibliography', *The Library*, 3rd ser. 1 (1910), 302–28, 396–423, who corrects the editors of the *DNB*, who schizophrenically split 'John Phillips', religious author, and 'John Philip', author of doggerel verse and blackletter tracts. For his output, see *STC* 19863–19877. Other examples may be Arthur Gurney, whose only recorded writings are *Fruitfull dialogue touching the doctrine of Gods providence, and mans free will* (see n. 33, above) and *A doleful discourse and ruthfull reporte of the great spoyle and lamentable losse, by fire, in the towne of East Dearham* (1581), and Samuel Saxey, another 'Student in Divinitie', who wrote *A straunge and wonderfull example of the judgement of Almighty God, shewed upon two adulterous persons in London* ([1583]). Neither appear to have matriculated at university.

[194] Cf. Watt, *Cheap Print*, 306–11.

[195] William Averell, *A wonderfull and straunge newes, which happened in the countye of Suffolke, and Essex, . . . where it rayned wheat* (1583); *A dyall for dainty darlings, rockt in the cradle of securitie* (1584), expanded as *Foure notable histories, appyled to foure worthy examples* (1590). According to Venn, an 'Avarell' was admitted fellow commoner of Corpus Christi College, Cambridge, in 1579.

[196] *Phillip Stubbes's Anatomy of Abuses in England in Shakspere's Youth. AD 1583*, pt. 1, ed. Frederick J. Furnivall (1877–9), 171, cf. 185. For his output see *STC* 23376–23399.7. Harvey, *Pierces Supererogation*, repr. in *Works*, ed. Grosart, ii. 280; and cf. Nashe, *The anatomie of absurditie* (1589) repr. in *Works*, ed. McKerrow, i. 19–21. See my ' "A Glose of Godlines": Philip Stubbes, Elizabethan Grub Street, and the Invention of Puritanism', in Caroline Litzenberger and Susan Wabuda (eds.), *Belief and Practice in Reformation England* (Aldershot, 1998), 177–206.

On the other side of the lay–clerical divide, for poor scholars training for the ministry and ordained clergymen with inadequate benefices, providential accounts of prodigies and miracles may well have been a fairly painless method of simultaneously refining one's preaching style and supplementing a meagre income. More than one rural vicar tried his hand at composing verses and tracts about recent calamities: the West Country rector John Carpenter wrote *A sorrowful song for sinful souls* about the earthquake in April 1580 and according to Thomas Nashe, Richard Harvey, pastor of Chislehurst, was 'wont to pen Gods judgements upon such and such and one, as thicke as Water-men at Westminster bridge'.[197] Sometimes we stumble upon ministers creatively commandeering this popular genre as a proselytizing tool. Peter Lake has shown how prison chaplains like Henry Goodcole used the format of the murder pamphlet to teach distinctively Protestant lessons about the machinations of Satan and the human propensity to sin, and as we shall see, similar glosses could be applied to stories about preternatural wonders and signs.[198] Just as metropolitan wits sometimes subjected the winning formula of 'strange newes' to merciless travesty and pastiche,[199] so too did committed Protestants attempt to tap the reading public's taste for sensation and turn it to an edifying end. Just as hack writers could assume the persona of puritanical indignation against national sins, the role of mock prophets crying out for instant amendment of manners and life, so too could the godly disguise their homilies with the meretricious veneer of wonderful news, hijacking topical journalism as a vehicle for arousing a response in otherwise unapproachable sectors of English society.

There will always remain a grey area in the interpretation of these short-lived ballad sheets and quarto and octavo books. It is intractably difficult to decide whether such texts are titillation under the pretence of religious admonition or homilies camouflaged as marvellous tales; whether they are auxiliaries or sacrilegious rivals of the clerical hierarchy. Sanctimonious, smug, or sincere; tongue-in-cheek or matter-of-fact; providential news invariably sold exceedingly well. Our inability to discriminate between 'originals' and 'imitations', between escapist

---

[197] John Carpenter, *A sorrowful song for sinful souls*, an octavo tract now lost, but listed in Andrew Maunsell, *The first part of the catalogue of English printed bookes* (1595), fo. 28b and Anthony à Wood, *Athenae Oxonienses*, rev. and augmented Philip Bliss, 4 vols. (1813–20), ii. 287–8. He later published *Remember Lots wife. Two godly and fruitfull sermons verie convenient for this our time* (1588). According to Nashe, Harvey had also 'writ' for the printer Henry Bynnemen on the 'miracles of the burning of Brustar with his wench': *Works*, ed. McKerrow, iii. 84.

[198] Peter Lake, 'Deeds against Nature: Cheap Print, Protestantism and Murder in Early Seventeenth Century England', in Kevin Sharpe and id. (eds.), *Culture and Politics in Early Stuart England* (Basingstoke, 1994), 257–83; id., 'Popular Form, Puritan Content? Two Puritan Appropriations of the Murder Pamphlet from Mid-Seventeenth-Century London', in Anthony Fletcher and Peter Roberts (eds.), *Religion, Culture and Society in Early Modern Britain: Essays in Honour of Patrick Collinson* (Cambridge, 1994), 313–34; and id., 'Puritanism, Arminianism and a Shropshire Axe-Murder', *Midland History*, 15 (1990), 37–64.

[199] e.g. Thomas Nashe, *Strange newes of the intercepting certaine letters* (1592), repr. in *Works*, ed. McKerrow, i, and Nicholas Breton, *Strange newes of divers counties, never discovered till of late, by a strange pilgrime in those parts* (1622). See also Shaaber, *Forerunners*, 215.

ephemera and sectarian propaganda, in itself suggests that sermons and cheap print are not monolithic categories which can only be positioned in sharp antithesis. Equally illuminating is the amphibious nature of their producers and the degree of collusion between the altruistic and the acquisitive which close attention to their publishing history so often reveals. If we are to use the concept of cultural brokerage here, it must be with an eye to moments of coalition between the godly and the ungodly no less than between the unlearned and the elite. Such texts are telling evidence of a complex equilibrium between the forces of the market-place and those of the Church.

Certaine Sermons

All this implies that we should not be too quick to accuse Protestant ministers of unwillingness to modify their evangelizing strategy and descend to the level and cater for the cultural preferences of their semi-literate parishioners. And yet it has been the received opinion of some advocates of the 'slow' and precarious Reformation—indeed one of the cornerstones of the revisionist case—that Calvinist clerics remained largely impervious to the rational capacities and real spiritual and material needs of the majority of the populace. Sermons have sometimes been presented as the quintessence of what the English people found most repugnant about Protestantism—as intellectually demanding and morally oppressive discourses force-fed to uncooperative congregations by intransigent preachers, 'time-wasting additions to already tedious and spartan reformed services' which engendered widespread irritation, resentment, and contempt.[200]

Too much significance has been attached to the despondent appraisals made by hypercritical puritan clergymen themselves, to their perennial complaint that most of the laity regarded sermons as 'Vinegar' to their teeth and 'smoake' to their eyes, esteemed them as little as 'an egge shell' or 'a gally-halfe-penny', and wished with all their hearts 'that the Pulpitte would fall'. There has been a tendency to treat the incorrigibly pelagian figures who inhabit dialogues like George Gifford's *Countrie divinitie* and Arthur Dent's *Plaine-mans path-way to heaven* less as polemically distorted stereotypes than objective anthropological descriptions, and to assume that the articulate resistance to preaching they personify was merely the tip of an iceberg of discontent. Surely 'honest and quiet men' would be saved, say Atheos and Asenutus impatiently, 'without all this running to sermons, and pratling of the scriptures'; it was not true that none were 'indued with Gods spirite' except those who gadded three or four miles in search of the rightly preached

---

[200] See esp. Haigh, 'Puritan Evangelism', esp. 46–50, quotation at 47; id., 'Introduction', 'The Recent Historiography of the English Reformation', and 'Anti-Clericalism and the English Reformation', all in id. (ed.), *The English Reformation Revised*, esp. 24, 73–4; id., 'Church of England, the Catholics and the People', 206–9. But cf. the more balanced account in his *English Reformations*, ch. 16. Note Patrick Collinson's critical remarks in 'Shepherds, Sheepdogs, and Hirelings: The Pastoral Ministry in Post-Reformation England', in W. J. Sheils and Diana Wood (eds.), *The Ministry: Clerical and Lay*, SCH 26 (Oxford, 1989), 199–213.

Word. To Theologus and Zelotes, the grave divines who are their fictional adversaries, all this is evidence that 'popish dung doth stick stil between your teeth'.[201] Notwithstanding the efforts of a generation of 'skilfull and painefull Husbandmen', lamented William Harrison, King's Preacher at Huyton, Lancashire, most were 'like bottomless barrels, which let water runne out as fast as it is powred in', deaf adders who deliberately stopped up their ears. In the country 'publike pyping' and 'open and lascivious dancing' drew the people from their duty. In the city, thundered the Kentish schoolmaster John Stockwood in 1578, 'Wyll not a fylthye playe, wyth the blast of a trumpette, sooner call thyther a thousande, than an houres tolling of a Bell bring to the Sermon an hundred?'[202] These rhetorically conditioned statements and commonplaces have not always been regarded with the dose of healthy scepticism which they deserve. As Stuart Clark has reminded us, they ought not to be treated as 'ethnographic reports'.[203]

Excessive attention has likewise been paid to isolated incidents and colourful remarks which reached the ears of ecclesiastical officials and entered into the records of the courts: the behaviour, for example, of one exasperated Yorkshireman who pelted dispersing churchgoers with snowballs in the winter of 1615, grumbling 'it was never good world since there were so many sermons', and the sentiments expressed by James Nicholson of Asygarth, Richmondshire who declared insolently in 1633 that 'the preaching of the gospel is but bibble bubble and I care not a fart of my tail for any black coat in Wensleydale and I had rather hear a cuckoo sing'. Whenever the minister of Susan Kent's Wiltshire parish mounted the pulpit, she knew that she was about to be bombarded with such a lot of irrelevant nonsense that 'I am weary to hear it and I can then sit down in my seat and take a good nap'.[204] Such vocal outbursts have repeatedly been cited in support of claims about the essential unpopularity of a religion which swept away familiar images and symbols and elevated the sermon on a pedestal.

There can be no doubt that preaching occupied a unique position in the Protestant economy of salvation: the spoken Word was believed to be the supreme engine of theological conversion, the 'ordinary' instrument and mechanism by which the Lord unfolded the intrinsic mystery of saving faith.[205] Investing it with

---

[201] Dent, *Plaine mans path-way*, 25–67, 137, 151; Gifford, *A briefe discourse of certaine pointes of the religion, which is among the common sort of Christians, which may be termed the countrie divinitie* (1583 edn.), fos. 26^{r-v}, 28^r.

[202] William Harrison, *The difference of hearers. Or an exposition of the parable of the sower* (1614), sigs. A4^v–5^r, p. 200, sigs. A6^r–7^v respectively; John Stockwood, *A sermon preached at Paules Crosse on Barthelmew day* (1578), 23–4. See James Bisse, *Two sermons preached, the one at Paules Crosse the eight of Januarie 1580* (1581), sig. A8^r.

[203] Clark, *Thinking with Demons*, 511.

[204] Cited in, respectively, M. Palliser, *Tudor York* (Oxford, 1979), 259; Philip Tyler, 'The Church Courts at York and Witchcraft Prosecutions 1567–1640', *Northern History*, 4 (1969), 102 n; Ingram, *Church Courts*, 121.

[205] For some statements to this effect, see Miles Mosse, *Justifying and saving faith distinguished from the faith of the devils* (Cambridge, 1614), sig. ¶¶2^r; Thomas Bell, *Thomas Bels motives: concerning Romish faith and religion* (Cambridge, 1593), sig. ¶¶3^r.

almost sacramental efficacy, Calvinists made the sermon the critical climax and focus of liturgical worship, the very hinge upon which the post-Reformation church service hung.[206] Without 'prophecy', declared the presbyterian leader Thomas Cartwright gravely, 'the kingdome off heaven ys as yt were locked': 'bare reading' from the Bible and Homilies was useless in the absence of 'living oracles' of the Logos.[207] Conformist divines like Richard Hooker condemned this 'superstitious conceipt . . . concerning Sermons', but therein lay the basis of the puritan preoccupation with 'settling' and maintaining a learned and university-trained preaching ministry.[208]

Nor can it be denied that most Protestant ministers selected rigorously diagrammatic structures for their pulpit discourses, shunning linguistic craft and metaphysical conceit in favour of an austere and sometimes rather arid Ramist division of doctrine, reason, and application or use.[209] Technical manuals did urge the clergy to strip their texts of 'ridiculous' tales and to avoid histrionic mannerisms; experts like William Perkins insisted that it was 'not meete, convenient, or laudable for men to move occasion of laughter in sermons'.[210] As a matter of principle, the godly preacher eschewed 'painted eloquence' and refrained from trimming his 'plain-style' sermons with the 'ornaments and laces of Ægypt' and sweetening them with 'the Frankincense and myrrhe of the Christian Synagogue'.[211] He stressed that he stood not as a 'smoothing Rhetorician' intent on pleasing the 'vayne Humour of Curious eares' and 'worldly wittes', but as the commissioned herald of his Maker, the envoy of a bitter penitential message dictated by the deity.[212] It followed logically that sacred awe was accorded to actual utterance, to the physical act of expounding Holy Writ.

This may explain why so many Elizabethan and early Stuart clergymen had such mixed feelings about committing their sermons to the confining straitjacket of print. It has sometimes been argued that the Reformation rode boldly on the back of the late medieval invention of movable type, that its apostles exploited

---

[206] See Horton Davies, *Worship and Theology in England from Cranmer to Hooker 1534–1603* (Princeton, 1970), ch. 8, esp. 294–7; Paul Seaver, *The Puritan Lectureships: The Politics of Religious Dissent, 1560–1662* (Stanford, Calif., 1970), 15–22.

[207] Thomas Cartwright, *The second replie . . . agaynst Maister Doctor Whitgiftes second answer touching the churche discipline* ([Heidelberg], 1575), fos. 380ʳ, 381ʳ, cf. fos. 383ʳ, 393ʳ, and 373ʳ–402ᵛ *passim*.

[208] Richard Hooker, *Of the lawes of ecclesiastical politie* ([1593]), bk. v, §21–2, esp. p. 43.

[209] On 'plain style' preaching, see W. Fraser Mitchell, *English Pulpit Oratory from Andrewes to Tillotson: A Study of its Literary Aspects* (1932), ch. 4; J. W. Blench, *Preaching in England in the Late Fifteenth and Sixteenth Centuries: A Study of English Sermons 1450–c.1600* (Oxford, 1964), 168–78; John F. Wilson, *Pulpit in Parliament: Puritanism during the English Civil Wars 1640–1648* (Princeton, 1969), esp. 139–46; Barbara Kiefer Lewalski, *Protestant Poetics and the Seventeenth-Century Religious Lyric* (Princeton, 1979), 214–31.

[210] Perkins, *The arte of prophecying*, in *Workes*, ii. 759; id., *The whole treatise of the cases of conscience* (Cambridge, 1608 edn.), 117; Richard Bernard, *The faithfull shepheard amended and enlarged* (1609 edn.), 89.

[211] Bernard, *Faithfull shepheard*, 19; Robert Abbot, *Bee thankfull London and her sisters; or, a sermon of thankfulnesse* (1626), sig. A2ᵛ. See also Perkins, *Arte of prophecying*, in *Workes*, ii. 759.

[212] Webbe, *Gods controversie*, 13; John Stockwood, *A very fruiteful sermon preched at Paules Crosse the tenth of May last* (1579), fo. 52ʳ; Carpenter, *Remember Lots wife*, sig. A2ʳ.

Gutenberg's device as a God-given gift, attaching such exalted importance to reading as a conduit to divine grace that they virtually made literacy a precondition for membership of the predestinate elite.[213] In fact, early modern Protestants were often deeply suspicious of this newfangled medium, and, at least initially, rather reluctant to mobilize it as a means of accomplishing the Church's mission on earth. They dismissed it as a poor substitute for oral performance: print could never adequately reproduce the kinetic, ravishing, and 'patheticall' effect of the preacher's animated voice or '*Viva vox*'.[214] To exchange one's tongue for a quill, 'laying aside the gesture and countenance of a livinge man', said John King, later bishop of London, was to bury one's words in a coffin or sarcophagus, to petrify them in 'a dead letter of lesse effectuall perswasion'. '[A] Sermon once delivered, goeth afterward to the Presse as to execution', reflected Isaac Bargrave, chaplain to Prince Charles and minister of a large Westminster parish.[215] It was but a feeble shadow of the original; to those who had heard it, declared Thomas Jackson of Canterbury, it was as superfluous as 'Lettise twice sod'.[216] John Barlow, rector of Godalming, Surrey, feared that ignorant and ill-informed lay people might use this as an excuse to absent themselves from Common Prayer and 'sit at home, with a printed paper, dreaming that will suffice to get faith for salvation'.[217]

Accordingly, a large contingent of ministers claimed that they came unwillingly and even against their express wishes into print. Some protested their arms had been twisted by overbearing patrons,[218] or that they had been categorically commanded by the ecclesiastical powers-that-be—preachers ordered down to London to perform at Paul's Cross, tacitly as spokesmen for the status quo, could hardly say no.[219] It was also a polite and self-deprecating convention to insist that the 'importunity' and 'sollicitation' of ardent and 'well-affected' listeners had compelled the author to translate his 'rude and raw meditations', modestly intended for a particular audience, into a written text suitable for public dissemination by

---

[213] See e.g. A. G. Dickens, *Reformation and Society in Sixteenth Century Europe* (New York, 1968), 51; Eisenstein, *Printing Press*, esp. i. 303–11, but cf. 374. This is also implicit in Haigh, 'Introduction', in id. (ed.), *English Reformation Revised*, 24. But note the caveats of Richard Gawthrop and Gerald Strauss, 'Protestantism and Literacy in Early Modern Germany', *P&P* 104 (1984), 31–55.

[214] John Lawrence, *A golden trumpet to rowse up a drowsie magistrate* (1624), sig. A4^{r-v}; Mosse, *Justifying and saving faith*, sig. ¶¶2^r. Many of the issues discussed in this and the following paragraphs are examined in D. F. McKenzie, 'Speech-Manuscript-Print', *Library Chronicle of the University of Texas at Austin*, 20 (1990), 87–109. Arnold Hunt's Cambridge PhD thesis, 'The Art of Hearing: English Preachers and their Audiences, 1590–1640' (1998), is the most comprehensive and illuminating discussion of these matters to date.

[215] John King, *Lectures upon Jonas, delivered at Yorke in the yeare of our lorde 1594* (Oxford, 1599), sig. *4^r; Isaac Bargrave, *A sermon preached before the honorable assembly of knights, cittizens, and burgesses, of the lower house of parliament* (1624), sig. A3^{r-v}.

[216] Jackson, *Londons new-yeeres gift*, sig. A2^v. See also Thomas Gataker, *Two sermons: tending to direction for Christian cariage, both in afflictions incumbent, and in judgements imminent* (1623), sig. A3^{r-v}.

[217] John Barlow, *Hierons last fare-well* (1618), sig. A4^r.

[218] e.g. Thomas Baughe, *A summons to judgement* (1614), sig. A3^v; William Hampton, *A proclamation of warre from the lord of hosts, or Englands warning by Israels ruine* (1627), sig. A2^v.

[219] e.g. Robert Johnson, *Davids teacher, or the true teacher of the right-way to heaven* (1609), unpaginated dedication; Jackson, *Londons new-yeeres gift*, title-page.

the press.[220] The 'poore Infant' Elias Petley delivered at Paul's Cross in Michaelmas 1622 was destined to have but a brief 'breathing', except that 'when 'twas gon', the clamorous requests of 'som Shunemites' 'would have it fetcht' forth and resuscitated.[221] As Robert Johnson admitted, by the early Jacobean period such apologetic overtures were hackneyed and 'overworne', but that does not necessarily mean that they were hollow and insincere.[222] Preachers like Richard Stock and George Webbe were compelled to send off their own manuscripts in order to forestall the unauthorized publication of their compositions in some 'more indigested manner', out of 'unperfect copies' taken down in shorthand by impatient enthusiasts and fans.[223] John Preston, Master of Emmanuel College, Cambridge, was so anxious that his sermons should not come forth into the world as 'vagabonds' that he took pains on his deathbed to see that they were properly 'setled & provided for'. And only at length and 'with much ado' did Samuel Ward of Ipswich consent to let a trusted colleague undertake the 'Midwive-like office' of editor of his *Balme for Gilead* (1617).[224] These printed texts seem to have been intended chiefly for the benefit of those present when they were initally preached, 'to bee and remayne to and for the use of them that had before tasted of the same'.[225]

These reservations and misgivings were counterbalanced by awareness of the distinct advantages print possessed over evanescent speech. Clerics who overcame their inhibitions conceded, sometimes rather grudgingly, that publishing, for all its limitations, should still be accounted 'a kinde of Preaching'. Typography might lack the lustre and vivacity of oratory, but it was more permanent, of 'longer continuance' and 'larger extent'. It could carry the minister's injunctions to a much wider, invisible auditory, and this was particularly important in the context of a national emergency—no medium could be ignored as an organ for spreading the message that only collective repentance and heartfelt prayer would stave off further manifestations of God's just anger and wrath.[226] Sermons were 'but nine dayes wonder', said William Jackson, term lecturer at Whittington College in London;

---

[220] This pretext for printing is so ubiquitous that it seems invidious to select examples, but see Sampson Price, *Ephesus warning before her woe* (1616), sig. A2ʳ; Thedore Hering, *The triumph of the church over water and fire* (1625), sig. A4ʳ; John Jones, *Londons looking backe to Jerusalem, or Gods judgements upon others, are to be observed by us* (1633), 3; Abraham Gibson, *The lands mourning, for vaine swearing: or the downe-fall of oathes* (1613), sig. A3ᵛ; William Procter, *The watchman warning* (1625), sig. A3ʳ.

[221] Elias Petley, *The royal receipt: or, Hezekiahs physicke* (1623), sig. A2ʳ⁻ᵛ. The 'shunemites' to which he refers were probably the pious hostesses who served him during his stay in the capital.

[222] Johnson, *Davids teacher*, unpaginated dedication.

[223] Webbe, *Gods controversie*, sigs. A3ᵛ–4ʳ; Richard Stock, *A sermon preached at Paules Crosse, the second of November. 1606* (1609), sig. *8ʳ.

[224] Thomas Ball, *The Life of the Renowned Doctor Preston . . .*, ed. E. W. Harcourt (Oxford, 1885), 173; Ward, *Balme from Gilead to recover coscience*, ed. Thomas Gataker (1617), sigs. A3ʳ–5ᵛ.

[225] Carpenter, *Remember Lots wife*, sig. A3ᵛ. Cf. Gabriel Price, *The laver of the heart; or bath of sanctification* (1616), sig. A7ʳ; Webbe, *Gods controversie*, sig. A6ᵛ.

[226] Thomas Jackson, *Judah must into captivitie. Six sermons on Jerem. 7. 16* (1622), sig. A1ʳ⁻ᵛ. Cf. Robert Bedingfield, *A sermon preached at Pauls Crosse the 24. of October. 1624* (1625), sig. ¶2ᵛ; Daniel Featley, *Clavis mystica* (1636), sig. *2ᵛ.

precious labours, 'fit for the time' and vital for the public good, should not be suffered to perish at birth and to 'have the funerall so soone'.[227] It was 'an holy desire that the eye may second the eare in any thing that may helpe the soule', remarked Joseph Hall, 'and we, that are fishers of men, should be wanting to our selves, if we had not baits for both those sences'.[228] Oral discourses, observed Samuel Ward, were 'as showers of Rayne that water for the instant', while books were 'Snow that lyes longer on the earth'.[229] Print could also preserve 'monuments' and 'parcellreliques' of 'painefull' ministers who had passed away: failure to publish them posthumously was equivalent to 'defrauding the store-house of Religion'.[230]

Puritan enthusiasm for the press as an alternative proselytizing tool grew less half-hearted as the seventeenth century progressed. This was only partly due to Laudian and later persecution, which drove banished and silenced preachers to divert their didactic and prophetic energies into the production of practical divinity instead. 'We are now willing to make some worke for the Presse because we have no imployment in the Pulpit', professed John Dod and Robert Cleaver in the preface to a biblical commentary published in 1606, after both men had been deprived of their Oxfordshire livings for liturgical nonconformity. Encouraging their molested brethren to copy them, they declared 'that as their faithfull labours were formerly like pure fountaines, which did only refresh their particular congregations: so now, by meanes of printing, they may be made like great and comfortable rivers, to water the whole Land'. Dr Sebastian Benefield hoped to 'redeeme the time past' 'by my writing by my pen'—to compensate for the decade and a half in which his academic post had hindered him from the vital task of teaching.[231] And in his *Christian directory* published in 1673 Richard Baxter insisted that while 'Vocal preaching' had 'the preheminence in moving the affections', books were better in other respects. They were 'domestick, present, constant, judicious, pertinent, yea, and powerfull'; they could be read 'at every hour and day', 'kept at a smaller charge than Preachers', and help make up for the shortcomings of 'ignorant, ungodly or dull' ministers.[232] As literacy penetrated to the lowest seam of lay society, active pastors began to exploit ever more systematically and imaginatively popular deference to the authority and delight in the novelty of the printed word.

It remains probable that the body of printed sermons that survives is a tiny and unrepresentative specimen of the true range and character of preaching available

---

[227] William Jackson, *The celestiall husbandrie: or, the tillage of the soule* (1616), sig. *2ʳ.

[228] J[oseph] H[all], *An holy pangyrick* (1613), sig. A3ᵛ.

[229] Samuel Ward, *The happinesse of practice* (1621), sig. A3ʳ.

[230] Edward Gee, *Two sermons. One, the surse and crime of Meroz . . . The other, a sermon of patience* (1620), sig. A2ʳ⁻ᵛ; John Rainolds, *The prophecie of Obadiah opened and applyed in sundry learned and gracious sermons preached at All-Hallowes and St. Maries in Oxford*, ed. William Hinde (1613), sigs. A2ᵛ–3ʳ. Cf. Matthias Milwarde's unpaginated epistle to John Milwarde, *Jacobs great day of trouble, and deliverance* (1610); Gataker, *Two sermons*, sigs. A3ᵛ–4ʳ.

[231] John Dod and Robert Cleaver, *A plaine and familiar exposition of the ninth and tenth chapters of the Proverbs of Salomon* (1612), sig. A3ʳ; Benefield, *Commentary . . . upon . . . Amos*, sig. ¶4ʳ.

[232] Richard Baxter, *A Christian directory: or, a summ of practical theologie, and cases of conscience* (1673), 60.

in Elizabethan and early Stuart England. We can only speculate how many over-worked clergymen could never spare time for the arduous task of reconstructing their texts for the press—busy curates limping under their parochial responsibilities, high-ranking prelates and divines like Archbishop Tobie Matthew of York who led exhausting lives as itinerant circuit preachers in their dioceses on the side.[233] It is possible that many ministers shared the convictions of Thomas Pestell, who published a visitation sermon in 1630 following 'vehement entreaties' by the mayor and aldermen of Leicester. In the preface he confessed that 'in my youth, among other weaknesses, I yeelded to the tentation of printing Sermons,' but 'since I grew both an elder man, and a poore retired Vicar in an obscure angle of the Countrey, I resolv'd against any more such adventures' and set them aside as ado-lescent vanities. William Attersoll, parson of Isfield, Sussex, also gave over the ancillary occupation of writing to devote himself wholly to 'the more necessary duty' of preaching.[234] Others with ample opportunity to publish their utterances may have disapproved so strongly of the upstart medium of print that they vowed never to meddle with it, or, conscious of the 'stigma' which this intimidating new technology conferred, preferred to circulate them scribally, in manuscript, instead.[235]

The scores of sermons framed for rustic villagers and country congregations are especially elusive. Only rarely did these unassuming homilies on the lectionary reach the ears of any other than their 'rude' original auditory.[236] The degree of learned sophistication presupposed by many published discourses, their margins weighed down with erudite Latin annotations, is probably entirely atypical of the intellectual level at which most parochial preaching was pitched. Many of the godly preachers immortalized in Samuel Clarke's influential collections of *Lives* were renowned for 'stooping to the meanest capacity' and for avoiding 'hard and un-usuall English' and phrases that were 'too spruce and trim'. The Gloucestershire rector Richard Capel even spoke to the 'poor Country people in their own proper dialect, so as they could not but even see, and feel, and find out God'.[237] The ele-mentary catechetical instruction and basic drilling in Protestant tenets which must have formed the backbone of the average pastor's output was unsuitable for public

[233] Collinson, *Religion of Protestants*, 48–9 and Nicholas W. S. Cranfield, ' "Must the Fire Either Goe Out, or Become all Wildfire?": A Collection of Oxford Sermons 1634–1638', *Bodleian Library Record*, 13 (1989), 123.

[234] Thomas Pestell, *Gods visitation: in a sermon preached at Leicester, at an ordinary visitation* (1630), sig. A2r–v; William Attersoll, *Three treatises. 1. The conversion of Nineveh. 2. Gods trumpet sounding the alarum. 3. Physicke against famine* (1632), unpaginated dedication.

[235] On this subject see J. W. Saunders, 'The Stigma of Print: A Note on the Social Bases of Tudor Poetry', *Essays in Criticism*, 1 (1951), 139–64; Harold Love, 'Manuscript versus Print in the Transmission of English Literature, 1600–1700', *Bibliographical Soc. of Australia and New Zealand Bulletin*, 9 (1985), 95–107; id., 'Scribal Publication in Seventeenth-Century England', *Transactions of the Cambridge Bibliographical Soc.* 9 (1987), 130–54; id., *Scribal Publication in Seventeenth Century England* (Oxford, 1993); McKenzie, 'Speech-Manuscript-Print', esp. 94–6.

[236] An interesting exception is H[ugh] R[oberts], *A godly and necessary sermon anainst fleshly lustes; and against certaine mischievous May-games*, adjoined to his *The day of hearing . . .* (Oxford, 1600).

[237] Samuel Clarke, *The lives of thirty two English divines* (1677 edn.), 176, 331, 305.

consumption: such slim pickings could hardly be expected to sell to prospective purchasers well advanced in the faith. The sermon literature which was printed clearly constituted a higher stratum, a second tier.[238] Much of it grew out of combination lectures and voluntary 'exercises';[239] much was the natural by-product of semi-official preaching on civil, political, and providential occasions.[240] What appeared in print is hardly a reliable guide to what was ordinarily dished up in the parishes, but lazy, less talented, and 'rawe' young curates not infrequently adopted these 'showpiece' sermons as models, cribbing their Sunday disquisitions from the canonical works of renowned divines. According to William Cupper, such books enabled 'divers idle and truantly Preachers' to 'vaunt themselves with other mens feathers'.[241]

Uprooted from their original contexts and imprisoned in a constraining cage of characters, individual sermons were robbed of much of their identity, especially when they became incorporated in bulky omnibus volumes. Clearly the literary creation designed for devout reading only vaguely approximates to the verbally delivered discourse, a fact which many older scholars intent on taxonomic analysis of preaching styles and rhetorical techniques were prone to overlook.[242] Although textbooks like Richard Bernard's *The faithfull shepheard* expostulated against 'the vanitie of preaching extempore', they also reprehended reading aloud from elaborately prepared manuscripts. Ministers were urged to learn their sermons by heart, recalling them only with the aid of sketchy summaries and headings.[243] Far from being facsimiles of the speaker's address, printed texts stood at several steps remove from what the congregation had actually heard. If the author had retained the cursory notes he had carried into church, it might be reasonably easy to reassemble the sermon; if not, he would have to rely entirely on his fallible memory.[244] George Webbe endeavoured to 'set forth' his 'with no other coat,

---

[238] See Harry S. Stout, *The New England Soul: Preaching and Religious Culture in Colonial New England* (New York, 1986), Cf. D. L. D'Avray's discussion of 12th-cent. French model sermon collections: *The Preaching of the Friars: Sermons Diffused from Paris before 1300* (Oxford, 1985), esp. 6, 65, 82.

[239] See Patrick Collinson, 'Lectures by Combination: Structures and Characteristics of Church Life in 17th-Century England', in *Godly People: Essays on English Protestantism and Puritanism* (1983), 495–6.

[240] Notably Paul's Cross sermons, on which see Millar Maclure, *The Paul's Cross Sermons 1534–1642*, University of Toronto Dept. of English Studies and Texts, 6 (Toronto, 1958).

[241] Cupper, *Certaine sermons*, sig. A4ʳ. See also John Earle's depiction of 'A young rawe Preacher' in *Micro-cosmographie*, 22: 'His Collections of Studie, are the notes of Sermons, which taken up at St Maries [Oxford] hee utters in the Country. And if he write brachigraphy, his stocke is so much the better.'

[242] e.g. Blench, *Preaching in England*; Horton Davies, *Worship and Theology . . . 1534–1603*, chs. 6, 8. Alan Fagan Herr, *The Elizabethan Sermon: A Survey and a Bibliography* (Philadelphia, 1940), esp. chs. 6–7, and Mitchell, *English Pulpit Oratory* are more sensitive to the gap between sermon and printed text, but the latter still takes the notion of preaching 'schools' as axiomatic. Some of the issues discussed in this paragraph are addressed by H. S. Bennett in *English Books and Readers 1558–1603* (Cambridge, 1965), 150–6, and *English Books and Readers 1603–1640* (Cambridge, 1970), 115–17.

[243] Bernard, *Faithfull shepheard*, 12, 82–5; Perkins, *Arte of prophecying*, in *Workes*, ii. 758.

[244] See e.g. Thomas Gataker, *A sparke toward the kindling of sorrow for Sion* (1621), sig. A4ʳ; Thomas Bilson, *The effect of certaine sermons touching the full redemption of mankind* (1599), sigs. A4ᵛ–B1ʳ. LRO DP 353 ('Severall Sermons upon divers occasions by Christopher Hudson Preacher of Gods wo[rd] at

then wherewith it was clothed in the pulpit, without addition or detraction . . . in every circumstance thereof, as neare as my pen could be the register to my tongue'. But few preachers could resist the impulse to revise, alter, and expand, or to rein-sert passages they had been obliged to omit as the sand in the hourglass slipped inexorably away.[245] George Benson of New College, Oxford, restored to mint con-dition a sermon which had come 'mangled' and 'maimed' to the ear, observing 'we cannot digest our matters by the clocke'. Robert Wakeman introduced material that had been 'cut off by the unseasonablenes of the weather, and shortnesse of the time' on the day he preached at the open air cross under the eaves of St Paul's Cathedral in June 1602. Michael Wigmore, a fellow of Oriel, meanwhile, had the text of his *The way of flesh* mutilated by the censor, who 'exempted' some sections as unacceptably choleric and 'bitter'.[246] Some considered it appropriate to polish their prose and garb their discourses in a more gracious exterior dress, but others adjusted them in the opposite direction, making them 'more plaine in printing' than they were in the preaching, 'to the end' they 'might not be obscure to any'.[247] Manuscripts sent to press not by the prophet but his dedicated colleagues or lay devotees often derived from notes 'taken from the mouth' of the preacher accord-ing to the ingenious stenographic system of 'characterie' or 'brachygraphie' for-malized by Dr Timothy Bright in 1588.[248] The Lincolnshire curate Francis Marbury, for instance, yielded to the publication of 'cursorie notes' taken from his 'swift speech' 'without anie reforming of mine own', because he had no leisure to look over them. Even though such texts were 'not altogether verbatim the same' as the actual peroration, they may have come closer to the sermon as preached than those produced by the orator himself, boasting an accuracy which their progen-itors often did 'greatly marvell thereat'.[249]

These forms of mediation and collaboration suggest that the enterprise of pub-lishing sermons by no means involved all 'push' and no 'pull'. The market for such

Preston in Lancashire. 1641') seems to be either a MS prepared for the press or a transcription of a lost printed text.

[245] Webbe, *Gods controversie*, sig. A5ʳ. Cf. Daniel Donne, *A sub-poena from the star chamber of heaven* (1623), unpaginated epistle 'To the Reader'. pp. 1–52 was preached 'word for word, as it is Printed'; the rest was an enlargement of 'a briefe Paraphrasticall Explication of the Particulars that remained'.

[246] George Benson, *A sermon preached at Paules Crosse the seaventh of May, M.DC.IX.* (1609), sig. A2ʳ⁻ᵛ; Robert Wakeman, *Jonahs sermon and Ninevehs repentance* (Oxford, 1603), sig. ¶2ᵛ; Michael Wigmore, *The way of flesh* (1619), sig. A3ʳ.

[247] See e.g. Lawrence, *Golden trumpet*, sig. a1ʳ⁻ᵛ; Gibson, *Lands mourning*, sig. A4ʳ.

[248] University of London Library, Senate House, Carlton MSS Box 17/8 ('Certaine sermons godley & learnedley preached by Mr Nicholas Felton Doctor of Divinitie and taken from his mouth by ——'). The title-page of this MS is set up like a printed page and includes 'London Anno Domini 1606'. Timothy Bright, *Characterie. An arte of shorte, swifte, and secrete writing by character* (1588). See also Edmond Willis, *An abbreviation of writing by character* (1618).

[249] Francis Marbury, *Notes on the doctrine of repentance. Delivered . . . by way of catechising* (1602), sig. A2ʳ⁻ᵛ; Thomas Gataker's editorial remarks in Ward, *Balme from Gilead*, sig. A4ʳ; Thomas Hopkins, *Two godlie and profitable sermons earnestly enveying against the sinnes of this land in generall, and in particular, against the sinnes of this citie of London* (1611), sig. A2ᵛ. The sermons of John Preston, Richard Sibbes, and Henry Smith are good examples of printed texts which derived from notes taken by devoted auditors.

items was apparently glutted: there was so great a surfeit, observed Robert Burton and Thomas Gataker, 'that whole teemes of Oxen cannot drawe them' and 'even Printers themselves complaine, that the Presse is oppressed with them'. There were more abroad in the world, admitted Dr Sebastian Benefield, 'then we can well use'.[250] Yet this does not seem to have stopped city stationers from launching forth more: as statistical analysis of imprints in this period reveals, the thirst of English readers for religious books was almost unquenchable.[251] The very fact that unscrupulous publishers like John Wolfe were prepared to bypass obtaining the minister's consent and print manuscripts procured by underhand methods confirms that sermons were a going concern.[252] Preachers and printers made use of imaginative marketing techniques. Some adorned their texts with titles as 'phantasticall' as those that advertised 'strange newes', calculated to catch the eye of idle buyers loitering around London bookstalls, who 'will tarry & stand gasing like silly passengers, at an Anticke picture in a painters shoppe that will not looke at a judicious piece', and bring them to 'the better beholding and consideration of the matter contained'. Samuel Ward illustrated his sermons with intriguing emblems of his own invention.[253]

Nor was it unusual for particular favourites to run through multiple editions. Arthur Dent's *Sermon of repentaunce* preached at Lee in Essex was reprinted thirty-seven times between 1582 and 1638, as well as translated into Welsh. More than one publisher risked infringing the rights of his rivals in order to acquire a slice of the profits. Dent's *Platforme, made for the proofe of Gods providence* was only slightly less successful: seven impressions dating between 1608 and 1629 survive. William Perkins's exposition of the prophet Zephaniah was republished every year from 1604 to 1609.[254]

These best-sellers are excellent examples of sermons issued in tiny blackletter formats, unbound booklets cheap enough to find a place in the travelling chapman and pedlar's pack. High quality folio editions of an author's collected works were obviously beyond the reach of humble villagers, but not so some small quartos and maybe most octavos. In 1585, Roger Ward's Shrewsbury bookshop stocked nearly two hundred 'sticht' sermons priced at between $2\frac{1}{2}d$. and $3d$.; Dent's popular trea-

---

[250] Burton, *Anatomy of melancholy*, 11; Gataker's editorial pref. to Ward, *Balme from Gilead*, sig. A4ʳ; Benefield, *Commentary . . . upon . . . Amos*, sig. ¶3ʳ⁻ᵛ.

[251] See Edith L. Klotz, 'A Subject Analysis of English Imprints for Every Tenth Year from 1480 to 1640', *Huntington Library Quarterly*, 1 (1938), 418. Klotz's figures suggest that 44% of publications were on 'religion or philosophy'. Herr estimates that in the reign of Elizabeth 1,000 sermons were printed in 500 separate publications: *Elizabethan Sermon*, 27, 117. Bennett, *English Books and Readers 1603–1640*, 107–9, estimates 2,000 for the early Stuart period.

[252] See Herr, *Elizabethan Sermon*, 70–1; Bennett, *English Books and Readers 1603–1640*, ch. 4.

[253] Burton, *Anatomy of melancholy*, 5; John Stockwood, *A Bartholomew fairing for parents, to bestow upon their sonnes and daughters, and for one friend to give unto another* (1589), sig. A3ʳ. *Woe to drunkards* (1622) provides a good example of Ward's emblematic title-pages.

[254] Arthur Dent, *A sermon of repentaunce* (1583 edn.), *STC* 6649.5–6670. The Welsh trans. is *STC* 6671. Roger Ward, Nathaniel Butter, and Edward Wright were all fined for illegally printing copies. Dent, *Platforme* (*STC* 6646.7–6649.3). William Perkins, *A faithfull and plaine exposition upon the two first verses of the second chapter of Zephaniah* (1604), *STC* 19706.5–19708.

tise on repentance was valued at just twopence in an inventory from York dated 1616.[255] The seventeenth-century owner of one extant copy of F. S.'s *Jerusalems fall, Englands warning* (1617) paid 4*d.* for this prophetic lecture published the following year—costly for a cottage labourer or craftsman who earned from 8*d.* to 12*d.* a day, but perhaps not way out of range.[256] Some of the popular 'penny godlies' in which the resourceful ballad partners began to specialize in the 1620s likewise began life in the pulpit. Printing sermons obviously made sound business sense: they were a financially viable sector of a flourishing industry.[257]

If preaching in print won the approval of readers across the social spectrum, was preaching in practice so very objectionable to the vast bulk of the English people? We need to balance our knowledge that sermons grated sharply on the nerves of some with the recognition that to others they were like an addictive and intoxicating drug. The vogue for voluntary memorization and repetition of the substance and 'heads' of the speaker's address and the obsession of well-disposed auditors with jotting them down in their pocket diaries and notebooks both suggest as much.[258] Account must be taken of those who petitioned on behalf of muzzled ministers suspended from their posts, alleging their loss was to the immense 'daunger and unspeakable griefe' of those who had formerly enjoyed the 'singuler Commodity' of their godly sermons.[259] Neither should we ignore the 'great companies' who flocked '(as Doves to the windows)' to isolated hamlets to hear famous preachers like Julines Herring, pastor of Calke in Derbyshire.[260] Those who made demonstrative progresses in search of spiritual refreshment from pulpits further afield, opting for lectures, fast days, prophesyings, and semi-separated conventicles rather than the ersatz, second-rate homilies on offer in their own parishes may well have belonged to an ostracized 'puritan' minority whose eccentric practices earned them the odium and 'Derision of the Vulgar Rabble'.[261] But the religious subculture of sermon-gadding was hardly less distinctive than the irreligious

[255] See Alexander Rodger, 'Roger Ward's Shrewsbury Stock: An Inventory of 1585', *The Library*, 5th ser. 13 (1958), 259; Robert Davies, *A Memoir of the York Press, with Notices of Authors, Printers, and Stationers, in the Sixteenth, Seventeenth, and Eighteenth Centuries* (1868), 363. Eleven copies of Edmund Bunny's *A necessarie admonition out of the prophet Joël* (1588), were valued at 2*s.* (i.e. around 2¼*d.* each). See also Johnson, 'Notes on English Retail Book-Prices', 83–113.

[256] F. S., *Jerusalems fall, Englands warning* (1617), title-page. For wages, see Henry Phelps Brown and Sheila V. Hopkins, *A Perspective of Wages and Prices* (1981), 11.

[257] See Watt, *Cheap Print*, 288, 314, and pt. III, ch. 8 *passim*.

[258] Patrick Collinson, 'The English Conventicle', in W. J. Sheils and Diana Wood (eds.), *Voluntary Religion*, SCH 23 (1986), 240–4. Examples of sermon notebooks include: CUL Add. MS 3320 (a notebook from *c.*1614–29, including notes of sermons delivered in Cambridge between 1627 and 1629); BL Sloane MS 598 (notes of sermons delivered in Cambridge in the first half of the 17th cent.); University of London Library, Senate House, IHR MS 979 (anonymous notebook with notes of sermons delivered in 1628–9); CUL Add. MS 3117 (commonplace book of Robert Saxby, clothier of Brenchley in Kent). I owe my knowledge of the last MS to the generosity of Dr John Craig.

[259] These sentiments are expressed in a petition to the Privy Council by inhabitants of Bury St Edmunds, dated 6 Aug. 1582, preserved in PRO SP 12/155/5.

[260] Clarke, *Lives of thirty two English divines*, 160–1.

[261] As Richard Baxter noted in his autobiography, *Reliquiae Baxterianae*, ed. Matthew Sylvester (1696), 2.

subculture which mocked and disparaged it. What from the outside looking in appeared faddish, 'enthusiastic', even seditious, was a symbol of godly solidarity to those who adhered to it—'an apparent signe of Gods Elect' and an 'infallible marke of Christs sheepe'.[262] The devotional and recreational patterns encouraged by these religious peregrinations had more than superficial continuities with those fostered by late medieval Catholic practices dismissed by Protestants as 'popish superstition'. Adam Wyatt, the town clerk of Barnstaple, directly compared the 'divers as well men as women' who rode to Pilton to 'a trental of sermons' on St Luke's Day 1586 with pre-Reformation pilgrims, and the 'oftest Gossipings' of John Earle's 'Shee-Puritan' were her 'Sabaoth-dayes journeyes'.[263]

Moreover, recent research seriously undermines the assumption that the Protestant emphasis on sermons represented a radical disjuncture with Roman Catholic practice. Medievalists have shown that the ideal of vernacular preaching was well entrenched in the thirteenth century and by the fifteenth expected of, if not always achieved by, every beneficed priest.[264] Echoing Erasmus's *Ecclesiastes* (1535) Henrician reformers may have repudiated popish sermons as shallow, unscriptural, and full of foolish fictions, but the charismatic, colloquial, and intensely Christocentric preaching style of the Franciscan and Dominican friars exerted an enduring influence, especially on itinerant evangelists like Hugh Latimer who played such a vital role in spreading the 'new Gospel' in the first phase of the English Reformation. Early Protestants were not employing an innovatory tool to which the laity were naturally resistant so much as grafting a new theological message onto an already familiar medium.[265]

Nor was post-Reformation sermon-going confined to a precociously pious religious elite. Perhaps especially in London preaching was as much a communal gathering as a solemn spiritual event, to which restive and wayward youth eagerly swarmed.[266] As Henry 'silver tongu'd' Smith observed, congregations came with 'divers motions': some like the 'Athenian' that 'hearkeneth after newes'; others like

---

[262] Harrison, *Difference of hearers*, sig. A3ᵛ. On the culture of sermon-going, see Patrick Collinson, 'The Godly: Aspects of Popular Protestantism', in *Godly People*, 1–17; id., *Religion of Protestants*, ch. 6; id., 'The Elizabethan Church and the New Religion', in Christopher Haigh (ed.), *The Reign of Elizabeth I* (Basingstoke, 1984), esp. 189–94; id., 'Shepherds, Sheepdogs, and Hirelings', 203–7; id., 'Elizabethan and Jacobean Puritanism as Forms of Popular Religious Culture', in Christopher Durston and Jacqueline Eales (eds.), *The Culture of English Puritanism, 1560–1700* (Basingstoke, 1996), 47–50.

[263] [Adam Wyatt], *The Lost Chronicle of Barnstaple 1586–1611*, ed. Todd Gray (Exeter, 1998), 62; Earle, *Micro-cosmographie*, 63.

[264] See D'Avray, *Preaching of the Friars*, 6 and *passim*; H. Leith Spencer, *English Preaching in the Late Middle Ages* (Oxford, 1993); Larissa Taylor, *Soldiers of Christ: Preaching in Late Medieval and Reformation France* (New York, 1982), esp. 5, 53, 73, 79–80. See also William A. Hinnebusch, *The Early English Friars Preachers*, Dissertationes Historicae Fasciculus, 14 (Rome, 1951); Toivo Harjunpaa, 'Preaching in England during the Later Middle Ages', *Acta Academiae Aboensis, ser. A, Humaniora*, 29 (1965).

[265] Susan Wabuda, 'The Provision of Preaching during the early English Reformation: With Special Reference to Itineration, *c.*1530 to 1547', PhD thesis (Cambridge, 1991) and her monograph on the subject forthcoming from Cambridge UP. I am grateful to the author for allowing me to read chapters in MS and for helpful discussions.

[266] See Susan Brigden, 'Youth and the English Reformation', in Paul Slack (ed.), *Rebellion, Popular Protest and the Social Order in Early Modern England* (Cambridge, 1984), 100–2.

the 'Pharisie' hoping to hear backbiting against high ranking personages; one 'to gaze about the Church' lasciviously with 'an evill eye'; another to muse privately in 'a browne studie'.[267] Sermons could attract pleasure-loving and scandalmongering crowds, like the 'great concourse and conflux of people' who came to witness the public penance of a fornicator in the parish church of St Swithins and to hear Richard Cooke's denunciation of God's judgements on adulterers in 1629. There were also what James Balmford called 'winter hearers', who attended lectures on rainy days 'when they have nothing else to do'.[268] Indeed, some of those whom Calvinists uncharitably shovelled into the category 'reprobate' appear to have been zealous frequenters of sermons themselves. Ministers like William Ward and George Gifford often singled out 'carnall gospellers and dissembling hypocrites' for particular reproof: men and women who outwardly relished the Word, bragged of their prodigious love of preaching, and seemed 'stout and excellent professours', but fell away under the 'fiery triall or parching heate of persecution'.[269] These individuals had 'a kinde of itch in their eares' which 'carryeth them head-long all to Sermons, as to a meales meate': they might 'runne up and downe to heare' them with 'a Bible under their arme', but their consciences remained 'vast rooms unswept, with many dark corners' filled with schism, disobedience, and sin.[270] Even 'professed usurers, gripes, monsters of men, harpyes, divels in their lives to express nothing lesse', declared the conformist Robert Burton, kept in step with this ostentatious puritan trend, pretending to knock their breasts and roll their eyes as custom prescribed.[271] The point made by many clergymen was not that preaching was unpopular, but rather that, like pearls trampled by swine, it was being trodden by the profane underfoot.

As Patrick Collinson has reminded us, it would be unwise to assume that those who followed in the wake of edifying preachers and those who jaunted to dances and fairs were members of unassimilable and mutually hostile social groups and to rule out the possibility that these parallel forms of sociability ever converged.[272] It would be no less serious a mistake to suppose that those who bought and read prophetic sermons were denizens of a different religious and cultural universe from those who consumed pamphlets and ballads about sudden deaths, alarming prodigies, and destructive fires and storms. In practice, the distinction between these two publishing staples has a disconcerting tendency to dissolve.[273]

[267] Henry Smith, *The art of hearing*, in *The sermons . . . gathered into one volume* (1611), 308.

[268] James Balmford, *A short dialogue concerning the plagues infection* (1603), sig. A4ʳ; Richard Cooke, *A white sheete, or a warning for whoremongers* (1629), sig. A2ᵛ and p. 1.

[269] William Ward, *Gods arrowes, or, two sermons concerning the visitation of God by the pestilence* (1607), fos. 14ʳ, 15ᵛ; George Gifford, *Certaine sermons, upon divers textes of holie scripture* (1597), 17.

[270] John Gore, *A winter sermon* (1635), separately paginated in *Ten godly and fruitfull sermons preached upon severall occasions* (1646), 7; John Whalley, *Gods plentie, feeding true pietie* (1616), 16–17.

[271] Burton, *Anatomy of melancholy*, 28.

[272] Patrick Collinson, *From Iconoclasm to Iconophobia: The Cultural Impact of the Second English Reformation*, Stenton Lecture 1985 (Reading, 1986), 7; id., *Religion of Protestants*, 220.

[273] See e.g. John Field, *A godly exhortation, by occasion of the late judgement of God, shewed at Parris-Garden* (1583); Thomas Wilcox, *A short, yet a true and faithfull narration of the fearefull fire that fell in the towne of Wooburne* (1595); Th[omas] B[edford], *A true and certaine relation of a strange-birth . . . Together with the notes of a sermon, preached . . . at the interring of the sayd birth* (1635).

Not until the 1620s did a true bridging genre emerge, a penny-priced typo-graphical format which could accommodate plain-style sermons, merry stories, and entertaining miscellanies; sententious 'countrie divinitie', penitential advice, and sensational judgement tales—all with equal ease. As Tessa Watt and Eamon Duffy have shown, the chapbook was the offspring of a similar marriage between zeal and greed, a literature generated by passionate nonconformist Calvinists as well as 'marketplace theologians' who rarely so much as deigned to shadow the church door.[274] It was also during this decade that the coranto first appeared, heralding the gradual erosion of the ballad and pamphlet's journalistic role, and opening a hairline crack between the newspaper and the novel.[275] In the meantime we must explore the quarto and octavo sermon and the broadside and stitched tract in tandem and side by side.

[274] Watt, *Cheap Print*, pt. III, esp. ch. 8; Duffy, 'Godly and the Multitude', esp. 47–8.

[275] See esp. Frearson, 'English Corantos' and Joad Raymond, *The Invention of the Newspaper: English Newsbooks 1641–1649* (Oxford, 1996). See also Matthias A. Shaaber, 'The History of the First English Newspaper', *Studies in Philology*, 29 (1929), 551–87; Laurence Hanson, 'English Newsbooks, 1620–1641', *The Library*, 4th ser. 18 (1938), 355–84; Joseph Frank, *The Beginnings of the English Newspaper 1620–1660* (Cambridge, Mass., 1961).

2

'The Theatre of Gods Judgements': Sudden Deaths and Providential Punishments

In February 1576, a widowed artisan woman suffered an unspeakable death in a tow merchant's warehouse situated in Wood Street in the commercial heart of the City of London. Leaving this establishment in possession of six pounds of textile fibre for which she apparently had no intention of paying, Anne Averies was hastily pursued by the irate proprietor, who accused her of shoplifting and indignantly demanded that she settle her outstanding account. Vehemently denying the charge, Mrs Averies returned to the scene of her petty crime and furiously 'rapt out two or three terrible oathes', desiring 'vengeance at Gods handes, that she might presently sinck where she stoode' if the shopkeeper's allegations were true. '[S]hee had not so soone spocken these woords', but the Lord Almighty 'accorded therunto'. In front of the astonished bystanders the guilty widow was 'immediatly stroke to the earth' and rendered speechless, casting up at her blasphemous mouth 'in great abboundance, and with horrible stinke, that matter which by natures course should have been voided downewards' and evacuated 'at the lower partes'. In this unenviable condition, uncontrollably vomiting up her own excrements, two days later Anne Averies died, 'to the terrour of all perjured and forsworne wretches'— or so declared the author of *The theatre of Gods judgements*, the Huntingdon schoolmaster Dr Thomas Beard.[1]

THE ENGLISH JUDGEMENT BOOK

This sordid Elizabethan anecdote of retributive justice found its way into most of the late sixteenth- and seventeenth-century encyclopedias of providential punishments inflicted upon shameless sinners which are the subject of this chapter. The habit of collecting and recounting such grisly stories of supernatural justice is

[1] The first extant account of the Anne Averies case is in Edmund Bicknoll's *A swoord agaynst swearyng* (1579), fo. 36ʳ⁻ᵛ, which was based on a now lost pamphlet published by John Alde in 1576. It can also be found in A[nthony] M[unday], *A view of sundry examples. Reporting many straunge murthers, sundry persons perjured, signes and tokens of Gods anger towards us* ([1580]), sig. B2ᵛ; Stephen Batman, *The doome warning all men to the judgemente* (1581), 401; Stubbes, *Anatomy*, pt. 1, ed. Furnivall, 136; Rogers, *General session*, 80; T. I., *A world of wonders. A masse of murthers. A covie of cosonages* (1595), sig. E1ʳ; Beard, *Theatre*, 178; John Stow, *The annales of England* (1605), 1152; Vaughan, *Spirit of detrac-tion*, 153–4; Gibson, *Lands mourning*, 51; and Shrewsbury School, MS Mus X. 31, fo. 120ᵛ. The story remained a favourite among later 17th-cent. compilers, see Samuel Clarke, *A mirrour or looking-glasse both for saints, and sinners . . .* (1657 edn.; 1st pub. 1646), 427; [Nathaniel Crouch] (R[ichard/Robert] B[urton]), *Wonderful prodigies of judgment and mercy* (1682), 26. Quotations are from the accounts by Beard, Munday, and the author of Shrewsbury School, MS X. 31.

widely regarded as an eccentricity of the hotter sort of Protestants. It was indeed customary for puritan clergymen and laypeople like Ralph Josselin, Lady Margaret Hoby, and Richard Baxter to record not merely the divine mercies and 'crosses' that had blessed and blighted their own lives, but also the prodigious accidents which had overtaken others. In his standard guide for pious diarists, the Essex rector John Beadle insisted that it was the spiritual duty of every 'thankful Christian' to register and meditate upon the exemplary ends of notorious offenders.[2] Out of these exercises in personal edification sprang handwritten anthologies of judgements and deliverances prepared to share with relatives, neighbours, and friends, and to be left as a religious legacy to one's descendants, a 'memoriall' of God's anger against malefactors for the benefit of children and grandchildren unborn. This was the purpose behind the hundreds of cautionary tales which the London artisan Nehemiah Wallington 'took notis off' and inscribed in a remarkable series of 'writing books' during the 1630s and 1640s.[3] Manuscript catalogues of the unsavoury fates of vile livers and evildoers were also assembled by ministers such as the Cheshire vicar Edward Burghall and probably circulated widely among like-minded parishioners, who supplied additional examples and copied out cases unknown to them in their own private compilations. Progressively augmented, some such compendia eventually passed into print.[4]

Beard's *Theatre*, first published in 1597, holds pride of place in this revered literary tradition. Expanded and reissued twice more in the author's lifetime, in 1612 and 1631, it was also abridged by Edmund Rudierd in 1618 as *The thunderbolt of Gods wrath against hard-hearted and stiffe-necked sinners*. It appeared posthumously in 1648 in an even bulkier folio edition, yet further enlarged by Beard before his death in 1632, in collaboration with Dr Thomas Taylor, minister of the metropolitan parish of St Mary Aldermanbury. Godly preachers repeatedly drew on the *Theatre* as a rich treasury of illustrative material for their weekly sermons: cited in the margins of countless devotional works, it was evidently a well-thumbed cler-

---

[2] J[ohn] B[eadle], *The journal or diary of a thankful Christian* (1656), 22–5, cf. William Gouge, *The churches conquest over the sword*, in *Gods three arrowes*, 304–5. Von Greyerz, *Vorsehungsglaube und kosmologie* supersedes all previous discussions of providential autobiography and related genres. Josselin, *Diary*, ed. Macfarlane; *Diary of Lady Margaret Hoby 1599–1605*, ed. Dorothy M. Meads (1930), esp. 193; Baxter, *Reliquiae Baxterianae*. See also *The Reverend Oliver Heywood, B.A. 1630–1702; His Autobiography, Diaries, Anecdote and Event Books . . .* , ed. J. Horsfall Turner, 4 vols. (Brighouse, 1882–5), esp. iii. 76–103, 186–213.

[3] BL Add. MS 21935 ('Historical Notices'), fos. 22ᵛ–38ʳ, printed in [Nehemiah Wallington], *Historical Notices of Events Occurring Chiefly in the Reign of Charles I . . .* , ed. R. Webb, 2 vols. (1869); BL Sloane MS 1457 ('A Memorial of God's Judgements upon Sabbath Breakers, Drunkards and Other Vile Livers, 1632'); FSL MS V. a. 436 ('Extract of the passage of my life; a collection of my written treatises'), esp. fos. 30–40, 145–50. On Wallington, see Seaver, *Wallington's World*, esp. ch. 3.

[4] Edward Burghall, 'Providence Improved', printed in T. Worthington Barlow, *Cheshire: Its Historical and Literary Associations, Illustrated in a Series of Biographical Sketches* (Manchester, 1852), 150–89. Burghall's MS was begun in 1628 and ended in 1663. Nehemiah Wallington refers to a collection of 'Examples of Gods Judgments in Halifax parish upon Sundry Aduleres and profaine parsons in the vicaridge of Hallifax since January the first 1598 as they were left in writting by that Reverent Docter Favor the Late Rector there (in the Rigistor Bookes)': FSL MS V. a. 436, fo. 150.

ical reference book. A classic text that can lay claim to rival John Foxe's *Actes and monuments* in the affections of the late Tudor and Stuart laity, it was part of the staple literary diet of devout Protestant families.[5] But it is above all upon Oliver Cromwell, Beard's own grammar school pupil, that its formative influence has always been detected and felt. To many of the Lord Protector's biographers, this was the very ABC and primer of the providential doctrine that runs like a connecting thread through Cromwell's radical political thinking.[6] As late as 1746, an evangelical pastor from Dundee was recommending it to Scottish presbyterians as compulsory Sunday reading: 'next to the Holy Bible', this was one of 'the most generally useful, instructing, awakening, soul-searching and heartwarming pieces' ever written.[7]

The *Theatre*, moreover, is often regarded as the grandfather of a distinctive and uniform genre of judgement books. It is accorded a key position in a pedigree which begins with Foxe's lengthy appendix to the *Actes and monuments* (1563) listing the gruesome penalties inflicted upon 'popish' persecutors,[8] and then descends through such works as Edmund Bicknoll's *A swoord agaynst swearing* (1579, 1609, 1611, 1618) and the Surrey rector and episcopal chaplain Stephen Batman's *The doome warning all men to the judgemente* (1581), both of which incorporated numerous cases of the 'just and visyble punishments' meted out to heinous sinners. Beard is also perceived to be the inspiration behind the Exeter merchant John Reynolds's *The triumphs of Gods revenge against the crying and execrable sinne of (wilfull and premeditated) murther*, printed in instalments between 1621 and 1635 and destined to become a seventeenth-century best-seller.[9] Next in the genealogy lies the Ipswich preacher Samuel Ward's *Woe to drunkards* (1622), followed by William Prynne's *Histrio-mastix. The players scourge* (1633), which amassed many divine providences as proof that theatrical entertainment was inherently evil. Henry Burton's *A divine tragedie lately acted* (1636) consciously located itself in a line extending back through Foxe, Reynolds, and Beard. '[D]esiring to tread in their pious footsteps', the famous rector of St Matthew's, Friday Street, collected

[5] William Prynne, John Bunyan, and Nehemiah Wallington all evidently either possessed or were able to borrow copies of the *Theatre* on a regular basis: William M. Lamont, *Puritanism and the English Revolution*, i. *Marginal Prynne, 1600–1669* (Aldershot, 1991 edn.), 31; *The Works of John Bunyan*, ed. George Offor, 3 vols. (Glasgow, 1859), iii. 587; Seaver, *Wallington's World*, 219n. Wallington certainly owned Rudierd's abridgement of the *Theatre*: FSL MS V. a. 436, fo. 145.

[6] Hill, *God's Englishman*, 39–40, 51, 234; Paul, *Lord Protector*, 24–7; Oliver Cromwell, *The Writings and Speeches of Oliver Cromwell*, ed. Wilbur C. Abbott, 4 vols. (Cambridge, Mass., 1937–47), i. 22–7; Maurice Ashley, *Oliver Cromwell and his World* (1972), 8.

[7] John Willison, *A treatise concerning the sanctification of the Lord's Day* (1746), in *The Practical Works of John Willison* (Glasgow, [1844]), 57–8.

[8] John Foxe, 'The severe punishment of God upon the persecutors of his people and enemies to his word, with such, also, as have been blasphemers, contemners, and mockers of his religion', in *The Acts and Monuments of John Foxe*, ed. S. R. Cattley, 8 vols. (1853–9), viii. 628–71. In later edns. adulterers, drunkards, and other sinners swelled the ranks of Catholic oppressors.

[9] John Reynolds, *The Triumphs of Gods revenge* . . . (1621, 1622, 1623, 1635). The last was the first complete edn. including all six books. On its publishing history, see Charles C. Mish, 'Best Sellers in Seventeenth-Century Fiction', *Papers of the Bibliographical Society of America*, 47 (1953), 369.

fifty-six 'domesticke examples' of 'Gods avenging Justice upon Sabbath-breakers' and 'other like libertines'.[10] *A mirrour or looking-glasse both for saints, and sinners* appeared from the pen of Samuel Clarke, curate of St Bennet Fink, in 1646, sprawling from a small octavo into two hefty volumes by 1671. The Newcastle non-conformist Samuel Hammond followed suit in 1659, confining himself to 'the most choyce' specimens of heavenly fury, 'such only as bear the strongest remark of Gods displeasure'.[11] During the Interregnum the presbyterian minister Matthew Poole attempted to coordinate an ambitious 'Designe for Registring of Illustrious Providences' observed throughout the British Isles. This elaborate scheme was stillborn, but it survived in blueprint to inspire a transatlantic project initiated by Increase Mather in New England in the early 1680s.[12] Rather more crassly polemical were the anecdotes about the ghastly ends of Royalist 'malignants', 'God-haters', and cowardly 'newters' gathered for 'the ungodlies horrour' by John Vicars in 1643, and the prodigy stories recounted in the baptist Henry Jessey's *The Lords loud call to England* and its anonymous continuation *Mirabilis annus*, a trilogy of pamphlets issued after the Restoration as sectarian propaganda against the newly reinstated Stuart monarchy and the re-established Anglican Church.[13] The tradition lingered on, though it shed some of its more extravagant controversial overtones. The judgement tale left its mark upon a compilation of stories illustrating *The glory of God's revenge against the bloody and detestable sins of murther and adultery* put together by a scholar of Peterhouse, Cambridge, Thomas Wright, in 1685.[14] And the Sussex vicar William Turner's *Compleat history of the most remarkable providences* (1697) testifies to the continuing vitality of the genre at the very end of the seventeenth century. Intended to furnish 'Topickes of Reproof and

---

[10] Ward, *Woe to drunkards*; William Prynne, *Histrio-mastix. The players scourge, or, actors tragaedie* (1633), esp. fos. 552ᵛ–565ʳ; [Henry Burton], *A divine tragedie lately acted, or a collection of sundry memorable examples of Gods judgements upon sabbath-breakers, and other like libertines* ([Amsterdam], 1636), sigs. A2ᵛ–3ʳ. Prynne also contributed the anonymous preface to Burton's book, as noted in *A briefe polemicall dissertation concerning the true time of the inchoation and determination of the Lords Day-sabbath* (1655), sigs. A2ᵛ–3ʳ. A shorter collection along the same lines is A. B., *The sabbath truly sanctified* (1645).

[11] [Samuel Hammond], *Gods judgements upon drunkards, swearers, and sabbath-breakers* (1659), quotation on contents page.

[12] CUL MS Dd. 3. 64 (Letters of Matthew Poole), fos. 136ʳ–141ᵛ; Increase Mather, *An essay for the recording of illustrious providences* (Boston, 1684), preface. A later American example is Nathan Fiske's *Remarkable providences to be gratefully recollected, religiously improved, and carefully transmitted to posterity* (Boston, 1776).

[13] John Vicars, *A looking-glasse for malignants: or, Gods hand against God haters* (1643; 1645); id., *Dagon demolished: or, twenty admirable examples of Gods severe justice and displeasure against the subscribers of the late engagement* (1660). In FSL MS V. a. 436, fo. 145, Wallington refers to another publication along the same lines: *Signs from heaven of the wrath of God . . . whereunto are annexed examples of most fereful judgments of God upon churches & upon sabbath breakers and upon such as have reviled those that are truly zealous of Gods glory calling them Roundhead in reproch & derision*. This may be an edn. of John Vicars, *Prodigies & apparitions or Englands warning pieces* ([1642–3]). H[enry] J[essey], *The Lords loud call to England. Being a true relation of some late, various and wonderful judgments, or handy-works of God* (1660); *Eniautos terastios. Mirabilis annus, or the year of prodigies and wonders* (1661); *Mirabilis annus secundus, or the second year of prodigies* (1662); *Mirabilis annus secundus, or, the second part of the second years prodigies* (1662).

[14] Thomas Wright, *The glory of God's revenge against the bloody and detestable sins of murther and adultery, express'd in thirty modern tragical histories* (1685; 1686; 1688; 1691).

Exhortation' for ministers and to edify 'Private Christians' in their closets and sitting rooms, this monumental tome presented itself as a powerful bulwark against the 'abounding Atheism' of the late Stuart age.[15]

All of these anthologies had overtly didactic aims. Graphic accounts of the draconian penalties which befell those who violated divine law were believed to be singularly effective in inculcating conventional lessons about contemporary ethics. There was no better method of moral indoctrination, argued Thomas Beard, no more reliable technique for rousing the 'drousie consciences of Gods children' and confounding 'the desperat hearts of the wicked' than setting signal examples of divine justice before their bleary eyes. To teach virtue by juxtaposing it with 'the contrarie and repugnant vice' was, after all, the Lord's own favoured technique, who 'useth oftner negative prohibitions than affirmative commandments in his law'. Providential histories were 'an easie and profitable apprentiship or schoole for every man to learne to get wisdome at another mans cost', a 'looking glasse' reflecting back the likely fate of the viewer should he or she fail to repent and amend.[16] They were like 'a burning Beacon', remarked the Kentish preacher Robert Abbot in 1636, a visible warning to forgetful humanity of the treacherous consequences of persisting in iniquity and sin.[17]

While their 'respectable Puritan ancestry' is rarely questioned,[18] works like Beard's *Theatre* have been presented as a pious distortion and 'corruption' of Calvinist orthodoxy: a 'regrettable' second-generation modification and vulgarization of the doctrine of providence as outlined definitively in the *Institutes*.[19] For in boldly claiming to be able to extrapolate God's purpose from historical events, and in predicating morality upon His meddlesome interferences in the terrestrial world, Beard and later compilers effectively belied the scriptural axiom that the Lord's ways were beyond human comprehension. They gave merely lip-service to the tenet that any attempt to unravel the meaning of particular providential events was high presumption and 'monstrous madness'.[20] Here, it has been inferred, were the intellectual origins of a distinctively English contribution to posthumous developments within the Genevan reformer's thought.

But careful analysis reveals that collections of cautionary tales were less the end-product of a one-sided process of theological transformation and/or degeneration than the outcome of an ongoing dialogue between age-old Christian and pre-Christian convictions and the new religious ideology ushered in by the

---

[15] William Turner, *A compleat history of the most remarkable providences, both of judgment and mercy, which have hapned in this present age* (1697), quotation at sig. b^v.

[16] Beard, *Theatre* (1597 edn.), sig. A3^r (dedication to Sir Edward Wingfield); (1631 edn.), sigs. A4^{r-v}, A5^r.

[17] Richard Abbot, *The young-mans warning-peece: or, a sermon preached at the buriall of William Rogers, apothecary* (1639; 1st pub. 1636), 92 and 87–100 *passim*.

[18] Donagan, 'Providence, Chance and Explanation', 389n.

[19] G. F. Waller, 'The Popularization of Calvinism: Thomas Beard's *The Theater of Gods Judgements*', *Theology*, 75 (1972), 177–8, 185–7 and 176–87 *passim*; Vander Molen, 'Providence as Mystery, Providence as Revelation', esp. 39–47; Seaver, *Wallington's World*, 45–8, 219–20.

[20] Calvin, *Institutes*, bk. I, ch. 17.

Reformation, and of two-way traffic between oral tradition and the world of literacy, learning, and print. Not only is this corpus of writings altogether more heterogeneous and syncretic than is generally implied, but its authors, editors, and readers, far from being a cohesive puritan fraternity, were a decidedly motley crew. The genre of God's judgements witnesses not so much to the 'percolation' of a diluted strain of Calvinism down into popular consciousness,[21] as to the cross-fertilization of an eclectic body of opinions and beliefs. It attests to interactions between different layers of culture and to processes of adaptation and assimilation which go some way to explaining how Protestantism was implanted in England.

MEDIEVAL EXEMPLA AND MODERNE AND HOME-BRED EXAMPLES

Thomas Beard and his celebrated book have themselves been much misunderstood. As John Morrill has recently demonstrated, despite his canonization as a seminal figure in the 'making' of Oliver Cromwell's puritanism, Beard did not come from typically 'godly' stock. A greedy conforming pluralist who acquired a royal chaplaincy and a cathedral prebend through the patronage of King James I, interfered officiously in municipal affairs, and survived William Laud's administration of the local archdeaconry without so much as a severe ticking off, he can scarcely be situated in the serried ranks of 'paineful' preachers with scruples of conscience and grievances about a Church 'but halfly reformed'. It was not Beard who ignited the fire in the young Cromwell's belly; far from a friend and ally, he was very probably one of his fiercest adversaries in the bitter factional clashes and disputes which racked the borough of Huntingdon.[22]

Nor, inspected more closely, does the *Theatre* live up to its reputation as an archetypally puritan text. This was no original composition, but, as the title-page of only the 1597 edition admits, for the most part a slavish translation from the French. Beard's magnum opus and '*tour de force*' turns out to be a piece of wholesale plagiarism—a fact historians have almost universally overlooked.[23] His unnamed source was a similar encyclopedia compiled by a Calvinist minister from Metz, Jean Chassanion.[24] Published in Switzerland in 1581, *De grands et redoutables jugemens et punitions de Dieu* was itself heavily indebted to the Lutheran pastor of Saxony Andreas Hondorff's *Promptuarium exemplorum. Historienn und exempel buch*, which first appeared from a Leipzig press in 1568. Translated into Latin as

---

[21] Waller, 'Popularization of Calvinism', 177. The argument of this chapter reinforces David Hall's interpretation of the religious culture of early New England, *Worlds of Wonder*, ch. 2, esp. pp. 71–80.

[22] John Morrill, 'The Making of Oliver Cromwell', repr. in id., *The Nature of the English Revolution* (1993), 124–5, 126–30, 132–3. For the older orthodoxy, see Benjamin Brook, *The Lives of the Puritans*, 3 vols. (1813), ii. 396–7; *DNB*; and the works cited in n. 6, above.

[23] Waller, 'Popularization of Calvinism', quotation at 186.

[24] Jean Chassanion, *Des grands et redoutables jugemens et punitions de Dieu advenus au monde principalement* (Morges, 1581), repub. as *Histoires memorables des grans et merveilleux jugemens et punitions de Dieu avenues au monde* (n.p., 1586). See *Dictionnaire de biographie française*, ed. J. Balteau *et al.* (Paris, 1933–), viii. 705–6.

Theatrum historicum by Phillip Lonicer in 1575 and running through some thirty editions before 1687, Hondorff's huge tome clearly left a lasting imprint on the European literary scene.[25] Beard's *Theatre* was only one of the many offspring this 700-page compendium of moralizing stories spawned.

Arranged according to the two Mosaic tables of the Ten Commandments,[26] all three works quarried a wide range of writings for dramatic cases of wicked men and women upon whom the avenging arm of God had swooped. They ransacked pagan, classical, and patristic writers, Italian humanist scholars and medieval Catholic monks no less, indeed, if anything more comprehensively than those of Protestant reformers and ecclesiastical historians—and with surprisingly little doctrinal discrimination. Examples gleaned from Pliny, Plutarch, and Socrates, Herodotus and Ovid jostled for space with episodes culled from Josephus, Tertullian, and Theodoret, Cyprian, John Chrysostom, and the Bible itself; Guicciardini and Pico della Mirandola rubbed elbows with Sleidan and the Magdeburg Centurians, Luther, Melanchthon, Beza, and the Brandenburg chronicler Johannes Carion.

Neither did Hondorff, Chassanion, and Beard consider it ideologically unsound to plunder the principal collections of Latin exempla dating back to the early thirteenth century, the cautionary tales which had animated the vernacular sermons of the mendicant friars.[27] They found much that was grist to their mill in these concordances of pulpit anecdotes, which, as the Russian scholar Aron Gurevich has argued, were themselves the consequence of a continuing dialectic between

---

[25] Chassanion probably used the Latin edn.; both he and Beard cite it frequently in their margins. See Heidemarie Schade, 'Andreas Hondorff's *Promptuarium Exemplorum*', in Wolfgang Brückner (ed.), *Volkserzählung und Reformation: Ein Handbuch zur Tradierung und Funktion von Erzählstoffen und Erzählliteratur im Protestantismus* (Berlin, 1974), 646–703. Other Lutheran exempla books include: [Johann Herold], *Exempla virtutum et vitiorum, atque etiam aliarum rerum maxime memorabilium* (Basel, [1555]); Zacharius Rivander, *Der ander theil promptuarii exemplorum* (Frankfurt, 1581), repub. as *Promptuarium exemplorum: historien und new exempulbuch* (Frankfurt, 1592). Hondorff also produced a *Historical calendar* (1575) which bears an equally close relationship to medieval lives of the saints such as the *Golden Legend*: Robert Kolb, *For all the Saints: Changing Perceptions of Martyrdom and Sainthood in the Lutheran Reformation* (Macon, Ga., 1987), 30–1.

[26] Beard and Chassanion followed the Calvinist division of the Decalogue into two books of four and six commandments, while Hondorff adhered to the pre-Reformation convention of splitting them into three and seven.

[27] Surviving MS exempla collections in the BL are calendared in J. A. Herbert, *Catalogue of Romances in the Department of Manuscripts in the British Museum*, iii (1910). Modern edns. of notable examples include Caesarius of Heisterbach, *The Dialogue on Miracles*, trans. H. Von E. Scott and C. C. Swinton Bland, 2 vols. (1929); Jacques de Vitry, *The Exempla or Illustrative Stories from the Sermones Vulgares*, ed. Thomas Frederick Crane, Folklore Soc. 26 (1890); Etienne de Besançon, *An Alphabet of Tales. An English 15th Century Translation of the Alphabetum Narrationum of Etienne de Besançon*, ed. Mary MacLeod Banks, EETS, os 126–7 (1904–5); Sidney J. Herrtage, *The Early English Versions of the Gesta Romanorum*, EETS, extra ser. 33 (1879). The last was translated into English by Richard Robinson, *A record of auncient histories, intituled in Latin: Gesta Romanorum* (1595). See T. F. Crane, 'Mediaeval Sermon-Books and Stories', *Proceedings of the American Philosophical Soc.* 21 (1884), 49–78; Joseph Albert Mosher, *The Exemplum in the Early Religious and Didactic Literature of England* (New York, 1911); G. R. Owst, *Preaching in Medieval England: An Introduction to Sermon Manuscripts of the Period c.1350–1450* (Cambridge, 1926), ch. 7.

'official doctrine and folkloric consciousness', between the ecclesiastical and the oral.[28] Probably the best-known such compilation circulating widely on the eve of the Reformation in both manuscript and print was the alphabetical *promptuarium* or 'storehouse' of stories which the Dominican prior of Basel Johannes Herolt (*Discipulus*) appended to his *Sermones de tempore et de sanctis*, completed *c*.1435–40.[29] Beard and his precursors did make modest efforts to winnow the chaff from the wheat, discarding the transparently 'popish' and 'superstitious' elements they found in the legends of the saints and other works of moral complaint. But a fair amount that was theologically dubious managed to creep in all the same. Sometimes they had to bend over backwards to vindicate particular cases they chose to include.[30] There is no gainsaying the direct line of descent from these medieval preaching aids to *The theatre of Gods judgements* and its European cousins. Consciously or unconsciously their authors were adapting and prolonging a homiletic genre rooted firmly in the proscribed Catholic past.

Hondorff's *Promptuarium exemplorum* and its progeny had intimate links with another closely related Lutheran tradition. They preyed on and fused with the apocalyptic wonder literature that began to proliferate in Germany in the 1550s— exhaustive chronological listings of portents, marvels, and other occult phenomena interpreted as evidence of impending cosmic disaster and signs of civilization's Last Days. Particularly influential were the *Wunderzeichen* of Job Fincelius (1556) and Caspar Goldwurm (1557)[31] and the Alsatian humanist Conrad Lycosthenes's *Prodigiorum ac ostentorum chronicon* (1557). Based on a fourth-century text by Julius Obsequens, the latter filtered into English in the form of Stephen Batman's *The doome warning all men to the judgemente* (1581).[32] The German *Wunderbuch* also reached audiences across the Channel via Huguenot France: two notable examples translated into English were Pierre Boaistuau's *Certaine secret wonders of nature* (1567) and Simon Goulart's *Admirable and memorable histories containing the wonders of our time* (1607).[33] Beard's book of dreadful obituaries was merely one more symptom of this cross-Continental literary drift.

---

[28] Aron Gurevich, *Medieval Popular Culture: Problems of Belief and Perception*, trans. János M. Bak and Paul A. Hollingsworth (Cambridge, 1988), see esp. foreword, pp. xv–xx, and ch. 1, quotation at p. 5.

[29] Johannes Herolt, *Sermones discipuli de tempore [et] de sanctis: et quadragesimale eiusdem: cum promptuario* (1510). There were as many as 48 German edns. of the book before 1520.

[30] A good example occurs in Beard, *Theatre*, 46–7.

[31] Job Fincelius, *Wunderzeichen. Warhafftige beschreibung und gründlich verzeicnus schrecklicher wunderzeichen und geschichten* (Jena, 1556); Caspar Goldwurm [or Goltwurm], *Wunderwerck und wunderzeichen buch* (1557). There are helpful discussions of this tradition in Robin Bruce Barnes, *Prophecy and Gnosis: Apocalypticism in the Wake of the Lutheran Reformation* (Stanford, Calif., 1988), 87–93; Rudolf Schenda, 'Die Deutschen Prodigiensammlungen des 16. und 17. Jahrhunderts', *Archiv für Geschichte des Buchwesens*, 4 (1963), 638–710; Clark, *Thinking with Demons*, ch. 24; and in the articles by Heinz Schilling and Bernward Deneke in Wolfgang Bruckner (ed.), *Volkserzählung und Reformation: Ein Handbuch zur Tradierung und Funktion von Erzählliteratur im Protestantismus* (Berlin, 1974), 325–92 and 124–77 respectively.

[32] Conrad Lycosthenes, *Prodigiorum ac ostentorum chronicon* (Basel, 1557), trans. into German as *Wunderwerck, oder Gottes unergründtliches vorbilden* (Basel, 1557); Batman, *Doome*.

[33] Pierre Boaistuau, *Certaine secrete wonders of nature*, trans. Edward Fenton (1569); Simon Goulart, *Admirable and memorable histories containing the wonders of our time*, trans. Ed. Grimeston (1607). On

A further strand in the development of these dictionaries of providential biography were the *de casibus* tragedies which comprised the Renaissance Florentine writer Giovanni Boccaccio's immortal *Decameron*. Reworked in the 1430s by John Lydgate as *The falle of princis* and again in the mid-Tudor period as *The myrrour for magistrates*, these verse narratives about the unhappy fates of the high and mighty were transitional works, in which the Christian paradigm of an omnipotent providence merged with classical notions of nemesis and fortune. Sometimes employed to demonstrate the 'slypery deceytes of the waveryng lady' and sometimes the just deserts of hubris and prodigality, the pattern of meteoric rise and ruinous undoing always held within it the seeds of causal ambiguity. Yet, for all its awkward pagan connotations, didactic storytelling of this type also left traces on the Protestant exempla book, which continued to place particular emphasis on the humiliating ends of high-ranking transgressors.[34]

Even Foxe's *Actes and monuments* (from which, predictably enough, Thomas Beard borrowed liberally) was modelled on a hagiographical genre already over a millennium old. In recounting the unearthly punishments which had overtaken the tormentors and executioners of the Marian martyrs, Foxe was revitalizing a tradition which stretched back through the ecclesiastical histories of Eusebius, Rufinus, and the Venerable Bede to the fourth-century apologist Lactantius Firmianus's *De mortibus persecutorum*, a collection of fabulous tales of the deaths of the persecutors of the infant Church from Nero to Diocletian. There was far less of a discrepancy between the miraculous stories which infiltrated these works and the providential anecdotes recounted in Protestant classics than their authors would have cared to admit.[35]

The vast bulk of the Huntingdon schoolmaster's encyclopedia, then, was the culmination of centuries of cultural absorption and accretion. Not only is there

the French connection, see Rudolf Schenda, *Die Französische Prodigienliteratur in der Zweiten Hälfte des 16. Jahrhunderts*, Muncher Romantistische Arbeiten, 16 (Munich, 1961), esp. pt III, chs. 1, 4.

[34] Giovanni Boccaccio, [*De casibus illustrium virorum.*] *Here beynneth the boke calledde John Bochas descrivinge the falle of princis*, trans. John Lydgate (1494). Another trans. of the *Decameron*, by [J. Florio?], appeared in 1620. William Baldwin *et al.*, *A myrrour for magistrates* (1563 edn.; 1st pub. 1559), quotation at sig. A1[r]. This was a rev. edn. of *A memorial of suche princes, as . . . have been unfortunate in the realme of England* ([1554?]). See also John Carr, *The ruinous fal of prodigalitie . . .* (1573); Richard Robinson, *The rewarde of wickednesse* (1574); Anthony Munday, *The mirrour of mutabilitie . . . Describing the fall of divers famous princes* (1579). This genre also had a German counterpart: see Georg Lauterbeck, *Regentbuch aus vielen . . . alten und newen historien . . . zusammen gezogen* (Leipzig, 1557). See the introd. to Lily B. Campbell's edn. of *The Mirror for Magistrates* (Cambridge, 1938) and William Farnham, *The Medieval Heritage of Elizabethan Tragedy* (Oxford, 1956), chs. 7, 9.

[35] Beard, *Theatre*, bk. I, chs. 12–13. Lactantius Firmianus' *De mortibus persecutorum* was not translated into English until the late 17th cent. by Gilbert Burnet: *A relation of the death of the primitive persecutors* (Amsterdam, 1687). See Patrick Collinson, 'Truth and Legend: The Veracity of John Foxe's Book of Martyrs', in A. C. Duke and C. A. Tamse (eds.), *Clio's Mirror: Historiography in Britain and the Netherlands* (Zutphen, 1985), 35–6. Some modern commentators persist in hailing Foxe's *Actes and Monuments* as representative of an 'age of revolt against supernaturalism': Helen White, *Tudor Books of Saints and Martyrs* (Madison, 1963), 164; John R. Knott, *Discourses of Martyrdom in English Literature, 1563–1694* (Cambridge, 1993), 41–6. Forthcoming work by Dr Thomas Freeman endorses the interpretation presented here. See also Ch. 5 below, p. 231.

astonishingly little about this class of texts which can be identified as indigenously English, but their recent genealogy, far from being exclusively Calvinist, was indisputably Lutheran.

The first edition of the *Theatre*, in fact, contained no more than a handful of divine judgements which had occurred within living memory. Once its popularity had been established Beard began to add more providences which had fallen out in recent times, episodes 'fresh and famous', 'prophane, yet probable, and more neere'.[36] These were often lifted almost verbatim from other printed texts. They were poached from sermons and tracts composed by his professional colleagues; from the chronicles of Raphael Holinshed and John Stow; and from the journalistic ephemera which fed off and into such annals and also, paradoxically, contributed to their disappearance and demise.[37] Many of Beard's 'moderne and home-bred examples' were precisely those reported in the sensational yellow press, precisely those which helped to fill the coffers of profit-seeking publishers of weird and wonderful news.[38] It was to cheap print that he owed the engrossing story of Anne Averies's ill-considered oath and the tale of Simon Pembroke, the Southwark figure-setter struck to the ground 'rattling in the throat' in 1577 after denying that he practised the 'divelish' and 'abhominable' art of conjuring.[39] In all likelihood, a broadsheet or pamphlet was also the source of that vivid cameo about the accidental or rather providential death of the playwright Christopher Marlowe for which Beard's book has since been renowned: his graphic account of the fatal wound the atheistical 'Marlin' inflicted with his own dagger during a drunken brawl in 'London streets' in 1593.[40]

It is in this frame of the kaleidoscope that the relationship between the *Theatre* and the cut-and-paste publications of Anthony Munday, Philip Stubbes, and other freelance writers and hacks comes more clearly into focus and view. Stubbes reinforced later editions of his scathing attack on Elizabethan manners, *The anatomie of abuses*, with several episodes which had already been narrated in ballads

---

[36] Beard, *Theatre*, 548, 228 respectively.

[37] For examples of Beard lifting material from the writings of other ministers, see *Theatre*, 560–1 and 555–6, where he cites from Ward, *Woe to drunkards* and Lewis Bayly, *The practise of pietie directing a Christian how to walke that he may please God* (1613). On the decline of the chronicle, see D. R. Woolf, 'Genre into Artifact: The Decline of the English Chronicle in the Sixteenth Century', *SCJ* 19 (1988), esp. 323, 333, 354.

[38] Beard, *Theatre*, 151.

[39] Ibid. 178, 126–7 respectively. For Anne Averies, see n. 1, above; for Simon Pembroke, see *A most strange and rare example of the just judgement of God executed upon a lewde and wicked conjurer* ([1577]). A ballad on the subject is transcribed in the Hall Commonplace Book (FSL MS V. a. 339, fo. 172[r–v]), but, along with 82 other ballads in the MS, seems to have been forged by the 19th-cent. scholar J. P. Collier: see Giles E. Dawson, 'John Payne Collier's Great Forgery', *Studies in Bibliography*, 24 (1971), 1–26. Beard's report of the 'wonderfull discoverie' of the assassins of Thomas Arden of Faversham in 1551 (p. 294) also probably came from a lost pamphlet or ballad: see Raphael Holinshed, *The first volume of chronicles . . . The laste volume of chronicles of England, Scotlande and Irelande*, 2 vols. (1577), ii. 1703–8; M[unday], *View of sundry examples*, sigs. C4[v]–D1[r].

[40] Beard, *Theatre*, 149–50. The phrase 'London streets', which was a manifest error, since the incident occurred in Deptford, occurs only in the 1597 edn. (pp. 147–8) and has the authentic ring and rhythm of doggerel verse.

or 'sticht' paperback books: a tract about the prodigious fire which consumed the London haberdasher William Brustar and his harlot had appeared in 1583 and songs about the seven Swabian drunkards procured to death by the devil and the pair of impious swillers from Neckarhausen mysteriously cemented to the tavern floor were published in 1579 and 1581.[41] Nor could he resist including the story of a foul-mouthed serving-man from Lincolnshire who came to an equally implausible end, 'whose tragicall discourse I my self penned about two yeares agoe'.[42] Here collections of judgement tales begin to shade into the rough-and-ready summaries of recent homicides, perjuries, monstrous births, and celestial omens which Grub Street journalists glued with a pious preamble and the minimum of moral commentary into a conglomerate whole—items like Munday's *A view of sundry examples* and T. I.'s *A world of wonders*, which included anecdotes ranging from Arthurian and Norman times right up to the present. They blur with the patchwork compilations of obsolete news-pamphlets which poorly paid wordsmiths hastily updated and cobbled together at the behest of unscrupulous publishers such as the notorious John Trundle.[43] Stories of the sudden deaths of impenitent offenders were part of the entrepreneur's as well as the preacher's stock-in-trade.

Beard's *Theatre*, then, blends like a chameleon into a variety of literary environments. It harmonizes as readily with the commercial world of cheap print as it does with the clerical world of evangelism and exegesis. And it is to a closer examination of the structure and significance of the providential anecdotes retold in both that this chapter now turns.

CAUTIONARY TALES

The tales of God's judgements recounted in blackletter ballads and pamphlets share the same characteristics as those which made up massive anthologies like Thomas Beard's. Both intermingled gratuitous circumstantial detail with stern spiritual admonition; both enclosed a ghoulish and prurient fascination with all manner of medical, sexual, and excremental excess within a homiletic shell. Each contained a quotient of violence certain to send a shiver down the spine and admitted semi-pornographic vignettes of rape, incest, and adultery guaranteed to create an erotic frisson. Recurrently the reader was allowed to succumb to a voyeuristic curiosity not just about the dire penalties inflicted upon sinners but also about their

[41] Stubbes, *Anatomy*, pt. 1, ed. Furnivall, 100–1, 111–14. Saxey, *A straunge and wonderfull example*. The ballads about the drunkards (now lost) are listed in *SR* ii. 354, 400 (26 June 1579 and 22 Aug. 1581). On the Swabian tipplers, see also Batman, *Doome*, 405.

[42] Stubbes, *Anatomy*, pt. 1, ed. Furnivall, 135. The ballad is one of two in the blackletter tract, *Two wunderfull and rare examples. Of the undeferred and present approching judgment, of the lord our God* ([1581]), sigs. B1ʳ–2ᵛ. J. P. Collier claimed to have owned a copy of the original broadside, subscribed P. S., which he repr. in *Broadside Black-letter Ballads* (1868), 42–7, but this may be another instance of Collier sleight of hand.

[43] M[unday], *View of sundry examples*; T. I., *World of wonders* and T. I., *Miracle, of miracles*. The latter was published by Trundle, who may well be the mysterious T. I.

blood-curdling crimes and sickening deeds. At the heart of Samuel Saxey's heavily moralized report of the incineration of the whoremonger Brustar and his Bridewell 'concubine', for instance, lay a lurid account of the 'grievous spectacle' of singed flesh and charred limbs that confronted eyewitnesses who burst into the seedy bedsit in Fleet Street which rivals anything to be found regularly in the pages of the *Sun* and *Daily Mail*.[44] Under the seventh commandment, Beard included a steamy academic scandal involving a law lecturer's illicit affair with the wife of a university proctor. Catching them naked in the bath, the outraged husband 'so curried the lecherous Doctor with a curry-combe, that he scraped out his eyes, and cut off his privie members; so that within three days after hee dyed'—this was how the Lord saw fit to punish so flagrant an offence against the holy institution of matrimony. The unfaithful spouse was spared out of compassion for the innocent, unborn child she was carrying, 'otherwise she should have tasted the same sauce'.[45]

Equally typical is a telescoped time-frame between wicked act and heavenly revenge, a strategy employed to enhance the teleological link between cause and effect. Deft ellipses in the narrative conceal any untidy lag between the commission of sin and God's wrathful response, which is invariably said to have occurred 'presently', 'straight away', or as quick as a flash. In a late sixteenth-century ballad about Jasper Coningham, a gentleman from Aberdeen who shocks his godly sister by declaring that Christianity is but 'a tale of Robin Hood' and hell a mere fable devised 'to keep poor fooles in feare':

> No sooner had he spoken
> this foul blasphemous thing,
> But that a heavy judgment
> upon him God did bring . . .

Instantaneously the disbelieving Scotsman is surrounded by a circle of flames and suffers an excruciating death.[46] Artificial climaxes of this kind pervade Beard's *Theatre* too: in one anecdote a 'cholericke father seeing his sonne slacke about his businesse' in Meissen on 11 September 1552 'wished he might never stirre from that place: for it was no sooner said, but done, his son stucke fast in the place' and remained immovably fixed 'with a post at his backe for his ease' for over seven years.[47] The author of the pamphlet about the suburban magician Simon Pembroke almost spoilt the effect: having forsworn himself in the local ecclesiastical court the amateur wizard 'sank down sodeynly amongst them starke deade'—'albeit somewhat sickely before, as it must truly be confessed'.[48]

---

[44] Saxey, *Straunge and wonderfull example*, sigs. B2ʳ, B2ᵛ–3ᵛ.
[45] Beard, *Theatre*, 400.
[46] *The wonderfull example of God shewed upon Jasper Coningham, a gentleman borne in Scotland* ([c.1600]). The ballad was entered among the ballad partners's stock in 1624: *SR* iv. 131–2.
[47] Beard, *Theatre*, 194. Also in Bicknoll, *Swoord agaynst swearyng*, fos. 44ᵛ–45ᵛ.
[48] *Most strange and rare example . . . upon a lewde and wicked conjurer*, sigs. A4ᵛ–5ʳ.

Another standard feature is an improbable correspondence between the mode of punishment and the nature of the crime, frequently to a degree that stretches if not beggars belief. Poetic justice is repeatedly satisfied when wicked miscreants ironically receive payment in kind. As in medieval exempla, sinners are afflicted in the actual limbs and organs they have so monstrously misused. Perjurers die with blackened tongues protruding from their gaping jaws; the pilfering fingers of thieves rot and drop off; lightning bolts hit the genitals of lechers and fornicators.[49] In one Jacobean song, a proud German merchant's wife is castigated for her vanity when she gives birth to 'a most deformed broode', a bicephalous infant whose flesh resembles the fashionable garb in which she once took such wanton pleasure, symbolically holding a mirror and a switch.[50] According to a pamphlet published in 1618, a northerner who exercised his evil imagination devising terrible oaths was sent a 'canker' that soon ate out 'the very instrument where with he blasphemed'.[51] Many of the stories incorporated in the *Theatre* carried this patterning to even more ludicrous lengths. The fate of the uncharitable governor of a French town who refuses to sell his store of grain to the famished peasants, protesting he has 'scarce enough for his owne hogs', is especially far-fetched:

which hoggish disposition the Lord requited in it owne kind; for his wife at the next litter brought forth seven pigs at one birth to encrease the number of his hogs: that as he had preferred filthie and ougley creatures before his poore brethren . . . so he might have of his owne getting more of that kind to make much of, since hee loved them so well.[52]

Only slightly less preposterous is an anecdote from Theodoret about the sacrilegious uncle of Julian the Apostate, who contemptuously 'pissed' against a communion table and thereafter expelled his urine and faeces via his throat, 'because when they passed naturally, hee abused them to the dishonour of God'.[53] Preachers

---

[49] For thieves whose hands rot, see J. C., *A warning for swearers. By the example of God's judgements shewed upon a man born near the town of Wolverhampton* ([1677]), probably a later edn. of the ballad entered to Thomas Lambert, 8 Nov. 1633: *SR* iv. 307. For blasphemers with blackened and protruding tongues, see *A looking-glasse, for murtherers and blasphemers; wherein the[y see] Gods judgement showne upon a keeper neere Enfield C[hase]* ([1626]) and *Two most strange and notable examples, shewed at Lyshborne the 26. day of Januarie now last past* (1591), sig. B2ʳ⁻ᵛ. The motif of punishment fitting the crime can easily be traced back to medieval exempla with the help of Frederic C. Tubach, *Index Exemplorum: A Handbook of Medieval Religious Tales*, FF Communications 204 (Helsinki, 1969). See e.g. nos. 674, 2103, 3704, 4906. A tale in Caesarius of Heisterbach, *Dialogue on Miracles*, ii. 196–7, concerns lightning setting fire to the genitals of a fornicating priest from Trier.

[50] *Pride's fall: or a warning to all English women, by the example of a strang monster, borne of late in Germany by a proude marchant's wife in the city of Geneva [sic Jena]*, 1609, printed in Clark (ed.), *Shirburn Ballads*, 134–9. A book on the subject was entered in *SR* on 15 Aug. 1608: iii. 388. The ballad became part of the partners' stock and several Restoration edns. survive.

[51] *A true relation of two most strange and fearefull accidents, lately happening, the one at Chagford in Devonshire, by the falling of th[e] stanary court-house* (1618), sigs. B1ᵛ⁻2ʳ.

[52] Beard, *Theatre*, 478–9. Cf. the canine-faced child case on p. 210, which is listed in Tubach, *Index Exemplorum*, no. 646.

[53] Beard, *Theatre*, 181–2. See *The ecclesiastical history of Theodoret bishop of Cyrus*, trans. R. Cadwaller, ed. G. E. ([St Omer], 1612), bk. III, ch. 12, pp. 219–20. There are obvious echoes of this exemplum in the tale of Anne Averies.

like John Downame and Joseph Caryl stressed that judgements were often fitted and proportioned according to the offence: they so manifested 'the image and superscription of sin' that anyone might read it written 'as it were in great text letters set over their heads'.[54] When it came to demonstrating how this maxim worked in practice, it was obviously very tempting to embellish the episode in hand.

No less arresting is the stereotyped quality of the capital punishments purportedly dealt out by the Lord. Biblical echoes and resonances abound: the earth yawns to swallow Anthony Painter, the 'Blaspheming Caryar' from Genoa (Plate 4), Dorothy Mattley, a Derbyshire liar, and the horses of a cornhoarding Buckinghamshire farmer, just as it had engulfed the Old Testament rebels Korah, Dathan, and Abiram thousands of years before. In an Elizabethan ballad about Queen Eleanor, the Spanish consort of Edward I, the carriage in which this autocratic lady is travelling sinks into the ground at Charing Cross to rise up again in shame at Queenhithe.[55] Herod's slow inward consumption by lice and worms frequently reappears, as does the intestinal disease which engulfed the heretic Arius, causing his entrails to be violently disgorged from his body.[56] Another popular theme was that of the reprobate stricken with apoplexy in the midst of a gluttonous meal and taken from the table choking on his meat—a distant allusion to King Belshazzar's feast. This was the miserable fate ascribed to the Anglo-Saxon robber baron Earl Godwin of Kent, suffocated by a crumb of consecrated bread after solemnly appealing to God to exonerate him from guilt.[57] Foxe's account of the 'poisoned life' and stinking' death of the 'grand butcher' Stephen Gardiner was skilfully trimmed to fit this template, as was the tale of Thomas Miles, a 'forsworne wretch' who died at his dinner plate in August 1635 with a morsel of food 'sticking fast in his throate'.[58] There was, indeed, a relatively limited repertoire of untimely and exemplary ends.

Commonly, then, tradition and topicality coalesce. Accounts of ostensibly current events assimilate layers of ecclesiastical legend and historical myth. Not

---

[54] Joseph Caryl, *An exposition with practical observations upon the book of Job*, 2 vols. (1676; 1st pub. 1645), col. 291; John Downame, *Foure treatises, tending to dissuade all Christians from foure no lesse hainous then common sinnes* (1609 edn.), 46, 74. Cf. John Gore, *A summer sermon upon Eliahs prayer* (1638), repr. in his *Ten godly and fruitfull sermons*, 26; Beard, *Theatre*, 222, 389.

[55] Num. xvi. 31–2. *Anthony Painter. The blaspheming caryar*, sig. B1ᵛ. *A most wonderful and sad judgement of God upon one Dorothy Mattley late of Ashover in the county of Darby* ([1661?]). This story was a classic incorporated in every Restoration judgement book and immortalized in John Bunyan's *The Life and Death of Mr. Badman* ... (1680), ed. James F. Forrest and Roger Sharrock (Oxford, 1988), 32–3. *A looking glasse for corne-hoorders, by the example of John Russell a farmer dwelling at St Peters Chassant in Buckingham shire, whose horses sunke into the ground the 4 of March 1631* ([1631?]). *The lamentable fall of Queene Elnor, who for her pride and wickednesse, by Gods judgment, sunke into the ground at Charing Crosse, and rose up again at Queene hive* ([c. 1600?]).

[56] Beard, *Theatre*, 28–9, 98–9. One example of the Arius paradigm is the notorious case of Grimwood in Foxe, *Acts and Monuments*, viii. 630–1, discussed below.

[57] Beard, *Theatre*, 177–8.

[58] Foxe, *Acts and Monuments*, vii. 592–3; viii. 628, recounted by Beard, *Theatre*, 62. L[awrence] P[rice], *A wonderfull wonder: being a most straunge and true relation of the resolute life and miserable death of Thomas Miles* ([1635]).

ANTHONY PAINT
THE
Blafpheming Caryar.

Who funke into the ground up to the neck, and there ftood two day
two nights, and not to bee drawne out by the ftrength of Ho
or digged out by the help of man: and there dyed the
3. *of Nouember*. 1613.

Alfo the punifhment of *Nicholas Mefle* a moft wicked blafphemer,
Reade and tremble.
Publifhed by Authoritie.

Thou art mine.

I am Damn'd.

At London printed for *Iohn Trundle* : and are to be fold at
Chrift Church Gate. 1614.

PLATE 4 *Anthony Painter. The blaspheming caryar* (London, 1614), title-page. By
permission of the Bodleian Library, University of Oxford. Shelfmark: 4° 16 Art. Bs (48).

only did authors inherit their overall narrative matrix and an arsenal of colourful
motifs from the pulpit anecdotes of the preaching friars; sometimes they embedded entire stories from these discarded sources within texts that professed to be
reports of contemporaneous news. An illuminating example of this process at work
is Philip Stubbes's atrocious poem about the 'lewde' young fellow who incessantly
swore by 'Gods wounds' and 'Gods bloud' and subsequently expired with his own
gushing and streaming from all his bodily orifices and joints. This incident
allegedly took place in June 1581 in the home of 'one Maister Frauncis Pennell,
Gentleman, dwelling at Boothbie', but it was in fact a medieval topos. The

Brigittine monk of Syon Richard Whitford had rehearsed a Henrician version of this exemplum in his *Werke for housholders*, first printed fifty years earlier, the tale of one 'mayster Baryngton' of Hertfordshire who peppered his speech with the same inveterate oath and died in an identical fashion 'but small tyme before'.[59] Something similar occurs in a ballad about two parricide sons who dispatch their Dutch father and then gamble away their patrimony at dice: the story of the unlucky gamester who throws his dagger wildly into the clouds in a futile attempt to assassinate his Maker can be discovered in almost all the major pre-Reformation *promptuaria*, as well as in Beard's *Theatre*, where the setting is German-speaking Switzerland in 1533. In the seventeenth-century broadside the murderer is devoured by a hole which instantly opens in the floor of the gaming house; in earlier permutations the knife returns like a boomerang to descend upon the scoundrel's own head, enacting the proverb 'who spits against heaven, it falls in his face'.[60]

Another case in point is a pamphlet relating how an innocent Antwerp youth executed for theft in Bonn at Christmas 1612 was supernaturally preserved on the gallows for the space of five days after the Lord placed beneath his dangling feet an invisible stool (Plate 5). The story of 'the hanged man miraculously saved' was no less firmly rooted in the hagiographical literature of the late Middle Ages. Here, however, the incorrigible criminal rescued by virtue of his passionate devotion to the Virgin Mary or St James has been replaced by a pious Protestant adolescent who attributes his deliverance solely to the mercy and sovereignty of God. And as Roger Chartier has shown, this legend was also revamped by publishers and propagandists in Tridentine France.[61] Catholic exempla collections supplied the basic storyline for other early modern pamphlets and songs, including a ballad first published in 1586 about a rich businessman who heartlessly snubbed his starving father and had his own lavish dinner strangely transformed into a dish of 'loathsome Toades'. In a thirteenth-century precursor of this tale, a son who has deceived his simple mother and driven her from home finds a serpent rather than a chicken coiled up on his plate. By the Restoration, this ancient fable had acquired a sharply

[59] Stubbes, *Two wunderfull and rare examples*, title-page and sigs. B1ʳ–2ᵛ; Richard Whitford, *A werke for housholders* (1533 edn.), sigs. C3ᵛ–4ʳ. Whitford's example is also recounted in Batman, *Doome*, 418; and Stubbes's in Perkins, *Direction for the government of the tongue*, 36; Gibson, *Lands mourning*, 72–3. The latter was still remembered as late as 1680 when it appears in a broadside entitled *The theatre of Gods judgements. Or the vialls of wrath poured out upon obstinate and resolute sinners, in 18 remarkable examples* ([1680]), no. 6.

[60] *The fearefull judgement of Almighty God, shewed upon two sonnes who most unnaturallye murthered their naturall father*, printed in Clark (ed.), *Shirburn Ballads*, 164–9; Tubach, *Index Exemplorum*, no. 2936, cf. 324. See also Beard, *Theatre*, 482.

[61] *True relation of Gods wonderfull mercies, in preserving one alive, which hanged five dayes*. A ballad also survives in MS: *A most miraculous, strange, and trewe ballad, of a younge man of the age of 19 yeares, who was wrongfully hangd at . . . Bon*, printed in Clark (ed.), *Shirburn Ballads*, 159–63. For medieval antecedents, see Tubach, *Index Exemplorum*, nos. 2234–6, 3796; Caesarius of Heisterbach, *Dialogue on Miracles*, ii. 60–1, 74; Johannes Herolt, *Miracles of the Blessed Virgin Mary*, trans. C. C. Swinton Bland (1928), 22–3. Roger Chartier, 'The Hanged Woman Miraculously Saved: An *Occasionnel*', in id. (ed.), *The Culture of Print: Power and the Uses of Print in Early Modern Europe*, trans. Lydia G. Cochrane (Cambridge, 1989), 59–91.

PLATE 5 *A true relation of Gods wonderfull mercies, in preserving one alive, which hanged five dayes, who was falsely accused* (London, [c.1613]), title-page. By permission of the British Library. Shelfmark: C. 143. b. 19.

sectarian edge: the scoundrel now disowns his destitute parent as a 'Presbyterian knave'.[62]

A particularly problematic aspect of these anecdotes is the precise mechanism by which providential retribution is engineered. Dozens of individual episodes

---

[62] *A most notable and worthy example of an ungratious sonne, who in the pride of his hart denied his owne father: and how God for his offence turned his meate into loathsome toades* ([c.1610?], [c.1625], [1638?]). First entered to Edward White on 8 Aug. 1586: *SR* ii. 452. The phrase 'Presbyterian knave' occurs in

exploit the device of the rash, just, or malicious wish which comes alarmingly true. In *A lanthorne for landlords* (*c*.1630), for instance, a courageous young woman struggling to bring up her orphaned twins and pay her weekly rent is pitilessly evicted by the miser who owns her humble abode. Aggrieved at her cruel treatment, she cries to heaven for revenge:

> That all the world may know,
> How you have forst a Soldiers wife
> a begging for to goe.

Her two undernourished toddlers perish, but the Almighty remembers her importunate plea and the hard-hearted 'Caitiffe' is driven raving mad by an astonishing succession of family scandals and disasters and eventually drowns himself in a shallow ditch barely deep enough to submerge 'a silly mouse'. This is reminiscent of another ballad based on an apocryphal story about a barren thirteenth-century countess from Holland punished for slandering a pauper blessed with a pair of 'pretty babes'. The insulted mother earnestly beseeches the Lord to send the pampered Madam as many children at one birth 'as dayes be in the yeare' and nine months later 'the lamenting lady' is duly delivered of 365 tiny 'ympes' (Plates 6*a* and *b*).[63] A similar petition brings down divine judgement upon several grasping fathers from a village near Grimsby who deny the local poor their customary right to glean pease: according to *Thunder haile, & lightni[ng] from heaven*, printed in 1616 (Plate 8), the injured parties pray to God to soften the hearts of their callous employers, who not long afterwards find their crops flattened by a violent storm.[64] Lurking behind all three examples is the idea of the beggar or widow's curse, that biblically sanctioned weapon of the helpless, impotent, and oppressed.[65] As these anecdotes suggest, there was always a fine line between the legitimate petition for supernatural aid and protection and the malevolent incantation or spell, between black magic and *maleficia* and forms of commination condoned by the Reformed Church of England.[66]

Other writers referred to the ritual maledictions still pronounced by some contemporary parents against their wayward and disobedient children. The spendthrift son who scoffs at his parents' admonitions features in several stories

a considerably modified Restoration version: *The ungrateful son; or, an example of God's justice upon the abusefull disobedience of a false-hearted and cruel son to his aged father* ([1682–95]). The story was recounted in prose in William Averell's *Dyall for dainty darlings*, sigs. C1ᵛ–D1ʳ. Caesarius of Heisterbach, *Dialogue on Miracles*, i. 432–3. See also Tubach, *Index Exemplorum*, nos. 970, 4891.

[63] *The lamenting lady, who for the wrongs done by her to a poore woman . . . was by the hand of God most strangely punished* ([1620?]).

[64] *Thunder haile, & lightni[ng] from heaven* ([1616]), esp. sig. B2ᵛ.

[65] Exod. xxii. 22–3; Deut. x. 18; Prov. xxviii. 27.

[66] On cursing, see Thomas, *Religion and the Decline of Magic*, 599–611, esp. 607–11; Alan Macfarlane, *Witchcraft in Tudor and Stuart England: A Regional and Comparative Study* (London, 1970), 171–6, 196–7; Hunt, *Puritan Moment*, 54–8. For ecclesiastically sanctioned cursing, see 'A Commination against Sinners, with Certain Prayers, to be Used Divers Times in the Year', in William Keating Clay (ed.), *Liturgical Services: Liturgies and Occasional Forms of Prayer set forth in the Reign of Queen Elizabeth*, Parker Soc. (Cambridge, 1847), 239–45.

PLATE 6 *The lamenting lady, who for the wrongs done by her to a poore woman . . . was by the hand of God most strangely punished* (London, [1620?]), woodcuts. By permission of the Pepys Library, Magdalene College, Cambridge. Shelfmark: Pepys Ballads I. 44–5.

a (*left*) A barren countess insults a poor beggar woman blessed with twins.

b (*below*) She is 'strangely punished' by the hand of God who causes her to give birth to 365 babies the size of newborn mice.

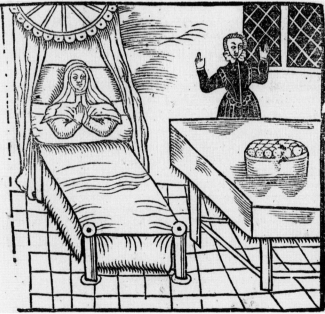

emphasizing the dangers of defying patriarchal authority and neglecting one's obligations to elderly relatives and kin. In a ballad dated 1633, for instance, a delinquent youth breathes his last gasp on a dunghill after his mother begs the Lord to send him a shameful death for consorting with 'strumpets and other lewd livers'.[67] No less familiar is the oath that recoils upon the utterer's own head, the curse that quite literally comes home to roost. One broadside printed around 1625 tells of a light-fingered London maidservant who repudiated the accusations levelled against her whenever her master and mistress's personal belongings were 'mist' and

> Wisht before God and men that she might rot,
> If that such things she ever saw or got.

Conveyed to Smithfield prison and then St Bartholomew's hospital, gangrenous decay 'presently' proves to be 'her heavy lot'.[68] In *A spectacle for usurers* (1606), a dishonest French pawnbroker who insists he would sooner be devoured by rats than defraud his clients is eaten by vermin, as he has decreed.[69] Edmund Bicknoll made a name for himself collecting cases of depraved persons who lived to rue the day they unadvisedly called upon the Lord to witness and avenge their evil deeds, and Thomas Beard allocated an entire chapter to the macabre deaths of individuals whose habitual expletive was 'the devil take me' or some execration to the like irreverent effect. One of these was an anecdote first related by the Edwardian bishop Nicholas Ridley about a Cornish gallant who spurred his horse on a bridge so aggressively that it 'sprange cleane over', carrying the 'lustie yonker' to a watery grave yelling this terrible oath as he fell.[70] Equally common are cases of frustrated mothers who foolishly wish that Satan would relieve them of their whingeing children.[71]

Latent in all these tales are theologically questionable assumptions about the physical efficacy of enunciating threatening words. Whether spoken in the heat of temper or solemnly pronounced upon the knees, curses implied an ability on the part of human beings to summon and manipulate divine power which was at odds with the idea that God preordained and actively brought about each and every

---

[67] L[awrence] P[rice], *A warning for all lewd livers. By the example of a disobedient child, who . . . died most miserably on a dunghill* ([1633]). See also *A most excellent new ballad, of an olde man and his wife, which in their olde age and misery sought to their owne children for succour, by whom they were disdained & scornfully sent away succourlesse, and how the vengeance of God was justly shewed upon them for the same* ([c.1600] and [c.1620]); *Most notable and worthy example of an ungratious sonne*; and Beard, *Theatre*, bk. II, ch. 1.

[68] H. I., *Example for all those that make no conscience of swearing and forswearing.* This news story made its way into the 1631 edn. of Beard, *Theatre*, 548.

[69] *A spectacle for usurers and succors of poore folkes bloud* (1606), 4–5.

[70] Bicknoll, *Swoord agaynst swearyng*, fos. 43ʳ–45ᵛ; Beard, *Theatre*, bk. I, chs. 30–1. For the 'lustie yonker' see p. 195. Also related in Foxe, *Acts and Monuments*, viii. 644–5; Perkins, *Direction for the government of the tongue*, 35–6; Gibson, *Lands mourning*, 72.

[71] Beard, *Theatre*, 189–90, 193–5. Such tales are extremely common in medieval devotional literature: see e.g. *Robert of Brunne's Handlyng Synne, AD 1303*, ed. Frederick J. Furnivall, EETS, OS 119 (1901), 45–7.

event. Such imprecations could only be squared with Calvinist providentialism if it was understood that He executed them independently and not at His creatures' whim or command, and that their fulfilment had been encompassed in the eternal plan formulated before the beginning of time. But what is most striking about these stories—and there is no discernible difference between those recounted in sermons and those reported in the ephemeral press—is the fact that they can easily be interpreted in oblivion and even contradiction of this Protestant gloss.

Something similar can be said about those post-Reformation exempla in which the devil plays a prominent role. He is especially ubiquitous in news pamphlets about shocking murders and suicides, instigating potential killers to commit brutal homicidal crimes and inciting the desperate to take the inexcusable step of doing themselves in. There is often considerable ambivalence about the scope and character of diabolical activity in these horrific events: is Satan a closely supervised instrument of divine justice or an immanent supernatural being; is he the Lord's hangman and executioner or an autonomous Manichaean force? Some writers gave their narratives an orthodox Augustinian slant, stressing that Lucifer could only carry out his pernicious designs in so far as he was authorized to do so by God. He could not seduce mankind to evil unless it was consistent with divine will and it served the deity's purposes to give over a particular person to 'a reprobate sence'.[72] They presented every act of self-destruction as a providential judgement, the chief aider and abettor of which was the Archfiend. Thus the devil urges an unprincipled widow to throw herself from an upper storey window in Cornhill in 1574; thus the cut-throat Thomas Hill submits to similar inducements and suspends himself 'with v points of his hose . . . on an olde hedlesse naile' in a cell in Canterbury gaol.[73] The author of *The bloudy booke*, a report of the suicide of Sir John Fites, a serial killer, in 1605, suspected that the devil had materialized, so menacing him with damnation in hell that he deliberately fell on the point of his sword.[74] Beard collected more than twenty examples of wrongdoers lured by the Father of Lies to take their own lives, in all of which he is portrayed as an agent and lieutenant of heavenly wrath.[75]

Elsewhere, however, Satan operates with disturbingly unbridled freedom and vigour—with all the ebullience of medieval demons and fiends. Far from being a meek and faithful messenger of the Almighty, he often appears a formidable warrior in his own right, intent upon seducing and destroying mankind. The woodcut pictures accompanying many pamphlets and ballads reinforced this by depicting the Prince of Darkness in the corporeal forms he had already assumed

---

[72] I. T., *A horrible creuel and bloudy murther, committed at Putney in Surrey* (1614), sig. A4ᵛ. For other Protestant glosses, see *The godly end and wofull lamentation of one John Stevens, a youth that was hang'd . . . at Salisbury* ([1633]); *Spectacle for usurers*, 3; *Murder upon murder, committed by Thomas Sherwood, alias Countrey Tom* ([1635]) and the fuller account in Henry Goodcole's pamphlet, *Heavens speedie hue and cry sent after lust and murther* (1635).

[73] M[unday], *View of sundry examples*, sigs. B2ʳ and D1ʳ.

[74] *The bloudy booke. Or, the tragicall and desperate end of Sir John Fites (alias) Fitz* (1605), sig. D3ᵛ.

[75] Beard, *Theatre*, bk. II, ch. 12, see esp. p. 307. See also pp. 30, 65, 75, 215–16.

for centuries—as a black dog or bear, or a mythical beast complete with horns, serpent's tail, and cloven hooves (Plate 7). In one such cartoon, he crows over a humiliated sinner, declaring triumphantly 'Thou art mine' (Plate 4).[76] In the ballad version of *Dr Faustus*, the professor of divinity who mortgages his soul to Mephistopheles in return for immortal powers, the 'Divell' similarly seems less a servant and pawn than a spiritual coequal with God. Always ready to take advantage of the least opportunity to increase his infernal kingdom, he takes positively sadistic pleasure in ripping Faustus's body to bits.[77] As we saw in Chapter 1, such tensions were inbuilt in Protestant demonology itself: the reformers faced the problem of having to reconcile a renewed emphasis on Satan's power to corrupt humanity with the claim that he could only work within well-defined limits. Their conviction that the devil was launching a fresh assault on the forces of good in the world, in league with an army of witches whom he had bound to his service by means of a pact, coexisted a little uneasily with the full logical consequences of their belief in divine omnipotence. In this respect, as in others, Protestantism had the potential to reinforce rather than undercut older assumptions.[78]

A related issue was whether submission to Satan's wily influence was the cause of vicious impulses or rather the unhappy result. Protestant ministers contended that succumbing to such temptations and committing suicide was 'not onely a punishment of sinne past, but a fearefull sinne it selfe': the Almighty had to forsake an individual before the devil could begin his all-out assaults, but those who then yielded did so culpably, out of their own free will. The offender was thus doubly condemned.[79] Hence Francis Spiera, the Italian apostate whose tragic history became a Protestant trope, is tormented to a point of extremity not just for recanting the Reformed religion, but for despairing of divine mercy and persuading himself that he is eternally doomed.[80] Yet it was simple enough to ignore these

---

[76] *Anthony Painter. The blaspheming caryar.* See also *The unnaturall wife: or, the lamentable murther of one Goodman Davis, who was stabbed to death by his wife* ([1628]). On the iconography of the devil in pamphlet literature, see Davies, *Reflections of Renaissance England*, 202–5.

[77] *The judgement of God shewed upon one John Faustus, Doctor in Divinity* ([1658–64]). First entered to Richard Jones, 28 Feb. 1589 (*SR* ii. 516) but no copy of the Elizabethan broadside survives. For another story modelled on Faustus, in which a woman who bargains with the devil has her head torn from her body, see L[awrence] P[rice], *Strange and wonderfull news of a woman which lived neer unto the famous city of London, who had her head torn off from her body by the divell* ([*c.*1630]).

[78] As has been argued by Michael MacDonald, *Mystical Bedlam: Madness, Anxiety, and Healing in Seventeenth Century England* (Cambridge, 1981), 167–8, 174–5; id. and Terence R. Murphy, *Sleepless Souls: Suicide in Early Modern England* (Oxford, 1990), 31–41. See also the remarks of Lake, 'Deeds against Nature', 268–9, 277–83. Cf. Fernando Cervantes, *The Devil in the New World: The Impact of Diabolism in New Spain* (New Haven, 1994), esp. 18–19, 128–33, who agrees that the devil was part of popular as well as elite belief but stresses the extent to which the new emphasis on providence by demonologists on both sides of the Reformation divide marked a departure from traditional theology.

[79] Beard, *Theatre*, 317, cf. 308. See e.g. *Thunder haile, & lightni[ng] from heaven*, sigs. C1ʳ–3ʳ.

[80] Two prose tracts about Spiera were printed: Matteo Gribaldi, *A notable and marveilous epistle . . . concernyng the terrible judgemente of God, upon hym that for feare of men, denieth Christ and the knowne veritie* (1550, [1570?]) and Nathaniel Bacon, *A relation of the fearefull estate of Francis Spira, in the yeare, 1548* (1638). BL Sloane MS 397 is a copy of the latter. A ballad on the subject entered in *SR* on 15 June 1587 is now lost: ii. 472. Spiera's story is summarized in Beard, *Theatre*, 73–4. See also Michael

PLATE 7 *The unnaturall wife: or, the lamentable murther of one goodman Davis, who was stabbed to death by his wife* (London, [1628]), woodcut. By permission of the Pepys Library, Magdalene College, Cambridge. Shelfmark: Pepys Ballads I. 122.

doctrinal niceties and view self-murderers as the unwitting victims of diabolical aggression of a type which no ordinary person could be expected to successfully repel. Moreover, as Richard Godbeer has recently argued, in practice Protestant teaching on the question of moral responsibility was ambiguous and open to mis-interpretation: it could as easily justify locating the source of evil and sin outside as inside the self. There was thus ample room in these anecdotes for ideological and hermeneutic confusion. They highlight how far Calvinist theology was capable of accommodating, if not encouraging, aspects of popular belief.[81]

We also see cultural continuities tempering and at the same time facilitating cultural change in *A strange and fearefull warning* (1623), a pamphlet about poltergeist activity in the household of John Barefoote, a tailor of the Wiltshire town of Sunning, in 1622. The havoc wrought in his home is interpreted as divine retribution for his failure to execute his father's will and misappropriation of property left to his sisters. The noisy, mischievous spirit is 'Gods Angell' in the guise of the devil, to whom He had given sufferance and 'leave unto, to bee a punisher of the said false Steward'. Despite its author's irreproachably Protestant account of these eerie events, this news report still reads suspiciously like a medieval ghost story—

MacDonald, 'The Fearefull Estate of Francis Spira: Narrative, Identity, and Emotion in Early Modern England', *JBS* 31 (1992), 32–61; M. A. Overell, 'The Exploitation of Francesco Spiera', *SCJ* 26 (1995), 619–37.

[81] Godbeer, *Devil's Dominion*, ch. 3, esp. 85–108.

another case of a restless soul returning from the dead to ensure the proper disposition of his legacies and bequests. The Reformation may have done away with purgatory, but it could not and did not eliminate capricious spectres: it merely redefined them as demons.[82]

Traces of Christian and pre-Christian convictions from an earlier age likewise linger on in accounts of the 'marvailous operation of Gods finger' in the 'admirable discoverie' of hidden murders and their wicked perpetrators.[83] In both Beard's *Theatre* and the ephemeral literature produced by London journalists and hacks, it is neither chance, coincidence, nor human intuition but providence which magnetically draws murderers back to the scene of their secret crimes, thwarts their escape across the sea by sending stormy and unseasonable weather, and induces their horses to trip on stretches of ground where there is 'scarce a pibble to resist' their 'hast'.[84] And who else inclines a farmer to dredge his pond at considerable expense and a mischievous boy to throw a mongrel into a privy, thereby unearthing mangled bodies which had long remained concealed?[85] Foul play frequently comes to light by even more frankly 'miraculous' means. Culprits are uncloaked by the deaf, blind, and dumb; in a case from Hertfordshire dated 1606, God restores the faculty of speech to a hideously mutilated 10-year-old schoolgirl with only a stump for a tongue.[86] Stories in which buried carcasses are dug up by dogs, or in which crows, swallows, pigeons, and cranes conspire to reveal the villains to the investigating authorities looked back to classical sources like Plutarch and Pliny, betraying ancient convictions about the way nature manifested its outrage about human

---

[82] *A strange and fearefull warning, to all sonnes and executors* (1623), sigs. A8ʳ, A3ʳ, and *passim*. For other exempla involving poltergeists, see *The most rare, strange and wonderfull example of Almightie God, shewed in the citie of Telonne in Provence, on a cruell papisticall bishop* (1592), 3–4; Beard, *Theatre*, 572–82. Some of the most perceptive work on ghost beliefs after the Reformation has been done by folklorists, see Theo Brown, *The Fate of the Dead: A Study in Folk-Eschatology in the West Country after the Reformation* (Cambridge, 1979), esp. chs. 2–3 and p. 83; Gillian Bennett, 'Ghost and Witch in the Sixteenth and Seventeenth Centuries', *Folklore*, 97 (1986), 3–14. See also Natalie Zemon Davis, 'Ghosts, Kin, and Progeny: Some Features of Family Life in Early Modern France', *Daedalus*, 106 (1977), 87–114; Thomas, *Religion and the Decline of Magic*, 701–18, esp. 715–16; Ronald Finucane, *Appearances of the Dead: A Cultural History of Ghosts* (1982), esp. ch. 4. I have also benefited from discussing the subject with Dr Peter Marshall.

[83] Quotations from *A true report of the horrible murther, which was committed in the house of Sir Jerome Bowes, knight* (1607), sig. C2ᵛ and Beard, *Theatre*, 295. As Philippa C. Maddern notes, the idea that God would infallibly discover and punish was commonplace among the medieval laity: *Violence and Social Order: East Anglia 1422–1442* (Oxford, 1992), 79–80.

[84] *The araignment, examination, confession and judgement of Arnold Cosbye: who wilfully murdered the Lord Burke, neere the towne of Wansworth* (1591), sigs. B2ᵛ–3ᵛ; *True report of the horrible murther . . . committed in the house of Sir Jerome Bowes*, sig. C2ʳ⁻ᵛ; *Two most unnaturall and bloodie murthers* (1605), 16. Beard added a new chapter on the subject in the 1612 and subsequent edns. of his *Theatre*, bk. II, ch. 11.

[85] Thomas Cooper, *The cry and revenge of blood* (1620), 60 [*vere* 40]–43; *Deeds against nature, and monsters by kinde* (1614), sig. A4ʳ⁻ᵛ.

[86] *The most cruell and bloody murther committed by an inkeepers wife, called Annis Dell* (1606), sigs. B4ʳ–C2ᵛ; *The horrible murther of a young boy of three yeres of age, whose sister had her tongue cut out* (1606), 5–9. See also *A most horrible & detestable murther committed by a bloudie minded man . . . most strangely revealed by his childe that was under five yeares of age* (1595). For murder revealed by the deaf and dumb, see *Three bloudie murders*, sig. C2ʳ⁻ᵛ.

misdeeds.[87] Others incorporated phenomena that originated in medieval ordeals and taboos. In a ballad from the 1630s, for example, the dying victim of the ruthless Buckinghamshire highwaywoman Susan Higges spits three drops of blood in her face, which she tries in vain to wash away. This scripturally based belief, familiar from Shakespeare's *Macbeth*, also features in the report of a Lincolnshire innkeeper's wife who slays an unsuspecting traveller for his cash—no amount of scrubbing will remove the tell-tale dark stains on her smock.[88] In *Sundry strange and inhumaine murthers* (1591), the corpses of three children bleed afresh in the presence of the assassin hired by their widowed father to rid him of his unwanted burden, who promptly owns up, considering himself caught in the act. The same kind of sympathetic magic occurs when a Rutlandshire shoemaker is dragged before an exhumed body, which prises open one of its eyes to mesmerize the murderer.[89] Post-Reformation commentators as prominent as King James I sanctioned the judicial ritual of compelling a suspect to approach and touch a lifeless cadaver as a proof of his or her innocence or guilt and it continued to feature in trials and coroners' inquests throughout the sixteenth and seventeenth centuries. A few sceptics were beginning to explain away such spontaneous effects physiologically or psychologically, but as late as 1691 Richard Baxter was still celebrating well-documented cases as 'stupendous signs' of God's wrath against those who infringed the sixth commandment.[90] Like the curse, this was a type of supernatural trial in which God was prevailed upon to reveal His justice in a manner apparently incompatible with Calvinist insistence upon its inscrutability.[91] Yet it too knitted with Protestant belief in the inexorability of divine justice and in a world ruled over by an omniscient and interventionist deity.[92]

At the same time, there was a growing tendency for providence to work internally through the malefactor's own conscience and for divine retribution to take the more intangible form of mental torment. In 'the infancy of the world', declared the preacher Thomas Adams, 'Gods blowes were most outward', but 'in this ripe (or rather rotten) age of it, they are most inward and spirituall'. Intransigent sinners should not fear fire and brimstone, thunderclaps, or fiery vipers so much

---

[87] For examples, see *Sundrye strange and inhumaine murthers, lately committed* (1591), sigs. B1ʳ, B4ᵛ; *Thunder haile, & lightni[ng] from heaven*, sig. C3ʳ. See also Edward Topsell, *The historie of foure-footed beastes* (1607), 156–7 and the lost ballad and pamphlet published by John Trundle in Mar. and Sept. 1615: *SR* iii. 564, 572. The latter was entitled *Newes out of Lancashire or the strang[e] and miraculous revelacon of a murther by a ghost a calf a pigeon &c.*

[88] *A true relation of one Susan Higges, dwelling in Risborow, a towne in Buckinghamshire* ([*c.*1640?]); T. I., *World of wonders*, sig. F3ᵛ. See Gen. iv. 9–10.

[89] *Sundrye strange and inhumaine murthers*, sig. A4ʳ⁻ᵛ. See also *Araignment, examination, confession and judgement of Arnold Cosbye*, sig. B3ʳ; M[unday], *View of sundry examples*, sigs. C4ᵛ–D1ʳ.

[90] James VI and I, *Daemonologie, in the forme of a dialogue* (1603 edn.), 79. Thomas Ady was one of those who tried to explain away this effect psychologically: *Candle in the dark*, 131. Baxter, *The certainty of the worlds of spirits* (1691), 105–7.

[91] For valuable comments on the theology of ordeals, see Robert Bartlett, *Trial by Fire and Water: The Medieval Judicial Ordeal* (Oxford, 1986), esp. 73–87.

[92] Cf. Lake, 'Deeds against Nature', 269–74.

as a troubled and accusatory state of mind. The heaviest of all chastisements, stressed Bishop Lewis Bayly, was 'a heart that cannot repent'.[93] Some storytellers reflected this paradigm shift by elaborating upon the psychic torture that afflicted the wicked, and the pangs and twinges of guilt which led them to come clean, incriminate themselves, or slit their own throats. A favourite example was Father Lea of Foster Lane who disembowelled himself with 'an olde rustie knife', overcome with remorse after hiring himself out as a false witness in 1576.[94] Yet, like the decline of hell as a concrete place and reified concept, the interiorization of temporal punishment and the rise of what John Stachniewski has called the 'persecutory imagination' did not occur overnight.[95] Beard's *Theatre* lies in limbo between a physical and a subliminal notion of providential justice. In it, anecdotes about anguished, self-accusing criminals and sinners driven into 'a franticke bedlam' and out of their wits sit side by side with 'strange, yet not incredible' tales of butchered calves' heads mysteriously metamorphosed into murdered men's and of pennies extorted from peasants which transform themselves into snarling and poisonous snakes.[96]

The vengeful Jehovah delineated in these judgement stories was no more than a caricature of the arcane, transcendent, and imponderable deity delineated by Calvin in the *Institutes*. Indeed, the title-page illustrations of many pamphlets continued to represent Him anthropomorphically (Plates 8, 9), in a manner utterly inimical to iconophobic Protestants to whom anything other than that forbiddingly abstract symbol, the Hebrew Tetragrammaton, was abominable idolatry (Plate 10).[97] This is a God who behaves more like a feudal warlord jealously engaged in a personal vendetta than a stern but benevolent Father and Redeemer; He behaves in fact very much like the punitive saints to be found in every pre-Reformation collection of sermon exempla. He is just as impetuous in pursuing those who mock His majesty, just as vindictive towards those who neglect to carry out promises to their exacting divine patron, just as ready to resort to slaps and blows to convince the contumacious as the proud and sometimes imperious holy personages who won the affections of the late medieval laity.[98] There is not so great a gulf between the

---

[93]   Thomas Adams, *The gallants burden* (1612), repr. in *The Workes . . .* (1630), 5; Bayly, *Practise of pietie*, 259–60.

[94]   This example can be found in Bicknoll, *Swoord agaynst swearyng*, fos. 37ʳ–38ᵛ (summarizing a lost pamphlet printed by John Allde); M[unday], *View of sundry examples*, sigs. B2ᵛ–3ʳ; T. I., *World of wonders*, sig. E1. Francis Godlif or Godly published a pamphlet in 1577 entitled *Judgement of God uppon a perjured person, dwelling in Gunne Alley in the parishe of Saint Buttolphs, who ripped his belly*, which may also be about Father Lea. This is recorded in Maunsell, *Catalogue*, fo. 113a. See also *Two horrible and inhumane murders done in Lincolneshire . . .* (1607), sig. A4ʳ⁻ᵛ; *A fearefull example. Shewed upon a perjured person. Who . . . did . . . desperatly stabbe himselfe* (1591), 4.

[95]   D. P. Walker, *The Decline of Hell: Seventeenth Century Discussions of Eternal Torment* (1964); Stachniewski, *Persecutory Imagination*, ch. 2, esp. 23–4 and 36, and 93–4. See also Margaret Aston, *England's Iconoclasts*, i. *Laws against Images* (Oxford, 1988), 465.

[96]   Beard, *Theatre*, 52 and 304 respectively.

[97]   On the iconography of God in pamphlet literature, see Davies, *Reflections of Renaissance England*, 195–8.

[98]   On the aggressive behaviour of medieval saints see Gurevich, *Medieval Popular Culture*, ch. 2, esp. 46–8, and 202–5; Duffy, *Stripping of the Altars*, 185; Ronald C. Finucane, *Miracles and Pilgrims: Popular*

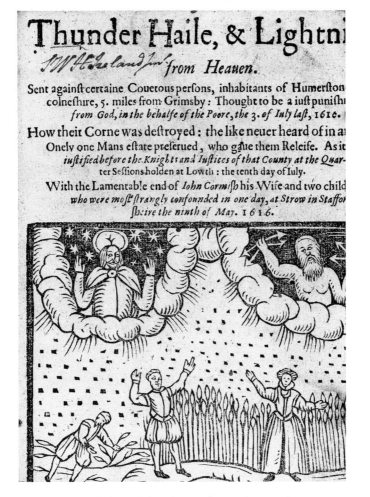

PLATE 8 *Thunder haile, & lightni[ng] from heaven. Sent against certaine covetous persons, inhabitants of Humerstone [Lin]colneshire* (London, [1616]), title-page. By permission of the British Library. Shelfmark: C. 115. d. 6.

savage retaliatory tactics adopted by the Almighty in many of the cautionary tales collected by Protestant ministers and the conduct of John the Baptist in an anecdote recounted by the German Cistercian Caesarius of Heisterbach dating from *c.*1220–35: dishonoured by a dissolute cathedral canon, the saint angrily rebukes him in a dream, lifting his celestial foot to give the wretched cleric a swift and sharp kick in the belly. Nor are they too far removed from stories of the Virgin Mary boxing the ears of a nun with lecherous thoughts and Christ striking the cheek of

Beliefs in Medieval England (1977), 34–5; David Gentilcore, *From Bishop to Witch: The System of the Sacred in Early Modern Terra d'Ottranto* (Manchester, 1992), ch. 6, esp. 184–5.

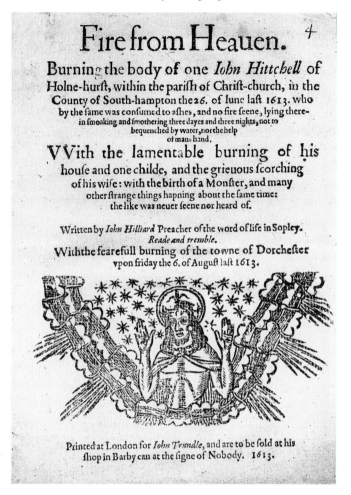

PLATE 9 John Hilliard, *Fire from heaven. Burning the body of one John Hitchell of Holne-hurst* (London, 1613), title-page. By permission of the Bodleian Library, University of Oxford. Shelfmark: Wood D 28 (4).
Recycled pre-Reformation woodcut of Christ in majesty.

a monk who goes to sleep during the nightly office when he should be keeping the vigil.[99] It is no less difficult to reconcile this tit-for-tat mentality with Protestantism than with the Christianity of the thirteenth-, fourteenth-, and fifteenth-century Church.

[99] Caesarius of Heisterbach, *Dialogue on Miracles*, i. 234, ii. 52–3; Tubach, *Index Exemplorum*, no. 746. See also nos. 190, 216, 1946, 2734, 3470.

PLATE 10 Thomas Gataker, *A sparke toward the kindling of sorrow for Sion. A meditation on Amos. 6.6.* (London, 1621), detail from p. 1. By permission of the British Library. Shelfmark: 4474. bb. 31.
Hebrew Tetragrammaton.

Protestants did quietly edit out of medieval exempla elements emphasizing submission to priestly authority and compliance with ecclesiastical regulations regarding Roman Catholic ritual and liturgy; they suppressed stories in which divine beings indulgently overlooked the moral lapses of their devotees; and they naturally replaced the earlier focus on cloistered religious with a new stress on ordinary laypeople. But more than a residue of the tendency to domesticate and personalize the sacred remained.

And when it comes to doling out mercies and rewards to the faithful and good, providence seems to engross all the therapeutic properties previously divided among a host of heavenly deputies. It is in the Lord rather than the Blessed Virgin, the traditional protectress of seafarers in peril, that eight English sailors left behind in Greenland in 1630 place their sole trust;[100] He alone who sustains a pious Elizabethan widow and her seven children on a burnt sixpenny loaf of bread for nearly two months in Copthall in Kent; who causes pease to grow upon rocks on the Suffolk coast to sustain the poor; and who nourishes the family of a Worcestershire debtor on a single udder of mare's milk for several weeks.[101] It is

---

[100] Edward Pellham, *Gods power and providence: shewed, in the miraculous preservation and deliverance of eight Englishmen, left by mischance in Green-land anno 1630* (1631), esp. sig. A3ʳ, pp. 16, 35. This incident also generated a ballad: *A wonder beyond mans expectation, in the preservation of eight men in Greenland* (1632). For a similar example of a shipwrecked sailor who attributes his deliverance to providence, see *Lamentable newes, shewing the wonderfull deliverance of Maister Edmond Pet sayler* (1613). For a miraculous cure attributed to God's mercy see *Two most remarkable and true histories . . . The one relating how God most miraculously restored to health Elizabeth Goossens Taets* (1620).

[101] *The Kentish wonder: being a true relation how a poor distressed widow, in the wild of Kent, was, by the providence of the Almighty, miraculously preserved in her necessity* ([1672–80]) and *The Kentish miracle; or, a strange and miraculous work of Gods providence* ([1684]). These ballads were based on an Elizabethan broadside entitled *The poore widowe of Copthall in Kent and her seaven children how wonderfullie the Lord fed them in their wante*, entered in *SR* to Thomas Millington on 31 Oct. 1594 and re-entered to Henry Gosson on 12 Nov. 1608: ii. 664; iii. 394. A ballad entitled *Gods mercye showed to the poore at Orford and Albourowe in Suffolk shewinge the soden growth of peaze uppon the sea rock* was entered in *SR* iii. 67. The story is summarized in Batman, *Doome*, 402–3. This was an updated version of an old marvel which had apparently occurred in 1554. For the Worcestershire debtor, see T. I., *World of wonders*, sig. E1ᵛ.

very tempting to see this thaumaturgic, wonder-working God as an emotional substitute for a hierarchical network of miracle-mongering saints, as filling the substantial vacuum left by the official abolition of their cults.

There is also a degree of overlap with the past with regard to the types of sinners targeted for exemplary punishment. John Bossy has argued that in the late Middle Ages the Decalogue slowly displaced the Seven Deadly Sins as the dominant moral system. An ethical code in which transgressions against society—against charity and solidarity—had pre-eminence was eclipsed by one which placed greater emphasis on spiritual and sexual offences, above all adultery and idolatry. The obligations of individual Christians towards God gradually took precedence over their responsibilities towards their community.[102] The moral economy which emerges from a study of cheap print and clerical encyclopedias, however, cannot be situated securely on either side of this divide. In Beard's *Theatre* retributive episodes which probably would have slotted more comfortably into the traditional septenary schema of the Seven Deadlies have been thrust into chapters organized around the Ten Commandments. Extant ballads and newsbooks do sometimes reflect the preoccupation with carnal lust and religious apostasy which allegedly hallmarked the early modern era, but they no less frequently give expression to an 'old-fashioned' concern with vices like pride and sumptuary excess which undermined the established social and gender hierarchy. The Almighty bears down heavily upon liars, cursers, blasphemers, fornicators, and magicians, but He also brandishes His sword against covetous usurers, misers, and cornhoarders, negligent relatives and stony-hearted daughters and sons. No class of evildoer is immune. This was a genre which could as easily accommodate a report of five sabbath-breaking drunkards who caroused the night away and drowned when their water taxi overturned in the Thames, as the saga of a lover who returned from the dead to abduct the faithless maiden who broke his heart along with her engagement vow. Providence could be appropriated to teach a plebeian lesson about marital etiquette no less effectively than a clerical one about sabbatarianism.[103] Of course, even anecdotes about the divine wrath visited upon those who failed to keep Sunday holy cannot be regarded as unequivocally Protestant, let alone puritan. Stories about blood flowing from loaves kneaded on the Lord's Day and husbandmen whose hands are paralysed when they repair ploughs on the sabbath can be found scattered throughout late medieval homiletic and devotional literature.[104]

---

[102] John Bossy, *Christianity and the West 1400–1700* (Oxford, 1985), 35–42; id., 'Moral Arithmetic: Seven Sins into Ten Commandments', in Edmund Leites (ed.), *Conscience and Casuistry in Early Modern Europe* (Cambridge, 1988), 214–34.

[103] *A dolefull dittye of five unfortunat persons that were drowned in their drunkenes in crossing over the Thames . . . set forth for an example for all such prophaners of the Lord's sabaoth daye* ([1616]), printed in Clark (ed.), *Shirburn Ballads*, 68–71; *A warning for maidens; [or, Young Bateman]* ([1650?]), one of a number of 17th-cent. edns. of the ballad, *A warning for fayre maides by thexample of Jarmans wyfe*, entered to Edward Alde on 8 June 1603: *SR* iii. 236.

[104] See Tubach, *Index Exemplorum*, no. 4135 and Kenneth L. Parker, *The English Sabbath: A Study of Doctrine and Discipline from the Reformation to the Civil War* (Cambridge, 1988), p. 11 and ch. 2 *passim*.

What emerges, then, is a relatively crude providentialism in which suffering and misfortune are simplistically equated with immorality and sin. Preachers might constantly remind their congregations that adversities befell the godly as well as the degenerate and wicked, that God had sound reasons for suffering his 'owne deerest servants' to be humbled and tried. They might explain away the glaring anomalies in divine justice by asserting that the Lord had a logic, albeit opaque and enigmatic, of His own: He struck down some sinners in their prime as a terrible advertisement, 'a Parable or warning peece' to the rest, but spared others so that mankind would live in godly awe and fear of the final Day of Doom.[105] But in the context of Protestant exempla books, as of cheap print, we rarely catch sight of this cryptic reasoning or of the rhetoric of Job. And although the danger of seeking to deduce the identity of the elect and the reprobate from external events was a constant refrain of the clergy, in practice temporal punishment and eternal torment were readily confused. The unspoken supposition underlying the vast majority of these stories is that the disastrous ends that overtake impenitent offenders in this world accurately prefigure their hideous fate in the next—providing, in the words of Beard himself, but 'a taste and a scantling' of the tribulations in store for them in the inferno below.[106] A stricken Lincolnshire serving-man, for instance, dies commending his spirit to 'th'infernall gulfe, and Laberinth of hell'; Anthony Painter, the 'Blaspheming Caryar', cries with dreadful certainty 'I am damnd, I am damnd to all the divels of hell' (Plate 4); and John Mesnier, a Parisian persecutor of the Huguenots, breathes his last 'beginning to feele in this life, both in bodie and soule, the rigour of eternall fire'.[107] Less explicit but no less illuminating are those anecdotes in which the corpses of sinners become as black as pitch, too heavy for the pall-bearers to lift, or exude an odious stench, symbolizing the corrupt and accursed state of their souls.[108] These motifs were vestiges of an outmoded eschatology in which, at least in the popular mind, there was a mathematically straightforward relationship between salvation and merit and damnation and sin.[109] Most tales of God's judgements could be understood in complete ignorance, even pelagian negation, of the soteriological paradoxes high Calvinist divinity contained.

Despite Dr Parker's demonstration that a mature doctrine of the sabbath predated the Reformation, the sabbatarianism which emerged in the work of Nicholas Bownd and other puritan ministers in the mid- and late 1590s was theologically different and distinct. See Patrick Collinson, 'The Beginnings of English Sabbatarianism', in id., *Godly People: Essays on English Protestantism and Puritanism* (1983), 429–43.

[105] Quotations from Williams, *Best religion*, 150; Vaughan, *Spirit of detraction*, 274. On these themes see also Beard, *Theatre*, bk. II, chs. 51–4; Rogers, *General session*, chs. 12–13.

[106] Beard, *Theatre*, 539.

[107] Stubbes, *Two wunderfull and rare examples*, sig. B2ʳ; *Anthony Painter. The blaspheming caryar*, woodcut on title-page and sig. B2ʳ; Beard, *Theatre*, 53.

[108] For some examples, see Beard, *Theatre*, 64; *A new ballad, intituled, a warning to youth, shewing the lewd life of a marchants sonne of London* ([1628–9]); *The devils conquest: or, a wish obtained: shewing how one lately of Barnsby-street wisht the devil fetch her . . . and her body was found as black as pitch all over* ([1665]); Thomas Broke, *An epitaphe declaryng the lyfe and end of D. Edmund Boner &c* ([1569?]); Stubbes, *Anatomy*, pt. I, ed. Furnivall, 72.

[109] For their medieval heritage, see Tubach, *Index Exemplorum*, nos. 723, 1256, 1257, 1264, 1265, 1270, 1416, 5029.

A revealing exception to this general rule is a pamphlet published by the Hampshire preacher John Hilliard in 1613 (Plate 9). *Fire from heaven* is ostensibly a thoroughly conventional example of sensational news—a graphic account of a tragic accident which befell John Hitchell, a sleeping carpenter from Holdenhurst in Dorset struck by a flash of lightning during a midsummer thunderstorm and consumed to ashes by a mysterious, unquenchable flame. But once the misleading title-page has been turned the tract bears far more resemblance to a funeral sermon. As Hilliard was at pains to stress, Hitchell was no notorious libertine and sinner, no idle and debauched tippler in the local tavern, but a man of honest and upright demeanour who laboured 'truely and painefully' in his vocation and was a considerate husband and conscientious father. Not even 'the nearest or the worst affected of his neighbours' avowed otherwise. God had sent this strange example to underline Christ's caveat to the Jews in Luke xiii.1-5: 'let us not thinke that those on whome the Tower in Siloam fell, were greater sinners then all those that dwell in Jerusalem, but rather let us assure our selves, that unlesse we repent, we shall also perish.' If this happened in 'a green tree', asked Hilliard, 'what shall become of us, that are drie and withered?', 'what shall become of us vile wretched creatures that delight in nothing but sinne?'[110] Here a case of sudden and drastic death has been used to drive home a more subtle and sophisticated theological message. Deceptively packaged by our old friend John Trundle, who plastered a moth-eaten woodcut of Christ in majesty on the title-page and added his trademark 'Reade and Tremble', *Fire from heaven* was a curious hybrid—the product of a fruitful partnership between piety and profit.

This, therefore, was no unambiguously Protestant genre. But nor was it more than residually Catholic. The reservoir of providential stories into which both preachers and publishers constantly contributed and dipped testifies instead to an intermingling and fusion of elements of the old cosmology with aspects of the new. This process of osmosis adds weight to Peter Lake's recent claims that we need to discard the assumption that Protestantism was antipathetic to the basic mental structures of traditional religion.[111]

PROVERBIAL WISDOM AND AUTHENTYCKE REPORTS

The cautionary tales reported in cheap print and recounted in judgement books, then, had a venerable heritage, a cultural existence which predated the advent of print. Circulated scribally among secular clergy and monks, Latin exempla betray sure signs of infection by, or rather intermixture with, a semi-autonomous vernacular culture which flourished beyond the church and cloister wall.[112] As many scholars are now recognizing, the revolution in communications which coincided

---

[110] Hilliard, *Fire from heaven*, sigs. B1ᵛ, B1ʳ, B2ʳ.
[111] Lake, 'Deeds against Nature', 283.
[112] See n. 28, above.

with the Reformation did not, at least in the short term, eliminate this culture, but, on the contrary, enriched and reinforced it.

Certainly, ideas about the inexorability of supernatural justice seem to have remained deeply embedded in oral tradition in early modern England. They were, for example, an integral part of proverbial wisdom. Plenty of short pithy sayings then widely in use encapsulated a bleak realism about the impossibility of evading either one's destiny or one's just deserts: 'As you bake so shall you brew', 'God's mill grinds slow but sure', 'The Lord comes with leaden feet but strikes with iron hands', 'Pride will have a fall', 'Murder will out'. Equally commonplace was the notion that punishments were doled out to mirror exactly the character and gravity of the crime.[113]

The same assumptions are inherent in many topographical legends current in the Elizabethan and early Stuart period. Embodying a sense of the past still focused more on space than time and more on sites than dates, tales about the origin of geological features and prehistoric monuments functioned as a vehicle for teaching social norms, moral taboos, and Christian truths. They embodied a belief that God literally inscribed His judgements on the landscape. Thomas Fuller recorded in his *History of the worthies of England* (1662) a local tradition explaining how the Hanging Stone near Combe Martin in Devon had acquired its name: it was said that a sheep thief resting on the rock had been providentially strangled to death by the stolen ewe tied around his neck. A story associated with 'The Hurlers', a group of standing stones in the parish of St Cleer near Liskeard, likewise found its way into Richard Carew's *Survey of Cornwall* (1602). According to 'the country people's report', these megaliths had once been men, 'so metamorphosed' because they had profaned the sabbath by the Cornish game of hurling.[114] Other upright slabs were alleged to be petrified dancers and lakes were sometimes regarded as the consequence of iniquitous towns and cities sinking into a hole in the earth and being submerged under water. Both sets of legends have Old Testament prototypes—the transformation of Lot's wife into a pillar of salt and apocryphal versions of the destruction of Sodom and Gomorrah.[115] By the late seventeenth century, the educated elite were dissociating themselves from such 'vulgar errors'

---

[113] Morris Palmer Tilley, *A Dictionary of the Proverbs in England in the Sixteeenth and Seventeenth Centuries* (Ann Arbor, 1950), nos. B52, G270, G182, P581, M1315, F114. See also Bartlett Jere Whiting, *Proverbs, Sentences, and Proverbial Phrases from English Writings mainly before 1500* (Cambridge, Mass. 1968), nos. B529, G264, M806–7, P385–6, P391, P393. On proverbs, see James Obelkevich, 'Proverbs and Social History', in Peter Burke and Roy Porter (eds.), *The Social History of Language* (Cambridge, 1987), 43–72; Fox, 'Aspects of Oral Culture', ch. 3.

[114] Thomas Fuller, *The history of the worthies of England* (1662), 1st pagination, 247–8; Richard Carew, *The Survey of Cornwall*, ed. F. E. Halliday (1969), 203.

[115] See Herbert Halpert, 'Supernatural Sanctions and the Legend', in Venetia J. Newall (ed.), *Folklore Studies in the Twentieth Century: Proceedings of the Centenary Conference of the Folklore Society* (Woodbridge, 1980), 226–33; Jacqueline Simpson, 'Beyond Etiology: Interpreting Local Legends', *Fabula*, 24 (1983), 223–32; ead., 'God's Visible Judgements: The Christian Dimension of Landscape Legends', *Landscape History*, 8 (1986), 53–8; ead., 'The Local Legend: A Product of Popular Culture', *Rural History*, 2 (1991), 25–35.

and 'popular antiquities' and beginning to erect a barrier between 'authentic' written records and unreliable verbal ones which not only gave rise to the modern distinction between 'history' and 'folklore' but redefined various traditions which had hitherto been part of the cultural mainstream as 'superstitions'.[116] Ironically, many of the adages and tales they marginalized can be traced back to learned and literary sources.[117]

Some of the outlandish stories with Latinate roots popularized in Elizabethan and early Stuart ephemera seem themselves to have been handed down from generation to generation by word of mouth. Sebastian Muenster's *Cosmography* was probably the immediate source for a ballad published in 1586 about Archbishop Hatto, the cruel tenth-century prelate who burnt the poor of Mainz in a barn claiming they deserved to be exterminated like mice and was soon after plagued by an army of voracious rodents who relentlessly pursued him to his refuge in a tower on the Rhine and there gnawed him slowly to death. But this fable, like other stories about man-eating rats of similar vintage preserved in post-Reformation sermons and tracts, bears clear marks of oral transmission: a condensed and imprecise sense of chronology, a palpable degree of exaggeration, and above all the existence of multiple variants of the central narrative theme.[118] The captivating tale of 'the lamenting lady' also drew upon a pan-European motif: this medieval anecdote about Marguerite of Henneberg had English counterparts linked with locations in the West Country and Wiltshire. Distilled into English in Thomas Coryate's *Crudities*, by 1635, even in a small Devon village, it was said to be 'notorious' and on every inhabitant's lips.[119] The fate of wicked Earl Godwin, father of King Harold II, was a piece of Kentish folklore preserved by William Lambarde in his *Perambulation* of the county published in 1596. As Lambarde realized, this tradition (like those already discussed) had been contaminated and ossified by its inser-

[116] D. R. Woolf, 'The "Common Voice": History, Folklore and Oral Tradition in Early Modern England', *P&P* 120 (1988), 26–52. See also Keith Thomas, *The Perception of the Past in Early Modern England* (1983), 5–9.

[117] See Obelkevich, 'Proverbs and Social History', 45, 55–7; Natalie Zemon Davis, 'Proverbial Wisdom and Popular Errors', in her *Society and Culture in Early Modern France* (Stanford, Calif., 1975), 230–3.

[118] On Hatto, see Sebastian Muenster, *A briefe collection and compendious extract of straunge and memorable thinges, gathered oute of the Cosmographye of Sebastian Muenster* (1572), fos. 16ᵛ–17ʳ. A broadside entitled *The wrathfull judgement of God upon Bishop Hatto* was entered to Henry Carr on 15 Aug. 1586: *SR* ii. 454. The ballad survives in a 17th-cent. edn.: *Bloudy news from Germany; or, the people's misery by famine. Being an example of God's just judgement on one Harto [sic], a nobleman in Germany* ([1672–95]). For a similar story about King Popiel or Pompilius, Cromer, *Notable example of Gods vengeance, uppon a murdering king*, also issued as pt. 2 of Arsanes, *Orations, of Arsanes agaynst Philip the trecherous kyng of Macedone . . .* [ed. T. Norton] ([1560?]); Batman, *Doome*, 190–1. For a different version, see Muenster, *Briefe collection*, fos. 25ᵛ–27ʳ. Both of these tales appear in Beard, *Theatre*, 273–4 and in Boaistuau, *Certaine secrete wonders of nature*, fos. 8ʳ–9ʳ. On oral transmission, see Gwyn Prins, 'Oral History', in Peter Burke (ed.), *New Perspectives on Historical Writing* (Oxford, 1991), esp. 119–25.

[119] *Lamenting lady*. Thomas Coryate, *Coryats crudities. Hastily gobled up in five moneths travells* (1611), 646–8. Ellen Ettlinger, 'Seven Children at One Birth', *Folklore*, 81 (1970), 268–75. The notoriety of the tale in Devon is attested by B[edford], *True and certaine relation of a strange-birth*, 12. See also James Howell, *Epistolae Ho-Elianae. Familiar letters domestic and forren* (1645), 16–17.

tion into the literature of the elite: 'Neither were these things continued in memorie, by the mouthes of the unlearned people onely, but committed to writing also, by the hands and pens of Monks, Frears, and others of the learned sort: so that in course of time, the matter was past all peradventure, and . . . beleeved for undoubted veritie'.[120] Like proverbs and legends, they did not spring unpolluted from the font of popular memory.[121] Such stories were clearly capable of penetrating and circulating in a range of social milieux.

So too were the tragic mishaps and accidents which befell their friends and enemies, neighbours and peers. There was a general tendency, by no means confined to narrowly puritan circles, to see sudden death in terms of vengeance visited from above—especially, as Thomas Fuller observed, if the victim had led an overtly licentious life.[122] Arthur Dent's Essex parishioners were wont to interpret any suicide in a providential light: 'we use to say, if a man hang himselfe, drowne himselfe, or any manner of way make away himselfe, that hee was cursed of God, that Gods hand was heavy against him, that the divel ought him a shame, and now hee hath paide it him.'[123] Fear of some dire heavenly penalty for perjury evidently induced a Wiltshire servant girl to confess to lying in an ecclesiastical court in 1635, acknowledging that the Lord had 'justly punished her for her foul and false accusation by taking from her the use of her limbs'.[124] When a man was found dead at Holywell in Wales in 1630 after making disparaging remarks about the marvellous healing properties of the spring a local jury seems to have brought in a verdict of death by divine judgement.[125] This example may be unusual—many coroners' inquests accounted for tragic accidents in terms of 'misadventure' or 'misfortune'—but it does indicate that providence was part of the mental furniture of the early modern mind, an explanatory tool which contemporaries could employ at will.[126] So do the number of court depositions in which eyewitnesses described corpses bleeding in the presence of the murderer: in a case from Hertfordshire in 1629, the body of a presumed suicide was officially exhumed and bled afresh in front of her guilty sister, who was subsequently tried for the crime.[127] There are a significant number of entries in parish registers recording fatalities attributed by the local clergyman and members of his morbidly inquisitive

---

[120] William Lambarde, *A perambulation of Kent . . .* (1596 edn.), 105. Lambarde believed this to be a 'devised tale' contrived to make Godwin and his sons 'hatefull to all posteritie after their death'. See Beard, *Theatre*, 177–8. See also Prins, 'Oral History', 132; Ruth B. Bottigheimer, 'Fairy Tales, Folk Narrative Research and History', *Social History*, 14 (1989), esp. 344–5, 348–9, 352.

[121] See Thomas, *Perception of the Past*, 7.

[122] Thomas Fuller, *The church-history of Britain* (1655), bk. LXV, ch. 28.

[123] Dent, *Plaine mans path-way*, 66–7.

[124] Cited in Ingram, *Church Courts*, 330.

[125] 'Documenta de S. Wenefreda', *Analecta Bollandiana*, 6 (Paris, 1887), 330.

[126] See the examples cited in Macfarlane, *Witchcraft in Tudor and Stuart England*, 179.

[127] Malcolm Gaskill, 'Reporting Murder: Fiction in the Archives in Early Modern England', *Social History*, 23 (1998), 11 and 9–13 *passim*. For the decline of such techniques and beliefs in legal procedure, see id., 'The Displacement of Providence: Policing and Prosecution in Seventeenth- and Eighteenth Century England', *Continuity and Change*, 11 (1996), 341–74.

congregation to the direct intervention of an infuriated deity. In the early 1580s, for instance, Owyn Tonny of Dorking in Surrey, 'scoffing at thunder, standing under a beech was stroke to death, his clothes stinking with a sulphurious stench'; on 6 August 1638 Katherina Stockman, in the act of stealing apples from a Cotswold squire's orchard, 'fell downe from the tree beinge the sabbath day at night and brake her necke'.[128]

Rumour about calamities of this kind ran rife in close-knit rural communities and carried with the wind, often travelling via the private correspondence of merchants and gentlemen to outlying rural locations. Sir William Masham, for instance, reported to Lady Barrington in a letter dated 1631 that a Mr Pennington of Gray's Inn, who customarily blustered 'the devil take me', had been much troubled on his deathbed by the spectre of a black dog: his body, when discovered, was 'much torn and distorted, his eyes clawed out, as some think by the divell'.[129] One of the weekly London newsletters received by Joseph Mede, fellow of Christ's College, Cambridge, in February 1625 included an account of a lady who crossed her fingers and fibbed only to see them become 'coale black and mortifyed' eight hours later and fall from her hands the following day.[130] The West Country justice Walter Yonge did not hesitate to transcribe into his journal a juicy snippet of hearsay which reached his ears later the same year: the story of one Mrs Bartlett who denied pinching a child's pinafore from an Axminster hedge with the oath that 'she might never be able to open her mouth or speak more'—a wish, which, of course, almost instantly transpired.[131] Not even the serious young law student Simonds D'Ewes could resist noting in his cipher diary the fate of Richard Sackville, the lascivious third earl of Dorset, who expired in 1624 surfeiting on 'a potato pie which meate hee had often eaten as was reported', as an aphrodisiac, 'to endkindle his lust'.[132]

Distorted and embroidered as they travelled along the grapevine, such anecdotes were the stuff of which clerical anthologies of God's judgements were made. Authors supplemented their own laborious literary researches with incidents sent to them by acquaintances, colleagues, and virtual strangers from across the country, 'friendly imparted' in the course of conversation, or overheard in idle market-place chat.[133] Foxe's *Actes and monuments* swelled in size in subsequent editions in large part because readers bombarded him with 'additional historyes' which they hoped

---

[128] J. Charles Cox, *The Parish Registers of England* (1910), 128, 130–1, and ch. 8 *passim*. Even the death of Dorothy Mattley (see n. 55, above), the liar who sank into the ground, has a formal record in the register for Ashover: 133–4. See also *VCH Sussex*, ed. William Page, ii (1907), 32.

[129] HMC, *Seventh Report. Part I* (1879), 548.

[130] BL Harleian MS 389, fos. 400ᵛ–401ʳ.

[131] Yonge, *Diary*, ed. Roberts, 83. The truth of the tale had been personally affirmed to him by one Tristram Andrew of the town on 12 June 1625.

[132] *The Diary of Sir Simonds D'Ewes (1622–1624): Journal d'un étudiant Londonien sous le règne de Jacques Iᵉʳ*, ed. Elisabeth Bourcier, Publications de la Sorbonne Littératures 5 (Paris, 1975), 189.

[133] Quotation from Clarke, *Mirror or looking-glasse*, sig. A5ʳ. There are interesting traces of East Anglian dialect in some of Samuel Ward's examples in *Woe to drunkards*, e.g. p. 22 where 'quackle' is used for 'choke'.

he might find some future occasion to use, 'thoghe your booke ys paste the prynte'. Archdeacon John Loude or Louthe of Nottingham reported what he had 'creably herd' from 'authentycke' sources concerning the 'strawnge and hasty dethe' of John Williams LL D and the 'venjance' poured out on Mr Cooke, registrar of the diocese of Winchester and a fierce 'enymye' of the Protestant martyr John Philpot.[134] Behind Henry Burton's *Divine tragedie* stands a network of puritans keeping a watchful eye open for telling examples of divine wrath against those who had engaged in idle recreations and seasonal pastimes on the sabbath. One example conveyed to the London preacher from Somerset concerned a maypole which toppled in the centre of Glastonbury crushing the child of the churchwarden, reputedly 'the cheefe stickler in the businesse'; another from Gloucestershire told how fire had razed the home of a miller who celebrated a Whitsun ale with music, cider, and no less than 'three score dozen of cheescakes', all in defiance of his vicar's admonitions.[135] Beard inserted in the 1631 edition of the *Theatre* a case communicated to him in the handwriting of Master George Nelson, 'a worthie Minister' from nearby Godmanchester: the example of John Bone, a coachman from Ely who drank himself into a stupor during sermon-time in 1629, tumbled off his box, and was trampled to death under the feet of his team. He took on the trust of unnamed but 'very credible persons' the story of a wealthy Berkshire gentleman, 'a profest Atheist and a scorner of the Word of God and Sacraments', who, being a witness at an infant's christening 'would needs have it called *Beelzebub*', and for this blasphemous jest was afflicted with a heart attack while out riding, as a deterrent to all epicures and unbelievers. Nor was Beard above recounting a 'common and vulgar storie . . . which is almost in every childes mouth' of a condemned criminal who, desiring to speak to his mother in her ear before his execution, bit it off with his teeth like an animal instead, claiming a bad upbringing was to blame for his disgraceful life and shameful death.[136]

In fact, so much that smacked of inaccurate reminiscence, if not blatant fabrication, obtruded into these encyclopedias that it became necessary to preface them with protestations that 'no fained miracles, no fabulous stories, nor ould wives tales' had been included within, only meticulously documented providences which

---

[134] John Gough Nichols (ed.), *Narratives of the Days of the Reformation, Chiefly from the Manuscripts of John Foxe the Martyrologist*, CS, os 77 (1859), 18, 20–2, 49–51. For another judgement story supplied by a correspondent, see BL Harleian MS 416, fo. 188ʳ (Francys Halle to Mr Felde, dated 13 Sept. 1569). This example, which concerned Richard Rausse alias Child, a 'synging man' and an 'impudent papist' and 'greate persecutor' who was struck by apoplexy during the reign of Mary I, was not inserted in subsequent edns. of the *Actes and monuments*. I am grateful to Damian Nussbaum for bringing this letter to my attention.

[135] [Burton], *Divine tragedie lately acted*, sigs. A2ᵛ–3ʳ, pp. 15, 4 respectively. One of his suppliers may have been the rich clothier John Ashe of Freshford, near Bath, who distributed 200 copies of the book to selected ministers: HMC, *Third Report* (1872), 191 (21 Dec. 1636, Examination of John Rowsewell, a Somerset vicar, and others before Bishop Piers).

[136] Beard, *Theatre*, 561–2, 150–1, 225–6 respectively. On 212, Beard alludes to a judgement on sabbath-breakers, but adds 'The just report thereof I passe over heere to set downe, untill such time as I shall bee better instructed'.

would 'abide the triall and search' of time and which many 'yet living' were prepared to ratify with their hand on the Bible. But Henry Burton's earnest assertions
failed to allay the suspicions of some of the godly themselves: writing to John
Winthrop in Massachusetts in 1637 one 'feared that there is a great fayling in many
and chiefe circumstances in the Instances alleaged' and believed that 'some few of
them alsoe were not taken too suddenly on trust and heare-say without well looking
after the truth'.[137] And it was the 'great mixture of false and foolish and unwit-
nessed fictions', not to mention 'foule impostures', published alongside properly
authenticated accounts which convinced mid- and late seventeenth-century
compilers like Matthew Poole of the need for quasi-scientific techniques of
verification.[138] Such concerns may be testimony less to deliberate artifice than to
the Chinese whispers effect of oral communication.[139]

We can scent the same kind of spontaneous improvisation in the historical material John Foxe accumulated for his martyrology in the 1550s and 60s. More than
a few of his grisly descriptions of the fates of Marian persecutors were supplied
by otherwise anonymous individuals who relied upon such untrustworthy sources
as childhood memory, local folklore, and alehouse gossip. Foxe professed to have
separated out and rejected mere rumour, not daring to 'lean too much upon public
speech' and 'the voice of the people', but some of his edifying exempla still read
very much as though they are based on little more than unkind conjecture and
malicious surmise.[140] The story of the escaped bull which made a beeline for a
Catholic official who had just presided over the burning of a Gloucestershire
heretic and gored him to death was third-hand information, already sixty years old
when it was passed on to Foxe. It was also almost certainly a myth: the chancellor
in question outlived the alleged accident by a decade and a half.[141] The anecdote
about 12-year-old Dennis Benfield of Walthamstow who came to grief the very day
after declaring that God was 'an old doting fool' should surely also be taken with

---

[137] [Burton], *Divine tragedie lately acted*, 3–4. *Winthrop Papers*, ed. Ford *et al.*, iii. 400. Commenting
on an oral report about a woman from a Devon village bitten fatally by an adder as she gathered foliage
to adorn the parish maypole in 1634, Walter Yonge reproved the wild excesses of the popular imagination, saying 'shee dyed not of this nether was yt to decce [deck?] the maypole': BL Add. MS 35331,
fo. 59ᵛ.

[138] CUL MS Dd. 3. 64, fo. 136ʳ⁻ᵛ. Cf. fos. 137ʳ and 139ᵛ, where an anonymous commentator on Poole's
'Designe' says 'I have often observed that assoone as the first wonder rebateth those that at first over-
spoke the truth, doe in the end by multiplications of falls surmisalls and devised causes eclipse and
affront the truth.' See also Mather, *Essay*, preface. On these projects, see Winship, 'Theater of God's
Judgments', 171–87.

[139] Cf. Adam Fox's discussion of how rumours about the monarch and politics were whipped up and
embellished in the act of transmission: 'Rumour, News and Popular Political Opinion', 613–19.

[140] Foxe, *Acts and Monuments*, vii. 53. Foxe was less cautious about recounting these reports in the
1563 edn. and sometimes he did not even bother to alter the coarse, racy, and indelicate expressions
employed by his eager eyewitnesses.

[141] Ibid. iv. 127–9. Recounted in Beard, *Theatre*, 60–1. On Foxe's errors in respect of this case, see
J. F. Mozley, *John Foxe and his Book* (1940), 163–4. Similar examples include the notorious Grimwood
tale, referred to below, and the story of the death of the bishop of St Davids, Henry Morgan: *Acts and
Monuments*, viii. 629, recounted in Beard, *Theatre*, 62–3. On Foxe's errors, see Wood, *Athenae
Oxonienses*, ii. 788–90.

a moderate pinch of salt.[142] So too 'the stinking death' of Burton, the apostate Lincolnshire bailiff who perished after a crow flying overhead deposited the poisonous contents of its bowels on his head, the 'scent and savour whereof so noyed his stomach' that he never ceased vomitting until he gave up the ghost. According to the martyrologist, this was 'testified, for a certainty, by divers of his neighbours, both honest and credible'.[143] Such tales have been regarded as casting a shadow on Foxe's integrity as a historian,[144] but they probably reveal more about the degree to which providential beliefs shaped the storytelling skills which helped his illiterate as well as literate contributors make sense of unexpected events and build coherence into their immediate experience.[145] In at least some cases, they reflect the crystallization of pre-existing oral tradition in print.

Indeed, the godly found reason to reprove, as well as occasion to regret, the curiosity of their contemporaries about the divine causes of the misfortunes which befell those that dwelt within their midst. It was the settled 'opinion of the common people', lamented clergymen like Henry Smith and Thomas Rogers, 'to censure them worst whom they see most afflicted', to jump automatically to the 'rash, and sinister' conclusion that disaster and adversity was always a sign and 'Kains marke' of heavenly displeasure.[146] It was a consequence of 'our corrupt nature', observed Thomas Cooper and William Ward, that 'when wee see any notable plague or misery sent to a man, by and by with great rigour we condemne him as a very evil man' and 'give sentence upon him that he is . . . a reprobate'.[147] 'Every fearefull accident', bewailed Robert Abbot in 1636, bespoke 'the language of damnation' to the average parishioner. Too many lost no time in announcing that the Lord came 'as a swift witnesse' against the victims to 'make his sword drunke with their bloud' and in branding them 'bastards, and not for Gods rest'.[148] To make this 'descanning of other mens destinies' a topic of conversation, said the Welsh magistrate William Vaughan, was arrogant and unwarrrantable, for these decisions were 'among the secrets of his government, and past our cognizance'. This was how 'detracting busibodies' went 'about to overthrow' the doctrine of predestination.[149]

---

[142] Foxe, *Acts and Monuments*, viii. 640, recounted in Beard, *Theatre*, 184; Perkins, *Direction for the government of the tongue*, 35.

[143] Foxe, *Acts and Monuments*, viii. 632–3, recounted in Beard, *Theatre*, 75.

[144] See e.g. J. M. Stone, 'Foxe's Book of Errors', in id., *Studies from Court and Cloister* (Edinburgh, 1905), 250–76; James Gairdner, *Lollardy and the Reformation in England: An Historical Survey*, 4 vols. (1908–13), i. 343–56. Thomas Freeman has recently criticized the tendency to regard Foxe's providential stories as an embarrassing aberration from the rest of his text and argued that to do so is to misunderstand his purposes and activities as a historian. I am grateful to him for sharing with me his unpublished paper on this subject: 'Grimwood's Guts: Faction and Fiction in Foxe's "Book of Martyrs"'.

[145] Cf. the comments of Davis, *Fiction in the Archives*, esp. 3–4, 111–12.

[146] Henry Smith, *Two sermons of Jonahs punishment* (1602), repr. in *Sermons*, sig. C1ᵛ; Rogers, *General session*, 86; Robert Gray, *An alarum to England, sounding the most fearefull and terrible example of Gods vengeance* (1609), sig. B5ᵛ and sigs. B4ᵛ–8ʳ *passim*.

[147] Cooper, *Certaine sermons*, 169, cf. 170; Ward, *Gods arrowes*, fo. 37ʳ⁻ᵛ.

[148] Abbot, *Young-mans warning-peece*, 88, 98, and 87–100 *passim*.

[149] Vaughan, *Spirit of detraction*, sig. A1ʳ, pp. 239, 271–4; Abbot, *Young-mans warning-peece*, 97.

'If God bring any strange thing to passe,' admonished William Perkins, 'speak not boldly of it, but rather in silence wonder'; 'if we speak anything we must judge charitably'.[150] Protestant preachers also did their best to subvert the 'popish' error that a quiet, penitent, and 'lamb-like' death was a guarantee of everlasting happiness and an impatient and uncomfortable one a 'passage to endlesse woe and misery'—a legacy of the medieval *ars moriendi*.[151]

Yet this was a state of affairs for which Reformed ministers were arguably partly responsible themselves. At the pastoral level they seem to have studiously avoided discussing the more arcane aspects of predestinarian theology: most of the catechisms examined by Professor Ian Green either drew a discreet veil of silence over the issue or implied that salvation was available to every Christian who fervently embraced the Gospel.[152] It was perilously tempting to 'Arminianize' when addressing unlearned laypeople incapable of wrapping their minds around the complexities of the double decree and this can only have reinforced the prevalent assumption that sinners who came to bad ends were eternally damned. Moreover, as R. T. Kendall has demonstrated, second-generation Calvinists reacted against the antinomian tendencies latent within the Genevan reformer's original thought by veering sharply back in the direction of voluntarism. They ameliorated the harsh precept that no individual could ever know whether he was destined for paradise or ordained to the bottomless pit by placing increasing emphasis on the outward tokens by which the elect were 'assured' and 'sanctified'.[153] Their assertion that saving faith found expression in holiness of life held within it not only the nucleus of a new works-righteousness, but the corollary that immoral conduct was 'a prophecie of torment' and an emblem of spiritual rejection.[154] It brought early seventeeth-century puritanism, it might be suggested, closer to the natural bias and tenor of traditional belief.

Furthermore, whether or not they realized it, ministers who illustrated their sermons with providential anedotes were helping to maintain a measure of continuity with the pre-Reformation methods of preaching which they so vociferously denounced. Together with a host of early reformers, William Perkins had nothing but contempt for 'foolish lying legends' and 'fond and friarish tales' about miracles and in his manual for preachers he sternly banished them from the pulpit.[155] And

---

[150] Perkins, *Direction for the government of the tongue*, 31–2.

[151] See e.g. Dent, *Sermon of repentaunce*, sigs. D7ᵛ–8ʳ; Robert Bolton, *A discourse about the state of true happiness* (1638 edn.), in *The workes . . .* (1641), 61–2, and *Instructions for a right comforting afflicted consciences* (1640 edn.), in *Workes*, 239–47; Thomas Jackson, *The raging tempest stilled* (1623), 195–6. See also Philippe Ariès, *The Hour of our Death* (1981), 10–11, 108; Duffy, *Stripping of the Altars*, ch. 9.

[152] Ian Green, *The Christian's ABC: Catechisms and Catechizing in England c.1530–1740* (Oxford, 1996), ch. 8.

[153] Kendall, *Calvin and English Calvinism*, *passim*, esp. 3, 146–8, 209–13 and chs. 3–4. See also Wallace, *Puritans and Predestination*, 7–11, 51; Lake, *Moderate Puritans*, 151–3, 160–5, 167–8.

[154] Henry Smith, *The fall of King Nebuchadnezzar* (1591), in *Sermons*, 184.

[155] Perkins, *Arte of prophecying*, in *Workes*, ii. 759. For early Reformation complaints, see Wabuda, 'Provision of Preaching', ch. 3, esp. pp. 77–81. A good example of a medieval preacher who wove such tales into his sermons is John Mirk, *Mirk's Festial: A Collection of Homilies*, ed. Theodor Erbe, EETS, extra ser. 96 (1905).

yet we find divines like Nicholas Bownde, Lewis Bayly, and Thomas Rogers rein-
serting medieval exempla into their lectures, sometimes in a no more than
superficially Protestantized form.[156] This too they did in deference to the intellectual capacities of those under their charge: 'home-observed' providences were a
proven method for capturing the attention of listless parishioners recommended
by Richard Bernard, author of another handbook for clerical professionals.[157]
George Herbert's 'Countrey Parson' girded himself with the judgements of God,
for his audience was 'very attentive at such discourses', heeding them better than
the most vehement exhortations: rural congregations were 'thick, and heavy, and
hard to raise to a poynt of Zeal, and fervency, and need a mountaine of fire to
kindle them; but stories and sayings they will well remember'.[158] This was no doubt
why William Perkins himself related the tale of a Cambridgeshire man who
mocked at thunder, saying '(as report was) it was nothing but a knave cooper
knocking on his tubbes', and soon after 'fell downe starke dead' having been
'strooke ... about the girdlestead'. 'Behold here the fruit of good fellowship',
Hugh Roberts announced to his Sussex parishioners on the first Sunday in May
1598, describing the compound fracture sustained by a football player during a
match played on the sabbath two weeks before, which had taken him to his grave
a 'senight' since. This, he said, was 'a spectacle sufficient to terrifie all'.[159]

Of course, sermons about God's judgements did not always have the desired
result. As a young curate in Northamptonshire Hugh Clark had little success in
persuading the 'generality' of 'ungodly people' to leave off morris dancing on the
Lord's Day. Even after a series of 'sad dispensations' from heaven, these 'obdurate
persons soon shaked off their fears, and returned to their vomit again'. Only when
they smelt fire and brimstone in the air and heard chains rattling up and down the
town did they begin to give better heed to their long-suffering preacher, convinced
that 'the devil was come to fetch them away quick to hell'.[160] No clergyman
could ultimately dictate the moral his listeners derived from cautionary tales, as
Sir Thomas More recognized when he recalled the witty words of 'a good felow'
who heard news of a church in Beverley that had collapsed suddenly during
evening prayer: 'lo quod he now maye you see what yt ys to be at evensong
whan ye shold be at the bere baytynge.'[161] The London hacks who churned out
pamphlets and ditties about sensational punishments had even less control over the

[156] Nicholas Bownd, *The doctrine of the sabbath, plainely layde forth* (1595), 129–30; Bayly, *Practise of pietie*, 549; Rogers, *Generall session*, 79–80; and see also Perkins himself, *Direction for the government of the tongue*, 14, 34.

[157] Bernard, *Faithfull shepheard*, 68. For other examples of preachers recounting providences, see Bolton, *Instructions*, in *Workes*, 60–1; Downame, *Foure treatises*, 46; Andrew Willet, *Hexapla in Exodum* (1608), 442–3.

[158] Herbert, *A priest to the temple*, in *Works*, ed. Hutchinson, 233.

[159] Perkins, *Exposition*, in *Workes*, i. 140; R[oberts], *A godly and necessarie sermon*, appended to *The day of hearing*, sig. K3ʳ.

[160] Clarke, *Lives of thirty two English divines*, 127–8.

[161] Thomas More, *A Dialogue Concerning Heresies* (1529), repr. in *The Complete Works ...* ed. Thomas M. C. Lawler *et al.*, vol. vi, pt. 1 (New Haven, 1981), 258.

response of their diverse and invisible readership. After hearing a ballad about a moneylender's wife 'brought to bed of twenty money-bags at a burden', Shakespeare's gullible shepherdess Dorcas exclaims 'Bless me from marrying a usurer!'—ingenious, but probably not the lesson the rhymster intended![162] It is clear that such texts could be read at several different levels. They might be taken at face value and accepted as literally true; they might be recognized as semi-fictional constructs but interpreted as an allegory or parable teaching an important ethical truth; or they might be dismissed as ridiculous tales dreamt up by a canny stationer as a device to make money. It would also be unwise to dismiss the possibility that many were immune to the moralizing providentialism of ministers and scribblers and purchased such ephemera simply because they found it entertaining. Nevertheless, there remains much to suggest that beliefs about divine intervention against heinous transgressors were deeply rooted in the religious outlook of most contemporaries.

TAUNTING TABLE-TALKE

Correlating success and prosperity with divine approval and poverty and sorrow with the opposite was a trap into which the 'saints' themselves not infrequently fell. Even Calvin himself took note of judgements on sabbath-breakers and persecutors, declaring that 'if God should set up scaffolds to execute his chastisements upon: wee could not perceive them more evidently'. Notwithstanding his stern caveats about divine inscrutability in the *Institutes*, he seems to have had no scruples about denouncing the untimely and accidental deaths of Henri II and François II of France as a punishment for molesting Protestants.[163] But the godly were quick to condemn such tendencies as presumptuous in others, particularly when the misfortune happened to be their own. They knew by bitter experience that 'profane worldlings' and 'carnal Protestants' were all too capable of harnessing providence for their own impious objectives—to retaliate against those whom they in turn despised as self-righteous, hypocritical, and excessively 'precise'. After Elizabeth Vaughan was slain in her bed by a streak of lightning around 1611, her grieving husband lashed out against the 'Spirit of Detraction' which the catastrophe had kindled, against the prattling multitude who made 'a taunting table-talke of this heavenly visitation', 'usurping the Popish partes of Ghostly Confessors' and attributing it to 'some silent sinnes' of his late wife or his own officious efforts to eradicate local disorder, evil manners, and vice. They had used it to vent their spleen against 'a busie medler', 'a picke thanke', and 'a melancholike Monke'.[164] When the pious Lancashire gentlewoman Katherine Brettergh expired in her youthful prime at the turn of the sixteenth century, William Harrison likewise expostulated against 'country-Papists' who greeted sudden deaths with the jeer

---

[162] *The Winter's Tale*, IV. iv. 256–62, in *Complete Works*, ed. Alexander, 399.
[163] As noted by Winship, 'Theater of God's Judgments', 28–33.
[164] Vaughan, *Spirit of detraction*, sigs. *1ᵛ–2ʳ, §1ʳ⁻ᵛ. See also p. 286 and 'Circle 6' *passim*.

'there is a judgement of god, serving either to discover a hypocrite, or plague a wicked man', adding jubilantly 'see the effect of this religion, see the end of these men'.[165]

Obviously the 'ungodly' could effortlessly invert the providential rhetoric so often commandeered by committed Protestants upon their own heads. As the jurist John Selden remarked, 'Commonly we say a Judgment falls upon a man for something in him we cannot abide.' In the repertoire of contemporary insults, this was roughly equivalent to wishing upon an annoying neighbour a 'pox' or a 'plague'— and, as we have seen, contemporaries were convinced that such curses sometimes came true.[166] No doubt spite and irritation played a large part in generating such accusations, but they also grew out of a genuine sense of outrage against individuals who dared to infringe their community's unwritten conventions and rules. The discourse of divine justice might be seen as an extra-legal form of sanction, a 'species of popular disapprobation' which bears comparison with the rituals of rough music and the skimmington ride, and with the mocking rhymes and lampoons by which the 'meaner' sort of people reproved and wounded their superiors, as well as their peers.[167] Thus when fire engulfed the London home of the wealthy cloth merchant Sir William Cockayne in November 1623, destroying £10,000 worth of goods and merchandise, he received no pity from the urban populace, who rather made 'a judgement of God upon him, for undoing the City'.[168] Ballads about the supernatural penalties meted out to cornhoarders, enclosers, and rack-renting landlords betray a similar undercurrent of resentment and protest against greedy middlemen. It would be a mistake to interpret them as unmediated expressions of the grievances of a 'class-conscious' poor, especially since these tales were often repeated by clerical elites. However, they did very effectively perform the function of identifying and condemning conventional plebeian scapegoats for suffering during periods of dearth. In this regard the timing of such ephemera deserves particular scrutiny: many coincide with moments of agrarian crisis and riot like the Midland Revolt. This was the context in which a lost song about a rapacious German farmer who cordoned off common pasture and was 'strangely troden to death by his owne cattell' was published in September 1607, while the backdrop for a pamphlet entitled *The miraculous judgement of God shewn in Herefordshire, where a mightie barne filled with corne was consumed with fire* was the

[165] William Harrison, *A brief discourse of the Christian life and death, of Mistris Katherin Brettergh* (1602), bound with *Deaths advantage little regarded, and the soules solace against sorrow . . .* (1602 edn.), sig. N2ʳ.

[166] John Selden, *Table-talk* (1689), 26.

[167] See Martin Ingram, 'Ridings, Rough Music and Mocking Rhymes in Early Modern England', in Barry Reay (ed.), *Popular Culture in Seventeenth Century England* (1988), 166–97, quotation at 178; id., 'Ridings, Rough Music and the "Reform of Popular Culture" in Early Modern England', *P&P* 105 (1984), 79–113.

[168] BL Harleian MS 389, fo. 381ʳ. Cf. Chamberlain, *Letters*, ed. McClure, ii. 523–4. On the disastrous Cockayne project, which led to a severe trade crisis, see Astrid Friis, *Alderman Cockayne's Project and the Cloth Trade: The Commercial Policy of England in its Main Aspects 1603–1625* (London, 1927), esp. chs. 4–6.

succession of bad harvests in the mid-1590s.[169] It is possible that some such stories originated in insinuations bandied about on the ale bench: as Adam Fox has recently shown, it was by no means unusual for popular satires and rhymes to filter into print. In this indirect sense, the press could be a medium for subversive comment by those without political rights.[170]

Wrested from their original contexts, providential anecdotes can seem no more than harmless, diverting, even ludicrous fictions. But interpreting, publicizing, even simply retelling them was a risky business: making a neighbourhood scandal into a national scandal could lay one open to sustainable charges of criminal libel. A Suffolk parson by the name of Prick who read out one of John Foxe's gory judgement tales against persecutors from the pulpit was sued for slander by a member of his own congregation—by an unhappy coincidence, the very same Mr Grimwood of Higham whose bowels he had graphically described dropping from his body in the course of the sermon. The unfortunate clergyman escaped conviction by the skin of his teeth, after being acquitted of malicious intent at the next assize and following an appeal in the court of Queen's Bench.[171] Clearly contemporaries did not regard this type of imputation in the light of a hilarious dinner party joke: it was a stigma that could seriously damage one's reputation and credit. Indeed, as Tom Freeman has demonstrated, some of the stories subsequently incorporated in the *Actes and monuments* were part of carefully orchestrated campaigns of defamation: they could be deadly weapons of factional dispute and vehicles for perpetuating local vendettas and feuds. Foxe's account of the capture and execution of the Marian martyr George Eagles and the providential punishment of his betrayer Ralph Lurden, for example, seems to have originated in a sustained attempt to impugn Lurden's uncle Benjamin Clere, a leading Colchester merchant and magistrate with powerful enemies among the governing elite. Its construction and circulation in print was one manifestation of the muckraking municipal politics which accompanied the entrenchment of the Reformation in East Anglian market towns.[172]

---

[169] This ballad and pamphlet were entered on 4 Sept. 1607 and 21 Feb. 1595 respectively: *SR* iii. 359; ii. 671. Other lost ballads and pamphlets about judgements on cornhoarders include *The poores lamentacon for the price of corne with Godes justice shewed uppon a cruell horder of corne* (entered 16 Oct. 1594, *SR* ii. 662); *The juste judgement of God upon a myserable hard harted ffermour* (entered 18 Mar. 1587, *SR* ii. 466); *Newes from Antwerpe or a glasse for gredy fermours* (entered 3 Sept. 1607, *SR* iii. 359); *A ballad declaringe the greate covetousnes and unmercifull dealinge of one Walter Gray sometyme Archebisshop of Yorke whoe havinge greate abundance of corne suffred the needie in the tyme of famyne to die for wante of relief, and of the fearefull vengance of God pronounced againste him* (entered 1 Aug. 1581, *SR* ii. 398). On middlemen as scapegoats, see John Walter and Keith Wrightson, 'Dearth and the Social Order in Early Modern England', in Paul Slack (ed.), *Rebellion, Popular Protest and the Social Order* (Cambridge, 1984), esp. 114–18. For divines who repeated stories of curses on cornhoarders see William Woodwall, *A sermon upon the xii. xiii. and xiiii. verses of the xiiii chapter of Ezechiel* (1609), 45; Charles Fitz-Geffrey, *The curse of corne-horders: with the blessing of seasonable selling . . .* (1631), esp. 33–5.

[170] Adam Fox, 'Ballads, Libels and Popular Ridicule in Jacobean England', *P&P* 145 (1994), 47–83.

[171] Foxe, *Acts and Monuments*, viii. 630–1. On this case, see Mozley, *John Foxe and his Book*, 194–9.

[172] Freeman, 'Grimwood's Guts'. The dissemination of the story of Grimwood itself had distinctly factional purposes and undertones.

All this helps to explain why popular moralists took the precaution of obtaining signatures of witnesses willing to vouch for the truth of the incidents they recounted.[173] It may also account for a Privy Council order in May 1600 calling in 'a certaine pamphlette or ballade towching the death of William Doddington, esquire . . . which we thincke verie unmeete to be published'.[174] Beard and other compilers prudently concealed the names and addresses of persons whose exemplary ends they felt it their duty to divulge to the country at large, especially when they were men of 'great possessions'. Samuel Ward wisely withheld details of all the Suffolk alcoholics he listed in his sermon *Woe to drunkards* 'for the kinreds sake yet living': to save the relatives from further embarrassment about the family black sheep and, no doubt, also as an insurance policy against any nasty repercussions for himself.[175] And Heynes, a Cornish minister who acquainted Foxe with an example of a blasphemous young gallant borne away by the devil, would under no circumstances reveal his identity 'for dread of those (as he said) which yet remained of his affinity'.[176] Over time, such fears inevitably faded and attention shifted from the individual so disgraced to the universal moral to be derived from his or her fate.

Firmly entrenched in the consciousness of the unlearned and lettered alike, belief in divine justice lent itself well to sectarian struggle. When a clerical sympathizer of the Family of Love dropped dead shortly after recanting at Paul's Cross in 1575, both the Church of England and the followers of Henrik Niclaes requisitioned providence as a polemical weapon: John Rogers alighted upon this 'souden death' as a 'terrible example' of the punishments heretics could expect, while a courtier Familist writing a few years later drew a causal link between the Essex vicar's unexpected demise and his defection from this secretive sect.[177] Henry Burton circulated his stories of God's judgements on sabbath-breakers as part of the propaganda campaign against Charles I's reproclamation of the 'book of liberty' or Declaration of Sports in 1633. It was also during the 1630s that Sir Henry Spelman began to compile his *History and fate of sacrilege*, a systematic account of the signal punishments visited upon desecrators of sacred objects and spaces from Hebrew to Caroline times, with special reference to the misfortunes which had befallen the purchasers of monastic estates since the Dissolution. Although it remained locked in manuscript until 1698, this treatise helped convert

---

[173] As noted in Ch. 1, above, many ballads included lists of witnesses. In BL Lansdowne MS 819, fo. 87[r], there is a note of witnesses to the two incidents described in Philip Stubbes's *Two wunderfull and rare examples*. Contrary to the *DNB*, Stubbes was not prosecuted by Joan Bowser, one of the victims of the divine judgements he described.

[174] *APC 1599–1600*, 289.

[175] Beard, *Theatre*, 150 and see 316–17, 372 where he conceals names to avoid offending 'some that are alive' and so 'that none might thinke themselves disgraced thereby'. Ward, *Woe to drunkards*, 29. Also the remarks of an unknown commentor on Matthew Poole's 'Designe', CUL MS Dd. 3. 64, fos. 139[v]–140[r].

[176] Foxe, *Acts and Monuments*, viii. 645.

[177] Christopher W. Marsh, *The Family of Love in English Society, 1550–1630* (Cambridge, 1994), 94–5.

the notion of a hereditary curse on those who violated hallowed ground into a catchword of Anglicanism.[178] Once the Civil War itself had broken out, on both sides there was no holding back. Crudely partisan judgement stories proliferated: cautionary tales about Cavaliers and upholders of Prayer Book rites were countered by cases of providential wrath visited upon Roundheads and unruly iconoclasts. Royalists no less gleefully alighted on the casual accidents that afflicted their sworn enemies than Parliamentarians.[179]

Thomas Beard's *Theatre* itself was a two-edged sword: it could be used to bolster as well as undermine the divine right claims of the Stuart regime. There were chapters in his book detailing the disastrous ends of tyrants and despots, but there were also chapters advocating the passive obedience of subjects to oppressive rulers and inveighing against active resistance and rebellion in all situations without exception. It provided no sanction for withholding taxes and subsidies like ship money from an anointed ruler; nor did it offer any kind of blueprint for king-killing.[180] And far from acquiring a new 'anti-monarchial' tone when it was republished in folio sixteen years after Beard's death,[181] it was actually prefaced by an obsequious dedicatory epistle to the adolescent duke of York, later James II.[182] Those commentators who have seen Beard's *Theatre* as doing much of the spade-work for theorists of regicide and revolution are thus frankly wrong, or at least missing an essential point: no one sector of English society had a monopoly on providence.[183]

Subordination to the ends of interconfessional conflict and party political strife debased the cautionary tale, giving rise to the chorus of complaints that such punishments were invented which we have noted above. In the long run it perhaps assisted in transforming the still small stream of elite scepticism about the eruption of supernatural forces into the world into a fast-flowing river and in redefining literal belief in a punitive deity as 'superstition'.[184] But that is to look beyond the chronological endpoint of this book: before 1640 the idea of an interventionist deity was very much part of the intellectual and cultural mainstream.

---

[178] Henry Spelman, *The history and fate of sacrilege* (1698), written 1632. Spelman had incorporated material of a similar kind in *De non temerandis ecclesiis* (1613). See Thomas, *Religion and the Decline of Magic*, 114–21.

[179] See e.g. Vicars, *Looking-glasse for malignants*; id., *Dagon demolished*; BL Sloane MS 1457, fos. 68ʳ–76ʳ.

[180] Beard, *Theatre*, bk. I, chs. 3–4, 6; bk. II, chs. 2, 5.

[181] Vander Molen, 'Providence as Mystery, Providence as Revelation', 44.

[182] Beard, *Theatre* (1648 edn.), sig. A2ʳ⁻ᵛ. The editor was one M. Heron, who described himself as his 'Highnesse most Humble, and most obedient Servant'.

[183] Hill, *God's Englishman*, 39–40; Lamont, *Puritanism, i. Marginal Prynne*, 31, 111–12, 117, 201; Vander Molen, 'Providence as Mystery, Providence as Revelation', 42–4.

[184] Cf. the conclusions of Peter Elmer, '"Saints or Sorcerers": Quakerism, Demonology and the Decline of Witchcraft in Seventeenth Century England', in Jonathan Barry, Marianne Hester, and Gareth Roberts (eds.), *Witchcraft in Early Modern Europe* (Cambridge, 1996), 172–3 and *passim*.

TRAGICALL HISTORYES

Just as stories of divine retribution of indeterminable age were cemented and petrified in print, so did topical news reports written up by city hacks feed off and then back into the oral sphere. Some journalistic ballads about God's judgements on heinous sinners became part of the professional stock of specialist publishers and booksellers.[185] Periodically reissuing popular favourites, these entrepreneurs became the guardians and custodians of a newly emerging post-Reformation 'tradition'. Eighteenth- and nineteeth-century critics even admitted a handful into the classical literary canon, condescendingly labelling them fine specimens of 'plebeian' poetry and prose. And a significant fraction of the folktales and songs assembled by collectors earlier this century can themselves be traced to pamphlets, chapbooks, and broadsides published in the sixteenth and seventeenth centuries.[186] The sentimental fairy story *The Babes in the Wood*, for instance, seems to have started out as a fairly unexceptional Elizabethan broadside with the title *The Norfolk gentleman, his last will and testament*—an account of a corrupt uncle who conspires to murder his small wards for their wealth and in due course comes to a suitably sticky end. The stanzas relating how the children, abandoned by the soft-hearted ruffians recruited to kill them, die of hypothermia in each other's arms and are covered with leaves by the robins of the forest, were a heart-rending, if rather superfluous, addition. First published in 1595, re-entered in the Stationers' Register in 1624 and 1675, three hundred years later this tale still finds a place in children's picture books.[187] One of the most harrowing episodes in Thomas Hardy's *Jude the Obscure* has a similar antecedent in a 'true balett' dated *c.*1577. In it a poor man is wrongly accused of stealing a loaf of bread by his rich and pitiless neighbour, who throws it to the dogs rather than allow it to save the destitute family from utter starvation. The cold-blooded wretch is swallowed into a hole which opens beneath his feet, but not before two of the children hang themselves, followed, in this case, by their grief-stricken father. It looks very much as if this motif had rooted itself in the rural lore upon which the Dorset novelist drew.[188] No less enduring was *The Fair Maid of Clifton* or *Young Bateman*, the tale of a dead bridegroom who returned to carry off the disloyal lady to whom he had once plighted his troth: still betraying discernible traces of belief in purgatory, this story was also

---

[185] For the general background, see Watt, *Cheap Print*, ch. 3, esp. pp. 122–5; Cyprian Blagden, 'Notes on the Ballad Market in the Second Half of the Seventeenth Century', *Studies in Bibliography: Papers of the Bibliographical Soc. of the University of Virginia*, 6 (1954), 161–8.

[186] See Margaret Spufford, 'The Pedlar, the Historian and the Folklorist: Seventeenth Century Communications', *Folklore*, 105 (1994), esp. 20–1.

[187] *The Norfolke gentleman, his last will and testament* ([*c.*1635]). First entered to Thomas Millington on 15 Oct. 1595: *SR* iii. 50. Katharine M. Briggs, *A Dictionary of British Folk-Tales in the English Language incorporating the F. J. Norton Collection*, 4 vols. (1970–1), pt. B, ii. 390–1.

[188] *A true balett of Deniing a poore man a loffe of brede which he paid for 1577*, printed in Peter J. Seng (ed.), *Tudor Songs and Ballads from MS Cotton Vespasian A-25* (Cambridge, Mass. 1978), 117–21.

copyrighted by the ballad partners at regular intervals.[189] Such examples supply evidence of a symbiosis between the timeless and the topical and between oral culture and cheap print.

Both *The Norfolk gentleman* and *Young Bateman* also supplied the storyline for a contemporary play, Robert Yarington's *Two lamentable tragedies* appearing in 1601 and William Sampson's *The vow breaker* in 1636.[190] Many providential murder pamphlets likewise made their way onto the metropolitan stage. These were the raw materials out of which the late Tudor and early Stuart genre of domestic or homiletic tragedy grew—a genre which one scholar has aptly styled the 'dramatised sermon'.[191] Nor should it surprise us that thumbnail sketches of the plots of *Arden of Feversham* (1592) and John Webster's Italianate revenge play *The Duchess of Malfi* (1613–14) can be found in Thomas Beard's *Theatre of Gods judgements*, or that John Reynolds's *The triumphs of Gods revenge* was the chief source of Middleton and Rowley's *The changeling* (1621).[192] Despite mature puritanism's almost pathological distrust of the medium, commercial drama often had a religious cast and could be a vessel for Protestant, or at least Protestantized, beliefs and ideas.[193]

In many ways, then, encyclopedias of personal providences seem to have as much affinity with the world of clerical discourse as with that of sensational 'newes'. It has been suggested that Beard's *Theatre* is better situated 'on the borderline of theology and popular fiction', the fringes of fashionable ephemeral literature, than within the mainstream of puritan devotional writing.[194] If this is a fair assessment of the Huntingdon schoolmaster's compendium, it is even more true of the Exeter merchant John Reynolds's popular anthology of 'Tragicall Historyes', *The triumphs of Gods revenge* (Plate 11). There is often no more than parenthetical deference to the workings of providence in these absorbing novellas

---

[189] *A warning for maidens;* [*or, Young Bateman*]. The ballad was entered in 1603, see n. 103 above. See also Briggs, *Dictionary of British Folk-Tales*, pt. B, i. 449–50.

[190] Robert Yarington, *Two lamentable tragedies. The one, of the murther of Maister Beech . . . The other of a young childe murthered in a wood by two ruffins, with the consent of his unckle* (1601); William Sampson, *The vow breaker. Or, The faire maide of Clifton* (1636).

[191] Henry Hitch Adams, *English Domestic or Homiletic Tragedy 1575–1642* (New York, 1943), quotation at 113; Keith Sturgess (ed.), *Three Elizabethan Domestic Tragedies* (Harmondsworth, 1969), 7–47. Joseph Marshburn provides a comprehensive listing of plays based on murder pamphlets in *Murder and Witchcraft in England, 1550–1640 as Recounted in Pamphlets, Ballads, Broadsides, and Plays* (Norman, Okla. 1971).

[192] *The lamentable and true tragedie of M. Arden of Feversham in Kent* (1592) is repr. in Sturgess (ed.), *Three Elizabethan Domestic Tragedies. The Selected Plays of John Webster: The White Devil, The Duchess of Malfi, The Devil's Law Case*, ed. Jonathan Dollimore and Alan Sinfield (Cambridge, 1983), 135. The relevant references in Beard, *Theatre* are 294, 378–9. Middleton and Rowley, *The Changeling*, ed. Patricia Thomson (1964), p. x. Reynolds, *Triumphs of Gods revenge* (1635 edn.), bk. 1, history 4. See also Margot Heinemann, *Puritanism and Theatre: Thomas Middleton and Opposition Drama under the Early Stuarts* (Cambridge, 1980), 173.

[193] On mature Protestant attitudes to the theatre, see Collinson, *From Iconoclasm to Iconophobia*, 11–15; id., *Birthpangs*, 112–15. And note the remarks of Paul Whitfield White, *Theatre and Reformation: Protestantism, Patronage and Playing in Tudor England* (Cambridge, 1993), 173–4.

[194] Waller, 'Popularization of Calvinism', 185.

PLATE 11 John Reynolds, *The triumphs of Gods revenge against the crying and execrable sinne of (willfull and premeditated) murther* (London, 1640), title-page. By permission of the Syndics of Cambridge University Library. Shelfmark: Syn. 4. 64. 10.

about ambition, passion, and villainous intrigue, invariably set in exotic Mediterranean locations, and generously laced with all the ingredients of the modern paperback best-seller—sex, violence, and the occult. Reynolds prefaced the book with the assurance 'that the purest and most unstayned Virgin shall not need to make her beautifull Cheekes guilty of the least Blush in perusing it all over', but the heavy-handed intrusions of the omniscient narrator do little to counteract its salacious and bloodthirsty character, or the vocabulary of fortune and chance with which it is infused. He piously set forth these homicidal tales as 'very necessary to restraine, and deterre us' from 'the crying and execrable sinne, of (wilfull and premeditated) murther', consecrating his pen 'rather to Instruction then Eloquence', and urging his readers to 'forget the shaddowes, to remember the substance, and so looke from the Mappe, to the Morall'.[195] In encasing this bitter pill in an appetizing coating Reynolds had hit upon a winning formula, for the work ran through no less than ten editions before 1700, picking up a set of quaint copperplate engravings in 1657.[196] Reading this kind of literature was a leisure activity of which puritans with a deep-seated belief in the duplicity of fiction, in spite of themselves, could only approve.[197]

The tension between teaching and delighting, between edification and recreation, remained acute in the many later compilations which imitated Reynolds's and Beard's. Samuel Ward was careful to exclude ridiculous details that might rather 'move laughter' than serious meditation, deeming these 'not fit to relate' in 1622. But Samuel Clarke openly admitted to including 'more pleasant stories' when he wrote his *Mirrour or looking-glasse* in 1646, designed to 'prevent tediousnesse' and 'nauseousnesse'.[198] The distinction between novelistic didacticism and the didactic novel became even fuzzier as the seventeenth century progressed. In the 1680s, we find, on the one hand, Bunyan's *Life and death of Mr Badman*, and on the other, the prolific writings of the Restoration publisher Nathaniel Crouch, who haphazardly culled prodigy tales from existing collections and reissued them in inexpensive formats under the pseudonym Robert or Richard Burton or simply 'R. B.'. In his *Wonderful prodigies of judgement and mercy* and *Admirable curiosities, rarities & wonders* the balance shifts perceptibly from religious indoctrination to secular entertainment. Attacked by Cotton Mather as a 'sham-scribler', Crouch was certainly no puritan, but as a man in the business of selling his books he saw to it that they were lacquered with a thick providential veneer.[199] More romantic, swashbuckling tales along these lines were assembled in Thomas Wright's *The glory of Gods revenge* (1685), together with 'Eminent Examples and Delightful Histories' of the 'Triumphs of Friendship and Chastity'. The book was presented as 'An Antidote to Vice from others woe', a 'Mirrour to the vitious' which would by 'Chymistry Divine . . . depraved Faculties refine', but the moral lesson has been

---

[195] Reynolds, *Triumphs of Gods revenge* (1635 edn.), bk. I (1621 edn.), sig. B2ᵛ; unpaginated 'Re-advertisement to the Judicious Christian Reader'; title-page; bk. II (1622 edn.), 220. He claimed responsibility only for the 'illustration and pollishing' of these 'deplorable' biographies: bk. II (1622 edn.), sig. A3ʳ.

[196] See Mish, 'Best Sellers', 369.

[197] See e.g. Sibbes, *Works*, vol. i, ch. 13 ('Of imagination, sin of it, and remedies for it') and William Perkins, *A treatise of mans imaginations* (1607), in *Workes*, ii. 521–52.

[198] Ward, *Woe to drunkards*, 24; Clarke, *Mirrour or looking-glasse*, sig. A5ʳ.

[199] [Nathaniel Crouch] R[ichard/Robert] B[urton] (pseud.), *Admirable curiosities, rarities, & wonders in England, Scotland, and Ireland* (1682) and *Wonderful prodigies of judgment and mercy* (1682). On Crouch, see Hall, *Worlds of Wonder*, 52, 112–14; Robert Mayer, 'Nathaniel Crouch, Bookseller and Historian: Popular Historiography and Cultural Power in Late Seventeenth-Century England', *Eighteenth-Century Studies*, 27 (1994), 391–419.

condensed into a short paragraph tacked on, almost as an afterthought, at the end of each tale.[200]

Exactly one hundred years later in 1786, Beard's *Theatre* was abbreviated and republished in Glasgow as a chapbook. One of a series of 'Small Histories' printed on the poorest quality paper, ranging from *Laugh and be fat* to *Jemmy Twitchers jests*, from *Moll Flanders* to *Don Quixote*, and from *Bucaneers of America* to *Hocus Pocus*, by the eighteenth century this collection of Protestant exempla had indisputably become a popular classic.[201]

To conclude: stories of divine retribution visited upon notorious sinners were by no means the exclusive property of puritans. They were aspects of an idiom capable of uniting godly and ungodly, literate and illiterate, privileged and poor. No less at home in ephemeral literature than in spiritual diaries, they flowed back and forth between print, script, and speech and up and down different levels in the social hierarchy with remarkable ease. Rooted as much in oral tradition as in academic discourse, shaped as much by a tangled skein of older religious convictions as by the predestinarian tenets propounded by Calvinist ministers, ballads, pamphlets, and anthologies of God's judgements bear witness to the gradual reconfiguration of a pre-existing set of beliefs in a new ideological climate and environment. Providentialism was one aspect of late medieval religious culture which Reformation doctrine and practical divinity served, in some respects, to stimulate rather than repress.

---

[200] Wright, *Glory of God's revenge*, unpaginated prefatory matter. The same cocktail of sanctimonious moralizing and the picaresque can be seen in a serial publication entitled *The Terrific Register; Or, Record of Crimes, Judgments, Providences, and Calamities*, 2 vols. (1825).

[201] Thomas Beard and Thomas Taylor, *The theatre of God's judgments* (Glasgow, 1786), 107.

3
'*Visible Sermons*':[1]
Divine Providence and Public Calamities

Preaching in a Sussex parish in 1598, the Welsh clergyman Hugh Roberts delivered a stern lecture on the practical and theological lessons to be derived from catastrophic events:

everie plague, everie calamitie, sudden death, burning with fire, murther, strange sicknesses, famine, everie flood of waters, ruine of buildings, unseasonable weather: everie one of these and of the like adversities, as oft as they happen in the world, are a sermon of repentance to all that see them, or heare therof . . . a memento to every one of us to looke to our selves, and to call to remembrance our owne sinns, knowing that it is the same God that will take vengeance of everie sinne, and transgression of men, & that he will strike with a more heavie hand, if his warning, and example of his justice be not regarded.[2]

'What are al these but as it were great Cranes with beams, and Cable Ropes, to drawe us up to the Lord by Repentance?', declared Arthur Dent, addressing a congregation in Essex in 1581.[3] The providential significance of what we now call 'natural' disasters was a perennial homiletic theme. No Protestant minister could pass up the opportunity afforded by a major conflagration, blizzard, drought, inundation, or epidemic to deliver a thundering diatribe on the doctrine of divine judgements. Nor could the host of ballad-mongers and hacks who eked out an existence writing journalistic ephemera. Hundreds of soberly moralizing news reports about the terrible calamities visited upon cities, towns, and villages in England, Continental Europe, and the New World issued from London publishing houses—'mournfull ditties' and 'doleful sonets', 'lamentable' discourses and 'woefull' relations of the misery and devastation wrought by the untameable elements at the instigation of an angry deity. Echoing the preachers, pamphleteers piously insisted that such 'strange alterations of times & seasons' were '*Flagella Dei*', 'fearfull representations of the dreadfull trumpets of Gods wrath' against incorrigible sinners.[4] Each of these 'visible Judgements', affirmed one unknown author, was 'a Sermon preached from Heaven by the Lord himselfe' to 'awaken and affright' unrighteous humanity to heartfelt contrition.[5]

---

[1] This phrase was used by a correspondent of Joseph Mede in a newsletter dated 12 Feb. 1627, reporting violent thunder and lightning in the vicinity of Boston, Lincolnshire, twelve days before: BL Harleian MS 390, fo. 205ᵛ.

[2] R[oberts], *Day of hearing*, 110.   [3] Dent, *Sermon of repentaunce*, sig. C7ʳ.

[4] *The wonders of this windie winter* (1613), sigs. A3ʳ, A4ʳ; *A most true relation of a very dreadfull earthquake . . . in Munster in Germanie*, trans. Charles Demetrius ([1613]), sig. B3ᵛ.

[5] *A true relation of those sad and lamentable accidents, which happened in and about the parish church of*

This chapter analyses contemporary responses to moments of acute corporate emergency and crisis, as refracted through the pulpit and press and as reflected in official policy and the conduct of the populace. In the face of the hostile forces periodically unleashed by a harsh environment, it was not just the rhetoric of Protestant ministers and metropolitan scribblers which merged and converged. Not everyone explained terrible calamities as the consequence of God's just wrath as readily or emphatically as the clergy, but providential beliefs did help to unite afflicted communities and to highlight areas of consensus between the outlook of different sections of English society. However, they also exacerbated latent conflicts and tensions within it.

HEAVY TYDINGS

Circumstantial accounts of destructive meteorological and geological phenomena were one of the mainstays of the Elizabethan and early Stuart book trade. The rhymsters and prose writers hired to produce such reports invariably assumed a persona of lugubrious woe and histrionic rhetorical lament.

> Compassion mooves me when I here recite,
> What with a quaking heart and hand I write

effused Martin Parker after an earthquake rocked the Neapolitan province of Calabria in March 1638. Who could hear the 'dolefull tale' of the magnificent Norwich church spire 'shaken downe by a thunder-clap' in 1601, wailed its narrator, 'and yet not shed a teare?'[6] Much emotive hyperbole was employed in evoking the distressing spectacle of market towns razed by fire and vast tracts of pasture and farmland laid waste by swollen rivers which had burst their banks. 'It might have made a stony hart to weepe', insisted one writer soon after Darlington in County Durham was ravaged in May 1585, 'to see how fiersily the houses burned of the foreside, and the goodes on the backside, how the yong infants sucking at their mothers brests in rufull maner sckriched'; 'whosoever' apprehended the horrific blaze which had devoured Tiverton within 'a twinkling of an eye' in 1598 would concede that the plight of its residents was 'most lamentable, and their sorrowe unspeakeable'.[7] So, too, those who vicariously witnessed the transmutation of 'famous' and flourishing Dorchester into a 'ruinated Troy, or decayed Carthage', 'a heape of ashes for travellers that passe by to sigh at'; or who heard the pitiful cries of the inhabitants of Bury St Edmunds 'ready to runne out of their

---

Withycombe in the Dartmoores (1638), 1, 5, 2 respectively. Cf. Anthony Anderson, *A sermon preached at Paules Crosse* (1581), sig. G1ᵛ, who called calamities 'Gods extraordinary Preachers from Heaven'.

[6] Martin Parker, *A true and terrible narration of a horrible earthquake, which happened in the province of Calabria* (1638), sig. A2ᵛ; *A newe ballad of the most wonderfull and strange fall of Christ's Church pinnacle in Norwitch* (c.1601), printed in Clark (ed.), *Shirburn Ballads*, 206. See also Richard Tarlton, *A very lamentable and woful discours of the fierce fluds, whiche lately flowed in Bedfordshire, in Lincoln-shire, and in many other places* (1570).

[7] *Lamentable n[ews] from the towne of Darnton in the bishopricke of Durham* (1585), 8; *The true lamentable discourse of the burning of Teverton in Devon-shire* ([1598]), sigs. A3ᵛ, B1ᵛ.

wits' as their homes were devoured by ravenous flames in April 1608 (Plate 12).[8]
'Behold the miserable estate of these poore drowned Creatures', implored one
pamphlet about the widespread floods in Norfolk, Somerset, and Gloucestershire
in 1607, directing attention to a crude woodcut of people clinging desperately to
trees and animals submerged up to their necks.[9] Heart-rending anecdotes of private
tragedy and personal 'mischance', astonishing stories of preservation and escape,
and 'strange Tragi-comicall Scaenes' abound: verbal snapshots of tiny schoolboys
discovered floating face down in ditches, sisters and brothers clasped arm in arm
having perished in each other's bosoms, orphaned babies carried to safety in their
cots, and gentlemen who 'rode' from one flood-stricken town to the next on the
ridges of dislodged rooves (Plates 13, 14).[10]

   This type of sentimentality sat rather uneasily alongside the heavy-handed providentialism with which the vast majority of these ballads and pamphlets were
thickly overlaid. God, the 'Omni-sufficiently skilfull Enginer', maintained the
author of a tract about an earthquake in the German town of Munster in 1612,
was 'at all times furnished with Thunder, Lightning & Tempest, (the Artillerie of
his vengeance)'; the 'smallest breath' of His nostrils, 'like a whirewind', could
'destroy the tottering globe of the whole earth'. Daily was the Lord provoked
'to powre forth the consuming vials of his incensed heavie Indignation, upon all
the misgoverned sonnes of sinfull men'. His 'extraordinarie Finger' could be
detected in every hurricane, hailstorm, and volcanic eruption.[11] Such events, said
John Chapman in his *A most true report of the myraculous moving and sinking of a
plot of ground . . . at Westram in Kent* ([1596]) were proof that 'veryly' there was a
deity who ruled the universe; they were 'a sencible testimony of his most certaine
beeing'.[12] The Irish city of Cork was said to have been 'suddainely' and 'horribly
consumed' by unquenchable flames which fell directly from heaven, like those
which had incinerated the biblical cities of Sodom and Gomorrah in the Old
Testament.[13] Most news reporters and preachers, however, stressed that God operated through secondary causes rather than by overriding the regular mechanisms
of nature. According to the presbyterian activist Thomas Wilcox, the conflagration which levelled Woburn in Bedfordshire in 1595 was kindled by an elderly cot-

---

[8] Hilliard, *Fire from heaven. . . . with the fearefull burning of the towne of Dorchester upon Friday the
6. of August last 1613*, sig. C4[v]. *The woefull and lamentable wast and spoile done by a suddaine fire in
S. Edmonds-bury in Suffolke* (1608), sig. B1[r–v].

[9] *More strange newes: of wonderfull accidents hapning by the late overflowings of waters . . .* ([1607]).

[10] Quotation from *1607. A true report of certaine wonderfull overflowings of waters*, sig. C1[r]. For examples of such anecdotes, see *Wonders of this windie winter*; *Gods warning to his people of England*; *Last terrible tempestious windes and weather; 1607. Lamentable newes out of Monmouthshire in Wales*; *The windie
yeare* (1613); *The cold yeare. 1614. A deepe snow* (1615).

[11] *Most true relation of a very dreadfull earth-quake*, sig. B3[r–v]; *Wonders of this windie winter*, sig. A4[r];
Last terrible tempestious windes and weather, sig. B2[r].

[12] Chapman, *Most true report*, sig. A4[r].

[13] *Relation of the most lamentable burning of the cittie of Corke*, sigs. A4[r], B2[r]. See also *Newes from
France. Or a relation of a marvellous and fearfull accident of a disaster, which happened at Paris . . . by
meanes of a terrible fire* (1618), sig. A3[v].

THE
Woefull and Lamen-
table waſt and ſpoile done by a
ſuddaine Fire in S. Edmondſ-bury
in *Suffolke*, on Munday the tenth of
Aprill. 1 6 0 8

LONDON
Printed for *Henrie Goſſon*, and are to be ſolde in Pater-
noſter rowe, 't the Signe of the Sunne.
1 6 0 8

PLATE 12 *The woefull and lamentable wast and spoile done by a suddaine fire in
S. Edmonds-bury in Suffolke, on Munday the tenth of Aprill 1608* (London, 1608),
title-page. By permission of the British Library. Shelfmark: C. 192. a. 128.

tager who changed her bed straw and laid the old in the chimney supposing that
there were no sparks in the grate.[14] Tiverton's 'great griefe' was similarly traced to
a mundane domestic mishap, 'a sillie flash of fier, blazing forth of a frying pan' in
which a beggar woman was cooking pancakes.[15] The fact that the Lord chose to

[14] Wilcox, *Faithfull narration*, 14. Wilcox was curate at Bovingdon, Hertfordshire, not too far distant,
during the 1590s.
[15] *True lamentable discourse of the burning of Teverton*, sigs. A3ᵛ–4ʳ. See also *Wofull newes from the
west-parts of England. Being the lamentable burning of the towne of Teverton* (1612), sigs. A3ᵛ–4ʳ, C3ʳ⁻ᵛ.
The fires at Tiverton were also noted in Bayly, *Practise of pietie*, 551–3, and Beard, *Theatre*, 555–6.

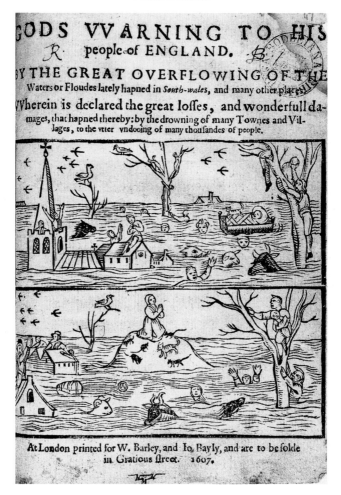

PLATE 13 *Gods warning to his people of England. By the great overflowing of the waters or floudes lately happened in South-wales and many other places* (London, 1607), title-page. By permission of the Bodleian Library, University of Oxford. Shelfmark: 4°C 16 Art. Bs (47).

bring about His purposes through such trivial accidents and humble instruments did not detract from His omnipotence—or the providential lesson He expected Englishmen and women to learn from these catastrophes. When William Whately preached in Banbury two days after much of the town was burnt to the ground in the spring of 1628, he too advised his auditors to avert their gaze from the human negligence which had immediately occasioned the holocaust and acknowledge the hand of the Almighty behind it.[16]

---

[16] William Whately, *Sinne no more* (1628), 50.

The last terrible Tempestious windes and weather. Truely Relating many Lamentable Ship-wracks, with drowning of many people, on the Coasts of England, Scotland, France and Ireland: with the Iles of Wight, Garsey & Iarsey. Shewing also, many great misfortunes, that haue lately hapned on Land, by reason of the windes and rayne, in diuers places of this Kingdome.

Imprinted at London for Ios: Hunt and are to be sold by Iohn Wright, 1613.

PLATE 14 *The last terrible tempestious windes and weather* (London, 1613), title-page. By permission of the Bodleian Library, University of Oxford. Shelfmark 4° E 17 (12) Art.

Some writers identified such disasters as harbingers of the Second Coming, the Last Judgement, and the final apocalyptic annihilation of mankind. They were the 'very neere fore-runners of that great and terrible Day of the Lord', declared the Northamptonshire minister Robert Bolton; the alarm bells by which 'he summons us to the doome', agreed a pamphleteer in 1592.[17] But freak storms,

---

[17] Bolton, *Discourse about the state of true happiness*, in *Workes*, 79; *A true relation of the French kinge his good successe . . .* , [*with*] *A most wonderfull and rare example . . . of a certaine mountaine in the Ile of Palme, which burned continually, for five or six weeks together* (1592), 15. Cf. *Hevy newes of an horryble earth quake whiche was in the cytie of Scharbaria* ([1542]); *1624. Newes from Holland, true, strange, and wonderfull* (1624), 9–10. All these pamphlets explicitly or implicitly drew on the Gospels of Matt. xxiv and Luke xxi.

torrential rain, and raging gale-force winds were more often thought of as ominous prognostications of the heavier temporal punishments God had in store, 'as a smoke in respect of a more terrible ensuing fire, and like a mustering of souldiers before the sad battell'. They were 'strange Edictes' and 'dombe warnings of Distruction', sirens sounding out the grievous judgements which hung like a louring cloud over the land.[18] The lightning bolt and fireball which swept through the parish church of Widecombe on Dartmoor during a service in 1638, killing several people at worship in their pews, was one such signal 'shot off from a Watch Tower, to give notice of an enemies approach'; the 'wonderfull overflowings of waters' in 1607 were 'the very diseases and monstrous byrthes of nature, sent into the world to terrifie it' of yet greater cataclysms waiting in the wings.[19] In His infinite mercy the Almighty fired flares of danger before He inflicted fatal blows.

But what were the grounds of the Lord's 'celestiall quarrell' with England? What were the 'outragious Enormities' which incited Him to holy violence against an 'impenetrable unrepenting perfidious people'? According to the author of *The windie yeare* (1613), they were 'writ upon every mans forehead'.[20] Most pamphleteers contented themselves with a general assault on the 'millions of varieties of transgressions' and 'abhominable hell hatchd impieties' by which contemporaries seemed 'to batter the glorious frame of Heaven'.[21] Some ran through a conventional catalogue of endemic offences—gluttony, adultery, pride, insobriety, and sumptuary excess; covetousness, usury, injustice, and oppression; swearing, blasphemy, idleness, and spiritual apathy. Others singled out specific vices for particular censure: Cork was indicted for moneylending; Tiverton for her 'horrible prophanation of the Lords day' and her penny-pinching disregard of the poor; Banbury for sabbath-breaking, abuse of the Eucharist, and drunkenness—'that fertill broody big bellied sinne'.[22] Like the ancient Israelites, the English had an 'innated hereditary perversenes' which induced them to shrug off their adversities and ignore the deity's repeated calls for moral renewal.[23]

God chastised communities like an affectionate father, declared Thomas Wilcox in the aftermath of the Woburn fire, to win them away from the vicious and depraved habits to which they were addicted.[24] He was 'loathe to chide, and more loath to strike us', asserted a journalist commenting on the severe winter of 1613,

[18] *Woefull and lamentable wast and spoile done . . . in S. Edmonds-bury*, sig. B2ʳ; Gurney, *Doleful discourse*, sig. C3ᵛ; *Gods warning to his people of England*, sig. A2ʳ.

[19] *True relation of those sad and lamentable accidents, which happened in . . . Withycombe*, 2; *1607. A true report of certaine wonderfull overflowings of waters*, sig. A3ʳ. The Widecombe incident is also narrated in *Second and most exact relation of those sad and lamentable accidents*; and *Newes and strange newes from St Christophers* (1638). A similar accident occurred two years later in Cornwall: *The voyce of the lord in the temple* (1640).

[20] *Windie yeare*, sig. A4ᵛ; *Last terrible tempestious windes and weather*, sigs. B2ʳ, 3ᵛ.

[21] *Last terrible tempestious windes and weather*, sig. B2ʳ.

[22] *Relation of the most lamentable burning of the cittie of Corke*, sig. B1ʳ; *True lamentable discourse of the burning of Teverton*, sig. B2ʳ⁻ᵛ and Bayly, *Practise of pietie*, 552; Whately, *Sinne no more*, 35.

[23] *Last terrible tempestious windes and weather*, sig. B1ʳ.

[24] Wilcox, *Faithfull narration*, 41–3.

'but if like foolish haire-braind children, we provoke him too often and too much to anger, he wil take up his Triple mace of hot vengance, and bruse us in peeces with the same'.[25] Rather than igniting isolated blazes like the one in Bury St Edmunds in 1608, He would 'make of the world one geernall bone-fier'.[26] The Lord 'has lovingly smitten us', 'the roaring boy' told his Banbury parishioners in 1628, but if the town did not 'wax better' by these mild stripes and vow to 'sinne no more' He would assuredly bring some greater evil upon it.[27] Such gentle strokes and lashes were, in fact, encouraging signs: they indicated that the Almighty had not yet given up hope of reclaiming a village or city from its Babylonian captivity in sin. It was when He ceased to castigate a locality and allowed it to wallow in its own wickedness that the inhabitants should really begin to worry and prepare themselves for the worst.

God's ultimate aim, therefore, was to reform rather than completely confound: 'the Almighties handy-workes' were 'never sent, but for our Instruction', maintained Henry Holland in *Motus Medi-terraneus*, a relation of the 'prodigious earth-quake' in Coventry in 1626, to 'rouse up our selves from the Cradle of Securitie, wherein wee have beene long rocked asleepe'.[28] They were 'easie messengers to call us homewards', that every individual might 'learne to strike saile to his sinnes, and put his soule into the safe harbour of Penitence'.[29] The Lord did not punish communities like Stockbury in Kent or Beccles in Suffolk because they had incensed Him more than the rest. Christ's caveat following the massacre of the Galileans and the collapse of the Tower of Siloam was no less relevant here: 'Unless you repent you shall likewise perish.' No corporation should flatter itself that it might be immune. To assume that Tiverton or any other unlucky municipality was populated by more heinous transgressors than those who inhabited one's own was utterly unwarrantable. These were merely the 'myrrours' in which the Lord reflected the likely fate of 'goodly' cities and towns which failed to learn from the penalties inflicted upon their iniquitous neighbours.[30] When an entire bench of assize judges and JPs died during an outbreak of gaol fever in Lincoln in 1590, it was likewise

> For our examples that remaine behind,
> To cleere our eyes that Sathan so did blind.[31]

Nor should one suppose that the victims of shocking disasters were predestined to eternal torment. In the judgements God executed on earth, observed the author

---

[25] *Windie yeare*, sig. C3ᵛ, cf. sig. B2ʳ.

[26] *Woefull and lamentable wast and spoile done . . . in S. Edmonds-bury*, sig. A4ʳ.

[27] Whately, *Sinne no more*, 3, cf. 5.   [28] [Holland], *Motus Medi-terraneus*, sigs. A4ᵛ, B1ᵛ.

[29] *Woefull and lamentable wast and spoile done . . . in S. Edmonds-bury*, sig. B3ᵛ.

[30] This scriptural passage is tacitly or overtly referred to in many pamphlets and ballads: see e.g. *A most true and lamentable report, of a great tempest of haile which fell upon a village in Kent, called Stockbery* (1590), 7; D. Sterrie, *A briefe sonet declaring the lamentation of Beckles, a market town in Suffolke which was . . . pitifully burned with fire* ([1586]).

[31] *A mournfull dittie on the death of certaine judges and justices of the peace . . . who died immediatly after the assises, holden at Lincolne last past* (1590).

of *1607. Lamentable newes out of Monmouthshire*, 'neyther the elect alone are preserved, nor the reprobate onely are destroyed'.[32]

The necessity of viewing communal afflictions through 'spirituall eyes' and transforming them into 'godly sorrowes', then, was the basic message of ballads, pamphlets, and sermons alike.[33] Wherever men and women saw such 'legible Characters' of the Lord's wrath, they should 'learne to spell out his meaning' touching themselves, striving to decipher these 'so lively documentes' of divine admonition.[34] The concluding refrain was always the same: zealously repent and amend 'least a more fearefull punishment, and a longer whip of correction draw blood of us'; put on sackcloth and ashes and implore the Lord to withdraw His hovering sword.[35]

NINE DAYS' WONDERS

Yet preachers and pamphleteers concurred in thinking that the bulk of the populace robbed God of his providence by imputing wild weather conditions to forces 'measurable by philosophicall reason', to conjunctions of the planets and stars, or to the erratic operations of fortune and chance.[36] The 'most part of men judge very fondly and corruptly' in this regard, lamented the London minister William Cupper in 1592: 'there is, say they, a continuall alteration or chaunge of things in the world'.[37] [T]emporizing naturallists' took no notice of the 'strangenesse' of such occurrences and 'more like unto Atheists, then Christians' accounted them 'common, and usuall', 'charactering' the 'sorest judgements' but 'customary accidents'.[38] Men and women were 'so farre bewitcht and gone in woe', complained Arthur Gurney in the wake of a fire in East Dereham, Norfolk, in 1581, that whenever the Lord imprinted his warnings in the sky and upon the earth, they were prone to 'dasell and devise' of Mother Nature, ascribing 'eche thing unto her lawes' and thereby making her into an idol.[39] Too many who witnessed the 'great Floods' in 1607 likewise turned 'the matter of their sins behind their backes', resorting to a meteorological explanation instead.[40] When the steeple of Olveston church was struck by lightning in 1606, the local Gloucestershire schoolmaster lamented that 'scarce one or two' among the multitude that flocked to see the charred remains 'but this was his complaint, what a mishap is this, what a mis-

---

[32] *1607. Lamentable newes out of Monmouthshire*, sig. C3[r].

[33] Whately, *Sinne no more*, 12, 53–4.

[34] *True relation of those sad and lamentable accidents, which happened in . . . Withycombe*, 2–3; Wilcox, *Faithfull narration*, 25.

[35] *1607. A true report of certaine wonderfull overflowings of waters*, sig. A2[r].

[36] Chapman, *Most true report*, sig. A4[r]. See also Whately, *Sinne no more*, 51; Wilcox, *Faithfull narration*, 31–2, 38.

[37] Cupper, *Certaine sermons*, 95–6, cf. 197.

[38] *Wonders of this windie winter*, sig. B2[r–v]; *1624. Newes from Holland*, 19–20.

[39] Gurney, *Doleful discourse*, sig. C3[v].

[40] *Miracle upon miracle. Or a true relation of the great floods which happened in Coventry, in Lynne, and other places* (1607), 5–6.

chance is here, what hard hap, what bad fortune, with such heathenish speeches, as if the spheres of heaven were the wheeles of fortune, and the clouds, hayle, lightning, thunder, and all the terrors of God else, were but a cast at hazard'. Most bewailed 'the losse of their sweet ring of Bels' more earnestly than their own spiritual infirmities.[41]

Certainly many parish registers, private diaries, and journals record gale-force winds and hailstones 'as bigge as walnottes', tennis balls, or turkeys' eggs without any pious comment whatsoever. Such entries are hardly evidence that an agnostic and morally neutral view of climatic anomalies prevailed, though they do beg questions about how many educated—and uneducated—people acknowledged a general providence without subscribing to the view that the hand of the Almighty could be traced in every particular terrestrial disaster.[42] To ascribe the cold winter of 1608 to chance, wrote the gentleman astrologer Sir Christopher Heydon to the Cambridge divine Samuel Ward, was 'with the Epicure [to] erect temples to blind Fortune'. Yet he no less firmly rejected the hypothesis that it was an act of God as 'unworthy of a scholar'.[43] The wide circulation of almanacs and prognostications linking extreme weather conditions with planetary movements and of classical writings on natural philosophy, especially those of Aristotle and Pliny, also suggests that contemporary attitudes were highly eclectic.[44] Learned puritans such as William Fulke and Thomas Gataker were themselves beginning to distinguish more sharply between the primary and secondary causes of events and moving towards developed concepts of casualty and contingency. It is striking to find Fulke complaining in a scholarly treatise that too many contemporaries thought that storms were 'immediate miracles, without any naturall meane . . . to procure them' and discussing the atmospheric effects of temperature differentials at length. Nevertheless, he insisted, only the impious denied that tempests were sent by the deity to declare His power and move men and women to amendment of life.[45]

Fires and violent gales which led to maritime disaster were sometimes attributed to the evil machinations of witches. Margaret Byx, alias Elwin, for instance, was convicted in 1615 of plotting to burn the Norfolk town of Wymondham by means of conjuration: she confessed to raising a blustery wind so that the flames 'should not be staied nor quenched in hast'.[46] According to the parish register of

---

[41] P. S., *Fearefull newes of thunder and lightning, with the terrible effects thereof, which Almighty God sent on a place called Olvestone, in the county of Glocester* (1606), sig. D1^r.

[42] See e.g. Shrewsbury School, MS Mus. X. 31, fo. 182^v, cf. 150^v; BL Egerton MS 784, fo. 33^r; BL Harleian MS 389, fo. 350^v; BL Add. MS 38599, fo. 50^v; Suffolk RO (Ipswich), FC 62 D1/1 (Parish register of St Mary, Cratfield), entry dated 17 Aug. 1615.

[43] Cited in Margo Todd, 'Providence, Chance and the New Science in Early Stuart Cambridge', *HJ* 29 (1986), 703.

[44] See Capp, *English Almanacs*; S. K. Heninger, *A Handbook of Renaissance Meteorology: With Particular Reference to Elizabethan and Jacobean Literature* (Durham, NC, 1960), esp. chs. 2–3.

[45] Fulke, *A most pleasant prospect into the garden of naturall contemplation, to behold the naturall causes of all kind of meteors* (1639 edn.; 1st pub. as *A goodly gallerye* in 1563), fos. 44^{r-v}, 5^r–6^r, 46^{r-v}. See also Todd, 'Providence, Chance and the New Science'.

[46] *The Official Papers of Sir Nathaniel Bacon of Stiffkey, Norfolk, as Justice of the Peace 1580–1620*, ed. H. W. Saunders, CS, 3rd ser. 26 (1915), 31–2.

Wells fourteen sailors perished off the west coast in 1583 because of the 'detestable working' of one Mother Gabley 'by the boiling or rather labouring of certayn Eggs in a payle full of colde water': she was later tried for her crimes. More famously, Agnes Thompson was alleged to have stirred up the tempest which nearly wrecked the ship in which James VI of Scotland was returning from Denmark.[47] But what we rarely find in the English (by contrast with the Continental) context are claims that the laity attributed ferocious storms which destroyed crops and led to harvest failure and dearth to *maleficia*. In Germany and Switzerland Protestant and Tridentine ministers fought a running battle against the popular tendency to blame climatic aberrations on weather magic rather than accept them as punishments for wickedness. But in England the 'ordinarie course' of nature seems to have been more of an obstacle to a truly 'providential' understanding of subsistence crises.[48] Scarcity was not attributed to sorcery so much as to the callous greed of corn-hoarders and middlemen in the victualling trade.[49] Either way people impiously avoided internalizing the blame.

Equally commonplace was the age-old allegation that contemporaries treated such disasters as trifles, disregarding them as soon as the immediate danger was over. 'Alacke! we write our passed punishments upon the brest of Time, and when his backe is turned, it is like Childrens bookes claspt up, we forget what lessons we reade there' bemoaned the translator of a Dutch news tract in 1613, 'our escaped miseries are but our mockeries . . . we feele stripes to day, but forget the smarting tomorrow'. It was 'the fashion of too too many to question and talke, and make things of this nature, but a nine days wonder', wrote another journalist reprovingly.[50] As with all such shakings of the Lord's 'whips', a London shop-keeper tells a North Country traveller in a dialogue about the 'deepe snow' of 1614, 'so of this, wee make but a May-game'. It was also 'but too sufficiently' clear to Thomas Wilcox that town fires were usually regarded in the light of spilt milk—misfortunes which tears could do nothing to relieve or redeem.[51] However sinister the catastrophe of the hour, deplored dozens of pamphleteers, 'we scoffe and deride it as presaging any mischief to us', just as the Old World shunned the reprehensions of Noah and Sodom and Gomorrah scorned the predictions of Lot.[52]

Sometimes, however, it was not the 'senselesse stoicisme'[53] of the common sort which called for clerical reproof, but their superstitious speculation. When, for

[47] George Lyman Kittredge, *Witchcraft in Old and New England* (Cambridge, Mass., 1929), 160 (and ch. 8 passim); *Newes from Scotland*, sig. C1ʳ.

[48] See Wolfgang Behringer, 'Weather, Hunger and Fear: Origins of the European Witch-Hunts in Climate, Society and Mentality', *German History*, 13 (1995), 1–27; H. C. Erik Midelfort, *Witch-Hunting in Southwestern Germany 1562–1684: The Social and Intellectual Foundations* (Stanford, Calif., 1972), 37–9, 88–90.

[49] Walter and Wrightson, 'Dearth and the Social Order'.

[50] *Most true relation of a very dreadfull earth-quake*, sig. A4ʳ; *True relation of those sad and lamentable accidents, which happened in . . . Withycombe*, 13–14.

[51] *Cold yeare*, sig. B1ʳ; Wilcox, *Faithfull narration*, 47.

[52] *1624. Newes from Holland*, 11.   [53] Whately, *Sinne no more*, 3.

instance, the bells of the Surrey parish of Bletchingley melted during a fire which broke out on the anniversary of Elizabeth's accession, 17 November 1606, a number of observers did 'descant upon the day', seizing upon the disaster 'to take some colour of advantage' against the Protestant faith and proclaiming it a posthumous judgement against the last Tudor monarch. The vicar of Banstead, Simon Harward, swiftly dismissed such 'popish' conjecturing, pointing out that the carillon in question had been cast and hallowed long before the Reformation.[54] Bishop John Jewel was equally aware of the capacity of conservative laypeople to interpret coincidences over-curiously and wrest them against the new regime: had he arrived in Salisbury before the spire of the cathedral was shattered by a lightning bolt on 7 May 1560, he wrote to Peter Martyr, 'so foolish . . . are mens minds, that all this mischief would have been ascribed to my coming'.[55] Seventy years later William Whately warned the 'worldlings' of Banbury against using the town's calamity as an excuse to traduce the godly: 'let there be none, no not one amongst you, that out of a malicious desire to scourge pietie, so nicke-named, upon our sides, shall mocke at Puritanisme, upon occasion of this hand of God which he hath stretched out against us, whom the world hath pleased, but falsely, to terme Puritans'.[56] And when the weathercock at St James's Palace fell down during a midsummer thunderstorm in 1623, at the height of the controversy surrounding the Habsburg match, rumour transformed it into the heraldic shield of Prince Charles himself, 'upon which some did criticise or prognosticate that the armes of England should downe and those of Spaine bee sett up'—suggestions Simonds D'Ewes, among others, dismissed contemptuously as 'fopperyes'.[57] Often the problem was not that the 'vulgar multitude' saw no supernatural import in such accidents but rather that they saw too much.

Suddenly overtaken by catastrophe, many seem to have jumped to the conclusion that the end of the world was at hand. According to Henry Machyn, merchant-taylor, this was how Londoners instinctively reacted to a howling gale in July of 1561; the villagers of Hay-on-Wye in Herefordshire 'Expectid nothinge ells but the dysmall daye of doome' after a raging tempest battered their community in 1585; so did Richard Shanne's Yorkshire neighbours during a furious downpour the following year.[58] When severe storms created havoc in counties across England in August 1589, many 'did rise owt of their bedds and fell to prayenge and weepinge thinkinge sure that the later day' drew nigh, or so a Shrewsbury

---

[54] Simon Harward, *A discourse of the severall kinds and causes of lightnings* (1607), sigs. B1^v–2^r.

[55] *The Zurich Letters A.D. 1558–1579*, ed. Hastings Robinson, Parker Soc. (Cambridge, 1842), 78.

[56] Whately, *Sinne no more*, 23.

[57] D'Ewes, *Diary*, ed. Bourcier, 146. Cf. BL Harleian MS 389, fo. 350^r.

[58] *The Diary of Henry Machyn, Citizen and Merchant-Taylor of London, from A.D. 1550 to A.D. 1563*, ed. John Gough Nichols, CS, 1st ser. 42 (1848), 265; Shrewsbury School, MS Mus X. 31, fo. 161^r, summarizing *A most rare & true report, of such great tempests, straunge sightes, and wonderfull accidents, which happened by the providence of God, in Hereford shire, at a place called the Hay* (1585), sig. A3^r; BL Add. MS 38599, fo. 66^r. See also *Autobiography and Correspondence of Sir Simonds D'Ewes . . .* , ed. James Orchard Halliwell, 2 vols. (1845) i. 39.

burgess recorded in his semi-official civic chronicle.[59] The floods in South Wales in 1607 apparently instilled such 'an amazed feare into the hearts of all the inhabitants . . . that every one prepared himselfe ready to entertayne the last Period of his lives Destruction: Deeming it altogether to be a second deluge: or an universal, punishment by Water'.[60] More than a handful who felt the earth move beneath Coventry in 1626 were reported to have betaken themselves 'to their best meditations and devotions'—'especially the better sort', the pamphleteer added parenthetically.[61]

There is a risk of taking these trite commonplaces too much at face value, of forgetting how far such narratives were coloured and conditioned by the generic conventions of sensational 'newes', of ignoring the extent to which the authors of 'true' relations and reports overdramatized their subject matter in line with audience expectations. Nevertheless it is clear that calamitous occurrences had the ability to arouse inert beliefs about divine intervention in at least some sectors of the sixteenth- and seventeenth-century populace. Indeed, there was often little to distinguish the impulsive piety crisis generated in relatively uncommitted members of the established Church from that of their Catholic ancestors or contemporaries across the English Channel. William Vaughan deplored the alacrity with which rural labourers in Jacobean Wales resorted to Romish gestures: 'when our ignorant countriemen heare but the clap of a thunder, or see but a flash of lightning, they arme themselves forthwith with outward showes, with crossing their profane bodies'.[62] By all accounts, this stubborn hangover from the medieval past was by no means confined to the 'dark corners of the land'. William Perkins, based in Cambridgeshire, said that this 'charm' and 'enchantment' was 'a thing usuall even of latter times'.[63]

Nor did the clergy tire of griping about the 'hypocriticall prayers', 'counterfeite repentaunce', and 'copper conversion' of Christians whose faith and fervour lasted only as long as their misfortunes.[64] Perkins had obviously encountered the phenomenon of spontaneous but short-lived religious renewal all too often in the course of his labours: 'when crosses and calamities befall men . . . then with Ahab they outwardly humble themselves, and go softly: they use to frequent the place where the word is preached, and Gods name called upon: but alas . . . these things are but fits arising of uncertaine and flittering motions in the heart. For so soone as the crosse is removed, they returne to their old byas againe'. Such, he observed despondently, was 'the manner of the world'.[65] '[W]hen wee are either generallie molested, or particularly endangered', cried the rector of East Hoathly, Sussex,

---

[59] Shrewsbury School, MS Mus X. 31, fo. 176ʳ.
[60] *Gods warning to his people of England*, 4.
[61] [Holland], *Motus Medi-terraneus*, sig. B3ᵛ.
[62] Vaughan, *Spirit of detraction*, 238.
[63] Perkins, *Damned art of Witchcraft*, 151–2.
[64] Gifford, *Countrie divinitie*, fo. 75ᵛ, cf. fo. 69ᵛ; Francis Marbury, *A sermon preached at Pauls Crosse the 13. of June, 1602* (1602), sigs. C1ᵛ–2ʳ.
[65] Perkins, *Workes*, i. 231.

Edward Topsell, in a course of sermons preached in the lean and hungry years of the late 1590s, 'Howe doe we cleave to the churches, and turne over the bibles, and runne over the worde? but in times of more ease wee are more idle, and take libertie of sinning'.[66] Great judgements made 'more prayers in a day, more seeking to God, and that feelingly & hastily, then otherwise are ordinary in a weeke', George Abbot, later Archbishop of Canterbury, noted ruefully, 'but when his rod ceased', so did such zeal.[67] 'Wofull experience' had taught Adam Harsnet, rector of Cranham in Essex, to anticipate the same. Whilst the hand of the Lord was heavy upon his parishioners they 'exceedingly lamented their former lewd, and vile courses; cryed out upon their pot-companions, and such as have beene occasions of their sinne', and vowed to turn over a new leaf. But the minute their anguish was lifted they 'started' from such resolutions 'like broken bowes', reducing their 'faire promises' unto 'foule performances'.[68] As soon as the visitation was over, agreed Charles Richardson, most slid back to their licentious ways 'as the dog to his vomit', growing 'as jocund, and jolly as they were before'. They might hang down their heads like bulrushes for a day, but their good intentions wore away as quickly as their troubles.[69] 'Carnall' and cold statute Protestants, declared John Gore and Obadiah Whitbie, dealt with the Almighty and his ministers 'as boyes doe by Walnut-trees, and other fruit-trees, in faire weather throw cudgels at us, in foule runne to us for shelter'.[70] Richard Stock, preacher at Allhallows, Breadstreet, chose the simile of mariners who ardently supplicated their Maker in the midst of a storm, but reverted to their 'distempers and disorders' once the danger of ship-wreck had passed: 'so many men who are crept out of a judgement' relapsed into their accustomed 'dishonoring of God'.[71]

These clerical clichés need to be interpreted with no less care and circumspection than the florid and inflated statements of ballad-mongers and hacks. Yet what emerges from this long litany of pastoral complaints is evidence (albeit encased within a literary trope) that hardship and disaster gave rise to temporary surges of piety and remorse, even in individuals written off by the clergy as hardened sinners and irreclaimable reprobates. This was especially apparent during outbreaks of epidemic disease. As Thomas Dekker and other commentators reported, at such times the pews of provincial and metropolitan churches were filled to capacity. According to John Taylor the 'water poet', London churchwardens were even obliged to bar the doors to parish excommunicates whom they had hitherto done their utmost to drag in.[72] In his epic poem on the plague of 1625, *Britain's remembrancer*, the

---

[66] Edward Topsell, *Times lamentation: or an exposition on the prophet Joel* (1599), 172–3.

[67] George Abbot, *An exposition upon the prophet Jonah* (1600), 61.

[68] Adam Harsnet, *Gods summons unto a general repentaunce* (1640), 88–90 and see 136–40.

[69] Charles Richardson, *The repentance of Peter and Judas* (1612), 137–8; Harsnet, *Gods summons*, 252. See also Thomas Fuller, *A sermon intended for Paul's Crosse . . . upon the late decrease and withdrawing of Gods heavie visitation of the plague of pestilence from the said citie* (1626), 40.

[70] Gore, *Summer sermon*, in *Ten godly and fruitfull sermons*, 32; O[badiah] W[hitbie], *Londons returne, after the decrease of the sicknes* (1637), 17.

[71] Richard Stock, *The doctrine and use of repentance* (1610 edn.), 164.

[72] John Taylor, *The fearefull summer: or, Londons calamitie, the countries discourtesie, and both their*

dissident stationer George Wither described how theatres, inns, tennis courts, and gaming houses were virtually deserted: if some citizens forsook their familiar recreational haunts 'through servile terror; some, for fashion', some pharisaically, and only a few with 'true humiliation', this hardly diminished the sombre, penitential mood which seems to have gripped the populace.[73] 'Cambridge is wonderously reformed since the plague there', the Suffolk minister John Rous wrote in his diary in 1631. '[S]cholers frequent not the streetes and tavernes, as before', 'but', he noted laconically in the margin some time later, now 'doe worse'.[74] Such moments of providential panic and ascetic intensity may have been fleeting and brief, but they must not be dismissed as insignificant.

THE GREAT EARTHQUAKE

Few episodes in which *digitus dei* was discerned to be actively at work left a more enduring impression upon the collective memory of late sixteenth- and early seventeenth-century England than 'the Great Earthquake' of 6 April 1580. The minor tremor which shook various parts of the country, especially East Anglia, London, and Kent, in the late afternoon of Wednesday in Easter week lasted barely a minute. Chimneys toppled; masonry cracked; window frames, furniture, and crockery rattled; bells clamoured of their own accord. One of the pinnacles of Westminster Abbey was dislodged, and stonework falling from the roof of Christ's Hospital church near Newgate market 'brayned' a local shoemaker's apprentice by the name of Thomas Gray and fatally injured his fellow maidservant Mabel Everitt as they sat listening to an evensong sermon; others were 'sorely bruised' as they hastened to escape. Lawyers at supper in the Middle Temple were so alarmed that they apparently ran from the tables with their knives still in their fists. In Sandwich Bay the ocean foamed, nearly capsizing a number of ships; at Dover chunks of white cliff and castle wall fell into the sea. The aftershock was felt in Oxford, Norwich, and Saffron Walden, as well as Antwerp, Bruges, Rouen, and Calais.

Notwithstanding its negligible effects, the earthquake had an enormous impact upon Elizabethan minds. As Samuel Gardiner, chaplain to Archbishop Abbot, reflected in 1606, it 'shaked not only the scenicall Theatre, but the great stage and Theatre of the whole land'.[75] Printed items began to issue from the presses within twenty-four hours of the event. The Sussex physician Thomas Twyne produced a scholarly essay on seismology;[76] Abraham Fleming, later rector of St Pancras, Soper Lane, translated relevant sections of Friedrich Nausea's *Libri mirabilium*

miserie (1636 edn.), sig. B4ʳ. See also Richard Milton, *Londons miserie, the countries crueltie: with Gods mercie* (1625), 16; Thomas Dekker, *A rod for run-awayes. Gods tokens, of his fearefull judgements* (1625), sig. B3ᵛ; id., *The blacke rod: and the white rod* (1630), 13.

[73] George Wither, *Britain's remembrancer* (1628), fos. 108ᵛ, 65ᵛ respectively.

[74] John Rous, *Diary*, ed. Everett Green, 63.

[75] Samuel Gardiner, *Doomes-day booke: or, an alarum for atheistes, a watchword for worldlinges, a caveat for Christians* (1606), 28.

[76] Thomas Twyne, *A shorte and pithie discourse, concerning the engendring, tokens, and effects of all earthquakes in generall* (1580).

reptem (1532);[77] 'familiar letters' were exchanged between eloquent university wits;[78] Latin set pieces and pious commentaries flowed from the pens of puritanical laymen such as Arthur Golding and John Phillip;[79] Grub Street bards including Thomas Churchyard and the celebrated comedian Dick Tarlton rustled up moralistic books and broadsides. Some of these tracts and sheets have survived, but many more have been lost to mustard pots and backyard privies, including a song by William Elderton entitled 'Quake. quake. yt is tyme to quake when towers and townes and all doo shake'.[80] The tremor was clearly a godsend to publishers of providential ephemera: Gabriel Harvey jocularly suggested Edmund Spenser might send him 'some odde fresh paulting threehalfepennie Pamphlet for newes; or some Balductum Tragicall Ballet in Ryme, and without Reason, setting out the right myserable, and most wofull estate of the wicked, and damnable worlde at these perillous dayes, after the devisers best manner: or whatsoever else shall first take some of your brave London Eldertons in the Head'.[81] Recorded in bold and red letters in parish registers and account ledgers, documented in civic chronicles and private notebooks, the 'woonderfull yearthquacke' was obviously the subject of much heated discussion in the late spring and early summer of that year.[82] Providing the springboard for many a sermon, it also engendered a 'godly

[77] Abraham Fleming, *A bright burning beacon . . . conteining . . . a commemoration of our late earthquake* (1580).

[78] Spenser and Harvey, *Three proper, and wittie, familiar letters . . . touching the earthquake in Aprill last, and our English refourmed versifying*, in Harvey, *Works*, ed. Grosart, i.

[79] Phillip or 'Phillipes' is mentioned as the author of a report on the earthquake by Fleming, *Bright burning beacon*, sig. A4ᵛ. No copy of this tract, apparently entitled *Quedam de terre motu*, survives: it is listed in Charles Henry Cooper and Thompson Cooper, *Athenae Cantabrigienses*, 2 vols. (Cambridge, 1858–1913), ii. 99. See Ch. 1 n. 193, above, Arthur Golding, *A discourse upon the earthquake that hapned throughe this realme of Englande, and other places of Christendom, the sixt of Aprill. 1580* (1580). On the relationship between Golding's *Discourse* and the official homily composed after the earthquake, see Llewellyn M. Buell, 'Arthur Golding and the Earthquake of 1580', *Philological Quarterly*, 24 (1945), 227–32.

[80] Both their compositions can be found in Thomas Churchyard, *A warning for the wise . . . Written of the late earthquake chanced in London and other places, the 6. of April 1580* (1580). See Campbell, 'Richard Tarlton and the Earthquake of 1580', 293–301.

[81] Spenser and Harvey, *Three proper, and wittie, familiar letters*, in Harvey, *Works*, ed. Grosart, i. 62. For items licensed in the wake of the earthquake, see *SR* ii. 367–73. William Elderton's *Quake. Quake. Yt is Tyme to Quake* was registered on 25 Apr. In *Bright burning beacon*, sig. A4ᵛ, Fleming lists other lost publications by Francis Shakleton, Robert Gillins, and John Grafton. John Carpenter wrote *A sorrowfull song for sinfull soules, composed upon the strange and wonderfull shaking of the earth the 6 of Aprill, 1586* [*sic*], which also cannot now be traced (see Ch. 1 n. 197, above). Anthony Munday included a short account of the event in his *View of sundry examples*, sigs. D2ᵛ–3ʳ. A ballad on 'The great earthquake' is preserved in the Hall Commonplace Book, FSL MS V. a. 339, fos. 176ᵛ–177ᵛ, but may well be a Collier forgery (see Ch. 2 n. 39, above).

[82] See e.g. CUL MS Mm. 1. 29 (Notebook of Thomas Earl, St Mildred's Breadstreet, 1564–1600), fo. 46ᵛ; Shrewsbury School, MS Mus X. 31, fo. 135ᵛ; the 'Annals of Sandwich', printed in William Boys, *Collections for an History of Sandwich in Kent . . .* , 2 vols. (Canterbury, 1792), ii. 695–6; Merton College, Oxford, MS printed in Anthony à Wood, *The History and Antiquities of the University of Oxford in Two Books*, trans. John Gutch (Oxford, 1792–6), II. i. 198–9; the Norwich Roll printed in Francis Blomefield, *An Essay towards a Topographical History of the County of Norfolk*, 11 vols. (1805–10), iii. 355; Suffolk RO (Bury St Edmunds), FL 522/11/22 (Townwardens' accounts, Bardwell, Suffolk), fo. 9ʳ (I owe this reference to Mrs Jean Lock). The earthquake was also recorded in printed chronicles: see John Stow, *The chronicles of England . . .* (1580), 1210–11.

admonition' promulgated by the ecclesiastical authorities, along with orders for
biweekly fasting and prayer.[83]

Whatever his agenda, every author agreed that the earthquake was a 'bright,
burning beacon' forewarning of future desolating punishments should the English
people fail to take heed and 'retire home to the sheepefold' of their God.[84] It was
'a messenger and summoner of us to the dreadful Judgement-seate'. After twenty-
one years of courteous entreaties the Lord was losing patience with this ungrateful and iniquitous nation and beginning to lay His axe to the root of the tree. He
had mixed mercy with severity by limiting the tremor to less than sixty seconds,
'so rather shaking [His] rod at us, than smiting us according to oure deserts'.[85] If
it was ignored and treated as a 'toy', exhorted Fleming, 'shall we not heape upon
our heades the firie coles of his consuming furie'?[86] Richard Tarlton summed it all
up in one clumsy couplet:

> Our health of soules must hang in great suspence
> When earth and Sea doo quake for our offence.[87]

No one doubted that this was a sign sent from heaven; what was in dispute
among the learned was precisely how the Almighty had brought it to pass. Abraham
Fleming insisted that the earthquake had been created by the deity outside the
order of nature. He sternly counselled his readers not to be seduced by 'every vaine
Philosophers fansie' into searching for any other cause than the Lord's 'justly conceived indignation against the wickedness of the world': to do so was not merely
'atheisme' but 'open blasphemie'.[88] Arthur Golding also reproved those who would
'not stick to deface the apparent working of God' by ascribing 'this rare and unac-
customed miracle' to geological movements within the earth's core, in accordance
with Aristotelian theories.[89] Thomas Twyne and Gabriel Harvey, however, inclined
to the view that, although the tremor was a genuine token of wrath, it had been
generated by purely physical forces. '[V]ery seldome' in 'these latter dayes',
declared the Cambridge don, did the Lord exercise his providence 'myraculously
and extraordinarily', without 'the service and Ministrie of his Creatures, in the
atcheeving thereof'.[90]

Most preachers and pamphleteers did not hold out much hope that the episode
would have lasting regenerative influence upon the populace at large. It was 'sud-

---

[83] *The order of prayer upon Wednesdayes and Frydayes, to avert and turne Gods wrath from us, threatned
by the late terrible earthquake* ([1580]), repr. in Clay (ed.), *Liturgical Services*, 562–6.

[84] Fleming, *Bright burning beacon*, sig. D1^v.

[85] Golding, *Discourse upon the earthquake*, sigs. B3^v–4^r, D1^r.

[86] Fleming, *Bright burning beacon*, sig. D2^r.

[87] Tarlton, in Churchyard, *Warning for the wise*, sig. D3^r.

[88] Fleming, *Bright burning beacon*, sig. B4^v. See also sigs. E2^r, F2^v, G1^v.

[89] 'A Godly Admonition', in Clay (ed.), *Liturgical Services*, 570–2; Golding, *Discourse upon the earthquake*, sig. B2^v–3^v.

[90] Spenser and Harvey, *Three proper, and wittie, familiar letters*, in Harvey, *Works*, ed. Grosart, i. 54–5;
Twyne, *Shorte and pithie discourse*, esp. sigs. A3^v, B3^v. On the question of causation, see also Kocher,
Science and Religion, 111–13.

dainly feard and I stand in dout wil as suddainly be forgotten', Thomas Churchyard predicted two days later on 8 April.[91] Who had learnt the lessons encoded therein? demanded William Withers, an 11-year-old seer who created a sensation in the normally sedate Suffolk town of Walsham-le-Willows less than a fortnight after Christmas 1580. God had 'passed by you, as it were, but with one touche of his finger', this young husbandman's son told the crowd that assembled in his bedroom, and unless pride and infidelity were swiftly forsaken they would shortly 'feele & taste' of 'a farre greater Earthquake' than the tiny tremor eight months before.[92] Hugh Broughton was only one of his elders in holy orders to endorse the gloomy predictions of this precocious schoolboy, though he addressed a rather more distinguished audience—Queen Elizabeth's court.[93] James Bisse recollected it at Paul's Cross in January 1581; in a lecture at Ipswich seventeen years later Samuel Bird lamented that 'notwithstanding it was a most lively resemblance of the resurrection, yet who almost doth nowe remember it'?; it was in grave danger of being 'buried in oblivion', said Bishop Arthur Lake of Bath and Wells in a sermon delivered sometime before his death in 1626.[94] Despite the scepticism of the clergy 'the great earthquake' did linger on in the collective imagination. 'I never shall forget it', exclaims the Nurse fervently in Shakespeare's *Romeo and Juliet*, first performed around 1591.[95] Two generations later it was still being listed in the 'compendious chronolgies' of historic happenings appended to many almanacs.[96] And it had acquired almost titanic dimensions by 1638, when a newswriter recalled the hundreds of houses overturned and the 'great number' of helpless people who had been slain.[97]

Even once due allowance is made for journalistic exaggeration and licence, there is much to suggest that the earthquake left many who experienced it deeply perturbed. Londoners living in the districts of St Katherine's, Limehouse, and Ratcliff were 'so marvellously amazed', reported Churchyard, 'that it was pitifull to beholde how fearefully they ranne oute of their doores, and howe strangely one would beholde an other, thinking verilye, that the latter day hadde bene come'.[98] The consternation the earthquake caused in the capital, said Fleming, was 'needelesse to be named': 'the talking of Gods judgements, the fearing of his vengeance,

---

[91] Churchyard, *Warning for the wise*, sigs. C3ᵛ–4ʳ.

[92] Phillip, *Wonderfull worke of God shewed upon a chylde, whose name is William Withers*, sig. B1ʳ⁻ᵛ. This incident is further discussed in Ch. 4, below.

[93] H[ugh] B[roughton], *Moriemini. A verie profitable sermon preached before her majestie at the court* (1593), 9.

[94] Bisse, *Two sermons*, sig. B8ʳ; Samuel Bird, *The lectures . . . upon the 11. chapter of the epistle unto the Hebrewes, and upon the 38. Psalme* (Cambridge, 1598), 77–8; Arthur Lake, *Sermons with some religious and divine meditations* (1629), 372.

[95] Shakespeare, *Romeo and Juliet*, I. iii. 24–5, in *Complete Works*, ed. Alexander.

[96] See e.g. Edward Pond, *Enchiridion: or Pond his Eutheca: 1604. A new almanacke* (1604), sig. A3ʳ; Samuel Perkins, *A new almanacke and prognostication* (1627), sig. B6ᵛ; John Woodhouse, *An almanacke or prognostication* (1630), 'A briefe Chronologie of things past'; Jonathan Dove, *An almanack for . . . 1639* (Cambridge, 1639), sig. C7ʳ; Richard Allestree, *A new almanack and prognostication* (1640), sigs. C1ᵛ–2ʳ.

[97] Parker, *True and terrible narration of a horrible earthquake*, sig. A8ʳ.

[98] Churchyard, *Warning for the wise*, sig. B1ʳ.

the suspecting of great daunger, the prophesieng of Doomes day, the confessing of sinne, the blaming of all estates, the complaining against pride, the exclaiming against envie, the crieng out against the abuse of the Sabbaoth day, the finding fault with a thousand enormities . . . the inveieng against diverse disorders in these daies'; 'the peoples mouthes were full of common places at that instant'. Though 'devotion died when daunger ceased', their 'sudden zeale' was 'vehement'.[99] On 22 April Bishop Aylmer urged Lord Burghley 'to give some ordre and direccion to stire up' the urban multitude to religious observances, 'speciallie for that' they were 'presentlie much moved'.[100] But it was not merely 'the simpler, and unskilfuller sort' who were startled into making earnest intercessions: the newly married Saffron Walden gentlewomen in whose company Gabriel Harvey spent the evening let out unladylike screams, falling 'forsooth, very demurely' from flirting to praying, and beseeching their companions to 'leave off playing' and take to their knees.[101] It is hardly surprising that the earthquake led the parishioners of Debden in Essex to tremble—only the day before, Laurence Chaderton had preached to them all too prophetically on the text of Joel iii. 16 ('The heaven and the earth shall shake, but the Lord will be the hope of His people').[102] When a second tremor jolted Great Chart and Ashford at midnight on 1 May, the sleeping inhabitants seem to have regretted not taking more notice of the first, for they ran in their bed-clothes to the closest church to call importunately upon the Lord. According to John Stow, the wave of piety which washed the nation was 'wonderfull for the time', and a Coventry alderman commented drily in the city annals: 'this yeare was a disease all the land over called speedy repentance'.[103]

One sphere in which the events of 6 April 1580 may have marked something of a watershed was the stage. Occurring in the context of a battery of attacks upon the dramatic profession and medium from both pulpit and press, the earthquake appears to have provoked much soul-searching on the part of the civic authorities who had sanctioned the opening of commercial theatres in 1577, and among at least some of their patrons as well.[104] By all accounts, audiences at the Theatre, the

[99] Fleming, *Bright burning beacon*, sigs. O4^v–P1^r.

[100] BL Lansdowne MS 30, no. 49, fo. 145^r, printed in Clay (ed.), *Liturgical Services*, 562.

[101] Spenser and Harvey, *Three proper, and wittie, familiar letters*, in Harvey, *Works*, ed. Grosart, i. 41–2.

[102] Francis Dillingham, *Laurence Chaderton, D.D. (First Master of Emmanuel)*, ed. E. S. Shuckburgh (Cambridge, 1884), 14.

[103] Stow, *Annales*, 1163–4; R. W. Ingram (ed.), *Records of Early English Drama. Coventry* (Manchester, 1981), 294.

[104] For the anti-theatrical context, see William Ringler, 'The First Phase of the Elizabethan Attack on the Stage, 1558–1579', *Huntington Library Quarterly*, 5 (1942), 391–418; Jonas Barish, *The Antitheatrical Prejudice* (Berkeley and Los Angeles, 1981), ch. 4; Collinson, *Birthpangs*, 112–15. The theatre had been attacked in John Northbrooke, *Spiritus est vicarius Christi in terra. A treatise wherein dicing, dauncing vaine playes or enterludes with other idle pastimes . . . are reproved* ([1577]); Stephen Gosson, *The schoole of abuse, conteining a pleasaunt invective against poets, pipers, plaiers* (1579); and in a series of Paul's Cross sermons preached in the late 1570s. Anthony Munday's expanded edn. of Salvianus' treatise on the subject, *A second and third blast of retrait from plaies and theaters* (1580), was published a few months after the earthquake.

Curtain at Holywell, and other open air arenas where 'bawdie enterluds' and 'trumperies' had been enacted that afternoon were scared out of their wits. Some seriously injured themselves leaping from the stands; others were hurt in the ensuing stampede; 'not any', alleged Philip Stubbes, 'but they went away sore affraid, & wounded in conscience'.[105] Preachers and polemicists alighted upon the event for a renewed cry to the city fathers to 'pluck down these places of abuse' and to the people to abandon this diabolical pastime; the refrain of one lost ballad was 'comme from the plaie'.[106] Abraham Fleming ingeniously twisted the details of the incident to serve as a 'watchword' to 'all such as favour that damnable facultie', as every practised providentialist could: God had shown this judgement on Thomas Gray and Mabel Everitt as they were seated obediently in church 'to teach us what his out stretched arme can doe in prophane places, among an un-circumcised multitude', and on a weekday 'that wee might see his long suffering, in sparing us on the Sabbaoth'.[107] When the Lord Mayor wrote to the Lord Chancellor on 12 April recommending that plays be forbidden within and without the liberties, he explicitly referred to the earthquake the previous week. Nor was it sheer coincidence that the liturgical drama which had outlasted the political reformation in Coventry was decisively suppressed the same year; it was appar-ently as a direct result of the tremor that the town's famous Corpus Christi 'padgins' were permanently 'layd downe'.[108]

MORAL EMERGENCIES

Public calamities in general seem to have added much momentum to the cluster of interrelated campaigns to alter moral standards and behaviour which historians have come to refer to collectively as the 'Reformation of Manners'. Local disasters recurrently triggered new initiatives in those crusades against drunkenness and swearing, sexual promiscuity and sabbath-breaking, idleness and disorderly recre-ations traditionally associated particularly with puritanism. Ordained ministers and lay moralists were experts at exploiting and harnessing such periods of height-ened feeling to further the ends of their assault upon godlessness and vice: every catastrophe became the pretext for a renewed blitz upon the 'crying' and 'capitall' sins of the age.

They had a veritable field day against urban entertainments in January of 1583 when a gallery full of bear-baiting fans at Paris Garden on the south bank of the Thames collapsed one wintry Sunday afternoon, killing eight servants and artisans outright, and leaving at least 150 other spectators grievously maimed.[109] As Dr John

---

[105] Stubbes, *Anatomy*, pt. 1, ed. Furnivall, 180. See also Churchyard, *Warning for the wise*, sig. B2ʳ; J[ohn] G[reene], *A refutation of the apology for actors* (1615), 43–4; Prynne, *Histrio-mastix*, fo. 556ᵛ.

[106] Stubbes, *Anatomy*, pt. 1, ed. Furnivall, 180; *SR* ii. 368.

[107] Fleming, *Bright burning beacon*, sig. D3ᵛ.

[108] The mayoral letter is printed in E. K. Chambers, *The Elizabethan Stage*, 4 vols. (Oxford, 1923), iv. 279. Ingram (ed.), *Records of Early English Drama. Coventry*, 294.

[109] The accident was used as evidence of divine anger by Stubbes, *Anatomy*, pt. 1, ed. Furnivall, 179; [Alexander Leighton], *A shorte treatise against stage-playes* ([Amsterdam], 1625), 28; Beard, *Theatre*,

Dee noted in his diary, the godly were quick to 'expownd it as a due plage of God for the wickednes ther usid, and the Sabath day so profanely spent'.[110] The main issue at stake was less cruelty to animals than the spiritual peril of engaging in such 'carnall sports' and of unholy contempt for sabbatarian views. Within a week of this Elizabethan Hillsborough, the puritan publicist John Field had produced *A godly exhortation*, prefaced by a trenchant epistle to the Mayor, Recorder, and Aldermen, whom he boldly reproached for having failed to take sustained action to eliminate such nests and nurseries of intolerable impiety hitherto. He admitted that the pit itself was not within their jurisdiction ('whereby you might seeme to be cleared'), but because they had done nothing to restrain those under their charge from resorting there, he insisted, 'this transgression must needs also reach to you'.[111] Field was not a voice in the wilderness; nor were his words lost in the wind. London's chief magistrate was moved 'in consciens to beseche' Lord Burghley 'to give order for redress of suche contempt of gods service' and the incident did help induce the Privy Council to extend the prohibition against Sunday performances in the outer suburbs as well as within the city walls.[112]

The burning of the Globe and Fortune theatres in June 1613 and December 1621 inspired yet more appeals to 'stage-strutters' and playgoers to lay aside their depraved practices and thereby deflect the wrath of God. In each case, as Ben Jonson remarked, 'the brethren', no less than red-nosed rhymsters and profit-seeking publishers, 'straight nos'd it out for newes'.[113] Another windfall to the reformist cause was the tragedy which occurred in the Oxfordshire village of Witney on 3 February 1653, where a large crowd had assembled to watch a

---

212; Bayly, *Practise of pietie*, 550–1; Prynne, *Histrio-mastix*, fos. 556ᵛ–557ʳ; Fuller, *Church-history of Britain*, bk. IX, p. 165. There were undoubtedly other publications about the disaster: Henry Cave's *Narration of the fall of Paris Garden* (1588), referred to by Prynne, is now lost, and on 21 Jan. 1583, Richard Jones and William Bartlett were fined and imprisoned for printing without licence 'a thing of *The fall of the galleries at Paris Garden*': *SR* ii. 853. A ballad entitled 'Fatall fall at Paris Garden' is preserved in the Hall Commonplace Book, FSL MS V. a. 339, fos. 163ʳ–164ʳ, but may be a forgery. See Ch. 2 n. 39, above.

[110] *The Private Diary of Dr John Dee and the Catalogue of his Library of Manuscripts*, ed. James Orchard Halliwell, CS, 1st ser. 19 (1842), 18.

[111] Field, *Godly exhortation*, dedicatory epistle to the Lord Mayor, William Fleetwood, Recorder, and the Aldermen of the City, sig. [A]2ʳ⁻ᵛ and *passim*. On Field, see Patrick Collinson, 'John Field and Elizabethan Puritanism', in *Godly People: Essays on English Protestantism and Puritanism* (1983), 335–70.

[112] BL Lansdowne MS 37, no. 4, fo. 8ʳ, printed in Chambers, *Elizabethan Stage*, iv. 292. Another 'providence' against bear-baiting occurred in Bunbury in Cheshire on 26 July 1638 where people assembled for entertainment during a wake were injured when the churchyard wall fell on top of them. Burghall, 'Providence Improved', in Barlow (ed.), *Cheshire*, 157.

[113] Ben Jonson, 'Execration against Vulcan', in *Q. Horatius Flaccus: His art of poetry. Englished*, trans. Ben Jonson (1640), 36–7. For *A sonnett upon the pittiful burneing of the Globe playhouse in London*, preserved in a 17th-cent. MS from Yorkshire, see Chambers, *Elizabethan Stage*, ii. 419–23. This may be one of the ballads entered to Simon Stafford and Edward White on 30 June (*The sodayne burninge of the Globe on the Bankside in the play tyme on Saint Peters Day last 1613* and *A dolefull ballad of the generall overthrowe of the famous theater on the Bankesyde, called the Globe &c*, by William Parratt), *SR* iii. 328. See also Prynne, *Histrio-mastix*, fo. 556ʳ.

company of strolling players perform the popular Elizabethan comedy *Mucedorus* in an upstairs room of the White Hart Inn. The floor of the chamber gave way after the second act, carrying five of the onlookers to an early grave and injuring some sixty more. The local lecturer, John Rowe, needed no other excuse to deliver a sermon series on the depravity of this leisure activity, to say nothing of a string of other abominations he claimed ran rife thereabouts. To his mind the general impiety of the actors was compounded by a tiny piece of anti-puritan satire he found embedded in the script: God was clearly avenging those who had dared to scoff at His 'saints'.[114]

Every country town ravaged by fire received a similar tongue-lashing from its previously unheeded preachers, who having long threatened their parishioners with some draconian divine punishment, now had good reason to gloat. Was the generation which saw Stratford-upon-Avon razed to the ground twice on the same day twelve months apart entirely insensible to the repeated calls of its ministers for a sweeping moral revolution? Did the chief inhabitants of Tiverton still turn a deaf ear to the strictures of their vicar after the town was consumed by fire in 1598 and again in 1612? Or were they too convinced that it was high time to change their weekly market from Monday and so remove one principal occasion for profaning the sabbath?[115] Even if the effect was no more than a municipal facelift, a cursory clean-up of the streets, it should not be overlooked. David Underdown has demonstrated that the conflagration in Dorchester on 6 August 1613 resulted in 'a sort of spiritual mass conversion'. This was the catalyst that transformed an ill-governed 'provincial backwater' into a 'New Jerusalem', a Christian commonwealth and citadel akin to Calvin's Geneva. It helped harden the tepid Protestantism of the majority into the vibrant and militant religiosity practised by the 'hotter sort'. '[M]en lay frozen in the dregs', wrote the merchant William Whiteway, 'until it pleased God to awaken them by this fiery trial'. Inflamed by the rhetoric of John White, rector of the parish of Holy Trinity, the pious burgesses who controlled the corporation set about building 'a city on a hill' with missionary fervour, enforcing religious conformity and godly discipline, promoting comprehensive new measures for education and welfare, and creating effective mechanisms to channel the sudden upsurge in charitable giving. This radical programme for communal improvement inevitably met with some inertia and opposition, but it also enjoyed a degree of success which is surely testimony to the prevalence and potency of providential convictions. Commemorated annually until

---

[114] John Rowe, *Tragi-comoedia. Being a brief relation of the strange, and wonderfull hand of God discovered at Witny* (Oxford, 1653), esp. sigs. *1ʳ–*2ʳ. I owe my knowledge of this tract to Professor Patrick Collinson. Another disaster which lent itself to a providential reading was the collapse of a makeshift theatre in Riseley, Bedfordshire, in 1607, cited in Beard, *Theatre*, 212; Prynne, *Histrio-mastix*, fo. 557ʳ.

[115] See Bayly, *Practise of pietie*, 551–2; Beard, *Theatre*, 555–6. On Stratford, which burned in 1594, 1595, and 1614, see also Shrewsbury School, MS Mus X. 31, fos. 196ᵛ–197ʳ; on Tiverton, see *The true lamentable discourse of the burning of Teverton* and *Wofull newes from the west-parts of England*.

1634, the town's near annihilation by fire promoted an ongoing commitment to moral regeneration.[116]

Elsewhere, communal emergencies stimulated similar programmes for ethical and social rehabilitation. An epidemic in 1627 persuaded the godly aldermen of Salisbury to mimic the strict regime instituted by their Dorset brethren and declare war on the 'gross and foul sins' which had pulled divine vengeance down upon the city. Documents relating to similar reforms in Norwich in the 1570s, spearheaded by the city's 'apostle' John More, are also couched in what Paul Slack has called 'the Puritan language of collective paranoia': they too convey an urgent sense that personal, communal, and national salvation was inextricably linked with the effective repression of disorder, impropriety, and crime.[117] So do petitions like the one drawn up by the scandalized godly of Moston in 1655, calling for steps to be taken against swearing and other 'crying wickednesses . . . dayly committed in the tippling houses of the town' before 'some remarkable judgement' befell the community.[118] In 1590 a Southampton jury feared that if nothing was done to restrain unlawful games the plagues of God would continue to hang over the city.[119] MPs like Francis Davey who sponsored bills against drunkenness and swearing likewise warned the Commons that unless good laws were made the Lord would 'lay his heavy hand of wrath and indignation upon this land', and such concerns frequently found their way into the preambles of the resulting statutes.[120] Providentialism was a vital stimulus to voluntary self-regulation from above, and also perhaps from below. For, as Mark Byford's study of Elizabethan Essex suggests, the enforcement of sharp moral codes by local officials could and did win the support of plebeian townspeople: illicit lovers carted around Colchester in a tumbrel as part of a public shaming ritual akin to the popular skimmington were greeted with a chorus of approving jeers from those who lined the streets.[121]

Debate still rages about the driving force behind the late Tudor and early Stuart

---

[116] David Underdown, *Fire from Heaven: Life in an English Town in the Seventeenth Century* (1992), p. 5, ch. 4, and *passim*. The quotation from Whiteway, from a civic memorandum in Dorset RO, is cited on p. 90. See also Frances Rose-Troup, *John White: The Patriarch of Dorchester*, [*Dorset*], *and The Founder of Massachusetts 1575–1648* (New York, 1930), ch. 4.

[117] Paul Slack, *Poverty and Policy in Tudor and Stuart England* (1988), 149, 151–2. On Salisbury, see id., 'Poverty and Politics in Salisbury 1597–1666', in Peter Clark and id. (eds.), *Crisis and Order in English Towns 1500–1700: Essays in Urban History* (1972), 164–203; id., 'Religious Protest and Urban Authority: The Case of Henry Sherfield, Iconoclast, 1633', in Derek Baker (ed.), *Schism, Heresy and Religious Protest*, SCH 9 (Cambridge, 1972), 295–302. See also Collinson, *Religion of Protestants*, ch. 4 and Peter Clark, ' "The Ramoth-Gilead of the Good": Urban Change and Political Radicalism at Gloucester 1540–1640', in Peter Clark, Alan G. R. Smith, and Nicholas Tyacke (eds.), *The English Commonwealth 1547–1640* (Leicester, 1979), 167–87.

[118] Cited in Keith Wrightson, 'The Puritan Reformation of Manners with Special Reference to the Counties of Lancashire and Essex 1640–1660', PhD thesis (Cambridge, 1973), 175 and see ch. 8 *passim*.

[119] Quoted in David Underdown, *Revel, Riot and Rebellion: Popular Politics and Culture in England 1603–1660* (Oxford, 1987), 51.

[120] See Joan R. Kent, 'Attitudes of Members of the House of Commons to the Regulation of "Personal Conduct" in Late Elizabethan and Early Stuart England', *BIHR* 46 (1973), 43.

[121] Byford, 'The Price of Protestantism', ch. 5, esp. 397–404. See also Ingram, 'Ridings, Rough Music and the "Reform of Popular Culture" '.

'Reformation of Manners' at both the legislative and the local level, but the role played by anxiety about divine retribution has not always received the attention it deserves. Even in Ronald Hutton's *The Rise and Fall of Merry England*, which reverses the priorities of many previous studies by giving more weight to religious factors than population growth, price inflation, and the concomitant rise in poverty, it merits little more than a passing mention.[122] Social historians are inclined to be somewhat sceptical about the panic-stricken tones in which moral reformers spoke of the necessity of appeasing an angry deity and warding off impending plagues, preferring to emphasize the prudential motives of the rising 'middling sort'—the practical benefits to be derived from combatting lawless behaviour and suppressing traditional festive customs and the secular interests served by 'social control'. But it is never really possible to decide just where providentialism ends and pragmatism begins: concerns about the social order and reactions to the palpable effects of economic and demographic pressure cannot be understood outside the Christian frame of reference shared by the vast majority of early modern Englishmen and women.[123] Moreover, as scholars such as Martin Ingram are beginning to insist, fear of fire and brimstone cannot be regarded merely as a convenient ideological excuse.[124] It was arguably of overriding importance in fuelling the engine of ethical and cultural reform. When contemporary clergymen spoke of the sins that were hauling down judgements as with 'carte' or 'gable ropes' and 'cordes of vanitie' and compelling God to come against the English people with 'the beesome of utter desolation', they were giving expression to a deep-seated conviction.[125] 'Questionlesse', declared Arthur Dent, these were 'the very fire-brands' and 'touchwood' to kindle divine wrath against the whole land.[126]

To many minds it was the current crisis in human justice that forced the Almighty 'to take the matter into his owne hands' and execute punishment

---

[122] Hutton, *Rise and Fall of Merry England*, see esp. 111–12, 146, 261–2. Providential convictions are also barely mentioned in Anthony Fletcher's survey of such initiatives in *Reform in the Provinces: The Government of Stuart England* (New Haven, 1986), ch. 8.

[123] Cf. the attempt to uphold a distinction between spiritual considerations and concerns about the social order in Robert B. Shoemaker, 'Reforming the City: The Reformation of Manners Campaign in London, 1690–1738', in Lee Davison, Tim Hitchcock, Tim Keirn, and Robert B. Shoemaker (eds.), *Stilling the Grumbling Hive: The Response to Social and Economic Problems in England, 1689–1750* (Stroud, 1992), 99–120.

[124] Martin Ingram, 'Reformation of Manners in Early Modern England', in Paul Griffiths, Adam Fox, and Steve Hindle (eds.), *The Experience of Authority in Early Modern England* (Basingstoke, 1996), 47–88. See also Bruce Lenman, 'The Limits of Godly Discipline in the Early Modern Period with Particular Reference to England and Scotland', in Kaspar Von Greyerz (ed.), *Religion and Society in Early Modern Europe 1500–1800* (1984), esp. 128–9 and the very germane chapter on 'Witch-cleansing' by Stuart Clark in *Thinking with Demons*, ch. 25.

[125] For such phrases, which echo Isa. v. 18, see Wilcox, *Faithfull narration*, 21; Northbrooke, *Treatise*, 144; Bolton, *Discourse about the state of true happiness*, in *Workes*, sigs. A8ʳ–B1ʳ. See also *A treatise of daunses, wherin it is shewed, that they are as it were accessories and dependants . . . to whoredome* (1581), sig. C2ᵛ; Thomas Lovell, *A dialogue between custom and veritie concerning the use and abuse of dauncing and minstrelsie* ([1581]), sigs. A2ᵛ–3ʳ, A4ᵛ–5ʳ, A6ʳ; Salvianus, *A second and third blast*, 53, 85–6; Downame, *Foure treatises*, sig. A2ᵛ; Daniel Dent, *A sermon against drunkennes: preached at Ware* (1628), esp. 3, 12, 18, 20–2; Christopher Hudson's assize sermons 1631–2, in LRO DP 353, esp. fos. 46ʳ, 49ᵛ–53ʳ.

[126] Dent, *Plaine mans path-way*, 227.

Himself—to become, as it were, His own busy controller.[127] '[W]hen Magistrates sleepe and wincke at enormous crimes,' asserted John Downame, 'when as their sword . . . most rusteth in the scabberd, Then is the Lord most readie to draw out the terrible sword of his fearce vengeance'; when they were negligent and remiss, agreed Samuel Ward, then He was constrained to practise 'Marshall law'.[128] Where, on the other hand, God's deputies and vicegerents diligently fulfilled their judicial responsibilities He seldom played the policeman Himself. If parents, schoolmasters, and ecclesiastical and civil officials conscientiously corrected their subordinates, if men and women fraternally admonished their peers, the Almighty would have no reason to resort to what Bishop John Hooper of Worcester and Gloucester described as 'an extraordinary magistrate'—dearth, pestilence, or war.[129] There was no need for such special 'Sergjeants and Pursevants' in places where men upheld the spirit and letter of the Mosaic law, men like George Caldwell, mayor of Northampton, whose all-out assault upon dicing, carding, and alehouse-haunting in 1606 secured the cessation of the plague which had raged for over two years— or so it was claimed by one tireless campaigner against the demon drink.[130] It should also be noted that the targets of such initiatives were not just the poor.[131] The logic of providence was not class specific: on the contrary, in the eyes of God the heinousness of an offence increased with the rank and status of the perpetrator.

Those who were 'at the Sterne' could thus be 'a great meanes' to prevent the 'Ship-wracke' of the kingdom.[132] By imitating the exemplary zeal of biblical figures like the prophet Nehemiah they would alleviate the danger into which individual delinquents dragged society at large. If they meted out the penalties for adultery and fornication as righteously and passionately as Phineas had plunged his javelin into the copulating bodies of Zimri and his Moabite concubine then their own nation, like the Jews, might also be spared from God's all-consuming ire.[133] For,

---

[127] Dent, *Plaine mans path-way*, 232.

[128] Downame, *Foure treatises*, 174, cf. 161–2; Ward, *Woe to drunkards*, 18.

[129] John Hooper, *An homelye to be read in the tyme of pestylence, and a most presente remedye for the same* ([Worcester, 1553]), sig. B3ᵛ.

[130] James Godskall, *The kings medicine for this present yeere 1604* (1604), sig. E6ᵛ; Richard Rawlidge, *A monster late found out and discovered. Or the scourging of tiplers, the ruine of Bacchus, and the bane of tapsters* (Amsterdam, 1628), sig. F1ʳ⁻ᵛ.

[131] This is implicit in Wrightson and Levine, *Poverty and Piety*, esp. chs. 5–7 and 'Terling Revisited', 207–11; Hunt, *Puritan Moment*, esp. 79–84; Underdown, *Revel, Riot and Rebellion*, esp. chs. 2–3. This position is questioned from various angles by Patrick Collinson, 'Cranbrook and the Fletchers: Popular and Unpopular Religion in the Kentish Weald', in *Godly People: Essays on English Protestantism and Puritanism* (1983), 407–8; id., *Religion of Protestants*, ch. 5, esp. 239–41; Martin Ingram, 'Religion, Communities and Moral Discipline in Late Sixteenth- and Early Seventeenth-Century England: Case Studies', in Kaspar Von Greyerz (ed.), *Religion and Society in Early Modern Europe 1500–1800* (1984), 177–93; id., *Church Courts*, esp. 166–7; Robert Von Friedeburg, 'Reformation of Manners and the Social Composition of Offenders in an East Anglian Cloth Village: Earls Colne, Essex, 1531–1642', *JBS* 29 (1990), 347–85.

[132] Fuller, *Sermon intended for Paul's Crosse*, sig. A3ᵛ. See also LRO DP 353, fo. 46ʳ. See also Clark, *Thinking with Demons*, ch. 37, for some of these themes.

[133] On Nehemiah, see Henry Robrough, *Balme from Gilead, to cure all diseases, especially the plague* (1626), 21, cf. 80. On Phineas (Num. xxv. 11), see John Preston, *A sermon preached at a generall fast*

just as every Israelite had suffered for the sin of Achan, so would England smart for the sake of each swearer, drunkard, or other evildoer living within its midst. As several preachers put it, wilful sinners were nothing less than 'traytors' to the reigning monarch and state.[134] Any society that connived at iniquity laid itself open to a national catastrophe.[135] Hence the frenzy with which the godly denounced the royal Book of Sports in 1633: in their eyes, enforcing an injunction to break the fourth commandment and profane the sabbath was tantamount to pressing a button to self-destruct.

There can be no doubt that puritans were especially prominent in campaigns to purge England of sin. Internalizing the Pauline precept that Christians had an unshirkable responsibility to edify the faithful and avoid offending the weak, and imbued with the idea that they had a personal vocation and mission to protect the nation from divine visitation, they naturally became leading proponents of moral reformation.[136] To this extent Margaret Spufford is mistaken in dismissing 'puritanism' as 'a gigantic red herring'.[137] Nevertheless, as so much of the recent historiography on this subject has served to underscore, social discipline was not the preserve of 'precisians' alone. Protestants of all temperatures and complexions engaged in such crusades, animated by the belief that this was the key to appeasing God's displeasure with Britain. The vocabulary of patriotic providentialism is no less apparent in the propaganda issued by William of Orange and the Anglican Societies for the Reformation of Manners in the 1690s than in the statutes and ordinances of the Long Parliament and Cromwellian Protectorate.[138]

before the Commons-House of Parliament: the second of July, 1625. In the time of plague, in *The saints qualification: a treatise* (1633), 295 and 283–4.

[134] See Smith, *Two sermons of Jonahs punishment*, in *Sermons*, sig. A6ʳ and *passim*; Hering, *Triumph of the church over water and fire*, 41. For Achan, see Josh. vii, xxii. 20; 1 Chr. ii. 7. The quotation comes from MS notes of a sermon preached by Arthur Hildersham in Cambridge, probably sometime in the 1620s, on Luke xiii. 3: BL Sloane MS 598, fo. 10ʳ.

[135] See e.g. Ward, *Woe to drunkards*, 46; Prynne, *Histrio-mastix*, fo. 562ᵛ; Leighton, *Shorte treatise against stage-plays*, sig. A2ʳ.

[136] See the remarks of Peter Lake, 'Defining Puritanism – Again?', in Francis J. Bremer (ed.), *Puritanism: Transatlantic Perspectives on a Seventeenth-Century Anglo-American Faith* (Boston, 1993), 10–11.

[137] Margaret Spufford, 'Puritanism and Social Control?', in Anthony Fletcher and John Stevenson (eds.), *Order and Disorder in Early Modern England* (Cambridge, 1985), 57. The link with puritanism is upheld by Jeremy Goring, *Godly Exercises or the Devil's Dance? Puritanism and Popular Culture in Pre-Civil War England*, Friends of Dr Williams's Library 37th Lecture (1983). See also Keith Wrightson's judicious remarks in the 'Postscript' to the 2nd edn. (1995) of id. and Levine, *Poverty and Piety*, esp. 201–9.

[138] On the Anglican hierarchy, the societies, and William III, see Dudley W. R. Bahlman, *The Moral Revolution of 1688* (New Haven, 1957); Tina Isaacs, 'The Anglican Hierarchy and the Reformation of Manners 1688–1738', *JEH* 33 (1982), 391–411; John Spurr, ' "Virtue, Religion and Government": The Anglican Uses of Providence', in Tim Harris, Paul Seaward, and Mark Goldie (eds.), *The Politics of Religion in Restoration England* (Oxford, 1990), 29–47; id., *The Restoration Church of England, 1646–1689* (New Haven, 1991), ch. 5; id., 'The Church, the Societies and the Moral Revolution of 1688', in John Walsh, Colin Haydon, and Stephen Taylor (eds.), *The Church in England c.1689–c.1833* (Cambridge, 1993), 127–42; Craig Rose, 'Providence, Protestant Union and Godly Reformation in the 1690s', *TRHS*, 6th ser. 3 (1993), 151–69; Tony Claydon, *William III and the Godly Revolution* (Cambridge, 1996). On the Long Parliament and Republic, see Keith Thomas, 'The Puritans and Adultery: The Act of 1650 Reconsidered', in Donald Pennington and Keith Thomas (eds.), *Puritans and Revolutionaries: Essays in Seventeenth Century History Presented to Christopher Hill* (Oxford, 1978), 257–82; Derek Hirst,

Research in this field over the past decade has also emphasized that sixteenth- and seventeenth-century efforts to correct moral abuses were by no means as novel as older scholars supposed. As Bruce Lenman, Margaret Spufford, Marjorie McIntosh, and Martin Ingram have all stressed, spasms of activity against sexual licentiousness and idle sports, swearing and gambling, were a routine feature of English parochial life. The early modern struggle to police personal conduct was just one contribution to 'an ongoing dialogue, extending over centuries if not millennia, between varieties of official and popular culture', rather than a unique corollary of Protestant piety and doctrine. The 'puritan' urge to eradicate immorality had both medieval antecedents and Tridentine parallels, as did the belief that divine vengeance would be visited upon communities which failed to stamp out sin.[139] What still demands explanation, however, is the peculiar and unprecedented vigour, intensity, and scale of such offensives in the century and a half after the advent of Protestantism—the 'permanent tilt in the pattern of regulation' which coincided with the entrenchment of the English Reformation.[140] A crucial part of the answer is surely the greatly enhanced awareness of God's providence fostered by Calvinist theology.

PRAYERS FIT FOR THE TIME

One way of placating the Almighty, then, was to implement existing laws and edicts and pass new ones where there were glaring gaps. But the first recourse of a community paralysed by some appalling calamity was always public penitence, humiliation, and prayer. The custom of collective supplication at times of trouble and crisis was actively promoted and endorsed by the Elizabethan and early Stuart Church. Each successive emergency with implications for a complete diocese or the country at large—from dearth and plague to foreign military threats and domestic rebellions—prompted the political and episcopal hierarchy to print and distribute special liturgies designed to supplement the formularies laid down in the 1559 *Book of common prayer*. These consisted of carefully selected lessons and psalms, appropriately worded intercessions, and sometimes homilies tailored to fit the occasion as well. Attendance at additional weekday church services was usually decreed, often in association with abstinence and almsgiving.[141] During periods of

---

'The Failure of Godly Rule in the English Republic', *P&P* 132 (1991), 33–66; Christopher Durston, 'Puritan Rule and the Failure of Cultural Revolution, 1645–1660', in id. and Jacqueline Eales (eds.), *The Culture of English Puritanism, 1560–1700* (Basingstoke, 1996), 210–33.

[139] See Lenman, 'Limits of Godly Discipline', esp. 124–5; Marjorie McIntosh, 'Local Change and Community Control in England, 1465–1500', *Huntington Library Qriuarterly*, 49 (1986), 219–42, esp. 233; ead., *Autonomy and Community: The Royal Manor of Havering, 1200–1500* (Cambridge, 1986), ch. 6, esp. 260–1; ead., *A Community Transformed: The Manor and Liberty of Havering, 1500–1620* (Cambridge, 1991), 240–58; Ingram, 'Reformation of Manners'; id., 'The Reform of Popular Culture? Sex and Marriage in Early Modern England', in Barry Reay (ed.), *Popular Culture in Seventeenth-Century England* (1988) quotation at 131.

[140] Ingram, 'Reformation of Manners', 77.

[141] See *STC* 'Liturgies', 'Special Forms of Prayer on Various Occasions'. A number of those issued

acute suffering forms of meditation 'very meet to be daily used' in private house-holds were also published, requiring the paterfamilias to assemble his wife, chil-dren, and servants each evening before they retired to bed and recite in their presence a series of self-abasing petitions (Plate 15).[142] Popular poets and scrib-blers like Martin Parker jumped on the bandwagon and produced similar broad-sides combining prayers and petitions for divine mercy with statistics of the death toll (Plate 16).[143]

The practice of communal fasting owed much to puritan inspiration and pres-sure. Days of atonement, such as those enjoined during the major epidemic in 1563 and after the earthquake in 1580, borrowed their format from Genevan directories for worship, which were themselves based on the Hebraic observances outlined in the Book of Leviticus.[144] This scriptural institution, asserted Calvinist theoreti-cians like Thomas Cartwright, John Udall, Nicholas Bownde, and Arthur Hildersham, was not another aspect of Jewish ceremonialism abrogated by the Gospel. Nor could it be compared with the hollow hypocrisy of popish asceticism. The 'shamefull' and 'childish superstition' of Roman Catholic ritual was a form of 'belly service' which kindled divine wrath rather than assuaged it. 'The holy exercise of a true fast' was a solemn profession of repentance commanded by Christ to continue in perpetuity. Protestant fasts coupled outward abnegation with inward confession; the former had no merit, but was merely an exterior 'helpe' to draw the devout 'more effectually . . . unto the feeling of their sinnes, and the desert therof, that so they might powre out their praiers more effectually unto the Lord, for the remission of the same'. For the space of twenty-four hours adults should abstain from all comforts and pleasures, 'so farre as necessity and comeli-nesse' permitted, forgoing food, recreation, and a full night's sleep—not to mention the 'mutuall felowship' and 'company' of the marriage bed. Attired in 'old, homely and meaner apparell' (a symbolic counterpart of sackcloth and ashes and an antidote to pride) and refraining from bodily labour as if it were the sabbath, they were to occupy their time in devout prayer, psalm-singing, and above all, in hearing and reading God's Word. Another central feature of the proceedings was

during the Elizabethan period can be found in Clay (ed.), *Liturgical Services*. Official homilies were pro-duced by Alexander Nowell, dean of St Paul's, after the outbreak of plague in 1563, and by Arthur Golding following the earthquake of 1580. For an example of an episcopal initiative, see London, Inner Temple Library, MS Petyt 538, vol. 47, no. 199 (for the diocese of Ely, 1580). See also C. J. Kitching, ' "Prayers Fit for the Time": Fasting and Prayer in Response to National Crises in the Reign of Elizabeth I', in W. J. Sheils (ed.), *Monks, Hermits and the Ascetic Tradition*, SCH 22 (Oxford, 1985), 241–50.

[142] See William Keating Clay (ed.), *Private Prayers, put forth by Authority during the Reign of Queen Elizabeth*, Parker Soc. (Cambridge, 1851); *A praier very comfortable and necessary to be used of all Christians . . . that it would please the Lord God to be appeased in his wrath* ([c.1603]); [*Prayers*] *In the time of Gods visitation by sickenesse, or mortality especially, may be used by governours of families* ([1607?]).

[143] M[artin] P[arker], *Lord have mercy upon us. This is the humble petition of England unto Almighty God* ([1636]).

[144] Lev. xvi, xxiii; Joel ii. 12–13. For the orders for the fasts of 1563 and 1580, see Clay (ed.), *Liturgical Services*, 489–90, 563. The 1563 order was adapted for the outbreaks of plagues in 1593, 1603, 1625, and 1636: see *STC* 16524, 16532, 16540 and 16553.

In the time of Gods visitation by Sickenesse, or Mortality especially, may be vsed by Gouernours of Families

Firſt, A Confeſſion of ſinnes.

Eternall, Almighty, and iuſt God, mercifull, louing, and holy Father, wee thy humble ſeruants humbly confeſſe and acknowledge herein thy preſence, that all the imaginations of the thoughts of our hearts are onely euill continually, yea euery man in his beſt eſtate is altogether vanitie. And we (duſt and aſhes) haue grieuouſly ſinned, wee haue tranſgreſſed thine holy lawes and ordinances, we haue exceeded in meaſure, number and weight, the iniquities of our forefathers, and haue thereby iuſtly deſerued that thou ſhouldeſt in thy iuſt iudgement haue drawne forth the ſword of thy iuſtice, and executed vengeance, euen in the higheſt degree againſt vs, according to the meaſure, number and weight of our manifold ſinnes and haynous iniquities, we are not worthy of the leaſt of all thy mercies. Wee humbly alſo confeſſe and acknowledge (euen againſt our ſelues) that neither thouſands of Rammes, nor tenne thouſand riuers of oyle (if we were able and willing to yeeld them vnto thee) are ſufficient to ſatisfie thy iuſtice for the leaſt of the iniquities which we haue committed againſt thee, if thou ſhouldeſt turne thine eye of mercy and compaſſion away from vs; and theſe things heretofore we confeſſed (O Lord) but our liues we amended not. And yet notwithſtanding (O mercifull Lord, holy and louing Father) ſo great is thy louing kindneſſe towards vs, and ſo manifold are thy mercies, that thou (of thy fauour) haſt beene pleaſed (euen in pittie and compaſſion for thine owne ſake, without any deſert of ours) to pacifie thine owne wrath, by a few light and eaſie ſtrokes with thy rod of correction, and ſo for a time to ceaſe thine anger, to trie vs if we would ſeeke after thee, not ſuffering thy puniſhing Angel to paſſe through *Ieruſalem* and *Iudea, London,* and other theſe dominions, with a ſwift courſe and heauy hand, as in the dayes of King *Dauid.* And (finding vs a rebellious and ſtiff-necked people) haſt ſent out thine Angel to threaten and execute vengeance in greater weight, and in greater meaſure againſt vs, if we will not amend. And yet in fauor ſtayeſt from executing thy fierce wrath. What ſhall we then offer vnto thee (O Lord our God) for all the bleſſings which we haue receiued from thee? Thou haſt no neede to receiue of vs, all beaſts, all cattell, all ſheepe on mountaines; yea the earth is thine, and all that therein is, the world, and they that dwel therein, we our ſelues, and all that we haue are thine, what haue we that we haue not receiued of thee? We confeſſe (O Lord) euen againſt our ſelues, that we haue nothing to offer but the calues of polluted lippes, proceeding from vncleane & vncircumciſed hearts, that is, praiſe, thankes, and prayer, and the ſame (if thou ſhouldeſt conſider them as they are ours) very ful of vanities and corruptions.

Secondly, A thankſgiuing for deliuerances.

SVch as we haue (yet) O mercifull father, we (more humbly and more freely, and hartily, then heretofore) offer vnto thy Maieſtie. Wee praiſe thy holy, great and glorious name, and we yeeld vnto thee humble and hearty thankes for thy great & wonderfull deliuerances, deliuerances from peſtilence, famine, & ſword, heretofore worthily threatned againſt vs, & for other thy manifold fauors & bleſſings bountifully beſtowed vpon this Citty, and vpon this Land, & (now eſpecially Lord) for thy great mercie, in that thou art pleaſed, euen now at this preſent, once againe to touch the people of this Land for their triall, with thy louing rodde of fatherly correction, rather then in iuſtice to powre out the violls of thy wrath, vtterly to conſume vs for our vnthankefulneſſe and diſobedience.

Thirdly, A Prayer for continuance of Gods mercies.

ANd we humbly and hartily pray thee (O Lord) euen for thine owne names ſake, and for thy Sonne our Sauiour Ieſus Chriſtes ſake, lay not to our charge our offences paſt, forgiue vs our iniquities, couer our ſinnes, and impute them not vnto vs, and then wee ſhall be bleſſed. Purge, frame, and forme our hearts anew; ſoften them, and make them repentant and obedient, willing freely without backe-ſliding or halting to yeelde obedience vnto that ſpirite which faith: Giue me the hart; deliuer vs alſo (holy Father) not onely from periſhing by waters, according to thy mercifull and gratious promiſe made of olde, but alſo from that aboundance of waters, which may kill, hurt and hinder, the ſeede or fruits of the earth, and giue vs holy Father (as gratiouſly in great mercie thou haſt giuen vs) onely that former and that latter raine, commended in thy holy word, and other ſeaſonable and temperate weather, which may yeeld vnto the good ſeede of the ground, as now, ſo hereafter, (by thy bleſſing) in times conuenient life, growth and increaſe, ſo as we may by thy gracious fauour, as this yeare, ſo others alſo, at length reape the fruites of plentifull harueſts: And becauſe ſo it is (Lord) that thou makeſt a land barren for the wickedneſſe of them that dwell therein, change thou our hearts (we humbly beſeech thee) roote out the wickedneſſe from the hearts of the inhabitants of the land, and then we ſhall be ſure that the land ſhall yeeld her increaſe. Giue vs O Lord thy grace and holy ſpirit, to guide and gouerne vs, and to hold vs within the liſts and limites of thy holy precepts and ordinances, in ſuch ſort, as that we may for euer hereafter, vſe thy word as the onely wiſe, and al-ſufficient rule to ſquare our liues by, knowing that all vnwritten verities, and all tradiions, and inuentions of men, yea all the imaginations of the thoughts of our hearts are onely euill continually; let thy word be a lanthorne to our feete, and a light vnto our pathes, knowing that therein is the true Kings high-way to be found, that leadeth to euerlaſting life and ſaluation, and that all other wayes which haue not warrant from thence (if thou ſhalt in iudgement looke into them) will be found to be but by-paths, leading to eternall death and deſtruction. Giue vs (O Lord) a holy and earneſt deſire, often to heare thy holy and heauenly word : giue vs wiſe, vnderſtanding, faithfull and obedient hearts, that we may truely vnderſtand, & faithfully belieue; & may (not for feare, or faſhion, or for any other worldly reſpect whatſoeuer) but in a true obedience for conſcience ſake) fruitfully practiſe in our liues and conuerſations thine holy ſtatutes & ordinances. Continue thy grace, mercy, and accuſtomed louing kindneſſe (O Lord we beſeech thee for thine owne names ſake, and for thy Sonne our Lord and Sauiour Ieſus Chriſtes ſake) vnto King *Iames* our bleſſed *Dauid,* and vnto the Queene, and the Prince his ſonne, and to all his royall progeny. And grant (if it be thy good pleaſure) that he may attaine to the yeares of the eldeſt of his Fathers, in the dayes of their Pilgrimage, ſet vp his ſeede after him (Lord we beſeech thee) and ſtabliſh the throne of his Kingdome in his poſteritie in all ages, ſo as there may not want a man of his ſeede to ſit vpon his throne, to feede people in *Iacob,* and thine inheritance in *Iſrael,* ſo long as the heauen and the earth indure. Be mercifull alſo vnto all *Iſrael, Ieruſalem,* and *Iudea, London,* and all the Kings Dominions; and to the Magiſtrates and Miniſters of thy holy word and ſacraments. In their ſeuerall degrees, dignities, and callings, giue them (O Lord we beſeech thee) a true loue and zeale of the execution of thy holy lawes, that they may (according to thine owne appointments) faithfully, diligently, and with a religious care and conſcience, of the aduancement of the glorious goſpel of thy Sonne our Lord and Sauior Ieſus Chriſt, diſcharge that great charge and weightie burthen which thou haſt laide vpon them : and ſtop the entry and paſſage (O Lord) both to Magiſtracie and Miniſtery, ſo as neither rauening wolues deuourers, nor wily foxes deceiuers of thy flocke, nor any others, but ſuch onely as thou knoweſt to be furniſhed with gifts fit for the diſcharge of thoſe great and weighty callings, be ſuffered to enter or paſſe thereunto. We vſe meanes (O Lord) to preſerue health, and to auoide and expulſe infection : But we depend not vpon them, we truſt not in them, wee humbly confeſſe, that no good ſucceſſe, no bleſſing, can come but from thee, and by thee alone: and therefore we humbly and hartily pray thee to giue ſucceſſe, and to yeeld thy bleſſing thereunto, and to ſay once againe to thine Angel, Hold now thy hand. More particularly (O holy Father) continue alſo (we beſeech thee) thy mercy and louing kindeneſſe to the little flocke within this houſe, and to thy humble and vnworthy ſeruant whom thou (of thy fauor) haſt appointed to be ouerſeer thereof, and giue vnto them thy grace in ſuch meaſure that they may ſo walke euery of them in their ſeuerall places and callings, as may be agreeable to thy holy and bleſſed wil, through Ieſus Chriſt our Lord and onely Sauiour. In whoſe name wee humbly further pray vnto thee for theſe and all other things which thou in thy wiſdome knoweſt to be moſt meete for vs, and for thy whole Church, in that forme of prayer which he himſelfe hath taught vs. *Our Father which art in heauen, &c.*

Printed at London by Valentine Simmes, dwelling on Adling hill at the ſigne of the white Swanne.

PLATE 15 *In time of Gods visitation by sickenesse, or mortality especially, may be used by governours of families* (London, [1607?]). By permission of the Society of Antiquaries of London. Lemon Collection 119.

Broadside containing prayers to be used by households during outbreaks of plague.

PLATE 16 Martin Parker, *Lord have mercy upon us. This is the humble petition of England unto Almighty God* (London, [1636]). By permission of the Guildhall Library, Corporation of London.

the collection of money for distribution to the deserving poor or some other worthy cause, such as a relief effort for one's afflicted Protestant brethren abroad.[145] Official formularies recommended that the money saved by eating just one 'competent and moderate meal' without 'variety or delicacy' and by setting aside fine

---

[145] Quotations from Thomas Cartwright, *The holy exercise of a true fast* (1580), repr. in *Cartwrightiana*, ed. Albert Peel and Leland H. Carlson, Elizabethan Nonconformist Texts 1 (1951), 122, 127–8, 133, 135,

clothes should be bestowed upon the needy.[146] Government-sponsored fasts tended to be more modest and less austere variations on the model laid out in technical treatises—at least before the heyday of public fasting between 1642 and 1649, when the last Wednesday of every month was given over to compulsory humiliation and prayer. Their underlying function, however, was the same: to seek reconciliation with a justly incensed deity.[147]

In the century preceding the Revolution, a stream of petitions and pleas for public fasts flowed from the pens and mouths of godly preachers and laymen. 'Sundrie' had required one for confounding the 'cruell enemies of goddes gospell' in the wake of the St Bartholomew's Day Massacre in 1572. Six years later Lawrence Chaderton used the national pulpit of Paul's Cross to call upon the Mayor and bishop of London to order solemn assemblies for this purpose, 'for the better avoyding and turning away the judgements of God, which hang over our heades, namely this present plague, whereby the Lorde in mercie hath visited this Citie'. The puritan MP Paul Wentworth proposed a parliamentary fast in the context of Catholic intrigue and the Jesuit mission of 1580–1. And if we move forward to March 1627, a time when political tension was running high and news of Protestant defeats in the Thirty Years War was provoking much public anxiety, we find the House of Commons humbly beseeching the King to set aside a day for fasting and prayer 'upon a tender and compassionate sence, of the extreame calamities of the reformed churches abroad, and with much sorrowe apprehending the heavy displeasure of almightie God declared against ourselves in the manifolde evills already fallen upon us and in those which are further thretned . . . even to the utter destraction and subversion of the Churche and State'.[148] Sometimes such requests bore fruit, but there always remained a strong possibility that they might be ignored. In such cases, ruled Udall, the godly should not tarry for the magistrate. Particular ministers were not to 'meddle' with the jurisdiction of higher authorities but they could call their 'owne charge unto this same exercise', as should responsible heads of households—gatherings which unsympathetic bishops were liable to brand as seditious conventicles. In turn, individuals under the direction

---

153; John Udall, *The true remedie against famine and warres* (1586), fo.81ᵛ. Other theorists include Henry Holland, *The Christian exercise of fasting, private and publike* (1596); William Perkins, *A reformed catholike* (Cambridge, 1597), 220–9; Nicholas Bownd, *The holy exercise of fasting* (Cambridge, 1604); Arthur Hildersham, *The doctrine of fasting and praier. In sundry sermons at the fast in 1625* (1633).

[146] Clay (ed.), *Liturgical Services*, 94.

[147] On public fasting, see Roland Bartel, 'The Story of Public Fast Days in England', *Anglican Theological Review*, 37 (1955), 190–200; Winthrop S. Hudson, 'Fast Days and Civil Religion', in *Theology in Sixteenth and Seventeenth Century England: Papers Read at a Clark Library Seminar, February 6, 1971* (Los Angeles, 1971), 3–24; Christopher Durston, ' "For the Better Humiliation of the People": Public Days of Fasting and Thanksgiving during the English Revolution', *The Seventeenth Century*, 7 (1992), 129–49.

[148] BL Lansdowne MS 15, fo. 79ʳ; Laurence Chaderton, *An excellent and godly sermon, most needefull for this time* (1580), sigs. F2ᵛ–3ᵛ; Collinson, *Elizabethan Puritan Movement*, 217–18; BL Add. MS 35331, fo. 9ʳ. See also BL Add. MS 38492, fo. 98ʳ; BL Harleian MS 1221, fo. 87ʳ.

of negligent and 'careless Maisters' ought to betake themselves to their private chambers.[149]

Evidence of the less formal measures introduced by pastors, vicars, and civil officers in response to localized misfortunes is scattered, but far from scant. In August 1572, for instance, the mayor and jurats of Rye ordered the townspeople to repair to church to pray and hear sermons each Monday morning and afternoon 'till it please God to stay this unseasonable weather'—'a token' of His 'great displeasure'. '[F]or the better continuance of the people in godly fervency', they simultaneously proclaimed a fast to be kept 'by all sorts' between the ages of 16 and 60 ('sick folk' and harvest labourers excepted), who were 'to content themselves that day with bread and drink, that they might be more apt to prayer'.[150] The propitiatory rituals organized elsewhere were even more elaborately structured. Indeed, they frequently grew into demonstrative religious gatherings that drew a confluence of people to listen to three or four lectures in succession, followed by a hearty buffet supper: the Jesuit William Weston has left us with a memorable description of one such fast at Wisbech Castle in the late Elizabethan period. This type of fasting was a close cousin of the public preaching conferences known as 'prophesyings' to which Elizabeth took such singular exception in 1576, and of other ad hoc and voluntary religious activities which contrived to circumvent official prohibitions and survive inside the established Church well into the reign of James. In the summer of 1580 the public fast promulgated by the Privy Council gave impetus to such exercises and afforded them a measure of legal immunity, and the clergy who organized a puritan fast-cum-rally in Stamford paid little attention to the conditions laid down by the diocesan. Because they encouraged 'gadding' across ecclesiastical boundaries and sometimes became occasions for airing religio-political grievances such 'generall concourses' to crave divine pardon were regarded by the authorities with considerable unease and suspicion.[151] The rabidly anti-puritan Richard Bancroft saw to it that private fasts unauthorized by the local bishop were outlawed in the canons of 1604.[152]

During outbreaks of bubonic plague there were other reasons for recommending 'moderate assemblyes' within each individual parish.[153] Spiritual remedies for

---

[149] Quotations from Udall, *True remedie*, fo. 81ᵛ. Cf. Chaderton, *Excellent and godly sermon*, sigs. F2ᵛ–3ʳ. Cartwright cautiously evaded this question: *Cartwrightiana*, 140.

[150] HMC, *Thirteenth Report, Appendix, Part IV (MSS of Rye and Hereford Corporations)* (1892), 21.

[151] See Patrick Collinson, 'The Puritan Classical Movement in the Reign of Elizabeth I', PhD thesis (London, 1957), ch. 4; id., *Elizabethan Puritan Movement*, 214–19; id., *Religion of Protestants*, 260–3; Tom Webster, *Godly Clergy in Early Stuart England: The Caroline Puritan Movement c.1620–1643* (Cambridge, 1998), ch. 3. *William Weston: The Autobiography of an Elizabethan*, ed. and trans. Philip Caraman (1955), 164–5. The phrase 'generall concourses' occurs in a letter from Edmund Grindal to William Cecil on 30 July 1563: BL Lansdowne MS 6, fo. 156ᵛ.

[152] Edward Cardwell (ed.), *Synodalia: A Collection of Articles of Religion, Canons, and Proceedings of Convocations in the Province of Canterbury from the Year 1547 to the year 1717*, 2 vols. (Oxford, 1842), i. 288.

[153] BL Lansdowne MS 6, fo. 156ᵛ.

adversity had to be squared with increasingly sophisticated secular methods of checking the progress of what contemporaries erroneously supposed to be a contagious disease. 'Promiscuous meetings' might mollify God but they contravened the quarantine regulations and other precautions taken to prevent the spread of infection. As Edmund Grindal, then bishop of London, wrote to William Cecil in 1563, in this matter 'relygion and pollicie' were 'mixte': a modus vivendi between piety and pragmatism had to be reached.[154] Likewise, accepting a providential explanation for a devastating blaze or flood did not preclude the development of formal preventive measures, building by-laws, fire-fighting equipment, and other damage-limitation techniques.[155] 'Religious' interpretations and 'rationalist' reactions were by no means incompatible.

Protestants vocally dissociated their own penitential rites from those engaged in by their Roman Catholic neighbours and forebears, scornfully dismissing them as a form of incantatory magic or conjuration which it was absurd to imply could have truly propitious results. The translator of a pamphlet reporting the devastation caused by a violent storm in Barcelona in November 1617 had nothing but contempt for the manner in which the Spaniards endeavoured to mollify God. 'Loe here the refuge of superstitious and Idolatrous people', he annotated a page describing how the local clergy and laity had immediately organized symbolic displays of relics, crucifixes, and monstrances containing the transubstantiated host, and offered up special masses and oblations to the Virgin Mary and the city's patron saints: 'Rather shold you have fixed the eye of your Faith & Hope upon Christ sitting at the right hand of the Father.'[156] William Gouge likewise condemned such 'Popish toyes to pacifie God' as ineffectual 'humane inventions'. Processions of flagellants wearing hairshirts, walking barefoot, crying *misericordia*, and whipping themselves until the blood ran from the cuts would no more turn away divine vengeance than heathen sacrifice of humans and animals.[157]

But there was far less difference in practice than Protestants so energetically

---

[154] Wither, *Britain's remembrancer*, fo. 131ʳ; BL Lansdowne MS 6, fo. 168ʳ. See also *APC 1625–1626*, 125. Paul Slack explores the implications of this conflict in detail in *The Impact of Plague in Tudor and Stuart England* (1985), esp. pt. III. See also Richard Palmer, 'The Church, Leprosy and Plague in Medieval and Early Modern Europe', in W. J. Sheils (ed.), *The Church and Healing*, SCH 19 (Oxford, 1982), 79–99.

[155] See C. J. Kitching, 'Fire Disaster and Fire Relief in Sixteenth-Century England: The Nantwich Fire of 1583', *BIHR* 44 (1981), 171–87; Penny Roberts, 'Agencies Human and Divine: Fire in French Cities, 1520–1720' and Raingard Eßer, 'Fear of Water and Floods in the Low Countries', both in William G. Naphy and Penny Roberts (eds.), *Fear in Early Modern Society* (Manchester, 1997), 9–27 and 62–77 respectively.

[156] Rejaule, *Newes from Spain*, sigs. B3ʳ, A4ᵛ. For other contemporary descriptions of Catholic responses to disaster: BL Harleian MS 390, fo. 41ʳ; *Hevy newes of an horryble earth quake*, 3; *True relation of the French kinge his good successe*, 18; 'A trew & a perfecte discourse of woonderfull & straunge myracle & sygnes which apperyd in France the 5 of May 1573', transcribed from a lost pamphlet, in BL Cotton MS Vespasian A. XXV, fo. 42ʳ; PRO SP 12/283/45 ('A relation of the earthquake and prodigious accident that happenend in the City of Arechipa in Peru and the contry adjoyninge betweene the xviii th of February 1601 and the third of Marche the same yeare').

[157] Gouge, *Plaister for the plague*, in *Gods three arrowes*, 42–6.

alleged. Writing to Archbishop Matthew Parker on 2 January 1564 about the arrangements for a thanksgiving Eucharist at St Paul's to mark the cessation of the plague, Grindal was anxious to prevent the service becoming an overly emotional spectacle savouring of 'romish' sacramentalism, a communion service carried out 'tumultously and gazingly, by means of the infinite multitude that will resort thither to see'.[158] Especially for unlearned villagers and town dwellers whose lives straddled the religious upheavals of the mid-sixteenth century, ritual and liturgical continuity must have extenuated the radical theological changes they were obliged to digest. Viewed from this angle, Reformed liturgies for fasting and prayer look like direct substitutes for the corporate acts of contrition by which medieval and Continental communities sought to induce God to suspend hostilities against them—albeit without the aid of intermediary sacred beings. Like pilgrimages and votary promises, parades of relics and midwinter marches of weeping, near-naked parishioners, they too were communal attempts to bargain with the Almighty through preventive penance. To borrow a phrase from David Sabean, they too might be seen as 'a kind of collective rite of exorcism'.[159]

Such observations contradict the ingrained assumption that Protestantism was inherently unwelcoming to ritual forms. Without doubt the Reformers did contribute to what Edward Muir has recently described as 'a revolution in ritual theory', and to the emergence of 'a new theological metaphysics'. Especially in their assault on the mass, they reconceptualized sacramental rites in terms of representation, as forms of communication rather than procedures by and through which the divine and diabolical were made manifest.[160] Yet as vehemently as they repudiated prescribed patterns of religious observance at the outset, in the long run they could not resist the need to replace them. Thus, as Peter Burke has remarked, 'expelled at the door', ritual 'came back in through the window'. Especially in the second and later stages of the Reformation, fasting, psalm-singing, sermons, and rounds of rousing prayer played a vital role in binding together Protestant congregations, cementing their special corporate relationship with God, and strengthening confessional identity and the cohesion of the international Calvinist movement.[161] While some of the rites associated with the abolished Catholic calendar of feast days seem to have migrated into domestic contexts and become transmuted into essentially 'secular' customs and pastimes, these propitiary rituals bear out Leigh Eric Schmidt's insight that more than a few practices rooted in the Roman past were eventually resurrected in an acceptably reformed

---

[158] Petyt MS 47, fo. 525, printed in *The Remains of Edmund Grindal, D.D.*, ed. William Nicholson, Parker Soc. (Cambridge, 1843), 267.

[159] David Sabean, *Power in the Blood: Popular Culture and Village Discourse in Early Modern Germany* (Cambridge, 1984), 69, cf. 91.

[160] Edward Muir, *Ritual in Early Modern Europe* (Cambridge, 1997), ch. 5, quotations at 155, 181.

[161] Peter Burke, 'The Repudiation of Ritual in Early Modern Europe', in *The Historical Anthropology of Early Modern Italy* (Cambridge, 1987), 230. See also Hall, *Worlds of Wonder*, ch. 4; Bodo Nischan, 'Ritual and Protestant Identity in Late Reformation Germany', in Bruce Gordon (ed.), *Protestant History and Identity in Sixteenth-Century Europe*, 2 vols. (Aldershot, 1996), ii. 142–58.

guise.[162] Despite the sustained polemic of anti-Catholic propagandists against claims that supernatural power could be manipulated by humans, Protestantism in effect devised an ecclesiastical 'magic' of its own.[163]

UNLESS YE REPENT

Indeed, the unspoken assumption inherent in all such rituals and liturgies was that penitence and prayer could have near mechanical efficacy in holding back the Flood. Both clerical commentators and profit-seeking publishers of cheap print implied that moral regeneration and earnest invocation were an almost infallible means of diverting plagues and dissolving the menacing storm cloud hanging over-head. In providential news reports the notion that sincere and humble entreaty to heaven could have automatic effect sometimes took an alarmingly literal twist. Aware that a landslide was about to obliterate their Alpine village a pious Swiss family promptly fell to its knees, whereupon 'they perceived such fruit and profit of their prayers, that the earth which rowled . . . passed over their house in a manner as a huge wave, without any harme to the house, or any within it'.[164] And when a volcano in the Mediterranean Sea began to erupt in May 1592, the islanders 'instantlye besought the Lord that he would not enter into judgement with them, nor punish them according to their desertes: whiche done, the Lord in mercy with-drew his plagues'.[165]

The message which emanated from the pulpits was only slightly more muted. Prayer, observed John Gore, rector of St Peter's, Cornhill, in 1638, was an 'omnipotent grace', '*Fraenum Coeli*', 'the very bridle of Heaven'.[166] As Scripture showed, it could overpower the Almighty Himself: how else could Abraham, Moses, and Elijah have prevailed to avert and mitigate His ire against the Israelites? It was 'like a cord wherewith we binde the hands of God . . . with bands more indissoluble then those seven greene withs that bound the hands of Sampson', affirmed Griffith Williams, chaplain to Charles I and later bishop of Ossory.[167] John Squire, vicar of St Leonard's, Shoreditch, compared it with 'the Bow of Jonathan, which never turnes backe', 'the Sword of Saul which never returnes emptie'. It was victorious and invincible, 'that BATH-SHEBA . . . God will not say it nay'.[168] All three ministers actively embraced the legacy of Hooker and Whitgift and displayed sympathy with the policies of Laud, which may partly explain why they attached

---

[162] Hutton, 'English Reformation and the Evidence of Folklore'; Leigh Eric Schmidt, *Holy Fairs: Scottish Communions and American Revivals in the Early Modern Period* (Princeton, 1989), 213 and 215–16. On the Reformation as a ritual process, see R. W. Scribner, 'Ritual and Reformation', in his *Popular Culture and Popular Movements in Reformation Germany* (1987), 103–22.

[163] See the comments of Thomas, *Religion and the Decline of Magic*, 73, 89, 173–4, 318.

[164] *Gods handy-worke in wonders . . .* (1615), sig. B4ᵛ.

[165] *True relation of the French kinge his good successe*, 18.

[166] Gore, *Summer sermon*, in *Ten godly and fruitfull sermons*, 3.

[167] Williams, *Best religion*, 1097, cf. 1096. See Gen. xviii. 23–33, Exod. xxxii. 10, Deut. ix. 14, James v. 17–18.

[168] John Squire, *A thanksgiving for the decreasing, and hope of the removing of the plague* (1637), 12–14.

such a premium to prayer. Yet Protestants from all points on the ideological spectrum employed the same metaphors. They too likened prayer to a physician, 'asylum', or 'hospital', a sovereign antidote, 'catholicon', and medicinal balsam or balm; they too used the simile of 'manacles' and 'shackles' that could stay the Almighty from striking—'yea', added Henry Bullinger, and take His judgements 'clean away'.[169] The tears and supplications of the righteous, stressed Arthur Dent, were 'even able to doo all things'.[170] There were 'no better Halbards, and no trustier garde to preserve a King' and his subjects from physical and spiritual danger, echoed James Godskall in a treatise dedicated to the Lord Mayor, Sheriffs, and Aldermen and 'given as a new yeers-gift, to the honourable city of London' in 1604. These and not the 'counterfaite physicke' and 'Antichristian medicine' sanctioned by the Pope and 'prepared by the Divell his Apothecary' were the Christian's strongest weapons against the plagues which followed in the train of iniquity.[171] In a sermon delivered before 1628, Alexander Udny, minister at Hawking in Kent, supplied a concrete example to drive home his point about the benefits of fasting: 'we had experience hereof in our last humiliation, when God so miraculously (moved by our prayers) stayed the Pestilence raigning amongst us.'[172]

Ballad-mongers, pamphleteers, and sermon-writers constantly spoke of unfeigned repentance as a foolproof method of staving off the fatal consequences of sin. If men and women knuckled under, desisted from wickedness, and rectified their lives, 'then *no doubt* in stead of vengeance comes mercy, & in stead of plagues [we] shall receive blessings', averred one journalist in 1624; '*no doubt* but God . . . will turne his favourable countenance toward us', maintained another a decade later; '*no doubt*', echoed another, 'but wee shall have the threatning of Gods wrath removed and be the injoyers of the blisse of his Kingdome'.[173] Divine anger would certainly be slaked if people quickly abandoned the old Adam and amended their ways: 'for even as wooll-packs and other soft matter, beateth backe, and dampeth the force of all shot', said Dent, 'so penitent, melting, and soft hearts, do beat backe the shot' of the deity's rage.[174] 'Shall I put you in hope, that if yee presently repent and turn unto the Lord, the lord will forthwith stay his hande, and slay no more?', asked Thomas Pullein, vicar of Pontefract, in a sermon entitled *Jeremiahs teares* preached in York Minster in 1604. 'Beloved', he declared, 'I have no such commission'—and yet the whole tenor of his lecture was that a swift 'retrayt' from sin would secure rapid release from the current visitation.[175]

---

[169] Bullinger, *Decades*, ed. Harding, iv. 168 and 163–226 *passim*. See also Thomas Becon, *The Early Works* . . . , ed. John Ayre, Parker Soc. (Cambridge, 1843), 142–4; Gouge, *The churches conquest over the sword*, in *Gods three arrowes*, 258–63; Fuller, *Sermon intended for Paul's Crosse*, 35; Perkins, *Faithfull and plaine exposition upon . . . Zephaniah* (1605), repr. in *Workes*, iii. 422.

[170] Dent, *Plaine mans path-way*, 237, cf. 240.

[171] Godskall, *Kings medicine*, sigs. C1ᵛ, H8ᵛ–I1ʳ, I8ʳ⁻ᵛ.

[172] Alexander Udny, *The voyce of the cryer* (1628), 85.

[173] *1624. Newes from Holland*, 5; *Last terrible tempestious windes and weather*, sig. C3ᵛ; *Miracle upon miracle*, 12 (my italics).

[174] Dent, *Plaine mans path-way*, 252, cf. 255.

[175] Thomas Pullein, *Jeremiahs teares* (1608), sig. E1ʳ.

This kind of upbeat message was clearly what sermon-goers in times of adversity were anxious to hear. Indefatigable notetakers like the Kentish clothier Robert Saxby regularly recorded confident assertions of this kind. How far he subconsciously adjusted the tone and emphasis of the preacher's discourse in summarizing it is open to question, though the evidence already cited suggests that as a scribe he was probably fairly reliable. Moreover, equally bold claims about the remarkable power of prayer can be found in a manuscript volume of his sermons which the puritan divine Herbert Palmer appears to have copied out lovingly to present to his mother.[176]

'We must alwaies understand the denouncing of Gods judgements . . . not to bee absolute', Ralph Walker advised his auditors; they were 'ever made', agreed Alexander Hume, 'either with an expresse condition, or with a tacite and quiet condition which they include, To wit, if repentance followe not'.[177] The night of sorrow promised to sinners would 'as surely come, as ever Evening succeeded Day,' stressed Thomas Adams, 'but there is an Except, that shall save us, a seasonable and substantiall repentance: if we turne from those winding Labyrinths of sinne'.[178] Upholding the escape clause of 'unless ye repent' was orthodox Protestant doctrine—the biblical *locus classicus* being the conversion of Nineveh by the prophet Jonah, forcing the Lord to retract His former decision to wipe that iniquitous city off the face of the earth.[179]

In moments of crisis the clergy rarely bothered to explain how academic theologians contrived to reconcile the notion of instrumental repentance and prayer and apparent modifications of the Almighty's immutable decree with the axiom of His preordination and foreknowledge of every temporal event. They tended to tiptoe around the theological quagmire of the discrepancy between God's 'secret' and 'revealed' wills, and to avoid the thorny question of in exactly what sense He might be said to 'change His mind' or 'repent'—as it seemed in the cases of Nineveh and of good King Hezekiah, doomed to die and then, upon ardent intercession, given fifteen years respite. According to Calvin and his disciples, if God was 'persuaded' to resheathe His sword, this was no spontaneously improvised response to an alteration in human behaviour, but a choice foreseen from eternity and inbuilt into the original scheme.[180] In calling to repentance those

---

[176] CUL Add. MS 3117, e.g. fos. 30ʳ, 40ʳ; Herbert Palmer, 'Sermons concerning the necessity and manner of divine invocation', University of London Library, Senate House, MS 302, sermon 5 on Job xxvii. 10.

[177] Walker, *Learned and profitable treatise*, 71–2; H[ume], *Foure discourses*, 15. Cf. Udny, *Voyce of the cryer*, 16–17.

[178] Adams, *The gallants burden*, in *Workes*, 29.

[179] Jonah iii. 10 and see also 2 Ch. vii. 13–14 and Jer. xviii. 8. See e.g. Veron, *Fruteful treatise*, fos. 102ʳ–105ʳ; *The Works of James Pilkington, B. D., Lord Bishop of Durham*, ed. James Scholefield, Parker Soc. (Cambridge, 1842), 89; Corderoy, *Warning for worldlings*, 239–40; Abbot, *Exposition upon the prophet Jonah*, 494–6. This issue is further discussed in Chs. 1 and 6.

[180] On Hezekiah, see Isa. xxxviii, and see also 2 Sam. xxiv. 16. On distinctions between God's 'effectual' and 'signified' wills and the cases of Nineveh and Hezekiah, see e.g. Calvin, *Institutes*, bk I, ch. 17, § 12–14; bk III, ch. 3; Walker, *Learned and profitable treatise*, 71–3, 241–3; [Gerardus], *Speciall treatise*, sigs. K1ᵛ–2ᵛ; Vermigli, *Common places*, ch. 18; Cupper, *Certaine sermons*, 142–3.

'whom he hathe determined to spare', declared Jean Veron, 'he dothe rather make a way unto his devine providence, than otherwyse'.[181] That He already knew the outcome of every petition and prayer did not render them unnecessary.[182] These complex issues, claimed Jeremy Corderoy, were intended to be 'a stumbling block to men of perverse minds'.[183] In the context of calamity, it was far better not to refer to such technicalities at all. However much divines might quibble and equivocate in the schools, the compassionate pastor was bound to give his parishioners the impression that the Lord could in fact be browbeaten, brought round, and (as it were) corrupted by bribes.[184]

Another subtlety liable to fall by the wayside in an emergency was the principle that repentance was a gratuitous spiritual gift, 'no worke of nature, but a supernaturall worke of God'. '[I]t lyeth not in the power of man to repent when hee pleaseth' and 'whensoever' he wished, admonished a succession of Elizabethan and early Stuart preachers. It was not within the 'art' of any individual to make this healing 'confection of Repentance' himself, said the Essex minister Adam Harsnet; like faith itself, this was a grace bestowed upon one by the Holy Ghost. Via exposure to the 'Delphian sword' of his Word, God had to 'enter into the minde' of men and women, renew their determination to resist the temptations of sin, create in them a new and contrite heart, and inspire them to perform 'actions of holiness'. Without providence no such regenerating change could ever take place. True repentance was not granted to wilful sinners who lived in 'carnall securitie'; in short, it was only conferred upon the predestinate elect.[185]

However, according to George Gifford, Richard Stock, and many other incumbents of country livings, the vast majority of the population were 'as blind as beetles in this point'.[186] They 'popishly' misconceived repentance, supposing it consisted merely of crying 'from the teeth outward Lord have mercie on me, and so away'. The 'crooked cancre wormes of this worlde' contented themselves with 'the bare title and naked name', asserted Dent, with the shadow rather than the substance; with a 'legall' rather than 'evangelicall' demonstration of their mortification and grief.[187] 'In these dayes', sighed Udny, people were 'so carelesse in living, and wretched in sinning' that they supposed repentance was something

---

[181] Veron, *Fruteful treatise*, fo. 105ʳ.

[182] On prayer, Cradocke, *Shippe of assured safetie*, 174; [Gerardus], *Speciall treatise*, sig. G2ʳ⁻ᵛ; Walker, *Learned and profitable treatise*, 241; Robrough, *Balme from Gilead*, 132.

[183] Corderoy, *Warning for worldlings*, 240.

[184] Cf. Kocher, *Science and Religion*, 97–9; Donagan, 'Godly Choice', 313–15. See also Thomas, *Religion and the Decline of Magic*, 133–8.

[185] Quotations from Harsnet, *Gods summons*, 18–19; Udny, *Voyce of the cryer*, 23–4; and 'An homelye of repentaunce and of true reconciliation unto God', in *Certaine sermons appoynted by the quenes majesty*, fo. 291ʳ. See also Thomas Settle, *A catechisme briefly opening the misterie of our redemption by Christ* (1585), sigs. B6ᵛ–7ᵛ; Stock, *Doctrine and use of repentance*, 125–40, 167–9; William Perkins, *Two treatises. I. Of the nature and practise of repentance* (Cambridge, 1593), esp. ch. 1.

[186] George Gifford, *Foure sermons upon the seven chiefe vertues or principall effectes of faith, and the doctrine of election* (1582 edn.), sig. B5ʳ. Cf. William Case, *A sermon of the nature and end of repentance* (1616), 10 and *passim*; George Meriton, *A sermon of repentance* (1607), sig. B3ʳ and *passim*.

[187] Dent, *Sermon of repentaunce*, sigs. A7ʳ, A8ʳ; Harsnet, *Gods summons*, 28–33. Cf. Stock, *Doctrine and use of repentance*, esp. 7–8, 119–21.

they could simply take out of 'their pocket' when the need to use it arose. They imagined it to be 'a very light & easie thing, which they can have when they list' and which could be done 'in the turning of a hand, with a wet finger'.[188] As a result too many put it off until they were old and grey or regarded it as 'a death-bed duty', a last dying speech. In Adam Harsnet's opinion, deferring moral reformation was 'an epidemicall, and generall evill, whereof the most sort of people have a spice'. Nothing, lamented Stock, was more commonly mentioned by those with only a few hours to live than the passage from Luke xxiii about the thief crucified with Christ who was saved by repenting at the very end; such opinions also ran rife in the areas of Cambridgeshire in which William Perkins exercised his ministry.[189] This popular fallacy was linked with another about the placid personality of God. 'Profane worldlings' believed Him to be indulgent, soft-hearted, and 'easilie intreated by their pitifull moaning, to pardon their sinnes'. As Edmund Topsell observed, they 'thinke that the Lord is pinned to their sleeves; imagining him to be such a childe as might bee lost with an apple and wonne with a trifle againe'. The proverbial phrase Bartimaeus Andrewes had heard too often on the lips of the Suffolk laity was 'sweet & figgy'.[190]

Notwithstanding the profusion of complaints about eleventh hour repentance, when catastrophe struck the clergy could hardly avoid encouraging these pelagian attitudes themselves. When the Lord's sword was poised to smite, what else could they do but remind their congregations that Scripture said it was never too late to repent, and that all would be forgiven whenever, like the prodigal son, they returned to the fold?[191] Although they did their best to refute the notion that penitential gestures were 'meritorious' in 'blotting out our iniquities, and transgressions', although they loudly condemned the Catholic Church for making penance a formal and efficient cause of justification '*ex opere operato*', Protestant ministers continued to emphasize that true repentance (the 'fruit' and 'houshold sister' of faith) was a prerequisite for the remission of sins.[192] They had no desire to stifle the valuable side effects of communal misfortune by suggesting that, in and of themselves, such impulses were profitless. As both Peter Lake and Ian Green have remarked, inadvertently and sometimes even deliberately, they yielded ground in practice to the voluntarism which they repudiated in theory.[193] Moralistic ballads

---

[188] Udny, *Voyce of the cryer*, 59; Gifford, *Foure sermons*, sig. B5ʳ; Harsnet, *Gods summons*, 270, cf. 18, 274–5.

[189] Williams, *Best religion*, 189; Harsnet, *Gods summons*, 269–70, cf. sigs. A5ᵛ–6ʳ, pp. 291–3; Stock, *Doctrine and use of repentance*, 339; Perkins, *Workes*, i. 139, and id., *Foundation of Christian religion*, sig. A2ʳ. The fallacy of the over-forgiving God was a commonplace of medieval preachers too: Owst, *Preaching in Medieval England*, 335–6.

[190] Stock, *Doctrine and use of repentance*, 37; Topsell, *Times lamentation*, 184; Bartimaeus Andrewes, *Certaine verie worthie, godly and profitable sermons, upon the fifth chapter of the Songs of Solomon* (1583), 166.

[191] See Ezek. xviii. 21–4; 2 Pet. iii. 9.

[192] Harsnet, *Gods summons*, 215; Robrough, *Balme from Gilead*, 369–80, quotation at 369; Perkins, *Two treatises*, sig. ¶3ᵛ; Dent, *Sermon of repentaunce*, sig. A4ᵛ. See also Woodwall, *Sermon upon . . . Ezechiel*, 39–42.

[193] Lake, *Moderate Puritans*, ch. 7, esp. 153–65; Green, *Christian's ABC*, chs. 8–9.

and pamphlets about public calamities were permeated by the same ideological ambivalence. Even where they concluded with an impeccably Calvinist plea to God to *'give us* grace to amend our lives' and *'grant us* speedy repentance', it was quite possible to carry away the antithetical idea that this lay firmly within the scope and province of human volition.[194]

What cannot have escaped notice is the extent to which the language of corporate repentance and temporal deliverance overlaps with the language of individual redemption and eternal salvation. Theodore Bozeman has argued persuasively that in Elizabethan puritan thought the two dimensions were never separate: they were planes which shared the same matrix and calculus, and between which there was a constant dialectical flow.[195] Preachers subsumed self into society and macrocosm into microcosm. When William Whately addressed Banbury in 1628 'as a common bodie, one person', he was merely articulating what elsewhere went unsaid.[196] 'How often hath the Lord cried unto you in effect, Yarmouth, Yarmouth', William Yonger reminded a congregation of Norfolk fishermen during an invasion scare in 1599; 'O Witny, Witny', lamented John Rowe half a century later, 'the Lord is angry with thee'; 'Newport sin no more, lest a worst punishment befall the', warned a Shropshire minister in 1665; 'O England, England', implored the Paul's Cross lecturers we shall explore in Chapter 6.[197] Personification was a standard rhetorical device of hacks and rhymsters too. In *A proper newe sonet* published in 1586, for instance, Thomas Deloney adopted the identity of the fire-ravaged town of Beccles in Suffolk:

> With sobbing sighes and trickling teares,
> my state I doe lament
> Perceiving how Gods heavie wrath
> against my sinnes is bent
> Let all men viewe my woefull fall
> and rue my woefull case,
> And learne hereby in speedy sort
> repentaunce to embrace.[198]

The ballad-monger who moralized the plight of Cork in 1622 slid no less easily from admonishing other towns and corporations to warning each particular hearer

---

[194] *1624. Newes from Holland*, 20; *Wonders of this windie winter*, sig. A3ᵛ (my italics). Cf. *Windie year*, sig. D3ʳ; Harward, *Discourse of the severall kinds and causes of lightnings*, sig. C1ᵛ.

[195] T. D. Bozeman, 'Covenant Theology and "National Covenant": A Study in Elizabethan Presbyterian Thought', paper delivered at the 1991 Millersville University Conference on Puritanism in Old and New England. A foreshortened version, entitled 'Federal Theology and the "National Covenant": An Elizabethan Presbyterian Case Study', can be found in *Church History*, 61 (1992), 394–407. This matter is discussed further in Ch. 6, below.

[196] Whately, *Sinne no more*, 58.

[197] W[illiam] Y[onger], *A sermon preached at Great Yarmouth* (1600), sig. B4ʳ; Rowe, *Tragi-comoedia*, 45; T. Millington, cited in Cox, *Parish Registers*, 215.

[198] T[homas] D[eloney], *A proper newe sonet declaring the lamentation of Beckles in Suffolke, which was . . . most pittifully burned with fire* ([1586]).

and reader, and from emphasizing the fate of the wicked in this world to stressing their torments in the next:

> Corke to all Citties, may example bee,
> To know they are not from Gods Justice free:
> For being Sinner they may feare the like,
> As fell to Corke, God in his wrath will strike . . .

> God's mercifull to Sinners which repent,
> His Justice is towards lingring sinners bent:
> Who will take holde of mercy and of Grace,
> Let them repent whilest they have tune and space.

> Repentance onely pacifies Gods Ire,
> Preserves from sodaine, and Eternall Fire . . .[199]

And the author of a Restoration broadside which reported *Newes from Hereford* of 'a wonderfull and terrible earthquake' on 1 October 1661 likewise spoke simultaneously to the nation and every single one of its citizens:

> Old England of thy sins in time repent
> Before the wrath of god to thee is sent . . .[200]

To untrained ears, the penitential message of preachers and minstrels must have been almost indistinguishable.

GODS ARROWE OF THE PESTILENCE

There seem, then, to have been far more points of proximity and harmony between clerical Protestantism and the religion of the 'common sort of Christians', and between pre- and post-Reformation piety, than some historians of religious culture in this period have presumed. The picture is not, of course, all one of happy accord and mutual rapport; there were areas of friction and confrontation which it would be foolish and short-sighted to ignore. But providentialism appears to have been a conceptual framework flexible enough to absorb and accommodate discordant tendencies and bifurcating strands. The final section of this chapter tests this hypothesis by analysing responses to and explanations of the serious outbreaks of epidemic disease which regularly decimated urban and rural communities.

As Paul Slack has taught us, a set of diverse but interrelated assumptions about the nature and causes of 'the pestilence' circulated in Tudor and Stuart England. Theology, astrology, and Galenic humoral theory interlocked in an eclectic and multifaceted interpretation of its medical and metaphysical origins, at the core of which lay the concept of providence.[201] According to Protestant preachers and pamphleteers, plague was one of God's three 'mortall arrowes': along with famine and war, one of the three 'deadly weapons' He held in His quiver, one of the three

---

[199] *Lamentable burning of the citty of Corke.*

[200] W. K., *Newes from Hereford. Or, a wonderful and terrible earthquake: with a wonderful thunderclap, that happened on Tuesday being the first of October, 1661* ([1661?]).

[201] Slack, *Impact of Plague*, esp. ch. 2.

horses of death he periodically released to crush and trample sinners. These most grievous punishments were the Lord's last resort, His final strategy for reclaiming disobedient nations before He disowned them for ever.[202] Only His unsearchable will could satisfactorily explain why the disease was so severe, irresistible, and unpredictable and why some and not others survived and recovered. This was the common thread linking the large and diverse vernacular literature—scientific, devotional, and fictional, homiletic and ephemeral—produced during major periods of mortality and sickness, which there is no space to discuss in any detail here.[203] Nor is it my intention to trespass into territory which has already been fully and definitively explored—the intellectual shifts which facilitated the adoption of an ambitious administrative code of health regulations designed to arrest the spread of plague, and the controversy and opposition which these progressive policies often aroused.[204] What does warrant further exploration is the interface between the responses of learned Protestant clergymen and their less well-educated parishioners.

Every curate and vicar who mounted the steps of his pulpit during an epidemic was at pains to stress that the congregation assembled beneath him had no one else to blame for the present visitation but itself. If the moral abuses of the age were 'duly weighed', insisted William Gouge in 1630, 'we shall see cause enough to confesse that Gods wrath is justly gone out against us, and that we have deservedly pulled this Plague upon our owne pates'. '[Y]ou must thanke your selves, and your sins' for the sickness, Thomas Pullein told his audience in early Jacobean York.[205] The 'Spirituall Phisicke' and 'pretious preservatives' of repentance and prayer were the surest way of eluding and removing it, declared Henry Holland and William Cupper, and should be every Christian's first recourse.[206] '[I]t is not the cleane keeping, and sweeping of our houses and streetes, that can drive away this fearefull messenger', Laurence Chaderton exhorted an audience at Paul's Cross in October 1578, 'but the purging and sweeping of our consciences from all the stinking filth and drosse of synne'. This would 'prove a better antidote, than all the Pitch, Rue, and Franckincense in the World'.[207]

---

[202] Gouge, *Dearths death*, in *Gods three arrowes*, quotation at 134; John Sanford, *Gods arrowe of the pestilence* (Oxford, 1604), 38; [Holland], *Motus Medi-terraneus*, sig. C2^{r-v}; Jackson, *Londons new-yeeres gift*, fos. 8^v-9^r. The idea derives from 2 Sam. xxiv. 12–13.

[203] On plague literature, see Herbert G. Wright, 'Some Sixteenth and Seventeenth Century Writers on the Plague', in *Essays and Studies 1953* (1953), 41–55; Paul H. Kocher, 'The Idea of God in Elizabethan Medicine', *Journal of the History of Ideas*, 16 (1950), 3–29; Slack, 'Mirrors of Health'; Clark, *Elizabethan Pamphleteers*, 110–20. Apart from purely medical literature on the disease, there were many works of meditation and devotion in prose and verse, pious broadsheets and 'jestbook' type pamphlets such as those produced by the playwright Thomas Dekker. The morality of mirth, the ethics of escape, and the cold reception of fleeing Londoners in the country were frequently subjects for discussion.

[204] Slack, *Impact of Plague*, esp. pt. III.

[205] Gouge, *Plaister for the plague*, in *Gods three arrowes*, 82; Pullein, *Jeremiahs teares*, sigs. E2^v-3^r.

[206] Cupper, *Certaine sermons*, 44; Henry Holland, *Spirituall preservatives against the pestilence* (1593), title-page and *passim*.

[207] Chaderton, *Excellent and godly sermon*, sig. F3^r; W[hitbie], *Londons returne*, 28.

However, few ministers went so far as to deny that intermediary mechanisms were at work in corrupting and infecting the water and air, or to state that sanitary measures and herbal or pharmaceutical potions and elixirs were an utter waste of time. They trod a tightrope between two equally perilous extremes: the sickness could 'hardly [be] healed by naturall curatives' alone, but it was just as unwise to neglect completely 'lawfull ordinarie meanes'.[208] Indeed, they joined forces with the physicians to fight what appeared to be a resilient strain of popular fatalism— the ingrained idea that since the disease was directly inflicted by the finger of God it was not contagious at all. According to James Balmford, speaking from pastoral experience in Southwark in 1603, this 'bloody errour' was 'stiffely maintained by no small number of people', 'not onely by the rude multitude, but by too many of the better sort' as well.[209] As early as 1578, Thomas White, vicar of St Dunstan in the West, had taken a stand against this 'harde opinion', which, he announced, 'I utterlye mislike' and 'canne not allowe'; the same year the authorities attempted to deter the expression of such 'dangerous' views 'upon payne of imprisonment'.[210] In his *The haven of health* (1584) the doctor Thomas Coghan sharply reproached individuals who said it was 'needelesse or bootelesse to shunne the plague' and mocked those more prudent and circumspect than they were themselves.[211] Richard Greenham likewise condemned parishioners who rushed into infected places, desperately tempting God 'by an unadvised boldnes', and William Cupper reproved the 'Foolish hardinesse in some, not to feare the plague' when he lectured in the vicinity of Cripplegate in 1592. To 'audaciously thrust our selves' into this kind of danger, said John Sanford, chaplain of Magdalen College, Oxford, in 1604, was to 'become homicides and wilfull murtherers of our selves'.[212] These rash, 'adventurous', and madcap practices, it was widely agreed, sprang from the unsound notion that 'no person shall dye but at their tyme prefixed'. Balmford condemned this as the delirious persuasion of 'brain-sicke men', which they 'forge in their owne phantasticall braine-pans'.[213] George Wither thought that the false supposition that victims of the plague had been 'foredoom'd' grew out of 'misconceiving (to no small offence) | The doctrine of Eternall Providence'.[214]

Certainly there was the thinnest of dividing lines between 'foole-hardy presi-

[208] Holland, *Spirituall preservatives*, title-page; Chaderton, *Excellent and godly sermon*, sig. F3[r]. On this issue, see also Harley, 'Spiritual Physic'.

[209] Balmford, *Short dialogue*, sig. A2[v] and p. 38.

[210] Thomas White, *A sermon preached at Pawles Crosse on Sunday the thirde of November 1577. in the time of the plague* (1578), 79; *Orders thought meete by her majestie, and her privie councell, to be executed throughout the counties of this realme, in such townes, villages, and other places, as are, or may be hereafter infected with the plague, for the stay of further increase of the same* ([1578?]), sig. B2[v]. See also Theodore Beza, *A shorte learned and pithie treatize of the plague*, trans. John Stockwood (1580), sigs. ¶3[v], and A1[r]–B8[r]; Johann Ewich, *Of the duetie of a faithfull and wise magistrate, in preserving and delivering of the common wealth from infection, in the time of the plague or pestilence*, trans. John Stockwood (1583), sig. **4[r–v].

[211] Thomas Coghan, *The haven of health* (1584), 266.

[212] Greenham, *Works*, 251; Cupper, *Certaine sermons*, 110; Sanford, *Gods arrowe*, 50.

[213] *Orders thought meete by her majestie, and her privie councell, to be executed*, sig. B2[v]; Balmford, *Short dialogue*, 51 and see 59. See also Taylor, *Fearefull summer*, sig. C2[r].

[214] Wither, *Britain's remembrancer*, fo. 52[r–v].

dence and presumption' and a proper trust in God's protection, between Protestant providentialism and 'heathenish' determinism, between meek submission to the Lord's chastisement and careless stoicism in the face of an uncontrollable scourge.[215] But as Paul Slack has observed, we should be wary of assuming that popular opinion about epidemics was as coherent or uniform as the critical statements of their social superiors and spiritual mentors imply.[216] Educated observers interpolated the extreme views they attributed to their humble neighbours from their reluctance to obey the regulations designed for their own safety: from their stubborn resistance to precautionary measures which made them 'Gods prisoners' by incarcerating them in their own houses and banned customary recreational gatherings and traditional funeral rites. Such measures ran counter to the conviction that it was 'a matter of conscience' and charity to visit the sick—a basic moral principle to which the 'poorer sort' seem to have steadfastly clung.[217]

Yet it remains true that Protestant ideology could, on occasion, both fuse with and foster such assumptions. Strictly applied, providentialist tenets did inherently devalue secular schemes for plague control and buttress a distinctly fatalistic position. There were, furthermore, lay and clerical figures prepared to speak out boldly against the orders imposed by the civic and ecclesiastical hierarchy. In 1563, Grindal summoned metropolitan preachers before him to answer the charge that some of their number had 'perswadett' their flocks to defy the ordinances 'sette furthe'; the mayor of Norwich omitted to implement them in 1580, reputedly affirming such steps to be 'of no importance, seing God hath appointed and limited unto everie man a certaine tenure of life'. And a Spanish visitor to London in 1609 reported that 'The Puritans say that it should not be avoided, that it is good fortune to die of the plague, and that although they are close to it, it will not attack any but those already singled out by God, let them take what measures they may. That this is infallible and that it is false madness to try to guard against it.'[218]

No one aroused more disquiet and anxiety than Henoch Clapham, a cantankerous clergyman who, by his own account, had cast aside 'the vayne exercise of Poetrie' some twenty years before, betaken himself to serious study, and around 1591 entered the Church. His career thereafter was nothing if not chequered. In trouble with the authorities not long after his ordination, Clapham prudently

---

[215] *Certaine prayers collected out of a forme of godly meditations, set forth by his majesties authoritie: and most necessary to be used at this time in the present visitation of Gods heavy hand for our manifold sinnes* (1603), sig. D1ᵛ, and sigs. D1ʳ–2ʳ *passim*.

[216] Slack, *Impact of Plague*, 232. See also 285–303.

[217] Balmford, *Short dialogue*, 38, cf. 41. See HMC, *Tenth Report, Appendix, Part II (Gawdy Family of Norfolk)* (1885), 163 (William Davy to F. Gawdy on 9 May 1637): 'There is a strange opinion here amongst the poorer sort of people who hold it a matter of conscience to visit their neighbours in any sickness, yea tho' they know it to be the infection'; and BL Lansdowne MS 19, fo. 38ᵛ (Dr Andrew Perne to Lord Burghley, 21 Nov. 1574), among 'the poore folke in the Townes of Cambridge and Barnwell' were some 'of that perverse judgment that one Christian ought not to avoide the company of an other that is infected with that diseas of the plage'.

[218] BL Lansdowne MS 7, no. 63, fo. 143ʳ; *APC 1578–1580*, 437; Slack, *Impact of Plague*, 231.

withdrew to Amsterdam where he became embroiled in sectarian disputes among
the English Protestant exiles. On his return to England he actively exercised his
ministry in London, writing virulent anti-Catholic and anti-separatist polemic on
the side.[219] In November 1603, Clapham was committed to the Clink for preaching that the plague was not infectious and for publishing a pamphlet contradicting the official injunctions. This was his *Epistle discoursing upon the present pestilence*,
which he dedicated to his 'ordinarie hearers, for keeping them upright in this day
of tentation', preparing a second edition soon afterwards 'for strengthning the
joynts' of the first.[220]

Clapham dismissed scientific explanations and prescriptions for the disease, contending that both Scripture and experience amply demonstrated that the pestilence
was a mortal stroke by Jehovah's angel for sin: 'diverse so smitten, have felt and
heard the noyse of a blow; and . . . found the plain print of a blew hand left behind
upon the flesh'.[221] He did stress, however, that human cordials and medicines
should not altogether be disdained: to say 'I shall live so long as God hath
appointed, though I never use physicke; it is as good as this, I shall live so long as
God hath appointed, though I never eate nor drinke.'[222] This important
qualification rested on an implicit distinction between natural and supernatural
manifestations of the plague which Clapham would later refine. Unfortunately, it
was impossible to tell the two species apart (the one contagious while the other was
not), there being no 'essential differencing marke'.[223] But the most contentious part
of Clapham's teaching was his assertion that religious faith could preserve an individual from dying of the 'pest'. True believers who perished did so because they
lacked assurance, not of their eternal justification and salvation, but of their temporal deliverance from death, whereas reprobates who escaped were blessed with
a 'temporary' and 'bragging' apprehension of divine mercy and providence only
in this particular respect. This promise of immunity was extracted from Psalm xci:
'Because thou hast made the Lord, which is my refuge, even the most High, Thy
habitation; There shall no evil befall thee, neither shall any plague come nigh thy
dwelling.'[224]

Clapham was vigorously refuted by a prominent doctor, Francis Herring, who
attacked 'the strange, uncoth, and unreasonable Paradox, broched of late in this
city' as 'a monstrous and pernitious heresie' and 'a fond conceit'; and by James

---

[219] Henoch Clapham, *Doctor Andros* [*Lancelot Andrewes*] *his prosopeia answered* ([Middelburg], 1605),
4. Clapham alludes to some of his earlier activities and difficulties in *An epistle discoursing upon the
present pestilence* (1603), sig. A2ʳ, in the new dedicatory epistle to Sir Baptist Hicks in the 2nd edn.
(1603), sig. A2ʳ⁻ᵛ, and in the epistle appended to *Doctor Andros*, 76–82.

[220] Clapham, *Epistle* (1st edn.), sig. A2ᵛ; (2nd edn.), sig. A2ᵛ. Cf. Slack's account of this controversy
in *Impact of Plague*, 233–6.

[221] Clapham, *Epistle* (2nd edn.), sig. B1ᵛ.

[222] Ibid. (1st edn.), sig. B1ᵛ, cf. sigs. B1ʳ–2ʳ.

[223] Ibid. (2nd edn.), sig. B3ʳ; *Henoch Clapham his demaundes and answeres touching the pestilence*, ed.
Pere. Re. ([Middelburg], 1604), 6–15, quotation at 15; id., *Doctor Andros*, 12–30.

[224] Clapham, *Epistle* (1st edn.), sig. B2ʳ⁻ᵛ; (2nd edn.), sigs. B4ʳ–C1ᵛ; id., *Demaundes and answeres*,
17–24; id., *Doctor Andros*, 37–40, 46–8. Ps. xci. 9–10.

Balmford in a short and 'familiar' dialogue printed 'to preserve bloud, through the blessing of God'. Balmford, in turn, was answered by one W. T., whose concealed identity enabled him safely to adopt a stance for which Clapham was to languish in gaol for another eighteen months.[225]

Henoch Clapham may have been a maverick, but to a large extent he merely articulated ambiguities embedded in Calvinist theology all along. As he himself protested, he was not 'herein singular and odde by himselfe'.[226] Why were other ministers like Henry Holland, William Fulke, and Arthur Dent permitted to air the same opinions without being assailed with the cry of 'Treason' and 'haled out of the Temple' as 'false prophets' and 'seducers of their Hearers'?[227] '[A]ll that I did, was but a bringing of that doctrine, into distinct methode, which (for the most part) was taught over-confusedly'. According to the editor of *His demaundes and answeres*, written in prison in 1604, Clapham had simply 'distilled' the truth 'out of the cloudes' and disclosed 'the kernel of knowledge, which lay couched under the shell of obscuritie' and 'which others so long had masked'. Such attitudes were not his 'sole fancie'—they had hitherto been applauded and authorized by the powers-that-be.[228] At least in this regard, Clapham was partially right. His difficulties at the hands of Bishop Richard Bancroft, Lancelot Andrewes, and the High Commission probably owed as much to the changing character of the Church hierarchy, the current 'styrres' within the ranks of the London clergy, and his volatile and irascible temperament, as they did to the alleged heterodoxy of his views.[229]

The real problem may have been the way in which Clapham's rather opaque statements were interpreted—or misinterpreted—by the urban populace. Vicious rumours about his preaching had led 'unwise Spirits' to 'bruite abroad' that he

---

[225] Francis Herring, *A modest defence of the caveat given to the wearers of impoisoned amulets, as preservatives from the plague* (1604), preface, quotations at sigs. A2ᵛ, A3ᵛ; Balmford, *Short dialogue*, sig. A3ʳ and title-page; W. T., *A casting up of accounts of certain errors* (1603). Slack tentatively suggests 'W. T.' may be Walter Travers: *Impact of Plague*, 397 n. 30.

[226] *Epistle* (2nd edn.), sig. B3ᵛ. He added: 'They be rather odde that understand not themselves'. Cf. id., *Demaundes and answeres*, 12.

[227] Clapham, *Doctor Andros*, 60, 54 respectively. He was referring to Holland's *Spirituall preservatives*, William Fulke's sermon on 2 Sam. xxiv, *A godly and learned sermon, preached before an honourable auditorie . . .* ([1580]); and Dent's *Plaine mans path-way*, 103. In *Demaundes and answeres*, 7, he also cited William Cupper's *Certaine sermons*. There was certainly some justification in Clapham's retort. Cf. Hooper, *Homelye*, sig. A3ᵛ: 'the plage shall not touche hym that sytteth under the protection of the highest'.

[228] Clapham, *Demaundes and answeres*, 34; preface by 'Pere. Re.', sig. A1ᵛ and p. 16.

[229] In a petition to Prince Henry dated 1 June 1604 Clapham alleged that his imprisonment by order of the bishop of London was motivated not so much by his teachings on the plague as his overt opposition a few years earlier to Bancroft's connivance at the publication of polemical tracts by leading Appellants, notably William Watson's *Quodlibets (A decacordon of ten quodlibeticall questions concerning religion and state* (1602)). Since that time, alleged Clapham, 'he could never brooke me, and therefore [was] glad to take me any way nappinge'. In a letter to Bancroft himself dated 29 Apr. he had spoken of the bishop's 'ancient stomach, so conceived against him' and accused him of treating papists more gently than 'paynfull preachers of the Gospell'. See BL Royal MS 18A XIX, esp. fo. 3ʳ⁻ᵛ and BL Stowe MS 156, fos. 56ᵛ⁻57ʳ.

proclaimed that plague was not catching and that all who died of it were damned: he was arrested even as he was 'checking such false reportes'.[230] Too many had comprehended his sermons 'verie crookedly' and begun 'to expounde the doctrine themselves according to those parcels which they had gleaned by peece meale . . . never understanding the Author as he meant'.[231] Clapham deeply regretted that many 'tooke occasion' thereby 'to be over bold and ventrous in the sicknes tyme and so miscaried', but he could hardly be held responsible for the manner in which his audiences mutated and perverted his discourse in accordance with their own preconceptions.[232] These were shrewd rejoinders, and they may well have been true. As one of Clapham's own opponents remarked, if congregations completely understood what was expounded from the pulpits 'there would not be so many spiders to suck ranke poison out of sound doctrine'.[233]

As we saw in Chapter 2, confusion between an individual's earthly fortunes and his or her spiritual status and fate was always acute: many seem to have regarded sudden death as a sure sign that the victim was destined for damnation and hell.[234] Those who expired prematurely during epidemics were no exception. In his *Britain's remembrancer* (1625) George Wither alluded in passing to 'fooles' who thought that God inflicted plague upon reprobates alone and Henry Robrough, pastor of St Leonard's, Eastcheap, remonstrated against this common mistake a year later: 'if God smite a Minister, or one that is not just of our cut, in matter of judgement, we mark him with a blacke coale, we judge them before the time; we account them as those did rashly, Paul touched with a viper.'[235] It was wrong to suppose that the Almighty was carrying out a programme of ethnic cleansing or an exercise in moral eugenics. It was for suggestions of this kind that John Lowe, curate of St Benedict's, Norwich, found himself under episcopal scrutiny in 1603. Yet in declaring 'that all those whome the Lord had taken a way by the . . . pestilence were slayne by the lyon for transgressing of Gode's commaundement' and in 'making no difference but that all were wicked which the Lord tooke so away', he may not have been quite as 'heretical' and marginal as his godly accuser, a local weaver, alleged. Charged with adultery, alehouse-haunting, and embezzling parish funds and branded 'a sturrer upe of contention amongst his neighbores', Lowe was evidently an unpopular pastor who had clashed violently with his parishioners. It looks very much as if his enemies exploited the heightened sensitivity of the authorities to this issue in the wake of the Clapham cause célèbre to drag him

---

[230] Clapham, *Demaundes and answeres*, sig. A2ʳ; id., *Doctor Andros*, sig. A2ᵛ.

[231] Clapham, *Doctor Andros*, 55; id., *Demaundes and answeres*, sig. A1ᵛ.

[232] Clapham, *Doctor Andros*, 49.

[233] Balmford, *Short dialogue*, 42.

[234] See Ch. 2 above, pp. 95, 103–4.

[235] Wither, *Britain's remembrancer*, fo. 64ᵛ; Robrough, *Balme from Gilead*, 62. During the plague of 1630, Gouge reproved those who thought that no true believers died during a plague (this was 'too bold an assertion, unwarrantable, uncharitable'), as well as those who upheld Clapham's opinion that 'particular faith' in God's protection could provide immunity: *Plaister for the plague*, in *Gods three arrowes*, 21–2.

before the bishop and rub his nose in mud.[236] As it has been argued above, such distortions of predestinarian precepts were simply a logical consequence of central elements within mainstream puritan practical divinity.[237]

Plague became a source of rupture and recrimination on another level too. Providential interpretations of the pestilence gradually acquired a treacherously polemical edge. Until perhaps the 1620s, diagnosis of the transgressions fuelling God's choler had been a relatively uncontroversial enterprise, one which usually underwrote rather than undermined the status quo. It was moral and social failings—drunkenness, adultery, covetousness, pride, blasphemy, and religious apathy—which were deemed to have aroused divine indignation, and against which clergymen from across the confessional spectrum made common cause.[238] Thereafter, however, the whole project became far more inflammatory. The 'scapegoat' sins prophetic preachers claimed had precipitated catastrophe were no longer personal vices committed in private domestic contexts, but public offences played out on a platform in full view of the world. Outrage about the institutions condoning and licensing violations of divine law began to eclipse and outweigh outrage against individual delinquents. Above all, providence became a pawn in the internecine conflicts within the Caroline Church between ministers of an Arminian and Laudian persuasion and those Calvinists they were in the process of relabelling 'puritan' troublemakers. Thus, in 1630, William Gouge was daring to suggest to the godly of St Anne's parish, Blackfriars, that one chief provocation of God's current displeasure was the disturbing resurgence of Romish idolatry: for many years this thick and suffocating haze had been dispelled by the bright light of the Gospel, but now 'the cloud gathereth, and thickneth againe'. Inward and outward apostasy was an equally sinister trend: defection to the antichristian enemy under any guise could never be tolerated by heaven.[239] The same year an unknown Londoner confided to a clerical friend his conviction that the latest epidemic in the capital and the growth of Catholicism at Queen Henrietta Maria's court, especially the recent arrival of twelve Capuchin friars to serve her spiritual needs, were inextricably linked. '[I]t is to be feared we have much missory comming uppone us,' he wrote; 'popary did never so abounde among us as att this present it does'.[240]

---

[236] '1603. Answer of James Wilson to a sermon by John Lowe', in *The Registrum Vagum of Anthony Harison*, ed. Thomas F. Barton, 2 vols., Norfolk Record Soc. 32–3 ([Norwich], 1963–4), ii. 159–63, quotation at 163.

[237] See Ch. 2 above, p. 104.

[238] See e.g. Cupper, *Certaine sermons*, 208–16; Richard Leake, *Foure sermons, preached and publikely taught . . . immediatly after the great visitation of the pestilence in the foresayd countie* [*Westmorland*] (1599), 56–9; Ward, *Gods arrowes*, fos. 23ʳ–31ᵛ; Fuller, *Sermon intended for Paul's Crosse*, 1 [*vere* 9]–23; Robrough, *Balme from Gilead*, 7–23. On Leake, see Edward M. Wilson, 'Richard Leake's Plague Sermons, 1599', *Transactions of the Cumberland and Westmorland Antiquarian and Archaeological Society*, NS 75 (1975), 150–73.

[239] Gouge, *Plaister for the plague*, in *Gods three arrowes*, 79, 82.

[240] Gloucester Cathedral Library, MS 40, fragment of a letter (*c.*1630). It was reported that 'uppone the begenninge of this plagge the kinge does begin to tacke it to harte & will not suffer any to goe to masse butt the queens sarvants . . .'. I owe this reference to Arnold Hunt.

In November 1635 John 'Decalogue' Dod was declaring that 'the plague of God was in the land for the new mixtures of Religion that is commanded in the Churches', and Edward Sparhawke, a disaffected Coggeshall preacher, similarly taunted the authorities in a christening sermon delivered in March 1637, insisting that the railing of altars, the introduction of 'superstitious Adorations' like bowing at the name of Jesus, the officially sanctioned desecration of the sabbath by the Book of Sports, and 'the treading downe of Gods people' were prolonging and intensifying the present infection. '[U]ntill these Causes be removed', he observed tersely, 'the Plague will not cease'.[241]

Fasting too re-emerged as a bone of contention during the Personal Rule. Official fasts had been proclaimed to coincide with the days of prayer and humiliation observed by Parliament in the late 1620s to stave off the plague and in consideration of 'the present estate of the affaires of Christendome, and the deplorable condition of those who professe the true Reformed Religion' and presently suffered at the hands of ravaging Catholic armies.[242] Charles I proclaimed a weekly fast for the duration of the severe epidemic in 1636 and issued a special liturgy for the purpose, together with the particular instruction that such exercises were to be 'no otherwise Celebrated . . . then by a Devout and Religious use of the Prayers in the Printed Booke'. Ministers, it was most emphatically declared, were not to 'detaine their assemblies any longer time together to heare either Sermons or other Divine Service, because such detaining of the people so long together, may prove dangerous to the further increase of the Sickenesse'.[243] This evoked stinging criticism from discontented quarters of the early Stuart Church, including the outspoken rector of St Matthew's, Friday Street, Henry Burton and William Prynne, who secretly published an explosive leaflet entitled *Newes from Ipswich*, written under a pseudonym. In this corrosive piece of puritan propaganda masquerading as a 'coranto' he launched an immoderate assault on 'Luciferan Lord Bishops', 'these desperate Archagents for the Divell, and Pope of Rome, and Master underminers of our Religion', who had, he alleged, dismembered, emasculated, and 'gelded' the plague liturgy by prohibiting sermons ('the very life and soul of a Fast') in contaminated areas. By this diabolical device, these 'impious popish prelats' had created 'a dumb fast and a mock fast', a fast which had not abated but exacerbated the pestilence—as figures compiled from bills of mortality statistically proved.[244]

Laudians like John Squire and Obadiah Whitbie could not allow this 'rayling

---

[241] PRO SP 16/350/54 I. See also Harold Smith, 'An Objectionable Sermon', *Essex Review*, 26 (1927), 202–4; Hunt, *Puritan Moment*, 274.

[242] James F. Larkin (ed.), *Stuart Royal Proclamations*, ii. *Royal Proclamations of King Charles I 1625–1646* (Oxford, 1983), 46–8, 97–9, 193–4, 220–2.

[243] Ibid. 538–40. The liturgy itself is *STC* 16553, *A forme of common prayer, together with an order of fasting: for the averting of Gods heavie visitation* (1636).

[244] Henry Burton, *For God, and the king. The summe of two sermons preached on the fifth of November last in St Matthewes Friday-Streete. 1636* ([Amsterdam], 1636), sig. a2ᵛ, 141–9; [William Prynne] Matthew White (pseud.), *Newes from Ipswich* (Ipswich [Edinburgh], [1636?]), sigs. B1ᵛ, A2ᵛ, A3ʳ⁻ᵛ, A4ʳ⁻ᵛ respectively.

Newes-monger' and 'factious Libeller' to have the last word: sermons were an excellent ornament to a fast, they said, but not its vital essence. It was mere fanaticism to esteem the one without the other 'to bee but a Carkasse to be Buried, and Removed out of their sight, as an ugly spectacle'. '[T]o stop the black-mouth' of the 'schismaticall' Prynne, they presented evidence of a spectacular slide in the totals of those buried each week since the ordinance came forth. Any fractional increase was far more likely to have been triggered by the seditious slanders of Prynne and his 'over-uncharitable Abettours', they claimed, than by the suppression of preaching.[245]

In the provinces, unauthorized private fasts also took on ever more subversive and anti-establishment overtones. A solemn assembly of this kind involving large numbers of the 'meaner sort' held in London on St Andrew's Day 1626 prompted Bishop George Montaigne to take the guilty parties into safe custody 'for some undutiful and bold speeches' made in the course of the prayers. Apparently the preacher had implored God to reveal to Charles I what was necessary for the sound government of the kingdom and induce his queen to forsake idolatry and superstition.[246] Laud himself took action against the 'ill', 'unwarrantable', and 'unworthy custome' of fasting in December 1635, after hearing that the new bishop of Aberdeen had sanctioned a public day of humiliation throughout his diocese. The King, he wrote to Archbishop Spottiswood of St Andrews, was much displeased to hear of the continuance of this practice 'contrary to the rules of Christianity and all the ancient Canons', particularly while he was 'settling that Church against all thinges that were defective in it'. The Scottish prelate was to reprove the offending cleric sharply for overshooting himself and forbid further fasts unless they had express royal permission.[247] In September 1636 the Suffolk minister Robert Reyce complained to John Winthrop in Massachusetts that such observances were 'deemed as hatefull as conventicles' and 'the frute of vestry elders'; when nationwide exercises were ordered the next month a great many 'Absurd Disorderly people' and 'Out-lopers' apparently wandered miles 'to meet with a Fast minted after their owne Mindes'.[248] Preaching at a similar exercise at Easton in Huntingdonshire in November Giles Randall numbered the Forced Loan and ship money amongst the many sins which were causing the Lord's wrath to 'lye heavye' upon the land.[249] The following year Charles Chauncy, who had already made more than one appearance before the High Commission, was reported to the authorities for presiding over a similar exercise at Marston St Lawrence in

---

[245] Squire, *Thanksgiving*, quotations at 26, 27, 21, 24, 25–6 respectively. W[hitbie], *Londons returne*, 15–16, and 27, for an endorsement of the fast's efficacy.

[246] *CSPD Addenda March 1625 to January 1649*, 175.

[247] PRO SP 16/303/11.

[248] *Winthrop Papers*, ed. Ford *et al.*, iii. 306 (Robert Reyce, under pseud. of Laurence Browne, to John Winthrop, 9 Sept. 1636); Squire, *Thanksgiving*, 20–1.

[249] PRO SP 16/355/8 (Obadiah Coysh and John Sutton to Sir Capel Bedell, 1 May 1637). See also the investigation of a fast organized by John Sym, minister of Leigh, Essex, in 1636: PRO SP 16/327/101; 362/106.

Northamptonshire. In front of 'the whole tribe of Gad' (an audience of sixty local puritans, including Lord Saye and Sele), he and a colleague held forth for six to eight hours, pleading God to deliver his servants Prynne, Bastwick, and Burton from persecution. Chauncy, wrote Dr Samuel Clerke to Sir John Lambe, Dean of the Arches, 'doth mend like a Sowre Ale in Sommer'.[250] Instead of galvanizing and unifying the ranks of a loose and inclusive Church, the practice of collective repentance and the doctrine of providence were now threatening to tear them apart.

Paradoxically, then, the ideology of divine omnipotence could be both a source of cultural and communal solidarity and a catalyst of ecclesiastical and political discord and dissent. At critical junctures, when towns and villages, cities and districts struggled against hardship and disaster, the moral exhortations of preachers and pamphleteers and the penitential instincts of their hearers and readers had a tendency to coalesce. Social, cultural, and ideological differences in outlook and opinion faded as communities united against adversity and pulled together to stamp out vice and appease God's wrath. Providentialism underpinned coordinated religious responses to catastrophe and helped forge the temporary alliances between 'holy professors' and 'profane sinners' to which public calamities often gave rise. It needs to be seen not as a rigid and static collection of theological concepts but as a dynamic and adaptable body of beliefs with a deep taproot in the medieval past—a body of beliefs capable of coexisting quite easily with less overtly religious explanations of and reactions to distressing events. Ministers adjusted and glossed over the complexities of Protestant dogma as presented in the textbooks and ordinary laypeople found ways of reconciling what they heard in sermons with their pre-existing convictions about divine intervention in the earthly world. The long-term effect of these reciprocal processes was surely to anchor and entrench the Reformation. But the very elasticity of the discourse also promoted ominous divisions and antagonisms within English Protestantism which would ultimately endanger the structural integrity of the early Stuart state itself.

[250] PRO SP 16/361/67. On Chauncy, *DNB*.

4
'Tongues of Heaven':
Prodigies, Portents, and Prophets

> No natural exhalation in the sky,
> No scope of nature, no distemper'd day,
> No common wind, no customed event,
> But they will pluck away his natural cause
> And call them meteors, prodigies, and signs,
> Abortives, presages, and tongues of heaven,
> Plainly denouncing vengeance . . .

So declares a character in Shakespeare's *King John* (*c*.1584),[1] reflecting upon the grave fascination which strange celestial and terrestrial phenomena exercised over the minds of the early thirteenth- no less than the late sixteenth-century populace. Recounted in cheap print and sermons, recorded in the correspondence of academics and gentlemen, and broadcast across the country by word of mouth, monstrous births, blazing stars, frightening apparitions, and eclipses were widely acknowledged to be providential tokens of future misfortune, and contemplated with a mixture of anxiety, astonishment, and awe. In 1583, for instance, William Averell, student of divinity at Corpus Christi College, Cambridge, published a blackletter tract reporting the 'wonderfull and straunge newes' that it had rained wheat in the vicinity of Ipswich on Friday, 1 February. This prodigious downpour, he declared, was 'a notable example to put us in remembraunce of the judgements of God, and a preparative, sent to move us to speedy repentance': 'seying we regarde not his word, he will teache us by wonders'.[2] According to an anonymous journalist, mysterious hieroglyphical symbols discovered on a herring captured off the Norwegian coast in November 1597 had also been engraved there by *digitus dei* to 'figure forth' divine wrath against inveterate sinners—'a heavie sentence' recalling the handwriting on King Belshazzar's wall (Plate 17).[3] Three dead bodies resurrected from their graves in the German city of Holdt in September 1616 to prophesy hideous punishments were likewise reputed to be a terrible 'Praemonition' that 'the dreadfull day of doome drawes neere'.[4] A stranger caused

---

[1] III. iv. 153–9, in *Complete Works*, ed. Alexander, 431. Cf. Thomas Jackson, who described the comet of 1618 as 'that stately tongue of Heaven': *Judah must into captivitie*, 26.

[2] Averell, *Wonderfull and straunge newes*, title-page, sig. B2ʳ, cf. sig. A7ʳ.

[3] *A most straunge and wonderfull herring, taken on the 26. day of November 1597* . . . (1598), sigs. A2ᵛ, A3ʳ. Belshazzar's feast is in Dan. v.

[4] *Miraculous newes, from the cittie of Holdt . . . where there were plainly beheld three dead bodyes rise out of their graves*, trans. T. F. (1616), sig. A3ᵛ; *Miraculous newes from the cittie of Holdt in Germany, where there were three dead bodyes seene to rise out of their graves*, printed in Clark (ed.), *Shirburn Ballads*, 76–80.

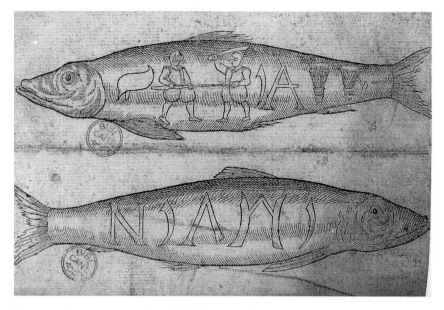

PLATE 17 *A most straunge and wonderfull herring, taken on the 26. day of November 1597. neere unto Drenton* (London, 1598), sig. A4ᵛ. By permission of the Syndics of Cambridge University Library. Shelfmark: Dd*. 3. 26 (14).

a stir at Whitehall in the summer of 1626 when he delivered 'strange tydings' of 'a generall darknes' throughout England for three days and three nights, to be followed by a widespread famine.[5] And when flashing lights and a fiery sword were observed in the sky above Axminster and Dartmouth in the autumn of 1638, Walter Yonge solemnly noted the occurrence in his diary under the heading '*portentum*'.[6]

   As we shall see, close scrutiny of these inauspicious signs of the times yields further evidence of the degree to which Calvinist theology not merely accommodated but arguably even enhanced aspects of pre-Reformation practice and belief. It reveals how some traditional cultural paradigms were subtly altered and rehabilitated rather than permanently effaced by the advent of an era of rapid doctrinal and devotional innovation and change. Protestant ministers vigorously attacked popular techniques of predicting the future as 'heathenish', 'superstitious', and incompatible with a true understanding of the doctrine of providence. In practice, however, it was not always easy to disentangle the two.

[5] PRO SP 16/32/114 (Thomas Cruse to Lady Carnsew, [July?], 1626).
[6] BL Add. MS 35331, fo. 72ʳ.

SIGNS OF THE TIMES

The disposition to see prodigies sprang from a theocentric view of the universe, an intensely moralistic cosmology. It rested on the premiss that the physical environment and human conduct were closely attuned: aberrations in the natural order literally incarnated the spiritual chaos and anarchy created by sin. As their etymology implied, *monstrum* and *prodigium* demonstrated and presaged divine will.[7] The earth was one huge emblem and hieroglyph, 'Gods great booke *in Folio*', and every creature 'a severall page, in which wee may reade some instruction to further us in heavenly wisedome'; it was 'a prospective glasse' through which Christians might behold their Maker and Judge.[8] Portents were the danger signals and 'domb warnings' of a world in moral crisis and on the verge of mechanical collapse— 'Ensignes of anger' and 'advertisements of afterclaps'.[9] The Lord sent such 'haroulds', 'trumpetters', and 'Pursuivants' because the cries of the clergy went unheeded.[10] 'The foure Elements have beene Preachers to us,' observed one pious pamphleteer, 'yet wee get (or at least, shew) little amendment by the Doctrin, they have Read unto us', stubbornly persisting in iniquity 'albeit God himself Holla in our Eares'.[11]

The early modern canon of providential signs and wonders was a mosaic and an amalgam of a cluster of superficially inconsistent intellectual traditions. First and foremost, it drew authority and inspiration from Scripture. The Old Testament told of many amazing prodigies shown to the Israelites: mysterious columns of cloud and combustible bushes; Moses transforming dust into lice; plagues of locusts, frogs, and caterpillars descending upon wicked nations and kings like the Philistines and Pharaoh. In the last days, foretold the prophet Joel, signs would be shown 'in the heavens and in the earth, blood, and fire, and pillars of smoke'. The Gospels of Matthew, Mark, and Luke likewise listed false prophets, wars, earthquakes, famine, pestilence, and empyreal sights among the forerunners of Christ's Second Coming.[12] Preaching in the early 1550s, Hugh Latimer was

---

[7] As noted by St Augustine, *Of the citie of God*, bk. XXI, ch. 8; and by the 7th-cent. Bishop Isidore of Seville, in his *Etymologiae*, bk. XI, ch. 3, §3 (*c.* AD 620), trans. by William D. Sharpe, 'The Medical Writings: An English Translation with an Introduction and Commentary', *Transactions of the American Philosophical Soc.*, NS 54 (1964), 51. Both works were printed in the early modern period.

[8] See L. Brinckmair, *The warnings of Germany. By wonderfull signes, and strange prodigies seene . . . betweene the yeare 1618 and 1638* (1638), sig. *2ᵛ; Topsell, *Historie of foure-footed beastes*, sigs. ¶3ʳ–¶4ʳ; Philemon Holland, 'Preface to the reader' of his trans. of Pliny, *The historie of the world . . .* (1601).

[9] *Strange newes out of Kent*, sig. B3ᵛ; *Wonder woorth the reading*, 3; [Fridericus Nausea], *A treatise of blazing starres in generall. As well supernaturall as naturall*, trans. Abraham Fleming (1618 edn.; 1st pub. 1577), sig. B3ᵛ.

[10] Boaistuau, *Certaine secrete wonders of nature*, sig. A4ʳ; *Looke up and see wonders. A miraculous apparition in the ayre, lately seene in Barke-shire at Bawklin Greene neere Hatford. April. 9th. 1628* (1628), 1.

[11] *Looke up and see wonders*, 3, 1. For the metaphor of prodigies as 'preachings from heaven', see also Thomas Day, *Wonderfull straunge sightes seene in the element, over the citie of London and other places* ([1583]), sig. 2ᵛ; Anderson, *Sermon*, sig. G1ᵛ.

[12] See Exod. xxxiii. 9–10, iii. 2, viii; Pss. lxxviii. 45–8, cv. 27–41; Joel ii. 30–1; Matt. xxiv; Mark xiii; Luke xxi; Acts ii. 17–20.

certain that the recent appearance of a curious ring around the sun signified 'that this fearful day is not far off', and Elizabethan and early Stuart ministers like Edwin Sandys, Francis Shakelton, and Stephen Batman readily applied these texts to their own unsettled times, concluding that shooting stars, double tides, and swarms of beetles and flies were the world's 'Ulcers', 'Biles', and 'blaines', which did 'verie notablie prognosticate . . . the universall dissolution, and destruction of the same'.[13] Scores of news writers lazily reiterated these biblical clichés, augmenting the chorus of warning that native and foreign marvels clearly betokened that the crack of doom approached.

Portents also had inherently apocalyptic overtones. Daniel and Revelation, along with the apocryphal book of 2 Esdras, insisted that occult phenomena would prefigure the overthrow of the present earthly order, the annihilation of Antichrist, and the vindication of the elect.[14] Scholars such as Joseph Mede and Robert Salter subjected sightings of meteors and parhelions to detailed eschatological analysis, scrutinizing them for fresh insights into the gnostic Hebrew prophecies and the mystical Seven Seals in the vision of St John.[15] A pamphlet published in 1589 similarly sought to decode the cryptic 'divine caracters' inscribed on four fish recently caught in Danish waters 'by considerations Poligraphicall, theologicall, thalmudicall & cabalisticall', and to calculate from them the exact year in which the King of Saints would return to vanquish the Beast and judge the quick and the dead.[16] Chiliastic expectation of an utopian thousand-year epoch of Messianic rule could be spliced onto such prodigy stories, but until the emergence of the Fifth Monarchists and other radical sects in the 1640s and 1650s, most cheap print and preaching about strange wonders seems to have been sombrely providential rather than euphorically millenarian in tone.[17] It saw them as foreshadowing interim temporal judgements rather than the final consummating act in the Lord's grand design.

[13] Hugh Latimer, *Sermons and Remains . . .* , ed. George Elwes Corrie, Parker Soc. (Cambridge, 1845), 51; Edwin Sandys, *Sermons . . .* , ed. John Ayre, Parker Soc. (Cambridge, 1841), 346–69; Francis Shakelton, *A blazyng starre or burnyng beacon, seene the 10. of October laste* (1580), quotations at sig. B3^r; Batman, *Doome*, 400 and *passim*.

[14] See esp. Dan. vi. 27; Rev. xiii. 13–14; 2 Esd. v. 4–8.

[15] Joseph Mede, *Clavis apocalyptica* (Cambridge, 1627), trans. Richard More as *The key of the Revelation, searched and demonstrated out of the naturall and proper characters of the visions* (1650 edn.), see esp. 80–120. For one set of mock suns which troubled Mede, see BL Harleian MS 389, fos. 147^r, 153^v. Salter, *Wonderfull prophecies from the beginning of the monarchy of this land . . . together with an essay touching the late prodigious comete* (1626), esp. 43–7. On Mede, see Paul Christianson, *Reformers and Babylon: English Apocalyptic Visions from the Reformation to the Eve of the Civil War* (Toronto, 1978), 124–8; Katharine R. Firth, *The Apocalyptic Tradition in Reformation Britain 1530–1645* (Oxford, 1979), 213–19; Frearson, 'English Corantos', esp. 322–8.

[16] *A briefe conjecturall discourse, upon the hierographicall letters & caracters found upon fower fishes, taken neere Marstrand in the kingdome of Denmarke* (1589), sig. B1^r, title. For a German broadsheet on this subject, see Walter L. Strauss (ed.), *The German Single-Leaf Woodcut 1550–1600*, 4 vols. (New York, 1975), iii. 1350.

[17] On Civil War millenarianism, see Bernard Capp, 'The Fifth Monarchists and Popular Millenarianism', in J. F. McGregor and B. Reay (eds.), *Radical Religion in the English Revolution* (Oxford, 1984), esp. 178–9.

Another important source of influence was the series of prodigies observed prior to the siege of Jerusalem *c.* AD 70, generally deemed to be a fulfilment of Christ's grim predictions in Luke xxi. Widely known from contemporary translations and abridgements of Flavius Josephus' *History of the Jewish wars*, these omens included a comet in the shape of a flaming sword, bright lights and voices in the temple, spectral armies, a lamb calved by a heifer, and a plebeian seer who trod the streets for seven years proclaiming the ghastly fate of the city.[18] Echoes of this text can be found in the medieval prophetic legend of the Fifteen Signs before Doomsday— a succession of portents it was believed would appear in the fortnight directly leading up to the Last Judgement. Associated with St Jerome, this tradition was widely diffused via pamphlets and ballads in the early modern period.[19]

This rich vein of Judeao-Christian thought was supplemented by the historical and philosophical writings of classical antiquity. The post-Reformation repertoire of omens and portents owed much to pagan mythology. Monstrous babies and beasts, falling stars, milk rains, and inanimate objects which spontaneously ignited or sweated droplets of blood filled the pages of Virgil, Plutarch, Seneca, Livy, and especially Aristotle, Cicero, and Pliny. Much of this material filtered into the works of Isidore of Seville and Albertus Magnus; it was also absorbed by the authors of medieval bestiaries, notably the thirteenth-century Franciscan friar Bartholomew Glanville. Renaissance humanism, assisted by the advent of print, infused this ancient divinatory tradition with new life, generating a spate of Latin and vernacular prodigy collections culled from the Romans and Greeks, an enterprise actively promoted by Continental reformers such as Philip Melanchthon and Job Fincelius.[20] Bulky didactic encyclopedias like those compiled by Conrad Lycosthenes blurred and merged with the publications of naturalists and physicians such as Ambrose Paré and Conrad Gesner. This literature made its way into English through the efforts of Edward Topsell, Stephen Batman, and other translators.[21] So did books of marvels and secrets of the kind assembled by Pierre

---

[18] Flavius Josephus, *The famous and memorable workes*, trans. Thomas Lodge (2nd edn. 1609) (entered 7 Mar. 1591: *SR* ii. 576), bk. VII, ch. 12, pp. 738–9. The octavo abridgement by 'Joseph ben Gorion' was probably more widely known than Lodge's folio: Joseph ben Gorion (pseud.), *A compendious and most marveilous historie of the latter times of the Jewes common weale*, trans. P. Morwyng (Oxford, 1575 edn.; 1st pub. 1558), 237–9. See also Ch. 6, below.

[19] See W. Woodhouse, *The .xv. fearfull tokens preceding I say, the generall judgement called domesday* ([1566]); William Heist, *The Fifteen Signs before Doomsday* (East Lansing, Mich., 1952).

[20] On anthologies of prodigies and their medieval and classical precursors, see Schenda, 'Deutschen Prodigiensammlungen'; Jean Céard, *La Nature et les prodiges: L'Insolite au XVI siècle en France* (Geneva, 1977), esp. ch. 7; Norman R. Smith, 'Portent Lore and Medieval Popular Culture', *Journal of Popular Culture*, 14 (1980), 47–59; Katharine Park and Lorraine J. Daston, 'Unnatural Conceptions: The Study of Monsters in Sixteenth- and Seventeeth-Century France and England', *P&P* 92 (1981), 35–43; Barnes, *Prophecy and Gnosis*, esp. 87–91; Dudley Wilson, *Signs and Wonders: Monstrous Births from the Middle Ages to the Enlightenment* (1993); and esp. Clark, *Thinking with Demons*, chs. 16–17, 24. See also Ch. 2, above.

[21] Lycosthenes, *Prodigiorum ac ostentorum chronicon* (1557), trans. and expanded by Batman as *The doome warning all men to the judgemente* (1581); *The workes of that famous chirurgion Ambrose Parey*, trans. Thomas Johnson (1634; 1st pub. in French 1573), bk. XXV; parts of Gesner's *Historiæ animalium* (Zurich 1551–8) were trans. by Topsell as *The historie of foure-footed beastes* (1607) and *The historie of serpents*

Boaistuau and Simon Goulart—a genre which enjoyed a growing vogue. Thomas Lupton's *A thousand notable things* is typical of the more popular of these catalogues of curiosities ranging from diabolical possession and Caesarean section to herbal remedies and insatiable appetites, interspersed with geological, astronomical, botanical, and anatomical freaks.[22]

The second-hand classical culture such works made accessible fused with and reinforced the indigenous, orally transmitted lore of the countryside.[23] In pre-Civil War England, the notion that there were analogies and correspondences between the various species and that human vicissitudes were sympathetically expressed by animal, vegetable, and mineral abnormalities was by no means restricted to the unlearned rural multitude. Individuals from all walks of life regarded red sky in the morning as a meteorological warning and the sight and sound of certain birds as omens of bad luck. It was a piece of proverbial wisdom that 'the croaking raven bodes misfortune',[24] and crows, owls, and magpies were also considered to be unpropitious, especially when they intruded into places of habitation, business, or worship. Such assumptions were shared by the inhabitants of bustling towns and the teeming metropolis. A heron which perched on the steeple of St Peter's Cornhill one afternoon was interpreted as a sign that the current epidemic was likely to spread and in 1604 the House of Commons rejected a bill after a speech by its puritan sponsor was interrupted by the flight of a jackdaw through the parliamentary chamber.[25] Primeval fears about the encroachment of the wild into the 'civilized' domain may also help to explain the horror with which the inhabitants of Wymondham in Norfolk watched a flock of 'owgely ravens' seize upon meat and fish in their butcher's shops and market stalls in 1595,[26] and the alarm and consternation caused on both sides of the Irish Sea by a battle between hundreds of starlings in the sky above Cork in the autumn of 1621—few failed to draw a direct connection when fire ravaged the city the following May (Plate 18).[27] No less

---

(1608). For a brief compilation of extracts from Pliny and Livy, see Thomas Churchyard, *The wonders of the ayre, the trembling of the earth, and the warnings of the world before the judgement day* (1602).

[22] Boaistuau, *Certaine secrete wonders of nature*; Goulart, *Admirable and memorable histories*; Thomas Lupton, *A thousand notable things* ([c.1590 edn.]; 1st pub. [1579]).

[23] The following paragraphs owe much to the insights of Thomas, *Religion and the Decline of Magic*, 745–9, and *Man and the Natural World: Changing Attitudes in England 1500–1800* (Harmondsworth, 1983), esp. 70–80.

[24] Tilley, *Dictionary of Proverbs*, no. R33.

[25] Thomas Nashe, *Christs teares over Jerusalem* (1593), repr. in *Works*, ed. McKerrow, ii. 172; *Journals of the House of Commons. From November the 8th 1547 . . . to March the 2d 1628* ([1742]), 983.

[26] Shrewsbury School, MS Mus X. 31, fo. 207ᵛ. A ballad on this subject was entered to Thomas Scarlet on 28 Oct. 1595: *SR* iii. 51.

[27] *Wonderfull battell of starelings*; *A battell of birds most strangly fought in Ireland* ([1621]); *Relation of the most lamentable burning of the cittie of Corke*; *Lamentable burning of the citty of Corke*. For contemporary comments on these events, see BL Harleian MS 389, fos. 166ʳ, 208ʳ; BL Egerton MS 784, fo. 22ʳ; BL Add. MS 38599, fos. 53ʳ⁻ᵛ, 54ᵛ; Yonge, *Diary*, ed. Roberts, 45. According to Simonds D'Ewes, 'Upon this newes tame hearneseies [hernshaws or herons] got out . . . and came upon Paules steeple; the people were at first frightened and feared burning of London': *Diary*, ed. Bourcier, 83.

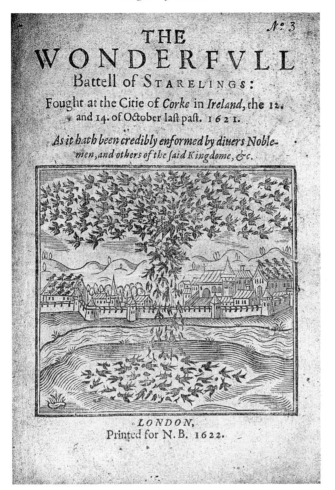

PLATE 18 *The wonderfull battell of starelings: fought at the citie of Corke in Ireland* (London, 1622), title-page. By permission of the Board of Trinity College Dublin. Shelfmark: Press A. 3. 36 no. 3.

perturbing was the temporary disappearance of a creature with sacred connotations: when not a single wren was sighted in Cambridge one winter later that decade, local people brooded about invasion from abroad, noting apprehensively that the same had occurred immediately prior to the Norman Conquest in 1066.[28] Strange foliage and mutant flowers or fruit were also interpreted as inauspicious

---

[28] Trinity College, Cambridge, MS O. 7. 3, fo. 6ʳ.

oracular tokens. A seven-headed cabbage found near Nuremberg provoked much concern in 1553 and when an oak tree in Lanhydrock Park began to produce speckled white leaves in the late Elizabethan period it was widely conjectured that the owner of the Cornish estate would die as soon as the variegation ceased. 'Certain it is that divers ancient families in England are admonished by such predictions', wrote Richard Carew in 1602.[29] The young Simonds D'Ewes was worried by 'the retrograde growth of beanes' in August 1622, when the 'black eye' grew unnaturally upwards, making him 'much to wonder' what it did portend. Reports of trees blossoming and confused birds laying eggs during an unseasonal spring in one of the Swiss cantons that November likewise led to much anxious speculation.[30]

Equally ingrained was the conviction that comets and eclipses heralded momentous events, particularly the subversion of kingdoms and the death of princes, statesmen, and peers. '[E]xperience hath taught men', said the West Country clergyman Thomas Bedford, that each 'super-terrestriall' blaze 'is in its kinde Doctrinal'.[31] Country squires habitually linked astronomical phenomena with political developments in their private memorabilia: Richard Shanne of Methley in Yorkshire, for example, related the appearance of Halley's Comet in 1618 to the outbreak of war in Bohemia and the decease of Queen Anne of Denmark, consort and 'bedfellowe of Kinge James', early the following year.[32] The same coincidences were no doubt noticed by well-informed artisans, yeomen, and tenant farmers, who may have scribbled them in the margins of their almanacs, those increasingly popular repositories of useful agricultural and astrological data.

Astrology itself is another thread that can be teased out of the complex tapestry that was the early modern culture of preternatural wonders and signs.[33] Amateur and professional stargazers studied celestial movements for information about future harvest failures, natural disasters, revolutions, and epidemics, anticipating planetary conjunctions with considerable excitement and dread. The meeting of Saturn and Jupiter on 9 July 1623 inspired much feverish discussion in London, especially among 'the common sorte of people', who seem to have awaited it in a state of trepidation and suspense, some predicting a heat wave with thunder and lightning, others fire and brimstone, others still the end of the world.[34] Multiple mock suns regularly inspired enquiries into the 'remarkeble occurrences' likely to ensue, and whenever new stars appeared in established constellations lay and clerical prognosticators set to work explicating the significance of their posi-

---

[29] Batman, *Doome*, 362. For a German broadsheet about the cabbage, see Strauss (ed.), *German Single-Leaf Woodcut*, i. 400. Carew, *Survey of Cornwall*, 215.

[30] D'Ewes, *Diary*, ed. Bourcier, 90–1; BL Harleian MS 389, fo. 265[r].

[31] B[edford], *True and certaine relation of a strange-birth*, sig. C1[v]. See also Hakewill, *Apologie*, bk. II, §6, 119–21. On comets, see Thomas Hill, *A contemplation of mysteries: contayning the rare effectes and significations of certayne comets* ([1574?]); T[homas] T[wyne], *A view of certain wonderful effects . . . now newly conferred with the presignifications of the comete, or blasing star* (1578).

[32] BL Add. MS 38599, fo. 49[r].   [33] On astrology, see Ch. 1 above, pp. 23–5.

[34] D'Ewes, *Diary*, ed. Bourcier, 145.

tion in relation to Libra, Scorpio, Sagittarius, or some other zodiacal sign.[35] Experts condemned the ten great plagues foretold by the Calabrian astronomer John Doleta after one such sighting in 1586 as 'frivolous newes', but his predictions about the dire catastrophes that would accompany the 'Climactericall yeare' when the moon was in Pisces, 'the watrie sign', were very nearly realized two years later in the guise of the Spanish Armada.[36] Such prophecies could be politically inflammatory, not least because they had the dangerous potential to become self-fulfilling. In 1601, for instance, the authorities called in a 'foolish prognostication' published by William Woodhouse declaring that the Essex rebellion was the effect of an eclipse the previous year and foretelling future upheavals and the demise of key figures in Church and State.[37] All too often popular forecasters crossed the fine line between suggesting that the stars simply signified divine intentions and implying that they exerted actual causal influence over human affairs.

Another set of prophetic traditions which became integrated into the mainstream of Elizabethan and early Stuart thinking about omens and portents were the obscure and adaptable pronouncements associated with such mythical figures as the Delphic Oracle, Merlin, and the Wandering Jew. The animal symbolism which characterized Galfridian prophecy, as codified by the eleventh-century Benedictine monk Geoffrey of Monmouth, was readily compatible with the rich zoomorphic imagery embedded in the Book of Revelation. Allegorical prophecies of this type had circulated widely before 1500, often in the form of illuminated pictures and scrolls. They ran rife during the early Reformation, when identifications of Henry VIII with the legendary Mouldwarp forced the government to place a law against them on the statute book in 1542.[38] Such predictions could, however, be transformed into pro- as well as anti-Protestant propaganda. In the reign of Elizabeth the German Lutheran preacher Paul Graebner presented the Queen with an elaborate painted prophecy about the future religious fortunes of Europe in which the Pope, Jesuits, and Catholic monarchs were depicted as snakes, frogs, and other frightful serpentine beasts. These speculations were resurrected

---

[35] See e.g. Bodleian Library, Oxford, MS Ashmole 174, fo. 420[r]; F. K., [lacks title-page, heading A2[r]] *Of the crinitall starre, which appeareth this October and November. 1580* ([1580]), esp. sigs. A3[r]–4[v].

[36] [John Doleta], *Straunge newes out of Calabria: prognosticated in the yere 1586. upon the yere 87* ([1586]), sig. A3[v]; answered by T. R., *A confutation of the tenne great plagues, prognosticated by John Doleta from the country of Calabria* ([1587]), fos. 1[v], 2[r], 11[r].

[37] *CSPD 1598–1601*, 585. Woodhouse's first extant almanac (*STC* 532) is dated 1602.

[38] On Galfridian and other forms of political prophecy, see Thomas, *Religion and the Decline of Magic*, ch. 13, esp. 462, 466; Howard Dobin, *Merlin's Disciples: Prophecy, Poetry and Power in Renaissance England* (Stanford, Calif., 1990). For the Henrician period, see M. H. Dodds, 'Political Prophecies in the Reign of Henry VIII', *Modern Language Review*, 11 (1916), 276–84; G. R. Elton, *Policy and Police: The Enforcement of the Reformation in the Age of Thomas Cromwell* (Cambridge, 1972), ch. 2; Alistair Fox, 'Prophecies and Politics in the Reign of Henry VIII', in id. and John Guy (eds.), *Reassessing the Henrician Age: Humanism, Politics, and Reform 1500–1550* (Oxford, 1986), 77–94; Sharon L. Jansen, *Political Protest and Prophecy under Henry VIII* (Woodbridge, 1991). For the resurgence of such prophecies in the Civil War period, see Harry Rusche, 'Prophecies and Propaganda, 1641 to 1651', *EHR* 84 (1969), 752–70; Jerome Friedman, *Miracles and the Pulp Press during the English Revolution: The Battle of the Frogs and Fairford's Flies* (1993), chs. 4, 11.

during the Thirty Years War and recast to fit the circumstances of the fall of Charles I and the erection of the godly republic in 1649.[39] Stephen Batman's *The doome warning all men to the judgemente* incorporated the utterances of the nine Hellenic Sibyls.[40] And, revived in the Jacobean period, the medieval anti-Semitic myth of Calebbe Shilocke—the shoemaker of Jerusalem condemned to endless peregrination as a penance for insulting Christ en route to Calvary—became another convenient device for rehearsing familiar warnings about the succession of miseries likely 'to fall upon the whole worlde by reason of sinne'.[41]

A final prophetic genre which enjoyed some popularity in this period was the fragment of text recovered from a formerly holy or otherwise historic site. Some of the manuscripts reputedly enclosed in earthenware pots in Derbyshire barrows and crumbling East Anglian monasteries alluded obliquely to current domestic and dynastic developments; others were vehicles for moral exhortation of an entirely uncontroversial kind.[42] A Hebrew parchment discovered wrapped in lead in the shape of a heart in the ruined wall of the Parisian church of St Denis in 1617, for example, contained a set of pessimistic premonitions about impending punishments for wickedness. Francis Bacon scoffed at such revelations as fit for nothing but 'Winter Talke, by the Fireside', not least because they perpetuated the idea that monks had special occult and magical powers. Yet more than one gentleman carefully transcribed into his diary the disasters this document declared would precede the General Assize, which it was believed would take place in just thirteen years time.[43] These were cultural relics of the Middle Ages which continued to infiltrate the early modern scene.

RATHER INCREDIBLE THEN PROBABLE

In view of their highly eclectic character, it is hardly surprising that prodigies and prophecies occupied something of a grey area in the Protestant doctrine of

[39] Trinity College, Cambridge, MS R. 16. 22. The prophecy was summarized in James Maxwell, *Admirable and notable prophecies* (1615), 87–8. See Barnes, *Prophecy and Gnosis*, 251; Thomas, *Religion and the Decline of Magic*, 468, 488.

[40] Batman, *Doome*, 36–7. On sibylline prophecy and the Oracula Sibyllina, a 2nd- or 3rd-cent. Christian imitation of the collection of oracular utterances preserved in Rome and consulted by the Senate, see Rupert Taylor, *The Political Prophecy in England* (New York, 1911), ch. 2, esp. pp. 28–38.

[41] [Andrea Buonaccorsi] Signior Valesco (pseud.), *Newes from Rome. Of two mightie armies . . . Also certaine prophecies of a Jew serving to that armie, called Caleb Shilocke . . .* , trans. W. W. ([1606]), quotation at sig. B4[r]; id., *A Jewes prophesy, with newes from Rome* ([1607]); *Calebbe Shillocke, his prophesie: or, the Jewes prediction* ([1607]). See also BL Add. MS 38599, fos. 51[v]–52[v]. The ballad of the Wandering Jew survived in the ballad partners' stock for over 25 years: Watt, *Cheap Print*, 337. See also George K. Anderson, *The Legend of the Wandering Jew* (Providence, RI, 1965), esp. ch. 2.

[42] Examples include BL Harleian MS 389, fo. 335[r] ('A prophecie found in the Abbey of St Benedict in Norfolk'); Bodleian Library, Oxford, MS Ashmole 174, fo. 495[r] (verses found in a pot in a Derbyshire barrow dated 1642). See also Thomas, *Religion and the Decline of Magic*, 463–4.

[43] *A prophesie of the judgment day. Being lately found in Saint Denis church in France, and wrapped in leade in the forme of an heart* ([1620?]); Francis Bacon, 'Of Prophecies', in *The essayes or counsels, civill and morall* (1625), 216; Yonge, *Diary*, ed. Roberts, 38; BL Add. MS 38599, fo. 58[v].

providence. They were topics which hovered on the borderline of theological respectability and which Reformed ministers and laypeople approached with varying degrees of cautious ambivalence. Dr Edward Cradocke, Lady Margaret Professor of Divinity at Oxford, cited Pierre Boaistuau's *Certaine secrete wonders of nature* (1569) without scruple or reservation as a valuable source.[44] But many of his colleagues were less sure about how much credence should be given to some of the more outlandish portents included in such collections, admitting that they often exceeded 'common sence and apprehension' and seemed 'not so absurde as altogither repugnant to naturall reasons', 'rather incredible then probable'.[45] In a period marked by the growth of empirical attitudes towards evidence and the gradual transformation of standards of proof,[46] well-educated contemporaries became increasingly wary of the prodigy stories which were a staple product of London publishers of inexpensive ephemera. Stephen Batman, for instance, omitted details of a black cockerel which had crowed in the lap of a Bristol woman in 1580 'for wante of sufficient testimony'; he also passed over a report of hounds barking in the air at Blonsdon in Wiltshire '[n]ot that I thinke [it] untrue' but because it was 'too slenderly printed, and without some one especiall Author'.[47] At least some readers of 'strange newes' seem to have shared the suspicions of the clergy. Joseph Mede carefully sifted trustworthy accounts from 'meere tales' and dozens of moralistic pamphleteers anticipated and deflected the charge that the omens and wonders they described were simply 'poeticall fictions'.[48]

In the final analysis, however, most committed Calvinists were too uncertain about the status of such phenomena to discard altogether the possibility that they had actually occurred. 'Things of this nature are lyable to fabulositie', remarked Mede, commenting on rumours that fire had rained from heaven on the Lincolnshire market town of Boston in February 1627, 'but all is not false which so many talke of & from divers places.'[49] After all, as the Bible revealed, the Almighty could and did operate in the most mysterious and mind-boggling ways— it would be the height of blasphemy to suggest that the metamorphosis of Aaron's rod into a serpent, the parting of the Red Sea, and the transmutation of the morning dew into manna were no more than allegories or myths.[50] Fantastic meta-

[44] Cradocke, *Shippe of assured safetie*, ch. 13, Boaistuau cited at p. 69.

[45] Goulart, *Admirable and memorable histories*, sig. A3ʳ, and cf. the unpaginated 'The Printer to the Reader'; Batman, *Doome*, sig. ¶3ᵛ; Averell, *Wonderfull and straunge newes*, sig. A5ʳ.

[46] See Barbara Shapiro, *Probability and Certainty in Seventeenth-Century England: A Study of the Relationships between Natural Science, Religion, History, Law, and Literature* (Princeton, 1983), esp. chs. 2–3; Lorraine Daston, 'Marvelous Facts and Miraculous Evidence in Early Modern Europe', *Critical Enquiry*, 18 (1991), 93–124.

[47] Batman, *Doome*, 412.

[48] BL Harleian MS 389, fos. 146ʳ, 153ᵛ, 166ʳ; *Wonderfull battell of starelings*, sig. A3ᵛ. See also *Miracle upon miracle*, 1–3; *Miraculous newes, from the cittie of Holdt*, 'The bookes Apologie', sigs. C2ʳ–3ʳ; *True and most dreadfull discourse of a woman possessed with the devill*, sig. A3ʳ⁻ᵛ.

[49] BL Harleian MS 390, fo. 211ʳ.

[50] Exod. vii. 12, xiv. 21–3, xvi. 13–18 respectively.

physical effects like the two dragons seen fighting over the Belgian town of Ghent in 1609 might be a product of satanical magic and trickery, but this too was a scripturally endorsed sign of the times, a prelude to the Second Coming attested to in 2 Thessalonians ii. Even if the seven-headed baby with dogs' ears and toads' feet begotten by a French harlot was 'a deepe illusion of the Devill' designed to lead the unwary astray, one was still advised to take it as a hint to repent and amend.[51] 'By such tokens, sometimes wonderful, sometimes ridiculous, doth God at his pleasure foreshew future accidents', concluded Richard Carew.[52] Prudent circumspection should always be tempered by a lively piety. Sometimes the best course of action was a willing suspension of disbelief.

It was often the case that the natural causes of improbable portents were simply hidden from the shallow and feeble understanding of ordinary women and men. Though they might seem to defy the regular mechanisms set in motion at the Creation, the vast majority were not in fact 'miracles': they only seemed so in the eyes of the ignorant.[53] God was 'the Originall and principall worker of such wonders', stressed Bishop Nausea's *Treatise of blazing starres*, but he usually brought them about not against, but in accordance with, physical processes and laws.[54] Thus Thomas Fuller declared that a parhelion which had been observed before a battle in Herefordshire in 1461 was 'nothing else but the Image of the Sun represented in an equal, smooth, thick and watery cloud', though he still recorded it as one of that county's memorable wonders.[55] William Fulke's *Goodly gallerye* (1563) also set out to reveal the natural causes of a wide range of ostensibly supernatural events, always taking care not to push the Almighty out of the cosmic picture completely. In a section concerning 'monstrous or prodigious rayne', he went to extraordinary lengths to account for the fall of a full-grown calf from the sky, without ever suggesting that it was too implausible to have happened at all.[56] As Stuart Clark has demonstrated so masterfully in his *Thinking with Demons*, the difficulty of assessing the precise character and origin of puzzling phenomena was compounded by the fact that the boundaries between the natural and non-natural, divine and demonic, real and illusory, were themselves highly unstable, porous, and fluid.[57] Clergy and laity alike were obliged to remain open-minded.

Protestant ministers, then, continued to acknowledge that prodigies of all kinds could be a medium for conveying messages from heaven. But they were anxious to restrain the popular impulse to derive specific, deterministic predictions from

---

[51] 2 Thess. ii. 9–11. The dragons fighting above Ghent were reported in a lost pamphlet published in Feb. 1609, though the incident in question had occurred in 1579: *SR* iii. 401. For the seven-headed baby, Batman, *Doome*, 407–8.

[52] Carew, *Survey of Cornwall*, 196.

[53] Brinckmair, *Warnings of Germany*, sig. *4ᵛ.

[54] Nausea, *Treatise of blazing starres*, sigs. B3ᵛ–4ʳ.

[55] Fuller, *Worthies*, 2nd pagination, 34.

[56] Fulke, *Most pleasant prospect* (1st pub. as *A goodly gallerye*), fos. 51ᵛ–52ᵛ.

[57] Clark, *Thinking with Demons*, esp. 153–5, 161–78, 262–6, 279.

such occurrences. Christians should exercise a self-denying ordinance, said Francis Shakelton, never presuming to probe too 'curiously into the secretes of almightie God'.[58] It was unwarrantable to undertake 'to write too broad and busie Comments on any such Textes as these', declared an anonymous pamphleteer in 1628; 'Let us not be so foolish, as turne Almanacke-makers, and to Prognosticate, Prophesie, Foredoome, or Fore-tell, what shall happen . . . to our owne Kingdome, or any other . . . for such giddy-brayn'd Medlers, shoote their arrowes beyond the Moone.'[59] Celestial and terrestrial aberrations were the Lord's riddles and conundrums, His providence being 'a perfect maze or Labyrinth' far beyond human comprehension.[60]

Preachers like William Perkins, George Gifford, and Bishop Gervase Babington of Worcester were also eager to eliminate 'superstitious' observation of mundane and purely casual events. It was 'fond', 'vain', and 'foolish' to suppose that a hare crossing one's path betokened bad luck and divination based on the examination of the entrails of beasts and the flight path of fowls was equivalent to 'wicked and damnable' wizardry. Some rural folklore regarding the weather was 'lawfull wisdome' but, according to Sir Thomas Browne, most 'auguriall conceptions' of this type were 'vulgar' and 'heathenish' errors. Denounced as diabolical 'devises' and 'abominations', they carried with them an inherent danger of idolatry.[61] Hence the frenzy with which puritan zealots chopped down the famous Glastonbury hawthorn tree, which flowered every Christmas, in the course of the Civil Wars.[62] Genuine communications from the Lord were not to be confused with the lamentable side effects of 'popish' credulity.

How far late sixteenth- and seventeenth-century congregations heeded these caveats is unclear, but it is important to note that Protestant ideology was sufficiently ambiguous about prodigies to enable pre-Reformation beliefs about them to persist. The technical distinctions emphasized by learned ministers may well have been quietly edited out or ignored by their parishioners. Even the godly themselves regularly succumbed to the temptation to read God's intentions inscribed in the physical environment and to use nature as a prescriptive guide to action and an aid in decision-making. It was a painful bite by a hornet which persuaded the Ipswich tailor John Dane to cease playing truant from church and a rumble of thunder which deterred him from indulging in a night of rowdy

---

[58] Shakelton, *Blazyng starre*, sig. B1ᵛ.

[59] *Looke up and see wonders*, 17.

[60] Brinckmair, *Warnings of Germany*, sig. **2ʳ, cf. sig. *4ʳ.

[61] See Perkins, *Damned art of witchcraft*, 66–73; Gifford, *Dialogue*, sig. F4ᵛ; Gervase Babington, *The workes* . . . (1615), bk. I, pp. 494–5; Scot, *Discoverie of witchcraft*, bk. XI, chs. 13–20; Howard, *Defensative*, sigs. T2ᵛ, Ff3ʳ⁻ᵛ. Thomas Browne, *Pseudodoxia epidemica: or, enquiries into very many received tenets and commonly presumed truths* (1646), 264–5. On the development of the concept of 'casual' events, see Todd, 'Providence, Chance and the New Science', esp. 705–8.

[62] John Aubrey, *Three Prose Works*, ed. John Buchanan-Brown (Fontwell, Sussex, 1972), 330. Thomas Fuller was 'loath' to specify the position of an oak tree in the New Forest which reputedly grew green leaves on Christmas day lest 'some ignorant zealot . . . under the notion of superstition . . . make Timber of this Oake': *Worthies*, 2nd pagination, 3.

dancing.[63] And when the puritan John Bastwick was banished to the Isles of Scilly in 1637 William Prynne reported that 'thousands of Robin Redbreasts' had assembled to greet this servant of the lord, 'none of which birds were ever seene in those Islands before'.[64] As Barbara Donagan has observed, 'the transition from superstitious signs to divine providences could be tricky'.[65] In practice there was probably far less of a gulf between Calvinist providentialism and the oracular, magical culture of rural England than many curates and vicars were prepared to concede. Loosely overlaid with a novel doctrinal matrix, many elements of the latter were allowed to linger on.

Furthermore, some popular methods of forecasting the future appear to have complemented rather than contradicted the more biblically orthodox brands of prophecy of which the hotter sort of Protestants unequivocally approved. Calvinists may have vociferously denounced the dubious fortune-telling techniques employed by 'judicial' astrologers, but they looked more kindly upon its less pretentious sister art, 'natural astrology' or astronomy. By acknowledging that the stars were simply the Lord's heralds and lieutenants, one could go about scrutinizing celestial bodies and heavenly movements in a manner strikingly similar to that which characterized proscribed branches of the science.[66] The dividing line between divinatory practices outlawed by the clergy and officially sanctioned strategies for interpreting omens and portents could thus be very permeable indeed. As Richard Godbeer has remarked, despite its utmost efforts, Protestantism failed to eliminate 'the spirit of promiscuity that suffused English supernaturalism'.[67]

The next three sections consider in more detail the resulting tension and interplay between Protestant theology and the pre-existing cultures of divination it sought to uproot and replace. It draws attention to the way in which preachers, pamphleteers, and eye- and earwitnesses consciously and unconsciously transformed unusual happenings into marvels by assimilating them with older models, prototypes, and motifs. They adapted ancient cultural patterns to serve as templates for the interpretation of current events, simultaneously throwing their own preoccupations into sharp and vivid relief.

---

[63] Dane, 'Narrative', 151. See also Michael Winship, 'Encountering Providence in the Seventeenth Century: The Experiences of a Yeoman and a Minister', *Essex Institute Historical Collections*, 126 (1990), esp. 33–6.

[64] [William Prynne], *A new discovery of the prelates tyranny* (1641), sig. *3ᵛ (between pp. 90 and 91).

[65] Donagan, 'Godly Choice', 319. Cf ead., 'Providence, Chance and Explanation', 397–8.

[66] See Godbeer, *Devil's Dominion*, ch. 4, esp. 126–7; Raymond Gillespie, 'The Religion of Irish Protestants: A View from the Laity, 1580–1700', in Alan Ford, James McGuire, and Kenneth Milne (eds.), *As by Law Established: The Church of Ireland since the Reformation* (Dublin, 1995), 95–6. Lutheranism seems to have been even more accommodating towards astrology. See Stefano Caroti, 'Melanchthon's Astrology', in Paola Zambelli (ed.), *'Astrologi hallucinati': Stars and the End of the World in Luther's Time* (Berlin, 1986), 109–21; Barnes, *Prophecy and Gnosis*, ch. 4; Sachiko Kusukawa, *The Transformation of Natural Philosophy: The Case of Philip Melanchthon* (Cambridge, 1995), ch. 4.

[67] Godbeer, *Devil's Dominion*, 53.

STRAUNGE SIGHTES

'Report in such distractions as these, hath a thousand eyes, and sees more than it can understand; and as many tongues, which being once set a going, they speake any thing'.[68] These were the words of an unknown journalist, reflecting upon the process by which 'strange newes' in early modern England was magnified, altered, and remade as it passed from one avid reader and inquisitive listener to the next. As Simonds D'Ewes observed in 1622, it grew 'with the cameleon to varye everye day into a new shape'.[69]

In no case can we detect the distorting effects of the bush telegraph so clearly at work as that of preternatural apparitions, voices, and sounds. In the Elizabethan and early Stuart period there was no shortage of sightings of glittering swords and troops of horses, angels wielding dangerous weapons, and phantom armies clashing in the heavens. In mid-1580, for example, 'worthy gentlemen' living in rural Somerset witnessed two fierce encounters between contingents of men robed in black mourning clothes, followed by a third skirmish involving several dozen figures in armour and harness.[70] At Bodmin and Fowey a castle flying flags and streamers and a galleon in full sail, together with a flotilla of smaller vessels, were said to have appeared out of the mist.[71] Inhabitants of the Cumbrian town of Cockermouth were terrified by a major battle in the northern sky two nights before Christmas 1598, in which regiments of soldiers marched upon their enemies from a river of blood, escorted by a 'great navie of shipps of hudge bignes'.[72] Sixteen or eighteen 'persons of credit' observed battalions of infantry and cavalry gathering for attack on a Welsh mountain near Chester in November 1602, which, upon further investigation, 'sodainly vanisht'.[73] Contemporaries also seem to have had a singular capacity for hearing muskets, guns, and cannons discharging in the air, and the slow, steady beat of the military drum commanding advance or retreat. Rumours about ominous noises circulated in the West Riding of Yorkshire in August 1618, Plymouth in January 1622, and Lincolnshire in February 1627.[74] Galloping steeds were heard in the vicinity of Stonehenge in the autumn of 1638, but nothing materialized except 'an empty coyche without any horses drawinge yt, which wente

---

[68] *Looke up and see wonders*, 16.

[69] D'Ewes, *Diary*, ed. Bourcier, 104.

[70] This incident is noted in Stow, *Chronicles*, 1211; Batman, *Doome*, 411; Shrewsbury School, MS Mus X. 31, fo. 135ᵛ; Robert Persons, 'Life of Edmund Campion', Stonyhurst College, MS Grene P, printed in Philip Caraman (ed.), *The Other Face: Catholic Life under Elizabeth I* (1960), 112. The source was a lost pamphlet by Thomas Churchyard entitled *Wonders in Wiltshire, and Somersetshire*.

[71] Batman, *Doome*, 409–10; Caraman (ed.), *Other Face*, 111; Stow, *Chronicles*, 1211.

[72] Shrewsbury School, MS Mus X. 31, fo. 216ʳ⁻ᵛ.

[73] Chamberlain, *Letters*, ed. McClure, i. 169; National Library of Wales, Aberystwyth, Plas Nantglyn MS 1, cited in G. Dyfnallt Owen, *Elizabethan Wales: The Social Scene* (Cardiff, 1962), 64–5.

[74] BL Add. MS 38599, fo. 49ᵛ; Yonge, *Diary*, ed. Roberts, 48–9; BL Harleian MSS 389, fo. 146ʳ; 390, fo. 205ᵛ.

of it self'.[75] In January of the same year 'strange and extraordinary coruscations' resembling brigades of marching pikemen seen in the air over Grimsby gave the antiquary Gervase Holles and several other local gentlemen pause for thought, notwithstanding the fact that they could discern a clear 'Naturall Cause'.[76] Aerial battles multiplied rapidly prior to and following the outbreak of fighting in Germany in 1618 and in England in 1642.[77]

Accounts of even more extravagant spectacles flooded in from foreign parts. The 'lycknes' of Atlas bearing the heavy burden of the 'rownde world' upon his weary shoulders and crying '*Vigilate & orate*, Watche and Praye', was seen at Montpellier in Languedoc in 1573.[78] Winged seraphs brandishing naked blades and flaming rods intoned 'woe, woe' above cities besieged by ghostly combatants in Poland, Bohemia, Silesia, and Picardy on four separate occasions during the following two decades.[79] A similar vision in Normandy in 1598 incorporated four black horsemen, a bloody cross, and a wagon which exploded in a burning cloud.[80] A series of ominous tokens observed by inhabitants of the German city of Rosenberg around 1593 included two rainbows joined back to back, a curved sword, and a huge bleeding crucifix; and charging cavalry appeared against the backdrop of a scarlet sun and other strange symbols in Croatia in June of 1605 (Plate 19).[81]

Some such news reports were dismissed as papistical figments and 'phantasies'. Joseph Hall declared sternly that the tale of an angel which had alighted on an altar wielding a sabre and threatening 'instant destruction' to England in the year 1601 was a pretended vision to which no sober Protestant should yield a shred of credit.[82] The anonymous editor of *Good newes to Christendome* (1620) was no less convinced that an apparition of a woman in white thwarting the combined might

---

[75] BL Add. MS 35331, fo. 72[v].

[76] BL Lansdowne MS 207C, fos. 192[v]–193[v].

[77] Numerous Continental examples can be found in Brinckmair, *Warnings of Germany*, which was summarized in a ballad entitled *A lamentable list, of certaine hidious, frightfull, and prodigious signes* ([1638]). For England, see e.g. *A signe from heaven: or, a fearefull and terrible noise heard in the ayre at Alborow in the county of Suffolke . . . Wherein was heard the beating of drums, the discharging of muskets, and great ordnance* (1642).

[78] This lost pamphlet, entitled *A trew & a perfecte discourse of woonderfull & straunge myracle & sygnes which appreyd in France the 5 of May 1573, beinge . . . a certen syghne & togen, that the day of judgement draweth nye*, is transcribed in BL Cotton MS Vespasian A. XXV, fos. 41[r]–42[v]. For a German broadsheet on this subject, see Strauss (ed.), *German Single-Leaf Woodcut*, i. 412.

[79] Batman, *Doome*, 400, 408–9; Shrewsbury School, MS Mus X. 31, fos. 117[r], 171[v], 193[r–v]. A lost pamphlet with the title *A booke of newes of twoo angels that came before the cytie of Droppa in S[i]lesia* was licensed on 22 Nov. 1593: *SR* ii. 640.

[80] *True newes from [Mecare:] and also out of Worcestershire*, sig. A2[r–v].

[81] *Strange signes seene in the aire, strange monsters behelde on the land, and wonderfull prodigies both by land and sea, over, in, and about the citie of Rosenberge* (1594); *Strange fearfull & true newes, which hapned at Carlstadt, in the kingdome of Croatia*, trans. E. Gresham ([1606]). Other pamphlets about armies, bloody swords, and crosses in foreign skies include *Abstene fra sin or ze sal fal under, for the day of the Lord is befoir the dur.* ([Edinburgh, 1579?]); *The miserable estate of the citie of Paris at this present, with a true report of sundrie straunge visions, lately seene in the ayre upon the coast of Britanie* (1590).

[82] Joseph Hall, *The great mysterie of godliness* (1652), 159.

PLATE 19 *Strange fearful & true newes, which hapned at Carlstadt . . . Declaring how the sunne did shine like bloude nine dayes together, and how two armies were seene in the ayre*, trans. E. Gresham (London, [1606]), title-page. By permission of the British Library. Shelfmark: C. 143. a. 19.

of the Turks, Persians, Arabians, and Moors had been forged in the 'shop of invention'; and Joseph Mede gave many poorly documented prodigy stories shipped in from Continental Europe very short shrift indeed. 'Esteeme it no further then it deserves', he scribbled in a note to Sir Martin Stutevile enclosing a full transcription of a lost pamphlet about the appearance of three spectres in East Friesland in 1622, the first brilliantly illuminated, the second an emaciated skeleton, and the third a soldier dripping in gore, each uttering a macabre message of imminent devastation and slaughter.[83] But it would be a mistake to overstate the wariness with which learned Protestants approached mysterious apparitions. Stephen Batman had no hesitation in including in his *Doome warning all men to the judgemente* an account of a vision of Christ seated on an arch above Fribourg in 1553.[84] The appearance of double suns and an inverted rainbow perturbed a reverend divine in Sussex in 1636, who noted a similar occurrence recorded in Foxe's *Actes and monumentes* under the year 1554 ('before religion was subverted in this kingdome') and passed on news of this worrying coincidence to a 'fellow laborer in the Lords Wyneyard'.[85] And the Zurich minister Ludwig Lavater devoted a substantial chapter of his treatise *Of ghostes and spirites* to sinister sights of this type.[86] Clearly there was still room for them within the Reformed universe.

However we choose to explain away such strange phenomena, as thunderclaps or sunspots, peculiar cloud formations, or the aurora borealis, they open up a window into the collective subconscious. There are unresolved problems in extending psychoanalytical techniques from individuals to groups, but, like ghosts, nightmares, and dreams, apparitions betray hints about the latent and unarticulated anxieties of the age in which they are seen.[87] Visions of militant hordes surely reflect widespread expectations that England would soon have to fight off hostile invaders, become sucked into the horrific conflicts which had already engulfed the Continent, or, worst of all, find herself embroiled in a gruesome civil war. We can safely suggest that those who saw celestial bodies, muddy streams, stagnant ponds, and even shellfish turn the colour of blood shared the same awful apprehensions.[88] While it is not always easy to unravel the actual reactions of onlookers from the poetic embellishments added by proto-Grub Street hacks, some such eerie audiovisual experiences seem to have been interpreted as forerunners of Armageddon and 'the ennd of all fleashe'.[89] Men, women, and children who beheld armies fighting above villages in the Vale of the White Horse one spring day in 1628, accompanied by the hissing of bullets and the rumbling of heavy artillery, apparently 'fell on their knees, and not onely thought, but sayd, that verily the day of Judgement was come' (Plate 20).[90]

Equally illuminating is an iconographical approach. As both Keith Thomas and Ottavia Niccoli have noted, hallucinations afford an incomparable opportunity to

[83] Cortano, *Good newes to Christendome*, sig. A3ʳ, pp. 13–15; BL Harleian MS 389, fos. 282ʳ–285ᵛ, 292ʳ.

[84] Batman, *Doome*, 369.

[85] BL Sloane MS 648, fos. 61ʳ–62ʳ.

[86] Lewes [Ludwig] Lavater, *Of ghostes and spirites walking by nyght, and of strange noyses, crackes, and sundry forewarnynges*, trans. R. H. (1572), pt. I, ch. 17.

[87] See Jacques Le Goff, 'Dreams in the Culture and Collective Psychology of the Medieval West', in his *Time, Work, and Culture in the Middle Ages*, trans. Arthur Goldhammer (Chicago, 1980), 201–4.

[88] For only a handful of examples, see Day, *Wonderfull straunge sightes*, sig. 2ʳ⁻ᵛ; BL Add. MS 35331, fo. 72ʳ.

[89] Shrewsbury School, MS Mus X. 31, fo. 216ᵛ.

[90] *Looke up and see wonders*, 15–16.

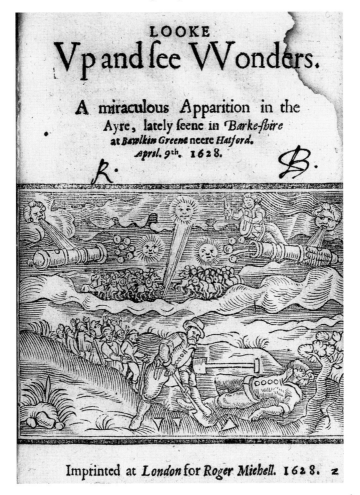

PLATE 20 *Looke up and see wonders. A miraculous apparition in the ayre, lately seene in Barke-shire at Bawklin Greene neere Hatford April. 9th. 1628* (London, 1628), title-page. By permission of the Bodleian Library, University of Oxford. Shelfmark: 4 °C 16 Art. Bs (6).

study the inherited stereotypes by which sensory perception in any given era is governed. Imagined acoustic effects are clearly no less historically and culturally conditioned.[91] Spectral armies, for instance, have antecedents in medieval and classical literature, as well as in Norse and Germanic mythology—not least the cluster of

---

[91] Thomas, *Religion and the Decline of Magic*, 104; Ottavia Niccoli, *Prophecy and People in Renaissance Italy*, trans. Lydia G. Cochrane (Princeton, 1990), 62 and ch. 3 *passim*.

legends surrounding the 'Wild Hunt' or 'Furious Horde', the saga of dead warriors who annually return to their former battlefields led by Odin, the deity of war.[92] The apparition of a wild man near Frankfurt in 1600 is another case which highlights how folklore helped eyewitnesses digest and control frightening experiences.[93] And visions of supernatural beings provide us with a rare glimpse of what puritans like William Perkins called the 'idols of the mind': the concrete images of other-worldly personages which sixteenth- and seventeenth-century people continued to visualize long after murals on church walls were whitewashed and acres of stained glass were destroyed.[94] As William Fulke noted, the common people referred to beams and streams of light appearing through a cloud as 'the descending of the holy Ghost, or our Ladies Assumption, because these things are painted after such a sort'.[95] Heavenly intermediaries and arms descending from the clouds flourishing switches, swords, and spears likewise have many cousins and counterparts in late medieval sermon exempla and stories linked with the lives of the saints.[96] In the woodcuts hastily plastered onto the title-pages of news pamphlets, as well as the vivid descriptions inside, the suspect pictorial heritage of the Catholic past found a kind of sanctuary and asylum. Some printers iconoclastically altered pre-Reformation blocks in line with Calvinist dictates (Plate 21), but others blatantly ignored the informal taboo on representations of the deity. Indeed, given the frequency with which accounts of aerial battles and angry spectres were imported from abroad and the parallel sub-genres which burgeoned in pre-Tridentine Italy, Lutheran Germany, and Valois France, it is scarcely astonishing that much providential journalism is theologically ambidextrous and opaque.[97] And yet these stories consistently crept into the homiletic discourse of zealously Protestant clerics.

BLACK DOGS AND OUGLIE FIENDS

Similar remarks might be made about the related phenomenon of diabolical apparitions. Tales of the devil trespassing into private houses and ecclesiastical buildings

---

[92] Rudolf Simek, *Dictionary of Northern Mythology*, trans. Angela Hall (Woodbridge, 1993), 240–6, 372–3. See also Niccoli, *Prophecy and People*, 66–71; ead., 'The Kings of the Dead on the Battlefield of Agnadello', in Edward Muir and Guido Ruggiero (eds.), *Microhistory and the Lost Peoples of Europe: Selections from Quaderni Storici* (Baltimore, 1981), 71–100. For another manifestation of the 'Furious Horde', and its diabolization, see Carlo Ginzburg, *The Night Battles: Witchcraft and Agrarian Cults in the Sixteenth and Seventeenth Centuries*, trans. John and Anne Tedeschi (1983), esp. ch. 2.

[93] *A most straunge and wounderfull accident, happened at Weersburch by Franckford* (1600), 4–5. On the Wild Man as an element of pre-Reformation culture and its manipulation by Lutheran propagandists, see Scribner, *For the Sake of Simple Folk*, 62, 135–6, 163, 169, 233–4, 241.

[94] William Perkins, *A warning against the idolatrie of the last times and an instruction touching religious or divine worship* (1601), repr. in *Workes*, i. 671. See also Aston, *England's Iconoclasts*, I. 452–65.

[95] Fulke, *Most pleasant prospect*, fo. 40[r–v].

[96] See e.g. the story of a vision of 'our Lord Ihesu holdyng thre speres yn his hond, redy forto schote to the world for vengeans . . .'. from the life of St Dominic recounted in *Mirk's Festial*, ed. Erbe, 73.

[97] On Italy, Niccoli, *Prophecy and People*, ch. 3; for Germany, many examples can be found in Strauss (ed.), *German Single-Leaf Woodcut*; on France, Jean-Pierre Seguin, 'Notes sur des feuilles d'information relatant des combats apparus dans le ciel (1575–1656)', *Arts et traditions populaires*, 7 (1959), 51–62, 256–70, and id., *Information en France avant le périodique*.

PLATE 21 *True newes from* [*Mecare:*] *and also out of Worcestershire* (London, [1598]), title-page woodcut. By permission of the Syndics of Cambridge University Library. Shelfmark: Syn. 7. 59. 84.

Modified pre-Reformation woodcut. Several 'idols in the frontispiece' have been removed, probably figures of God the Father, Christ, and the Virgin Mary.

ran rife. In May 1584, for instance, Satan manifested himself to concerned relatives and friends who had gathered around the sickbed of a delirious yeoman's wife at Ditcheat, Somerset, in the guise of a headless and tailless black bear. Lifting the prostrate lady, this horrible beast somersaulted her through three rooms and down a long flight of stairs, where it disappeared, exuding a sulphurous stink (Plate 22).[98] The poltergeist which haunted the home of Oxfordshire gentleman George Lee for four months in 1591–2 made himself known to the servants of the family in the form of a large coal-coloured dog.[99] A nearly identical sight had confronted 'diverse credible persons' in Herefordshire six years before: they were paralysed with fear when the dreadful creature proceeded to rip up whole trees by their roots.[100] And a succession of rural congregations seem to have encountered the Prince of Darkness during violent electrical storms, the wicked spirit sweeping through the nave at high speed. This occurred, for instance, at Eckington in

---

[98] *True and most dreadfull discourse of a woman possessed with the devill.* This pamphlet was updated by John Trundle and repub. in T. I., *Miracle, of miracles* in 1614.

[99] *A true discourse of such straunge and woonderfull accidents, as hapned in the house of M. George Lee of North-Aston, in the countie of Oxford* (1592).

[100] *Most rare & true report, of such great tempests . . . at a place called the Hay*, sig. A3[r].

A Miracle, of Miracles.

As fearefull as euer was feene or heard of in the memorie of M A N.

Which lately happened at *Dichet* in Sommerfetfhire , and fent by diuers credible witneffes to be publifhed in L O N D O N.

Alfo a Prophefie reuealed by a poore Countrey Maide, who being dead the firft of October laft, 1613. 24. houres , reuiued againe, and lay fiue *dayes weeping, and continued prophefying of ftrange euents to come, and fo died the 5. day following.*

Witneffed by M. *Nicholas Faber*, Parfon of the Towne, and diuers worthy Gentlemen of the fame countrey. 1613,

Withall, Lincolnefhire Teares. For a great deluge, in which fiue Villages were lamentably-drowned this prefent month.

At London printed for *Iohn Trundle*: and are to be fold at Chrift Church gate. 1614.

PLATE 22 T. I., *A miracle, of miracles. As fearefull as ever was seene or heard of in the memorie of man* (London, 1614), title-page. By permission of the British Library. Shelfmark: C. 39. d. 5. A pamphlet published by John Trundle containing an 'updated' version of *A true and most dreadfull discourse of a woman possessed with the devill . . . At Dichet in Sommersetshire* (London, [1584]).

Derbyshire in 1595 and at Great Chart in Kent in 1613, where the devil materialized 'a most ugly shape out of the ayer like unto a broad eyed bul'.[101] When the Father of Lies made personal visits to particular individuals he adopted the same corporeal forms. A Norfolk miller who consulted the astrological physician Richard Napier in 1603 told how the devil had appeared to him as a man dressed in black, transmuted himself into a black dog and bear, and then vanished away.[102]

[101] On Eckington, see the extract from Stonyhurst College, MS Grene F, printed in Caraman (ed.), *Other Face*, 283, and Henry Foley (ed.), *Records of the English Province of the Society of Jesus*, 7 vols. in 8 (1877–83), iii. 227–8; on Great Chart, *Wonders of this windie winter*, sig. C2ᵛ. For other examples, see Kittredge, *Witchcraft*, ch. 5.

[102] Bodleian Library, Oxford, MS Ashmole 207, fo. 59ᵛ, quoted in Sharpe, *Instruments of Darkness*, 75. See also MacDonald, *Mystical Bedlam*, 107–10, 200–4, 208–10; Lavater, *Of ghostes and spirites*, pt. II, ch. 17, pp. 167–71.

Again, close scrutiny of the imagery involved is highly revealing. All of it has roots in medieval demonology and reflects the eclectic assortment of Christian, rabbinical, pagan, and even Oriental symbols for Satan which had long been part of popular consciousness.[103] As Reginald Scot observed, 'ouglie' fiends with horns, fangs, forked tails, cloven feet, and fiery tongues were the 'bugs' with which early modern nursemaids terrified their recalcitrant charges into submission. Although he himself condemned belief in such spectres as 'wretched and cowardlie infidelitie',[104] the advent of Protestantism served on the whole to enhance awareness of diabolical interference in human affairs and reinforce pre-existing stereotypes.[105] So, for that matter, did cheap print and dramatic entertainment on the professional stage. When the youth Alexander Nyndge suffered fits and convulsions as a result of possession by a demon in 1573, spectators thought that he looked 'much like the picture of the Devill in a play, with an horrible roaring voyce, sounding Hell-hound'.[106] In whatever guise the devil appears—dragon, serpent, or lizard; furry wild mammal or dark shaggy dog—uncertainty about his status, as the Lord's executioner or the Tempter, is usually acute. In *Strange newes from Antwarpe* (1612), Lucifer sets fire to St Michael's priory, a notorious centre of 'papisticall' idolatry. Perched on the steeple, he drops a huge stone on top of the monks, before swooping down to lacerate the sumptuous altarpiece by Peter Paul Rubens with his savage talons.[107] This satanic iconoclast is unquestionably the agent of an implacably Calvinist God, but the demons who are the dramatis personae of such visions frequently break out of this deferential mould.[108]

This is particularly true when biblical representations are displaced by folkloric prototypes like the Black Hound or Dog. This phantom of Anglo-Saxon and Scandinavian ancestry was widely regarded as an augur of fatal disaster. Associated with prehistoric burial sites and graveyards, it was believed to inhabit the underworld, that mythical abode of the dead.[109]

---

[103] On the iconography of the devil, see Davies, *Reflections of Renaissance England*, 202–5. On medieval and early modern popular demonology, J. A. MacCulloch, *Medieval Faith and Fable* (1932), ch. 4; C. L'Estrange Ewen, *Witchcraft and Demonianism: A Concise Account from Sworn Depositions and Confessions obtained in the Courts of England and Wales* (1933), 48–54; Thomas, *Religion and the Decline of Magic*, 559–69.

[104] Scot, *Discoverie of witchcraft*, bk. VII, ch. 15.

[105] See Keith L. Roos, *The Devil in 16th Century German Literature: The Teufelsbücher* (Frankfurt, 1972).

[106] Edward Nyndge, *A true and fearefull vexation of one Alexander Nyndge: being most horribly tormented with the devill* (1615 edn.; 1st pub. [1573?]), sig. B1[r].

[107] *Strange newes from Antwarpe*, trans. I. F. (1612), esp. 4–8.

[108] See Ch. 2 above, pp. 85–6.

[109] See Theo Brown, 'The Black Dog', *Folklore*, 69 (1958), 175–92 and 'The Black Dog in English Folklore', in J. R. Porter and W. M. S. Russell (eds.), *Animals in Folklore* (Ipswich, 1978), 45–58. For black dog folktales, see Kevin Crossley-Holland, *Folk-Tales of the British Isles* (1985), 145–9; Barbara Allen Woods, *The Devil in Dog Form: A Partial Type-Index of Devil Legends* (Berkeley and Los Angeles, 1959), esp. chs. 3–4.

A further complicating factor is the affinity such spectres bear to the physical forms conventionally assumed by witches' familiars: it is often difficult to distinguish the devil from the subservient demons he placed at the disposal of those human beings whom he managed to seduce. The practice of employing maumets or imps was an idiosyncrasy of English sorcerers and these companion spirits frequently took on the semblance of common domestic pets. Elizabeth Sawyer of Edmonton, executed for murdering a neighbour by means of *maleficium* in 1621, for instance, enjoyed intimate relations three times each week with a black dog by the name of Tom.[110] As Clive Holmes and Jim Sharpe have suggested, this was an aspect of popular magical belief which Protestant demonology appears to have successfully assimilated by the early seventeenth century.[111] Diabolical apparitions highlight the extent to which Calvinist theology and traditional culture were able to mesh.

With hindsight it is easy to understand how a rare but perfectly natural occurrence could be transformed in the perception of disturbed observers into a frightening communal encounter with the archenemy of Christ in disguise. In the dimly lit interior of a consecrated building, globular lightning might well seem to be something altogether more sinister. It is instructive to compare accounts of the ingression of the devil into places of worship during tempests and hurricanes with descriptions of thunderstorms which struck parish churches in which no mention whatsoever is made of an uninvited fiend. When 'Sodayne darknes' descended during morning prayer at a chapel near Helston at Epiphany 1604 or 1605, heralding the entrance of a 'Bousterous and fyerye whyrlewind' which killed one member of the congregation and scorched several more, no one seems to have suggested this was the Father of Lies, though it was interpreted as an 'Embassage and Revelatyon' from heaven.[112] Nor did eyewitnesses of the fireballs which raced through the churches of Antony, in Cornwall, on Whitsunday 1640, and of Widecombe-in-the-Moor eighteen months before (Plate 23). In the latter example, it was only long afterwards that allusion was made to the appearance of the devil on horseback, by which time the calamity had become a well-known Devonshire legend.[113]

---

[110] Henry Goodcole, *The wonderfull discoverie of Elizabeth Sawyer a witch, late of Edmonton* (1621), esp. sig. C2ᵛ. The case inspired a play by William Rowley, Thomas Dekker, John Ford, *et al.*: *The witch of Edmonton: a known true story* (1658). For other examples, see L'Estrange Ewen, *Witchcraft and Demonianism*, 70–6.

[111] See Clive Holmes, 'Popular Culture? Witches, Magistrates, and Divines in Early Modern England', in Steven L. Kaplan (ed.), *Understanding Popular Culture: Europe from the Middle Ages to the Nineteenth Century* (Berlin, 1984), 97–9; Sharpe, *Instruments of Darkness*, 71–5; id., 'The Devil in East Anglia: The Matthew Hopkins Trials Reconsidered', in Jonathan Barry, Marianne Hester, and Gareth Roberts (eds.), *Witchcraft in Early Modern Europe* (Cambridge, 1996), 244–50.

[112] *The Trevelyan Letters to 1840*, ed. Mary Siraut, Somerset Record Soc. 80 (Taunton, 1990), 72.

[113] *Voyce of the Lord in the temple*; *True relation of those sad and lamentable accidents, which happened in . . . Withycombe*; and *A second and most exact relation of those sad and lamentable accidents*. For the legend of the devil on horseback, see 'An Auld Wife's Story', in Robert Dymond, *'Things New and Old' concerning the Parish of Widecombe-in-the-Moor and its Neighbourhood* (Torquay, 1876), 68–70, 88–109.

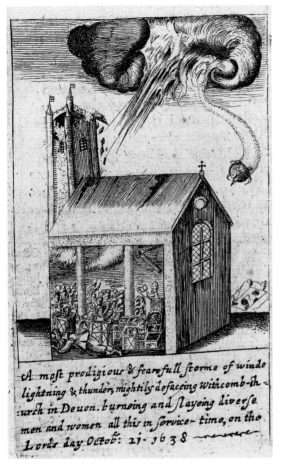

PLATE 23 John Vicars, *Prodigies & apparitions or Englands warning pieces* (London, [1642-3]), 30. By permission of the British Library. Shelfmark: C. 27. a. 15.
A depiction of the fireball which swept through the parish church of Widecome-in-the Moor in 1638.

How, why, and by whom were such incidents transfigured into myths? Under what circumstances were people predisposed to perceive the personification of all wickedness in their midst—what one journalist termed that 'most rare and terrible stratagem and perfect paterne of our impietie'?[114] Too often we can only speculate about the role parochial friction and turmoil played in creating a suitably receptive frame of mind. It may not be irrelevant that the parishioners of Great Chart were thought to have 'an evil custome among them' of 'conferring & talking of worldly affaiers' in the aisles rather than attending to the sermon, behaving as if they were in a fair or market instead of a church, 'to the great griefe' of

The incident was fictionalized in R. D. Blackmore's *Christowell: A Dartmoor Tale*, 3 vols. (1882), vol. iii, chs. 17–18.

[114] *Most rare & true report, of such great tempests . . . at a place called the Hay*, sig. A3ʳ.

the godly.[115] Nor that the evensong congregation at Wells Cathedral which observed 'a dark and unproportionable thing of the bigness of a football' burst in through the west window one December day in 1596 was listening to a lecture concerning spirits and their properties, which evidently involved a stern rebuke of certain local disorders. Upon recovering their senses, many were said to have found themselves 'pryvely' marked with 'bloudy signes and shewes of Gods wrath' resembling suns, moons, crosses, and stars.[116] A tempest at Mansfield in Nottinghamshire, in which lightning hit the steeple and the church was filled with 'a pestilent perfume' of brimstone, was blamed on the vicar, whose 'evil life' was alleged to be 'the cause of that evil sent'.[117]

In the case of the 'strange and terrible wunder' of the Black Dog of Bungay in Suffolk, however, the process can be traced with greater precision. On Sunday 4 August 1577, a violent storm hit St Mary's Church, 'as never was sene the lyke' and 'never to be forgotten'. Flashes of lightning struck two men sitting in the belfry stone dead, seriously injured another, and caused major structural damage to the tower and clock. The parish records contain no reference to any mysterious beast; nor does the brief entry about the accident in Holinshed's chronicle.[118] Yet a black dog features prominently in a providential news pamphlet about the catastrophe prepared by the prolific translator and author Abraham Fleming (Plate 24). According to this account, a 'moste horrible similitude and likenesse' of the devil 'moved such admiration in the mindes of the assemblie, that they thought doomes day was already come'. They watched in shock as it wrung the necks of two of their neighbours 'clene backward' and gave a third 'such a gripe on the back' that he shrivelled like 'a peece of leather scorched in a hot fire' or a purse 'drawen togither with a string'. The truth of this report was not merely confirmed 'by the mouthes of them that were eye witnesses of the same', but by the scratches of Satan's claws and nails visible on the masonry and north porch door. Fleming apparently derived his version of the story from a manuscript prepared by leading parishioners, appropriating it as a paradigm of the divine indignation kindled by sin.[119]

But the tale also has an intriguing context and subtext. Bungay was a community fractured by deep religious divisions and the church building itself seems to have been the main arena and focus of factional dispute. Only three months previously the conservative vicar Christopher Smythe and his supporters had clashed

---

[115] *Wonders of this windie winter*, sig. C2^v.

[116] Stow, *Annales*, 1249; Shrewsbury School, MS Mus X. 31, fo. 211^r; Churchyard, *Wonders of the ayre*, sig. C2^v.

[117] Foley (ed.), *Records of the English Province*, iii. 228.

[118] The quotation is from a marginal note in St Mary's churchwardens' accounts: Suffolk RO, Lowestoft, 116/E1/1. Raphael Holinshed, *The first and second volumes of chronicles*, 3 vols. (1587), iii. 1270–1. All the relevant documents are printed in Christopher Reeve, *A Straunge and Terrible Wunder: The Story of the Black Dog of Bungay* (Bungay, 1988), 25–6.

[119] Fleming, *Straunge, and terrible wunder*, quotations at sigs. A5^{r-v}, A6^r, A7^r.

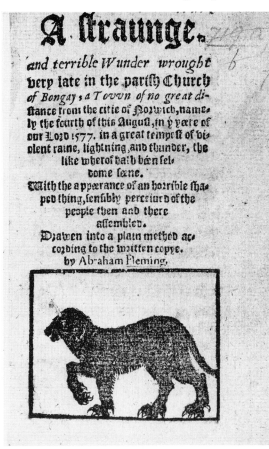

A ſtraunge.

and terrible VVunder wrought
very late in the pariſh Church
of Bongay, a Tovvn of no great di-
ſtance from the citie of Norwich, namely the fourth of this Auguſt, in ẏ yeare of
our Lord 1577. in a great tempeſt of violent raine, lightning, and thunder, the
like whereof hath been ſel-
dome ſeene.
With the appearance of an horrible ſha-
ped thing, ſenſibly perceiued of the
people then and there
aſſembled.
Drawen into a plain method according to the written coppe.
by Abraham Fleming.

PLATE 24 Abraham
Fleming, *A straunge, and
terrible wunder wrought
very late in the parish
church of Bongay*
(London, [1577]), title-
page. By permission of
the British Library.
Shelfmark: C. 27. a. 4.

with the hot Protestants of the parish over the question of removing 'popish' furnishings and trappings. Tired of tarrying for the magistrate, the two church reeves had taken matters into their own hands and defaced an elaborately decorated rood-screen, which they considered too graphic a reminder of Roman Catholic idolatry. This piece of godly vandalism resulted in the immediate ejection of the insubordinate pair from office and their replacement by candidates from the enemy camp—in short, an anti-puritan coup.[120] In this atmosphere of mutual hostility and distrust, is it surprising that some worshippers feared that their dissension had

---

[120] Reeve, *Straunge and Terrible Wunder*, 14–16, and ch. 1 *passim*. In the parish register, Thomas Edwards, the local shoemaker, described the ill-fated screen as 'very comlyn & decentlyn made, accord-ing to the queen her maiesties Laws', but a marginal note in another hand declares 'Thom. Edwards here Lye for it was full of Immagery not defaced'.

opened the way for the Adversary to intrude or prompted God to send the devil
to punish a parochial hierarchy which obstinately resisted further reform?
Nebulous impressions sharpened by panic, antagonism, and guilt inevitably crys-
tallized in accordance with regional folklore—the East Anglian variation of a pan-
European archetype, Black Shuck.[121] Still remembered in the village, the incident
was readily integrated into a time-honoured oral tradition, which print, in tandem
with Protestantism, helped to preserve. It highlights how a progressive message
could be superimposed upon a cultural mode of much greater antiquity, and suggests ways in which the Reformation rejuvenated and sustained older patterns of
thought by clothing them in a new ideological coat.

MONSTEROUS CHYLDREN AND BEASTS

Monstrous creatures and human misbirths are another class of prodigies in which
Protestant attitudes to portents interacted dialectically with miscellaneous convictions of considerable vintage.[122] Early modern England was saturated with reports
of Siamese twins, misshapen infants, piglets, goslings, calves, and whales washed
up from the deep to die on the beach. The assumption that such aberrations of
nature were metaphysical signs was common to both blackletter ballads and pamphlets and the erudite teratological writings of physicians, cosmographers, and
divines. Monsters were objects of the fascination and dread of learned clergymen
no less than the rural crowds who journeyed to obscure locations to see these
strange sights. Ralph Josselin, vicar of Earls Colne, recorded in his diary of divine
providences the disturbing news of a curious set of triplets born near Colchester
in May 1646—a child, a serpent, and a toad which lapped. The country people
who 'came in great aboundance' to gaze upon a leviathan stranded in shallow
waters at the mouth of the Humber River in 1595 knew not 'what to saye or judge
therof, but onely resolveth them selves that it was sent of God for some great
purpose'.[123]

   The idea that morality and embryology interlocked could nevertheless lead
interpreters in several different directions. According to many commentators,
grotesquely deformed babies and animals were not 'simple or meere mistakings in
God as if like a bungler in some common trade, he were not his Crafts-master' and
had badly botched the job.[124] These unsightly spectacles unveiled His glory no less

---

[121] Ibid. ch. 6; Brown, 'Black Dog'. A similar synthesis of folklore and topical concerns is
evident in songs and stories concerning the appearance of dragons and serpents. See David Hey,
'The Dragon of Wantley: Rural Popular Culture and Local Legend', *Rural History*, 4 (1993), 23–40.
There may be a similar tale behind John Trundle's infamous pamphlet about the Sussex serpent,
True and wonderfull. See Jacqueline Simpson, *British Dragons* (1980), 48, 113–14; ead., 'Local Legend',
25–35.
[122] On monstrous births, see Park and Daston, 'Unnatural Conceptions'; Niccoli, *Prophecy and
People*, chs. 2, 5; Scribner, *For the Sake of Simple Folk*, 127–36; Wilson, *Signs and Wonders*.
[123] Josselin, *Diary*, ed. Macfarlane, 60; *A most certaine report of a monster borne at Oteringham in
Holdernesse . . . Also of a most strange and huge fish, which was driven on the sand at Outhorn*, sig. B1ᵛ.
[124] *Gods handy-worke in wonders*, sig. A3ʳ.

clearly than perfect human specimens. They were 'larum-bels sent from our gentle redeemer', 'lesons & scholynges for us all', a physiological expression of the degeneracy of contemporary ethics.[125] God sometimes encoded a particular message in the contorted limbs and tumorous growths of these unfortunate infants, projecting onto their diminutive bodies a silhouette of the sins which had infested the body politic.[126] In striving to decipher the significance of their distorted anatomical features Elizabethan and early Stuart moralists externalized their own prejudices and obsessions.

Fleshy protuberances and flaps often took on the appearance of the fashionable accessories and garments against which so many preachers directed their fulminations about vanity and sumptuary excess. As one chronicler observed, it was 'as if nature would upbraide our pride in artificiall braverie, by producing monsters in the same attires'.[127] The pleated folds of skin around the neck of a baby girl delivered in the parish of Mickleham, Surrey, in the summer of 1566 were construed as a divine remonstrance against starched ruffs (Plate 25); a boy born with long curly locks in Southhampton in 1602 led to equally vehement attacks on this latest barber shop fad.[128] Similar concerns induced all who saw pictures of seven unusual wildfowl captured in Lincolnshire in 1586 to compare their neck feathers and quills with the elaborate collars and frizzled hairstyles flaunted by 'gallant dames' and fops—revealing, incidentally, that by the late sixteenth century ruffs were already something of a rarity.[129] Few could resist the temptation to read deeper meaning into two infants joined at the breastbone and belly whose tiny arms clasped in embrace—this was undoubtedly an exhortation against the decline of Christian charity and the decay of brotherly love.[130] Whenever a monstrous pig was farrowed trite remarks were made about filthy and swinish manners (Plate 26)[131] and babies whose heads, hands, or feet vaguely resembled those of a rat, mole, crab, or some other bird, reptile, crustacean, or beast also lent themselves

---

[125] *Strange newes out of Kent*, sig. B4ᵛ; *The true discription of two monsterous chyldren borne at Herne in Kent . . .* ([1565]).

[126] For statements to this effect, see *The true reporte of the forme and shape of a monstrous childe, borne at Muche Horkesleye* ([1562]); John Barker, *The true description of a monsterous chylde, borne in the Ile of Wight* ([1564]).

[127] John Hayward, *Annals of the First Four Years of the Reign of Queen Elizabeth*, ed. John Bruce, CS, 1st ser. 7 (1840), 107. He was commenting on the baby described in John D., *A discription of a monstrous chylde, borne at Chychester in Sussex* (1562), around whose neck grew a collar of flesh and skin 'pleighted and foulded like a double ruffe'.

[128] H. B., *The true discripcion of a childe with ruffes borne in the parish of Micheham, in the countie of Surrey* (1566); *A most strange and trew ballad of a monst[r]ous child borne in Southampton*, printed in Clark (ed.), *Shirburn Ballads*, 293–6.

[129] *A most wonderfull, and true report, the like never hearde of before, of diverse unknowne foules . . . latelie taken at Crowley in the countie of Lyncolne. 1586* ([1586]). For a German version, see Strauss (ed.), *German Single-Leaf Woodcut*, i. 139.

[130] *True discription of two monsterous chyldren borne at Herne in Kent*; B[edford], *True and certaine relation of a strange-birth*, 20–1.

[131] *The description of a monstrous pig, the which was farrowed at Hamsted besyde London* ([1562]); W[illiam] F[ulwood], *The shape of .ii. monsters* ([1562]); I. P., *A mervaylous straunge deformed swyne* ([1570?]); *This horryble monster is cast of a sowe in Eestlande in Pruse* ([Germany, 1531]).

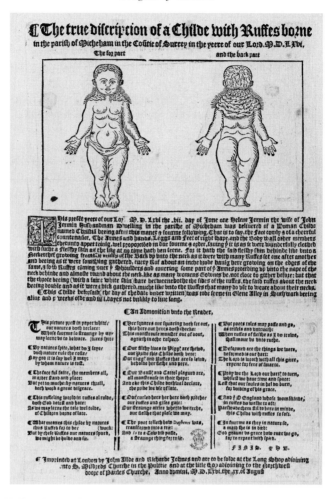

PLATE 25 H. B., *The true discripcion of a childe with ruffes borne in the parish of Micheham, in the countie of Surrey, in the yeere of our lord M.D.LXvi* (London, 1566). By permission of the British Library. Shelfmark: Huth 50 (34).

readily to figurative exposition.[132] So did those with ear lobes, lumps, and membranes which looked like the vestments worn by Catholic friars, pontiffs, and mass priests—copes, mitres, and cowls abound (Plate 27).[133] The cuttlefish allegedly captured off the Dutch coast in 1566 with scales like beggars' bowls, owls'

---

[132] See e.g. *Most certaine report of a monster borne at Oteringham*, sig. A3ᵛ; *Gods handy-worke in wonders*, sig. B1ᵛ.

[133] e.g. *An example of Gods judgement shew[n] upon two children borne in high Dutchlan[d] in the citie of*

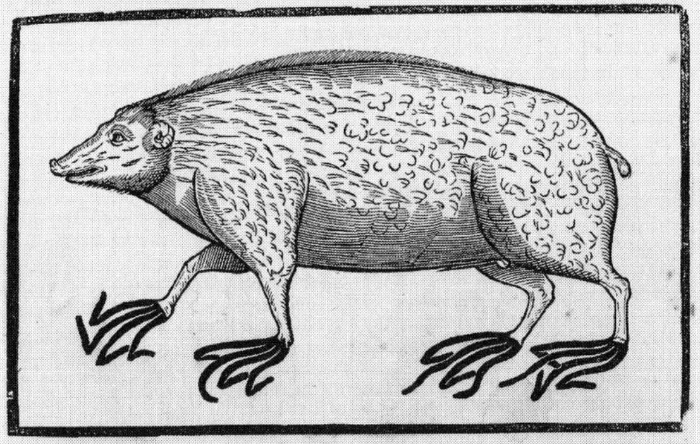
A meruaylous straunge deformed Swyne.

Here Good Reader shalt thou beholde a straunge and deformed Swyne, farowed and brought foorth in Denmarke, and there bought and brought ouer by an Englishman, which hath it at this present, & is to be seen a liue, the proportion wherof is wonderous straunge to beholde and vew: the forepart therof from the Snoute beneath the foreshoulders are in al pointes like vnto a Swine, except the Eares only, which resemble ye eares of a Lion, the hinder parte (contrarie to kinde) is proportioned in all pointes like vnto a Ram, hauing softe wooll both white and blacke mixed monge the hard Heare, and so groweth from the shoulders downewarde, all the body ouer, and it is a Boare Pyg, howbeit, there doth nothing appeare outwarde, but onely the Pysell vnder his Belly, but if a man list to feele & gripe it in the Grindes, there ye may feele his Coddes within his belly: and the most straungest thinge of all, is the misshapen and deformed Feete, wheron grow certayne Tallents and very harde Clawes, doubling vnder his Feete, euery Claw so byg as a mans Fynger, and blacke of colour, and the length of euery of them are full .x. inches, very straunge and wonderfull to beholde, it feedeth and eateth diuers and sundrie thinges, aswell Haye and Grasse, as Breade and Apples, with such other thinges as sheepe and Swyne do feede on.

An exhortacion or warnynge to all men, for amendment of lyfe.

Come neere good Christians all,
beholde a Monster rare:
Whose monstrous shape (no doubt) fortels
Gods wrath we should beware.
His wondrous works we ought not iudge,
as toyes and trifles vaine:
Whither it be Childe or brutish Beast,
forwarnings they are playne.
As now, this mingled brutish Beast,
Gods creature is we see:
Although as straunge of shape and forme
as possyblie may be.
For if you do way well ech poynt,
his nature and his shape
I feare resembles some of those,
as on the same do gape.
For why most Swinish are our liues,
and monstrous (that is sure:)
Though we resemble simple Sheepe,
or Lambes that be most pure.
But euery Tree it selfe will try,
at last by his owne Fruite:
Though on our Backs we cary Woll,
our conscience is pollute,
Though smilingly with flattering face,
we seeme Gods word to loue:
Contrary wise som hate the same,
as well their deedes did proue.
Who ment the ruine of our Realme,
as Traytours to our Queene:

Som white fasse Lambs haue sought to do
(nay, monstrous Swine) I weene.
I meane not here at large to showe
offences as they bee:
In whom they raigne, in hie or low,
I name here no degree.
But generally, I say to all,
repent amend your life:
The greedy rich, the needy poore,
yea, yongman, Maide, and Wife.
The Protestant, the Papist eke,
what secte so that ye be,
Gripe your own conscience, learne to do
as God commaundeth ye.
For all are sinners Dauid saith,
Yea, do the best we may,
Unprofitable seruaunts still we be,
we can it not denay.
Judge ye therfore how far amisse,
all those their liues do frame:
That outwardly professe Gods truth,
and inward hate the same.
Judge ye againe that hate your Prince,
and seeke the Realme to spoyle:
What monstrous Swine you proue at length,
for all your couert coyle.
Experience late by Felton false,
and Norton two I weene:
Their Treason known were wondred at
as they had Monsters been.

And surely I can iudge no lesse,
but that they Monsters were:
Quite changed from true subiects shape,
their deedes did so appere.
Then let their deedes example be,
to vs that Subiects are:
For treason ends by shamfull death,
therfore by them beware.
I speake not here of monstrous Pride,
in Man, in Mayde, and Wife:
Nor Whoredom which is daily vsde,
in England ranke and rife.
Of Couetousnesse, what should I say,
or Usery daily don:
It booteth not to speake therof,
so much therby is wonne.
But if they well do count their Cardes,
how God they do offend:
I wis their sweete ill gotten gaines,
hath sowre and bitter end,
From the which end deliuer vs Lord,
and graunt both hie and low,
To become thy seruaunts iust and true
and then our end we know.
God graunt our gracious souerain Queen
long ouer vs may raigne:
And this life past, with Christ our Lord,
Heauens ioyes she may attaine.

FINIS I. P.

Imprinted at London by VVilliam Hovv, for Richard Iohnes: and are to be solde at his Shop ioyning to the Southwest doore of Paules Church.

Plate 26 I. P., *A mervaylous straunge deformed swyne* (London, [1570?]). By permission of the British Library. Shelfmark: Huth 50 (42).

eyes, a parrot's beak, and a red, four-cornered tail like a clerical biretta clearly encapsulated a covert attack on the moral bankruptcy and rapacity of the Church of Rome (Plate 28).[134]

There was obviously a fine line between simply accentuating the exemplary character of a monstrous birth and totally refashioning it by adding one or two suitable motifs. Others, no doubt, were purely fictitious: hybrid creatures pieced together by crusading pamphleteers prepared to resort to artifice and pastiche to forward their cause. Luther and Melanchthon's exploitation of the 'papal ass' and

Lutssolof ([1582?]), sig. A4[r]; *Strange signes seene in the aire*, sig. A4[r]; Batman, *Doome*, 405; Shrewsbury School, MS Mus X. 31, fos. 170[v]–171[r].

[134] *The discription of a rare or rather most monstrous fishe taken on the east cost of Holland* ([1566]). For a German version, see Strauss (ed.), *German Single-Leaf Woodcut*, i. 202.

PLATE 27 *An example of Gods judgement shew*[*n*] *upon two children borne in high Dutchlan*[*d*] *in the citie of Lutssolof, the first day of Julie* (London, [1582?]), title-page. By permission of the Huntington Library, San Marino, California. Monstrous child with bishop's mitre, sword, and switch.

'monk calf' as Protestant propaganda in 1523 are cases in point.[135] Owing much to techniques of divination inherited from classical antiquity, the urge to pin down the exact meaning of particular prodigies was somewhat at odds with Calvin's stern caveats about divine inscrutability. Yet, as we have already seen, it was one to which the Genevan reformer and his followers repeatedly fell prey.

In insisting that malformed babies embodied a generic warning, ministers were struggling to subvert the deeply seated assumption that the conception of such children was a variety of retributive justice directed against their begetters. They sharply reproved the 'common custome' of charging the mother and father with sexual misconduct and gross moral turpitude, doing their best to exonerate them from the allegations of adultery, incest, and even bestiality to which misbirths invariably gave rise.[136] Reference was recurrently made to John ix, where Jesus ex-

---

[135] See Scribner, *For the Sake of Simple Folk*, 127–32. This pamphlet was published in England in 1579: Philipp Melanchthon and Martin Luther, *Of two woonderful popish monsters*, trans. J. Brooke (1579).
[136] *True discription of two monsterous chyldren borne at Herne in Kent.* For the ubiquity and persistence of such beliefs, see Ernest W. Baughman, *Type and Motif-Index of the Folktales of England and North*

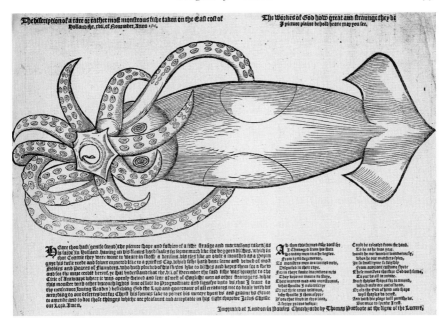

PLATE 28 *The discription of a rare or rather most monstrous fishe taken on the east cost of Holland the .xvii. of November, anno. 1566* (London, [1566]). By permission of the Huntington Library, San Marino, California.
Broadsheet depicting a cuttle fish captured off the coast of Holland. The Dutch print on which it was based was a piece of anti-Catholic propaganda issued during the 'wonder year' of 1566.

plains to his disciples that the blind man they meet by the wayside does not bear the marks of hereditary guilt but the glory of divine omnipotence. Thomas Bedford cited this scriptural passage in a sermon preached at the burial of two inseparable siblings in Plymouth in 1635, insisting that their disfigurement was 'meerely *Ex Dei bene-placito*, the good pleasure of God'.[137] So did the author of a broadside (Plate 29) about a brother and sister sharing the same ribcage born to a sober Buckinghamshire husband and wife in the spring of 1566, anticipating that

> . . . some proude boastyng Pharisie,
> the parents wyll detect:
> And judge with heapes of uglie vice
> their lives to be infect.[138]

America, Indiana University Folklore Series 20 (Bloomington, Ill., 1966), nos. G303.25.21.–21.5, Q552.5–5 (d), M411.3(a).

[137] B[edford], *True and certaine relation of a strange-birth*, 18–20.
[138] John Mellys, *The true description of two monsterous children . . . borne in the parish of Swanburne in Buckynghamshyre* ([1566]).

PLATE 29 J. Mellys, *The true description of two monsterous children, laufully begotten betwene George Stevens and Margerie his wyfe, and borne in the parish of Swanburne in Buckynghamshyre the iiij. of Aprill, anno domini 1566* (London, [1566]). By permission of the British Library. Shelfmark: Huth 50 (35).

Pamphleteers and preachers constantly emphasized that such babies had been 'laufully begotten' within the bonds of holy matrimony and sometimes statements to this effect were even inserted in parish registers.[139] A Chichester butcher and his wife who produced an unsightly monster in May 1562 were declared to be 'of

[139] See Allison E. Barker, 'The Kelsdale Wonder', *Local Population Studies*, 26 (1981), 43.

honest and quiet conversation', as were John and Elizabeth Rawling of Ottringham in Holderness after the birth in 1595 of a dark-skinned baby with a head like a rabbit which had caused 'terror to all the beholders'.[140] At village level, infants with appalling congenital defects evidently cast a terrible shadow over the morals of married couples who had the misfortune to bring them into the world. It left them a permanent stigma, a halo of scandal and shame which news-sheets emblazoned with their names did nothing to dim.

However, when imputations about depraved and promiscuous behaviour had some basis in fact, the providentialism of the clergy and laity was apt to converge. Monstrous births which were the product of pre- or extra-marital sex or some other unspeakable act were universally viewed as personal judgements. Pious journalists rarely refrained from pointing a self-righteous finger at parents who had conceived Siamese twins or deformed babies in sin. Margaret Mere of Maidstone, who gave birth to a hideous monster in 1568, was 'unmaryed' and had 'played the naughty packe'; Richard Southern, father of an ill-proportioned infant 'born out of Wedlocke' in Northamptonshire three years earlier, had fled, apparently unable to face up to public disgrace; Annis Figge, who bore a child with a prickly black beard and an encephalous head in Chichester in 1582, was branded a wicked adulteress.[141] Janus-faced twins born in Adlington, Lancashire, in 1613 were proof that the Lord punished flagrant transgressors down to the third and fourth generation: the mother herself was a bastard, while her lover was a man of 'very lewde carriage and conditions'. The anatomical freak delivered to the daughter of a Herefordshire yeoman who slept with her first cousin in 1599 supplied an excuse for inveighing against 'amorous yonkers', 'lewde huswives', and dissolute youth, and for reiterating the forbidden unions listed in the official table of kindred and affinity.[142] And a hideous, half-human hybrid sired by a Sussex man who copulated with a mare in the early 1670s was nailed up in the porch of the local church as a 'monument' of the Lord's just wrath against sodomy.[143] The notion that physical malformity was the outward manifestation of private immorality likewise taints a report about an elderly lady from Montgomeryshire from whose forehead grew a cranial bone tumour in the shape of a cuckold's horn: the pamphlet was full of parenthetical innuendoes implying that she had been unfaithful to her husband (Plate 30).[144] As Thomas Beard's tale of the canine-faced baby conceived by a

---

[140] John D., *Discription of a monstrous chylde*; *Most certaine report of a monster borne at Oteringham*, sig. A3ʳ.

[141] *The forme and shape of a monstrous child, borne at Maydstone in Kent* ([1568]); William Elderton, *The true fourme and shape of a monsterous chyld, whiche was borne in Stony Stratforde, in North Hamptonshire* ([1565]); G. B., *Of a monstrous childe borne at Chichester . . . with a short and sharpe discourse, for the punishment of whoredome* ([1581?]), sig. A2ᵛ.

[142] *Strange newes of a prodigious monster*, sig. B1ʳ; I. R., *Most straunge, and true discourse, of the wonderfull judgement of God*, 9.

[143] Turner, *Compleat history*, pt. II, p. 25.

[144] *Myraculous, and monstrous, but yet, most true, and certayne discourse of a woman.*

PLATE 30 *A myraculous, and monstrous, but yet, most true, and certayne discourse of a woman . . . in the midst of whose fore-head . . . there groweth out a crooked horne* (London, 1588), title-page woodcut. By permission of the Huntington Library, San Marino, California.
Mrs Margaret Owyn, the 60-year-old Welsh housewife who allegedly sprouted a four-inch horn in her forehead in 1588.

sabbath-breaking nobleman so memorably attests, all too often such presuppositions slipped into the writings of the clergy themselves.[145]

Immoderate coitus, carnal frenzy, and intercourse during menstruation were also thought to be causes of monstrous conceptions. According to the French surgeon Ambrose Paré, abnormal births occurred when parents 'lye and joine themselves together without law and measure, or luxuriously and beastly, or at such times as they ought to forbeare by the command of God and the Church'.[146] The role of monsters in reinforcing traditional conjugal values and condemning blatant infringements of conventional sexual taboos thus complicated and partially annulled their function as forewarnings of the punishments soon to fall upon

[145] Beard, *Theatre*, 210.
[146] Paré, *Workes*, 962. The relevant biblical passages are Lev. xv. 24, xviii. 19, xx. 18; Ezra v. 8. See also Ottavia Niccoli, ' "Menstruum Quasi Monstruum": Monstrous Births and Menstrual Taboo in the Sixteenth Century', in Edward Muir and Guido Ruggiero (eds.), *Sex and Gender in Historical Perspective* (Baltimore, 1990), 1–25.

iniquitous England. But it also underlines the fact that Protestantism encouraged tendencies already inherent in the intensely moralistic religious culture of the late medieval parish.[147]

Like other prodigy tales, stories of the marvels of early modern obstetrics and marine biology were often impregnated by ideas of mythological and magical origin. Minds steeped in Celtic folklore instinctively transformed a seal observed off the Carmarthenshire coast in 1604 into the legendary siren or mermaid, half-woman, half-fish, regarded by sailors as an omen of maritime disaster. The author of *A most strange and true report* of this 'dreadfull woonder' interpreted it as a warning to the Welsh and English people to repent and amend.[148] Monstrous birth narratives also absorbed the theologically problematic concepts of the beggar's curse, witch's hex, and self-fulfilling oath. In a case reported by Stephen Batman dating from 1575, a Dutch woman whose drunken husband rashly wishes she might bear a devil is duly delivered of a human incubus.[149] Tannakin Skinker, the hog-faced lady from Holland who caused a sensation when she visited London in the late 1630s, was said to have been bewitched while in her mother's womb, a spell which could be reversed if a man professed himself willing to marry such an eyesore—as in the classic fairy tale *The Beauty and the Beast*.[150] Such stories reflect assumptions about the power of maternal fantasy and the harm that could be exerted by a malevolent imagination from afar.[151] Once again we see the orthodox doctrine of providence helping to shelter and countenance ideas which Reformed theologians theoretically rejected as relics of popery and paganism.

Our study of aerial battles, diabolical visions, and monstrous creatures suggests that too much emphasis has been placed on Protestantism's intolerance of rival explanatory systems like sorcery and astrology, and upon the violent rupture which the Reformation effected with traditional belief. It has revealed elements of late medieval piety which its successor almost involuntarily enlisted and enveloped. The continuing appearance of popular prophets and seers represents a further set of variations on these interesting themes.

PROPHETS, MESSIAHS, AND SEERS

Scripture taught sixteenth- and seventeenth century Christians to expect the appearance of false prophets and pseudo-messiahs immediately prior to the Second Coming.[152] Early modern England nurtured a sizeable brood of bogus Christs and

---

[147] Cf. Byford, 'Price of Protestantism', ch. 5.

[148] P. G., *Most strange and true report of a monsterous fish, who appeared in the forme of a woman, from her waste upwards*, quotation at sig. A3ᵛ. On mermaids, see Topsell, *Historie of foure-footed beastes*, 452–5.

[149] Batman, *Doome*, 401; M[unday], *View of sundry examples*, sig. C3ʳ⁻ᵛ; Shrewsbury School, MS Mus X. 31, fo. 123ʳ. There is an updated version of this story *in Gods handy-worke in wonders*, sigs. A4ᵛ–B1ᵛ.

[150] *Certaine relation of the hog-faced gentlewoman called Mistris Tannakin Skinker*, sigs. A4ʳ–B1ʳ; Price, *Monstrous shape*.

[151] See Gen. xxx. 37–42; Paré, *Workes*, 978.

[152] Matt. xxiv. 5, 11, 24; Mark xiii. 6; Luke xxi. 8. Some of the prophets mentioned in this paragraph are discussed briefly by Thomas, *Religion and the Decline of Magic*, 151–73, and Richard

obscure persons claiming to be Enoch, Elijah, or some other ecstatic figure foreshadowed in the Bible. Many of these pretenders to heaven have left no perceptible mark on the historical record; others, especially those who clashed with the
civil and ecclesiastical authorities, are rather better documented.

In 1561, for instance, one William Geffrie had been whipped from the
Marshalsea to Bedlam because he professed a certain John Moore to be Christ.
Less than twelve months later a Manchester draper by the name of Elizeus Hall
assumed the title of Eli, the carpenter's son, after experiencing a series of strange
dreams and extraterrestrial journeys.[153] During the 1570s and 1580s, dozens of
would-be seers pestered the royal court, calling for repentance, warning of imminent calamity, and claiming to have a special 'embassage' from heaven. Lord
Burghley's remarkable dossier of letters from these religious enthusiasts includes
a petition from an Emmanuel Plantagenet, who declared he was the son of God
the Father and Elizabeth I, from whom he had been taken at birth by the angel
Gabriel. Another importunate prophet was the glover Robert Dickins, who told
the Queen and her Privy Council in 1588 that the Lord would 'smite the earthe
with . . . famine swoord and pestelens' if England did not take swift steps to slake
His wrath. He derived his authority from a series of angelical visions in the course
of which he had been commissioned to sound a trumpet before the Day of
Judgement and live a life of chastity and obedience, 'fleeing & abhorring all the
filthy lusts of the flesh'.[154] In 1586 an Essex shoemaker called John White or
Snelling had proclaimed himself to be a new John the Baptist and the following
year one Ralph Durden, a clergyman who exercised his ministry in the same part
of East Anglia, insisted that God had endowed him with unique insight into the
opaque prophecies of the Apocalypse and allocated him a special role in fulfilling
them. He saw himself as an Elijah figure and interpreted a little round spot on his
left thigh as a sign that he would be the next king of the world.[155] The most famous
of Elizabethan false prophets burst onto the scene in 1591: William Hacket, the
illiterate Northamptonshire maltmaker, who, together with two puritan gentlemen
who volunteered to act as his lieutenants, created an enormous commotion in the
capital. Executed as a traitor and an agent of Satan, this self-proclaimed Messiah
had confidently predicted the plagues that would consume the nation if thorough-
going reformation of the Church along Genevan lines was not quickly commenced.[156] Hacket's fate did little to deter others convinced that they too had a

Bauckham, *Tudor Apocalypse: Sixteenth Century Apocalypticism, Millenarianism and the English
Reformation*, The Courtenay Library of Reformation Classics, 8 (Appleford, 1978), ch. 10.

[153] Holinshed, *Chronicles*, iii. 1194. PRO SP 12/23/39; John Strype, *Annals of the Reformation and
Establishment of Religion . . .* , 4 vols. in 7 (Oxford, 1824), I. i 433–5; and the MS described in *Bernard
Quaritch Ltd. Sale Catalogue of Manuscripts and Printed Books*, no. 914 (1971), item 4. Attempts to trace
this MS through Bernard Quaritch and Sotheby's have unfortunately failed.

[154] BL Lansdowne MS 99, fos. 13ʳ⁻ᵛ, 18ʳ–20ᵛ.

[155] PRO SP 12/194/57. BL Lansdowne MS 101, fos. 177ʳ–182ʳ ('A writing of one Durden, who
called himself Elias').

[156] See Richard Cosin, *Conspiracie, for pretended reformation* (1592); [Richard Bancroft], *Daungerous*

divine vocation. In 1594 a 'poor fool' who fancied he was a greater prophet than Moses wrote to the pastors and elders of the French Church in London, enclosing a letter of exhortation to the Queen. A few years later, in 1601, a certain John Richardson implored the ageing Tudor monarch to allow him to carry out his errand to the Almighty and deliver her a message from the Holy Ghost; and in 1619 James I was troubled at Theobalds by 'a pretty young fellow' called Weekes bearing further admonitions from God.[157] The 1630s and 1640s saw a fresh wave of messiahs and seers, including Richard Farnham and John Bull, two Cockney weavers who announced they were the witnesses spoken of in Revelation xi. 3 in 1636.[158] Some of these prophets attracted a small circle of spellbound followers, but most were ignored, dismissed, or imprisoned.

In denouncing such spurious Christs and Elijahs, Protestants usually protested that the gift of prophecy had passed away when the primitive Church came of age. Prophesying in the simple sense of preaching and expounding God's word was, of course, perpetual, but individuals endowed with second sight, the ability to reveal secrets, and foretell future events, so Arthur Dent declared, were 'an extraordinary function' with which God had long since dispensed.[159] '*Donum Propheticum*', the gift of 'breathing new Scripture', echoed Stephen Denison, minister of the London parish of St Katherine Cree, addressing an audience at Paul's Cross in 1627, 'certainly and infallibly, is finally ceased'.[160] When Christianity was still in its infancy, fighting an uphill battle against heathen idolatry and 'Greekish gentilitie', prophets had been needful—a special instrument vouchsafed to ensure evangelical success. But once the triumph of the Gospel was no longer in question, such crutches and props had been systematically removed.[161] In these days when books and teachers of the Word were widely diffused, mankind could not expect to be fed with 'mylke like babes' and to be 'trained up like Infidels, or Ethniques'. Even the Catholic nobleman Henry Howard declared that to crave such 'helpes', 'staffes', and 'spectacles' was rather 'a signe of wa[n]tonnesse, then an argument of constauncie'.[162]

Many of these emphatic declarations were directed towards the authors of astrological prognostications, predictions associated with figures like Merlin,

positions and proceedings (1593), ch. 6; Henry Arthington, *The seduction of Arthington by Hacket especiallie, with some tokens of his unfained repentance and submission* ([1592]). A detailed discussion of the episode can be found in my '"Frantick Hacket": Prophecy, Sorcery, Insanity and the Elizabethan Puritan Movement', *HJ* 41 (1998), 27–66.

[157] HMC, *Salisbury. Part XIII* (1915), 519 and *Part XI* (1906), 219; Thomas Birch (ed.), *The Court and Times of James the First*, 2 vols. (1849), ii. 159–60.

[158] T[homas] H[eywood], *A true discourse of the two infamous upstart prophets, Richard Farnham weaver of White-Chappell, and John Bull weaver of Saint Butolphs Algate* (1636); *A curb for sectaries and bold propheciers* (1641); *False prophets discovered* (1642).

[159] Arthur Dent, *The plaine-mans path-way to heaven. The second part* (1612 edn.), 185. See also Scot, *Discoverie of witchcraft*, bk. VIII, ch. 2.

[160] Stephen Denison, *The white wolfe. Or, a sermon preached at Pauls Crosse* (1627), 5.

[161] Vermigli, *Common places*, 18, 23–4.

[162] Howard, *Defensative*, sig. Ee2ʳ; John Harvey, *A discoursive problem concerning prophecies* (1588), 50.

Nostradamus and the Sibyls, and the 'Anabaptisticall revelations' of familists. But the clergy were also concerned to discredit individuals who alleged they were Enoch and Elijah redivivus. Most ministers dismissed the notion that these prophets would return to earth in person before the Last Judgement as a 'Jewish fable'. They insisted that Ecclesiasticus xliv. 16 and Malachi iv. 5 had already been fulfilled, the latter in the guise of John the Baptist. As for the two witnesses in Revelation xi, this text was to be interpreted allegorically and not 'corporally after the lettre': it referred to all post-Reformation preachers against the papal Antichrist rather than any specific set of individuals.[163] People who persisted in such claims were either 'cogging imposters' and 'cosenors' itching after worldly fame; witting or unwitting victims of demonic delusions; or simply deranged, 'brainsick', and insane. It was well known that Lucifer could 'apishlie counterfeit' the Holy Spirit, and, as William Perkins and others observed, men and women possessed with 'raving furie' or overcome by 'melancholy fumes' often suffered from 'strong phantasies' of this kind.[164]

Nevertheless, not all Protestant ministers were wholly convinced that prophets as a race were completely extinct. '[P]erhaps there be some now a daies in the church,' Peter Martyr Vermigli conceded cautiously, 'yet I thinke there be not manie'. It was only in exceptional circumstances, when 'the ordinarie ministration at anie time . . . be out of course', that God raised up prophets 'extraordinarilie to restore things into order'.[165] According to the presbyterian leader Thomas Cartwright, 'th'erection of a church out of the dust' was one such emergency.[166] Although rare, then, seers sent from heaven might still be wandering around in one's midst. The real problem was distinguishing them from the servants of the devil and the mentally sick. Charles Odingsells lectured on this subject at Langar in Nottinghamshire in 1619 and in a dialogue published in 1587 William Perkins had supplied a checklist of the 'notes' and 'marks' by which false prophets could be correctly differentiated from true ones.[167]

The clergy thus carved out a small but significant niche for divinely inspired personages in post-Reformation theology. At the level of the laity, many seem to have remained amenable to the idea that if ordained ministers failed to win English society to sincere repentance the Lord might well make humbler personages the

---

[163] Perkins, *A fruitfull dialogue betweene the Christian and the worldling, concerning the ende of the world* (1587), in *Workes*, iii. 468; Vermigli, *Common places*, 382–4; Henry Bullinger, *A hundred sermons upon the Apocalips of Jesu Christe* ([1561]), 312.

[164] Harvey, *Discoursive problem*, 34–5, 50; Scot, *Discoverie of witchcraft*, bk. VIII, ch. 2; Perkins, *Damned art of witchcraft*, 26; id., *Fruitfull dialogue*, in *Workes*, iii. 468; Vermigli, *Common places*, 19, 21; Howard, *Defensative*, sigs. I1ʳ–K1ᵛ.

[165] Vermigli, *Common places*, 18, 22, 24.

[166] Quoted in Cosin, *Conspiracie*, 18; and see Thomas Cartwright, *A brief apologie . . . against all such slaunderous accusations as it pleaseth Mr Sutcliffe in severall pamphlettes most injuriously to loade him with* (Middelburg, 1596), sig. B2ᵛ.

[167] Charles Odingsells, *Two sermons lately preached at Langar in the Valley of Belvoir* (1620), esp. 6–13; Perkins, *Fruitfull dialogue* in *Workes*, iii. 468.

mouthpieces of His wrath. Just as He sent comets, monsters, and apparitions to spell out His threats to those who scoffed at the fire and brimstone sermons of godly preachers, so did He sometimes commission the socially marginal, sexually subordinate, and politically inarticulate to speak and to teach: children and women, paupers and pensioners.[168]

Evidence of at least vestigial belief in this kind of divine ventriloquism is not difficult to find: a steady stream of ephemera about prophetic infants and elderly oracles issued from late Tudor and early Stuart presses. There are many reports of foetuses crying inauspiciously from the womb and newborn babies uttering menacing forewarnings before making a premature exit from the earthly realm. A 'manechild' delivered to a 'goodwyfe' at the Sign of the Hedgehog in Paul's Churchyard in 1555 exclaimed 'Rise and pray' before it 'departed the worlde'.[169] An infant was heard to wail in its mother's belly in Purmerend, a Calvinist citadel in the Netherlands, on New Year's Eve 1599, as did a baby born in Hammersmith in 1638.[170] Deformed triplets delivered to Flemish parents in 1608 announced the catastrophes that would precede the Last Judgement and then gave up the ghost; a set of Siamese twins and their negroid sibling had made similar predictions in the Dutch city of Lutssolof in 1579.[171] A 77-year-old woman in Ferrara gave birth to a three-legged boy who warned of 'greate plagues' and calamities before 'spuing forth flames of fyre from his mouth'; in 1580 three prophetic children were delivered to a lady in Prague at the relatively youthful age of 59.[172] And a toddler dressed in a green gown discovered beneath a hedge in Holland in 1624 heralded God's three arrows of famine, sickness, and war and then disappeared without trace.[173] Stories of visionaries over 80 years of age are only slightly less common. In one pamphlet, a white-haired gentleman deaf and dumb since his birth suddenly breaks his lifelong silence by leaping across a laden dinner table and urging fellow guests

---

[168] The discussion which follows focuses on the young, the aged, and the poor, since female prophets have already received considerable attention from historians, notably Phyllis Mack. See her 'Women as Prophets during the English Civil War', *Feminist Studies*, 8 (1982), 19–45, and *Visionary Women: Ecstatic Prophecy in Seventeenth-Century England* (Berkeley and Los Angeles, 1993). The most recent study is Diane Watt, *Secretaries of God: Women Prophets in Late Medieval and Early Modern England* (Woodbridge, 1997). For an illuminating parallel in late 16th-cent. Spain, Richard L. Kagan, *Lucrecia's Dreams: Politics and Prophecy in Sixteenth Century Spain* (Berkeley and Los Angeles, 1990).

[169] BL Harleian MS 353, fo. 145ʳ; Machyn, *Diary*, ed. Nichols, 88.

[170] *A strange and miraculous accident happened in the cittie of Purmerent . . . Of a yong child which was heard to cry in the mothers wombe before it was borne* (1599); BL Add. MS 35331, fo. 72ʳ.

[171] *True relation of the birth of three monsters in the city of Namen in Flanders*, sig. B1ʳ; *Example of Gods judgement shew[n] upon two children borne in high Dutchlan[d]*. See also the case from 1564 in PRO SP 15/28/58ᵛ and Staffordshire RO, D641/3/P/4/13/3, a reference I owe to Alison Shell.

[172] For the 77-year-old from Ferrara, see Batman, *Doome*, 406. The other example is the subject of a fragmentary ballad in the Bodleian, *STC* 1325 [Ballad describing natural portents, including a woman of 59 years giving birth in Prague] ([1580?]), summarized in M[unday], *View of sundry examples*, sig. C4ʳ⁻ᵛ.

[173] *1624. Newes from Holland*, 11–16. See also *Vox infantis. Or, the propheticall child. Being a true relation of an infant that was found in a field, neere Lempster, in Herefordshire* (1649).

at the feast to fall to heartfelt contrition. According to a ballad dated 1657 'strange speeches' uttered by 155-year-old Margaret Hough from Rainow in Cheshire foretold the fall of the Cromwellian Commonwealth, while two Frenchmen who appeared in Toulouse around 1680 preaching repentance were veritable Methuselahs, having allegedly been born an entire millennium before.[174]

Some of these may have been mere tales, but itinerant artisans did actually wander the streets of Elizabethan and early Stuart London and provincial towns droning 'woe, woe to England'. William Hacket, who travelled to York and Lincoln in the 1580s convinced he was John the Baptist 'sent thither . . . to prepare the way of the Lord', was whipped and banished by the civic authorities.[175] Others were mocked by the populace and escorted swiftly to bedlam. But when a tailor by the name of Spering arrived in Dorchester in February 1622, cursing 'Rome that bloody citty', Jesuits, and papists in accordance with the commands of 'one that met him in a red cap', no one seems to have tried to restrain him. Some 'accompted' him 'distracted', but his anti-Catholic diatribe apparently struck a chord with those dismayed by the negotiations for the Spanish match and England's unseemly neutrality in the context of the Thirty Years War—including William Whiteway, merchant and city worthy.[176]

Such prophets joined a long line of juvenile, geriatric, and plebeian seers. This was another cultural paradigm carried over into the post-Reformation era and Protestantized. One prototype to which accounts of peripatetic oracles adhered was the rustic crier immortalized in Josephus' *History of the Jewish wars*.[177] This lonely figure had left his stamp on the succession of unlettered lay evangelists, hermits, and priests who roamed European cities throughout the Middle Ages, especially in intervals of serious economic crisis and political unrest. The most famous of the Italian market-place prophets who preached repentance and doom was the Florentine Dominican friar Girolamo Savonarola;[178] perhaps his best known counterpart in rural Germany is the Drummer of Niklashausen, a young shepherd and minstrel who summoned the people to turn from unrighteousness to a sanctified life in 1476.[179] Other sources of inspiration for these celestial ambassadors were penitential visions of the Virgin Mary and saints: dozens of cases of

---

[174] *A true reporte of three straunge and wonderful accidents, lately hapened at Pernaw, a cittie in Lifflande* (1603), sigs. ¶3ᵛ–4ʳ; *A new prophesie: or some strange speeches declared by an old woman living now in Cheshire, in Ranna* ([1657]); *The worlds wonder: giving an account of two old men, lately known and seen in the city of Tholouze, in France, who declare themselves to be above a thousand years old a peice, and preach repentance to the world* ([1675–80]).

[175] Cosin, *Conspiracie*, 7–8.

[176] BL Egerton MS 784, fo. 24ᵛ.

[177] Josephus, *Famous and memorable workes*, 738–9; Joseph ben Gorion (pseud.), *Compendious and most marveilous historie*, 237–9.

[178] On Savonarola and other seers, see Donald Weinstein, *Savonarola and Florence: Prophecy and Patriotism in the Renaissance* (Princeton, 1970); Richard C. Trexler, *Public Life in Renaissance Florence* (New York, 1980), 35–6, 462–90; Niccoli, *Prophecy and People*, ch. 4, esp. 91–8.

[179] Norman Cohn, *The Pursuit of the Millennium: Revolutionary Millenarians and Mystical Anarchists of the Middle Ages* (1970 edn.), ch. 12; Richard Wunderli, *Peasant Fires: The Drummer of Niklashausen* (Bloomington, Ill., 1992).

apparitions who instruct servants, farm labourers, and adolescents to admonish their impious communities have been uncovered in records from thirteenth-, fourteenth-, and fifteenth-century Spain, Italy, and France.[180] These oral and narrative traditions were reinforced by the prophetic writings generated by followers of the Calabrian mystic Joachim of Fiore, the revelations of St Bridget of Sweden, and the even older legend of the Heavenly Letter, an apocryphal epistle enjoining moral regeneration, purportedly composed by Jesus Christ Himself.[181] They also interwove with ingrained beliefs about the origin of the prophetic gifts exercised by rural soothsayers and amateur astrologers. Many cunning men and women supposed they derived their fortune-telling skills from God's angels, the Holy Ghost, or the souls of biblical oracles like Samuel and Moses, and the faculty of second sight was widely supposed to be a hereditary gift.[182]

The notion that the very old and the very young were especially likely to be charged with the office of prophet had an equally venerable heritage. 'Out of the mouth of babes and sucklings . . .', said the Psalmist; 'your sons and your daughters shall prophesy, your old men shall dream dreams, your young men shall see visions', so it was written in Joel.[183] Certain secular, pagan, and magical convictions likewise implied that individuals at the extreme ends of the age spectrum were capable of closer spiritual communion with the Almighty than those in the middle. In this gerontocratic society, longevity was linked with wisdom and authority and treated with reverence and respect. The Seven Sages and Old Father Time stood alongside King Solomon as models; white witches and wizards were often in the winter of their years; and, in the ecclesiastical art which rabid Calvinists did their best to obliterate, God was always depicted as the bearded Ancient of Days.[184] Virginity and innocence, on the other hand, were also considered to be a key to clairvoyance: village sorcerers frequently employed children to gaze into crystal balls and make telepathic contact with the spirits of the dead.[185] Reports of prophetic orphans found under walls and in woods and fields have more than superficial similarities with fairy stories involving the abduction of human babies

---

[180] See William A. Christian, *Apparitions in Late Medieval and Renaissance Spain* (Princeton, 1981) and Diana M. Webb, 'Penitence and Peace-Making in City and Contado: The *Bianchi* of 1399', in Derek Baker (ed.), *The Church in Town and Countryside*, SCH 16 (Oxford, 1979), 243–56.

[181] On Joachim, Marjorie Reeves, *The Influence of Prophecy in the Later Middle Ages: A Study in Joachimism* (Oxford, 1969), esp. 174, 176, 180, 252, 309, 474, 491, 496. For Bridget of Sweden, *The Revelations of Saint Birgitta*, ed. William Patterson Cuming, EETS, os 178 (1929), esp. 38–9, 97–9, 104–117. On the Heavenly Letter, Cohn, *Pursuit of the Millennium*, 129–32, 134.

[182] On diviners and cunning folk, see Gifford, *Dialogue*, sig. F1ᵛ, and Bodleian Library, Oxford, MS Ashmole 1491, fo. 884ʳ. On second sight, see Aubrey, *Three Prose Works*, 113–19.

[183] Ps. viii. 2; Joel ii. 28; cf. Acts ii. 17.

[184] Keith Thomas, 'Age and Authority in Early Modern England', *Proceedings of the British Academy*, 62 (1976), 205–48.

[185] e.g., a Southampton wizard observed in 1631 that 'when a spiritt is raised none hath power to see yt but children of Eleaven or Twelve yeares of age or such as are true maides': R. C. Anderson (ed.), *The Book of Examinations and Depositions, 1627–1634*, Publications of the Southampton Record Soc. 31 (Southampton, 1931), 104–5. See also Thomas, *Religion and the Decline of Magic*, 255–6, 319–20.

and their replacement by starveling elves and changelings.[186] And in the case of elderly matrons who bring forth precocious preachers the parallel with John the Baptist's aged mother Elizabeth is transparently clear.

Nor was the concept of the child and early adolescent as an inherently sacred and psychic being, a kind of aerial and antenna for receiving special transmissions from heaven, in any sense novel. Late medieval Catholicism clung tightly to the idea that children and teenagers were more often chosen as divine envoys and inter-cessors than adults. Regions as diverse as fifteenth-century Tuscany, Castile, and Catalonia[187] and Henrician England yield instances of popular prophets and seers on the verge or in the middle of puberty. The celebrated case of Elizabeth Barton, the Holy Maid of Kent, executed for treason in 1534, was only one example of a well-established devotional pattern, a classic expression of feminine piety which accidentally became caught up in the controversy surrounding the royal divorce.[188] The same combination of convulsive fits, cataleptic revelations, and mystical visions exhibited by a young lady in Ipswich in 1516 had led to the revival of a local Marian cult.[189] Neither was this type of 'enthusiastic' activity anathema to the streamlined religiosity enjoined by the clerical agents of the Counter-Reformation. In February 1580, a 13-year-old girl from Flint claimed to have been favoured with a sequence of apparitions confirming the doctrine of purgatory, the mass, and the intercessory powers of the Virgin Mary and the saints, the contents of which she expounded to an assembled company of church papists while in a trance. Elizabeth Orton also took advantage of her dreamlike state to revile the current ecclesiasti-cal regime, crying 'fie upon the naughtie Religion now used, fie upon their wicked and accursed Churche, moste abhominable in Gods sight'. She subse-quently confessed to having fabricated her raptures under the orders of the crypto-Catholic Welsh schoolmaster of her parents' own parish, but the very form her imposture took betrays the vigour of the native ecstatic tradition she and her mentor attempted to mimic.[190] Thirteen years later, in 1593, a young Hampshire girl who slept for fifteen days and nights awoke much wiser and 'more comly then before' and told how she had seen both Mary Tudor and Mary Queen of Scots in heaven and Henry VIII and the earl of Leicester in hell. It was probably her prophecy that Elizabeth I would die before Michaelmas which resulted in her

---

[186] On changelings, see Thomas, *Religion and the Decline of Magic*, 728, 731–2.

[187] See Christian, *Apparitions*, esp. 215–220; Trexler, *Public Life*, ch. 11, and id., 'Ritual in Florence: Adolescence and Salvation in the Renaissance', in Charles Trinkaus and Heiko A. Oberman (eds.), *The Pursuit of Holiness in Late Medieval and Renaissance Religion* (Leiden, 1974), 200–64.

[188] A. Denton Cheney, 'The Holy Maid of Kent', *TRHS*, NS 17 (1904), 107–29; Alan Neame, *The Holy Maid of Kent: The Life of Elizabeth Barton, 1506–1534* (1971); Watt, *Secretaries of God*, ch. 3.

[189] BL Harleian MS 651, fos. 194ᵛ–196ᵛ; More, *Dialogue concerning heresies*, repr. in *Complete Works*, ed. Lawler *et al.*, vol. vi, pt. 1, pp. 92–4. A similar case in Leominster in the reign of Henry VII was exposed as a fraud: see ibid. 87–8. On the Ipswich case, see also Diarmaid MacCulloch, *Suffolk and the Tudors: Politics and Religion in an English County 1500–1600* (Oxford, 1986), 143–5.

[190] The scurrilously anti-Catholic account by Barnaby Rich, reprints a pamphlet describing the visions anonymously penned by some 'Archpapiste' and secretly published: *The true report of a late practise enterprised by a papist, with a yong maiden in Wales* (1582), quotations at sig. D1ʳ.

imprisonment in Winchester and the spread of rumours that she was really a witch.[191]

And yet this was a tradition which zealous Protestantism not merely failed to suppress but even, on occasion, annexed. At least one child prophet who attracted attention in the Elizabethan period was the product of an intensely puritan upbringing. On Christmas Eve, 1580, 11-year-old William Withers of Walsham-le-Willows in Suffolk descended into a deep coma, regaining consciousness ten days later to deliver a series of alarming predictions about the apocalyptic fate of iniquitous England. News of his week-and-a-half-long swoon carried with the wind, for there was soon 'mutche resort of people' from villages further afield. But it was not only the credulous 'common sort' who flocked to his bedside. 'Thither came' James Gayton, godly preacher at St Mary's Church, Bury St Edmunds and 'divers worshipful Gentlemen' of credit and rank. Reiterating the threatenings of God in the Bible 'in such sorte as though he were a learned Divine', this hus-bandman's son admonished his 'deaf-eared'—and dumbfounded—social superiors that unless 'spedie repentance' was swiftly forthcoming, the earth would shake, gape, and swallow them alive.[192]

Ironically his audience included three of the most progressive magistrates in the county, Sir Robert Jermyn, Robert Ashfield, and Sir William Spring, whose patronage of leading clerical figures in the campaign for further reformation was to bring them into headlong conflict with the conservative bishop of Norwich the following year.[193] The so-called 'Bury Stirs' inevitably spilt over into the sur-rounding district, indeed into Walsham-le-Willows itself, where an obstinately nonconformist preacher, Ezechias Morley, crossed swords with a faction of pow-erful 'enemyes', who succeeded in driving him from the parish at Michaelmas 1582.[194] Morley may not have been implicated in the extraordinary events eighteen months before, but his tribulations are nevertheless testimony to a seriously divided community, a microcosm of the animosity and confrontation fervent Protestant evangelism could provoke. William Withers's outbursts apparently occurred in the context of bitter wrangling between passionate advocates of moral and spiritual revolution and diehard defenders of an older religious and cultural order. They

---

[191] *The Letters and Despatches of Richard Verstegan (c.1550–1640)*, ed. Anthony G. Petti, CRS 52 (1959), 176–7.

[192] Phillip, *Wonderfull worke of God*, quotations at sigs. B1ᵛ, B1ʳ, A8ᵛ, B1ʳ, A8ᵛ respectively. A ballad on the same subject was entered to Edward White on 16 Jan. 1581: *SR* ii. 386. For a fuller account of this episode, see my essay '"Out of the Mouth of Babes and Sucklings": Prophecy, Puritanism, and Childhood in Elizabethan Suffolk', in Diana Wood (ed.), *The Church and Childhood*, SCH 31 (Oxford, 1995), 285–99.

[193] See BL Egerton MS 1693, fos. 87ʳ⁻ᵛ, 89ʳ–90ʳ, 91ʳ–100ʳ; BL Lansdowne MS 33, fos. 26ʳ⁻ᵛ, 40ʳ, 41ʳ⁻ᵛ; BL Lansdowne MS 37, fos. 59ʳ–62ᵛ. For discussion of the 'Bury Stirs', see most recently J. S. Craig, 'The Bury Stirs Revisited: An Analysis of the Townsmen', *Proceedings of the Suffolk Institute of Archaeology and History*, 37 (1991), 208–24.

[194] For Morley's 'troubles', see Dr Williams's Library, London, MS Morrice A, fo. 166ʳ⁻ᵛ. He had similar difficulties at the hands of the bishop of London in the Essex parish of Ridgewell: Dr Williams's Library, MS Morrice B(2), fo. 91ᵛ.

were representative of a wider crusade against drunkenness and adultery, sabbath-breaking and swearing, luxurious dress and profane sports and pastimes. Eyeing a fashionably attired servingman by his bedside, this 11-year-old Jeremiah fiercely reprehended his 'great and monstrous ruffes', advising him 'it were better for him to put on sackcloth & mourn for his sinnes, then in such abhominable pride to pranke up himselfe like the divels darling', the 'very father' of lies. At this the shamefaced manservant 'sorrowed & wept for his offence, rente the bande from his necke, tooke a knife and cut it in peeces, and vowed never to weare the like againe'—or so, at least, it was said.[195]

According to John Phillip, the pious journalist who edited and no doubt embroidered a manuscript account of the affair for that daredevil puritan publisher of the Marprelate tracts, Robert Waldegrave,[196] God had thus 'raised up a second Daniel' in the guise of a meek Suffolk child. William Withers was 'an instrument given to us by the providence of God . . . to waken us out of the perilous slumber of our sinne'. Because preachers were unable 'to pearce our stonye stubberne & flintie hearts', he declared, 'to our shame thou hast opened the mouth of a childe to foreshewe unto us the fulnesse of thy furie'.[197]

Historians, however, are inclined to be more sceptical and 'scientific' when it comes to assessing the source of Master William's verbal revelations. Was he in the grips of a physical or psychosomatic illness, aggravated by the emotional turmoil of an early adolescence? Or was the entire episode an ingenious fraud, a rehearsed performance carried out by a devout and clever pupil in collusion with an ecclesiastical coach? Had some enterprising minister co-opted an accomplice in an imaginative scheme to galvanize the local people into adopting godly habits? The 'spontaneous' conversion of the pretentiously dressed servant certainly seems more like a brilliantly stage-managed dramatic moral tableau. Or might this be no more than a schoolboy prank, a trick played by a young mischief-maker on his unsuspecting elders? Perhaps the lad was roguishly imitating his clerical betters, but it is equally possible that he was impudently mocking them, subconsciously reacting against the repressively patriarchal religious culture in which he had clearly been reared. Children, who, like women, were denied access to more conventional vehicles for expression—the pulpit and the printed text—were obliged to bypass them and represent their utterances as divine revelations. This was a carnivalesque inversion of the established social order which simultaneously reinforced it.[198] Whichever theory is closest to the truth, we have here indirect but compelling evidence of the impact which puritanism could have upon an impressionable youth.

William Withers is an intriguing example of a phenomenon which seems to have

---

[195] Phillip, *Wonderfull worke of God*, sig. B2ʳ.
[196] On Phillip and Waldegrave, see Ch. 1 above, pp. 48–9.
[197] Phillip, *Wonderfull worke of God*, sigs. A8ʳ, B6ᵛ, and *passim*.
[198] Cf. Thomas, *Religion and the Decline of Magic*, 163–4, 177; Mack, 'Women as Prophets', esp. 27–8, 32, 35, 37–8.

reached near epidemic proportions in late sixteenth- and early seventeenth-century Lutheran Scandinavia and Germany. Documentation relating to hundreds of popular Protestant prophets survives, most instances involving an encounter between angels and uneducated laypeople, who are instructed to exhort their contemporaries to repent or face a terrifying fate. Impeccably Protestant in theology, these apparitions represent a creative adaptation of the pre-Reformation vision.[199] Such stories were widely diffused: the tale of a country maid of Melwing who was briefly resurrected from the dead in January 1580 to deliver a penitential address was nothing less than a European best-seller. By August the pamphlet had been published in English and in November it was summarized in a blackletter ballad.[200] It is quite possible that reports of this Saxon Cassandra provided our young Suffolk oracle with some kind of role model and script, though he may merely have been imitating the fire and brimstone preaching on which he had presumably been weaned. Either way, print and Protestantism can be seen to have instilled new vitality into the essentially Catholic paradigm of the lowly personage set apart from his or her peers by virtue of a sacred commission.

Cases from the 1640s and 1650s strongly reinforce these points. The Melwing prophetess was reinvented in the guise of a pious teenager from Worksop in 1641 and a 20-year-old Cornish girl called Christian James in 1656, and during the Interregnum several young puritan virgins gave expression to their evangelical and millennial zeal through inspired speeches delivered in a trance-like state induced by prolonged fasting and physical weakness.[201]

As these examples suggest, experimental Protestantism continued to find an outlet for that austere set of late medieval behaviour patterns which Rudolph Bell has labelled 'holy anorexia'. Self-starvation as part of a personal quest for sainthood was not totally stifled by the onset of the Reformation, though it was fundamentally redefined. The miraculous fasts of early modern women like the Dutch maiden Eva Fliegen, who lived off the smell of a rose between 1597 and 1611, were now presented as manifestations of the marvellous providence of God, rather than meritorious acts attributable to human free will. Immortalized in woodcuts and

---

[199] See Jürgen Beyer, 'A Prophet in Lübeck seen in the Local and the Lutheran Context', in Bob Scribner and Trevor Johnson (eds.), *Popular Religion in Germany and Central Europe, 1400–1800* (Basingstoke, 1996), 166–82 and David Sabean, 'A Prophet in the Thirty Years' War: Penance as a Social Metaphor', in his *Power in the Blood*, 61–93. I am grateful to Jürgen Beyer for many valuable discussions on this subject.

[200] Schlichtenberger, *Prophesie uttered by the daughter of an honest countrey man. SR* ii. 375, 383. The event was updated to 1613 in T. I., *Miracle of miracles*, sigs. B4ʳ–C4ʳ. For a case with even more striking similarities to the Withers affair, involving a 7-year-old boy who fell into a trance in a Swedish village in the 1530s, see Batman, *Doome*, 318–19.

[201] See *The wonderfull works of God. Declared by a strange prophecie of a maid, that lately lived neere Worsop in Nottingham-shire* (1641); L[awrence] P[rice], *A wonderful prophecy. Declared by Christian James, a maid of twenty years of age* ([1656]); Nigel Smith, 'A Child Prophet: Martha Hatfield as the Wise Virgin', in Gillian Avery and Julia Briggs (eds.), *Children and their Books: A Celebration of the Work of Iona and Peter Opie* (Oxford, 1989), 79–93; Susan Hardman Moore, ' "Such Perfecting of Praise out of the Mouth of a Babe": Henry Jessey and the Case of Sarah Wight', in Diana Wood (ed.), *The Church and Childhood*, SCH 31 (Oxford, 1995), 285–99.

engravings, such figures helped satisfy the craving of the populace for Protestant martyrs, prophets, and saints (Plate 31).[202]

But Protestantism's passive acceptance and even active endorsement of ascetics and seers must not be exaggerated. Probably the majority of self-proclaimed prophets were regarded by the clergy with suspicion and stigmatized as witches, demoniacs, lunatics, or charlatans. Their status and identity was fluid, subjective, and above all situational: differentiating between divine ecstasy and diabolical frenzy, deceit and disease, was a question of perspective and a product of the particular circumstances in which the oracle appeared. Prophets whose pronouncements enshrined an implicit or explicit critique of the current religious and political regime, clashed with the priorities of powerful pressure groups, or presented a serious threat to the male and clerical monopoly on authority, invariably became the targets of one or more of these strategies of demonization.

For instance, when the Leicestershire apprentice Robert Dickins set himself forth as a divine messenger sent 'to perfect some defects in the Prophesie of Malachy' in 1582—a self-consciously 'Anglican' Elias who affirmed that the Church of England had been thoroughly purged of all 'popish' ceremonies and rites—it is hardly surprising that the 'silver tongu'd' puritan preacher Henry Smith briskly denounced him as 'a young divell' and 'a child of perdition'. His request for permission to preach repentance in the presence of Elizabeth I six years later met with no better reception: his letter, now amongst the miscellaneous papers of Lord Burghley, is annotated in a contemporary secretary hand with the phrase 'a fond glover'.[203] A Cambridgeshire labourer and practitioner of physic by the name of Butler who predicted there would be great troubles in the land by fire, famine, and sword came under equally critical scrutiny by royal officials in 1605. Investigated as part of a wider enquiry into the activities of various East Anglican sorcerers and witches, one of his accomplices was dismissed as 'waywardly conceited but utterly unlearned', while he himself was declared to be 'a very poor creature'.[204] Jane Hawkins, a peddler from St Ives who fell into a 'rapture' or 'exstasie'

---

[202] For Eva Fleigen, see *Protestants and Jesuites up in armes in Gulicke-land. Also, a true and wonderfull relation of a Dutch maiden . . . who . . . hath fasted for the space of 14 yeares; Of a maide nowe dwelling at the towne of Meurs in Dutchland, that hath not taken any foode this 16 yeares*, printed in Clark (ed.), *Shirburn Ballads*, 55–9; *The pourtrayture of Eva Fliegen the miraculous mayd that lived at Muers in Cleveland without food* ([*c*.1620?]). Other accounts of Protestant fasting girls include *Notable and prodigious historie of a mayden*; Gurth, *Most true and more admirable newes*; François Citois, *A true and admirable historie of a mayden of Confolens, in the province of Poictiers: that for the space of three yeeres and more hath lived, and yet doth, without receiving either meate or drinke* (1603). See also Hyder E. Rollins, 'Notes on Some English Accounts of Miraculous Fasts', *Journal of American Folklore*, 34 (1921), 357–76. On the late medieval tradition of self-starvation, see Rudolph M. Bell, *Holy Anorexia* (Chicago, 1985) and Caroline Walker Bynum, *Holy Feast and Holy Fast: The Religious Significance of Food to Medieval Women* (Berkeley and Los Angeles, 1987).

[203] See Smith's notes of his interviews with Dickins and his sermon denouncing him as a false prophet, *The lost sheepe is found*, in *Three sermons* (1599), repr. in *Sermons*, 36–56, quotations at 47, 49; and Fuller, *Church-history of Britain*, cent. XVI, bk. IX, quotation at p. 142. For Dickins's later activities, see above and BL Lansdowne MS 99, fos. 18ʳ–20ᵛ.

[204] BL Add. MS 6177, fos. 199ʳ–200ʳ; HMC, *Salisbury, Part XVII* (1938), 22–5, 36. I owe these references to Malcolm Gaskill.

Within the engraving:

THE POURTRAYTURE OF ELia fliegen the miraculous

Mayd that liued at mucrs in cleueland without food &c:

Twas I that prayd I neuer might eate more,
(Cause my stepmother grutched mee my fed):
Whether on flowers I fed; as I had store:
Or on a dew, that euery morning stood.
Like honey on my lips, full seauenteene yeay
This is a truth, if you the truth will heare.

PLATE 31 *The poutrayture of Eva Fliegen the miraculous mayd* (London, [*c.*1620?]). © The British Museum. Department of Prints and Drawings. Engraving of a Dutch maiden who fasted for over fourteen years and was sustained by the providence of God.

in March 1629 and held forth in verse on sensitive 'matters of divinitie, and state' was likewise exposed as a shameless imposter—'a wittye and a craftie Baggage'. According to Bishop Williams of Lincoln, the revelations of this 'Riminge precheresse' and 'Eleventh Sibill' were not emanations of the Holy Spirit but the 'dotages and Reveries of a franticke weoman'.[205]

The most common method of discrediting prophetic children and adolescents was to allege that they were the victims of vexation by unclean spirits. For, like its alter ego prophecy, demonic possession was a malady to which children and young adults were particularly prone.[206] Characterized by fits, contortions, and tantrums,

---

[205] See PRO SP 16/141/63 and 142/19.
[206] The literature on demonic possession and exorcism in England alone is large. See esp. Thomas, *Religion and the Decline of Magic*, 569–88; D. P. Walker, *Unclean Spirits: Possession and Exorcism in France and England in the Late Sixteenth and Early Seventeenth Centuries* (1981); J. A. Sharpe, 'Disruption in the Well Ordered Household: Age, Authority and Possessed Adolescents', in Paul Griffiths, Adam Fox,

hypnotic trances and moments of startling lucidity, the clinical symptoms and side effects of these conditions were almost indistinguishable. Both these 'culture bound syndromes' regularly generated juvenile revival sermons and exhibitions of steadfast faith; both conditions were a means by which the child of a pious household could express forbidden impulses and engage in normally punishable conduct without fear of recrimination.[207] In some cases, the points of comparison are very striking indeed—not least that of the 13-year-old son of a Norwich alderman who vanquished the fiend who had tormented him for several weeks in 1574 by hurling forth relevant passages from Scripture.[208] No less compelling is the behaviour of two young patients of the famous puritan exorcist John Darrell in the mid-1590s: John Starkie of Cleworth in Lancashire and the 'Boy of Burton', Thomas Darling. The gestures and utterances of such demoniacs oscillated uneasily between blaspheming and preaching; their rantings and ravings often sound more like the divinely inspired speeches of a prophet than the perfidious discourses of the Archfiend masquerading as an angel of light. On one occasion Master Starkie spent two hours denouncing 'straunge sinnes' and warning of the 'fearful judgements' of God which were about to be visited upon England.[209] The diagnosis of demonic possession in these instances may have represented a defeat for the afflicted: the triumph of a clerical explanation of suffering as the chastisement of a sinner over a lay interpretation which saw it as a Job-like trial of the innocent or even a positive sign of a prophetic vocation.[210]

The problem of assessing the true source of inspiration for such zealous, preacherly speeches also exposed and aggravated divisions and frictions within the ranks of the Church of England. This is apparent as early as 1574, in connection with an episode involving two children, Rachel Pindar and Agnes Briggs, who exhibited the usual signs of pyschic disturbance and in due course were diagnosed

and Steve Hindle (eds.), *The Experience of Authority in England* (Basingstoke, 1996), 187–212; id., *Instruments of Darkness*, ch. 8; and Thomas Freeman, 'The Devil and John Foxe: The Genesis of Puritan Exorcism', *P&P* (forthcoming). For Europe, see most recently Clark, *Thinking with Demons*, chs. 26–8.

[207] To borrow a phrase from Michael MacDonald (ed.), *Witchcraft and Hysteria in Elizabethan London: Edward Jorden and the Mary Glover Case* (1991), p. xxxv.

[208] John Parkhurst, *The Letter Book of John Parkhurst Bishop of Norwich Compiled during the Years 1571–1575*, ed. R. A. Houlbrooke, Norfolk Record Soc. 43 ([Norwich], 1974–5), 86–7.

[209] George More, *A true discourse concerning the certaine possession and dispossession of 7 persons in one familie in Lancashire* ([Middelburg], 1600), 24–5. For Darling, see Jesse Bee, *The most wonderfull and true storie, of a certaine witch named Alse Gooderige of Stapen hill . . . As also a true report of the strange torments of Thomas Darling*, ed. J. Denison (1597), 2, 29–31.

[210] See David Harley, 'Explaining Salem: Calvinist Psychology and the Diagnosis of Possession', *American Historical Review*, 101 (1996), 311–12, 328–30, and *passim*; Walker, *Unclean Spirits*, 7, 17, 55; H. C. Erik Midelfort, 'The Devil and the German People: Reflections on the Popularity of Demon Possession in Sixteenth-Century Germany', in Stephen Ozment (ed.), *Religion and Culture in the Renaissance and Reformation*, Sixteenth Century Essays and Studies, 11 (Kirksville, Mo., 1989), esp. 112–18. The growing number of episodes which involved allegations of witchcraft, however, suggests that this victory was only very partial: to claim that demons had been sent into one by means of *maleficium* was to absolve oneself from moral blame. See Clive Holmes, 'Women: Witnesses and Witches', *P&P* 140 (1993), 63–4, and Freeman, 'Devil and John Foxe'.

to be victims of invasion by the devil and/or his minions. Archbishop Matthew Parker's campaign to discredit the girls as canny little schemers can only be understood fully in the context of his ruthless crackdown on clergy who refused to wear 'romish' vestments. As Thomas Freeman has shown, at least in part it was an attempt to publicly humiliate the martyrologist John Foxe, a revered spiritual physician who seems to have been intimately involved in the case from the beginning. Foxe was an adamant enemy of the surplice and had spearheaded efforts to persuade Parliament to revise the *Book of common prayer* in 1571: in this sense Parker's 'scepticism' about possession looks very much like a side-effect of the Vestiarian Controversy.[211] John Deacon, John Walker, and Samuel Harnset employed similar tactics in their celebrated clash with John Darrell at the turn of the century: the clients of this charismatic therapist were systematically reclassified as dissemblers who were incidentally suffering from some kind of psychosomatic complaint such as epilepsy or melancholia, while he himself was accused of active complicity. Harsnet levelled the same charges against a team of Jesuit exorcists headed by William Weston in his *Declaration of egregious popish impostures* in 1603—the damning comparison he drew between the fraudulent practices of the Romanist and puritan thaumaturges was designed to strike a simultaneous blow against both.[212] In 1602 Mary Glover, the godly teenaged daughter of a London shopkeeper became the focus of a fresh dispute between the Anglican hierarchy and its antagonists: Edward Jorden's *Brief discourse of a disease called the suffocation of the mother* redefined her affliction as hysteria compounded with deceit.[213] In all these instances a medical explanation was adopted in a deliberate attempt to deflate puritan pretensions. But the hotter sort of Protestants were also capable of assuming a sceptical standpoint when circumstances demanded such a stance. The pseudo-messiah William Hacket, for example, was loudly denounced as a stark raving madman by Thomas Cartwright and other presbyterians with whom the false Christ had forged incriminating links.[214] Differentiating between divine ecstasy, demonic possession, and natural disease was not only intensely subjective, it was also highly polemical.

The potential for confusing prophets, demoniacs, maniacs, and cheats and the possibility of reallocating them to a different category in the interests of a partisan cause highlight the degree to which nature and supernature, the satanic and the sacred, 'religion' and 'superstition', were divided by a movable line and a wafer-thin membrane. The tensions and ambiguities to which this and earlier sections

---

[211] See Freeman, 'Devil and John Foxe' and *The disclosing of a late counterfeyted possession by the devyl in two maydens within the citie of London* ([1574]). Foxe's involvement is established on sig. A6ᵛ.

[212] S[amuel] H[arsnet], *A discovery of the fraudulent practises of John Darrel bacheler of artes* (1599); John Deacon and John Walker, *Dialogicall discourses of spirits and divels* (1601); S[amuel] H[arsnet], *A declaration of egregious popish impostures* (1603). See also Walker, *Unclean Spirits*, 66–73; F. W. Brownlow, *Shakespeare, Harsnett, and the Devils of Denham* (Newark, NJ, 1993), esp. chs. 3–5.

[213] Edward Jorden, *A briefe discourse of a disease called the suffocation of the mother* (1603), reprod. in facsimile in MacDonald (ed.) *Witchcraft and Hysteria*. See introd., esp. pp. viii–ix, xlviii, liv.

[214] See Cartwright, *Brief apologie*, sigs. B2ᵛ, B3ʳ⁻ᵛ and my 'Frantick Hacket', 54–5.

have drawn attention testify to the eclecticism of contemporary mentalities and to the processes of negotiation by which Reformed theology and the religious culture of the laity reached an effective modus vivendi. They also demonstrate the extent to which Protestantism provided an environment within which pre-existing assumptions about the occult not only continued to survive but possibly even flourished.

CREDULITY, SCEPTICISM, AND SECTARIAN CONFLICT

As the post-Reformation period progressed, the interpretation of signs and wonders became increasingly politically charged. Simultaneously, attitudes towards preter- and supernatural phenomena were very slowly and barely perceptibly beginning to change. In the final few pages I want to suggest that these two developments may be closely linked.

As we shall see in more detail in the following chapter, bizarre events and unusual occurrences of all kinds were liable to be conscripted into the ongoing confessional war between the Churches of England and Rome. From 1559 onwards, following in the footsteps of Luther and Melanchthon, Protestant reformers and publicists enthusiastically exploited omens and portents as powerful symbols of the spiritual corruption and doctrinal deformity of their Catholic opponents. William Woodwall's allegorical poem about the reign of Elizabeth I explicated a succession of monstrous creatures as augurs of subsequent popish plots and conspiracies: the rebellion of the earls of Northumberland and Westmoreland in 1569 had been prefigured by the birth of a two-headed foal eight years before and Siamese twins born in 1585 foretold the recantation of the Jesuits Tyrrell and Tedder at Paul's Cross three years later.[215] J. L.'s *A true and perfecte description of a straung monstar borne in the city of Rome* (1590) was no less blatantly propagandist. Here the author used the standard format of the providential news pamphlet to launch an intemperate attack on the evil machinations of the papacy: the 'monstar' of the title was no more than a metaphor for Pope Sixtus V's Holy League, a bastard 'begotten of the divel upon the forenamed whor'.[216]

By the reign of James I we find prodigies and prophecies becoming pawns and weapons of sectarian conflict within the Protestant establishment, and the journalistic genre of 'strange newes' being hijacked as a vehicle for articulating topical grievances.[217] *A wonder woorth the reading*, a blackletter tract reporting the birth of

---

[215] Bodleian Library, Oxford, MS Eng. hist. e. 198, fos. 6ᵛ–7ʳ, 80ʳ.

[216] J. L., *A true and perfecte description of a straunge monstar borne in the city of Rome in Italy, in the yeare of our salvation. 1585* (1590), 2. Stephen Batman recorded among many 'monsters' born in 1570 'A Bul, without hide and hornes' hung outside the bishop of London's palace in London, i.e. Pope Pius V's excommunication of Queen Elizabeth: *Doome*, 395. On monsters as polemical metaphors, see also Kathryn M. Brammall, 'Monstrous Metamorphosis: Nature, Morality, and the Rhetoric of Monstrosity in Tudor England', *SCJ* 27 (1996), 3–21.

[217] For other examples of these strategies, see Anne Jacobson Schutte, ' "Such Monstrous Births": A Neglected Aspect of the Antinomian Controversy', *Renaissance Quarterly*, 38 (1985), 85–106; Lake, 'Puritanism, Arminianism and a Shropshire Axe-Murder'.

a deformed baby in Kent Street in August 1617, is a striking example. Published by the puritan printer William Jones on the eve of the turmoil stirred up by the Book of Sports, this 'true and faithfull relation' takes a sharp sideswipe against those who 'slight off' the 'fearefull sinne of prophaning the Saboth' with 'the title of Recreation': in the eyes of the writer, this abomination is one of the chief reasons why the Lord has sent forth his 'ensign of anger' in the guise of a grotesquely mis-shapen child.[218] An anonymous account of the parhelion observed above the Cornish market town of Tregony in December 1621 may also be less harmless than it initially seems: the author of the report of 'this fearefull and preternaturall ostent' (as entered in the Stationers' Register) was none other than that Jacobean firebrand John Everard, DD, lecturer at St Martin-in-the-Fields. A professional troublemaker whose virulently anti-Catholic sermons against the Spanish Match had landed him in gaol more times than contemporaries could count, it is highly unlikely that Everard's pamphlet did not have some kind of hidden agenda. Written at the height of the furore surrounding the Hapsburg marriage negotiations, it opened with an apocalyptic exhortation about the rising influence of Antichrist which surely enshrined a subtle critique of the policies of the current regime.[219] Equally deceptive at first sight is a reprint of three tiny Protestant tracts dating from the late Henrician period allegedly discovered encased in sailcloth in the stomach of a codfish gutted in Cambridge market on Midsummer's Eve 1626. In the unsigned preface to the volume (ingeniously titled *Vox piscis*), Thomas Goad, episcopal chaplain and committed Calvinist, expounded the significance of this strange prodigy, using it to mount an oblique but pointed attack upon the growing influence of Arminianism in England. Resituated in the context of widespread unease about constitutional innovations associated with that popular *bête noire* and the newly appointed chancellor of the University, the Duke of Buckingham, the book must clearly be regarded as something more than a bibliographical curiosity.[220] Such publications look very much like clever attempts to pull the wool over the eyes of the censor, to camouflage religious and political manifestos as scholarly antiquarianism and sensational ephemera.

The pronouncements of prophets also ceased to be ideologically innocuous. Jane Hawkins, the Cambridgeshire seer whose unflattering reflections on the status quo provoked concern among leading politicians and churchmen in 1629, had apparently been trained in the part by the precisian vicar Reverend Tokey and his curate Mr Wise, who seem to have intended to print her utterances and circulate them as propaganda.[221] Arise Evans, a Welshman who claimed to be 'God's secretary',

---

[218] *Wonder woorth the reading*, sigs. A4ᵛ–B1ʳ. On Jones, see Ch. 1 above, p. 48.

[219] [John Everard], *Somewhat: written by occasion of three sunnes seene at Tregnie in Cornewall, the 22. of December last* (1622), quotation at 11. Entered 16 Feb. 1622: *SR* iv. 64. On Everard, *DNB*, and Julia Frances Merritt, 'Religion, Government and Society in Early Modern Westminster, *c.* 1525–1625', PhD thesis (London, 1992), 349–51.

[220] See *Vox piscis: Or, the book-fish. Contayning three treatises which were found in the belly of a cod fish in Cambridge market . . .* (1627). Thomas Goad's authorship of the preface is established in BL Harleian MS 390, fo. 171ʳ. I discuss this episode in detail in ' "Vox Piscis: or the Book-Fish": Providence and the Uses of the Reformation Past in Caroline Cambridge', *EHR*, 114 (1999), 574–606.

[221] PRO SP 16/141/63 and 142/19.

beseiged Charles I's court in the 1630s, predicting the death of the King and lamenting the insidious rise of popery at the highest political levels.[222] Dame Eleanor Davies's equally impertinent prophecies against William Laud and the Stuart monarchy during the Personal Rule led to her confinement in Bethlehem Hospital, London's most famous mental asylum; not surprisingly, when the Long Parliament assembled she was rocketed to stardom.[223]

As control of the press began to disintegrate in the early 1640s, the literature of wonders also became more overtly and crudely polemical. The diabolical apparitions which had accompanied the violent electrical storms at Widecombe and Antony a few years earlier were used as evidence of divine outrage against the exploits of the bishops,[224] and on the eve of the Civil War portents of every description were being harnessed as signs of God's anger with the Laudian and Caroline regime. Once the fighting had begun, Royalist and Parliamentarian prodigy stories proliferated with predictable speed: stories of battles between regiments of frogs and batallions of flies; monstrous babies with Cavalier's locks or the pudding-basin haircut preferred by the Roundheads; elderly oracles and prognosticating children who fly off mysteriously into the sky.[225] Prophets, omens, and the pamphlets and ballads in which they were described thus have much to tell us about the ways in which public opinion before, during, and after the English Revolution was moulded and polarized.

There are grounds for suggesting that at least in the short term such news reports served to foster contemporary fascination with prodigies, and to reinforce the eclectic set of assumptions which enabled early modern Englishmen and women to make sense of them. Print invested orally transmitted wonder tales with a permanence and authority which enhanced their premonitory quality. Indeed, Thomas Nashe complained that they positively encouraged the credulity of 'gaping rurall fooles':

the Country Plowman feareth a Calabrian floodde in the midst of a furrowe, and the sillie Sheephearde committing his wandering sheepe to the custodie of his wappe, in his field

---

[222] After 1647 Evans switched his allegiance to the royalist cause. See Christopher Hill, 'Arise Evans: Welshman in London', in *Change and Continuity in Seventeenth-Century England* (New Haven, 1991 edn.), 48–77; id. and Michael Shepherd, 'The Case of Arise Evans: A Historico-Psychiatric Study', *Psychological Medicine*, 6 (1976), 351–8.

[223] Esther S. Cope, *Handmaid of the Holy Spirit: Dame Eleanor Davies, Never Soe Mad a Ladie* (Ann Arbor, 1992); Watt, *Secretaries of God*, ch. 5.

[224] Lewis Hughes, *Certaine greevances, well worthy the serious consideration of the right honorable and high court of parliament* (1640), 31–7.

[225] On the post-1640 period, see Bernard Capp, 'Popular Culture and the English Civil War', *History of European Ideas*, 10 (1989), esp. 31–4; Rusche, 'Prophecies and Propaganda'; Jerome Friedman, 'The Battle of Frogs and Fairford's Flies: Miracles and Popular Journalism during the English Revolution', *SCJ* 23 (1992), 419–42; id., *Miracles and the Pulp Press*, esp. ch. 3; Chris Durston, 'Signs and Wonders and the English Civil War', *History Today*, 37 (1987), 22–8; Andrew Warmington, 'Frogs, Toads and the Restoration in a Gloucestershire Village', *Midland History*, 14 (1989), 30–42. Typical examples include Vicars, *Prodigies & apparitions*; J[essey], *The Lords loud call to England*; and the *Mirabilis annus* pamphlets. See also Joad Raymond (ed.), *Making the News: An Anthology of the Newsbooks of Revolutionary England 1641–1660* (Moreton-in-Marsh, 1993), ch. 4.

naps dreameth of flying Dragons, which for feare least he should see to the losse of his sight, he falleth a sleepe; nor star he seeth in the night but seemeth a Comet; hee lighteth no sooner on a quagmyre, but he thinketh this is the foretold Earthquake, wherof his boy hath the Ballet.[226]

In the long run, however, the mass circulation of such leaflets and broadsheets and their manipulation by unscrupulous propagandists probably contributed to under-mining the credibility of both the discourse and the genre. Familiarity with the 'strange but true', in other words, may at length have bred contempt. Learned letter-writers and academics like John Chamberlain and Joseph Mede were apt to dismiss 'pedlarie pamflets' about portents as foolish trifles contrived by printers and their hacks, 'toyes to passe away the time'.[227] Readers in general grew increas-ingly suspicious about the authenticity of individual prodigies, especially those which were commandeered to buttress an enemy cause. Together with astrology, ecstatic prophecy, possession, and witchcraft, signs and wonders became tainted by their enslavement to the ends of party and faction and subject to spiralling allegations of forgery, fabrication, and fraud.

And yet this is a context in which it would be premature to speak of 'scepti-cism' as a coherent outlook and to imply that cynical attitudes towards the super-natural existed on an extensive scale at any level of English society. As much recent research has served to underline, even some of the most celebrated statements of 'scientific rationalism' turn out to be not so much the consequence of the onward march of mechanical philosophy and clinical medicine as by-products of the polemical circumstances in which they were conceived.[228] Historians have likewise exaggerated the degree to which prodigies cast off their sombre religious associa-tions and were demythologized in the course of the sixteenth and seventeenth cen-turies. For some contemporaries these intriguing anomalies do seem to have been no more than occasions for titillating gossip and 'table-talk'. Many of those who flocked to inspect 'strange fishe' displayed in London taverns, stared at 'Bartlemew faire babies' conveyed 'up and downe the country . . . to make a gaine', and paid a penny to see travelling circus acts and freak shows like 'The Two Inseparable Brothers', the Siamese twins from Italy who toured the British Isles between 1637 and 1642, may have derived more ghoulish amusement than moral edification from

[226] Thomas Nashe, *Nashes Lenten stuffe* (1599), sig. I2ᵛ, and *Anatomie of absurditie*, repr. in *Works*, ed. McKerrow, i. 23.

[227] Chamberlain, *Letters*, ed. McClure, i. 55, 69; BL Harleian MS 389, fos. 146ʳ, 153ᵛ, 166ʳ.

[228] Note MacDonald (ed.), *Witchcraft and Hysteria*, pp. xliv–vi. See also above, p. 217. Historians are increasingly arguing that the rise of 'scepticism' about the supernatural and its repudiation as vulgar 'superstition' was in large part a consequence of the way it became engulfed in political conflicts: Curry, 'Astrology in Early Modern England'; Elmer, 'Saints or Sorcerers', esp. 172–3; Ian Bostridge, 'Witchcraft Repealed', in Jonathan Barry, Marianne Hester, and Gareth Roberts (eds.), *Witchcraft in Early Modern Europe* (Cambridge, 1996), 309–34; Roy Porter, *Mind-forg'd Manacles: A History of Madness in England from the Restoration to the Regency* (1987), esp. 78–81; Michael MacDonald, 'Insanity and the Realities of History', *Psychological Medicine*, 11 (1981), 11–25. For similar suggestions in respect of providentialism, see Winship, 'Theater of God's Judgments', 4–5 and ch. 3.

these spectacles and sights.[229] Others, meanwhile, were coming to regard monstrous infants and beasts less as menacing tokens than examples of the benevolence of the Creator and the fecundity of Nature, specimens suitable for anatomical and embryological analysis, objects of a complex curiosity largely divorced from pious apprehension.[230] But it is still too early to conclude that belief in an interventionist deity was on the wane and 'secularization' well under way. Experimental investigation of strange medical, celestial, and terrestrial phenomena was by no means inconsistent with eschatalogical awe. Theology and biology, natural history and divinity, were still inextricably linked, and on balance, Baconian empiricism seems to have been more of a spur to, than a brake upon, fervent providentialism. Moreover, as Stuart Clark has taught us, it is entirely artificial and anachronistic to place them in bitter opposition.[231] Nor should we overstate the extent to which these embryonic intellectual trends reflected and encouraged an emerging split and dissociation between the sensibilities of the educated elite and those of the 'vulgar multitude': such a divergence was still far in the future.

Prodigies and portents need to be seen as part of a polyvalent discourse capable of operating on more than one social and rhetorical plane. Convictions about the divine origin and significance of such occurrences transcended the barriers erected by education and rank, though they took on different colours and complexions according to the cultural milieux within which they circulated.[232] When 'a great Arch of Fire' appeared in the sky above the English capital on 4 August 1571 the Spanish ambassador commented on the consternation it caused among the lower orders, who 'are so timid and greedy of wonders'.[233] Yet the evidence reviewed in this chapter suggests that such visions disturbed substantial citizens no less than their plebeian inferiors. If malformed babies drew crowds of inquisitive onlookers

[229] For references to these practices, see B[edford], *True and certaine relation of a strange-birth*, 12–13, 18; *Wonder woorth the reading*, 5. The shark described in C. R., *The true discription of this marveilous straunge fishe* ([1569]) could be seen 'at the red Lyon in Fletestreete'. [Martin Parker], *The two inseparable brothers* ([c.1634]). The twins had a licence from the Master of the Revels: Hyder E. Rollins (ed.), *The Pack of Autolycus* (Cambridge, Mass., 1927), 8. For examples of travelling freaks, see BL Egerton MS 784, fo. 110ʳ; Shrewsbury School, MS Mus X. 31, fo. 136ʳ. The Coventry Chamberlains' Accounts record payments made to one 'Walter Neare that went about to shew a child borne without armes' in 1637: John Tucker Murray (ed.), *English Dramatic Companies 1558–1642*, 2 vols. (1910), ii. 253.

[230] See Thomas, *Man and the Natural World*, ch. 2; Park and Daston, 'Unnatural Conceptions', esp. 43–54.

[231] As recent work has stressed: see Kusukawa, *Transformation of Natural Philosophy*; William B. Ashworth, 'Natural History and the Emblematic World View', in David C. Lindberg and Robert S. Westman (eds.), *Reappraisals of the Scientific Revolution* (Cambridge, 1990), 303–32. Clark, *Thinking with Demons*, pt. II, esp. chs. 10–11. Michael Winship explores the subtle adjustments late 17th-cent. New England puritans made in response to intellectual developments in 'Theater of God's Judgments' and 'Prodigies, Puritanism, and the Perils of Natural Philosophy: The Example of Cotton Mather', *William and Mary Quarterly*, 3rd ser. 51 (1994), 92–105.

[232] Cf. Madeleine Doran, 'The "Credulity" of the Elizabethans', *Journal of the History of Ideas*, 1 (1940), 151–76; Llewellyn M. Buell, 'Elizabethan Portents: Superstition or Doctrine?', in *Essays Critical and Historical Dedicated to Lily B. Campbell* (Berkeley and Los Angeles, 1950), 27–41.

[233] *Calendar of Letters and State Papers Relating to English Affairs (of the Reign of Elizabeth, 1558–1603), Preserved Principally in the Archives of Simancas*, 4 vols., ed. M. A. S. Hume (1892–9), ii. 327.

of low status and class, they also arrested the attention of prelates like James Pilkington and John Jewel, and sometimes members of the court and royal family as well.[234] Perhaps the 'thousandes' of post-Reformation pilgrims who travelled to see an Essex river which reputedly ran 'halfe water and halfe bloade' in November 1638 were mostly rural labourers, servants, and craftsmen,[235] but reports of a prodigious pond in Cambridge two years later induced a genteel lady living near Ware to write to the future archbishop of Canterbury, William Sancroft, entreating him to confirm the truth of this perturbing rumour: 'pray send us worde whether the watter continueth read still ye or noe'. Sancroft himself copied into one of his notebooks the contents of several news pamphlets, including the story of 'a strange Monster, or serpent found in the left ventricle of the heart' of John Pennant, a young man who died in 1637.[236] Mrs Margaret Owyn, the 60-year-old Welsh housewife who sprouted a four-inch horn in 1588 was not only ogled at by her neighbours and peers. Examined by local JPs, who referred the case to the Council of the Marches, she was subsequently sent to London for further investigation by the Privy Council.[237] 'That greedy seagull ignorance is apt to devoure anything', remarked Thomas Nashe, making a joke at the expense of unlearned Londoners who thought that 'the bubbling of Moore-ditch' was a 'myracle', expected a 'bedlam hatmakers wife' to bring forth 'a new Messias', and followed in the train of the latest artisan who 'proclaymes hymselfe Elias, and sayeth he is inspired wyth mutton and porredge'.[238] But child prophets and teenage demoniacs were honoured by the presence of provincial worthies as well as their less educated tenants and dependents. And in Caroline Cambridge town and gown alike considered the 'book-fish' 'a special Admonition' and 'a presage of further misery'. Stallkeepers and their customers struggled for a glimpse of this piscatorial prodigy; Joseph Mede, fellow of Christ's, dissected the slimy parcel; and James Ussher, archbishop of Armagh, feared that it embodied 'too true a Prophesy of the State to come'.[239]

Signs and wonders, then, were important points of contact between the multiple religious and social subcultures of early modern England. As such they provide unique insights into the collective consciousness of the Elizabethan and early

[234] See Jewel's letter to Henry Bullinger on 14 Aug. 1562, in *Zurich Letters*, ed. Robinson, 116; and William Garnett's letter to Pilkington regarding Siamese twins born near Newcastle in Feb. 1562: PRO SP 15/11/48. For babies brought to court, see Machyn, *Diary*, ed. Nichols, 284; BL Add. MS 35331, fo. 54[r].

[235] BL Add. MS 35331, fo. 72[v].

[236] Bodleian Library, Oxford, MS Tanner 467, fo. 71[r]; MS Sancroft 28, fos. 34–5. See also MS Sancroft 51 (notebook entitled 'Divination: Dreams, predictions, prophecies fullfilld'). I owe these references to Patrick Collinson. The latter prodigy was probably summarized from a pamphlet by Edward May, *A most certaine and true relation of a strange monster or serpent found in the left ventricle of the heart of John Pennant, gentleman* (1639).

[237] *Myraculous, and monstrous but yet, most true, and certayne discourse*, sig. A2[v].

[238] Nashe, *Lenten stuffe*, sig. I2[v].

[239] BL Harleian MS 390, fos. 82[r–v], 171[r]; Trinity College, Cambridge, MS O. 7. 3, fo. 5[v]; Richard Parr, *The life of the most reverend father in God, James Usher* (1686), 344–5.

Stuart populace. If we deliberately sidestep the positivist question of cause and treat them as products of subjective perception, they can be exceptionally revealing about the characteristics and inner contradictions of the culture that has engendered them, a sensitive barometer of its deepest preoccupations and fears. Historians have interpreted reports of curious cloud formations, fireballs, comets, beached whales, and Siamese twins as external projections of the instability of Italy in the wake of the invasion by Charles VIII, the volatility of France during the Wars of Religion, the turmoil created by the early Reformation in Germany, and the vulnerability of the young Dutch Republic.[240] The very fact that contemporaries from all points on the ideological spectrum believed that prodigies were proliferating in late sixteenth- and seventeenth-century Britain likewise alerts us to a growing sense of ecclesiastical and political disequilibrium. For, as Joseph Mede recognized, the apparent profusion of preternatural phenomena was partly a function of heightened sensitivity to their incidence: 'either we have more strange accidents then was wont', he wrote in 1627, 'or we take more notice of them or both'.[241] Preaching in Newcastle-upon-Tyne around the same time, the Laudian divine Dr Thomas Jackson feared that 'the first drops of Gods displeasure against the Nation' which such 'prognostiques' embodied would soon swell into a current, a river, a flood, and then into 'an ocean of publique woe, and tragique miseries'.[242] Indexing widespread anxieties about impending crisis and catastrophe, they suggest that the mental preconditions for Civil War were already in place.

[240] See Niccoli, *Prophecy and People*, esp. 19; Schenda, *Französische Prodigienliteratur*, esp. 136–9; Barnes, *Prophecy and Gnosis*; Simon Schama, *The Embarrassment of Riches: An Interpretation of Dutch Culture in the Golden Age* (1987), ch. 3, pt i.

[241] BL Harleian MS 390, fo. 211^r.

[242] Thomas Jackson, *A treatise concerning the signes of the time, or Gods forewarnings*, separately paginated in *Diverse sermons, with a short treatise befitting these present times* (Oxford, 1637), 8.

5
'Miracles of this Latter Age': Providence, Confessional Politics, and Patriotism

As the preceding chapters have shown, it would be a grave mistake to suppose that the discourse of divine providence was in any sense a monopoly of the hotter sort of Protestants. By enhancing the doctrine of a vigilant and interventionist deity, Calvinist theology merely intensified a cluster of assumptions which had long been part of the machinery of pre-Reformation minds. Far from rejecting the notion that supernatural forces intruded into human affairs and effecting a paradigm shift in conceptions of the relationship between the sacred and secular spheres, Protestantism actually served to reinforce the idea of a 'sacramental' and 'moralized' universe.[1] In this sense early modern Catholics and Protestants shared the same frame of reference: providential beliefs cut across the invisible iron curtain which contemporary polemic erected between Geneva and Rome.

This chapter examines how these rival proselytizing organizations appropriated and deployed providence as an intellectual weapon in their struggle to win converts, reinforce the commitment of their existing constituencies, and undermine the morale and credibility of their 'heretical' or 'antichristian' enemies. It explores the degree to which the task of interpreting God's actitivies in the temporal world became implicated in sectarian controversy and confessional strife prior to the outbreak of the Civil War, fuelling the perennial conflict between Catholics and Protestants, and, by the 1620s, exacerbating rifts and frictions within the established Church itself. Propagandists on either side of the Reformation divide were adept at exploiting out-of-the-ordinary events to promote and vindicate their cause, but it was Protestant polemicists who made the repeated interventions of the Almighty in English history the centrepiece of an enduring and chauvinistic national myth. Fusing anti-Catholic providentialism with patriotism, they invented a tradition of prejudice which not only took firm root in the imagination and the culture of the populace, but as David Cressy has demonstrated, was creatively mutated and warped as it was absorbed.[2] As effective as it was in bolstering loyalty to the Elizabethan and early Stuart state, providence also contributed to the development of a dangerously polarized and potentially explosive political scene.

---

[1] See Robert W. Scribner, 'The Reformation, Popular Magic, and the "Disenchantment of the World"', *Journal of Interdisciplinary History*, 23 (1993), 474–7 and *passim*.
[2] Cressy, *Bonfires and Bells*, p. xiv and *passim*.

MIRACLES HAVE CEASED

The working of miracles, maintained a host of late sixteenth- and early seventeenth-century Protestant writers and preachers, had long since ceased. As the Bible recorded, in the far distant past it had pleased God 'extraordinarilie to shew miracles amongest his people': hence the parting of the Red Sea to allow the Israelites to escape Pharaoh's army, hence manna falling from heaven to sustain them in the desert, hence the prophet Aaron transforming his rod into a serpent.[3] Prodigious feats above, against, or beyond the regular mechanisms of nature had also been performed by Christ and his Apostles before and immediately after his death, 'the exigence of the times so requiring', remarked Dr Robert Tynley, Archdeacon of Ely in 1609, 'when the doctrine of the Gospell was strange, new, and incredible', even 'a stumbling block' to the benighted Jews.[4] According to the convert Richard Sheldon's *Survey of the miracles of the Church of Rome* published in 1616, God had endowed Peter and Paul with special powers to help guide the first believers through 'the wildernes of Gentilisme' and the thickets of 'Pharasaicall pride'.[5] Signs and wonders, agreed the Spanish Calvinist Ferdinando Texeda, writing in 1625, were 'the seales and testimonials of Evangelicall Faith', the mother's milk on which the infant Church was weaned.[6] But this 'gift', stressed Calvin and his disciples, was 'only of temporary duration', 'soon lost, in some measure, by the ingratitude of men'.[7] Citing the Fathers Augustine and Chrysostom they insisted that although miracles had been necessary for the 'first begetting, breeding and nourcing' of Christianity, once it became established these props and aids, like a baby's walking frame, had been removed as redundant. To look for them 'in the cleere Sun-shine light of the Gospell' was to 'tempt' and 'doe injurie' to God. In the post-Apostolic age, declared Edward Dering in the 1570s, the Lord expected His people to embrace the truth without the help of any visible spectacles, and not, like doubting Thomas, to refuse to believe unless they could see. It was on the ark and anchor of the Word that Christians should ground their belief, not these 'poore and childish conceits'. Such wonders were a positive hindrance to real saving faith in the latter days of the world.[8] As John Jewel con-

---

[3] Scot, *Discoverie of witchcraft*, bk. VIII, ch. 1; Perkins, *Damned art of witchcraft*, 13. For helpful discussions of some of the issues raised in this section, see Kocher, *Science and Religion*, 104–10; D. P. Walker, 'The Cessation of Miracles', in Ingrid Merkel and Allen G. Debus (eds.), *Hermeticism and the Renaissance: Intellectual History and the Occult in Early Modern Europe* (Washington, 1988), 111–24.

[4] Robert Tynley, *Two learned sermons* (1609), 59–60, and 58–65 *passim*. Tynley was answering the arguments advanced by the exiled priest Robert Chambers in the preface to his trans. of Philips Numan, *Miracles lately wrought by the intercession of the glorious Virgin Marie, at Mont-aigu, nere unto Sichem in Brabant* (Antwerp, 1606).

[5] Richard Sheldon, *A survey of the miracles of the Church of Rome, proving them to be antichristian* (1616), 51.

[6] Ferdinando Texeda, *Miracles unmasked* (1625), 4–5. See also Edward Dering, *XXVII lectures or readings, upon part of the Epistle written to the Hebrues* (1576), repr. in *Workes*, 116–17.

[7] Calvin, *Institutes*, bk. IV, ch. 19, §18–19.

[8] Richard Baddeley, *The boy of Bilson: or, a true discovery of the late notorious impostures of certaine Romish priests in their pretended exorcisme . . . [of] William Perry* (1622), 2; Tynley, *Two learned sermons*, 65; Dering, *XXVII lectures*, in *Workes*, 116–17; Sheldon, *Survey*, 35, 49. See also John Downame (ed.), *The summe of sacred divinitie first briefly & methodically propounded* ([1620?]), 377.

cluded in a defence of his famous *Apologie of the Churche of England*, miracles were not 'evermore undoubted proofs' and 'perpetuall companions' of orthodox dogma.[9]

Most of these statements were made in the context of overt or oblique attacks on the Roman Catholic thaumaturgic cult. The marvels associated with saints, pilgrimages, relics, shrines, and exorcizing priests were condemned as inherently meretricious, counterfeit, and false, either a cunning variety of ecclesiastical fraud or the consequence of the 'secret collusions of infernal feyndes'.[10] Romish priests devised such 'coosening tricks', 'juggling knaveries', and 'crafty legerdemaines' to delude the gullible laity for 'their own lucre and gayne'.[11] Richard Sheldon attacked the 'copper Fables' incorporated in the famous *Golden Legend* as 'a packe of humane inventions', 'phantastick dotages' dreamt up by that 'Voraginous prelate', the thirteenth-century archbishop of Genoa, Jacobus de Voragine. The Jacobean minister John Gee echoed him, denouncing 'Popish Tales and fittens' as the 'poore shifts' to which Catholics were driven 'for the keeping of their weather-beaten cause aflote'.[12] According to Dering all Rome's doctrinal errors had been engendered by 'lying wonders', and 'the verie dregges of miracles, in milkepannes and greasie dishes, by Robin goodfellowe, and Hags, and Fayries' continued to underprop their idolatry and 'idle superstitions'.[13] If such anomalies could not be explained away as 'papisticall' sleight of hand, they could always be ascribed to diabolical artifice and malice—in other words to witchcraft. Sometimes God permitted the devil to simulate supernatural affects to lead the reprobate to spiritual destruction or to test and try the elect.[14] These were the 'snares of Sathan', demonic stratagems of which the godly were advised to beware.[15] The Pope's miracles, then, were Satan's miracles, 'signed with his counterfet seale'. And their very abundance and 'over-plus' in the Roman Catholic Church was patent proof that it was the antichristian synagogue foreshadowed in the Apocalypse. For, as Sheldon explained, with the advent of Antichrist true wonders had been largely withdrawn, leaving a proliferation of false ones in their place, the 'lying wonders' of the last days warned of in Matthew xxiv and 2 Thessalonians ii.[16]

Such arguments were an integral part of the conventional Reformation assault on popery as a faith based on the hypocrisy and deceit of the priesthood and the blind ignorance and credulity of the laity; they were central to Protestantism's

[9] John Jewel, *A defence of the apologie of the Churche of England* (1567), in *The Works . . .* , ed. John Ayre, 4 vols., Parker Soc. (Cambridge, 1845–50), iii. 197; Texeda, *Miracles unmasked*, 4.

[10] Numan, *Miracles*, sig. B5ʳ. See also Texeda, *Miracles unmasked*, 6 and *passim*.

[11] Numan, *Miracles*, sig. C2ᵛ; Deacon and Walker, *Dialogicall discourses*, 326, cf. 326–8. See also Jewel, *An exposition upon the two epistles of St Paul to the Thessalonians* (1583) in *Works*, ed. Ayre, ii. 922.

[12] John Gee, *The foot out of the snare: with a detection of sundry late practices and impostures of the priests and Jesuites in England* (1624), 25; Sheldon, *Survey*, 62–3, 119.

[13] Dering, *XXVII lectures*, in *Workes*, 116. See also Thomas Pickering's 'Epistle Dedicatorie' to Perkins, *Damned art of witchcraft and Miracle upon miracle*, 1–3.

[14] Tynley, *Two learned sermons*, 59–60.

[15] Dering, *XXVII lectures*, in *Workes*, 114.

[16] Sheldon, *Survey*, 9–10, 43–4, 59, 111, 225, and *passim*.

attempt to align itself with the forces of rationality and enlightenment.[17] They were also a direct response to Catholic controversialists like Richard Bristow, John Floyd, and Cardinal Robert Bellarmine who vigorously upheld the continuing validation of the visible Church and its members by 'personall' and 'dogmaticall' miracles. Wonders wrought both through the ministry of holy men and women and immediately by God numbered among the perpetual marks which distinguished the true religion from perfidious heresy. At a time when false doctrine, prophets, and sects were rife and scepticism was eating away at the heart of society such manifestations of divine power were deemed to be particularly needful—to validate beliefs and practices rejected by Protestants as superstitious and idolatrous and to assist the struggle of the Catholic missionaries to reverse the Reformation.[18] Robert Chambers, an English seminary priest based in Brussels, contemptuously dismissed the contention that 'the benefits which have descended down upon us from heaven, are certain pestilent pernicious contagions that are vamped out of the accursed dungeon and pitt of hel': apparitions, amazing cures, and retributive punishments were tokens of comfort to God's persecuted children and they rendered heretics who refused to 'woork their owne conversions' utterly inexcusable. To his mind, the reformers' assertion that this class of supernatural happening had disappeared when Christianity declined from its primitive purity was a transparent apologetic ploy: how else could they counteract Rome's claim to a direct and unbroken line of descent from the first-century Church?[19]

There was more than a grain of truth in this disarming allegation. The principle that miracles had ceased allowed Protestants to demolish all modern Catholic marvels at a single stroke: it relieved them of the responsibility of proving both that every individual case was either the product of trickery or sorcery and that Roman Catholicism was the Scarlet Whore and Seven Headed Beast identified in the Book of Revelation. Their insistence that God never gave the glory of His power to His creatures might be seen as equally expedient: again it automatically undercut the thaumaturgic pretensions of popish saints and priests.

These precepts also proved to be polemically useful in other debates and disputes. They were often invoked by Protestant demonologists intent on contradicting the common assumption that witches had an intrinsic ability to inflict harm upon their victims. And conformist propagandists engaged in the campaign to discredit the activities of the puritan exorcist John Darrell and his associates frequently reiterated these axioms in their attack upon the possibility of expelling unclean spirits by fasting and prayer, in the process making it something of a shib-

---

[17] See Peter Lake, 'Anti-Popery: The Structure of a Prejudice', in Richard Cust and Ann Hughes (eds.), *Conflict in Early Stuart England: Studies in Religion and Politics 1603–1642* (1989), 74–7.

[18] Richard Bristow, *A briefe treatise of divers plaine and sure waies to finde out the truth in this doubtfull and dangerous time of heresie* (Antwerp, 1599), §v and vi (pp. 15a–32b); John Floyd, *Purgatories triumph over hell* ([St Omer], 1613), ch. 5, esp. pp. 131–5; Robert Bellarmine, *Disputationum . . . de controversiis Christianae fidei, adversus huius temporis haereticos* (Ingolstadt, 1601 edn.; 1st pub. 1586), vol. i, bk. IV, ch. 14. See also Walker, 'Cessation of Miracles', 117–19.

[19] Numan, *Miracles*, quotations at sigs. B5[r], F2[r] and see sig. A6[r-v].

boleth of what (with mild anachronism) might be called 'Anglicanism'. By brand-ing the 'pestilent opinion' that miraculous events still occurred in modern times 'the liverie and badge' of Antichrist's 'brood', Samuel Harsnet, John Deacon, and John Walker were able to dismiss Darrell's dispossessions in the same breath as the 'counterfeit crankes' of the 'cogging' Catholic clergy.[20] Carrying the logic of anti-popery through to its natural conclusions thus significantly reduced the scope of spiritual agency in the physical world: indeed, as the contemporary response to Reginald Scot's *Discoverie of witchcraft* revealed, it could even lay one open to charges of atheism.[21]

But it is important to remember that all of these categorical assertions were made in the heat of controversy, by commentators braced for combat in the confessional boxing ring. Anthony Milton's *Catholic and Reformed* has taught us to be sensitive to the circumstances in which dogmatic statements were articulated, and high-lighted the extent to which English Protestant doctrine was 'shifting and pluralis-tic, varying in tone and content' in different situations.[22] The point certainly rings true in relation to the cessation of miracles: when the clergy addressed the ques-tion in other discursive contexts their answers were not always quite so cut and dried. As we saw in Chapter 1, very few were prepared to declare that God never interrupted or overrode the laws of nature. To do so would be to imply that the Lord had tied Himself exclusively to the use of secondary causes and this would derogate seriously from His supreme majesty. And, *pace* the polemicists, there was nothing in Scripture to confirm unequivocally the claim that miracles had ceased when the primitive Church cast off its swaddling bands.[23]

Theologians thus preserved room in Reformed cosmology for events that occurred 'beside the order so appointed' at Creation: they simply subsumed them into the category of 'special' or 'extraordinary providences'. 'By a metonymy of the effect', conceded William Ames, an occurrence of this kind could be 'called a Miracle'.[24] But the concept was hedged about with a number of significant qualifications. 'Special providences' and miracles were not spontaneous or im-promptu interventions; they were events for which God had foreseen the need and

---

[20] Deacon and Walker, *Dialogicall discourses*, unpaginated preface 'To the godly affected Reader' and dialogue 10; H[arsnet], *Discovery*, sig. A2^r-v. Harsnet used the same arguments against Catholic exor-cists in his *Declaration of egregious popish impostures*. See also Walker, *Unclean Spirits*, 66–9.

[21] See Sharpe, *Instruments of Darkness*, 53–5; Leland Estes, 'Reginald Scot and his *Discoverie of Witchcraft*: Religion and Science in the Opposition to the European Witch Craze', *Church History*, 52 (1983), 444–56. Sydney Anglo in 'Reginald Scot's *Discoverie of Witchcraft*: Scepticism and Sadduceeism', in id. (ed.), *The Damned Art: Essays in the Literature of Witchcraft* (1977), 106–39, shows that in the 'Discourse on divels' appended to the *Discoverie* Scot explicitly denied the intervention of both divine and demonic forces in human affairs.

[22] Anthony Milton, *Catholic and Reformed: The Roman and Protestant Churches in English Protestant Thought 1600–1640* (Cambridge, 1995), 542 and *passim*.

[23] As John Darrell noted, *An apologie, or defence of the possession of William Sommers* ([Amsterdam, 1599?]), fo. 11^v and *A briefe narration of the possession, dispossession, and repossession of William Sommers* ([Amsterdam?], 1598), sig. C1^v.

[24] Sibbes, *Works*, i. 205; Pemble, *Workes*, 279; Ames, *Marrow of sacred divinity*, 41. See also Walker, *Learned and profitable treatise*, 52–4; Hill, *Life everlasting*, 481–5.

built into His plan for humanity before the beginning of time. Nor could they be brought about at human behest, through the intercession of dead martyrs and saints. The Lord had stopped bestowing the gift of working wonders upon individual persons. According to William Perkins, the Apostles and Old Testament prophets had worked miracles as instruments of the Almighty only, and not of their own right, and even Christ's cure of the leper and raising of Lazarus from the dead proceeded directly from the omnipotence of His Father in heaven.[25] As for the assumption that consecrated objects had inherent thaumaturgic properties, in the eyes of Protestant divines this was tantamount to heathen idolatry. No less erroneous was the suggestion that Satan had the capacity to perform truly supernatural acts. In sixteenth- and seventeenth-century thinking, the devil was no more than a master of illusion and disguise, a skilled practitioner of natural magic and science. He could not challenge or subvert the fundamental order of things: God had the monopoly on all transactions of this kind.[26]

Nevertheless the vast majority of Protestant clergymen agreed that real miracles were exceedingly rare. Most examples of providential interference were *miranda* not *miracula*, preternatural wonders brought about by divine manipulation of secondary causes and elemental forces.[27] Calvinist theoreticians insisted that these two types of occurrence were generically distinct, but in practice, application, and above all collective perception, the line of demarcation between miracles, providences, and prodigious but entirely natural events was very hazy indeed. No less problematic was the task of deciding whether bizarre and puzzling phenomena should be attributed to diabolical guile, human cunning, the creativity of Nature, or the ingenuity of the Almighty. As contemporaries recognized, there was plenty of potential for confusion, especially on the part of ill-educated individuals ignorant of intellectual advances taking place in academic circles and unaware of the basic foundations of natural philosophy.[28]

It is probably safe to say that most ordinary laypeople were oblivious to the subtleties of the scholars' hairsplitting, technical definitions. Strange occurrences of all types were liable to be assigned the wrong causal label: destructive fires, storms, and floods; earthquakes and outbreaks of plague; monstrous births and eerie apparitions in the skies; tragic accidents and sudden deaths. Were those who wrote and read sensational news pamphlets emblazoned with titles like *Miracle upon miracle* or *Miraculous newes* alive to the controversy which this term generated in the studies and lecture rooms of the learned?[29] Did people who flocked to mineral

---

[25] Perkins, *Damned art of witchcraft*, 15–17 and see also sig.¶6ᵛ; Scot, *Discoverie of witchcraft*, bk. VII, ch. 1.

[26] Clark, 'Rational Witchfinder', 222–7; id., *Thinking with Demons*, pt. II, ch. 11.

[27] Darrell, *Apologie, or defence*, fo. 14ʳ⁻ᵛ and id., *A brief apologie proving the possession of William Somers* ([Middelburg], 1599), 33. See also H[arsnet], *Discovery*, sig. A4ʳ⁻ᵛ; Deacon and Walker, *Dialogicall discourses*, 312–14.

[28] See Clark, *Thinking with Demons*, esp. 153–5, 161–78, 262–6, 279.

[29] See e.g. *Myraculous, and monstrous, but yet, most true, and certayne discourse; Miracle upon miracle;* T. I., *A miracle, of miracles; Miraculous newes, from the cittie of Holdt*.

springs and newly discovered spas in the post-Reformation period gratefully attribute their medicinal properties to the beneficence of divine providence working through chemical and geological processes? Or did they regard these watering places in the same hallowed light as medieval pilgrims had revered healing wells dedicated to regional saints? In a tract about a spa established at Newnham Regis in Warwickshire in the mid-1580s, Dr Walter Bailey, Regius Professor of Physic at Oxford, complained that too many were carried away by the opinion that 'the faculties and vertues of them, were supernaturally given from God without any ordinarie meanes'—'Much like unto the superstition of our forefathers'.[30] And we may well ask whether those who assembled to witness the expulsion of demons from possessed children and adolescents acknowledged any difference in kind between those accomplished by puritan preachers and those performed by Tridentine priests. Despite the protestations of Darrell and others to the contrary, exorcism by fasting and prayer could develop into a ritual claiming near mechanical efficacy, and it is not surprising that prominent spiritual therapists, including the martyrologist Foxe, were canonized by the 'vulgar Sort' as 'Diviner[s] of signes and of wonders'.[31] Similar questions arise with regard to the *Actes and monuments* itself: the eyewitness accounts of Protestants burning at the stake which Foxe absorbed into his narrative include stories of incombustible organs and spectral tokens which bear a remarkable resemblance to those embedded in traditional hagiography and recounted in the histories of Eusebius and Bede—sources which the reformers denounced vociferously. This was a contradiction upon which the Douai controversialist Thomas Stapleton was all too quick to capitalize: 'Ar there not also in that donghell heaped a number of miserable miracles to sette forth the glory of their stinking martyrs?', he asked; 'Iff the Crosse of saint Oswalde seme a superstitious tale, how much more fonde and fabulous is the tale of one that suffred at Bramford, with a greate white crosse, appearing in his brest?'[32] The essential disparity between spurious 'popish' wonders and bona fide Protestant

---

[30] Bailey, *Briefe discours*, 4 and sig. A3[r–v]. On the problem of holy wells and miraculous cures after the Reformation, see my 'Reforming the Waters: Holy Wells and Healing Springs in Protestant England', in Diana Wood (ed.), *Life and Thought in the Northern Church, c.1100–c.1700*, SCH Subsidia 12 (Woodbridge, 1999 227–55).

[31] See Darrell, *Breife narration*, sig. C1[v]; id., *Apologie, or defence*, fos. 14[v]–18[v]. Deacon and Walker, *Dialogicall discourses*, 'To the godly affected Reader'. Bristow made much of the parallel: *Briefe treatise*, fo. 27b. See also Thomas, *Religion and the Decline of Magic*, 150–1 and Freeman, 'Devil and John Foxe'. A book of miracles supposedly performed by the presbyterian leader Thomas Cartwright allegedly circulated among his admirers: Cartwright, *Brief apologie*, sig. B5[r].

[32] Stapleton's preface to Bede's *The history of the church of Englande* (Antwerp, 1565), fos. 8[v]–9[r]. Cf. Floyd, *Purgatories triumph*, 138–42; [Nicholas Harpsfield], Alan Cope, (pseud.), *Dialogi sex* (Antwerp, 1566), dialogue 6; Robert Persons, *A treatise of three conversions of England from paganism to Christian religion*, 3 vols. ([St Omer], 1603–4), pt. II. See also Patrick Collinson, 'Truth, Lies, and Fiction in Sixteenth Century Protestant Historiography', in Donald R. Kelley and David Harris Sacks (eds.), *The Historical Imagination in Early Modern Britain: History, Rhetoric, and Fiction 1500–1800* (Cambridge, 1997), 55–7, and R. W. Scribner, 'Incombustible Luther: The Image of the Reformer in Early Modern Germany', in id., *Popular Culture and Popular Movements in Reformation Germany* (1987), 323–53. As noted above, Ch. 2 n. 35, such evidence contradicts the views of earlier scholars like Helen White and John Knott on Foxe's attitude to the miraculous.

ones may well have escaped the undiscriminating. To the untrained and relatively
unbiased eye they probably seemed one and the same.

'[G]odly credulitie', a senior Counter-Reformation missionary allegedly declared around 1586, 'doth much good, for the furthering of the Catholique cause,
and for the defacing of our common enemies, and their proceedings'. This incriminating admission extracted by the ecclesiastical authorities from the prominent
apostate Anthony Tyrrell was designed to prove just how unscrupulous the 'impos-
turizing renagadoes' of the Church of Rome really were.[33] Yet ardent Protestants
could hardly claim the high moral ground, for they were no less ready to utilize
the general fascination with the occult and to exploit the ambiguity surrounding
the question of whether or not miracles had ceased. Both sought to press providence into the service of confessional propaganda, and competed to control the
way in which contemporaries interpreted unexpected events.

STRANGE CONJECTURES OF VAYNE EVENTS

No incident from the early part of Elizabeth's reign illustrates this contest more
clearly than the devastating fire, ignited by a bolt of lightning, which consumed
the steeple, bells, and timber roof of St Paul's Cathedral on the eve of the abolished feast of Corpus Christi, 4 June 1561.[34] '[S]trooke with amazement', crowds
'filled all places with tumult and confusione, expecting a generall calamity of the
city'. 'Hereuppon', John Hayward recorded in his annals, 'strange conjectures wer
conceived, as of secret causes, soe of vayne events' which never came to pass.[35]
'[F]ond talkes' about the origin and significance of this 'rufull' accident filled the
air and several ballads on the subject were immediately published. Some blamed
the negligence of plumbers melting lead to repair the guttering; some suggested a
conspiracy involving 'wildfyer or gunpowder'; others suspected the nefarious practices of ill-affected conjurers and sorcerers, especially when 'certein charmes
or inchauntments, and devises of witchcraft' were discovered 'hydde in the
grownde'.[36] Many seem to have considered this catastrophe in the national capital
less than two years after the Queen's accession highly inauspicious. To impres-

---

[33] H[arsnet], *Declaration of egregious popish impostures* (1604 edn.), 251 and sig. A3ʳ, and see 246–56.
[34] The most extensive account can be found in *The true report of the burnyng of the steple and churche of Poules in London* (1561), sigs. A2ʳ–6ᵛ. *STC* attributes this item to James Pilkington, but as he is referred to in the third person throughout this may be incorrect. It was published in Latin as *Exemplum literarum amici cuiusdam ad omicum quendam suum, de vera origine conflagrationis pyramidis, & templi Paulini Londinensis* (1561), a copy of which is preserved in PRO SP 12/17/28. The official version entered in Bishop Grindal's register by the diocesan registrar Peter Johnson is printed in W. Sparrow Simpson (ed.), *Documents Illustrating the History of S. Paul's Cathedral*, CS, NS 26 (1880), 113–19. See also Patrick Collinson, *Archbishop Grindal 1519–1583* (1979), ch. 8.
[35] Hayward, *Annals*, ed. Bruce, 87–8.
[36] *True report of the burnyng of . . . Poules*, sig. A6ᵛ; Robert Persons, *An epistle of the persecution of Catholickes in Englande* (Douai [Rouen], [1582]), 148–9. The three ballads on the subject entered in the Stationers' Register (*SR* i. 202, 210, 263) seem now to be lost. The ballad entitled 'The burning of Powles', transcribed in FSL MS V. a. 339, fos. 132ᵛ–133ʳ, should be treated as a probable Collier forgery.

sionable minds, the fact that nothing remained of the Protestant communion table but a heap of smouldering coals no doubt spoke for itself.

In a sermon the next Sunday Bishop James Pilkington of Durham declared that the true source of the fatal spark was the Lord and exhorted his audience to view the visitation as a general warning to the whole realm of 'some greater plage to folow, if amendmente of lyfe in all states did not ensue'. He rebuked those who made a scapegoat of some 'perticuler' sector of society rather than acknowledge their own faults and sins and sharply reproved the 'prophanatyon' of Christ's temple during service time by 'walking, jangling, brawling, fighting, bargaining, &c'. Pilkington was especially anxious to scotch rumours spread by 'evil tunged persons' that the blaze was a divine punishment for the recent 'alteracion, or rather reformacion of religion': to neutralize this damaging allegation he rehearsed a long list of calamities which had befallen English churches while Romish 'supersticion and ignorance' had reigned.[37]

The chief target of Pilkington's attack was John Morwen, chaplain to Bishop Edmund Bonner and a former cathedral prebendary, who had written and disseminated 'in the stretes of West Chester' a 'seditious libel' in manuscript concerning the 'brinnynge of Paules'.[38] It was 'no marvaile', insisted Morwen, that God had sent fire from heaven to engulf the grandest church in a kingdom which had brazenly abolished the mass and abandoned its ancestors' faith. He agreed with Pilkington that this consecrated building had been polluted and abused, but alleged that it had been desecrated less by the congregation than by 'blasphemous' Protestant preachers and bishops. It was their 'newe fanglet doctrine' and the concomitant 'deformation' of morals and manners which had precipitated this providential judgement. He admonished his readers to ignore the 'faire wordes' of 'false Prophetes' and tread in the footsteps of their fathers, 'els Gods vengeance hanges over your heades'.[39]

Morwen's impertinent assertions could hardly be left unanswered and in due course a vigorous counterblast against popery appeared from the pen of a third polemicist. Only 'worldlynges' judged 'their religyon' 'by their bellye' and by random accidents, the author stressed, urging his readers to ignore the propaganda of the 'scavenger', frame their lives in accordance with the Gospel, or find themselves consumed by supernatural plagues.[40] But on this occasion it was probably

[37] *True report of the burnyng of . . . Poules*, sigs. A7ʳ–8ᵛ.

[38] [John Morwen], 'An addicion with an apologie to the causes of brinnynge of Paules Church . . . ', printed for refutation in *The burnynge of Paules church in London in the yeare of oure Lord 1561* (1563), quotations at sigs. A6ᵛ, A2ʳ respectively. On Morwen, see also PRO SP 15/11/45.

[39] [Morwen], 'Addicion with an apologie', in *Burnynge of Paules church*, sigs. A3ʳ–6ʳ. Catholics on the European mainland drew a similarly anti-Protestant moral: see the letter from Cardinal Commendone to Cardinal Borromeo, quoted in Henry Hart Milsom, *Annals of S. Paul's Cathedral* (2nd edn. 1869), 281 n. 9.

[40] 'A confutacion of an Addicion, wyth an Appologye . . . agaynst the causes of burnyng Paules Church in London', in *Burnynge of Paules church*, quotations at sigs. O8ᵛ, A7ʳ, and see sigs. P2ᵛ–3ʳ. The 'Confutacion' has always been ascribed to Pilkington, and is repr. in *Works*, ed. Scholefield, but again

the crude providentialism employed by his opponents which made more impact on that large segment of the populace as yet only half-heartedly committed to the Protestant regime.

The Almighty also appeared to be patronizing the papists in July of 1577, a few months before the execution of the proto-martyr of the English missionaries, Cuthbert Maine. At the summer assizes in Oxford, Rowland Jenkes, a defiant Catholic bookseller and binder, was indicted for publicly railing against the established religion, and for possessing and dispersing scandalous pamphlets and papal bulls against the Queen and state. For these 'high crimes and misdemeanours', the stationer was condemned to have his ears nailed to the pillory and to release himself by cutting them off with his own right hand. This celebrated treason trial coincided with an outbreak of typhus or 'gaol fever', during which almost the entire judicial bench and jury, together with several hundred other inhabitants of the university town, appear to have perished.[41]

Catholic writers eagerly seized upon this 'mortal distemper' as a divine reprisal for the barbarous treatment ordered to be meted out to Jenkes, suggesting that there was a direct causal relationship between his conviction and the onset of this mysterious contagious disease. '[T]he judge had hardly delivered the sentence' when the deadly pestilence descended upon the court, drawing its unjust proceedings to an abrupt and untimely halt—or so the Louvain theologian Dr Nicholas Sander asserted in a Latin survey of the rise and growth of the 'Anglican schism' which later became an international best-seller.[42] Equally partisan accounts of this 'ingens miraculum' or 'mighty miracle' were published by Robert Persons in his *Epistle of the persecution* (1581), subsequently incorporated in the compilation of documents known as *Concertatio ecclesiae Catholicae* (1593), and in a Spanish history of the sufferings of the English Catholics written by Bishop Yepez of Taraçona, confessor to King Philip II. All four works were components of a political campaign launched by clerical exiles on the Continent to highlight the plight of the faithful under the oppressive policies of the 'Calvino-papistas' and 'puritanos' in England.[43]

The 'solemn assize' had similar reverberations at home. Recusants and church

---

the fact that he is referred to at several points in the third person must cast a shadow of doubt on this attribution.

[41] Contemporary accounts can be found in Holinshed, *Chronicles*, iii. 1270; Stow, *Annales*, 1154; William Camden, *Annales. The true and royal history of the famous empresse Elizabeth queene of Englande France and Ireland &c* (1625), 376; Fuller, *Church-history of Britain*, bk. IX, pp. 109–10.

[42] Nicholas Sander, *Rise and Growth of the Anglican Schism*, trans. David Lewis (1877), 307–8, quotation at 308. This was the first English edn.

[43] Persons, *Epistle of the persecution*, 149–51; John Gibbons and John Fen (eds.), *Concertatio ecclesiae Catholicae in Anglia* (n.p., 1588), 37–8; Yepez, Bishop of Taraçona, *Historia particular de la persecucion de Inglaterra* (Madrid, 1599), 75. See also Pedro Ribadeneira's appendix to the Latin edn. of Sander's *Rise and Growth of the Anglican Schism* of 1610: *Nicolai Sanderi . . . De origine ac progressu schismatis anglicani* (n.p., 1610), ch. 13, pp. 59–64. A short notice of the incident was inserted in the register of Douai College in Aug. 1577: T. F. Knox (ed.), *The First and Second Diaries of the English College, Douay, and an Appendix of Unpublished Documents* (1878), 127.

papists in the vicinity of Oxford seem to have dispersed anti-Protestant interpretations of the epidemic in and around the prison. An eyewitness signing himself 'W. B.' prepared an authoritative report to stifle the 'flieng rumors' of those who had 'spoken untrulie in this behalfe', circulating 'their owne fantasies' concerning the 'venemous maladie'.[44] Some of these may have concerned the confessional identity of the dead: conspicuous among the victims were Sir Robert Bell, Speaker of the House of Commons and Chief Baron of the Exchequer, and Nicholas Barham, serjeant-at-law, 'both great enemies of the Popish religion'—a detail committed adherents of the Church of Rome are hardly likely to have left unremarked.[45] Lugubrious Protestant ballads lamenting the victims' demise seem to have been countered by the Catholic underground with rhymes and songs reflecting bitterly on the circumstances surrounding the Black Assize. The Welsh priest Richard White or Gwynne composed a carol in his native tongue which referred to Judge Bell as a wicked persecutor of God's people and suggested that the calamity had been sent 'to strike terror' into the heart of Queen Elizabeth herself.[46] An unlicensed pamphlet 'towching the late mortallitie' whose publication came under episcopal scrutiny in September may also have betrayed suspiciously 'popish' sympathies.[47] More than 150 years later, Richard Challoner, bishop of Debra, was still allocating the story of the prodigious infection a prominent place in his catalogue of martyrs, *Memoirs of Missionary Priests*: it slotted smoothly into his quasi-sacred chronicle of the Catholic community's triumph over terrorism and death.[48]

Most contemporary Protestants resorted to fairly lame and unoriginal explanations of the strange sickness in reply. There was much speculation about the suffocating effect of the nauseating stench emanating from the criminal-infested cells, but even more talk of black magic and biological warfare perpetrated by the agents of Antichrist. A few muttered about spells cast by the bookseller himself.[49] While some insisted that it was unwise to search divine providence too narrowly, others could be as ingenious as their assailants when it came to decoding the cryptic message encapsulated in temporal events. Ferocious enemies of Rome like Stephen

[44] Now lost, but cited by Abraham Fleming in Holinshed, *Chronicles*, iii. 1270.

[45] As Anthony à Wood noted in his account in *History and Antiquities of . . . Oxford*, ii. 188–92.

[46] See the lost ballads entered to Richard Jones on 6 and 30 Aug.: *SR* ii. 317, 336. The incident was also referred to in an updated version of Thomas Hill, *The doleful daunce and song of death: intituled, dance after my pipe* (1st pub. 1568–9). This popular ballad, which was part of the 1624 stock (*SR* iv. 132), survives in a later 17th-cent. edn. (Wing H2014). For White's carol, see J. H. Pollen (ed.), *Unpublished Documents Relating to the English Martyrs, i. 1584–1603*, CRS 5 (1908), 97.

[47] *APC 1577–1578*, 25–6. Bishop John Aylmer of London was ordered to investigate the publication of this pamphlet, as well as one concerning the 'straing accident' at Bungay (see Ch. 4 above, pp. 192–4). The Lords of the Privy Council did 'not a litle mervaile at the folly of the authors and the bouldnes of the printers'. It seems likely that both involved a critique of the Protestant status quo.

[48] Richard Challoner, *Memoirs of Missionary Priests*, 2 vols. (n.p., 1741–2), i. 6–10.

[49] Wood, *History and Antiquities of . . . Oxford*, ii. 190; Fuller, *Church-history of Britain*, bk. IX, p. 109. Fuller cited Francis Bacon's *Sylva sylvarum or a naturall history in ten centuries* (1627 edn.), 246, as evidence that the epidemic had natural causes. For the rumours about black magic, see Persons, *Epistle of the persecution*, 150; Thomas, *Religion and the Decline of Magic*, 613.

Batman and James Bisse insisted that the disease 'foreshewed Gods heavie displeasure, for delaying punishment on such wilfull Papists' so long and said that the Lord had 'smot down' not Philistines, idolaters, and murmurers but the 'godliest' men in Oxford at the time.[50] A newswriter who recalled the episode in 1618 argued that Jenkes's own 'blasphemous speeches' had incited the Lord to raise this 'sodaine stinking dampe', prudently omitting to mention the fact that the defendant had escaped the infection unscathed.[51]

In both instances Catholic propagandists might be said to have had the upper hand. But the tables were turned in August 1607, when a polemical play performed at the Jesuit college in Lyons went horribly wrong. This two-day theatrical extravaganza involving nearly 100 amateur actors, realistic sound effects, and pyrotechnic displays ended prematurely when a violent summer thunderstorm broke over the outdoor arena, striking nine or ten of the schoolboy comedians dead, and leaving the adult stars of the show in a state of shock, if not dangerously ill. More than half a dozen panic-stricken spectators were smothered in the frantic rush for safety that followed.

Five books and ballads about this ironically tragic conclusion to the 'Jesuits comedy' rolled off English presses during October,[52] and exaggerated oral reports filtered into southern ports directly from France. Grossly inflated estimates of the number of casualties reached the ears of Devonshire justice Walter Yonge from London and Lyme Regis: 'the greatest part of the people that came to behold and see' the dramatic spectacle had reputedly been slain.[53]

The catastrophic pantomime was both a journalist's scoop and a Protestant publicist's dream. It provided a perfect opportunity for caustic remarks about the evil doctrine espoused by the 'ravening wolves' of the Society of Jesus and the 'rabble of the seditious' whom they had seduced. One pamphleteer described it as a divine 'preservative' against the poison of popery, 'a warning peece shot off, to admonish thee that thou fall not into the presumption into which these Jesuites and their Disciples run headlong'. This was 'a certaine presagement, that ere long the glory of their Romish pride will conclude'.[54] At a second level, the disaster sharply reinforced the puritan outcry against mimetic representations on the stage, providing the godly with further proof that the Lord shared their abhorrence of the duplicity and dissimulation inherent in plays. But it was the theme of the didactic pageant which really clinched the Protestant case: the comedy was nothing less than 'a counterfeiting of the finall judgement', in which the Pope and his adherents were allotted places in a 'wooden paradise', while the Lutherans, Huguenots, and their

[50] Batman, *Doome*, 404; Bisse, *Two sermons*, sig. B7ᵛ.
[51] *True relation of two most strange and fearefull accidents*, sig. B3ᵛ. See also Coghan, *Haven of health . . . with a short censure of the late sicknes at Oxford*, 281.
[52] *SR* iii. 361–4. Two of these have survived: *The Jesuites comedie. Acted at Lyons in France* (1607); R. S., *The Jesuites play at Lyons in France* (1607).
[53] Yonge, *Diary*, ed. Roberts, 15–16.
[54] R. S., *Jesuites play*, 13, 23, sig. A3ʳ, and 24 respectively. In France, the incident was used to endorse calls for the Jesuits to be banished as 'unfit subjects to have hospitality in any Christian commonwealth'.

rulers were relegated to the gaping mouth of hell. Other scenes celebrated Jesuit complicity in the assassination of Henri III and conspiracies against the English monarchy including the Spanish Armada and the Gunpowder Plot, with a series of dumb shows contrasting the eternal felicity with which traitors like Parry, Campion, and Babington were rewarded with the everlasting torment to which Elizabeth I and Edward VI had been condemned.[55] Not only did this pedagogic drama embody a soteriology which Calvinists rejected as scripturally unsound, not only did it make dead Protestant princes an object of the derision of 'bald-pate Friars' and 'the papisticall multitude',[56] it also entailed idolatry of the very highest order—the impersonation of the Almighty Himself, that humanly inconceivable celestial being. It suited such commentators to imply that the lightning bolt had struck as soon as the verdict of damnation against the heretics was announced, 'even as' the 'first cracke of Jesuiticall thunder' heralding their excommunication had been discharged, knocking the prefect of the college who had usurped His throne directly from his seat. Inevitably, the disaster was presented as a paradigm of the divine punishment that would overtake Catholicism itself. Popery too made 'a mockerie of God'. A mere caricature and travesty of the true religion, it converted the cosmic drama of salvation and reprobation into 'a pastime, a vaine scarre-crowe', and 'a May-game'.[57]

English Catholics seem to have greeted these imputations with a dignified or stupefied silence, but French Jesuits tried to salvage the respectability of their society by reputing it 'an especiall miracle' that the actors were 'not smitten with the lightning downe to hell indeed' and insisting that this paradoxically was 'a verie visible marke of the perfection of their newe sect'.[58] This time, however, it was surely the 'heretics' who had the last word.

Protestants, then, could be as opportunistic as their theological opposites in taking tactical advantage of terrible accidents to score a point at their adversaries' expense. And when Catholics found themselves prey to plausible allegations of heavenly rage they responded with the same expedient retorts in which their Reformed enemies generally sought refuge themselves. They too might emphasize the casual or coincidental nature of calamities that occurred, declare them the outcome of diabolical deception or machiavellian treachery, or sweep them aside as 'liying libels, 'cogged miracles', 'faigned wonders', 'Rowling lyes', the 'verie rakinges of the sinke & cannels of filthie detraction'.[59] Alternatively they might avail themselves of the rhetoric of Job, piously observing that the Lord's ways were past finding out. Propagandists from each camp made shrewd and selective use of

[55] *Jesuites comedie*, sig. A3ʳ. See also R. S., *Jesuites play*, 17–21; [Leighton], *Shorte treatise against stage-playes*, 28.

[56] R. S., *Jesuites play*, 21. See also Prynne, *Histrio-mastix*, fo. 558ᵛ.

[57] R. S., *Jesuites play*, 21–2; *Jesuites comedie*, sigs. A3ʳ–4ʳ.

[58] *Jesuites comedie*, sig. A4ʳ.

[59] For such allegations from Catholics, see Stapleton's preface to Bede, *History of the church of Englande*, fo. 9ʳ; Persons, *Epistle of the persecution*, 148, 151; from Protestants, H[arsnet], *Declaration*, 166; R[obert] P[ricket], *The Jesuits miracles, or new popish wonders* (1607), sig. C4ʳ.

circumstances which fell out in their favour, and turned a blind eye to those which did not.

ROWLING LYES AND HELLISH SLANDERS

Both also busied themselves collecting anecdotes about the exemplary ends of implacable foes of their respective religions. It was relatively simple to make sensational reports of suicide and sudden death a vehicle for corrosive anti-popery, as John Foxe's famous appendix of divine judgements visited upon 'popish' persecutors eloquently attests.[60] Much less attention has been paid to the stories of providential justice which circulated among stalwart supporters of the Church of Rome: Catholic ministers and laypeople were as skilled in this form of rhetorical warfare as Foxe, Beard, Clarke, and their contributors and they drew upon the same treasury of ancient, semi-fictional motifs.

Cautionary tales about the terrible penalties inflicted upon bloodthirsty Protestant justices and barristers began to proliferate almost as soon as the proselytizing activities of the Tridentine priesthood were made a capital crime. Elizabethan and early Stuart recusants and church papists soon acquired their own martyrologies, and these works were no less liberally replenished with accounts of government spies, pursuivants, and executioners who came to sticky and unsavoury ends than Foxe's *Actes and monuments*. In his *Relation of sixteen martyrs*, for instance, Thomas Worthington described the supernatural discipline dealt out to the presiding judge at the trial of Thomas Sprott and Thomas Hunt, both executed in July 1600: 'riding abroad for his pleasure' a few days later, he fell from his horse in a fit of apoplexy, 'his braines straingely coming forth, both at his nose and mouth' and 'his right shoulder sore scorched, like burnd leather, as blacke as pitch'.[61] The 'strainge death' of one Mr Henberry, a former Catholic servant at Scotney in Kent who betrayed Father Richard Blount to the authorities, was likewise regarded as 'a just punishment for his perfidious villanie': visited not long afterwards with a 'loathsome disease', the sight and smell of which repelled even medical professionals, he languished and died.[62] The punitive hand of God quite literally fell upon Sir Henry Yelverton, who passed judgement upon Edward Arrowsmith in 1629 and watched his execution from a distance with the aid of a telescope: while he was sitting at supper he felt a fatal blow on his head as if he had been struck by an invisible fist.[63] Embroidered by eyewitnesses and publicized

---

[60] Foxe, *Acts and Monuments*, vol. viii, 'The severe punishment of God upon the persecutors of his people and enemies to his word'. On Foxe, see Ch. 2, above.

[61] Thomas Worthington, *A relation of sixtene martyrs: glorified in England in twelve monethes* (Douai, 1601), 89–90.

[62] Foley (ed.), *Records of the English Province*, iii. 486–8. For other judgement stories on persecutors, see Yepez, *Historia particular de la persecucion de Inglaterra*, ch. 9 and the chapter on 'God's Judgements' in an anonymous MS recounting the persecution of Catholics in the West Midlands printed in John Morris (ed.), *The Troubles of our Catholic Forefathers Related by Themselves*, 3 vols. (1872–7), iii. 57–9. Extracts from a later compilation in the same tradition dating from the 1680s are printed in Foley (ed.), *Records of the English Province*, v. 74–5.

[63] Philip Caraman (ed.), *The Years of Siege: Catholic Life from James I to Cromwell* (1966), 74.

both verbally and scribally, such narratives only occasionally achieved apotheosis in print. A chaotically scattered mass of edifying examples accumulated in manuscript, to await the exhaustive efforts of the late seventeenth-century penitentiary Christopher Grene to reduce this rich ragbag of martyrological documents to some sort of logical order.[64] No less rapidly disseminated was news of the gruesome fates which befell unruly iconoclasts, rabid Calvinists who compelled their recusant relatives and neighbours to receive communion or attend Sunday services, and puritans who defiantly ploughed their fields or performed other servile works on the abrogated holy days of the Virgin Mary and saints.[65] John Gerard incorporated in his autobiographical memoirs the story of a Protestant visitor to St Winifred's well in Wales who sniggered at some pilgrims bathing in the pool and leapt in to profane it with his dirty boots, only to be instantly paralysed by the water at whose miraculous powers he had just so insolently mocked.[66] In late sixteenth-century Shropshire Catholics exchanged accounts of the dreadful deaths of individuals who dared to infringe traditional ecclesiastical taboos, including the tale of Onslow, the royal solicitor who died after devouring fried bacon for breakfast during Lent.[67] Such anti-Protestant obituaries were a regular feature of the internal memoranda of the English Province of the Society of Jesus. Especially compelling was the case of the elderly cobbler who avidly read the vernacular Bible while he sat mending worn-out shoes: driven to desperation by this over-indulgence in Holy Writ, he hung himself in the bell tower of the local parish church. This, remarked the editor of the annual letter of the Jesuit mission for 1624, 'may well rebuke the rashness of heretics in handling the sacred pages'.[68]

Counter-Reformation priests also regaled the laity with anecdotes about the grievous punishments inflicted upon apostates, renegades, and 'schismatics'. Stories of the psychological torment suffered by Catholics who defied their consciences and participated in reformed services were one manifestation of the campaign for recusancy, powerful propaganda for the claim that conformity was a mortal and damnable sin. The clergy had a vested interest in spreading rumours about the mental anguish which had seized 16-year-old Thomas Fitzherbert when he gave way to the temptation to attend a Protestant sermon and afflicted a lady who consented to marry a heretic according to the order laid down in the Book of Common Prayer; it suited their purposes to repeat the tale of a young noblewoman who attempted to slash her throat and stab herself to death after receiving the Calvinist communion and swearing the Oath of Allegiance.[69] Compiling collections

---

[64] Grene's martyrological 'Collectanea' are now preserved at Stonyhurst College, Lancashire, and St Mary's College, Oscott, Sutton Coldfield.

[65] For examples, see Morris (ed.), *Troubles*, iii. 57–9; and Foley (ed.), *Records of the English Province*, vol. vii, pt. 2, pp. 1100, 1142.

[66] *John Gerard: The Autobiography of an Elizabethan*, ed. and trans. Philip Caraman (1951), 47. Similar stories about those who scoffed at the miracles at Montaigu in the early 17th cent. are recounted in Numan, *Miracles*, 57, 207–8, 276–9.

[67] Foley (ed.), *Records of the English Province*, iv. 494.

[68] Ibid. vol. vii, pt. 2, p. 1105.

[69] Ibid. ii. 210; iv. 287; vol. vii, pt. 2, p. 1121. See also 'Father Persons' Memoirs', ed. J. H. Pollen, in *CRS Miscellanea IV*, CRS 4 (1907), 141–3.

of judgements was also a favourite technique for discrediting those who deserted or divided from Rome and in 1598, on the eve of the Archpriest Controversy, Robert Persons prepared a list of the supernatural penalties meted out to the 'fautors of that faction' who had dared to oppose Jesuit policies.[70]

Protestant preachers, prelates, and political figures came in for the same kind of castigation: Bishops William Barlow and John Jewel reputedly ended their lives as ignominiously as Stephen Gardiner and Edmund Bonner; the sin-ridden body of the Secretary of State, Francis Walsingham, allegedly stank so much that one of his pall-bearers was poisoned by the 'noisome smell'; and according to John Chamberlain, the death of Queen Elizabeth herself was 'diversely related' by the papists in a manner 'as utterly voyde of truth, as of all civill honestie or human-itie'.[71] Several priests compiled catalogues of the unhappy fates of heretics throughout Christian history, from Pharaoh, Herod, and Arius, to Luther, Carlstadt, Calvin, and Zwingli.[72] Most of the exempla in a private collection dis-covered in the closet of the eminent Catholic convert Benjamin Carier around 1615 were lifted straight from the pages of Robert Bellarmine's *Disputationum*, with the notable exception of an intriguing report of the vengeance visited upon a group of Dover merchants, tradesmen, and town councillors who participated in a 'lewde' procession in derision of the Catholic liturgy and rite in 1559.[73] George Hakewill, chaplain to Prince Charles and Carier's erstwhile colleague, accounted this anec-dote 'no better then a meere Canterburie tale, or to speake in the Romish dialect, a godly fraud, or lie devised for the advantage of his holy Mother'. He rejected the defamatory stories about the reformers as 'hellish slander[s]' derived from tainted sources written by sworn enemies who sought 'this base kind of revenge'—a charge which could, of course, be ricocheted straight back at Protestant publicists themselves.[74]

---

[70] 'An Observation of Certayne Aparent Judgments', printed in 'The Memoirs of Father Robert Persons', ed. J. H. Pollen, *CRS Miscellanea II*, CRS 2 (1906), 202–11. A similar list of punishments on 'Deserters from the order' prepared by the Spaniard Pedro Ribadeneira survives in the Jesuit archives in Rome. See Thomas H. Clancy, 'Priestly Perseverance in the Old Society of Jesus: The Case of England', *Recusant History*, 19 (1989), 287.

[71] For Barlow, see Foley (ed.), *Records of the English Province*, vol. vii, pt. 2, p. 1073; for Jewel and Walsingham, see Yepez, *Historia particular de la persecution de Inglaterra*, 72, 92; and Morris (ed.), *Troubles*, iii. 59. Chamberlain, *Letters*, ed. McClure, i. 188.

[72] Ch. 17 of bk. IV ('The unhappy ends of such as have oppugned the Church') of Bellarmine's *Disputationum* became the prototype for collections of this kind. On the origin of polemical Catholic accounts of the death of Luther, see Michael B. Lukens, 'Luther's Death and the Secret Catholic Report', *Journal of Theological Studies*, NS 41 (1990), 545–53.

[73] Benjamin Carier, *A copy of a letter, written by M. Doctor Carier beyond seas . . . Whereunto are added certaine collections found in his closet . . . of the miserable ends of such as have impugned the Catholike church* ([Eng. secret press], 1615). For the fates of the participants in the Dover to Canterbury procession, see 41–2. Carier also listed examples 'Of the Temporall Prosperitie and Felicitie of them which have defended the Church'.

[74] George Hakewill, *An answere to a treatise written by Dr Carier* (1616), 26, 18, 15. Like their Protestant counterparts, Catholics also continued to use providential anecdotes to reprove immoral behaviour: see e.g. Philippe d'Outreman, *The true Christian Catholique or the maner how to live christianly*, trans. John Heigham (St Omer, 1622), bk. I; Edward Weston, *A triple cure of a triple malady . . .* ([St Omer, 1616]).

Monsters and other anomalies of nature were also harnessed to support the Catholic cause. When a Leicestershire butcher's daughter by the name of Agnes Bowker gave birth to a cat in January 1569, hostile commentators believed it to be 'a pleasaunt practise of papistrie, to bring the people to new wonders': the discovery of straw and congealed pieces of bacon inside its belly were regarded by the commissary Anthony Anderson and Christopher Pollard, curate of Harborough, as definitive evidence that the portent was in fact a fraud.[75] The symbol of a crucifix found in the trunk of an old ash tree which had blown down during a storm on the Glamorganshire estate of Sir Thomas Strading proved rather more difficult to explain away. Pictures of the image circulated in surrounding villages, along with rumours to the effect that God strongly disapproved of the Elizabethan Settlement, and in June 1561 a large company of pilgrims from the neighbouring town of Cowbridge gathered 'to gaze upon' the said 'St Donats Cross'. The Privy Council considered this resurgence of 'popish superstition' serious enough to appoint a special commission of enquiry and imprison the gentleman in question in the Tower of London. Five years later, in 1566, Nicholas Harpsfield, former archdeacon of Canterbury, incorporated an account of it in his *Dialogi sex*, published under the pseudonym of Alan Cope.[76]

Crudely polemical providentialism was thus as much a part of the cultural heritage and patrimony of Roman Catholics as of Protestants; it was an ideological legacy which the clerical leaders of both Reformations employed as confessional ammunition with equal expertise and alacrity. But adducing evidence of divine wrath against one's adversaries could not on its own convince people to embrace or retain a particular faith: it was equally imperative to establish God's positive endorsement of that community and creed.

The inheritors of a tradition which maintained that confirmation by miracles was an infallible mark of the institutional body of the faithful on earth, early modern Catholics were understandably anxious to demonstrate that the Lord's willingness to work wonders for the solace and exoneration of His afflicted people had not waned. They recorded the 'admirable providences' God vouchsafed to His pious servants almost as diligently as puritans: Lady Magdalen Montague was 'taken up without the least hurt, as if a bed of feathers' rather than a heavy marble altar had fallen upon her; Thomas Pounde no less astonishingly escaped injury when an ornamental ceiling collapsed, except a section above his head which hung in the air like an umbrella.[77] Anthologies of cures and conversions wrought by holy water, relics, and rosary beads, paternoster prayers, Agnus Dei, and the sacramental

[75] BL Lansdowne MS 101, fos. 21ʳ–33ʳ; William Bullein, *A dialogue bothe pleasaunt and pietifull, wherein is a godlie regiment against the fever pestilence* (1573), 106–7. For a detailed account of the case, see David Cressy, 'De la fiction dans les archives? ou le monstre de 1569', *Annales: Économies, sociétés, civilisations*, 48 (1993), 1309–29.

[76] PRO SP 12/17/19 and 20; [Harpsfield], *Dialogi sex*, 360–1, 369.

[77] [Richard Smith], *An Elizabethan Recusant House Comprising the Life of the Lady Magdalen Viscountess Montague (1538–1608)*, ed. A. C. Southern (1954), 56–7 and ch. 13 *passim*; Foley (ed.), *Records of the English Province*, iii. 597.

host were exported from Tridentine strongholds in the Netherlands. 'Doost thou not see how our Catholik doctrin by the same powerful hand at this present is upholden and fostered', urged Philips Numan in his account of the miracles accomplished by the intercession of the Virgin at Montaigu in Brabant before 1604, 'by which at the beginning it was planted and took root?'[78] Stories of prodigious infants whose merest touch healed the most hopeless patient and of raging fires extinguished by crucifixes thrust into the flames were propagated orally along clandestine communication routes.[79] Manuscript tracts spread the word about successful exorcisms, in which the dramatic ritual of ejecting devils evolved into the theatrical expulsion of the evil spirit of Calvinism itself. Father Weston's disposessions in Buckinghamshire in 1585–6 were described in a 'penned book of miracles', as was the famous Jacobean case of William Perry, 'the boy of Bilson'.[80] Protestants who condemned them as 'plain lie[s] invented to win grace to the popish faction' betrayed anxieties about their influence which cannot have been entirely unfounded.[81] Counter-Reformation evangelists made wildly exaggerated claims about the harvest of souls they thereby reaped, but by the mid-Elizabethan period, as Susan Brigden has remarked, it was popery rather than Protestantism which enjoyed the appeal of 'an exotic and forbidden fruit' and skilful publicity about preternatural phenomena does seem to have played a part in sustaining the notable revival of Roman Catholicism in urban centres in the early seventeenth century.[82]

Nor should historians be too sceptical about the evangelical potential of the miraculous happenings alleged to have accompanied the martyrdoms of Jesuit and secular priests. As Peter Lake and Michael Questier have shown, these were liminal occasions on which Catholic missionaries competed with Protestant ministers to channel spiritual power and charisma and win new converts to the faith.[83] Stories of wells and streams near scaffolds and gallows which ceased to flow and of the menacing postures and expressions assumed by quartered limbs and severed heads displayed on city gates travelled along the established channels of the Catholic underground, along with accounts of crows which feasted on sanctified flesh and then fell lifeless to the ground.[84] Patches of grass stepped upon by Father Oldcorne

---

[78] Numan, *Miracles*, 295. See also Bristow, *Briefe treatise*, fos. 17a–27a and the many examples in the annual letters of the Jesuit mission in Foley (ed.), *Records of the English Province*, vol. vii, pt. 2.

[79] The story of the 'wondrous child' circulated around 1607: see the hostile account by P[ricket] *Jesuits miracles*, sig. B4ᵛ. For anecdotes about fires extinguished by consecrated objects, see Foley (ed.), *Records of the English Province*, vol. vii, pt. 2, pp. 1100, 1136; and Trinity College, Cambridge, MS O. 7. 3, fo. 6ᵛ (a tale which this Protestant diarist thought fit only to be put in 'ther lying log').

[80] H[arsnet], *Declaration of egregious popish impostures*, 1 and *passim*; Baddeley, *Boy of Bilson*, 54. Many other examples are recorded in the Jesuit annual letters, see Foley (ed.), *Records of the English Province*, i. 223; iii. 446–7; vol. vii, pt. 2, pp. 1071, 1137–8, 1143.

[81] Yonge, *Diary*, ed. Roberts, 13.

[82] See Brigden, 'Youth and the English Reformation', 106–7.

[83] Peter Lake and Michael Questier, 'Agency, Appropriation and Rhetoric under the Gallows: Puritans, Romanists, and the State in Early Modern England', *P&P* 153 (1996), esp. 95–107.

[84] On wells and streams, see Challoner, *Memoirs of Missionary Priests*, ed. J. H. Pollen (1924), 164, 600; on heads and limbs, ibid. 158. For the crow, see Stonyhurst College, MS A. IV. 7, no. 5.

sprouted in the shape of imperial crowns; a flame was seen over the house of Thomas Sherwood's parents on the day of his execution in 1577; the heart of William Freeman was said to have jumped out of the flames twice in 1595.[85] No prodigy acquired more fame or notoriety than Henry 'Garnet's straw': a blood-stained ear of wheat on which a minute but perfect effigy of the Gunpowder Plot martyr's face allegedly appeared several months after his execution in May 1606. All England was reputedly 'belittered with the news'.[86] Catholics insisted that only the finger of God could have executed so exquisite an image, proclaiming the relic incontrovertible proof of the convicted traitor's innocence. Protestants attributed the picture to either necromancy or artistic genius, making much of the fact that Garnet—the arch-equivocator—was portrayed as double-faced. The 'painted straw' was the subject of a mocking pamphlet by Robert Pricket (Plate 32) and Thomas Coryat ranked the legend 'amongst the merry tales of Poggius the Florentine',[87] but the incident also caused consternation at the highest political levels. Richard Bancroft investigated it at the behest of Robert Cecil, and in 1613 Robert Abbot, Regius Professor of Divinity at Oxford, denounced it at length in a learned Latin treatise.[88] On the Continent the 'Spica Jesuitica' became a touchstone for Tridentine piety and anti-Stuart propaganda, with iconic engravings of the item circulating for sale in Cologne, The Hague, and Rome.[89]

Celebrated by Catholic hagiographers as signs of heavenly favour, the impending overthrow of heresy and the imminent ascendancy of the papacy, such marvels did much to foster the cult of Counter-Reformation martyrs and confessors of the faith, just as they had helped to canonize Marian Protestants burnt at the stake in the perception of the preceding generation.

ENGLANDS HALLELU-JAH

As far as Reformed ministers were concerned 'miracles' were no longer the insignia of Christ's single true Church, but 'special providences' met the continuing need

---

[85] On Oldcorne, see BL Add. MS 21203, fo. 24[r]. For Sherwood, 'Memoirs of Father Robert Persons', ed. Pollen, 83. For Freeman, Pollen (ed.), *Unpublished Documents*, 359.

[86] Fuller, *Church-history of Britain*, bk. x, pp. 40–1. On this incident, see BL Add. MS 21203, fos. 22[r]–23[v]; Gerard, *Autobiography*, ed. and trans. Caraman, 202; Henry More, *Historia missionis Anglicanae societatis Jesu* (St Omer, 1660), bk. VII, §35; Foley (ed.), *Records of the English Province*, iv. 121–33, 195–201; Philip Caraman, *Henry Garnet 1555–1606 and the Gunpowder Plot* (1964), 443–7. PRO, SP 14/21/5 is a narrative by a Catholic eyewitness of Garnet's execution, with a portrait of the straw engraved by Johann Wierix.

[87] P[ricket], *Jesuits miracles*, sigs. B1[v]–3[v]; Coryate, *Coryats Crudities*, 625.

[88] Robert Abbot, *Antilogia adversus apologiam Andreae Eudaemon-Joannis Jesuitae pro Henrico Garneto Jesuita proditore* (1613), fos. 197[r]–201[v]. He was refuting a tract written by the Cretan Jesuit Andreas Eudaemon-Joannes [André L'Heureux]: *Ad actionem proditioriam Edouardi Coqui, apologia pro R. P. Henrico Garneto Anglo* (n.p., 1610). See esp. ch. 14.

[89] As noted in a letter from Sir Charles Cornwallis to the Privy Council on 9 Apr, 1607, printed in Edmund Sawyer (ed.), *Memorials of affairs of state in the reigns of Q. Elizabeth and K. James I. Collected (chiefly) from the original papers of the Right Honourable Sir Ralph Winwood*, 3 vols. (1725), ii. 300; Coryate, *Coryats Crudities*, 625; and Fuller, *Church-history of Britain*, bk. x, P. 41. A Dutch print of 'Garnet's straw' survives in the BM DP&D, file marked 'English History 1606'.

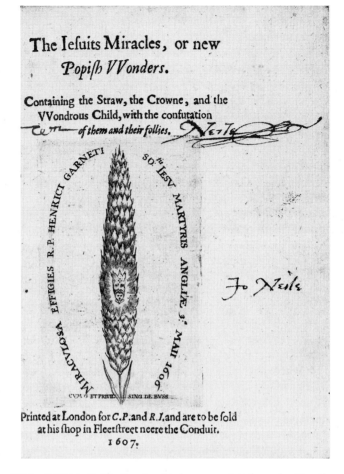

PLATE 32 R[obert] P[ricket], *The Jesuits miracles, or new popish wonders* (London, 1607), title-page. By permission of the British Library. Shelfmark: C. 117. b. 13.
'Garnet's straw', a bloodstained ear of wheat on which the face of Henry Garnet, the Jesuit executed for complicity in the Gunpowder Plot, 1605, miraculously appeared.

for supernatural sanction admirably well. Godly preachers and laymen pointed to the benefits showered upon England since the reintroduction of the Gospel in 1559: her peace, prosperity, material abundance, and agricultural plenty were 'plaine arguments' that this was unquestionably the brand of Christianity preferred by the Lord. His 'exceeding goodnes' to this small island proved just how 'well pleased' He was with a nation which had officially embraced the Protestant faith.[90]

[90] See e.g. Bailey, *Briefe discours*, sig. A2[r–v].

As the seminary priest Chambers with some justice complained, the 'benedictions' Protestants alleged the Lord 'hath heaped upon the Realme' were a means by which they could have their cake and eat it too: by insisting that miracles had ceased they could deny the authenticity of Catholic wonders en masse, while in the guise of 'special providences' they could simultaneously claim essentially the same kind of divine approbation for the Church of England.[91] Determined 'to stop the mouths of our insolent adversaries', Robert Tynley went so far as to insist that the real 'miracle' of the early modern era was the Reformation itself. '[T]he restoring of the purity of religion . . . from the drosse and corruptions of Antichrist' could not have been effected without 'the extraordinary and powerful working of almighty God'.[92] Such 'blessings' were a familiar and infinitely expandable theme, the subject of hundreds of ebulliently patriotic sermons—and of David Cressy's *Bonfires and Bells*.[93]

As Cressy has shown, anti-Catholic providentialism became closely entwined with the political integrity and the Protestant identity of the late Tudor and early Stuart state. English reformers supplanted the religious cult of saints with a quasi-religious cult of royalty and nationhood. They substituted the old cycle of ritual observances revolving around medieval holy days with a new calendar which hinged upon the anniversaries of celebrated moments in the recent historical past. Pre-eminent among these 'icon events' destined to be preserved in collective post-Reformation memory were the defeat of the Spanish 'Armado' in the 'Climactericall yeere' 1588 and the discovery of what Samuel Garey, preacher at Wynfarthing in Norfolk, called that 'Quintessence of all impiety' and 'confection of all villany', the Gunpowder Plot, in 1605.[94] Along with Queen Elizabeth's accession, Prince Charles's return from Madrid in 1623 without a Habsburg bride, and a handful of other critical episodes during the reigns of James I and his son, they constituted key links in a chain of astonishing deliverances from the malign forces of Rome and Spain, tangible seals of the Lord's special covenant with the elect English people, as with the Israelites of old. These were what the young Simonds D'Ewes termed the 'great miracle[s] of our latter age'—it was a vocabulary into which loyal Protestants all too often involuntarily slipped.[95]

In the Jacobean period, the memorialization of God's benevolence to Great Britain became a flourishing industry. Preachers annually retold the legendary tales of the nation's last-minute rescues from Catholic treachery and oppression in sermons delivered to keep their 'thankfull remembrance' eternally fresh: they

---

[91] Chambers' preface to Numan, *Miracles*, sig. A6ʳ.

[92] Tynley, *Two learned sermons*, 66–8. See also P[ricket], *Jesuits miracles*, sigs. E2ʳ–3ʳ.

[93] These sermons are the subject of Ch. 6, below. Cressy, *Bonfires and Bells*. For a summary of his argument, see 'The Protestant Calendar and the Vocabulary of Celebration in Early Stuart England', *JBS* 29 (1990), 31–52.

[94] Quotations from George Carleton, *A thankfull remembrance of Gods mercy* (1624), 119; and Samuel Garey, *Amphitheatrum scelerum: or the transcendent of treason: for the fifth of November*, pt. 3 of id., *Great Brittans little calendar: or, triple diarie. In remembrance of three daies* (1618), 184.

[95] D'Ewes, *Diary*, ed. Bourcier, 164.

ignored human frailty, freak weather conditions, and clever detective work in rousing narratives which emphasized the overpowering providence of God. Thomas Gataker's *Anniversarie memoriall of Englands delivery from the Spanish invasion* (1626), delivered at St Pancras, Soper Lane, in August 1625, was one of three yearly lectures endowed to the parish by Thomas Chapman in 1616: predictably, the other two commemorated the 'detestible Gunpowder Plot' and the 'joyfull entrance of our late most gracious soveraigne Lady queene Elizabeth' onto the throne on 17 November 1558. Humphrey Walwyn, a wealthy citizen and grocer who had bequeathed money to support a sermon on 5 November at St Martin Orgar four years earlier, gave detailed instructions about the tone and content of the address: the preacher was to 'open unto' the congregation 'the cruelty of those bloud thirsty papistes whose religion and deedes and practizes do declare from whence their religion is sprung which is from the Devill who was a murderer from the begynning and the father of all heresyes and lyes'.[96]

An ever-widening range of publications gave expression to this intoxicating mixture of jingoism, xenophobia, and anti-popery welded together by providentialism. Amateur versifiers and annalists like the London schoolmaster John Vicars celebrated the merciful interventions of the Almighty in 'gratulatory treatises' and poems which harped upon Catholic barbarities and sounded the trumpet of 'Englands hallelu-jah' for her timely preservation.[97] Ballads, broadsides, and chapbook-sized collections of prayers and psalms distilled this inspiring historiography into a format suitable for consumption by the semi-literate and '[f]it to instruct the simple and ignorant heerin'. Godly ditties flowed from the pens of ordained ministers and drunken scribblers alike and *Crummes of comfort*, a bestselling book of private devotions containing an account of 'Gods Wonderfull Deliverances of this Land', was the brainchild of the stationer Michael Sparke. From at least 1619 puppet plays popularized them among urban apprentices, servants, and the young.[98] Whatever form these chronicles of the Lord's eleventh-

---

[96] For Thomas Chapman and Humphrey Walwyn's bequests, see Guildhall Library, London, MS 5020 (The 'Great Book' of the parish of St Pancras, Soper Lane, 1616–1740), fos. 91^r–94^v and MS 959/1 (Vestry minutes and Churchwardens' accounts, St Martin, Orgar, 1471–1615), fo. 391^v. For only a handful of other examples, see William Leigh, *Great Britaines, great deliverance, from the great danger of popish powder* (1606); Samuel Hieron, *The ruine of Gods enemies: preached upon the commemoration-day of the deliverance from the gun-powder treason*, in *Three sermons* (Cambridge, 1609); Daniel Dyke, *Certaine comfortable sermons upon the 124. Psalme: tending to stirre up to thankefulnesse for our deliverance from the late gunpowder-treason* (1616); John Prideaux, *Higgation & Selah: for the discovery of the gun-powder plot*, in *Eight sermons* (1621). See also Ch. 6 n. 44, below.

[97] J[ohn] V[icars], *Englands hallelu-jah. Or Great Brittaines gratefull retribution, for Gods gratious benediction* (1631). Vicars also translated and expanded Francis Herring's *Pietas pontificia, seu, conjurationis illius prodigiosae* (1606) under the title *Mischeefes mysterie: or, treasons master-peece, the powder-plot* (1617). Another example is John Wilson, *A song or story, for the lasting remembrance of divers famous works, which God hath done in our time* (1626).

[98] Michael Sparke, *Crumms of comfort* (1627 edn.). This was entered in *SR* on 7 Oct. 1623: iv. 105, and by 1635 had already been reissued twenty times. The 42nd edn. was published in 1656. See also J[ohn] R[hodes], *The countrie mans comfort. Or religious recreations, fitte for all well disposed persons* (1637 edn.; 1st pub. 1588). Ballads on these subjects include John Awdely, *A godly ditty or prayer to be song*

hour interventions took, they embodied a swaggering self-confidence about Protestant England's privileged status, tinged with anxiety about the potentially catastrophic consequences of its stubborn continuance in sin. They were also almost invariably imbued with a virulent strain of apocalyptic hostility towards the adherents of the Pope. If a man looked upon these extraordinary intercessions with 'an unpartiall eye', declared Bishop George Carleton of Chichester in 1624, 'though he be an enemie, though he be a Jesuite, he must needes confesse that God was on our side'.[99]

As Peter Lake and others have argued, this was a species of bias and bigotry which struck a sympathetic chord in the psychology of the populace at large. Just as the popery/no popery dichotomy implicit in the mythology of England's 'miraculous' deliverances harmonized with the polarizing tendencies inherent in popular thinking,[100] so did the providentialism with which it interlocked cohere with time-honoured beliefs about divine interference in earthly affairs. Even if the apparent spontaneity of the festivities associated with such anniversaries and victories peels away to reveal a marked degree of orchestration by the authorities,[101] their durability over time testifies to the success with which these new Protestant rituals eventually wormed their way into the consciousness of the English people. As Ronald Hutton's exhaustive survey of churchwardens' accounts has shown, corporate rejoicing in the form of bonfires and bells, parades, and spectacular firework displays spread slowly and patchily, taking firm root only in the 1620s. Sponsored and financed by town corporations, it was part of a new civic-cum-martial festive culture designed to reinforce the power of governing oligarchies and bolster urban pride.[102] But that should not blind us to the extent to which these calendrical customs became the property of the crowd, a pattern of observance which helped compensate for the loss of rites abolished by the reformers because they savoured of idolatry. Belying its origins in the high politics of Whitehall and Westminster,

---

unto God for the preservation of his church, our queene and realme, against all traytours, rebels, and papisticall enemies ([1569?]); John Pits, *A prayer, and also a thanksgiving unto God, for his great mercy in giving and preserving our noble Queene Elizabeth to live and reigne over us . . . to be sung the xvii day of November 1577* ([1577]); T. S., *A song or psalme of thanksgiving, in remembrance of our great deliveraunce from the gun-powder treason* (1625). For puppet plays, see Ben Jonson, *Bartholomew fayre: a comedie, acted in the yeare, 1614*, v. i. 11–14, repr. in *Three Comedies*, ed. Michael Jamieson (Harmondsworth, 1966); Alan Haynes, *The Gunpowder Plot: Faith in Rebellion* (Stroud, 1994), 103.

[99] Carleton, *Thankfull remembrance*, 146.

[100] Lake, 'Anti-Popery', esp. 92–6; Robin Clifton, 'The Popular Fear of Catholics during the English Revolution', in Paul Slack (ed.), *Rebellion, Popular Protest and the Social Order in Early Modern England* (Cambridge, 1984), 129–61, esp. 161; id., 'Fear of Popery', in Conrad Russell (ed.), *The Origins of the English Civil War* (1973), esp. 165; Underdown, *Revel, Riot and Rebellion*, 129, 140–1; Hunt, *Puritan Moment*, 306–10.

[101] Cressy, *Bonfires and Bells*, esp. pp. xiv, 101. See also the Privy Council's orders for 'bonfires in every ward and such other joy and thankfulness to God as hath been in such cases accustomed' in the wake of the defeat of the Turks in 1571: Inner Temple Library, London, Petyt MS 538, vol. 52, fos. 4–5.

[102] See Hutton, *Rise and Fall of Merry England*, 182–5; id., *The Stations of the Sun: A History of the Ritual Year in Britain* (Oxford, 1996), ch. 39; Underdown, *Revel, Riot and Rebellion*, 68–72.

celebration of God's providential mercies operated as a kind of cultural cement, a ligature linking the learned culture of Protestant elites with the street culture of those they condemned as the 'carnal multitude'.

But it could also precipitate confrontations and collisions. Under Charles I commemoration of these red-letter days started to lose its unifying character and take on an increasingly strident and partisan tone. The recreational activities which were already part and parcel of 'remembering the fifth of November' and giving thanks for Elizabeth's accession on the seventeenth began to incur official irritation. The burning of effigies of the devil and Pope in the capital was regarded as offensive to the King's consort, the French Catholic Princess Henrietta Maria, and indeed it has been argued that the intensification of interest in these festivals after 1625 was in part an indictment of the marriage—a match only marginally more acceptable to public opinion than the aborted one with the Habsburg Infanta.[103] The rehearsal of England's deliverances from the Armada and Gunpowder Treason became embarrassing and distasteful to an episcopal hierarchy seeking to draw closer to European superpowers whom committed Calvinists still regarded as their confessional enemies. Preachers who hijacked these anniversaries to emphasize the hazards of relapsing into popery and to condemn recent innovations as the thin end of the wedge were relentlessly pursued and detained. The Ipswich preacher Samuel Ward was hauled before the High Commission for suggesting in a sermon on 5 November 1633 that the best way of demonstrating 'thanckfullnes' was 'a more stricte observacion of the Ten Commandments', including the fourth. Innocuous enough on the surface, in the context of the onslaught on sabbatarianism enshrined in the Declaration of Sports, his comment was construed as implicitly seditious.[104] Lecturing on the same day three years later Henry Burton launched a scathing attack on the 'creeping gangrene' infiltrating England and the 'usurping Antichristian Mushromes' seeking 'tooth and nayle' to re-erect 'the throne of the Beast in this Land', rebuild that tottering 'Babilonian Tower', and reinstate 'the great God of the Hod'. Unlike the original Gunpowder plotters, he warned, these schemers would not fail to overthrow both the true religion and the state. These scandalous allegations cost Burton a portion of his ears.[105]

In the late 1620s and 1630s, then, the vituperative anti-popery which had always been considered integral to the proper solemnization of these patriotic dates became the victim of repression and censorship. Once a rallying cry capable of uniting all parties within the Elizabethan Church, it came to be viewed as one of the outrageous excesses of a fanatical sectarian fringe, a trademark of 'puritan'

---

[103] Cressy, *Bonfires and Bells*, 59–60; Hutton, *Rise and Fall of Merry England*, 185–6.

[104] PRO SP 16/278/65 (Answers of Samuel Ward to 43 articles objected against him by the Commissioners for Causes Ecclesiastical, 19 Dec. 1634), fo. 144ʳ.

[105] Burton, *For God, and the king*, 34, 83, 66, 103, 84, 105 respectively. PRO SP 16/335/69 (Articles objected by the Commissioners for Causes Ecclesiastical against Henry Burton, 17 Nov. 1636). For another politically sensitive Gunpowder Plot sermon, see Thomas Hooker, *The Church's deliverances*, repr. in *Thomas Hooker: Writings in England and Holland, 1626–1633*, ed. George H. Williams *et al.*, Harvard Theological Studies, 28 (Cambridge, Mass., 1975). See also Cressy, *Bonfires and Bells*, 152–5.

deviance and schism. The opportunities it afforded to criticize the new 'popish' virus infecting English Protestantism eliminated it as a sphere of discourse into which radical Calvinist zeal could safely be channelled. As Anthony Milton has demonstrated, this devaluation of impassioned polemic against Antichrist was one tell-tale sign of the changing theological complexion of the ecclesiastical hierarchy, an index of the emergence of a more irenic and conciliatory attitude which transformed relations between Canterbury and Rome from an 'immortal fewde' to a cordial truce. Traditional clichés about Catholicism as a false religion and the 'very mystery of iniquity' were jettisoned and Laudian scholars and apologists quietly set aside the apocalyptic framework for ecclesiastical history which underpinned Foxe's *Actes and monuments*. They stressed instead the Church of England's jurisdictional continuity with her medieval predecessor, which they no longer denounced as the Scarlet Whore of Babylon but embraced as their Reverend Mother.[106]

There can be no doubt that providential landmarks like 1588 and 1605 were caught up in this attempt to reshape the past in line with the ecumenical priorities of leading prelates. Especially indicative are the terms in which Laud's chaplain, Samuel Baker, allegedly couched his refusal to license a second edition of John Vicars's translation of Francis Herring's Latin epic about this 'Master-peice of treachery' in 1637. When asked why a treatise against 'an act so odious and detestable' could not be approved for republication, he replied 'that we were not so angry with the Papists now, as we were about 20 yeares since, and that there was no need of any such Bookes as these to exasperate them, there being now an endeavour to winne them to us by fairnesse and mildnesse'.[107] But Laudians did not seek to extinguish the memory of these episodes completely: to do so would have been deeply disrespectful to the Stuart monarchy they served. They sought, rather, to muffle and remould it. Bishops like Matthew Wren still enquired about the observance of this holy day in their visitation articles, but the anniversary sermons preached by protégés of Laud avoided older xenophobic and polemical commonplaces and presented the conspiracy more as a political crime than an antichristian device to undermine the Protestant Reformation. In the dedicatory epistle to an address delivered at St Mary's in Oxford in 1638, for instance, Jeremy Taylor declared himself 'willing to consider' the possibility that the plotters had

---

[106] Milton, *Catholic and Reformed*, pt. 1. See also his 'The Church of England, Rome and the True Church: The Demise of a Jacobean Consensus', in Kenneth Fincham (ed.), *The Early Stuart Church, 1603–1642* (Basingstoke, 1993), 187–210; Bernard Capp, 'The Political Dimension of Apocalyptic Thought', in C. A. Patrides and Joseph Wittreich (eds.), *The Apocalypse in English Renaissance Thought and Literature: Patterns, Antecedents and Repercussions* (Manchester, 1984), 93–124; and for a subtle critique of some aspects of Milton's argument, Damian Nussbaum, 'Laudian Foxe Hunting: William Laud and the Status of John Foxe in the 1630s', in R. N. Swanson (ed.), *The Church Retrospective*, SCH 33 (Woodbridge, 1997), 329–42. The 'two famous deliverances of our English Nation' from the Armada and Gunpowder Plot were incorporated into the 1610 and later edns. of Foxe.

[107] Francis Herring, *November the 5. 1605. The quintessence of cruelty, or master-peece of treachery, the popish powder-plot*, trans. John Vicars (1641), sig. A3^r. This was the 2nd edn. of *Mischeefes mysterie* (1617). William Prynne, *Canterburies doome* (1646), 184.

been driven to this desperate measure by the excessively severe penalties for recusancy on the statute books. Although he ultimately rejected the argument that they were 'rather exasperated then perswaded', he did admit that this was 'a materiall consideration'.[108] Mr Kempe, a fellow of Queen's College, Cambridge, was said to have similarly 'extenuated the fact of the powder traitors' in 1637 and, preaching sometime before 1633, Thomas Taylor, pastor of Aldermanbury in London, voiced concern about contemporaries who could not 'endure our solemnities, and daies of publike joy for our deliverances against the bloody Papists'. He pointed a critical finger at the 'vipers' who 'swell[ed] with poyson and griefe' at the sentiments conventionally expressed on such occasions and pined when they saw 'Gods revenge powred on the heads of his adversaries'.[109] And when the liturgy for 5 November was reissued in 1635, the wording was subtly but significantly tempered to stress the sin of rebellion in general rather than the wickedness of Catholics in particular. To William Prynne and Robert Burton these 'perversions' and 'expurgations' were witness to a despicable scheme to 'gratifie' the papists and consign the true story of God's mercies to undeserving England to permanent oblivion. They maintained that Laud and his accomplices had 'treacherously Metamorphosed' the prayer to wash the 'Blackamore' of Roman Catholicism white and 'turn the edge of [it] upon the Puritanes'.[110]

    The plot to erase these 'icon' events from the historical record may have existed more in the minds of outspoken critics of the Caroline regime than it did in practice and fact, but such incidents do highlight how far the Protestant calendar became a political football in the years leading up to 1642. In the context of the evolution of two structurally similar but mutually exclusive conspiracy theories, these anniversaries ceased to be symbols of Protestant orthodoxy and unity and became sources of division, friction, and recrimination. The next section traces this process into the realm of material culture and pictorial art.

PICTURES THAT WERE DUMBE ENOUGH BEFORE[111]

In anniversary sermons ministers solemnly insisted that it was an unshirkable duty of the generation which witnessed national deliverances to engrave them with 'a Penne of Iron, with the Point of a Diamond, on the Tables of our hearts, on the

---

[108] Jeremy Taylor, *A sermon preached in Saint Maries Church in Oxford. Upon the anniversary of the gunpowder-treason* (Oxford, 1638), sig. A4[r–v].

[109] BL Harleian MS 7019, fo. 78[r]; Thomas Taylor, *Christs victorie over the dragon: or Satans downfall*, ed. William Jemmat (1633), 488–91. I owe both these references to Anthony Milton.

[110] *Prayers and thanksgiving to be used . . . for the happy deliverance of his majestie, the queene, prince, and states, of the parliament, from the most traiterous and bloody intended massacre by gun-powder, the fift of November. 1605* (1635). The modifications are on sig. D4[v]. William Prynne, *A quench-coale* ([Amsterdam], 1637), 12–18; id., *Canterburies doome*, 246–7; Burton, *For God, and the king*, 130–2.

[111] The argument of this section has been anticipated in my 'Impolitic Pictures: Providence, History, and the Iconography of Protestant Nationhood in Early Stuart England', in R. N. Swanson (ed.), *The Church Retrospective*, SCH 33 (Woodbridge, 1997), 307–28. A fuller and more extensively referenced discussion of the iconographical background can be found in my PhD thesis: 'Aspects of Providentialism in Early Modern England' (Cambridge, 1995), 210–24.

Postes of our Houses, on the Hornes of our Altars, in . . . Capitall Letters' and 'characters indeleble'. Men and women must erect 'eternall Trophees' in their souls, declared Thomas Taylor and Daniel Dyke, as well as 'an everlasting record of the utter ruine of Romish Amaleck' in books. To bury these 'monstrous births' of the papal 'harlot' in 'the dark pit of oblivion' was an unforgivable sin: nothing made the Almighty more irate than ingratitude for the mercies he so magnanimously bestowed. The memory of these Protestant passovers ought to be preserved in 'a Monument of Marble' for all ages to come.[112]

At least some contemporaries took the preachers' instructions quite literally. In the second and third decades of the seventeenth century, a vogue began to grow for engravings of the special providences already enshrined in the mythology of English nationhood, above all the defeat of the Spanish Armada and the discovery of the Gunpowder Plot.[113] These patriotic prints were the result of collaboration between English designers and stationers and highly skilled Dutch technicians and they owed a profound debt both to the emblem book and to commemorative pictures and medals manufactured in Protestant citadels in the Netherlands.[114] Crowded with complex symbols and littered with Latin phrases and biblical tags, these densely allegorical images were relatively expensive items aimed at an emerging market of urban 'middling sort' buyers—upwardly mobile shopkeepers, artisans, and tradesmen. At around sixpence a sheet, they were too costly to be peddled profitably in the countryside and probably beyond the means of regular consumers of the cheapest types of print.[115] But, repeatedly modified and plagiarized, they did in the long run become part of the specialist printsellers' popular stock. Produced and sold by puritan publishers like Thomas Jenner and Michael Sparke (men who used their profession as a springboard for a moral and religious crusade,

---

[112] See Hering, *Triumph of the church over water and fire,* 'To the Reader'; Dyke, *Certaine comfortable sermons,* 9; Thomas Taylor, *Two sermons: the one a heavenly voice . . . The other an everlasting record of the utter ruine of Romish Amalek* (1624), esp. 24; Francis Herring, *Popish pietie, or the first part of the historie of that horrible and barbarous conspiracie, commonly called the powder-treason,* trans. A. P (1610), sig. A3ʳ. This was another trans. of his *Pietas pontificia,* cited in n. 97, above.

[113] Most examples of this genre surviving in the British Museum are listed in BM *Satires.* Others can be traced through A. M. Hind, *Engraving in England in the Sixteenth and Seventeenth Centuries,* 3 vols. (Cambridge, 1952–64). For patriotic and anti-Catholic prints, see M. Dorothy George, *English Political Caricature to 1792: A Study of Opinion and Propaganda* (Oxford, 1959), introd. and ch. 1; David Kunzle, *The Early Comic Strip: Narrative Strips and Picture Stories in the European Broadsheet from c.1450 to 1825* (Berkeley and Los Angeles 1973), ch. 5. Some of these engravings are reproduced in John Miller, *The English Satirical Print 1600–1832: Religion in the Popular Prints 1600–1832* (Cambridge, 1986) and Michael Duffy, *The English Satirical Print 1600–1832: The Englishman and the Foreigner* (Cambridge, 1986).

[114] On emblems, see Margery Corbett and Ronald Lightbown, *The Comely Frontispiece: The Emblematic Title-Page in England 1550–1660* (1979) and Michael Bath, *Speaking Pictures: English Emblem Books and Renaissance Culture* (1994). For medals, see Edward Hawkins *et al., Medallic Illustrations of the History of Great Britain and Ireland to the Death of George II,* 2 vols. (1885), esp. [Elizabeth I], nos. 111, 112, 113, 116, 127, 128, 180, and [James I], no. 19; *Medallic Illustrations of the History of Great Britain and Ireland* (1904), pl. XII, nos. 2, 4, 10, 11, 12; pl. XIV, no. 18; pl. XV, nos. 3, 4, 12; pl. XVII, nos. 8, 9, 13. See also BM *Satires,* 48–55.

[115] Watt, *Cheap Print,* 141–2, 159.

proffering their services to the Parliamentary cause in the 1640s),[116] there is a strong
case for describing some of these engravings as early political cartoons, 'engines of
agitation' designed to swing and shape public opinion.[117] They may represent a
deliberate attempt to counteract the influence of the 'superstitious' and subversive
images seeping in from Antwerp, Brussels, and other Catholic centres, images
like those produced by the exile Richard Verstegan depicting the atrocities perpetrated by Protestant persecutors and satirizing Calvinist doctrine in a manner calculated 'to put an heretyke in doubte of his owne religion'.[118] However, the main
function of these prints seems to have been mnemonic. Invariably described as
'monuments', they were intended as visual remembrancers, images which pious
householders might hang in pride of place above their mantelpieces to remind them
of historic events with whose religious significance they were already deeply
imbued.

Excluded from Tessa Watt's pioneering study of broadside pictures on the basis
of price, these artefacts lend further weight to her suggestion that the iconophobic bias of second-generation Protestantism has been exaggerated and overstated.
There can be no doubt that Swiss-style divinity was inherently hostile to traditional devotional imagery, but it is wrong to infer that it effectively stifled all
aesthetic impulses and left late Tudor and early Stuart England languishing in
an 'artistic vacuum' and suffering from what Patrick Collinson has memorably
described as 'severe visual anorexia'.[119] Calvin and his disciples conceded that there
was and 'ever hath been a lawfull and laudable civill use of Pictures . . . both for
adornation of houses and convenient places, and for commemoration of persons
and things'.[120] Like the 'godly tables' and narrative 'scripture stories for walls' discussed by Dr Watt, prints of providential deliverances were utilitarian items which

---

[116] On Jenner, see Leona Rostenberg, *English Publishers in the Graphic Arts 1599–1700* (New York,
1963), 25–36. Some of his pre-1640 output can be traced through the 'Printers' and Publishers' Index',
in *STC* iii. 92. On Sparke, who endured public humiliation in the pillory for publishing Prynne's
Histrio-mastix, see *DNB*.

[117] Roy Porter, 'Seeing the Past', *P&P* 118 (1988), 191.

[118] On the trade in polemical Catholic prints, see the comments of [Thomas Scott], *Boanerges. Or
the humble supplication of the ministers of Scotland, to the high court of parliament in England* (Edinburgh
[London], 1624), 23; *Something written by occasion of that fatall and memorable accident in the Blacke
Friers on Sunday, being the 26. of October 1623* (1623), 17. For Verstegan, *Letters and Despatches*, ed.
Petti, 115, 117–18. Verstegan's *Theatrum crudelitatum haereticorum nostri temporis* (Antwerp, 1587) went
into four Latin and two French edns. between 1587 and 1602 and was also published in the form of a
series of separate prints. These are discussed in Anne Dillon, 'The Construction of Martyrdom in the
English Catholic Community to 1603', PhD thesis (Cambridge, 1999), chs. 3–4.

[119] Watt, *Cheap Print*, pt. 2, 'The Broadside Picture', esp. 134–9. On Protestant iconophobia, see
Collinson, *From Iconoclasm to Iconophobia*, 22–6; id., *Birthpangs*, 115–21, quotation at 119; and Karl
Josef Höltgen, 'The Reformation of Images and Some Jacobean Writers on Art', in Ulrich Broich *et
al.* (eds.), *Functions of Literature: Essays Presented to Erwin Wolff on his Sixtieth Birthday* (Tubingen,
1984), 123, and 119–46 *passim*. For the broader English and European context, see Aston, *England's
Iconoclasts*, vol. i, p. vii and *passim*; Carlos Eire, *War against the Idols: The Reformation of Worship from
Erasmus to Calvin* (Cambridge, 1986); Sergiusz Michalski, *The Reformation and the Visual Arts: The
Protestant Image Question in Western and Eastern Europe* (1993), esp. ch. 2.

[120] Calvin, *Institutes*, bk. 1, ch. 11, §12; Perkins, *Warning against the idolatrie of the last times*, in *Workes*,
i. 670.

must be placed against the broader backdrop of Elizabethan and Jacobean interior decoration on paper, plaster, and cloth.[121] And they too were congruent with the ideological priorities of the religion of the Word. If icons of the holy family and saints were instantly recognizable emblems of Roman Catholicism, the printed portraits of martyrs and reformers, tables of the ten persecutions of the primitive Church, and 'monuments' of national miracles which Protestants placed in their parlours and sitting rooms 'to stir them up to stand to the Faith' gave equally graphic and self-conscious expression to their confessional identity.[122]

The earliest of the small handful of these ephemeral items to have survived is *The powder Treason*, dating from around 1615 (Plate 33).[123] This lavishly detailed depiction of 'Jehovahs Prevention' of 'Antichrists Intention' to blow up the Houses of Parliament in November 1605 is an altar on which the religious householder is invited to offer up his own personal sacrifice of praise and thanksgiving to God. God Himself is represented by the all-seeing eye of *'providentia divina'*, encircled by the mysterious hieroglyph of the Tetragrammaton—the Hebrew name of the Lord spelt in four letters. For Calvinists hot under the collar about the perils of idolatry, this abstract symbol was the only acceptable way of signifying the transcendent presence of the Almighty: traditional anthropomorphic representations of a bearded patriarch enthroned in a bolster of clouds were condemned as the height of blasphemy and sacrilege.[124] From beneath the elaborately crested canopy of this shrine drops a panel displaying James I seated regally in Parliament, surrounded by the deferentially assembled ranks of his Privy Council, bishops, and peers.[125] In the vaults of the building 'Faux' prepares to ignite the casks of gunpowder which will explode the British monarchy and nobility into smithereens; a lunette below reveals the menacing mouth and bottomless pit of hell, where the devil, flanked by inferior demons, darkly conspires. Twelve portraits of the plotters ('The Popes salt-peeter Saints'), arranged around an oval miniature of the 'Arch prest' Henry Garnet, parody Christ and the Apostles. Copious inscriptions explain the sophisticated hermeneutics of the scene, glorifying the deliverance of Great Britain and its illustrious sovereign from a 'Swarme of Jesuited Locusts' with 'smouthe flattering Faces & scorpion'd stings'. 'Contrarie to all humane

---

[121] Watt, *Cheap Print*, ch. 5; and Anthony Wells-Cole, *Art and Decoration in Elizabethan and Jacobean England* (New Haven, 1997).

[122] The quotation, which refers to the fold-out tables of the ten persecutions in Foxe, is cited in Watt, *Cheap Print*, 158–9. Robert Chambers was quick to point out the apparent inconsistency between the iconoclastic principles of Protestants and the continuing proliferation of these kinds of images in practice: epistle to the 'Christian Reader', in Numan, *Miracles*, sigs. D6ᵛ–7ʳ.

[123] Richard Smith, *The powder treason*, engr. Michael Droueshout ([c.1615]). BM *Satires*, 67; Hind, *Engraving*, ii. 342.

[124] On the taboo against anthropomorphic representations of the deity, see Calvin, *Institutes*, bk. 1, ch. 11, §12; Perkins, *Warning against the idolatrie of the last times*, in id., *Workes*, i. 660, 677. See also Aston, *England's Iconoclasts*, vol i, pp. 452–7 and ead., 'The Bishops' Bible Illustrations', in Diana Wood (ed.), *The Church and the Arts*, SCH 28 (Oxford, 1992), 267–85.

[125] This part of the engraving is copied from the frontispiece to [Robert Glover], *Nobilitas politica vel civilis*, ed. Thomas Milles (1608) or Thomas Milles's trans. entitled *The catalogue of honor or tresury of true nobility peculiar to Great Britaine* (1610).

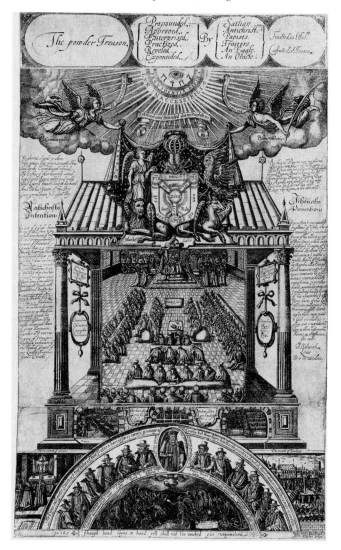

PLATE 33 Richard Smith, *The powder treason, propounded, by Sathan. Approved, by Antichrist. Enterprised, by papists. Practized, by traitors. Reveled, by an eagle. Expounded, by an oracle. Founded in hell. Confounded in heaven* ([London, *c.*1615]). © The British Museum. Department of Prints and Drawings, *Satires*, 67.

reason, & hellish expectation', God had redirected 'the fiery darts of this Luciferaine audacious enterprize' to return upon the perpetrators' 'owne paits', to His 'everlasting glory, our unspeakable Joy, & there infernall shame'. The scroll above the 'Helmet of Salvation' ('Tutch not mine Annointed doe my Prophete no harme') situates this engraving firmly within the context of the Jacobean doctrine of the divine right of kings.

Equally luxuriant in imperial imagery is a roughly contemporary print entitled *The papists powder treason*, now known only from a later seventeenth-century impression (Plate 34).[126] Crowded with Old Testament typology and classical allusion, this is another two-dimensional memorial, a triumphal arch recording on paper rather than in marble a signal victory won solely through the goodness of God. Here the artist sidesteps the interdict against visualizing the divine by resorting to allegory: a female personification of Bonita Divina sits astride 'Jacob's Stone Erected in aeternal memorie' of England's deliverance from the 'hellish' scheming of her Romish foes, with the Book of the Seven Seals lying open on her lap. Below, James I deciphers Lord Monteagle's letter, kneeling with his queen and heirs in this temple or pantheon of prayer. In the dimly lit left-hand niche, 'Guy Faux', masked and cloaked, casts a pool of light from his lantern on the faggots and barrels, with swift-footed Nemesis hot on his heels, assisted by an omniscient eye. Under the central aperture, the wheels of 'Justice's' chariot crush the 'male-contented crue' to death. Ten stanzas explicate the emblems embedded in every inch of this imposing edifice, while cherubim hold the corners of musical scores for two four-part psalms appropriate for the private devotions of the Protestant family on the anniversary of 5 November. Like the previous example, this 'monument' powerfully interlaces patriotism, royalism, and providential anti-popery as mutually reinforcing creeds. Both are compelling iconographical expressions of the prevailing political theology of the day, anti-Catholic images to which the civil and ecclesiastical establishment was scarcely likely to take exception.

In the following decade, however, circumstances began to turn the same themes decidedly sour, as Samuel Ward discovered when he published a thoroughly conventional print in 'memorye' of his nation's 'double deliveraunce from the invincible navie and the unmatcheable powder treason' in 1621 (Plate 35).[127] With the Habsburg marriage negotiations at a critical stage, it is not surprising that a picture portraying the intervention of providence (again in the irreproachable guise of the Jewish Tetragrammaton and the 'never slumbring' eye) against the Pope contriving with Satan and the Spanish King 'some rare stratagem' by which 'Great Brytanes State ruinate should bee' was construed as a personal insult to Philip IV. It was a tactless display of artistic talent which permanently tarnished Ward's reputation and seriously blighted his subsequent career. Provoking a formal protest

---

[126] *The papists powder treason* ([1679?]). The engraver is unknown, but the print was produced and sold by Richard Northcott, a publisher of historical works between 1677 and 1691. See Hind, *Engraving*, ii. 394–5. The original print can be dated to *c.*1612 because of the 'Palatina' inscription above Princess Elizabeth: she was betrothed to the Elector Palatine in May 1612 and married him in 1613.

[127] Samuel Ward, *Deo trin-uniBritanniae bis ultori In memoriam classis invincibilis subversae submersae / Proditionis nesandae detectae disiectae. To God, In memorye of his double deliveraunce from the invincible navie and the unmatcheable powder treason* (Amsterdam, 1621). BM *Satires*, 41; Hind, *Engraving*, ii. 393–4. I am grateful to Dr John Blatchly, formerly headmaster of Ipswich School, for valuable discussions and correspondence on the subject of Ward's print and its posthumous history.

PLATE 34 *The papists powder treason* (London, [1679?]). By permission of the Huntington Library, San Marino, California. RB 283000 IV. 21. A late seventeenth-century edition of an engraving first published *c.*1612.

from Count Gondomar, this ingenious artefact engraved in Amsterdam earned the Suffolk minister an extended term in prison. In a petition to James I the following spring, Ward claimed to have invented this 'embleme' 'five yeeres since in imitacion of auntient rites . . . without anie other sinister intencion, especiallie of meddling in any of your Majesties secrett affaires'. Any topical resonances were entirely inadvertent: far from seeking to interfere in *arcana imperii* he had merely coupled those 'two grand blessings' which divines 'daylie joyned' in anniversary sermons and intercessions without any molestation whatsover.[128]

Like its generic predecessors, this 'most remarkable Monument' was advertised as 'necessary to be had in the House of every good Christian, to shew Gods living and wonderfull providence, over this Kingdome, when the Papists twise sought

---

[128] PRO SP 15/42/76. Ward promised 'to be more cautelous for the future'. See also John Bruce, 'The Caricatures of Samuel Ward of Ipswich', *Notes and Queries*, 4th ser. 1 (1868), 1–2.

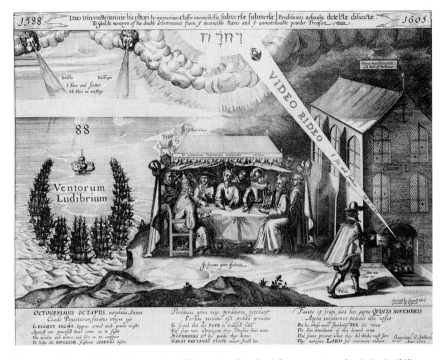

PLATE 35 Samuel Ward, *Deo trin–uniBritanniae bis ultori In memoriam classis invincibilis subversae submersae / Proditionis nesandae detectae disiectae. To God, In memorye of his double deliveraunce from the invincible navie and the unmatcheable powder treason* (Amsterdam, 1621). © The British Museum. Department of Prints and Drawings, *Satires*, 41.
Samuel Ward's 'monument' of England's 'Double Deliveraunce'.

their utter ruine & subvertion'.[129] Indeed, Ward had done little more than refine and juxtapose three pre-existing images. The crescent Armada dispersed by a heaven-sent wind has a prototype in a silver medal struck at Middelburg in 1588, inscribed 'Flavit [Jehovah] Et Dissipati Sunt.' (He blew and they were scattered.)[130] The cabbalistic council of machiavellian politicians was undoubtedly another frequently recycled motif and we have already encountered Guy Fawkes in his flowing cape and spurs sneaking towards the cellar beneath Parliament House to effect his 'deed of darkenes' only to be exposed by a great shaft of light on which is inscribed 'Video Rideo, I see and smile'. What was provocative was Ward's decision to release

---

[129] As it was advertised in a bookseller's notice to the reader at the end of Samuel Ward's *The life of faith* (1621 edn.).

[130] Hawkins *et al.*, *Medallic Illustrations*, no. 112, reprod. in M. J. Rodríguez-Salgado *et al.*, *Armada 1588–1988* (1988), fig. 16.12. The medal was struck at Middelburg, probably on the orders of Prince Maurice.

this 'facete and befitting picture' for public consumption in 1621.[131] Like Thomas Scott's *Vox populi*, it may well have been an ingenious attempt to sabotage the Spanish match by triggering a wave of anti-Catholic and hispanophobic feeling—and according to one London newsmonger, it was 'not good rubbing on that sore'.[132] Clearly the iconography of providence was no longer politically benign. As the Black Knight in Thomas Middleton's equally inflammatory play *A game at chesse* observed, 'pictures that were dumbe enough before' had become barking dogs which the authorities were clearly determined to muzzle.[133]

Such imagery did, however, enjoy something of an Indian summer after the ignominious collapse of the marriage talks in Madrid in October 1623 and the 'blessed revolution' in foreign policy the following February—the rapprochement between King and Parliament regarding Protestant England's military obligations to her Continental brethren.[134] Like other manifestations of exuberant anti-popery, 'monuments' to the Armada and Gunpowder Plot benefited from the disintegration of the Anglo-Spanish entente. One product of this period of reprieve was George Carleton's *A thankfull remembrance of Gods mercy*, a chronological account of the nation's deliverances from Catholic conspiracies since 1558 prefaced by a 'comely frontispiece' dominated by 'Ecclesia Vera' trampling upon 'Ecclesia Malignantium', a four-headed hydra comprising the Pope, a cardinal, a priest, and the devil, beneath her feet. The flags unfurled behind her by Deborah and Solomon, Elizabeth and James, bear simplified versions of the deliverances 'per aquas' and 'per ignem', by water and fire, twinned by Ward three years before (Plate 36).[135] An almost identical pair of salvation scenes appeared on the title-page of Christopher Lever's *The history of the defendors of the Catholique faith* (1627)[136] and the same engraver also prepared nineteen copperplate illustrations for the third edition of Carleton's book,[137] adapting the designs from a double folio sheet first published in 1625 (Plate 37).

Sold separately or as a folding synopsis of the text, this pillar was a pedagogic device by which godly parents could instruct their children in the fundamental principles of anti-popery and providential history. The obelisk is a mock papal bull

---

[131] [Scott], *Boanerges*, 25. He refers to another satirical cartoon, unfortunately now lost, which was also suppressed, its plate cut in pieces and its sellers imprisoned. It depicted James I holding the pope's nose to a grindstone turned by two archbishops.

[132] Chamberlain, *Letters*, ed. McClure, ii. 349. [Thomas Scott], *Vox populi. Or newes from Spayne* (1620). On Scott, see P. G. Lake, 'Constitutional Consensus and Puritan Opposition in the 1620s: Thomas Scott and the Spanish Match', *HJ* 25 (1982), 805–25.

[133] Thomas Middleton, *A Game at Chess* (performed 1624), ed. J. W. Harper (1966), III. i. 102–3.

[134] On the political context, see Thomas Cogswell, *The Blessed Revolution: English Politics and the Coming of War, 1621–1624* (Cambridge, 1989).

[135] Carleton, *Thankfull remembrance*, pub. May 1624 (*SR* iv. 116). Hind, *Engraving*, ii. 297–9; BM *Satires*, 98. The engraver was the Dutch immigrant William van de Passe.

[136] Christopher Lever, *The historie of the defendors of the Catholique faith* (1627). Hind, *Engraving*, iii. 214; BM *Satires*, 9. The engraver Frederik van Hulsen, also from the Netherlands, spent several months in London in 1627.

[137] Hind, *Engraving*, ii. 298–9. The engraved illustrations were inserted in the 3rd edn.

PLATE 36 George Carleton, *A thankfull remembrance of Gods mercy. In an historicall collection of the great and mercifull deliverances of the church and state of England, since the gospell began here to flourish, from the beginning of Queene Elizabeth* (London, 1624), title-page. By permission of the Syndics of Cambridge University Library. Shelfmark: SSS 32. 15.

promulgating sixteen articles or 'popish' treasons from the Northern Rising in 1569 to the Gunpowder Plot in 1605, with Prince Charles's heroic homecoming in 1623 occupying the final compartment in the base of the pyramid. Each of the crimes committed by the 'Devils instruments' is adjoined by a banner showing the divine retribution which ensued. This picture was to 'serve for strengthening of our hearts when we shall bee called to the like trials: For in these dayes of peace it is good to prepare against a storme'—a sentence which may well have acquired fresh significance in the 1630s, when zealous Calvinists were convincing themselves

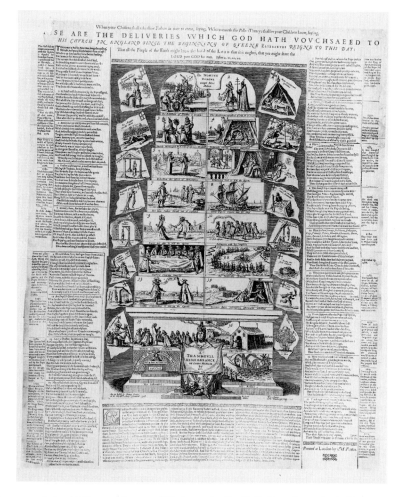

PLATE 37 *A thankfull remembrance of Gods mercie. By G. C.* (London, 1625). By
permission of the Ashmolean Museum, Oxford. Sutherland Collection, Large vol. III.
Fold-out plate designed for the second impression of George Carleton, *A thankfull
remembrance of Gods mercy* (1624), also sold separately as an engraved print.

that Laudian innovations amounted to a new Catholic conspiracy to bring England
under papal thraldom.[138]

Another monument dating from the 1620s, *To the glory of God in thankfull
remembrance of our three great deliverances*, also had a dual existence as a broadside

---

[138] *A thankfull remembrance of Gods mercie* (1625), engraved by Cornelius Danckersz of Amsterdam
and sold by Thomas Jenner. *SR* iv. 129. See Hind, *Engraving*, ii. 299. A later 17th-cent. edn., entitled
Popish plots and treasons, from the beginning of the reign of Queen Elizabeth (sold by John Garrett) is BM

and a series of plates for Michael Sparke's *Crumms of comfort* (Plate 38).[139] Uniting picture and prose, it was a memorandum of three national miracles, the scattering of the 'Spanish Armado', the prevention of the 'hellish and horrible Powder-Treason', and the cessation of the major outbreak of bubonic plague in 1625. The upper frames of this picture show the semicircular Spanish fleet off English shores; the timely discovery of the treacherous Faux, egged on by a pair of demons dancing in glee; and the devastation wrought by the grim reaper and the skeleton of death. Below are scenes of the corporate humiliation and thanksgiving the Lord expected from a covenanted people. Designed to prick the consciences of its viewers about the 'crying sinnes' that were pulling down 'the fourth Judgement, that is likely to fall upon us by the Sword', this print was a sobering pictorial reminder that contempt of God's admonitions and abuse of His mercies would soon transform the nation from 'a spectacle' of His 'ineffable goodnesse' into 'a spectacle' of His 'unsupportable wrath'.

The providential themes of these ephemeral engravings left an even more lasting legacy in silk, metal, paint, and stone. Pasted in paper above the fireplaces of middling-sort homes, the same patterns can also be found on tapestries and cushion covers embroidered by wealthy gentlewomen: at least two pieces of needlework based on Ward's *Double deliveraunce* have been preserved (Plate 39).[140] Relatives of Dame Dorothy Selby, the 'Dorcas' whose nimble fingers stitched one of these anti-Catholic samplers, had the scene incised in slate on a funeral monument erected

Satires, 13. Garrett was Jenner's successor, and worked between 1676 and 1697. This print bears a remarkable resemblance to a Dutch engraving disseminated as Counter-Remonstrant propaganda around the time of the Synod of Dort in 1618: Simon de Vries [*et al.*?], *t'Arminiaens testament* ([Holland], 1618), BM, DP&D. See Kunzle, *Early Comic Strip*, 57–60 and fig. 2–21 and see also fig. 2–28, *Piramis pacifica*, which commemorated the Dutch-Spanish Truce of 1609.

[139] *To the glory of God in thankefull remembrance of our three great deliverances unto etern[al] memory* (1627), engraved by Jan Barra and printed for sale by Michael Sparke. Hind, *Engraving*, iii. 101. Sparke, *Crumms of comfort*, as cited in n. 98, above. Frederick Van Hulsen engraved another pair of illustrations for the 1627 edn. of this book (between sigs. A8 and A9). They depicted 'The night of Popish superstition' and 'The returne of the Gospells light'. See Hind, *Engraving*, iii. 215.

[140] Lady Lever Art Gallery, Liverpool, LL5292 (dated after 1621), described in Xanthe Brooke, *The Lady Lever Art Gallery Catalogue of Embroideries* (Stroud, 1992), 18–20. Dame Dorothy Selby's needlework picture is now preserved in a private collection in Cardiff, but it is reproduced in J. L. Nevinson, 'English Domestic Embroidery Patterns of the Sixteenth and Seventeeth Centuries', *Walpole Society*, 28 (1939–40), 10 and pl. VI (b). A third piece of needlework based on Ward's print is described in the will of James Carcase dated 1637: 'long pillowe of tenteworke wherein is the Story of 88 and the Powther plott of the fiefte of November': PRO PROB 11/182/f5, cited in Brooke, *Catalogue*, 20. See also Katharine A. Esdaile, 'Gunpowder Plot in Needlework: Dame Dorothy Selby, "Whose Arte Disclos'd that Plot"', *Country Life*, 93 (June 1943), 1094–6, who reproduced another of Dame Selby's embroideries, which is clearly based on Richard Smith's *The powder treason*. Mid-17th-cent. printsellers like Peter Stent and John Garrett are known to have sold patterns for 'Gentlewomens works', and almost certainly their predecessors did the same. See Alexander Globe, *Peter Stent London Printseller circa 1642–1665* . . . (Vancouver, 1985), 12, 17, 21; and Garrett's advertisement in the right-hand corner of *Popish plots and treasons*, cited in n. 138, above. On the extent to which prints influenced tapestry and embroidery, see also Wells-Cole, *Art and Decoration*, chs. 13–14. A number of domestic artefacts were produced in celebration of the 1588 campaign, including the Armada fireback, probably made in Sussex: see Rodríguez-Salgado *et al.*, *Armada 1588–1988*, fig. 16.18.

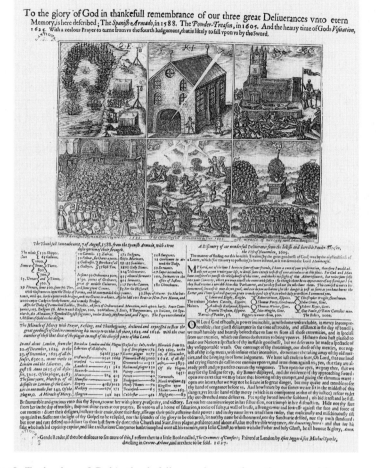

PLATE 38 *To the glory of God in thankefull remembrance of our three great deliverances unto etern[al] memory, is here described* (London, 1627). By permission of the Society of Antiquaries of London. Lemon Collection 266.
Engraved print based on illustrations in Michael Sparke, *Crumms of Comfort* (first published 1623).

in Ightham parish church in Kent to mark her death in 1641.[141] Inscriptions placed in Preston St Mary near Lavenham closely echo the same print and the Somerset family of William Strode, one of Charles I's fiercest opponents in the Long Parliament, seems to have had part of it engraved on brass, adding a divine ear

[141] Edward R. Harrison, *The History and Records of Ightham Church* (Oxford, 1932), 16–18 and the drawing of the incised slab reproduced at the back.

PLATE 39 Cushion cover, dated after 1621. By permission of the Board of Trustees of the National Museums and Galleries on Merseyside (Lady Lever Art Gallery, Port Sunlight).
One of a number of pieces of needlework based on Samuel Ward's 'Double Deliveraunce'.

eavesdropping on the villains labelled 'I hear and laugh'.[142] By the late 1620s many London churches contained tablets to Elizabeth I, 'Britaine's Blessing, Englands Splendor, Religions Nurse, The Faiths Defendor', and at St Mildred Bread Street a local worthy by the name of Captain Nicholas Crispe commissioned a stained glass window for the chancel with five 'artfull and curious' panels depicting the Armada, the Virgin Queen, the Powder Plot, the terrible epidemic, and lastly the pious benefactor and his dependants.[143] The defeat of 'Spaines proud Armado' with divine assistance was portrayed in an allegorical oil painting executed by Robert Stephenson for a Lincolnshire church around 1610, in which the crescent-shaped fleet in the guise of a dragon is vanquished by the forces of St George,

[142] *Suffolk in the XVIIth Century: The Breviary of Suffolk by Robert Reyce, 1618* (1902), 201–4. Philip Whittemore, 'A Brass Plate Commemorating the Defeat of the Gunpowder Plot', *Transactions of the Monumental Brass Society*, 13 (1985), 549–57; John Blatchly, 'The "Gunpowder Plot" Plate: A Postscript', *Transactions of the Monumental Brass Society*, 14 (1986), 68–9. One poor and fragile rubbing is all that has survived.

[143] John Stow, *A survey of London*, expanded by A. M[unday], H. D[yson], *et al.* (1633), 859–60 and note the 'Queen Elizabeth Monuments' described in the 'Perambulation or Circuit-Walke foure miles about London'. I owe this reference to Dr Julia Merritt. See also the monument to Elizabeth at All Hallows at the Wall noted in Lambeth Palace Library, London, MS 1485, fo. 33ʳ.

leaving its 'guts like Pharaos scattered hoast . . . splitt and drown'd upon the Irish coast'. This historic victory accomplished by the 'holy arme' of the Lord, together with the frustration of Guy Fawkes and his accomplices, inspired two remarkable paintings bequeathed to St Faith's, Gaywood, near King's Lynn, by its rector Thomas Hares in 1634.[144] The fifth of November 1605 was also commemorated in a painted version of *The papists powder treason* commissioned by Richard Haydocke, physician and brass engraver, for New College, Oxford, for the silver jubilee of the conspiracy in 1630.[145] Such memorials to the special providences God had conferred upon His people physically filled the gaps left by the 'table-monuments of miracles' removed from chapels and churches in the 1530s and 1540s in accordance with official instructions.[146]

Was the iconography of English nationhood a casualty of the broader ecclesiastical trends in the 1620s and 1630s we have already explored? Did it become one more target of the clampdown on rabid anti-Catholicism? Early modern censorship was never wholly effective and in the absence of adequate evidence, it would be unwise to do more than hypothesize. But, quite apart from Ward's print, there are several hints to the effect that by the second quarter of the seventeenth century these potent images of providential interventions had indeed become ideologically charged. When James I gave audience to the Spanish ambassador in the gallery at Whitehall in November 1620, for instance, he ordered several pieces which reflected badly upon Don Gondomar's countrymen to be cut out of pictures on the walls. Might the Armada have been among the sensitive subjects thus suppressed? It is worth remembering that 'hangings of 88' had been installed in the House of Lords.[147] Even more suggestive is the fact that John Vicars's suppressed pamphlet on *The quintessence of cruelty* included illustrations adapted from the relevant portions of Michael Sparke's broadsheet and book: vulgar depictions of 'Heavens All-seeing-Eye' thwarting the fatal designs of 'Fauks and his Father-Satan' can hardly have been aesthetically pleasing to the Laudian regime.[148] And

---

[144] Stephenson's painting was lent privately for display in the National Maritime Museum's Armada exhibition in 1988 and is reproduced in Rodríguez-Salgado *et al., Armada 1588–1988*, fig. 16.30. The Gaywood painting of the Armada is fig. 16.31. I am grateful to the Royal Commission on the Historical Monuments of England for assistance in locating a photograph of the other half of the diptych.

[145] Reproduced in L. G. Wickham Legg, 'On a Picture Commemorative of the Gunpowder Plot, Recently Discovered at New College, Oxford', *Archaeologia*, 84 (1934), 27–39; Karl Josef Höltgen, 'Richard Haydocke: Translator, Engraver, Physician', *The Library*, 5th ser. 33 (1978), 15–32. I am obliged to the Warden and Fellows of New College for permitting me to inspect this painting and to Mr Ralph Weller for allowing me to read relevant portions of his unpublished MS on Haydocke. For *Papists powder treason* see n. 126, above.

[146] See W. H. Frere (ed.), *Visitation Articles and Injunctions of the Period of the Reformation*, 3 vols. (1910), iii. 6, 68, 126.

[147] PRO SP 14/117/71 (Thomas Locke to Dudley Carleton, 11 Nov. 1620). The 'hangings of 88' are depicted in the frontispiece to Prynne's *Canterburies doome*.

[148] Herring, *Quintessence of cruelty*, trans. Vicars, sig. A1ʳ and p. 77. It may be more than an interesting coincidence that Thomas Jenner sold Vicars's *Englands hallelu-jah*. Also noteworthy is the fact that the only surviving 'monument' which can even tentatively be dated to the 1630s is a set of exhor-

most striking of all are the instructions Laud gave William Kingsley, archdeacon of Canterbury in April 1636 regarding a tablet to the Armada and Gunpowder Treason in the city parish church of either St Gregory or St George: inscribed 'In perpetuam Papistarum infamiam, &c', it too must have been modelled on Ward's ubiquitous print. If this stood in the east end of the chancel it was to be dismantled and erected elsewhere, so as not to profane the sacred space set aside for the altar. Once relocated, a painter was to be employed to 'put out of the Monument, all that concernes the Fleet in 88, because that belongs to a Forreigne Nation'. To Prynne, who recorded it in his *Canterburies doome*, this iconoclastic act was further proof of a conspiracy 'to obliterate the memoriall of our happy deliverance[s]' from the treachery of Spain and the papacy.[149] Such monuments had clearly become political icons: in the eyes of the Laudians they may well have seemed boorish, crude, and a defiant badge of adherence to a dissident creed.

Emblematic miniatures of 1588 and 1605 continued to reappear in books of remembrance published throughout the Civil War, Interregnum, and Restoration,[150] and new impressions of broadside monuments were issued whenever collective anxiety about illicit Catholic activity grew acute, especially during the scares surrounding the 'popish plot' fabricated by Titus Oates in 1678, the Exclusion Crisis, and the Glorious Revolution.[151] This was unquestionably an image which entered into the visual imagination of the nation as a whole: adapted for insertion in octavo editions of the Prayer Book and Bible during the reign of Charles II, it was a picture which generations of Protestant children must have surreptitiously inspected in their pews and copied, traced, and coloured in their nurseries and schoolrooms (Plate 40).[152]

No providential moment managed to wedge itself more firmly in Protestant mythology than November the fifth. Others, though hardly less legendary in their

tatory verses 'To my Posterity' privately printed for one Matthew Haviland: *A monument of Gods most gracious preservation of England from Spanish invasion, Aug. 2. 1588. and popish treason, Novem. 5. 1605. To my posterity* ([c.1635?]).

[149] Prynne, *Canterburies doome*, 91–3. No churchwardens' accounts survive for either of these parishes for this period and the Royal Commission on the Historical Monuments of England has no record of the monument. St George's was badly damaged by bombs in W. W. II.

[150] See e.g. Samuel Clarke's *Englands remembrancer, containing a true and full narrative of those two never to be forgotten deliverances* (1657), and id., *Mirrour or looking-glasse* (1671 edn.). See also BM *Satires*, 45–7.

[151] Ward's print reappeared in 1740 and in the 19th cent. The detail was revived for political cartoons against Charles James Fox. See BM *Satires*, 42–4, 1223, 2456; George, *English Political Caricature*, 63–4, 105 and pl. 29(a). Ward's print was part of Peter Stent and John Overton's stock in the 1650s and 1660s: Globe, *Peter Stent*, 135–6, 174, 177. As noted above both *Papists powder treason* and *Popish plots and treasons* are later 17th-cent. impressions. For crude woodcut reproductions of these images, see the anti-Catholic catechism published by Benjamin Harris: *The Protestant tutor. Instructing children to spel and read English, and grounding them in the true Protestant religion and discovering the errors and deceits of the papists* (1679), title-page, 52, 62. I owe this reference to Helen Weinstein.

[152] See *The book of common prayer*, octavo and duodecimo edns. of 1676, 1678, and 1711. John Sturt and G. L. Adams adapted this design for the same purpose in 1717 and 1787. See the octavo edn. of *The holy bible* (1669), pl. facing Pss. x–xiv.

PLATE 40 *The book of common
prayer* (London, octavo edn. 1676).
By permission of the Syndics of
Cambridge University Library.
Shelfmark: Adams 7. 67. 14.
Illustration facing 'A Form of
Prayer with Thanksgiving, to be
used yearly upon the Fifth day of
November; For the happy
Deliverance of the King, and the
Three Estates of the Realm, from
the most Traiterous and Bloudy
intended Massacre by
Gunpowder'. This copy has been
coloured in.

own time, have faded into oblivion and sunk without trace. The final section of
this chapter is a case study of how one forgotten providence became entangled in
confessional politics in the decades preceding the Civil War, both at street level and
in the circles of the learned.

THE FATALL VESPER[153]

On the afternoon of Sunday, 26 October 1623, a tragic accident occurred in the
London district of Blackfriars. A large garret adjoining the French ambassador's
residence, in which a congregation some three hundred strong had assembled to
hear Robert Drury, a celebrated Jesuit preach, suddenly and spectacularly col-

---

[153] For a fuller account of the Blackfriars accident, see my ' "The Fatall Vesper": Providentialism
and Anti-Popery in Late Jacobean London', *P&P* 144 (1994), 36–87.

lapsed. In the midst of the sermon the floor of the makeshift chapel gave way, plummeting the preacher, a fellow priest, and over ninety of his auditors to a ghastly death.[154] The disaster followed closely in the wake of the humiliating collapse of the protracted talks in Madrid for a marriage alliance between the heir to the English throne and the Habsburg Infanta Maria. It was an immediate sequel to the unprecedented outburst of popular royalist and anti-Spanish sentiment sparked off by the return of the prodigal young Stuart prince and his entourage.[155]

Instantly christened the 'fatall vesper' and 'dolefull even-song', it provoked an enormous furore. In the capital, there was 'much discoursing . . . of all the circumstances belonging to the busines';[156] in the country it quickly became the 'newes' on everyone's lips. Unreliable rumours and garbled hearsay ran rife; hastily scribbled accounts circulated in the city and passed with private correspondence into outlying provinces;[157] journalistic ballads and pamphlets poured forth from rival rhymsters, prose-writers, and printing presses within a matter of weeks;[158] and metropolitan preachers had a veritable field day—not least William Gouge, rector of the adjacent parish of St Anne.[159]

[154] The most detailed accounts of the accident, based on eyewitness reports, and including the coroner's list of the victims, can be found in W. C., *The fatall vesper* (1623) (often erroneously attributed to the puritan divine William Crashaw); Thomas Goad, *The dolefull even-song* (1623); and William Gouge, *The extent of Gods providence, set out in a sermon, preached in Black-Fryers church*, bound with *Gods three arrowes*, esp. 393–400. See also the London newsletters received by Joseph Mede and sent on to Sir Martin Stuteville: BL Harleian MS 389, fos. 372ʳ–374ᵛ. Many relevant extracts from printed tracts and MSS are printed in Foley (ed.), *Records of the English Province*, i. 76–97.

[155] See Thomas Cogswell, 'England and the Spanish Match', in Richard Cust and Ann Hughes (eds.), *Conflict in Early Stuart England: Studies in Religion and Politics 1603–1642* (1989), 107–33.

[156] PRO SP 14/154/17 (John Chamberlain to Sir Dudley Carleton, 8 Nov. 1623), printed in Chamberlain, *Letters*, ed. McClure, ii. 521. See also Gouge, *Extent of Gods Providence*, in *Gods three arrowes*, 392.

[157] See BL Harleian MS 389, fos. 372ʳ–377ʳ, 381ʳ; PRO SP 14/153/103, 104, 106, 108; 14/154/2, 17, 28 and 55; *The Knyvett Letters (1620–1644)*, ed. Bertram Schofield, Norfolk Record Soc. 20 (1949), 61–2. The accident was also recorded in a number of diaries: D'Ewes, *Diary*, ed. Bourcier, 167–8; id., *Autobiography and Correspondence*, ed. Halliwell, i. 238; BL Egerton MS 784, fo. 35ʳ; Yonge, *Diary*, ed. Roberts, 70; and in John Southcote, 'The Notebook of John Southcote, D.D., 1628–36', ed. J. H. Pollen, in *CRS Miscellanea I*, CRS 1 (1905), 99.

[158] In addition to the pamphlets by Goad and W. C. cited in n. 154 above, the following publications have survived: a ballad by Mathew Rhodes, *The dismall day, at the Black-Fryers* (1623); an anonymous pamphlet entitled *Something written by occasion of that fatall and memorable accident in the Blacke Friers . . .* (1623); a tract by the Jesuit John Floyd written under the initials I. R. P., *A word of comfort. Or a discourse concerning the late lamentable accident of the fall of a roome, at a Catholike sermon, in the Black-Friars at London* ([St Omer], 1623). Another Catholic account of the accident was published in Spanish: *Relacion de un caso en que murieron muchos Catolicos oyendo la palabra de Dios* (Valladolid, [1623]), a reference I owe to Alison Shell.

[159] Gouge's *Extent of Gods providence* was preached on 5 Nov. John Chamberlain had heard several sermons delivered shortly after the accident and commended 'our preachers cariage . . . for generally they do not dilate nor aggravate yt very much': PRO SP 14/154/17, printed in Chamberlain, *Letters*, ed. McClure, ii. 521. See also the epistle to Thomas Adams's sermon preached at Paul's Cross on the morning of the accident. *The barren tree* (1623), sig. A4ʳ⁻ᵛ. John Gee, who had attended the sermon and escaped unhurt from the rubble, discussed it in his recantation tract, *Foot out of the snare*, sigs. A4ʳ–Aa1ʳ, pp. 5–8 and in *Hold fast, a sermon preached at Pauls Crosse* (1624), 63–5. Goad, chaplain to Archbishop Abbot, interrogated Gee when he was summoned to Lambeth to explain his presence in the attic, and his own pamphlet probably derived from this examination.

To Protestant propagandists, the collapse of a house swarming with Catholics and their sympathizers was an open invitation to announce divine outrage against the Church of Rome. Vaunting claims were made about the symbolic overthrow of institutionalized impiety and idolatry: the catastrophe was declared to be conclusive proof of the treacherously unstable theological foundations of popery itself. Thomas Goad, chaplain to Archbishop Abbot, argued that 'a topicall inference' might be drawn 'from the fall of both the floares, namely, of the preaching, and the Massing roome, that both their Doctrine and Sacrifice are weakely and slenderly supported, and that God was displeased as well with their Pulpits, as altars'.[160] No less alluring was the hypothesis that the ceiling had buckled under the weight of Catholic iniquity, that a 'load of sinne pressed them down that fell'.[161]

Some private letter-writers dared to diagnose a rather more specific reason for this volcanic eruption of the Lord's wrath: the increasingly undisguised resurgence of popery during the preceding twelve months, of which this 'solemne assemblie' was all too overt and disturbing a sign. They implied that Jesuit insolence in launching a public mission in the capital was a direct consequence of the King's 'lenative courses', the pragmatic relaxation of the recusancy laws which had accompanied the delicate diplomacy surrounding the Habsburg match. Only behind the screen of anonymity could one risk expressing this opinion in print. The sole tract to do so was unlicensed and its author may well have been the irrepressible John Everard of St Martin-in-the-Fields. In suggesting that God had stormed in to thwart the unbridled boldness of the papists 'upon a litle connivence', such commentators were skating on extremely thin ice: it was but a small step to the seditious proposition that the accident embodied supernatural disapproval of the official policy of de facto toleration itself.[162]

Nor was it considered an uncanny coincidence that the calamity had occurred on 26 October. According to the Gregorian calendar used by Catholic countries on the Continent, this was none other than the anniversary of the Gunpowder Plot, 5 November. Few failed to notice the prodigious significance of the new style date—not even William Laud, then bishop of the Welsh diocese of St David's.[163] Some did 'descant much of the day'; others self-righteously reproved those who went 'so farre as to make a numerall inference of a second reflecting Tragedy', surrendering all such 'judiciary calculation' to their Maker. But the nexus was compelling: the visitation was confidently interpreted as an act of divine vengeance for

[160] Goad, *Dolefull even-song*, sigs. H2ᵛ, H3ʳ⁻ᵛ; See also *Something written*, 11, 28 and *passim*, and W. C., *Fatall vesper*, sig. F1ᵛ.

[161] Gee, *Foot out of the snare*, 5; Goad, *Dolefull even-song*, sig. H3ᵛ.

[162] PRO SP 14/154/17. Cf. Dudley Carleton's account, PRO SP 14/154/2, and Sir Simonds D'Ewes's reflections in *Autobiography and Correspondence*, ed. Halliwell, i. 238. *Something written*, 14–16. I am strongly tempted to identify the author of this pamphlet as John Everard. The similarity of the title with his *Somewhat: written by occasion of three sunnes seene at Tregnie in Cornwall . . .* (1622) is highly suggestive.

[163] *The Works of the Most Reverend Father in God, William Laud, D.D.*, ed. W. Scott and J. Bliss, 7 vols. (Oxford, 1847–60), iii. 143. See also BL Harleian MS 389, fo. 374ʳ.

the sinister 'mischiefe' miraculously prevented in 1605, a further reaffirmation of God's sacred contract with the Protestant nation.[164] John Persehowse, steward of the manor of Walsall in the West Midlands, whose own brother-in-law died in the disaster, declared it to be a 'second miracle . . . shewd upon the papistes', who had thus been justly punished for their 'devilish plott', 'according to their deserts'.[165] A conspicuous omission from David Cressy's *Bonfires and Bells*, Blackfriars was another 'icon event' which anchored itself securely in the annals of patriotic Protestant history.

The tale, moreover, grew much in the telling. Existing details were embroidered and muddled, and a set of fantastic anti-Catholic accretions sprang up. Many seem to have been under the mistaken impression that the service in progress had actually been a mass—a superstitious celebration of the Holy Eucharist. It took little to persuade one-eyed Protestants that the Lord had made it His personal business to debunk that central ritual of priestly deception, transubstantiation, and to exterminate credulous laypeople as they bowed sottishly in worship before the inanimate bread.[166] Equally preposterous suggestions circulated about the precise point at which Drury's sermon had been so rudely interrupted. Some stressed that in dilating his text the preacher had 'modelled out' popish doctrine in the form of the 'fantasie of Purgatory', the pseudo-sacrament of penance, and the heavenly merit one could accrue by performing good works. Thomas Goad did not 'curiously enquire' into the matter, 'as making interpretation of Gods judgement in stopping the currant of his speech at that instant', but others all too eagerly did.[167] Walter Yonge was not alone in supposing that the Jesuit had been delivering a violent invective against the heretics, levelling his execrations against Luther, Calvin, and the late Dr Thomas Sutton, the vehemently anti-papal minister of St Mary Overy, Southwark, who had drowned in tragic circumstances in September. Drury allegedly declared that the sea had 'swallowed' the latter, 'because hee was not worthie the earthe shoulde receve him, att which wordes', so the story went, the house immediately 'sancke'.[168] These rumours spread alongside fables to the effect that the oration underway that afternoon was the public recantation of an apostate priest. Recast as vengeance poured out upon a renegade in the very act of disavowing the Reformed religion, the disaster could serve as a cautionary tale for backsliding Calvinists.[169]

The Blackfriars accident was thus a windfall to the Protestant cause. It clumsily

---

[164] PRO SP 14/154/17; Goad, *Dolefull even-song*, sig. B2ᵛ; *Something written*, 12. According to the Jesuit Floyd this was a 'farre fetcht argument': *Word of comfort*, 37.

[165] Staffordshire RO, Stafford, D 260/M/F/1/5, fo. 122ʳ. I owe this reference to John Craig.

[166] See e.g. the entry in Eltham parish register by John Ford, printed in Daniel Lysons, *The Environs of London*, 4 vols. (1792–6), iv. 410. Cf. PRO SP 14/153/104.

[167] *Something written*, 24; Goad, *Dolefull even-song*, sig. C1ʳ⁻ᵛ. Cf. Floyd, *Word of comfort*, 37–8.

[168] BL Add. MS 28032, fo. 54ᵛ, printed in Yonge, *Diary*, ed. Roberts, 70. See also W. C., *Fatall vesper*, sig. D2ᵛ; Goad, *Dolefull even-song*, sig. H3ʳ; *Something written*, 17, 28. As Joseph Mede's London correspondent reported, Sutton's death had indeed been received with great rejoicing by the capital's 'Popelings': BL Harleian MS 389, fo. 355ʳ.

[169] PRO SP 14/154/2 and 14/153/104. Cf. BL Harleian MS 389, fo. 374ʳ.

buttressed the assertion that clinging stubbornly to popery was a perilous enterprise and that in the economy of salvation Catholics were heading along a high road to personal ruin. Those snatched from 'the very jawes of Death', admonished Goad, should reflect 'whether this sudden stroake and cracke be not the hand, and voice of God, to call them home from wandring after forraine Teachers, that . . . carry them hood-winked into the snares of danger, corporall, civill, and spirituall'.[170] Preachers like Thomas Adams grumbled about the obstinacy of 'our wilfull and bewitched Recusants', who 'from these legible Characters' refused to 'spell Gods plaine meaning', but individuals involved in the calamity who converted as a result became overnight heroes.[171] One such celebrity was the disillusioned Lancashire minister John Gee, whose scurrilous exposé of urban Catholicism, *The foot out of the snare*, was a 'monument' to his own narrow escape from extinction in the 'dolefull even-song' and to the divine grace which had plucked him back from the brink of the Babylonian pit.[172] Another edifying anecdote often repeated was the chronicle of the lame woman badly injured in the downfall who was thereby persuaded to make a textbook confession of the doctrine of salvation by faith alone: 'If God spare me now, I will never pray to Saints againe, but to my Lord and Saviour Jesus Christ, who onely is my Redeemer.'[173]

Catholics themselves were keenly aware that the disaster could only hinder their own proselytizing programme. 'O what advantage will our adversaries take at this', one lucky survivor bewailed; 'it would prove a great scandall to their Religion', foretold a precocious 10-year-old girl.[174] Private grief and sorrow, insisted the Jesuit John Floyd in the tract he wrote to console his dispirited co-religionists, must be subordinated to the 'publicke defence' of the beleaguered Church of Rome.[175]

One shrewd response was to impute the catastrophe entirely to the antiquity of the building and the decayed state of the wooden beam beneath the overcrowded upper room, emphasizing that such 'dreadfull mischances' were miseries 'indifferently incident unto mankind'.[176] But the reflex reaction of those who nursed a particular grudge against Protestants was to attribute the disaster to human malice and to detect behind it a cruel plot masterminded by malevolent members of the Church of England to massacre their recusant enemies. Calvinist conspirators, it was whispered in the city, had 'secretly drawne out the pins, or sawed halfe a sunder some of the supporting Timber'; Dr Price, 'a Popish Physician, stuck not falsely

---

[170] Goad, *Dolefull even-song*, sig. D2^{r-v}. See also Floyd, *Word of comfort*, 11.

[171] Adams, *Barren tree*, sig. A4^v. Cf. *Something written*, 13–14.

[172] Gee, *Foot out of the snare*, sig. Aa1^r, p. 6. Cf. id., *Hold fast*, 21–2, 63–5. *The foot out of the snare* ran through four edns. in 1624 alone. On Gee, see Michael C. Questier, 'John Gee, Archbishop Abbot, and the Use of Converts from Rome in Jacobean Anti-Catholicism', *Recusant History*, 21 (1993), 347–60.

[173] *Something written*, 14. See also BL Harleian MS 389, fo. 374^v.

[174] Goad, *Dolefull even-song*, sig. E2^{r-v} and W. C., *Fatall vesper*, sig. E4^{r-v}.

[175] Floyd, *Word of comfort*, 3–4.

[176] Ibid. 5, 11, cf. 12. See also More, *Historia missionis Anglicanae*, fo. 451^v (trans. in Foley (ed.), *Records of the English Province*, i. 87); *Something written*, 9; W. C., *Fatall vesper*, sigs. F1^v–2^r.

to say that the Puritans of Black Fryers had done it'.[177] Others proceeded to 'marshall the defunct in the inventory of Martyres', arguing that sudden death was a distinct asset to the members of a congregation devoutly at prayer: it ensured them celestial bliss and allowed them to bypass the pains of purgatory as well.[178]

John Floyd's *Word of comfort*, however, embodied a theologically more complex rejoinder to the claim that the accident demonstrated divine odium of popery. Protestants had no basis for being 'jolly and jocund, so puffed up with pride at the fall of a rotten chamber', he declared, since it was as much part of God's overarching providential plan to test and try the righteous through tribulation, as to discipline the wicked with draconian rigour. His 'holy purpose' was not to annihilate Catholics but to purge and refine their faith.[179] Though it might seem baffling, perverse, even sadistic to the feeble human intellect, 'to send strange disasters upon his servants hath been ever his custome'. Analysed from this angle, the calamity was a token of the Lord's good will towards a persecuted community and a harbinger of the 'speedy overthrow' of her 'hoater Adversaries'.[180] Floyd sarcastically rebuked heretical railing against popery 'in regard of a vulgar event', refuting 'their folly' who dared to scrutinize the 'darke mist of Gods unsearchable Counsels'. It was unwarrantable to 'judge of the sanctity of mens lives, by the hydeous shew of their deaths' and 'to make happy Event a note of Truth, or unlucky successe a signe of falshood'.[181]

But in the end Floyd was forced to fight back with the same blunt and undiscriminating instrument. He drew up a list of ominous calamities and prodigies which had occurred since the Henrician schism and parried Protestant taunts about the shameful death of Father Drury with stories of the unsavoury ends of Continental reformers including Calvin, whom he dubbed 'the Puritans Dad'. These tales were intended to deflate his enemies' 'insulting spirit' and dissipate their 'vayne and frivolous clamors'.[182] A pamphlet was reputedly published in Rome which even more literally returned the humiliating jeers of their enemies upon their own heads by relating the fall of a house in St Andrew's parish in Holborn, where a godly preacher and his 'Psalming Auditorie' had gathered for 'a Genevan lecture' the same evening—and so, one journalist remarked, 'by way of inversion' casting 'a lye upon us'.[183]

[177] *Something written*, 10–11; Goad, *Dolefull even-song*, sig. D1^{r–v}; W. C., *Fatall vesper*, sig. F1^{r–v}; *Knyvett Letters*, ed. Schofield, 62. On Dr Price, see BL Harleian MS 389, fo. 374^{r}.

[178] *Something written*, 10; Floyd, *Word of comfort*, 48; More, *Historia missionis Anglicanae*, fos. 451^{v}–452^{r} (trans. in Foley (ed.), *Records of the English Province*, i. 89); BL Harleian MS 389, fo. 374^{v}; PRO SP 14/154/17; Gee, *Foot out of the snare*, 7.

[179] Floyd, *Word of comfort*, 21, 48 and ch. 4 *passim*.

[180] Ibid. 8, 57 (and see 53).

[181] Ibid. 20, 4, 11, 27 (and see chs. 1–2 *passim*).

[182] Ibid. ch. 3, esp. pp. 27–32, quotations at 30.

[183] *1624. Newes from Holland*, sig. A2^{v}; Thomas James, *A manuduction, or introduction unto divinitie: containing a confutation of papists by papists* (1625), 127. See also the later account of the accident in Clarke, *Mirrour or looking-glasse*, 195.

Protestant ministers tried hard to restrain the response of the urban populace within the bounds of orthodox predestinarian belief. They prefaced their fulminations with the caveat that divine providence was ultimately unfathomable, reproaching those who rashly concluded that the victims were damned on no other grounds than their 'outward chastisement' and warning their audiences that 'unless ye repent, ye shall all likewise perish'.[184] Yet they too found it difficult to reconcile humanitarian compassion for the wretched plight of the wounded and dead with their passionately anti-Catholic convictions. '[W]here we see judgements executed on sinners when they are in their sinne, when they are impudent and presumptuous therein,' thundered Gouge, 'not to acknowledge such to be judged by the Lord, is to winke against a cleare light'.[185] In the context of the cosmic controversy between Christ and Antichrist, insisted another writer, 'wee may well use the language of Canaan' and no 'more mannerly . . . then the holy Ghost himselfe . . . plainly denuntiate what God threatens'. Failure to show 'a holy zeale in our anger' against the Roman whore and her followers bespoke an intolerably lukewarm commitment to the Reformed religion.[186]

In fact, anything but indifference had characterized the behaviour of the crowds which thronged to the scene of destruction in Blackfriars that autumn afternoon. The civic authorities were obliged to take immediate action to close off the site and 'to repress the insolencie and inhumanitie of the multitude', who not only assailed the survivors with curses and 'contumelious speech', but pelted them with mud and stones as they were carried off to surgeons and physicians through the streets. Angry mobs apparently went on the rampage, besieging the coaches of distressed recusant gentlewomen beating a hasty retreat and setting upon a young girl dragged unconscious from the wreckage, apparently intent on depriving her of what little life remained. According to the Venetian ambassador, the accident 'provided the occasion for a general and bloody riot' and a Dutch account of the disaster published in Antwerp in December reported that the rabble had boasted that 'they would that night cut the throats of all the Catholics in the City'.[187] Yet allegations about brutal and homicidal conduct did not come from hostile sources alone: John Chamberlain wrote to Sir Dudley Carleton that 'our people beeing growne so sauvage and barbarous' had not only refused to relieve the injured, 'but rather insulted upon them with taunts and gibes in their

---

[184] See the comments of W. C., *Fatall vesper*, sigs. B4ᵛ–C1ʳ; Goad, *Dolefull even-song*, sigs. A3ʳ⁻ᵛ, H2ᵛ⁻³ʳ; Gouge, *Extent of Gods providence*, in *Gods three arrowes*, 400; *Something written*, 1–3; Gee, *Hold fast*, 64. Adams who preached on Luke xiii. 3–5 declared that it 'pleased God Almighty' only a few hours later 'to make a fearefull Comment' on his unwittingly prophetic text. He had expounded in 'Characters of bloud' what 'His holy Pen had long since written . . . with inke': *Barren tree*, sig. A4ʳ.

[185] Gouge, *Extent of Gods providence*, in *Gods three arrowes*, 400.

[186] *Something written*, 4–7, quotation at 4–5.

[187] PRO SP 14/154/17; Floyd, *Word of comfort*, 42–3; Albert J. Loomie (ed.), *Spain and the Jacobean Catholics*, ii. *1613–1624*, CRS 68 (1978), 160 (A report of the archdeacon of Cambrai, 9 Nov. 1623); More, *Historia missionis Anglicanae*, fo. 451ᵛ (trans. in Foley (ed.), *Records of the English Province*, i. 88); *CSP Venetian*, xviii. 147; *Nieuwe Tijdinghen*, no. 136 (Antwerp, 1623), 5. I owe the last reference to Peter Arblaster.

affliction'—'[e]ven in Cheapside', he added reprovingly, 'where they sholde be more civill'.[188]

But the explosive response of the suburban poor to the 'fatall vesper' can hardly be described as random or irrational. There is a strong case for seeing it as a form of confessional conflict, and for comparing it with both the 'anti-popish panics' which periodically rocked towns and villages across the country and the animated outbreaks of hispanophobia which had swept the capital earlier that decade, when Spanish diplomats were subject to many indignities and much high-spirited verbal abuse at the hands of the 'inferiour and baser sort of people'.[189] In this instance, anti-popery was catalysed by providentialism: it was God's own aggression which stimulated the excesses of the local inhabitants, His own iconoclastic stroke against Catholics engaging in idolatrous rites which precipitated and legitimated the atrocities that followed. Perhaps the participants interpreted the catastrophe as a mandate and a cue to carry through the disciplinary process to completion, seeing themselves as collaborators in a programme of ethnic cleansing initiated by their enraged deity.[190] Their bold appropriation of the magistrate's sword may even have embodied an implicit protest against a government which refused to enforce the recusancy laws. The violence was certainly highly ritualized and judicial in character: stoning was sanctioned by the Mosaic law, cursing had a liturgical counterpart in the commination of sinners, and the dirt and refuse hurled at the victims might be interpreted as an ironic rite of purification through desecration.[191] These serious overtones should not blind us to the carnivalesque side of the proceedings: the accident obviously put some city dwellers in an exuberant holiday mood, providing an outlet for energies which all too readily spilt over into more sinister forms of revelry and sport.[192]

Who, then, were the actors in these street wars of religion? What was the confessional identity of the crowd? Catholics were convinced it was comprised of Calvinist fanatics—'infuriati Protestanti', to use the Venetian ambassador's

[188] PRO SP 14/154/17. See also *Something written*, 27; PRO, SP 14/153/103.

[189] For anti-popish panics, see Clifton, 'Fear of Popery', 144–67, and id., 'Popular Fear of Catholics', 129–61. For attacks on the Spanish ambassadors, see 'A Proclamation for suppressing insolent abuses committed by base people against persons of qualitie, as well Strangers as others, in the Streetes of the Citie and Suburbes of London' (8 Apr. 1621), repr. in J. F. Larkin and P. L. Hughes (eds.), *Stuart Royal Proclamations*, i, *Royal Proclamations of James I* (Oxford, 1973), 508–11, quotation at 509, and K. J. Lindley, 'Riot Prevention and Control in Early Stuart London, *TRHS*, 5th ser. 33 (1983), 111–12.

[190] Cf. Natalie Zemon Davis, 'The Rites of Violence', in *Society and Culture in Early Modern France* (Stanford, Calif., 1975), 159. Floyd condemned the crowd for usurping God's office 'as if he wanted eyther wisedome to know, or justice to hate, or power to punish sufficiently the grievousnes of mans sinnes': *Word of comfort*, 45.

[191] See Davis, 'Rites of Violence', 159, 179–80, and R. W. Scribner, 'Reformation, Carnival and the World Turned Upside-Down', in id., *Popular Culture and Popular Movements in Reformation Germany* (1987), 95–7. For stoning, see Lev. xx. 2, xxiv. 10–23; Num. xv. 32–6; Deut. xvii. 5, xxi. 21, xxii. 21, 24; Ezek. xvi. 40, xxiii. 47. Floyd drew attention to this too, denouncing the crowd's use of 'the instruments of Jewish cruelty': *Word of comfort*, 42. For ritualized cursing, 'A Commination against Sinners', in *The Book of Common Prayer* (1559), repr. in Clay (ed.), *Liturgical Services*, 239–45.

[192] On this aspect of religious violence, see Scribner, 'Reformation, Carnival and the World Turned Upside-Down', 87–9.

expressive Italian phrase.[193] The Jesuit Floyd did not attribute the barbarities to ordinary Protestants ('Heresy hath not made them so wild') but to puritans—the puritans of Blackfriars, that 'one particle of London' which they 'boast to be their speciall Nest'. These enormities were witness to the 'rudenes of their Pretended Holy Discipline', to the anarchic and antinomian tendencies encouraged by a radical internalization of presbyterian tenets.[194] To all appearances the mob was composed of individuals who exhibited more than a courteous distaste for the Roman Catholic faith. But puritan ministers were quick to dissociate themselves from the disorderly hordes and to deny all responsibility for rousing the rabble or stage-managing their terrorist attacks. One pamphleteer was horrified to hear such 'unruly voices crye out upon popery', aggrieved to see hooligans and thugs who 'feared neither God nor men' metamorphosed overnight into ardent 'professors of the Gospell, and detesters of Antichrist'. Their anti-Catholic zeal, in his opinion, was merely a convenient camouflage for vandalism, 'rifling', and 'spoile'.[195]

What we have been analysing is one occasion on which the culture of festive licence and the culture of a militant brand of Calvinism briefly converged, a fleeting moment when a precarious alliance was forged between those nicknamed 'puritans' and those they in turn deemed profane and impious. Based on a set of shared beliefs about the intervention of the sacred in the terrestrial realm, the temporary fusion of these groups reinforces recent suggestions that in times of crisis godly Protestants could influence and mobilize bodies of opinion far broader than that exclusive minority who called themselves the 'saints'.[196]

The anger of the London crowd, albeit intense, proved to be short-lived and the flurry of sensational ephemera about the 'fatall vesper' soon dwindled to a trickle, but the Blackfriars catastrophe retained its value as confessional propaganda long after it ceased to be headline news. It was probably not until several months later, for example, that an arresting engraving of the accident became available for sale (Plate 41).[197] This provocative print left its viewers in no doubt whatsoever that the disaster was an act of capital punishment executed by an irate Protestant deity. The finger of God points menacingly from the clouds, shooting a beam of supernatural light to pierce the preacher 'Drew(a)ry's' heart and silence his antichristian discourse for ever. Its uncompromising inscription, 'DIGITUS DEI HIC CONFV=', only adds to the macabre effect. All around him masonry crumbles and pillars topple, crushing the richly attired evensong crowd. The dismembered

---

[193] *CSP Venetian*, xviii. 147.

[194] Floyd, *Word of comfort*, 42–3, cf. 57. Floyd was here exploiting a rhetoric developed by conformist divines in the campaign against Puritanism in the 1590s and alluding to [Richard Bancroft], *A survay of the pretended holy discipline* (1593).

[195] *Something written*, 27.

[196] Lake, 'Anti-Popery', 93–6. See also Hunt, *Puritan Moment*, 306–10; Underdown, *Revel, Riot, and Rebellion*, 129, 140–1; Clifton, 'Popular Fear of Catholics', 161.

[197] *No plot no powder 1623* is BM *Satires*, 95. Engraver and artist unknown; sold by Thomas Jenner. This was not the only visual representation of the disaster: see the title-page of Richard Hord's Latin elegy on the subject *Black-Fryers* (1625); and the Dutch print entitled *Anno, 1623 . . .*, BM *Satires*, 63.

PLATE 41 *No plot no powder 1623* (London, [*c.*1623]). © The British Museum.
Department of Prints and Drawings, *Satires*, 95.
Engraving of the 'fatall vesper' in Blackfriars on 26 October 1623. This forms a
polemical triptych with plates 42 and 43.

bodies of the Jesuit's auditors are placed at excruciating angles, their faces stare
out bewildered and stunned. Some exclaim popishly in the midst of their ordeal,
'ora pro nobis', 'pray for us'. Others are clearly determined to desert Rome without
further delay: 'Masse is misery', one moans; 'Ile go no more to masse', another
fervently vows.

   No plot no powder seems to have been the third panel of a polemical triptych,
the final frame in a satirical cartoon designed along the lines of Samuel Ward's
Double deliverance. In *A plot with powder* (Plate 42) we are confronted by a

PLATE 42 *A plot with powder 1605* ([London, *c.*1623]). © The British Museum. Department of Prints and Drawings, mounted with *Satires*, 95.
Engraving of the discovery of the Gunpowder Plot, 5 November 1605.

familiar tableau: 'Faux' 'discovered' by divine omniscience as he steals towards the kegs of dynamite in the vault beneath Parliament House. Next, the curtain opens to reveal *A plot without powder* (Plate 43), a conclave of Jesuits and secular priests seated around a table littered with popish paraphernalia, intriguing to bring England back into the Catholic fold and under the subjection of Philip IV. In the third act of this divine drama truth is permitted to triumph once more: the perpetrators of plots with and without powder are violently surprised and overwhelmed. At 'Blackefriars' in 1623 God has at last revenged the 'Black Deeds' done in Westminster in 1605 and the 'Black Breed' that met in Fetter Lane, Holborn, around 1620. As the swallow-tailed pennants in the corners proclaim, there is neat poetic justice in the fact that the treachery of 5 November 'Old Stile' has been requited on 5 November 'New Stile'. The caption carried across from Guy

PLATE 43 *A plot without powder*
([London, *c.*1623]). © The
British Museum. Department
of Prints and Drawings,
Satires, 87.
Engraving of a conspiratorial
council of Jesuits and secular
priests.

Fawkes's cloak to Robert Drury's surplice also clumsily insists that this is a simple
case of cause and effect: 'Faux why Drew(a)ry'.[198]

The biblical verses engraved under each picture are from 2 Samuel xii. 11–12.
On one level, they amount to nothing more than a vulgar anti-Catholic brag, a
slogan of self-congratulation that the shady dealings of the papists behind closed
doors will eventually be brought to light and publicly punished. But the typological implications of this passage are problematical: God speaks here through the
prophet Nathan, delivering a chilling sentence against King David who has

---

[198] *A plot with powder 1605*, BM, DP & D (noted in Hind, *Engraving*, ii. 393); *A plot without powder*,
BM *Satires*, 87. These two prints have now been mounted together. Their connection with *No plot no
powder* has not previously been noticed. These copies seem to be specimens of different impressions
made from recycled plates in varying states of modification, deterioration, and decay.

committed adultery with Bathsheba, wife of Uriah the Hittite, and effectively murdered her husband by sending him to certain slaughter in battle: 'Thus saith the
Lord, behold, I wil raise up evil against thee out of thine owne house'. Is the divine
chastisement visited on the royal house of Israel an allegory of the future fortunes
of the Stuart line? Is it England's intended alliance with Antichrist, her licentious
liaison with the Habsburg Infanta, or her growing tolerance of Catholicism, which
has likewise kindled God's wrath? Should these engravings be interpreted as an
attack upon dynastic and ecclesiastical policies deemed to be prostituting the
integrity of the Protestant nation? Perhaps they contained no such clever political
riddles, but even as an entirely conventional expression of popular anti-popery they
were potentially inflammatory—as Samuel Ward's clash with the authorities two
years earlier had revealed. And given that the first print is a mirror image of the
third frame of the *Double deliveraunce*, and that the second was either based on or
the basis for an illustration for Thomas Scott's *Vox populi*, part 2, could it be that
Ward and/or Scott devised or commissioned all three?[199]

It certainly seems more than a coincidence that Thomas Scott preached and
published a subversive sermon about the Blackfriars catastrophe late in 1623.
Having already incensed the authorities with half a dozen pamphlets denouncing
the projected marriage alliance and stressing the moral necessity of English intervention in the Thirty Years War, it is no wonder that Scott took the precaution of
entrusting this vitriolic diatribe against Rome and Spain to the safety of a printing house in Holland. For even without the stigma of his name on its cover, *Digitus
dei* is unlikely to have escaped censorship at home.[200] Scott gave free rein to his
viciously satirical tongue in this apocalyptic exposition of the religio-political
significance of the recent tragedy. He asserted that it was 'the silence of all men at
that time and in that action' which had provoked God 'to speake and to doe'—the
tacit and near-universal sanction given to the current 'encrochments of Antichrist'.
He vigorously rebuked those who had held their peace for fear of being 'counted
factious, furious, and hot-headed fellowes' and rendered ineligible for 'preferment
and imployment', promising that God would find them out, and 'punish their falshood and faintnesse in his cause'.[201] This kind of Laodicean apathy could be
detected in official reluctance to implement the statutes against recusancy and in
the crypto-popery creeping into 'the heart and bosome' of the Stuart court and
state.[202] It was not 'the sodaine reentrance of Antichrist' that must be guarded

---

[199] T[homas] S[cott], *The second part of vox populi* (Goricom [London], 1624), 54, engraved by the
Utrecht craftsman Crispin van de Passe.

[200] [Thomas Scott], *Exod. 8. 19. Digitus dei. Esay. 59. 1. The Lords hand is not shortned. 2 Tim. 3. 8,
9* ([Holland, 1623]), repr. in id., *Vox populi. Vox dei. Vox regis. Digitus dei. The Belgick pismire. The tongue-
combat. Symmachia. The high-wayes of God and the king. The projector* ([Holland, 1624]), from which I
quote. It is unclear where Scott delivered this sermon. Early in 1621, having 'fore-notice of the pur-
sevant', he had prudently fled to Holland; BL Harleian MS 389, fo. 15ᵛ. It may have been preached at
Utrecht where he served as chaplain to the English garrison stationed there.

[201] [Scott], *Digitus dei*, 28–30, cf. 4–5.

[202] Ibid. 14–17, quotation at 17. Cf. [Scott], *Boanerges*, 26–8.

against, but 'his slye insinuation, and their wiles who pretend to worke reconcile-ment, and say that humour is too much stird upon both sides'. Accepting 'the least marke of the Beast which we have cast off, therby to buy our peace, and to endeare our entertainment', was 'to sinne with a high Hand' against the Holy Ghost.[203]

As the suppression of Middleton's *A game at chesse* in August 1624 revealed, unrestrained anti-Catholicism of this kind was still considered to be interna-tionally indiscreet.[204] Scott had the added temerity to redirect his venomous anti-popery inwards to dissect tendencies he believed were poisoning and debauching the political and ecclesiastical establishment from within. *Digitus dei* was one more symptom of the extent to which providentialism was evolving into a politicized discourse.

Elevated to the status of a sacred date in the epic tale of Protestant England's victory over popery, the 'fatall vesper' was assimilated into a historical tradition which, as we have seen, was itself emerging as a bone of contention between the Caroline government and its critics. The Harleys of Brampton Bryan, Herefordshire, gave heartfelt thanks for this among other 'publique deliverances' at household prayer meetings in 1633,[205] and by the end of that decade the 'BlackFrier Fall' was a standard entry in almanacs and a typical subject for Latin set pieces by young Oxbridge scholars.[206] John Vicars had re-emphasized the re-tributive connection between the 'Powder-Plott' and the 'Fatall Fall' in *Englands hallelu-jah* in 1631, declaring the disaster 'A Type of Justice on the Rabble of Rome', and it was also alluded to in Henry Burton's infamous *For God, and the king*: 'as the Lord hath made our Fifth of November a glorious day . . . So on the other side, Hee hath branded their fifth of November with the note of a perpet-uall curse and ignomy.'[207] In 1655 Thomas Fuller incorporated the catastrophe in his *Church-history of Britain* and it continued to appear in encyclopedic anthol-ogies of providences like Samuel Clarke's *Mirrour or looking-glasse both for saints, and sinners*.[208] Two years later Clarke appended an account of this seemingly indel-ible event to his *Englands remembrancer*, a cheap duodecimo tract recounting the 'never to be forgotten' deliverances of 1588 and 1605. He pirated William Gouge's

---

[203] [Scott], *Digitus dei*, 31, 33.

[204] Middleton, *Game at Chess*, ed. Harper, pp. xii–xiii.

[205] BL Add. MS 70062, no. 5. I am grateful to Jacqueline Eales for this reference.

[206] For just two examples, see Richard Allestree, *A new almanack and prognostication* (1630) and Thomas Kidman, *A new almanack for the yeare of our Lord God, 1634* (Cambridge, 1634). For Latin elegies, see Hord, *Black-Fryers*; John Robotham, *Omen Romae* (1627); Alexander Gil, 'In Ruinam Camerae Papisticae, Londini Octob. 26', in id., *Parerga* (1632), 10–13; and Edward Benlowes, quoted in Fuller, *Church-history of Britain*, bk. x, pp. 103–4. John Wilson celebrated it in *Song or story*, 31–7 and see the English poem in Bodleian Library, MS Eng. poet. e. 14, fo. 24ʳ.

[207] Vicars, *Englands hallelu-jah*, sig. B4ᵛ; Burton, *For God, and the king*, 102–3, see also PRO SP 16/354/176 and 180, 16/335/69. It was also recorded by Nehemiah Wallington: BL Add. MS 21935, fos. 23ʳ, 25ᵛ, and Sloane MS 1457, fos. 9ᵛ–10ʳ, 11ʳ; and by the Dorchester gentleman William Whiteway: CUL MS Dd. 11. 73, fo. 45ᵛ.

[208] Fuller, *Church-history of Britain*, bk. x, pp. 102–4; Clarke, *Mirrour or looking-glasse*, 394–9. It was also included in William Turner's *Compleat history*, ch. 99, p. 7 and in *The historians guide: or, Englands remembrancer* (1679 edn.), 8.

narrative of the calamity and added a crude fold-out copy of the *No Plot No Powder* print. Clarke published this pocketbook of history for the edification of the poor: he hoped it would resurrect the memory of mercies and judgements which 'some noted persons amongst us' seemed intent on extinguishing.[209] During the Interregnum republican leaders were ambivalent about commemorating the wonders which the Lord had wrought for the early Stuart regime, but the evidence assembled in this chapter suggests that these Protestant 'miracles' already had a tenacious grip on the consciousness of the English populace.

By the end of the Elizabethan period, then, anti-popery and providentialism had reacted to form a powerful but volatile compound. Religious intolerance nourished and was in turn nourished by a corpus of pre-existing convictions about the interposition of God in the earthly world, convictions rooted in classical natural philosophy and pagan belief as much as in the Bible and medieval theology. Providence lent itself to exploitation by the evangelists and propagandists of rival confessions precisely because it represented an area of relative cultural and ideological consensus. Protestants might insist that miracles had ceased to be a hallmark of the true Church on earth, but the concept of special providence released them from the crippling effects this precept had on their ability to convince wavering laypeople of the intrinsic rightness of their cause. It neatly extracted them from the polemical corner into which they had unwittingly backed themselves. Catholics manipulated this conceptual framework with no less flair and finesse than their confessional enemies, and, like them, discarded it as an interpretative tool when it suited them. Where they could not compete was in enlacing divine dispensations in their favour with the fortunes of the English, and after 1603 British, monarchy and state. The great deliverances from Spain and the Pope which became red-letter days in the post-Reformation calendar generated new symbols of identity—new rituals, myths, festive customs, and, notwithstanding the iconophobic tendencies inherent in Calvinism, new images too. These not only helped people adjust to the abolition of some of the richest aspects of traditional religion, but permanently cemented the link between Protestantism and patriotism. Anti-Catholic providentialism was thus a key chemical ingredient in the crucible in which, to echo Christopher Haigh's subtle distinction, a Protestant nation if not a nation of Protestants was gradually forged.[210] However, it also held within it the seeds of schism and fission. By the late 1620s, it was beginning to aggravate and intensify divisions inside the political and ecclesiastical establishment.

---

[209] Clarke, *Englands remembrancer*, 87–100, quotations at title-page, sig. F1ᵛ. The simplified *No plot no powder* print can be found in the BL copy (classmark G 3517) facing p. 67. There were new edns., expanded to incorporate more recent 'popish plots', in 1671, 1676, 1677, 1679, [1680?] and 1775.

[210] Haigh, *English Reformations*, 280.

6

'Englands Warning by Israel': Paul's Cross Prophecy[1]

'Israel and England, though they lye in a divers climat, may be said right Parallels; not so unfit in *Cosmographicall*, as fit in *Theologicall* comparison.' So declared that most poetic of Jacobean preachers Thomas Adams at the beginning of a conventional sermon diagnosing the symptoms and forecasting the course of his nation's terminal 'sicknesse' in sin.[2] This was so pithy and resonant an expression of the typological 'similitude'[3] between the ancient Hebrew and the modern English people that when John Jones, curate and lecturer at St Michael's Bassishaw, was summoned to perform at Paul's Cross in August 1630, he boldly stole it to enliven his own jeremiad, *Londons looking backe to Jerusalem*.[4]

This homiletic genre indisputably found its most mature and polished form in the tradition of national morality sermons delivered from the open air pulpit in the churchyard of St Paul's Cathedral, a rostrum contemporaries revered as the 'chiefest Watchtower', the central 'theater', and the very 'stage of this land' (Plate 44).[5] Yet preaching in the mould of the Old Testament prophets was also the staple fare of metropolitan, provincial, and rural congregations throughout the country. Alighting on key passages from Isaiah, Jeremiah, and Micah, Hosea, Amos, and Joel, Protestant ministers told a cheerless tale of England's dismal prospects if the current epidemic of iniquity continued unchecked. Although these thunderous addresses were often ebulliently patriotic in tone, self-congratulation was usually overshadowed by self-castigation, by anxiety about the consuming collective judgement which assuredly loomed.

The final chapter of this book analyses the providential thinking which underpinned the preaching of the Israelite paradigm in the eighty-year interval between

[1] The title of this chapter is taken from John Fosbroke's Paul's Cross sermon on 29 Nov. 1617, *Englands warning by Israel and Judah*, in *Six sermons delivered in the lecture at Kettering in the countie of Northampton, and in certain other places* (Cambridge, 1633). I borrow the phrase 'Paul's Cross Prophecy' from Patrick Collinson, 'Biblical Rhetoric: The English Nation and National Sentiment in the Prophetic Mode', in Claire McEachern and Deborah Shuger (eds.), *Religion and Culture in the English Renaissance* (Cambridge, 1997), 27. I am grateful to Professor Collinson for allowing me to read this essay prior to its publication. My debt to his work will be readily apparent: here it has been possible to explore in more detail many of the themes to which he draws attention.

[2] Thomas Adams, *Englands sicknes, comparatively conferred with Israels* (1615), repr. in *Workes*, 302.

[3] John Downame, *Lectures upon the foure first chapters of the prophecie of Hosea* (1608), 2nd pagination, 68.

[4] Jones, *Londons looking backe to Jerusalem*, 26.

[5] Webbe, *Gods controversie*, sig. A3ᵛ; D'Ewes, *Diary*, ed. Bourcier, 94; Stock, *Sermon preached at Paules Crosse*, sig. *3ᵛ. Cf. Procter, *Watchman warning*, sig. A3ᵛ.

PLATE 44 T[homas] B[rewer], *The weeping lady: or, London like Ninivie in sack-cloth* (London, 1625), sig. A3ᵛ. By permission of British Library. Shelfmark: C. 34. f. 20. Prophetic sermon at Paul's Cross, London.

Elizabeth's accession and the end of Charles I's Personal Rule. It examines the theology embodied in a representative sample of the tiny fraction of sermons exploiting this potent analogy which found their way into print, and it highlights the degree to which the preoccupations of prophetic preachers coincided with the habitual concerns of the authors and consumers of inexpensive ephemeral literature.[6] The static, typeset texts in which these fire and brimstone sermons are now constrained efface the fact that they were, above all, dramatic oral and physical performances. Indeed, this dynamic and charismatic brand of pulpit oratory provides compelling evidence that neither preaching nor providentialism was quite as alien and distasteful to the English people as some recent work has sought to persuade us they were.

---

[6] This chapter is based on a close study of Paul's Cross sermons preached between 1558 and 1640 and a wide sample of prophetic sermons preached at other locations during the same period. Millar Maclure's chronological register of Paul's Cross sermons in *The Paul's Cross Sermons 1534–1642* (rev. and expanded Peter Pauls and Jackson Campbell Boswell as *Register of Sermons Preached at Paul's Cross 1534–1642*, Centre for Reformation and Renaissance Studies Occasional Publications 6 (Ottawa, 1989)), is an invaluable tool, but his summaries of the sermons are not always a reliable guide to their overall content or character. On the history of Paul's Cross as an institution, see Maclure, *Paul's Cross Sermons*, ch. 1; Margaret E. Cornford, *Paul's Cross: A History* (1910). For an illuminating literary critical study, see Mary Morrissey, 'Rhetoric, Religion, and Politics in the Paul's Cross Sermons, 1603–1625', PhD thesis (Cambridge, 1997).

THE ENGLISH JEREMIAD

Until recently the English jeremiad has inhabited something of a scholarly lacuna. Easily eclipsed by the more exotic varieties of apocalyptic exegesis[7] and regularly passed over in favour of the searching evangelical preaching which probed and assuaged the afflicted consciences of the 'saints',[8] sermons which modelled themselves on the books of the major and minor Hebrew prophets may actually have been a more pervasive and influential form of clerical discourse than both.[9] The neglect of this genre is all the more astonishing in view of the thriving industry devoted to its North American counterpart, and this may help to explain why historians of puritan New England have been tempted to register the patent and copyright of the prophetic mode across the Atlantic, implying that it was an indigenous species of Massachusetts rather than an import from the Mother Country conveyed in the original cargo of the Pilgrim Fathers' ships.[10] Most students of the famous fast sermons preached to the Long Parliament between 1640 and 1649 have also ignored their ancestry in the searingly judgemental addresses delivered at Paul's Cross and other public venues.[11] When Stephen Marshall and Edmund Calamy mounted the pulpit of St Margaret's Westminster to admonish the House of Commons about the dangers of national apostasy and the threat of heavenly vengeance they were not merely rehearsing the grim warnings of early Caroline preachers before Parliament like John Preston and Jeremiah Dyke, but echoing a pessimistic message which had been resounding in the ears of city audiences for nearly a century.[12] Nor were such sermons a sudden innovation of the period after

---

[7] Christopher Hill, *Antichrist in the Seventeenth Century* (Oxford, 1971); Bauckham, *Tudor Apocalypse*; Christianson, *Reformers and Babylon*; Firth, *Apocalyptic Tradition*.

[8] William Haller, *The Rise of Puritanism . . .* (New York, 1938).

[9] Patrick Collinson and Michael McGiffert have now begun to correct this serious oversight, but we still lack a full-scale study of the genre of monograph length: Michael McGiffert, 'God's Controversy with Jacobean England', *American Historical Review*, 88 (1983), 1151–74; Patrick Collinson, 'The Protestant Nation', in *Birthpangs*, esp. 3–4, 17–27; id., 'Biblical Rhetoric'. See also Christopher Hill, *The English Bible and the Seventeenth-Century Revolution* (1993), esp. chs. 10–12. For the 'Anglican' jeremiads of the Restoration, see Spurr, 'Virtue, Religion and Government', 29–47; id., *Restoration Church*, ch. 5.

[10] Miller, *New England Mind*, esp. ch. 16; Sacvan Bercovitch, 'Horologicals to Chronometricals: The Rhetoric of the Jeremiad', in Eric Rothstein (ed.), *Literary Monographs*, 3 (Madison, 1970), 3–124; id., *The American Jeremiad* (Madison, 1978); David Minter, 'The Puritan Jeremiad as a Literary Form', in Sacvan Bercovitch (ed.), *The American Puritan Imagination: Essays in Revaluation* (Cambridge, 1974), 45–55; Emory Elliott, *Power and the Pulpit in Puritan New England* (Princeton, 1978); John F. Berens, *Providence and Patriotism in Early America 1640–1815* (Charlottesville, Va., 1978).

[11] E. W. Kirby, 'Sermons before the Commons, 1640–1642', *American Historical Review*, 44 (1939), 528–48; James C. Spalding, 'Sermons before Parliament (1640–1649) as a Public Puritan Diary', *Church History*, 36 (1967), 24–35; H. R. Trevor Roper, 'The Fast Sermons of the Long Parliament', in *Religion, the Reformation and Social Change* (2nd edn. 1972), 294–344; Stephen Baskerville, 'The Political Theology of the Fast Sermons of the Long Parliament', PhD thesis (London, 1987); Hill, *English Bible*, ch. 3. The most distinguished study to date is Wilson, *Pulpit in Parliament*.

[12] For entirely typical examples of the preaching of Marshall and Calamy, see respectively *Reformation and desolation: or, a sermon tending to the discovery of the symptoms of a people to whom God will by no meanes be reconciled* (1642) and *Englands looking-glasse, presented in a sermon, preached before*

1558: they have recognizable prototypes in the preaching of Edwardian reformers like John Hooper, Hugh Latimer, and Thomas Lever at court and the Cross.[13] With the restoration of Roman Catholicism under Mary I, this rousing prophetic rhetoric was forced into the alternative forum of print: its exiled exponents were obliged to exchange their lusty voices for the silence of the pen and the great national pulpit for a Continental press.[14]

Protestantism, moreover, in many respects merely provided a new ideological framework for an immemorial formulaic refrain. The dissection of vice, rebuke of estates, and summons to repentance had a venerable heritage in the vernacular preaching *apud sanctum Paulum* of the late Middle Ages.[15] In a sermon delivered beneath the cathedral in 1375, Thomas Brinton, Benedictine monk and bishop of Norwich, took up the cry of Hosea and Amos, suggesting that sin was so omnipotent that 'God who was accustomed to being English will abandon us' ('Deus qui solebat esse Anglicus a nobis recedit').[16] When the secular priest Thomas Wimbledon spoke from this podium in 1388 he too took on the mantle of a medieval Jeremiah and called upon all sorts of people to sanctify their lives. The fact that a printed version of this relic of popery, allegedly 'founde out hyd in a wall', ran through fifteen editions between 1550 and 1635 is not as surprising as it may initially seem: late Tudor and early Stuart prophetic preaching was no more than an elaborate set of variations on an ancient homiletic theme.[17] The pattern of

the honourable house of commons, at their late solemne fast (1642). For published fast sermons to parliament dating from the pre-1640 period, see Bargrave, *Sermon preached before the . . . lower house of parliament* (1624); Jeremiah Dyke, *A sermon preached at the publicke fast* (1628); John Harris, *The destruction of Sodome: a sermon preached at a publicke fast* ([1629]); John Preston, *A sermon preached at a generall fast*, in *The saints qualification* (1633). This is not to mention the prophetic sermons preached at puritan fasts, for which, see Collinson, *Elizabethan Puritan Movement*, 214–19; id., 'Puritan Classical Movement', 323–46; and William Sheils, 'Provincial Preaching on the Eve of the Civil War: Some West Riding Fast Sermons', in Anthony Fletcher and Peter Roberts (eds.), *Religion, Culture and Society in Early Modern Britain: Essays in Honour of Patrick Collinson* (Cambridge, 1994), 290–312.

[13] John Hooper, *An oversight, and deliberacion upon the holy prophete Jonas* ([1550?]); Hugh Latimer, *A most faithfull sermon preached before the kynges most excellente majestye, and hys most honorable councell* ([1550]), repr. in *Sermons*, ed. Corrie; Thomas Lever, *A sermon preached the thyrd Sonday in Lent before the kynges majestie, and his honorable counsell* (1550); id., *A fruitfull sermon made in Poules churche at London in the shroudes* (1550). See also Catharine Davies, '"Poor Persecuted Little Flock" or "Commonwealth of Christians": Edwardian Protestant Concepts of the Church', in Peter Lake and Maria Dowling (eds.), *Protestantism and the National Church in Sixteenth Century England* (1987), 78–102.

[14] See e.g. Bartholomew Traheron, *A warning to England to repente* ([Wesel?], 1558). For some discussion of this subject, see Joy Shakespeare, 'Plague and Punishment', in Peter Lake and Maria Dowling (eds.), *Protestantism and the National Church in Sixteenth Century England* (1987), 103–23.

[15] As noted by Maclure, *Paul's Cross Sermons*, 144. See also Spencer, *English Preaching in the Late Middle Ages*, 67. Sermons were preached at Paul's Cross from at least 1330.

[16] *The Sermons of Thomas Brinton, Bishop of Rochester (1373–1389)*, ed. Mary Aquinas Devlin, 2 vols., CS, 3rd ser. 85–6 (1954), i. 47. In another Paul's Cross sermon dated c.1383–4, Brinton referred to Hos. iv ('Non est veritas, non est misericordia, non est sciencia Dei in terra . . .'): ii. 500.

[17] Richard [Thomas] Wimbledon, *A sermon no lesse frutefull then famous. Made in the yeare of our Lord God. M.C. lxxxviii and founde out hyd in a wall* (1573 edn.), title-page, and see sig. A2[r-v]. His text was Luke xvi. 2 ('Give an account of thy stewardship'). See the introd. to the modern edn. by Ione Kemp Knight, *Wimbledon's Sermon: Redde Rationem Villicationis Tue: A Middle English Sermon of the Fourteenth Century*, Duquesne Studies, Philological Ser. 9 (Pittsburgh, 1967), esp. 22–6; Owst,

predicting imminent calamity and scourging immorality can be traced back even further, to the turn of the millennium. Archbishop Wulfstan of York's 'Sermon to the English' (*Sermo Lupi ad Anglos*), dated 1014, is an urgent call to a country left desolate by Viking raids to repent, appease the wrath of God, and thereby lift the threat of total subjugation by the Danes.[18]

'Ripping up' the 'raigning sinnes' of the age remained the 'usuall subject' of sermons at Paul's Cross throughout the Elizabethan and Jacobean period, as William Procter, vicar at Upminster, Essex, observed in September 1624.[19] There was no 'more seasonable' topic than the 'preventing of the further and future judgements of God upon us, and our posteritie', declared John Fosbroke, rector of the Northamptonshire parish of Cranford St Andrew, in the prologue to a withering exposition of Hosea v. 15 in 1617.[20] These were evidently the clichés the delegated speaker was expected to serve up each week, and few failed to satisfy the unadventurous appetites of the hundred- or thousand-strong crowd. According to Prebendary Thomas Jackson, lecturing at Canterbury cathedral in the early 1620s, there was 'no corner of the land, but for many yeeres hath rung with these warnings'.[21]

If such sermons followed an old-fashioned recipe, Protestant preachers can at least be accredited with refining it and adding flavour and spice. Elevating the art of scriptural typology to dizzy new heights, they pursued the comparison between England and the Old World prior to the Flood, the cities of Sodom and Gomorrah, the Assyrian capital Nineveh, the Asian Churches of Ephesus and Laodicea, and, above all, Israel far more systematically than ever before. Sixteenth- and seventeenth-century ministers treated their own nation and the Jews as exact contemporaries, close cousins, even identical twins. England had only to glance in the mirror of Holy Writ to see her own flaws and imperfections portrayed in stark relief and a terrifying premonition of her fate should she too disregard the Lord's fatherly chastisements and 'alarums'. Therein, asserted George Webbe, preacher at Steeple Ashton in Wiltshire, 'we may behold as in a glasse a lively picture of this our land in which wee live', a perfect allegory and emblem of her history and future.[22] After the accession of James I and the partial union with Scotland many ministers subtly adjusted this Anglocentric paradigm in a direction that was more politically correct. 'Therefore as Hosea said to Judah,' admonished Alexander Udny, chaplain to the king and minister at Hawking in Kent, 'loe I say to Britaine,

---

Preaching in Medieval England, 360–2. The allegation that the prophecy was 'founde out hyd in a wall' was probably an authenticating fiction: see Thomas, *Religion and the Decline of Magic*, 463–4. For other examples of prophetic sermons by John Bromyarde, Robert Rypon and John Mirk, see Owst, *Preaching in Medieval England*, 206–8.

[18] *Sermo Lupi ad Anglos*, ed. Dorothy Whitelock (1952).

[19] Procter, *Watchman warning*, 15. Cf. Lawrence, *Golden trumpet*, 42: 'this Pulpit hath sounded with these exclamations many times in your eares'.

[20] Fosbroke, *Englands warning by Israel and Judah*, in *Six sermons*, 1.

[21] Jackson, *Judah must into captivitie*, 26.

[22] Webbe, *Gods controversie*, 75–6. On the looking-glass theme, see also Calamy, *Englands looking-glasse*; A. W., *A fruitfull and godly sermon, preached at Paules crosse* ([1592]), sig. B3ᵛ; William Whately, *A caveat for the covetous* (1609), 86.

Heare the word of the Lord . . . for [he has] a controversie with the Inhabitants of the Land.'[23]

The clergy never ceased to be astounded at the accuracy with which the Hebrew prophets had delineated the appalling moral condition of a northern European island as remote from the biblical Middle East in miles as it was in millennia. It was 'as if', reflected Thomas Jackson, 'they had been sent unto us'.[24] The texts selected for such sermons might at first sight seem 'matters of another Meridian, aloofe from us as farre as Shiloh, or Jerusalem'.[25] But those who read the writings of Jeremiah and Ezekiel, Daniel Price told an audience of courtiers in November 1612, would 'beleeve that they prophecied purposely for this age, and this place wherein we breath'.[26] Preaching in St Paul's one wintry Sunday in 1637 soon after the cessation of the plague, Obadiah Whitbie suggested that if Hosea had 'uttered his Prophesie the last yeare, it would have beene hard to say, whether hee meant Israel or England: the Sceanes are the same, onely the Actors differ; both of us have beheld a Tragedy commenced in our owne blood: Jerusalem bore the first part, London the second'.[27] It was the assumed interchangeability of past and present which made the ghastly predictions of these preachers so sinister.

So too did their conviction that they were the direct heirs and successors of Isaiah, Micah, and other Old Testament remembrancers, specially commissioned to deliver a stern and timely rebuke to a 'sturdy and stiff-necked', 'obstinate and gaine-saying people'.[28] They too had a special mandate to 'strongly beate downe sinne' with a 'fierie tongue' using 'the terrible language of the law', to lift up their voices like trumpets to reprove transgressors without regard to status or place.[29] God's ministers must be Boanerges, sons of thunder, stressed the Berkshire clergyman Nathaniel Cannon in February 1613.[30] They must be 'plainedealing Amoses', declared Richard Stock, curate of Allhallows, Bread Street, in 1606— not 'flattring Amaziahs' and 'fawning Zedkiahs' who coddled froward offenders, sowing pillows under their elbows, stroking their spleens, and preparing lectures consisting only of the soothing lullaby of 'peace'.[31] According to the Oxford divine

[23] Udny, *Voyce of the cryer*, 14. For other examples of the expansion of the paradigm to accommodate the whole of Great Britain, see Lancelot Dawes, *Gods mercies and Jerusalems miseries* (1609), sig. I4[v]; Jones, *Londons looking backe to Jerusalem*, 38; James Rowlandson, *Gods blessing in blasting, and his mercy in mildew* (1623), 47.

[24] Jackson, *Judah must into captivitie*, 96.

[25] Jones, *Londons looking backe to Jerusalem*, 2.

[26] Daniel Price, *Sorrow for the sinnes of the time* (Oxford, 1613), 24.

[27] W[hitbie], *Londons returne*, 26.

[28] Pilkington, *Aggeus and Abdias prophetes*, in *Works*, ed. Scholefield, 128; Stock, *Sermon preached at Paules Crosse*, 7.

[29] Williams, *Best religion*, 153, cf. 1079–80; William Perkins, *The seconde treatise of the duties and dignities of the ministrie*, in id., *Workes*, iii. 455; Thomas Barnes, *Vox belli, or an alarme to warre* (1626), 5–6.

[30] Nathaniel Cannon, *The cryer* (1613), 24. His text was Isa. lviii. 1 ('Cry aloud, spare not, lift up thy voice like a trumpet, and shew my people their transgressions, and to the house of Jacob their sinnes'). Boarnerges was the name Christ gave to James and John, the sons of Zebedee: Mark iii. 17.

[31] Stock, *Sermon preached at Paules Crosse*, 13, 48; Gosson, *Trumpet of warre*, sig. F8[v]; Bolton, *Discourse about the state of true happinesse*, in *Workes*, 157–9.

Francis White, the preacher was a mere envoy and amanuensis, the puppet of a divine ventriloquist: 'God puts it into his mouth what hee shall say.'[32] His sermons should therefore be esteemed as 'vox Jehovae', 'the voyce of the everliving God', speaking through him.[33] Others described prophetic preachers as 'experienced Chirurgions' and 'Surgeons of soules', adept at lancing the 'festered sores' of the body politic and administering the 'sharpe Corrasives' and 'holdsome medicines' that would drag it back from its deathbed to a better state of health.[34] Nothing but 'bitter potions, a rough hand, and desperate remedies', stressed John Downame, rector of St Margaret's, Lothbury, could cure what was elsewhere described as the 'generall infection', 'Leprosie', and 'Gangraena' which was sweeping the nation.[35] 'Gods Deputy-Physicians' first reviewed England's blessings, then excoriated her sins, and finally delivered a gloomy prognosis for the debilitating moral disease that was consuming her.[36]

THE APPLE OF HIS EYE

Like the Jews before them, the English were deemed to be a uniquely favoured race. 'What had the Israelites that wee have not?', demanded the episcopal chaplain Robert Johnson in September 1609; 'our land is machable with theirs in every respect', he felt bound to reply.[37] The Lord had showered it with earthly commodities far surpassing those He had vouchsafed to her Continental neighbours, a veritable embarrassment of riches. Blessed with 'the dewe of heaven', it was as if He had set her in a new Garden of Eden, a terrestrial Paradise, an Elysium.[38] England, like Canaan, was a 'land flowing with milke and hony', 'wheat and barley'; it was 'the eye of Europe, and store-house of Christendome'.[39] Successively governed by three incomparable monarchs, she remained a haven and an oasis of peace. '[W]hereas other Nations doe ride even up into their horsebridles in blood,' Daniel Donne observed in 1622, 'wee through the great Goodnesse of God, sit every man under his owne Vine' in freedom.[40] While France, Germany, and Holland groaned under the sword and were 'overwhelmed with the Deluge and Inundation of Warre', reflected Thomas Fuller later that decade, 'this little fleece of ours hath

---

[32] Francis White, *Londons warning, by Jerusalem* (1619), 15 and 5–23 *passim*.

[33] Ibid. 6; Downame, *Lectures upon . . . Hosea*, 2nd pagination, 59, and see 171. Cf. Topsell, *Times lamentation*, 3: 'the sermons of the prophets are the sermons of the Lorde himselfe'.

[34] Procter, *Watchman warning*, 2; Gibson, *Lands mourning*, 6; A. W., *Fruitfull and godly sermon*, sig. B3ᵛ.

[35] Downame, *Lectures upon . . . Hosea*, 1st pagination, 41; Gray, *Alarum to England*, sig. I5ᵛ; William Whately, *Charitable teares: or a sermon shewing how needfull a thing it is for every godly man to lament the common sinnes of our countrie* (1623), 235; Dawes, *Gods mercies and Jerusalems miseries*, sig. A5ᵛ.

[36] Donne, *Sub-poena*, 39.

[37] Johnson, *Davids teacher*, sig. C4ᵛ.

[38] Field, *Godly exhortation*, sig. 4ᵛ. See also Gray, *Alarum to England*, sig. D8ʳ⁻ᵛ.

[39] Chaderton, *Excellent and godly sermon*, sig. F2ʳ; Johnson, *Davids teacher*, sig. C4ᵛ; Hampton, *Proclamation of warre*, 11. See also William Perkins, *Faithfull and plaine exposition . . . of Zephaniah*, in *Workes*, iii. 420.

[40] Donne, *Sub-poena*, 41. See also Jones, *Londons looking backe to Jerusalem*, 37–8; Samuel Buggs, *Davids strait* (1622), 57.

beene dry'.[41] Preachers rarely omitted to remind their listeners how lucky they were to be living in such 'Halcion-dayes' when countries across the Channel had become 'the cockpits for all Christendome to fight their battles in'.[42] England had been preserved like 'a cottage in a vinyard', 'a lodge in a garden of coucumbers'.[43] They always made space for a brief survey of the providential mercies the Almighty had bestowed upon His 'beleaguered isle' of Great Britain: Elizabeth's triumphant accession to the throne in 1558, the miraculous defeat of the Spanish Armada in 1588, and the nation's eleventh-hour deliverance from the 'gun-powder gulfe' on 5 November 1605.[44]

As far as spiritual privileges were concerned, England had been entrusted with that 'most precious jewell' and pearl, the Word.[45] Brought out of the Babylonish captivity of Roman Catholicism and retrieved from the 'Pharaolik persecutions' of the Marian regime, she now basked in the bright sunshine of Protestantism, surrounded, like the tiny land of Goshen, by a dark desert of Egyptian ignorance and superstition. According to Thomas Baughe, student of Christ Church, Oxford, there was 'no nooke, nor angle of this Ile, where the language of the gospel is not heard'.[46] What foreign country could boast 'a more joyfull supply' of learned ministers?, asked the London preacher Immanuel Bourne in June 1617; 'neither hath Asia, Africa, America, and the most parte of Europa such knowledge and preaching of his lawes' observed James Bisse.[47] Elsewhere the truth was too often 'mingled with the Cockle and Darnell of Popish errors and traditions', but at home only the pure essence would do.[48] In this respect, the English even outclassed the Hebrews: 'They were *Alphabetarii* and *Abecedarii*,' declared John Jones, 'young beginners, learning their ABC under the tutorship of the law'. They merely 'had the shadow, wee the substance,' echoed Dr Sebastian Benefield, 'they the candle-light, we the noone-day; they had the breakfast of the Law, fit for the morning of the world, we the dinner of the Gospel, fit for the high-noone thereof'.[49]

---

[41] Fuller, *Sermon intended for Paul's Crosse*, 32.

[42] F. S., *Jerusalems fall, Englands warning*, 3 [*vere* 5]; Benson, *Sermon preached at Paules Crosse*, 38.

[43] Bisse, *Two sermons*, sig. D4ʳ, alluding to Isa. i. 8.

[44] See e.g. White, *Londons warning, by Jerusalem*, 41–2; Hampton, *Proclamation of warre*, 10; Abbot, *Be thankfull London and her sisters*, 19. England's deliverances were, of course, the central theme of anniversary sermons: for examples at Paul's Cross, see Thomas White, *A sermon preached at Paules Crosse the 17. of November an. 1589* (1589); John Duport, *A sermon preached at Pauls Crosse on the 17. day of November 1590 . . . commonly called, the queenes day* (1591); Martin Fotherby, *The third sermon, at Paules Crosse, Novemb. 5. anno 1607. upon the day of our deliverance, from the gun-powder treason*, in *Foure sermons, lately preached* (1608); Tynley, *Two learned sermons* (preached 5 Nov. 1608); John Boys, *An exposition of the last psalme. Delivered in a sermon preached at Paules Crosse the fifth of November 1613* (1615), quotation at 20.

[45] Immanuel Bourne, *The rainebow, or, a sermon preached at Pauls Crosse* (1617), 44.

[46] Quotation from William Fisher, *A godly sermon preached at Paules Crosse the 31. day of October 1591* (1592), sig. A5ᵛ. For the parallel with Goshen, see Richard Jefferay, *The sonne of Gods entertainment by the sonnes of men* (1605), 24; Baughe, *Summons to judgement*, 33.

[47] Bourne, *Rainebow*, 44; Bisse, *Two sermons*, sig. D4ʳ.

[48] Donne, *Sub-poena*, 41.

[49] Jones, *Londons looking backe to Jerusalem*, 26; Benefield, *Commentary . . . upon . . . Amos*, 3rd pagination, 86.

England, maintained the Lincolnshire minister Robert Milles, was thus a 'Princesse among Provinces'; the Lord 'never was neerer to any', gloated John Lawrence, from the Creation to the present.[50] She was his 'Signet' and spouse, William Whately informed a congregation at Banbury in 1623, 'which he hath fostered as tenderly, and adorned as graciously as ever he did Judea'.[51] Preaching at Paul's Cross in January 1612, Dr Thomas Sutton proclaimed in his *Englands summons*: 'You are at this day, and long have beene, the astonishment and wonderment of all the world. God hath opened the windowes of Heaven wider, and offered more grace unto you . . . then to all the Nations under the canopy and roofe of heaven.'[52] Occasionally preachers issued a caveat about the dangers of arrogant conceit: 'wee are the people with whom he hath chosen to dwell for ever,' declared John Udall, yet we must not 'waxe insolent' because we 'excell others'.[53]

Such expressions of 'divine Anglophilia' certainly suggest that prophetic preaching helped to enhance the incipient nationalism of early modern England, promoting sentiments that could be insular, chauvinistic, and ethnocentric in the extreme.[54] In the privacy of their vestries and studies, the majority of Protestant ministers may have been scrupulously ecumenical in their outlook, the first to admit that their native country was only part of the vineyard of Christ, no more than a supporting actress in an apocalyptic drama being played out on the international stage. In the pulpit, however, it was all too easy to succumb to jingoistic hyperbole and accord her a starring role in the cosmic struggle against the papal Antichrist. Especially when they preached on patriotic holidays, many were apt to throw caution to the wind and imply that England was not merely one elect Church among many, but the Lord's own peculiar people and the very apple of His eye.[55] In practice, as opposed to the theory of academic elites, then, the balance

---

[50] Robert Milles, *Abrahams suite for Sodome* (1612), sig. B6^{r-v}; Lawrence, *Golden trumpet*, 17.

[51] Whately, *Charitable teares*, 244 and see sig. O1^r.

[52] Thomas Sutton, *Englands summons* (1612), in *Englands first and second summons. Two sermons preached at Paules Crosse* (1616), 30–1. For other exaggerated statements about England as God's chosen people, blessed above all other nations, see Bunny, *Necessarie admonition*, 68; Y[onger], *Sermon preached at Great Yarmouth*, sigs. B6^r, B7^r, E2^v; Adams, *Englands sicknes*, in id., *Workes*, 314; Donne, *Sub-poena*, 42; Procter, *Watchman warning*, 54; Jones, *Londons looking backe to Jerusalem*, 27, 49.

[53] Udall, *True remedie*, fos. 34^v–35^r.

[54] McGiffert, 'God's Controversy with Jacobean England', 1152 and *passim*. See also Collinson, 'The Protestant Nation', in *Birthpangs*, esp. 7–11; id., 'Biblical Rhetoric', esp. 23–4. McGiffert partially retracts his assertion that Jacobean Hoseads (esp. John Downame's *Lectures*) fostered and articulated the notion that God had a special relationship with England in response to criticisms made by Richard Greaves, in a communication to the editor of *American Historical Review*, 89 (1984), 1217–18. On Protestantism and patriotism, see also the essays in Peter Lake and Maria Dowling (eds.), *Protestantism and the National Church in Sixteenth Century England* (1987); Anthony Fletcher, 'The First Century of English Protestantism and the Growth of National Identity', in Stuart Mews (ed.), *Religion and National Identity*, SCH 18 (Oxford, 1982), 309–17; Hill, *English Bible*, 264–6; id., 'The Protestant Nation', in id., *The Collected Essays of Christopher Hill*, ii. *Religion and Politics in 17th Century England* (Brighton, 1986), esp. 29–31.

[55] The scriptural allusion is to Deut. xxxii. 10 and Ps. xvii. 8. Note, however, the careful discriminations of John Spenser, *A learned and gracious sermon preached at Paules Crosse* (1615), esp. 8, and Anderson, *Sermon*, sigs. B1^r–2^r.

was constantly being tipped. Uneducated listeners could be forgiven for thinking that the clergy were telling them that God was an Englishman, and their green and pleasant land His preferred place of abode.[56] John McKenna has argued that this pious myth had its origins in the political theology evolved during the Hundred Years War—a political theology which itself had been purloined from the Valois and Capetian publicists of thirteenth-century France. But Wulfstan's *Sermo Lupi ad Anglos* suggests it was already embryonic in the Anglo-Saxon era. A medieval commonplace brought out of mothballs to bolster every subsequent dynastic clash and crusade, this bellicose slogan continued to be confidently rearticulated long after the advent of Protestantism, whenever hostile invaders menaced British coasts.[57]

THE ACHANS TROUBLING ISRAEL

Having puffed up their auditors with patriotic pride, these Elizabethan and early Stuart Jeremiahs then proceeded to prick them with a pin. 'Our benefits have beene greater, then ever were bestowed upon any nation excepting neither one or other: & do we walke worthy of them?', asked the puritan activist John Field.[58] Manifestly no. 'England hath received much,' observed James Bisse, 'therefore of England much shalbe required.'[59] She had incurred a massive debt of gratitude which she made scarcely any effort to repay, returning not so much as a 'little mite' or tithe of the love and thanks she owed.[60] Just as the children of Israel had become sated with the taste of heavenly manna and turned back to the flesh-pots of Egypt, so had the children of England grown 'crop sicke' of God's Word and developed a partiality for the 'garlicke and onions' of sin.[61] Dozens of preachers used the parable of the barren fig tree to castigate their country's failure to yield the sweet fruits of righteousness and faith: this lovingly tended vineyard had bred sour grapes, weeds of disobedience, and the 'hellish bramble' of impiety instead.[62] In scale and enormity England's iniquities were 'no whit inferiour' to those of the Old World, Sodom, Gomorrah, Tyre, Nineveh, and Israel herself: 'surely ours are as impudent and sawcy as ever were theirs', John King asserted in York in 1594.[63]

---

[56] This is not the place to engage with the parallel question of whether or not Foxe's *Actes and monuments* presented England as 'the' or 'an' elect nation, as William Haller argued in *Foxe's Book of Martyrs and the Elect Nation* (1963). Katharine Firth and other scholars have demonstrated that Foxe's outlook was universal and ecumenical, not ethnocentric and nationalist, but how far these distinctions held up or broke down in the minds of contemporary readers remains unclear.

[57] John W. McKenna, 'How God became an Englishman', in Delloyd J. Guth and id. (eds.), *Tudor Rule and Revolution: Essays for G. R. Elton from his American Friends* (Cambridge, 1982), 25–43.

[58] Field, *Godly exhortation*, sig. B1ᵛ.

[59] Bisse, *Two sermons*, sig. D3ᵛ.

[60] Adams, *Englands sicknes*, in *Workes*, 314.

[61] Donne, *Sub-poena*, 41; King, *Lectures upon Jonas*, 442.

[62] Preachers who chose this text (Luke xiii. 6–7) include Anderson, *Sermon*, and Adams, *Barren tree*. On the vineyard (Isa. v. 4), see Spenser, *Learned and gracious sermon*. Quotation from Fisher, *Godly sermon*, sig. A8ᵛ.

[63] Gray, *Alarum to England*, sig. H2ᵛ; King, *Lectures upon Jonas*, 443.

According to Adam Hill, prebendary of Salisbury, they were even more inexcusable than those of the Jews: 'To stumble in the night it is dangerous, but to fall backward in the light of the Gospell is damnable.'[64] Sin was not confined to 'some private corners' but dared to 'jett up and downe the streets'; it was 'not onely committed', bellowed the Jacobean Boanerges Thomas Barnes, 'but also taught, as in a Schoole'.[65] Having swelled to giant size 'like unto Goliah', it now stank 'in the nosethrills of Almighty God', and the city of London was undoubtedly its 'Pontificall seat'—'a whirlpoole' and 'sinke' of every imaginable variety of evil and vice.[66]

What were the 'capitall crimes' of which these Paul's Cross prophets convicted England week after week?[67] It was conventional to divide her 'crimson', 'scarlet', 'darling', and 'crying sinnes' into two categories: 'privative' and 'positive'.[68] Echoing Hosea iv. 1, ministers opened the case for the prosecution by contending that there was 'no truth, nor mercy, nor knowledge of God in the land': injustice, corruption, and hypocrisy were endemic; charity and compassion had fled; ignorance and atheism prevailed.[69] Like lukewarm Laodicea, too many professed the Protestant religion with apathy rather than zeal.[70] As for transgressions of the Ten Commandments, they were 'more than can bee numbred by any Arithmetician' and 'greater then can be measured by any Geometrician'.[71] Most preachers rattled off a predictable list of moral offences—pride, adultery, idleness, gluttony, drunkenness, cursing, sabbath-breaking, covetousness, murder, theft, and oppression of the poor—disagreeing only about which should be labelled 'the very ringleader of the rest'. Thomas Barnes's *Wise-mans forecast* allocated this dubious honour to 'monstrous ingratitude and horrible unthankefulnesse for Gods favours', number one in a litany of twenty-two wrath-provoking sins.[72] Some examined each

---

[64] Adam Hill, *The crie of England* (1595), 105.

[65] Webbe, *Gods controversie*, 112; John Grent, *The burthen of Tyre* (1627), 35; Barnes, *The wise-mans forecast against the evill time* (1624), 37.

[66] Cannon, *Cryer*, 2; Gray, *Alarum to England*, sig. D2ᵛ; Jones, *Londons looking backe to Jerusalem*, 40.

[67] Downame, *Lectures upon . . . Hosea*, 2nd pagination, 49.

[68] For the distinction between 'privative' and 'positive', see ibid. 77; Sutton, *Englands summons*, in id., *Englands first and second summons*, 65–6. For the various adjectives: ibid. 2; Thomas Cheaste, *The way to life* (1609), 21; Gibson, *Lands mourning*, 101; Gray, *Alarum to England*, sig. D4ᵛ.

[69] As McGiffert has noted, the text was a favourite with Jacobean preachers: Downame, *Lectures upon . . . Hosea* (1608); Webbe, *Gods controversie* (1609); William Ward, *A sinners inditement* (1615 edn.), preached before 1612; Sutton, *Englands summons*, in *Englands first and second summons*, preached 1613; Samuel Torshell, *Gods controversie for sinne* (on Hos. iv. 1–2), in *The saints humiliation* (1633). Other hoseads include Samuel Smith, *An exposition upon the sixt chapter of the prophesie of Hosea* (1616); Fosbroke, *Englands warning by Israel and Judah* (1617) (on Hos. v. 15), in *Six sermons*; Daniel Featley, *Pandora's boxe; or, the cause of all evils and misery*, in *Clavis mystica* (on Hos. xiii. 9), preached *c*.1620; William Loe, *Vox clamantis* (1621) (on Hos. v. 1–2); Henry Leslie, *A warning for Israel* (Dublin, 1625).

[70] On Laodicea (Rev. iii. 15–16), see Thomas Sutton, *Englands second summons* (1615), in *Englands first and second summons*; Sampson Price, *Londons warning by Laodicea's luke-warmnesse* (1613).

[71] Lawrence, *Golden trumpet*, 74.

[72] Barnes, *Wise-mans forecast*, 17. Gray, *Alarum to England*, sig. F1ᵛ, uses the same phrase, but applies it to pride.

item in the inventory in exhaustive detail; others ran through the 'beaderowle' with 'a Laconicall brevitie'; the Suffolk parson Abraham Gibson devoted the entire two hours he was allocated at the Cross in 1613 to 'decyphering out' just one 'dangerous wound' and 'notorious impietie'—'vaine swearing'.[73]

In anatomizing such abuses preachers did not normally place themselves at political risk. Yet insofar as they maintained that 'the Lord regards not so much what the particular sins of a Nation or Church are, as what the action, the behaviour, the cariage of the state towards them is', the Israelite paradigm was intrinsically seditious.[74] Individuals who winked at prostitution, alehouse-haunting, or May games were as guilty as the offenders themselves, and this included magistrates and monarchs no less than the rude and vulgar multitude. 'Who (but a Cain)', cried Thomas Adams, 'is not his Brothers Keeper?'[75] It was during the 1620s and 1630s, when many Calvinists became convinced that the Caroline government was not merely conniving at popery and profanation of the Lord's Day but actively enjoining these abominations, that this sermon genre fulfilled its subversive potential. Mainstream puritan ministers like Daniel Featley began to open 'Pandora's boxe', and to use their scalpels to lance 'publicke sores' rather than 'pricke at . . . private wheales'.[76] Insisting that the real danger to England was not 'forraine foes' but 'home-bred sinnes', the enemy within,[77] dissident preachers adapted the jeremiad to attack the projected Spanish marriage, to berate royal policies that involved turning a cold shoulder upon embattled Protestants in the Palatinate and Bohemia, and to assail the creeping cancer of Arminianism—in the eyes of the godly, a kind of Counter-Reformation by stealth. Thomas Gataker sailed close to the wind in his *Sparke toward the kindling of sorrow for Sion* on Amos vi. 6 in 1621, suggesting that a country which showed no compassion for its afflicted brethren on the Continent could hardly expect pity at the hands of its God.[78] Provocative sermons like this induced James I to issue his *Directions* in August 1622, to repress the 'abuses and extravagances' which seemed to be running rife in contemporary preaching.[79] But these sharp measures did not keep the lid on this

---

[73] Milles, *Abrahams suite for Sodome*, sig. C4ᵛ; Webbe, *Gods controversie*, 80, and see 108; Gibson, *Lands mourning*, 6.

[74] Preston, *Sermon preached at a generall fast*, in *Saints qualification*, 295. See also Stock, *Sermon preached at Paules Crosse*, who preached on Isa. ix. 14–16 ('Therefore will the Lord cut off from Israel, head, and tayle, braunch, and rush, in one day. The Auncient and the Honourable man, he is the head: and the Prophet that teacheth lyes, he is the tayle. For the leaders of my people, cause them to erre: and they that are ledde by them, are devoured.')

[75] Adams, *Englands sicknes*, in *Workes*, 347, alluding to Gen. iv. 9.

[76] Featley, *Pandora's boxe*, in *Clavis mystica*, 90.

[77] Cheaste, *Way to life*, 4.

[78] Gataker, *Sparke toward the kindling of sorrow for Sion*, esp. 34–9. See also Thomas Barnes, *The court of conscience: or, Josephs brethrens judgement barre* (1623), esp. 145–8. See Cogswell, *Blessed Revolution*, 27–34; Hunt, *Puritan Moment*, 176–7, 198; Hill, *English Bible*, ch. 12, esp. 290–4. For the anti-Arminian implications of the sermons by Thomas Sutton and Sampson Price cited in n. 70, above, see my *Church Papists: Catholicism, Conformity and Confessional Polemic in Early Modern England*, Royal Historical Soc. Studies in History, 68 (Woodbridge, 1993), 116–17.

[79] Printed in J. P. Kenyon (ed.), *The Stuart Constitution: Documents and Commentary* (Cambridge, 2nd edn. 1986), 128–30.

volatile brand of biblical rhetoric for very long. Selected to address Parliament on the occasion of the public fast in April 1628, Jeremiah Dyke, vicar of Epping, dared to denounce 'the growth of Popery and Idolatry' and 'the departure of our old Truth in the increase of Arminanisme' as the source of the catastrophe looming over England. He urged his audience to carry out their duty as 'the publique Arke-wrights for the safety of this Church and state' and take immediate action to remove these 'nationall provocations' and 'Judasses'.[80] And John Preston had expected to receive 'Micaiah's enterteynment' (solitary confinement in prison) for a particularly searching prophetic sermon he planned to deliver at Whitehall the previous year, but he was muzzled before he mounted the pulpit at the behest of the bishops.[81]

Yet no one was more outspoken than Henry Burton, that well-known trouble-maker and agent provocateur. In a treatise entitled *Israels fast* dedicated to Charles I and that 'great Colledge of Physitians', the House of Commons, in 1628, he boldly took up the text of Joshua vii, the story of the sin of Achan and the tres-pass of the 'accursed thing'. Presenting it as 'a faire Precedent for these Times', he lashed out angrily against a faction which laboured 'under the seemely vaile and Matron like habit of the Church of England . . . to bring in that old Babylonish strumpet' Rome 'hoodwinkt' and 'to draw us to some friendly commerce and cor-respondence with that Whoore'. To his mind there were 'two maine Troublers of Israel', two reasons why the nation was teetering on the edge of 'a Precipice'—'to wit, Antichristian Idolatry, and Arminian Heresie'. Expressed through the medium of the clandestine press, Burton's opinions were already beyond the pale. This blunt and uncompromising indictment of the Stuart regime resulted in a rough interrogation before the High Commission at William Laud's instigation.[82] After the clampdown on political preaching prior to and during the Personal Rule, these incendiary themes largely ceased to find a safe outlet and conduit at Paul's Cross and became something of a rallying cry of the Caroline underground. Historically supplied by preachers appointed by the bishop of London and approved in times of crisis by the Privy Council, the Cross was always, to a greater or lesser extent, an organ of the authorities. In the 1630s, as Nicholas Tyacke has shown, it evolved into an increasingly accurate barometer of the current doctrinal climate and of prevailing ideological trends.[83]

[80] Dyke, *Sermon preached at the publicke fast*, esp. 25, 36, 38, 40, and see 43, 46.

[81] Ball, *Life of the Renowned Doctor Preston*, 160. The scriptural allusion is 1 Kgs. xxii. 27. The sermon was a sequel to his *A sensible demonstration of the deity*, printed in *Sermons preached before his Majestie; and upon other speciall occasions* (1630). See also Christopher Hill, 'The Political Sermons of John Preston', in id., *Puritanism and Revolution: Studies in the Interpretation of the English Revolution of the Seventeenth Century* (Harmondsworth, 1956), esp. 245–56.

[82] H[enry] B[urton], *Israels fast* . . . (La Rochel [London], 1628), sig. B1ʳ, title, sigs. B2ᵛ, B3ʳ, p. 32, sig. B1ʳ, p. 32 respectively. It is unclear where (and whether) this explosive sermon was actually preached. W. W. Greg (ed.), *Companion to Arber. Being a Calendar of Documents* (Oxford, 1967), 242–3. As Blair Worden has demonstrated the sin of Achan was to become an increasingly ominous motif: 'Oliver Cromwell and the Sin of Achan', in Derek Beales and Geoffrey Best (eds.), *History, Society and the Churches: Essays in Honour of Owen Chadwick* (Cambridge, 1985), 125–45.

[83] Nicholas Tyacke, *Anti-Calvinists: The Rise of English Arminianism c.1590–1640* (Oxford, 1987), app. I.

The identification of England's 'sword-procuring sinnes', then, often pushed prophetic preachers into direct confrontation with the ecclesiastical establishment.[84] Yet, at least before the ascendancy of Laud, it would be a mistake to suppose that 'puritans' completely monopolized this exegetical mode, or that the portions of the Bible upon which jeremiads were based were without exception employed as a 'yardstick' by which to judge and criticize the status quo.[85] In the Elizabethan and early Jacobean period, Hosea, Joel, and Amos were not 'a touchstone of dissent', the exclusive property of a nonconformist fringe.[86] Paul's Cross prophecy could in fact be a vehicle for vilifying the 'precise' and for celebrating the 'but halfly reformed' institution they maligned and decried. In September 1593, Adam Hill inveighed against Martin Marprelate, 'Anabaptisticall Schismatiques', and other young rebels who murmured against their spiritual fathers, the prelates. Three years later Stephen Gosson, reformed playwright and actor and now parson of Great Wigborough in Essex, reviled the 'wrangling humor of the Presbyterie', which 'with her belly full of barking libels' set out to disgrace the episcopal hierarchy: the printed text was dedicated, tellingly, to Bishop Richard Bancroft. And in 1607 Dr Martin Fotherby, archdeacon of Canterbury, denounced those who endeavoured by 'a colourable pretence of reformation' to undermine the 'blazing starre' and 'glorious beauty' of the early Stuart Church—as might have been expected from a royal chaplain, preaching on November the fifth. When Robert Johnson, who served Bishop William Barlow of Lincoln in the same capacity, addressed the Paul's Cross crowd in September 1609, he was even more scathing about 'lawlesse Sectuaries' who wrested 'the Scriptures as a nose of wax' to uphold their 'unchristian discipline' and christened their children with ludicrous names like 'More tryall', 'Free gift', and 'From above'.[87] A decade later the parameters of the debate were beginning to change, but we can still find Griffith Williams, dean of Bangor, condemning Thomas Cartwright and his disciples as a 'brood of vipers' in a sermon on *The mysteries of the rainbow* by which God had sealed His covenant with erring humanity after the Flood. Already notorious for his High Church sympathies, Williams would later apply the number 666 to the Solemn League and Covenant and denounce puritanism as an invention of Antichrist. During a series delivered partly at court and partly in Newcastle-upon-Tyne, Thomas Jackson, a grateful recipient of the patronage of William Laud and Richard Neile, adapted the allegory of the withered fruit tree (Luke xiii. 6–9) to expostulate against the 'misguided zeale' of those who considered extreme 'contrariety to Romish superstition' the very kernel of the Reformed religion:

---

[84] Quotation from Stephen Marshall, *A divine project to save a kingdome* (1644), 23.

[85] Hill, *English Bible*, 39, 41.

[86] As McGiffert notes, 'God's Controversy', 1171.

[87] Hill, *Crie of England*, 51–3, 82, 81 respectively; Gosson, *Trumpet of warre*, sig. F4[r]; Fotherby, *Third sermon*, in *Foure sermons*, 84–5; Johnson, *Davids teacher*, esp. sigs. F1[r]–3[r]. Cf. Jackson, *Londons new-yeeres gift*, fos. 23[r]–24[v] and Jefferay, *Sonne of Gods entertainment*, 35–8 (who attacked 'schismatics' and 'Brownists'); Benson, *Sermon preached at Paules Crosse*, 15–17 (who taxed itinerant preachers and sermon gadders).

'Antarcticks they are, & thinke they can never be farre enough from the North-pole untill they runne from it unto the Southpole, and pitch their habitation *in terrâ incognitâ* in a world and Church unknowne to the ancients.' Lecturing on another occasion in front of the King, he brusquely dismissed the transgressions which some malcontents 'conceive[d] to be the only cause of his displeasure with Britain: 'connivance' at Catholicism and 'to much favouring Arminianisme'.[88] Turning the tables, Laudians ranked ardent Calvinism and ferocious anti-popery at the top of the list of sins for which the Lord had a controversy with the inhab-itants of the land. Nevertheless, by the late 1630s, prophetic preaching had acquired distinctly sectarian connotations and overtones which the turmoil of the Civil War and Interregnum served both to reinforce—and also, as we shall see—to splinter and fragment.[89]

WITH CORDS OF VANITY AND CART ROPES

However they diagnosed their nation's failings, preachers from across the spectrum agreed that iniquity drew down a heavy retributive sentence from heaven, as with 'cords of vanity' and 'cart ropes'.[90] 'Mans sinne and Gods wrath', maintained Thomas Gataker, were as inseparable as 'needle and thred'.[91] Heinous transgres-sions put 'oyle to the flame' of the deity's displeasure; 'with a false key' they opened 'the doore to vengeance' and pulled down 'a sudden Babel of confusion' upon men's heads.[92] If God had not spared His 'owne darlings' of Israel, George Webbe demanded one summer morning in 1609, what hope did wicked England have of escaping scot-free? Did His adopted children have a greater privilege to sin than 'his owne inheritance, and peculiar people', the Jews?[93] If the Lord had lopped the 'natural branches' how could the 'wild olives' grafted on later evade the same fate?[94] As inevitably as its Old Testament prototype, the nation would be extirpated by a plague of apocalyptic proportions. For most Paul's Cross prophets, this was less a hypothesis than a fait accompli.

This biblical parallel became ever more menacing as the official Reformation receded further and further into the past. As their subjective sense of the scandal of popular contempt for the doctrinal tenets and ethical values of Protestantism intensified, so did the preachers' alarm about the hovering holocaust. James

---

[88] Williams, *Mysteries of the rainebow*, in *Best religion*, 11 and Milton, *Catholic and Reformed*, 119 n. Jackson, *Treatise concerning the signes of the time* and *Three sermons preached before the King* in *Diverse sermons*, 66 and 42 respectively. On the careers of Jackson and Williams, see *DNB*.

[89] The fourth style of preaching described in Abraham Wright's *Five sermons in five several styles; or waies of preaching* (1656) is 'the Presbyterian Way; before the Citie at Saint Paul's, London'.

[90] Isa. v. 18.

[91] Gataker, *Sparke toward the kindling of sorrow for Sion*, 4.

[92] Sutton, *Englands summons*, in *Englands first and second summons*, 131; Benson, *Sermon preached at Paules Crosse*, 41; Donne, *Sub-poena*, 90.

[93] Webbe, *Gods controversie*, 45–8.

[94] Rom. xi. 17–21. See e.g. Stockwood, *Sermon preached at Paules Crosse on Barthelmew day*, 14; F. S., *Jerusalems fall, Englands warning*, 3 [*vere* 5]; Hill, *Crie of England*, 100; Featley, *Pandora's boxe*, in *Clavis mystica*, 87.

Pilkington was already castigating his contemporaries for their 'cold slacknesse' and 'slothful negligence' in erecting the kingdom of Christ in the early 1560s;[95] a decade later Edward Bush pondered the consequences of 'our backslyding and backstarting from God';[96] 1578 saw John Stockwood, headmaster at Tonbridge School, deploring the unholy lifestyles of the majority after no less than twenty years of painful preaching;[97] Anthony Anderson and James Bisse were bewailing the fact that England was waxing weary of the Gospel and relapsing, with 'a catholike cooling' of its former zeal, into profanity and paganism in 1581.[98] Time ticked away and 1595 found William Perkins reproving a generation as perverse and unenlightened as its popish ancestors and rehearsing the familiar grievance that religion was made 'a by-word' and 'a mocking-stocke'.[99] Notwithstanding how many evangelists had been sent 'these foure and forty yeares togither, to instruct us', notwithstanding the thousands of sermons delivered, declared the Oxford divine Robert Wakeman in June 1602, 'yet we lie still frozen in the dregges of our iniquities'.[100] 'Never more Preaching and lesse practising', lamented Sampson Price in March 1616, parallelling apostate England with the unfaithful Church of Ephesus.[101] Such ministers were continually recalculating how long God had restrained His itching fingers, constantly adding days, weeks, and months to their mental tally of His forbearance and their country's contumacy.[102] 'I know, there was never age not complained of, not judged as worst', observed Thomas Adams, but he and his colleagues were convinced that in their case this homiletic platitude was true.[103]

The theme was as infinitely extendible as the nation's obstinate persistence in sin and the Lord's astonishing patience with it. For, like a tender-hearted father, He did not relish their destruction, but rather strove to reclaim them to the fold like the prodigal son, perpetually deferring the death sentence in expectation of a belated reformation. The clergy continued to 'marvaile' at such long-suffering.[104] More than once, stressed Perkins in a lacerating sermon on Zephaniah ii. 1–2 ('Search your selves, even search you, O Nation, not worthy to be beloved . . .'), God had prepared His sword for slaughter, and then, overcome with revulsion,

---

[95] Pilkington, *Aggeus and Abdias prophetes*, in *Works*, ed. Scholefield, 4, 11.

[96] E[dward] B[ush], *A sermon preached at Pauls Crosse on Trinity Sunday, 1571* (1576), sig. E1[r]. The copy in the Guildhall Library is attributed to Edmund Bunny, fellow of Merton College, Oxford, and chaplain to Edmund Grindal. See Maclure, *Register of Sermons*, rev. Pauls and Boswell, 52.

[97] Stockwood, *Sermon preached at Paules Crosse on Barthelmew day*, esp. 44–8.

[98] Anderson, *Sermon*, sigs. E6[v]–7[r], F8[v]; Bisse, *Two sermons*, sigs. D5[v]–6[r].

[99] Perkins, *Faithfull and plaine exposition . . . of Zephaniah*, in *Workes*, iii. 421.

[100] Wakeman, *Jonahs sermon and Ninevehs repentance*, 85, 93.

[101] Price, *Ephesus warning before her woe* (on Rev. ii. 5), 59.

[102] As F. S. noted in *Jerusalems fall, Englands warning*, 23, fault was increased by 'circumstance of the time'.

[103] Adams, *Englands sicknes*, in *Workes*, 345, and see 327.

[104] Dent, *Plaine mans path-way*, 174, 247. See also Milles, *Abrahams suite for Sodome*, sig. B5[v]. On God as a father and 'a spirituall Chirurgeon', see Fosbroke, *Englands warning by Israel and Judah*, in *Six sermons*, 14–21.

returned it to the sheath. He had 'stayed his birth even in the verie travell, and we have escaped, even as a man, whose necke hath beene upon the blocke' might be granted a last-minute reprieve.[105] Paradoxically, however, His procrastination only ensured that the general judgement, when it came, would be even more far-reaching and complete: the slower they were in starting the more terrible His swipes would be; the longer an arrow was held in the bow, the swifter the shot when it was eventually released. Arthur Dent summed this up in a piece of prover-bial wisdom: 'though God have Leaden feete, and commeth slowely to execute wrath, yet hath he an Iron hand, and will strike deadly when hee commeth.'[106] The Lord did not resort automatically to 'Martiall law' like some draconian dic-tator. He adopted 'a judiciall forme of proceeding', sending out His preachers to serve the people with a 'summons' and a 'sub-poena from the Star Chamber of Heaven', issuing them with a formal ultimatum and 'proclamation of warre'.[107] 'Gods Methode' could be compared with the tactics employed by the Tartar con-queror Tamburlaine before besieging a city: He too displayed three flags in suc-cession, white for mercy, red for threat, and black for imminent massacre and death.[108]

According to Jeremiah Dyke nothing riled the Almighty more than wilful dis-regard of the 'warning peeces' He fired in the 'whetting time' before the stubborn disobedience of a chosen people forced Him to discharge His 'murdering peeces'.[109] Ignoring the lesser punishments and prodigies by which He sought to coax a com-munity from sin was akin to collective suicide. No less assiduously than moralistic journalists did such preachers enumerate the providential omens and meteorolog-ical anomalies, strange wonders, and natural calamities that foreshadowed the far greater catastrophe to come; no less obsessively did they seek to decode the 'Monitory language' of these 'John Baptists of Judgement'.[110] England's Jeremiahs seem to have regularly plundered cheap newsprint for fresh evidence of God's escalating anger and fury. The burning of St Paul's Cathedral, the 'solemn assize'

---

[105] Perkins, *Faithfull and plaine exposition . . . of Zephaniah*, in *Workes*, iii. 423.

[106] Dent, *Plaine mans path-way*, 158. Cf. A. W., *Fruitfull and godly sermon*, sig. B1ʳ; Wakeman, *Jonahs sermon and Ninevehs repentance*, 40. For contemporary proverbs, see Tilley, *Dictionary of Proverbs*, nos. G182, G224, G270, P639, V25.

[107] For the legal metaphors, see Webbe, *Gods controversie*, 19, 9, and see 16–17; Sutton, *Englands summons*, in *Englands first and second summons*; Donne, *Sub-poena*; and the hoseads listed in n. 69, above. For the military metaphor, see Hampton, *Proclamation of warre*. See also F. S., *Jerusalems fall, Englands warning*, 2: 'God gives a Caveat before his Capias, and doth warne before he doth wound'.

[108] Dawes, *Gods mercies and Jerusalems miseries*, sig. H3ʳ⁻ᵛ; Sutton, *Englands summons*, in *Englands first and second summons*, 24–5; Wakeman, *Jonahs sermon and Ninevehs repentance*, 38–9. *Tamburlaine the Great* was the subject of a famous play by Christopher Marlowe (dated 1587), repr. in *The Complete Plays*, ed. J. B. Steane (Harmondsworth, 1969).

[109] Dyke, *Sermon preached at the publicke fast*, 4. Dyke seems to have been echoing Preston, *A sen-sible demonstration of the deity*, in *Sermons preached before his Majestie*, 89.

[110] Dyke, *Sermon preached at the publicke fast*, 9, 14, and see also 22–5. Cf. Anderson, *Sermon*, sig. G1ᵛ.

at Oxford, the 'great earthquake', Halley's comet, and the famous 'book-fish' all found their way into jeremiads.[111] Alluding to the annual crop of monstrous births, spectral armies, frightening sights, violent storms, double tides, desolating floods, and fatal accidents, John King declared in 1594 that 'the moneths of the year have yet gone about, wherein the Lord hath bowed the heavens, and come downe amongst us with more tokens and earnests of his wrath intended, then the agedest man of our land is able to recount of so small a time'. 'Wee have not altered the colour of the hayre of our heades, nor added one inch to our stature since all these things have been accomplished amongst us.'[112] The catalogue of alarming portents John Fosbroke compiled for *Englands warning by Israel and Judah* also included the untimely demise of 'that peerlesse Paragon of pietie, and all princely vertues, Prince Henry of happie memorie'.[113] After 1618, when military events on the Continent began to gather momentum, preachers began to meditate ever more anxiously on the fact that God had unleashed only two of His three lethal 'arrowes' against England. Having had first-hand experience of scarcity and pestilence, could there be any question that she too would taste of the bitter cup of a war of attrition? Only a small strip of water divided the island from the bloody battlefield which so much of mainland Europe had become. The Angel of the Lord had 'poured out his viall of red wine' on the Protestants of Germany and France, Daniel Featley proclaimed in the late 1620s: 'our sinnes as it were holloe to him to stretch his hand over the narrow sea, and cast the dregges of it on us, who have been long settled upon our lees: and undoubtedly this will be our potion to drinke'.[114] The Civil War, when it came in 1642, can have been no surprise to those who reiterated and internalized this menacing theme: it was simply the fulfilment of half a century of clerical predictions.

Yet all such subsidiary judgements, even armed conflict, were 'sweet'. They were 'Medicinale, not mortale', proof of the Lord's enduring paternal interest in the nation's welfare and health.[115] Returning full circle, preachers suggested that in 'al the store-house of Gods plagues' there was no sorer punishment, no more sinister 'prognosticant', than spiritual insensibility and sin. According to Alexander

---

[111] For only a handful of examples, see ibid. sigs. G1^v–3^r; Chaderton, *Excellent and godly sermon*, sig. F2^{r-v}; Bisse, *Two sermons*, sigs. B7^v–8^r; Perkins, *Faithfull and plaine exposition . . . of Zephaniah*, in *Workes*, iii. 424; R[obert] W[ilkinson], *Lots wife* (1607), 41; John King, *A sermon of publicke thanks-giving for the happie recoverie of his maiestie from his late dangerous sicknesse* (1619), 51–2; Dyke, *Sermon preached at the publicke fast*, 22.

[112] King, *Lectures upon Jonas*, 36. Cf. the almost identical passage in Gray, *Alarum to England*, sig. I7^{r-v}.

[113] Fosbroke, *Englands warning by Israel and Judah*, in *Six sermons*, 43.

[114] Daniel Featley, *A sermon preached at a publike fast*, in *Clavis mystica*, 892. For similar apprehensions, see Abbot, *Exposition upon the prophet Jonah*, 117–18; Hopkins, *Two godlie and profitable sermons*, 66–7; Thomas Hooker, *The Church's Deliverances* (a sermon for 5 Nov.), repr. in *Writings in England and Holland*, ed. Williams et al., 67; Robert Harris, *Davids comfort at Ziklag* (1628), 15–16; Jeremy Leech, *The trayne souldier* (1619), esp. 53–5. See also J. R. Hale, 'Incitement to Violence? English Divines on the Theme of War, 1578 to 1631', in id., *Renaissance War Studies* (1983), 487–517.

[115] Adams, *Barren tree*, 46. See also Preston, *Sermon preached at a generall fast*, in *Saints qualification*, 300.

Udny, England's intransigence was itself 'one evident token' of God's wrath.[116] When the Lord withdrew His restraining grace and left a country to wallow in its own iniquity, then was it all too clearly on the brink of extinction.

A FAMINE OF THE WORD AND THE LEAVEN IN THE LUMP

What was the supreme penalty which these jeremiads were designed to deflect and circumvent? Scripture offered a wide range of gruesome possibilities: the Flood which overwhelmed the Old World, drowning every living creature under fifteen cubits of water;[117] the brutal overthrow of the flourishing Phoenician mercantile city of Tyre by God's scourge, King Nebuchadnezzar;[118] the destruction of Sodom and Gomorrah, consumed to ashes by sulphurous flames and reduced to a breeding place of nettles and salt pits—so suddenly, said Robert Gray, that none of their citizens dreamt 'of such an hot service, as to have fire and brimstone to their breakfast'.[119] Naturally, however, it was on the fate of ancient Israel that most Paul's Cross prophecy tended to pivot. In Isaiah, Hosea, and Amos, Elizabethan and early Stuart ministers discovered a blueprint of the doom they believed would presently overtake England: the Almighty would pluck up the hedge of His vineyard, lay it open to the prey of its enemies, and then wipe it from the face of the earth. He would renounce His once preferred people, saying '*Lo-ammi* . . . I will not be your God', and inflict a debilitating famine of the Word upon the land.[120] Others alighted on the analogues of these stinging comminations in the New Testament: the Lord's curse against the Church of Laodicea (because 'thou art lukewarm, and neither cold nor hot, I will spue thee out of my mouth');[121] Christ's drastic verdict

[116] Adams, *Englands sicknes*, in *Workes*, 340; King, *Sermon of publicke thanks-giving*, 52; Udny, *Voyce of the cryer*, 14. Other preachers who employed this logic include Adams, *Gallants burden*, in *Workes*, 5; Stockwood, *Sermon preached at Paules Crosse on Barthelmew day*, 169; Downame, *Lectures upon . . . Hosea*, 2nd pagination, 266–7; and Hanibal Gamon, *Gods smiting to amendment, or, revengement* (1629), 29.

[117] Gen. vii. Preachers who chose the Flood include Bourne, *Rainebow* (on Gen. ix. 13); Dyke, *Sermon preached at the publicke fast* (Heb. xi. 7, 'By Faith Noah being warned of God . . . prepared an Arke . . .'); Williams, *Mysteries of the rainebow* (on Gen. ix. 13), in *Best religion*; Thomas Gataker, *Noah. His obedience, with the ground of it: or his faith, feare, and care* (on Heb. xi. 7), in *Two sermons*.

[118] Grent, *Burthen of Tyre* (on Isa. xxiii. 7–9).

[119] Gray, *Alarum to England* (sermons on the text of Gen. xix. 23–5), sig. B4ʳ. Other sermons on Sodom and Gomorrah include Hill, *Crie of England* (Gen. xviii. 21–2); Milles, *Abrahams suite for Sodome* (Gen. xviii. 32); Harris, *Destruction of Sodome* (Gen. xix. 24); W[ilkinson], *Lots wife*; Carpenter, *Remember Lots wife* (both on Luke xvii. 32); Christopher Hudson, 'The Preservation of the Godly in the greatest Perils. In a Sermon preached at Preston when the great Plague ceased in that towne. 1631' (on Rom. ix. 29, 'Except the Lord of Sabaoth had left us a seede, wee had beene as Sodome, & beene made like unto Gomorrha'), in LRO DP 353. John King, then rector of St Andrew's, Holborn, preached on the drowning of the Old World and the destruction of Sodom and Gomorrah on 24 Oct. 1602: Manningham, *Diary*, ed. Bruce, 64–72.

[120] Isa. v. 5; Amos ix. 8; Hos. i. 9; Amos viii. 11. It is invidious to single out particular examples, but for references to each of these passages, see respectively Hampton, *Proclamation of warre*, 12; Fosbroke, *Englands warning by Israel and Judah*, in *Six sermons*, 45; Downame, *Lectures upon . . . Hosea*, 1st pagination, 83; Baughe, *Summons*, 31.

[121] Rev. iii. 15–16. See the sermons by Sutton and Sampson Price listed in n. 70, above.

against the barren fig tree ('Cut it down');[122] and the threat that He would confiscate the golden candlestick of the Gospel and bestow it upon a more deserving race.[123] The idea that God had relinquished all hope of England's recovery and was preparing to dispossess it of this inestimable gift reverberated in urban and rural pulpits from the early days of the Reformation onwards, and the brief restoration of Roman Catholicism under Queen Mary provided later preachers of the paradigm with an ominous precedent. Would their tiny island ruin its second chance to prove itself a worthy guardian of Protestantism?[124] 'Can it be that the Lord wil trust us any longer with a Lease of his garden?', asked Bartimaeus Andrewes, vicar of the Suffolk parish of Wenham, in 1583.[125] If the English gave the true religion 'no better welcome & entertainment' than the Israelites and Romanists, warned Robert Wakeman in 1602, God would soon translate it to the Tartarians and Moors. He would instruct His prophets to arise, abandon their flocks in Yorkshire, Essex, and Kent, and travel to India, Turkey, and Barbary instead.[126] Like the seven famous churches of Asia, George Webbe suggested seven years later, their native country would become fit only for 'the Satyrs' and 'the Screechowle to lodge in, even a cage of uncleane and lothsome birds'—even, added John Downame, 'a Synagogue of Sathan'.[127]

As the seventeenth century progressed, the cry that God was leaving England for greener pastures was uttered in increasingly panic-stricken tones. As Arminianism secured a vice-like grip on the ecclesiastical hierarchy, as puritan preachers were silenced and deprived, as the godly watched their neighbours and pastors set sail for the Netherlands and North America, the theme of desertion swelled to a threnody.[128] Jeremiah Dyke traced the Lord's retreating 'foote-steps' in a parliamentary fast sermon in 1628, as did Thomas Hooker in a lecture delivered in Chelmsford on the eve of his own exodus, first to Holland and later to Boston, in 1631: 'I will deal plainly with you. As sure as God is God, God is going from England.' '[L]ook to it,' he told his devoted hearers, 'God is packing up of his gospel, because none will buy his wares'—perhaps no prophet warned of His departure more poignantly.[129] And it was a message which the Laudian hierarchy came to regard it as essential to suppress: one of the charges levelled against Samuel

---

[122] Luke xiii. 6–9. See Anderson, *Sermon* (Luke xiii. 6); Adams, *Barren tree* (Luke xiii. 7); Donne, *Sub-poena* (Luke iii. 9, 'Now is the Axe layd unto the root of the trees . . .').

[123] Rev. ii. 5 and Matt. xxi. 43. Examples include Price, *Ephesus warning before her woe* and Jones, *Londons looking backe to Jerusalem*, 28.

[124] See e.g. Abbot, *Exposition upon the prophet Jonah*, 9; Baughe, *Summons*, 31.

[125] Andrewes, *Certaine verie worthie, godly and profitable sermons*, 206. Cf. Ward, *Sinners inditement*, 7: 'What should a Carpender doe with a peece of Wood that will serve to no use in the building, but cast it into the fire'? So too would the Almighty 'cast us off to destruction'.

[126] Wakeman, *Jonahs sermon and Ninevehs repentance*, 64; King, *Lectures upon Jonas*, 21.

[127] Webbe, *Gods controversie*, 47; Downame, *Lectures upon . . . Hosea*, 2nd pagination, 133.

[128] See also Christopher Hill, 'God and the English Revolution', *History Workshop*, 17 (1984), esp. 21; id., *English Bible*, ch. 12.

[129] Dyke, *Sermon preached at the publicke fast*, 24; Hooker, *The Danger of Desertion* (1631), repr. in *Writings in England and Holland*, ed. Williams *et al.*, 244, 245, 246 respectively.

Ward of Ipswich when he was summoned before the High Commission in 1634 was his insistence in a sermon that 'religion and the gospel stood on tiptoes ready to be gone'.[130]

Yet this sentence of rejection, insisted the clergy, 'was pronounced with a condicion, reserved in the minde of the judge'.[131] It was provisional upon the failure of the English people to show themselves truly contrite—shedding 'a few Crocodile teares', said Thomas Cheaste of St Mary Hall sternly, would by no means suffice.[132] Heartfelt penitence was a 'shielde' and a bulwark against supernatural wrath; 'if wee can learne this spirituall language', John Sedgwick informed his audience at St Botolph's without Bishopsgate around 1624, 'we need not feare, the danger is past'.[133] In the pulpit few preachers troubled themselves to spell out the precise theological implications of the axiom that the Lord not merely foresaw but preordained all acts of repentance. As we saw in Chapter 3, all too frequently they slipped into a rhetoric which sounded distinctly voluntaristic.[134]

The destiny of the nation, then, balanced on the knife-edge of 'unless ye repent'. If England, like the imperial city of Nineveh, meekly humbled herself before the face of the Lord, He might just be induced to retract His awful decision to begin proceedings for divorce. A host of ministers—from Hugh Latimer to George Abbot—battered the ears of their auditors with the story of the lightning-quick conversion of the Assyrian capital, but the idea that their own nation might replicate its overnight transformation was beyond their wildest dreams.[135] After just a single 'pinching' sermon by Jonah and only three short days of preaching it, this depraved metropolis had responded with startling alacrity: 'many hundred Jonasses' had cried in England's streets since the reign of Edward VI and still she refused to rectify her ways.[136] Whereas the Ninevites had one 'witness', declared Jeremiah Dyke, we have had 'a cloude'; whereas they were warned once, 'we have beene warned unto wearinesse'; and while they were instructed by a stranger, the English had been admonished, not by some upstart Spaniard, but by their own

---

[130] Prynne, *Canterburies doome*, 361; Laud, *Works*, ed. Scott and Bliss, v. 328. But cf. PRO SP 16/278/65, fo. 146^{v-r} where Ward alleged he did not look 'through soe blacke spectacles as he that wrote [this]'. Curiously, the phrase was echoed by George Herbert, certainly no puritan, in his poem 'The Church Militant': 'Religion stands on tip-toe in our land, | Readie to passe to the American strand': *Works*, ed. Hutchinson, 196.

[131] King, *Lectures upon Jonas*, 458 [*vere* 452]. Cf. John Hoskins, *Sermons preached at Pauls Crosse and elsewhere* (1615), 33: 'Repentance is an ordinary revealed Evangellical condition to bee still supplied, whensoever God threatneth, and giveth space for repentance'.

[132] Cheaste, *Way to life*, 4.

[133] King, *Lectures upon Jonas*, 499; John Sedgwick, *Fury fiered: or, crueltie scourged* (1625 edn.), 71.

[134] See Ch. 3 above, pp. 150–6.

[135] See Latimer, *A most faithfull sermon*, repr. in *Sermons*, ed. Corrie; Hooper, *Oversight . . . upon the holy prophete Jonas*; King, *Lectures upon Jonas*; Abbot, *Exposition upon the prophet Jonah*; Smith, *Foure sermons*, in *Sermons*; Wakeman, *Jonahs sermon and Ninevehs repentance*; Attersoll, *The conversion of Nineveh*, in *Three treatises*. Also relevant is Thomas Tymme's trans. of the Lutheran Johann Brentz's *Newes from Ninive to Englande, brought by the prophete Jonas* (1570). See also the remarks of McGiffert, 'God's Controversy', 1155–6; Collinson, *Birthpangs*, 21–2.

[136] Latimer, *A most faithfull sermon*, in *Sermons*, ed. Corrie, 240; Wakeman, *Jonahs sermon and Ninevehs repentance*, 68.

countrymen and coreligionists.[137] '[E]nvironed' on every side by the truth, concluded Francis White, 'this little Iland of ours, is most without excuse'.[138] Sermon connoisseurs must have grown thoroughly sick of having 'ruffling Ninive, old and idolatrous Ninive' elevated on a pedestal as 'an example to us all' and of being told that she would rise up against them in judgement at the Last Trump.[139]

But the Calvinist eschatology espoused by the self-appointed prophets of Protestant England constrained them from thinking of the universal reformation of all its inhabitants as anything other than an unattainable ideal.[140] Sincere repentance was a grace God bestowed solely upon that virtuoso minority who were members of the invisible company of His predestinate elect. Therein lay the source of the conviction that the godly were the lifeblood of the nation, the leaven in the lump, the regenerate remnant who redeemed and validated a Church composed largely of hardened reprobates. Preaching at a public fast in 1628 Robert Harris used the metaphor of 'medulli mundi': honest men were 'to the world as marow is to the bones'.[141] Because their prayers were so successful in staving off temporal punishments, in binding the Lord's hands behind His back, they were said to be the 'buttresses and pillars' shoring up kingdoms and commonwealths— 'Bucklers to keepe away the force of the blow'.[142] Like Moses, these 'hedge-makers' stood in the gap and 'let downe the sluces, that the gushing streams of Gods vengeance may be stopt'. Like Phineas, their zeal helped deflect His wrath, at least temporarily.[143] At Paul's Cross in August 1611 Robert Milles retold the tale of how Abraham had bargained with the Almighty, first securing His promise that He would not destroy Sodom if fifty righteous persons could be discovered within it, and then craftily beating Him down to forty, thirty, twenty, and finally ten.[144] While even a handful of His servants remained intermixed with the impious multitude, the Lord would hold back His axe. According to Jeremiah v. 1, a single sound Israelite would have saved Jerusalem from utter destruction.[145] If the Lord had spared Israel for the sake of a small, undefiled band, declared John King in an optimistic mood, 'it may so stand with the goodnes of God, that a few innocent fooles' might preserve England too.[146]

---

[137] Dyke, *Sermon preached at the publicke fast*, 29. Thomas Gataker, *Two sermons*, 92 asked 'Had Jonas come to London, and there preached the like some fortnight or three weekes before that Powder-plot was to have beene executed, who would have beleeved it?'.

[138] White, *Londons warning, by Jerusalem*, 47 [*vere* 39].

[139] Smith, *Foure sermons*, in *Sermons*, sigs. C6ᵛ, C5ᵛ respectively.

[140] As noted by Collinson, *Birthpangs*, 22, the story of Nineveh was a type of Christ's death on the Cross for all men, not just for the elect.

[141] Harris, *Destruction of Sodome*, 21, and 17–22 *passim*. He also described the godly as '*sanguis mundi*, the bloud of the world'.

[142] Ibid. 18; Dawes, *Gods mercies and Jerusalems miseries*, sig. C2ʳ. Cf. Jackson, *Judah must into captivitie*, 47–58, 66–8.

[143] Dent, *Plaine mans path-way*, 237–44, quotation at 242; Marshall, *Divine project*, esp. 4. The scriptural allusions are to Ezek. xxii. 30, Ps. cvi. 23, and Num. xxv. 11.

[144] Milles, *Abrahams suite for Sodome*.

[145] Dawes, *Gods mercies and Jerusalems miseries* is a sermon on this text. Many preachers referred to the fact that God had not destroyed Sodom until Lot was safely in Zoar (Gen. xix).

[146] King, *Lectures upon Jonas*, 37.

Godly preachers like William Gouge proceeded to reproach the 'monstrous ingratitude' of 'prophane Atheists, Belly-gods, and Worldlings', who ought to hold themselves indebted to their 'precisian' neighbours for the very air which they breathed.[147] It was only because a 'competent number' kept themselves unspotted and mourned the sins of their unsanctified brethren that the latter enjoyed any share in the bounty of divine blessings at all.[148] At such moments, Protestant ministers came perilously close to reclaiming from medieval Catholicism the notion of vicarious penance, of a class of cloistered religious whose *raison d'être* was to make intercessions for the rest.

The argument that one Noah, Lot, or Nehemiah might ransom an entire community or nation was a natural corollary of the thesis that one Achan or Jonah could be the cause of its undoing.[149] As Patrick Collinson has taught us, it was here that prophetic discourse encountered difficulties as a catalyst and engine of patriotic feeling.[150] As preachers started imputing the blame for supernatural visitations to particular segments of society, as they began insisting that it was only because of the saints that sinners were even suffered to exist, the latent and unresolved tension between the English Church as an inclusive institution and the little flock of the faithful concealed within it showed distinct signs of exploding. As they overcame their reluctance to distinguish between the seed and the parasite, the yeast and the mould, the charitable assumption that the whole nation was a chosen people lost all credibility.[151] Providentialism may have fostered a religious sense of nationhood, but it simultaneously inhibited it, creating what Michael McGiffert has called 'a set of discriminations that dotted a line' along which both the civil and ecclesiastical establishments would later divide.[152]

One symptom of this changing dialectic was renewed discussion of the morality of mingling promiscuously with the visibly wicked. Puritans like John Downame, the acclaimed Tuesday lecturer at St Bartholomew Exchange, urged their followers to refrain from needless familiarity lest they be infected: the imminent danger of God's wrath, he said, 'should be an effectuall reason to perswade the faithfull to avoid their company'.[153] 'Come out of her my people,' echoed

---

[147] Gouge, *Plaister for the plague*, in *Gods three arrowes*, 27, and 26–7 *passim*; Jackson, *Judah must into captivitie*, 46, 57. For similar statements, see Field, *Godly exhortation*, sig. B1ʳ; Dent, *Plaine mans pathway*, 244–6; Harris, *Destruction of Sodome*, 18–19.

[148] Whately, *Charitable teares*, 216–17, id., and sig. O2ᵛ. Cf. Hooker, *The Church's Deliverances*, in *Writings in England and Holland*, ed. Williams *et al.*, 84–5.

[149] As Fosbroke noted in *Englands warning by Israel and Judah*, in *Six sermons*, 6, 'it be many times seen that a multitude are punished for one private mans offence, as the children of Israel were for the sinne of Achan'.

[150] Collinson, *Birthpangs*, esp. 21–7; id., 'Biblical Rhetoric', 33–6. Cf. Carol Wiener's argument about the ambivalence of anti-popery as a patriotic discourse in 'The Beleaguered Isle: A Study of Elizabethan and Early Jacobean Anti-Catholicism', *P&P* 51 (1971), 27–62.

[151] Collinson, *Elizabethan Puritan Movement*, 25. The narrowing of the paradigm in the late Elizabethan and early Stuart period can be compared with the way in which it opened out to embrace to the entire nation after the death of Mary in 1558. Aspects of this dialectic are explored in Lake and Dowling (eds.), *Protestantism and the National Church*, esp. the essays by Catharine Davies, Joy Shakespeare, Jane Facey, and Peter Lake.

[152] McGiffert, 'God's Controversy', 1152.

[153] Downame, *Lectures upon . . . Hosea*, 2nd pagination, 311, and see 294–6.

Thomas Barnes, 'that ye be not partakers of her sins, and that ye receive not of her plagues.'[154] The petrification of Lot's wife into a pillar of salt was a monument to the miserable fate of accessories after the fact.[155] Whether or not this antisocial ideology of shunning ultimately compelled its advocates to estrange themselves formally from the official Church, its sectarian and congregational resonances are nevertheless self-evident.[156] As they watched the integrity of the Protestant nation deteriorate in front of their eyes, England's Jeremiahs laboured to settle the pricking consciences of laypeople who wondered if it was callous and unpatriotic to forsake the unregenerate majority and separate or emigrate.[157] With a tremendously inflated sense of their own self-importance, they claimed that the Lord was beginning to fan and winnow the wheat from the chaff, shipping away His Noahs and Lots to safety before He released the full torrent of His fury.[158] Even Thomas Jackson, an overt critic of 'schism' comfortably ensconced in the lower echelons of the episcopal hierarchy, prophesied that 'if all these swallowes have once taken their flight, there will come the coldest and wofullest winter, that ever the Church amongst us felt and endured'.[159] A 'special immunity' from destruction was 'the patent of the priviledge' of the saints; God made sure there was a Zoar, an Ark, an Ararat, where His loved ones could take refuge.[160] In the 1630s, this 'retiring place' began to look very much like America.[161]

---

[154] Barnes, *Wise-mans forecast*, 62–4, echoing Rev. xviii. 4. See also William Attersoll, *Gods trumpet sounding the alarme*, separately paginated in *Three treatises*, 64 [*vere* 94]–97.

[155] Gen. xix. 26.

[156] On semi- and social separatism, see the discussions in Collinson, 'Voluntary Religion', in id., *Religion of Protestants*, 242–83; id., 'The Godly'; id., 'English Conventicle'; id., 'The Cohabitation of the Faithful with the Unfaithful', in Ole Peter Grell, Jonathan I. Israel, and Nicholas Tyacke (eds.), *From Persecution to Toleration: The Glorious Revolution and Religion in England* (Oxford, 1991), 51–76; and Murray Tolmie, *The Triumph of the Saints: The Separate Churches of London 1616–1649* (Cambridge, 1977).

[157] The question of whether or not it was permissible to flee during the plague was a parallel case of conscience, and discussion of this moral dilemma provided part of the theoretical underpinning for separation and emigration. See e.g. Gouge, *Plaister for the plague*, in *Gods three arrowes*, 23–6.

[158] See Hooker, *The Danger of Desertion*, in *Writings in England and Holland*, ed. Williams *et al.*, 246. For Elizabethan expressions of these ideas, see Fisher, *Godly sermon*, sig. D2ᵛ; Carpenter, *Remember Lots wife*, sig. F3ᵛ. See also the remarks of Gouge, *Plaister for the plague*, in *Gods three arrowes*, 17–21ᵛ; and Hudson, 'The Preservation of the Godly' (LRO DP 353). Both are in the context of discussion of the preservation of the godly from death of the plague.

[159] Jackson, *Judah must into captivitie*, 57.

[160] Price, *Sorrow for the sinnes of the time*, 2 (on Ezek. ix. 4, 'Set a marke upon the foreheads of them that sigh and that cry for all the Abominations'); Hooker, *The Danger of Desertion*, in *Writings in England and Holland*, ed. Williams *et al.*, 246.

[161] Thomas Cooper, *The blessing of Japheth, proving the gathering in of the gentiles, and finall conversion of the jewes* (1615), sig. A3ʳ. He reminded his distinguished audience, which included the Lord Mayor, Alderman, Sheriffs, and the Commissioners for the plantations in Ireland and Virginia, of the need 'to provide some retiring place for your selves, if so be the Lord, for our unthankefulnes should spue us out'. On motives for emigration, see also Susan Hardman Moore, 'Popery, Purity and Providence: Deciphering the New England Experiment', in Anthony Fletcher and Peter Roberts (eds.), *Religion, Culture and Society in Early Modern Britain: Essays in Honour of Patrick Collinson* (Cambridge, 1994), 257–89; Avihu Zakai, *Exile and the Kingdom: History and Apocalypse in the Puritan Migration to America* (Cambridge, 1992), esp. ch. 4.

COLLECTIVE ESCHATOLOGY[162]

Submerged in every jeremiad was the complex theological concept of the national covenant. Preachers repeatedly correlated the relationship between God and England with a legal contract or bond; a marriage pact between husband and wife; a bilateral agreement between mutually obligated parties; a diplomatic convention between countries at war.[163] The continuing flow of divine favour to a chosen nation was held to be dependent on its obedience to the old Deuteronomic law, on fulfilment of the terms of a compact similar to that which the Lord had made with Adam and ratified with Moses on behalf of the Jews.[164] A distinguished line of historians from the late Perry Miller to Michael McGiffert have maintained that this national covenant was quite distinct from the so-called covenant of grace which bound God to the elect scattered all over the globe—His testament, promise, and pledge to save them 'in return' for faith, which itself was a free and gratuitous gift. It has also been conventional to discuss the national covenant in isolation from the concurrent development of federal or covenant divinity—that subtle refinement of Calvin's soteriology, intended to safeguard it against both antinomianism and Arminianism, which unwittingly led Protestants back in the direction of moral legalism and a doctrine of meritorious deeds. By emphasizing the personal search for behavioural evidence of election, the covenant of works implicitly gave human beings more scope in their own redemption. How far this represented an 'epochal departure' from 'unadulterated Calvinism' remains the subject of heated dispute, but in helping to meet the psychological need for assurance and in depicting eternal deliverance as a quasi-conditional offer, covenant divinity did make predestinarian tenets more palatable and comprehensible to the unlearned laity.[165]

[162] I borrow this phrase and concept from Wilson, *Pulpit in Parliament*, 189.

[163] For the marriage metaphor, see Hooker, *The Danger of Desertion*, in *Writings in England and Holland*, ed. Williams *et al.*, 231; Featley, *Pandora's boxe*, in *Clavis Mystica*, 87; Spenser, *Learned and gracious sermon*, 10. For the metaphor of legal proceedings, see the hoseads listed in n. 69, above; Fisher, *Godly sermon*, sig. B1ʳ; Donne, *Sub-poena*. For the metaphor of war, see Hampton, *Proclamation of warre*.

[164] For explicit statements of the covenantal relationship between God and England, see F. S., *Jerusalems fall, Englands warning*, 20; Attersoll, *Gods trumpet*, in *Three treatises*, 115.

[165] There is a large literature on this complex subject: see Perry Miller, 'The Marrow of Puritan Divinity', *Publications of the Colonial Society of Massachusetts*, 32 (1937), 247–300; id., *New England Mind*, chs. 13, 16. Jens G. Moller traces the origins of federal divinity in the writings of William Tyndale and Swiss reformers including Zwingli and Bullinger in 'The Beginnings of Puritan Covenant Theology', *JEH* 13 (1962), 46–67; this theme is developed by Richard L. Greaves, 'The Origins and Early Development of English Covenant Thought', *The Historian*, 31 (1968), 21–35. Everett H. Emerson questions how far covenant theology departed from Calvin's thought in 'Calvin and Covenant Theology', *Church History*, 25 (1956), 136–44. But cf. Kendall, *Calvin and English Calvinism*, and Wallace, *Puritans and Predestination*, esp. 10–11, 197–8. See also Michael McGiffert, 'American Puritan Studies in the 1960s', *William and Mary Quarterly*, 3rd ser. 27 (1970), 47–50; id., 'Grace and Works: The Rise and Division of Covenant Divinity in Elizabethan Puritanism', *Harvard Theological Review*, 75 (1982), 463–502; id., 'From Moses to Adam: The Making of the Covenant of Works', *SCJ* 19 (1988), 131–55; id, 'God's Controversy', 1163–8; David Zaret, *The Heavenly Contract: Ideology and Organization in Pre-Revolutionary Puritanism* (Chicago, 1985); and notably David A. Weir, *The Origins of the Federal Theology in Sixteenth-Century Reformation Thought* (Oxford, 1990). Quotations in this

Theodore Bozeman, however, has argued persuasively that to draw a 'clean contrast between the individual and collective dimensions' is to misrepresent 'the overall dialectical weave of Puritan theology'. From the outset, the national covenant and the covenant of grace were tightly interlaced: an 'easy, instinctive transit' from the personal to the corporate, and from the evangelical to the temporal plane was a 'basic reflex' of English Protestant thought. In the jeremiad, there was a strong organic connection between society and self: the future of the community was fused with the fate of the private citizen's soul. Prophetic preachers shifted gear almost imperceptibly, speaking in the same breath of the earthly welfare of their country and the heavenly welfare of each Christian dwelling within her.[166] Thus, in a standard lecture on Jonah and Nineveh delivered in 1602, Robert Wakeman stressed that what he said of England and London at large, 'every man in particular may accompt as spoken unto himselfe'. 'What I say to all,' declared Robert Harris in *Gods goodnes and mercie* delivered in June 1622, 'I speake to every one now present.'[167] In contending that there could be no 'salvation' without repentance, preachers were referring not merely to preservation from epidemic disease, foreign conquest, and natural catastrophe, but also to emancipation from the everlasting desolation of spiritual rejection.[168] When Adam Hill told Elizabethan Londoners that their 'perpetuall damnation' was at hand; when Daniel Donne warned 'wee are so desperately sicke . . . that wee lye even at the doore of death, and there be scarce so much as a thresh-hold betweene us and eternall destruction', their words undoubtedly had amphibious significance.[169] Equally double-edged were the assertions of Thomas Hooker, who told his listeners that they deserved to descend 'a hundred times' to hell, adding that the Almighty would 'set his teeth at thee, and stamp thee down'. He closed with one final macabre prediction: 'Capernaum's place is England's place, which is the most scalding tormenting place of all . . . the poor native Turks and Infidels shall have a more cool summer-parlor in hell than England shall have.'[170]

Paul's Cross prophets inferred that temporal discipline was a 'type' of the endless punishment endured by reprobates in the 'bottomlesse pit'.[171] In *Tormenting Tophet*, preached in June 1614, the Essex vicar Henry Greenwood declared that 'the great destruction of the damned in hell, is livelily shadowed out

---

paragraph are from McGiffert, 'American Puritan Studies', 47; Miller, 'Marrow of Puritan Divinity', 258.

[166] Bozeman, 'Covenant Theology and "National Covenant"'; id., 'Federal Theology and the "National Covenant"', esp. 399. See Collinson's remarks in *Birthpangs*, 22–3, and 'Biblical Rhetoric', 27. Bozeman is partly anticipated by Wilson, *Pulpit in Parliament*, ch. 6, esp. 168–9, 185, 189–90.

[167] Wakeman, *Jonahs sermon and Ninevehs repentance*, 55; Robert Harris, *Gods goodnes and mercie* (1626 edn.), 22. Cf. Abbot, *Exposition upon the prophet Jonah*, 367.

[168] e.g. Wakeman, *Jonahs sermon and Ninevehs repentance*, 56; Y[onger], *Sermon preached at Great Yarmouth*, sigs. D7ᵛ–8ʳ, E2ᵛ–3ʳ.

[169] Hill, *Crie of England*, 75, cf. 3, 4, 36; Donne, *Sub-poena*, 39.

[170] Hooker, *The Danger of Desertion*, in *Writings in England and Holland*, ed. Williams *et al.*, 241, 242, alluding to Matt. xi. 21–4.

[171] Downame, *Lectures upon . . . Hosea*, 2nd pagination, 125. See Wilson, *Pulpit in Parliament*, 191.

unto us in the judgements of God on earth'.[172] '[T]he fire and brimstone which fell upon the Sodomites in this life', argued Robert Harris, 'was but a figure of that fire and brimstone which shall feed upon them in the life to come'. In suggesting that the providential penalties poured out on the unrighteous in the present were but 'preambles' and 'entrances into, not exemptions from ensuing miseries', the clergy were tacitly endorsing an innate tendency in popular eschatological thinking. They were encouraging the common assumption that sinners struck down by the hand of God were damned.[173] Even if, as Harry Stout has maintained in the context of colonial New England, ministers took scrupulous care to separate the 'contradictory logics of the two covenants' and give their audience clear 'rhetorical signals' about which they were employing in the course of a particular sermon, considerable potential for confusion remained. The ideological contortions required to grasp the difference cannot have been within the compass of all those listening—and the ambiguity was one which the clergy assuredly had an interest in exploiting.[174]

The prophetic mode, then, was predicated on the promise that through corporate repentance and reformation of life a covenanted people could actively shape and mould the future of their nation, and, by extension, their own personal fate. The calculus of 'unless ye repent' implicitly exalted human ability to exercise agency. In this it contrasted sharply with sermons inspired by the millennial visions embedded in Daniel and Revelation and fed by the speculations of Thomas Brightman and Joseph Mede. Apocalyptic preaching spoke of a glorious kingdom of Christ on earth erected by an all-powerful deity without any input from man whatsoever; it anticipated a revolutionary upheaval of the most basic structures of Christian society. But triumphant millenarianism was not common in the pulpits until after 1642: as John Wilson has argued, its emergence indexed the divisions evolving within mid-seventeenth-century puritanism. In the pre-Civil War period, most providential preaching embodied an eschatology that was reformist rather than transformist at root. It posited a relationship between the Almighty and England which rested on reciprocal rights and obligations and elided the distinction between individuals and collectivities.[175]

The symbiosis between microcosm and macrocosm which the jeremiad presupposed was reflected in the premiss that the audience addressed by the preacher was democratically representative of the commonwealth before God. Parliamentarians who gathered in St Margaret's Westminster for fast sermons in the 1620s and 1640s no more constituted a cross-section of English society than the King, Court, and Privy Council seated at St James or Whitehall, or undergraduates and academics who assembled weekly in the University Churches of Oxford

[172] Henry Greenwood, *Tormenting Tophet* (1615), 50 (on Isa. xxx. 30).
[173] Harris, *Destruction of Sodome*, 30. Cf. Gray, *Alarum to England*, sigs. B1ᵛ, B8ʳ. See Ch. 2 above, pp. 103–4.
[174] Stout, *New England Soul*, 27 and pt. 1 *passim*. See also Collinson, 'Biblical Rhetoric', 42 n. 50.
[175] Wilson, *Pulpit in Parliament*, ch. 7.

and Cambridge.[176] Congregations at Paul's Cross, however, were notoriously mongrel and 'mixt', a conglomeration of the 'better', 'middling', and 'meaner sorts' of people, of sightseeing foreigners, Londoners, and passing visitors from the country. This famous podium was a magnet and 'hive' which attracted the inquisitive no less than the devout. Francis Marbury, later rector of St Martin-in-the-Vintry, complained in June 1602 of disorderly hearers who habitually absented themselves from their own parish churches but regularly came to the Cross and there 'delude[d] the law with walking and talking'.[177] When the orator of the hour turned to denounce the sins of every rank, profession, and estate, he could thus be fairly confident that the crowd comprised members of each class, calling, sex, and age group against which he inveighed. George Webbe singled out the Lord Mayor, Aldermen, judges, ministers, citizens, and courtiers for particular criticism, while Thomas Baughe directed his diatribe against 'Gentles' and 'Gallants', 'beauteous Ladies', 'faire matrons, and damzels'. Daniel Donne's long roll-call included lawyers, tradesmen, married couples, parents, children, masters, and servants; and John Fosbroke appended an exhortation to that 'many-headed monster' 'the multitude' at the end.[178] The 'weekly "check-up"' conducted by the preachers may have been intended primarily to remind the city fathers of their duty 'to launce out all coruption and baggage' which was 'gathered in the bowels' of the metropolis, but it was simultaneously designed to provoke members of the audience to inspect and purge their own souls.[179]

Considered especially suitable for 'populous assemblies',[180] the jeremiad was delivered at a range of public venues from busy market places to the Spittle and the pulpits of provincial cathedrals. John Carpenter's *Remember Lots Wife* (1588) was originally prepared for the long nave of St Peter's in Exeter, while it was at Stourbridge Fair, in the presence of a motley crew of stallkeepers, customers, vagrants, and pickpockets, that William Perkins stepped into the shoes of Zephaniah in 1593.[181] It is less clear how frequently curates and vicars subjected

---

[176] Jeremiah Dyke described the House of Commons as 'an assembly of Noahs': *Sermon preached at the publicke fast*, 36. For sermons at court, see B[roughton], *Moriemini*; John Donne, *A sermon preached at Whitehall, March 3, 1619*, in *The Works . . .*, ed. Henry Alford, 6 vols. (1839), i. 291–306; Price, *Sorrow for the sinnes of the time.* For sermons at Oxford and Cambridge, see Robert Some, *A godly sermon preached in Latin at Great S. Maries in Cambridge* (1580) (on Hos. xiv. 3–4); Rainolds, *Prophecie of Obadiah.* See also Fulke, *Godly and learned sermon.*

[177] Gosson, *Trumpet of warre*, sig. A2r; Marbury, *Sermon preached at Pauls Crosse*, sig. E3r.

[178] Webbe, *Gods controversie*, 114–16; Baughe, *Summons to judgement*, 48–50; Donne, *Sub-poena*, 97–103; Fosbroke, *Englands warning by Israel and Judah*, in *Six sermons*, 33–8. A. W., *Fruitfull and godly sermon*, sig. A2v, acknowledges that the Paul's Cross congregation consisted of diverse degrees, conditions, and estates. For a moral rather than sociological taxonomy, see W[ilkinson], *Lots wife*, 49–55.

[179] Maclure, *Paul's Cross Sermons*, 121; *Sermon preached at Paules Crosse*, sig. F7r.

[180] John Wilkins, *Ecclesiastes, or, a discourse concerning the gift of preaching as it fals under the rules of art* (1647 edn.), quoted in Maclure, *Paul's Cross Sermons*, 154–5.

[181] Carpenter, *Remember Lots wife*; Perkins, *Faithfull and plaine exposition . . . of Zephaniah*, in *Workes*, iii. Other sermons in cathedrals include Jackson, *Judah must into captivitie* and *Raging tempest stilled.* See also Stanford E. Lehmberg, *The Reformation of Cathedrals: Cathedrals in English Society, 1485–1603* (Princeton, 1988), 275–7. For the Spittle, see Sandys, *Sermon made at the Spittle*, in *Sermons*, ed. Ayre.

rural parishes to this type of penitential preaching, thrusting these sobering Old Testament themes down the throats of captive audiences whose attendance at Sunday matins and evensong was constrained by the law. Few such homilies wriggled into print and, as Professor Stout's extensive study of early American manuscript sermons has shown, we cannot assume that those which were published are a reliable guide to what was dished up to parochial communities each week: the subject of discussion on the sabbath was almost invariably the personal pilgrimage of the individual Christian through life. Prophetic themes probably came to the fore in moments of national and communal emergency, reaching the ears of auditories enlarged by panic and fear. The congregations which heard William Whately urge fire-ravaged Banbury to 'Sinne no more' in March 1628 and the Lancashire preacher Christopher Hudson harangue Preston after the cessation of the plague in 1631, for instance, are likely to have been far larger and more heterogeneous than usual.[182] Such ministers may have had some grounds for upholding the conceit that the bustling 'country' town to which they spoke was an epitome of the entire 'country' in miniature.

On other occasions, the larger entity to which the prophet's listeners implicitly belonged was not England or Britain but the brotherhood of true believers dispersed throughout the world. Those who travelled considerable distances to attend combination lectures in Kettering, Cranbrook, or Mansfield hardly needed any reminder to repent and amend.[183] Nor perhaps did the sermon-gadders of seventeenth-century London—those, for instance, who implored the Worcestershire preacher Thomas Hopkins to publish their notes of two rousing addresses he had delivered during a visit to the city in 1608.[184] The parishioners of St Antholin's in Budge Row were evidently equally ardent 'professors of the faith': they had zealously repaired to Robert Gray's morning lectures on Genesis xix despite constant derision and scorn at the hands of their unregenerate neighbours.[185] So too the original audience of Robert Bolton's *Discourse about the state of true happinesse*: '(you are a people of understanding), I leave it to your owne consciences, to consider what must needs shortly befall us, except we gather our selves before the decree come foorth.'[186] The Gloucestershire villagers who sat through Sebastian Benefield's marathon run of sixty (tediously repetitive) sermons on Amos in the 1620s and 1630s must also have had the strong stomachs and heroic stamina of the prodigiously pious.[187] And George Abbot's series on Jonah was

[182] Stout, *New England Soul*, esp. introd., pp. 3–10; Whately, *Sinne no more*; Hudson, 'Preservation of the Godly' (LRO DP 353). Thomas Wilcox's *Faithfull narration* may also have originated as a sermon.

[183] See Patrick Collinson, 'Lectures by Combination', in *Godly People*, 467–98; id., *Religion of Protestants*, 136–40. Sermons preached during combination lectures include Bolton, *Instructions for a right comforting afflicted consciences . . . Delivered for the most part in the lecture at Kettering in Northamptonshire*, in *Workes*; and probably Whately, *Charitable teares*.

[184] Hopkins, *Two godlie and profitable sermons*, sig. A4ʳ ('To the Christian Reader').

[185] Gray, *Alarum to England*, sigs. A2ʳ–8ᵛ (dedications).

[186] Bolton, *Discourse about the state of true happinesse*, in *Workes*, 83.

[187] Benefield, *Commentary . . . upon . . . Amos*.

likewise absorbed by a select gathering of the godly of Oxford, who voluntarily assembled in St Mary the Virgin each Thursday on their way to work, summer and winter: he was 'rather induced to thinke, that everyone here belongeth to Gods election, for it standeth much with reason, that grace should have deepe roote in that people, who so early before day-light, come together with devotion, to heare what the Lord doth say concerning all of them'.[188] This was preaching to the converted, to a self-selected audience whose fault consisted less in committing offences than in quietly condoning them.

CHRISTS TEARES OVER JERUSALEM

The message of sin and judgement, plague and repentance, did not merely issue from the mouths of ordained ministers. As we have seen, these were also perennial themes of the providential ephemera churned out from London publishing houses throughout the Elizabethan and early Stuart period. Sensational ballads and pamphlets about floods, fires, earthquakes, and storms; deformed babies, diabolical apparitions, and sudden mishaps need to be interpreted as national morality sermons of a kind themselves. They too drew the parallel between biblical Israel and the 'faerie Iland' and 'unfruitfull Vineyard' of post-Reformation England, rehearsing her blessings, shortcomings, and impending punishments as solemnly as any Paul's Cross preacher.[189] Indeed, these news reports are saturated with prophetic rhetoric to a degree which suggests they were either composed by clergymen who regularly employed it in their pulpits, or written by versatile hacks sanctimoniously mimicking them, or, more probably, produced by a loose and unstable coalition of the two.[190]

The semi-professional writers who infested the capital often adopted the idiom of moral outrage and jingoistic patriotism in their attempt to eke out a livelihood by plying their pens. Metrical gloom was thus an established part of the repertoire of the early modern minstrel. There are dozens of Elizabethan songs affecting to be 'warnings', 'lanthorns', and death knells to a dangerously complacent and iniquitous nation. *A bell-man for England* sounded a siren to awake the people to their prayers before doomsday: first entered in 1586, this apocalyptic ditty sung to the ponderous tune of 'O man in desperation' survived in the ballad partners' stock for nearly a century.[191] Other 'alarums' extracted providential lessons from sacred

---

[188] Abbot, *Exposition upon the prophet Jonah*, 365 and 636. On 393 he spoke of 'common men', 'of whom we have little hope, that they have called for mercie'. John King's well attended *Lectures upon Jonas*, delivered in York, were preached to 'the most intelligent auditory of the place wherein I then lived': sigs. *3ᵛ–4ʳ.

[189] [Holland], *Motus Medi-terraneus*, sig. B2ʳ; Averell, *Wonderfull and straunge newes*, sig. B5ʳ. See also *Miracle upon Miracle*, esp. 10; *Most true and lamentable report, of a great tempest of haile which fell upon . . . Stockbery*, 3–5; *Gods warning to his people of England*, esp. 3–4; Parker, *True and terrible narration of a horrible earthquake*, sig. A6ᵛ.

[190] Lawrence Manley discerns a similar symbiosis between the discourse of preachers and pamphleteers in *Literature and Culture*, ch. 6, esp. 305–15.

[191] *A new ballad intituled, a bell-man for England, which night and day doth stand, to ring in all mens hearing, Gods vengeance is at hand* ([c.1620]) (entered *SR* 6 Dec. 1586: ii. 461). Copy in Clark (ed.),

and secular history: *Of the horrible and wofull destruction of, Sodome and Gomorra* was not quite as successful, but a ballad about Nineveh's timely conversion was a steady seller for at least fifty years.[192] And while only a few rhymsters alluded to the conquest of the ancient Greek metropoles of Alexandria and Troy, the sacking of Antwerp by the Spaniards in 1576 led to a spate of admonitions in verse.[193] Although most broadside jeremiads were addressed directly to London, a character in a Caroline comedy claimed he could give an excellent rendering of 'Jonas his crying out against Coventry'.[194]

No fallen city was more popular with the ballad-buying public than Jerusalem, besieged by Titus and Vespasian in AD 74. Around 1569 John Barker brought out a song about the storming of the city, set to the strains of 'the Queenes Almayne'. Drawing on the narrative by 'that prudent Jewe' Flavius Josephus, he also listed the preternatural tokens which had preceded this supreme act of vengeance for the assassination of Christ.[195] A new set of lyrics on this gripping subject appeared a decade later, this time to fit the rhythms of 'Bragandary',[196] but what Tessa Watt

---

Shirburn Ballads, 36–9. There were many versions of this ballad theme: William Birch, *A warnyng to England, let London begin: to repent their iniquitie, & flie from their sin* ([1565]) (entered *SR* 1564–5: i. 266); *Alarum to the true harted subjectes of London* (entered *SR* 1569–70: i. 412); *A warnynge or punysshement that Englonde shuld repente* (entered *SR* 1570–1: i. 438); *An alarme to England* (entered *SR* 17 Sept. 1578: ii. 338); John Carr, *A larum belle for London, with a caveat to England* (1573); *An ernest admonycon to repentance unto England especially to London* (entered *SR* 10/20 Apr. 1580: ii. 369); *The bell mans alarum* (entered *SR* 27 Nov. 1589: ii. 534); *A passing bell towling to call us to mind* ([1625?]); *Great Brittains arlarm [sic]* ([1667?]); Thomas Robins, *England's gentle admonition; or, a warning-piece to all sinners* ([1674–9]); *England's new bell-man* ([1690]). See Watt, *Cheap Print*, 90, 337. See also William Samuel, *A warnyng for the cittie of London* ([1550?]).

[192] *Of the horrible and wofull destruction of, Sodome and Gomorra* ([1570]) (entered *SR* 1568–9, 1570–1: i. 384, 439) and *The historie of the prophet Jonas. The repentance of Ninivie that great citie* ([c.1620]). This may be one of the following ballads: *Jonas* (entered *SR* 1562–3: i. 205); *The story of Jonas* (entered *SR* 1567–8: i. 355); *The mysse deades of Jonas &c* (entered *SR* 1569–70: i. 410); *Nowe have with ye to Ninive being a sonnet of Repentance* (entered *SR* 5 Sept. 1586: ii. 457). See also Watt, *Cheap Print*, 336.

[193] Rafe Norris, *A warning to London by the fall of Antwerp* ([1577?]). Other lost ballads include: *A warnynge songe to cities all to beware by Andwerps fall* (entered *SR* 25 Jan. 1577: i. 308); *Heavie newes to all Christendom from the wooful towne of Antwerp comme* (entered *SR* 1 July 1577: ii. 313); *A godlie exhortacon unto Englande to repent him of the evill and sinfull waies shewinge thexample and distruccon of Jerlm and Andwarp* (entered *SR* 15 Nov. 1578: ii. 341). See also R. Simpson's introd. to his edn. of the play *A Larum for London or The Seige of Antwerp. Together with The Spoyle of Antwerpe by George Gascoyne* (1872), 10. The 'moral' of the play, like Gascoyne's tract and Barnaby Rich's *Allarme to England* (1578), is that London should awake from its dangerous security and trust more to the protection of the professional soldier and less to its wealth.

[194] John Fletcher, *Monsieur Thomas. A comedy. Acted at the private house in Blacke Fryers* (1639), sig. H1ʳ.

[195] John Barker, *Of the horyble and woful destruccion of Jerusalem* ([1569?]) (entered *SR* 1568–9: i. 380). For Josephus, see Joseph Ben Gorion's abridgement *Compendious and most marveilous historie*, and Lodge's trans., *Famous and memorable workes of Josephus*. E. D. Mackerness has traced much of the material cited in this section in ' "Christs Teares" and the Literature of Warning', *English Studies*, 33 (1952), 251–4.

[196] *A warning or lanthorne to London. A dolefull destruction of faire Jerusalem*, printed in Clark (ed.), *Shirburn Ballads*, 31–4 (entered *SR* 8 June 1603: iii. 236; re-entered on 14 Dec. 1624: iv. 131). Other ballads on this theme include: *A newe ballad of the destruccon of Jerusalem* (entered *SR* 15 Aug. 1586: ii. 454); *A warning to all England by the dolefull destruction of Jerusalem &c* (entered *SR* 11 Oct. 1604: iii. 272).

has called the '*pièce de résistance* of this genre' was not composed until around 1593. Destined to remain in print for several generations, *Christs teares over Jerusalem. Or, a caveat for England*, was a clumsy summary of an uncharacteristically sombre tract by Thomas Nashe.[197] Thomas Deloney seems to have taken up the challenge a few years later, publishing a suspiciously similar allegorization of the episode entitled *Canaan's calamitie*.[198] All of these ballads linked a lugubrious account of how the Lord had wept bitterly as he approached the doomed city on Palm Sunday with an emotive description of the terrible famine which followed the actual siege forty years later:

> The vomit which one man did cast
> another man did eate.
> Their very dung they layd not wast,
> but made therof their meate.

Dogs, cats, mice, and rats they 'counted sweete', even devouring 'their shooes from of their feete'.[199] Every rhymster dwelt ghoulishly on the dreadful predicament of the noblewoman Miriam, forced to slay her baby son and roast him for her dinner, summing up the moral of this gory tale in one final refrain:

> Repent therefore O England,
> repent while thou has space,
> And doe not like Jerusalem,
> despise Gods proffered grace.[200]

'Jerusalems Fall, Englands Warning' was a favourite topos of prophetic preachers too. A succession of Elizabethan and early Stuart prophets took up the text of 'Christs teares' (Luke xix. 41–4) and squeezed out every last drop of typological significance.[201] John Stockwood could not resist incorporating morbid particulars of the miseries the Jews had endured in the wake of the Roman invasion, not least those of the cannabilistic mother Miriam, which, he said, 'were such as maye worthily cause an hearte of flint to weepe'.[202] When John Lawrence spoke at Paul's Cross in the spring of 1624, he too regaled his auditors with grisly details of how

---

[197] *Christs teares over Jerusalem. Or, a caveat for England, to call to God for mercy, lest we be plagued for our contempt and wickednesse* ([*c.*1640]) (entered to the ballad partners *SR* 14 Dec. 1624: iv. 131, but probably written *c.*1593). See Watt, *Cheap Print*, 98–9, 335. The ballad has been attributed to Thomas Deloney (*Works*, ed. Mann, 496), but this is doubtful. Thomas Nashe, *Christs teares over Jerusalem*, in *Works*, ed. McKerrow, ii.

[198] T[homas] D[eloney], *Canaans calamitie Jerusalems misery* (1618) (entered *SR* 5 Jan. 1598: iii. 100).

[199] *A warning or lanthorne to London*, printed in Clark (ed.), *Shirburn Ballads*, 33.

[200] *Christs teares over Jerusalem*.

[201] Sermons on Luke xix. 41–5 include John Stockwood, *A very fruitfull and necessarye sermon of the most lamentable destruction of Jerusalem* (1584); F. S., *Jerusalems fall, Englands warning*; Lawrence, *Golden trumpet*; Featley, *Sermon preached at a publike fast*, in *Clavis mystica*. See also Thomas Wilson, *Christs farewell to Jerusalem, and last prophesie* (1614) (on Luke xxiii. 27–31); Jackson, *A treatise concerning the signes of the time*, in *Diverse sermons*, esp. 42–8, 80–7.

[202] Stockwood, *Very fruitfull and necessarye sermon*, sigs. B8ʳ–C5ʳ. On Miriam, see sigs. C3ᵛ–4ʳ. Quotation at sig. B8ʳ.

aristocrats were obliged 'to eat the leather of their Coaches as they rid, Ladies to scrape in dunghils for their food, and many women to eat the fruit of their owne wombe'.[203]

Far from a distinctively post-Reformation motif, the siege and its hideous sequel had fascinated poets, prose-writers, and preachers since the days of the primitive Church. Drawn from apocryphal sources, the story was enshrined in alliterative verse, metrical romance, and a French *chanson de geste*;[204] it also infiltrated John Mirk's well-known *Festial* via Jacobus de Voragine's *Legenda Aurea*.[205] In the medieval legend, the battle and its aftermath were traditionally linked with an account of cures effected by the relic of the Holy Vernicle, St Veronica's veil, while the virtuous 'moder' Miriam, nauseated at the thought of eating her own infant's flesh, is enjoined to the horrible deed by an angel who appears to her in a dream. Protestants simply edited out these 'popish' accretions.

Regularly recounted from the metaphorical 'stage of the land', 'faire Jerusalem's' destruction also made its way onto the real stages of the land. A Latin play on this topic is credited to Thomas Legge, Master of Caius College, Cambridge, and it was the subject of an extraordinarily lavish production commissioned by the corporation and performed by the craft guilds of Coventry in 1584—an impeccably Protestant replacement for the Corpus Christi plays permanently 'layd downe' after the 'great earthquake' four years before. The taste for such civic entertainments and amateur 'pagens' continued: in 1591 the City Council granted permission for a revival of this spectacular piece of pseudo-biblical drama at Midsummer, on the condition that every maypole still standing was dismantled before Whitsun.[206] The taboo on dramatizing the Bible did not yet extend to the Apocrypha, which offered a scriptural setting without the taint of sacrilege. By the end of Elizabeth's reign, Coventry's reformed substitute for the old mystery cycle had itself come under the iconoclast's hammer, a symptom of the general hardening of attitudes towards the theatrical medium into which the English Reformation moved in its second generation.[207]

[203] Lawrence, *Golden trumpet*, 94–5.
[204] *The Siege of Jerusalem edited from MS. Laud. Misc. 656*, ed. E. Kölbing and Mabel Day, EETS, os 188 (1932) (an alliterative poem dating to the 1390s); *Titus and Vespasian or the Destruction of Jerusalem in Rhymed Couplets edited from the London and Oxford MSS*, ed. J. A. Herbert, Roxburghe Club (1905); *The dystruccyon of Jherusalem by Vaspazyan and Tytus* ([1513?]), trans. from a French *chanson de geste*.
[205] *Mirk's Festial*, ed. Erbe, 141–2; Jacobus de Voragine, *The Golden Legend or Lives of the Saints as Englished by William Caxton*, 7 vols. (1900), iii. 166–8.
[206] See G. C. Moore Smith, *College Plays Performed in the University of Cambridge* (Cambridge, 1923), 93; and the anonymous article entitled 'The Latin Plays acted before the University of Cambridge' in *Retrospective Review*, 12 (1825), 15. Details of the payments made to those involved in the Coventry play (apparently written by a Mr Smythe of Oxford) can be found in the City Annals, printed in Ingram (ed.), *Records of Early English Drama: Coventry*, 303–9. For the earthquake and the 1591 council decision, see pp. 294, 332.
[207] Murray Roston, *Biblical Drama in England: From the Middle Ages to the Present Day* (1968), 118–19. For the broader civic context in which these developments occurred, see Collinson, *Birthpangs*, chs. 2, 4, esp. pp. 99–106; id., 'Elizabethan and Jacobean Puritanism as Forms of Popular Religious Culture', 42–6.

But the abolition of paraliturgical drama did not see the total eclipse of these themes. Instead they were relocated to the commercial playhouses which began springing up on the outskirts of London in the late 1570s. William Heminge's *The Jewes tragedy or their fatal and final overthrow by Vespasian and Titus his son*, published posthumously in 1662, was one professional production about the siege of Jerusalem for which we have a printed script. First staged in the capital in 1590, Thomas Lodge and Robert Greene's *A looking glasse for London and England*, an elaborate dramatization of the Book of Jonah set in a Nineveh which bears more resemblance to Renaissance Italy than to ancient Assyria, appears to have been a box-office hit. This crudely plotted Protestant morality play quite literally involved the device of deus ex machina. In Act I an angel lowers the omniscient narrator and prophet 'Oseas' in a throne, who admonishes the city:

> London looke on, this matter nips thee neere,
> Leave off thy ryot, pride and sumptuous cheere.
> Spend lesse at boord, and spare not at the doore,
> But aide the infant, and releeve the poore.

A later stage direction indicates that other mechanical apparatus was flown: 'A hand from out a cloud, threatneth a burning sword'.[208]

These scriptural stories lent themselves readily to puppetry too. In Ben Jonson's *Bartholomew Fayre*, first performed in 1614, the hobby-horse seller Lantern Leatherhead boasts: 'O the motions that I . . . have given light to i' my time . . . *Jerusalem* was a stately thing, and so was *Ninevah*, and *The City of Norwich*, and *Sodom and Gomorrah* . . . but *The Gunpowder Plot*, there was a get-penny! I have presented that to an eighteen- or twenty-pence audience nine times in an afternoon'.[209] The inhabitants of Oxford and Norwich were regularly entertained by puppet shows and 'spectacula' on the subjects of 'Nineveh besieged & taken' and 'Hierusalem in its glory [and] destruction' in the 1630s—there was apparently sufficient interest from the public for the latter to be divided into five or six parts.[210] Notwithstanding the tirades of that puritan rabbi of Banbury, Zeal-of-the-Land Busy, the priorities of godly Protestantism and the trends of the professional theatre and literary market-place could sometimes converge. Playwrights and entertainers, like pamphleteers, were parasitical upon the homiletic patterns set by

---

[208] Thomas Lodge and Robert Greene, *A looking glasse for London and England* (1594), sigs. B1ʳ, B3ʳ, G2ʳ. Five quartos of this play survive, the last dated 1617. See Roston, *Biblical Drama*, 97–100.

[209] Jonson, *Bartholomew Fayre*, v. i. 6–13 repr. in *Three Comedies*, ed. Jamieson. See Patrick Collinson, 'Bartholomew Fair: The Theatre invents Puritanism', in David L. Smith, Richard Strier, and David Bevington (eds.), *The Theatrical City: London's Culture, Theatre and Literature, 1576–1649* (Cambridge, 1995), 157–69. In Jonson's *Every man out of his humour* (1599), ii. i, Fungoso says: 'There's a new motion of the city of Nineveh, with Jonas and the whale, to be seen at Fleet-bridge'. Quoted in Hyder E. Rollins (ed.), *A Pepysian Garland: Black-Letter Broadside Ballds of the Years 1595–1639* (Cambridge, 1922), 66.

[210] See *The Diary of Thomas Crosfield M.A., B.D. Fellow of Queen's College, Oxford*, ed. Frederick S. Boas (1935), 54, 71, 79, 135.

the clergy, with whom they competed as commentators on the vices of English society.[211]

PROPHECY IN PERFORMANCE

But it should not be forgotten that preachers were accomplished performers themselves. Indeed, they were obliged to be: as Thomas Wilson recognized in his best-selling treatise on rhetoric first published in 1553, unless they played to the tastes and 'tickle[d the] eares of their fleeting audience' they would very soon find themselves addressing 'bare walles' while their rivals at the Curtain and Globe enjoyed a full house—'for excepte men finde delight, thei will not longe abide'.[212] Like any other branch of oratory, stressed contemporary theoreticians like William Perkins and John Wilkins, 'prophesying' was an 'art' as well as a 'gift'. There can be no doubt that the jeremiad had much melodramatic and theatrical scope—perhaps no homiletic genre was better calculated to 'moove affection' and win 'the praise of teares, rather than of tongue'.[213] Ministers availed themselves of a variety of sophisticated rhetorical techniques. In this most bullying of sermon styles, the cross-examination and inquisition of England was a standard procedure. Let us eavesdrop on Edwin Sandys grilling Elizabethans who had gathered to hear him at the Spittle:

> Are we not as guilty of unrighteous dealing, of oppression, of extortion, are we not as covetous, are we not as proud as ever any people was? Is there not as much pride, belly-cheer, idleness, unmercifulness, in the city of London, as was in the city of Sodom? Do we not as much loath the true bread of heaven? Cleave we not as fast unto idolatry and super-stition? Commit we not adultery and fornication? Tempt we not God? Do we not mutter against the magistrates, as the Israelites did in the wilderness? Is there more truth, mercy, and knowledge of God, less swearing, lying, murder, theft, adultery, and bloodshed in England, than was in the land of Jewry? If kingdoms then be translated for wrongful dealing, for covetousness and pride; how can unrighteous, covetous and proud England stand long? If God spared not the flourishing city of Sodom, can he in his justice spare the sinful city of London? If God overthrew the mighty people of Israel in the wilderness for their sins, can he wink at our foul and manifold offences? If the land of Jewry was laid waste, and the elect Israel carried away captive for their ingratitude, will not God punish and plague our shameful contempt, our wilful disobedience?[214]

And John Downame interrogating the godly of Jacobean London:

---

[211] Manley, *Literature and Culture*, 310–11; Jeffrey Knapp, 'Preachers and Players in Shakespeare's England', *Representations*, 44 (1993), 29–59.

[212] Thomas Wilson, *The arte of rhetorique, for the use of all soche as are studious of eloquence* (1563 edn.), fo. 2^{r–v}.

[213] Quotations from Bernard, *Faithfull shepheard*, 81, and see 66; Jackson, *Judah must into captivitie*, sig. A3^v. See also Perkins, *Arte of prophecying*, in *Workes*, ii; Wilkins, *Ecclesiastes*; [Andreas Gerardus], *The practise of preaching, otherwise called the pathway to the pulpit*, trans. John Ludham (1577), esp. bk. 1, chs. 7 and 16.

[214] Sandys, *Sermon made at the Spittle*, in *Sermons*, ed. Ayre, 259.

hath not our long peace and prosperitie brought an universall sleepe of securitie upon the land? Have not our people greevously abused their great plenty, and the manifold blessings wherewith God hath inriched them, by mis-spending them in voluptuous pleasures, and in all manner of luxurious wantonnesse and intemperance? Was ever the land so defiled with the surfetting and drunkennesse, whordome, and all manner of uncleannesse? Was there ever the like greedy covetousnesse, oppression, bribing, extortion, and all manner deceitfull & cruel dealing? Were ever the hearts and hands of our Nation so effeminated, as in these times, wherein there is scarce any difference betweene men and women in nicenesse, wan-tonnesse, and soft luxuriousnesse, both in respect of diet and attire? Is not the manly courage, and able valour of this our Nation much decaied, and doth not foxe-like wilinesse take the place of true fortitude? Finally, were ever men more insolent in offering injuries, or more impotent in repelling deserved revenge?[215]

Or Thomas Sutton rising to a crescendo at Paul's Cross one cold Sunday in January 1612:

how long, shall the Preacher cry that sin is more to bee feared then any treason, and yet we practise it? How long shall the Preacher cry that sin is the onely Troyan-horse, whose womb can command a bloudy Armado, armed with cruelty and rage to work our overthrow, and yet we entertaine and welcome it? how long shall the Preacher cry in our streets, and wring it in your eares, that sin is the onely makebate betwixt God and us, & yet wee are in league and compact with it?[216]

Equally arresting were the daring metaphors and vivid similes these prophets habitually employed. As the late William Haller noted, theirs was a 'homely' idiom and an 'intensely imaginative hortatory prose'.[217] What could have made a greater impression on the prosperous grain merchants who heard William Perkins hold forth at Stourbridge Fair than his comparison of the English Church with a goodly heap of corn, so much worthless chaff and so little high-quality wheat?[218] And how better to engage the imagination of a nation of shopkeepers than to liken the Almighty to a pedlar packing away his wares, a tradesman closing 'the Shop-windowes of Heaven' and 'shutting up to be gone'?[219] Stephen Marshall, vicar of Finchingfield, Essex, who preached on the incendiary subject of *Meroz cursed* no less than sixty times on the eve of the Civil War, is said to have liberally salted his sermons with 'vulgar proverbs . . . odd country phrases and by-words, which . . . captivated people at a strange rate'.[220] Marshall's style may have been unusually

---

[215] Downame, *Lectures upon . . . Hosea*, 2nd pagination, 342.

[216] Sutton, *Englands summons*, in *Englands first and second summons*, 128–9. Another strategy for cap-turing attention was the use of emphasis, repetition, or a catchy phrase or refrain. Sampson Price e.g. punctuated each stage of his sermon on Rev. ii. 5, *Ephesus warning before her woe*, with a single word, 'Remember'.

[217] Haller, *Rise of Puritanism*, 23–4.

[218] Perkins, *Faithfull and plaine exposition . . . of Zephaniah*, in *Workes*, iii. 425.

[219] Hooker, *The Danger of Desertion*, in *Writings in England and Holland*, ed. Williams *et al.*, 246; William Fenner, *A treatise of the affections; or, the soules pulse* (1642), 189. Hooker's sermon was ascribed to Fenner (another Essex preacher) in a posthumous edition of his sermons.

[220] Capp, 'Popular Culture and the English Civil War', 31. See also Trevor Roper, 'Fast Sermons', esp. 307. Stephen Marshall, *Meroz cursed* (1641[1642]).

racy and colloquial, but prophetic preachers like 'silver tong'd' Henry Smith could be just as colourful when it came to 'picturing out' the sins which 'reigned' and 'revelled' in England.[221] Immanuel Bourne portrayed pride walking hand in hand with whoredom, with her mother drunkenness lagging behind, a trio which had begotten three venomous daughters, simony, sacrilege, and oppression.[222] Thomas Adams wielded his satirical pencil with particular vigour:

> I can point you to Usury, robbing, grinding, sucking bloud, cutting throates, whiles he sits in the Chimney corner, and heares of his Zanies, whelpes, underling-Theeves ending their dayes at the Gallowes. I can shew you Covetousnesse, swearing for gaine, crouching, ramping, playing Ape, Lion, or Devill, for Money: I can discover to you Drunkennesse, rising early to the wine, Malice making haste to the death of Ammon, Ambition running after honour, faster then Peter to the Sepulchre; Pride Whirling in her Chariot, Wantonnesse shutting up the windowes; Bribery creeping in at the Key-hole, even when the doore of Justice is locked up against her. Among all these I see not repentance: Doth she stay till the last act?[223]

In personifying vice, prophetic preachers were perpetuating the garish parade of the Seven Deadlies, the familiar rogues' gallery of malefactors so beloved by the medieval friars. They habitually fell back on the structures and motifs of traditional vernacular complaint.[224]

Such sermons were overloaded with anguished and impassioned particles of speech. 'O England, England', 'O London, London', implored preacher after preacher, imitating the sacred poetry of the canonical Scriptures. The 'emphatical language' of these apostrophes and interjections—part invocation, part plea, part lamentation—embodied an intimate address to a covenanted people, who, like the Israelites, had strayed from the path of righteousness into the wilderness of sin.[225] The same assumption underlay the use of terms of endearment: 'Beloved in the Lord', entreated Sebastian Benefield; 'Brethren, there must be some ende of these things', beseeched John King; 'alas, my Beloved', sighed Daniel Donne.[226]

---

[221] Quotation from Wakeman, *Jonahs sermon and Ninevehs repentance*, 59. See Henry Smith, *The trumpet of the soule sounding to judgement*, in *Foure sermons*, separately paginated in *Sermons*, sig. D2ʳ: 'when iniquitie hath played her part, vengeance leapes upon the stage, the Comedie is short, but the Tragedie is longer'. Bernard recommended that preachers 'picture out vice in his deformitie; and draw out vertue in her lively colours': *Faithfull shepheard*, 87, and see 68.

[222] Bourne, *Rainebow*, 46–8.

[223] Adams, *The gallants burden*, in *Workes*, 22–3. For similar parades, see Lawrence, *Golden trumpet*, 42; Jackson, *Londons new-yeeres gift*, fo. 19ᵛ; Jackson, *Celestiall husbandrie*, esp. 19–45; Benefield, *Commentary . . . upon . . . Amos*, 2nd pagination, 133.

[224] G. R. Owst, *Literature and Pulpit in Medieval England: A Neglected Chapter in the History of English Letters and of the English People* (Oxford, 1961), ch. 7; Morton W. Bloomfield, *The Seven Deadly Sins* (Michigan, 1952); John Peter, *Complaint and Satire in Early English Literature* (Oxford, 1956), esp. ch. 4.

[225] See J. H. Prynne, 'English Poetry and Emphatical Language', *Proceedings of the British Academy*, 74 (1989), 135–69 (I owe this reference and point to Patrick Collinson). See also George A. Kennedy, *Classical Rhetoric and its Christian and Secular Tradition from Ancient to Modern Times* (Chapel Hill, NC, 1980), ch. 7.

[226] Benefield, *Commentary . . . upon . . . Amos*, 1st pagination, 242 (cf. 255); King, *Lectures upon*

Many ministers resorted to the technique referred to in preaching manuals as '*prospopeia*': 'when wee bring in dead men speaking, or our selves doe take their person upon us'. Introducing the major and minor prophets appealing directly to the erring English nation was 'very pathetical', said Richard Bernard, 'and moveth much if it be rightly handled'.[227] Nor was it considered unacceptable to put words—or at least the Word—in the mouth of the Almighty Himself. The impersonation of God on the stage may have been branded the height of blasphemy, but in the pulpit it was regularly employed without the slightest reservation or reproof. Preaching at Paul's Cross in January 1581, James Bisse exclaimed:

The Lorde may nowe justly say to England, as hee somtimes spake unto Babylon. Come downe, and sit in the dust, O daughter Englande, thou shalt no more be called tender, and delicate, take the milstones, & grind meale, loose thy lockes, make bare thy feete, uncover thy legs and thighs, passe through the floodes, thy filthinesse shalbe discovered, thy shame shalbe seene, I will take vengeaunce, and will not meete thee as a man[228]

'Have I gotten so many victories for you (may God say) and no remembrance of me left among you?', demanded George Benson on 7 May 1609; 'he may say, and say truly to us, What more could I have done for you my people, then what I have not done?', John Lawrence affirmed one spring day fifteen years later. And here is the Elizabethan bishop of Lincoln Thomas Cooper addressing the nation in the late 1570s:

O Englande, Englande, how often times have I called thee? how sundrie wayes have I provoked thee? howe aboundantlye have I powred out my benefites and blessinges uppon thee? howe earnestlye have I by the mouth of my Preachers, clocked and cried to thee, as an Henne doeth to her Chickens, that thou mightest awake out of thy securitie, and by repentaunce, returne under the shadowe of my wings[229]

This was a mode of discourse which primarily sought to arouse and exercise its hearers' emotions rather than challenge their intellects. These Protestant Jeremiahs seem to have been no less adept at composing tear-jerking sermons than Spanish and Italian Catholic revivalists like St Bernadino of Siena, Diego de Cadiz, Vincent Ferrer, and the Jesuit missionaries of seventeenth- and eighteenth-century Naples and Bavaria. They too aimed to make their audiences physically weep with sorrow at their sins and demonstrate their collective mourning and contrition. The tears of the faithful stored up 'in the bottle of God' were an infallible means of staving off plagues and securing forgiveness, said the Kentish vicar Alexander Udny, and he was not just employing a figure of speech.[230]

Jonas, 467; Donne, *Sub-poena*, 96. Bernard recommended the use of 'loving terms' and 'mild exhortations': *Faithfull shepheard*, 75.

[227] *Faithfull shepheard*, 67, 77.

[228] Bisse, *Two sermons*, sig. D4ʳ.

[229] Benson, *Sermon preached at Paules Crosse*, 39; Lawrence, *Golden trumpet*, 61; Cooper, *Certaine sermons*, 188.

[230] William Christian, 'Provoked Religious Weeping in Early Modern Spain', in J. Davis (ed.), *Religious Organization and Religious Experience*, Association of Social Anthropologists Monograph, 21

It would also be difficult to deny that these preachers deliberately cultivated a prophetic demeanour and presence. How they conducted themselves on the rostrum is for the most part irrecoverable, but clerical handbooks do provide a few hints. Perkins insisted that godly solemnity should always grace the messenger of God; Bernard advocated a reverend, upright bearing and 'a comely countenance', not 'lumpish', 'frowning', or 'irefull', but sober, modest, and stern; George Abbot reminded his colleagues 'that in regard of his holinesse and righteousnesse whose person we represent, our cariage and behaviour should be framed to a resemblance of the immaculate Deitie'.[231] If the Old Testament visages which stare out from the engraved portraits in their posthumously published works are at all indicative, some ministers studiously modelled themselves on traditional depictions of the Hebrew patriarchs and prophets—not to mention anthropomorphic images of God the Father Himself. William Gouge was reputed to be the '*Effiges* of Moses' 'towards his latter end' and John More, the 'Apostle of Norwich' allegedly grew the longest beard of his generation so 'that no act of his life might be unworthy of the gravity of his appearance' (Plates 45 and 46).[232]

Only rarely do we catch sight of these overpowering personalities actually in the pulpit. According to John Manningham, London barrister and an inveterate attender of lectures, the preacher at Paul's Cross on 19 December 1602 had 'a long browne beard, a hanging looke, a gloting eye and a tossing learing jeasture', while Henoch Clapham was 'a blacke fellowe, with a sower looke . . . bold, and sometymes bluntly witty'. Augustine Baker, a young Welshman educated in the capital who later became a Benedictine monk, remembered Clapham as 'a mighty rabbin' who 'grew famous . . . by making strange faces and motions of his eyes, now up to heaven, and by and by down to the ground'. Such 'vehement and seemingly passionate actings . . . did take much with the simple sort'.[233] John Rogers was noted for his 'deep . . . trembling, quavering, singultive twang' and, according to the biographer Samuel Clarke, William Perkins 'used to pronounce the word Damn with such an Emphasis, as left a doleful Echo in his auditors ears' and was able to make their 'hearts fall down, and their haires almost to stand upright'.[234] Renowned

(1982), 97–114; David Gentilcore, ' "Adapt Yourselves to the People's Capabilities": Missionary Strategies, Methods and Impact in the Kingdom of Naples, 1600–1800', *JEH* 45 (1994), 269–96; Trevor Johnson, 'Blood, Tears and Xavier-Water: Jesuit Missionaries and Popular Religion in the Eighteenth-Century Upper Palatinate', in Bob Scribner and Trevor Johnson (eds.), *Popular Religion in Germany and Central Europe, 1400–1800* (Basingstoke, 1996), esp. 192–4. Udny, *Voyce of the cryer*, 86–92. See also Augustine Thompson, *Revival Preachers and Politics in Thirteenth Century Italy: The Great Devotion of 1233* (Oxford, 1992).

[231] Perkins, *Arte of prophecying*, in *Workes*, ii. 761; Bernard, *Faithfull shepheard*, 89; Abbot, *Exposition upon the prophet Jonah*, 409; [Gerardus], *Practise of preaching*, fos. 44[r], 177[r-v].

[232] Samuel Clarke, *A collection of the lives of ten eminent divines* (1662), 97, 114–15; *DNB, s.n.* John More. For More's portrait, see Henry Holland, *Herωologia Anglica hoc est clarissimorum et doctissimorum aliquot Anglorum qui floruerunt ab anno Cristi* (1620), facing 208.

[233] Manningham, *Diary*, ed. Bruce, 104–5; J. McCann and H. Connolly (eds.), *Memorials of Father Augustine Baker and Other Documents relating to the English Benedictines*, CRS 33 (1933), 56–7.

[234] According to a hostile source, quoted in Patrick Collinson, 'Lectures by Combination', in *Godly People*, 493; Samuel Clarke, *The marrow of ecclesiastical history* (1654), 851.

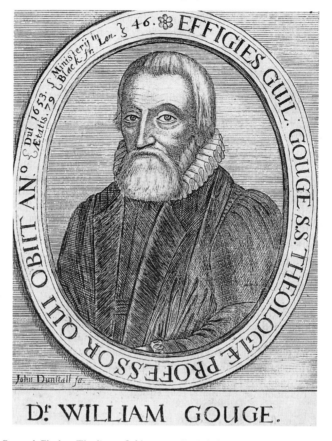

Dr WILLIAM GOUGE.

PLATE 45 Samuel Clarke, *The lives of thirty-two English divines* (London, 1677), 234.
By permission of the Syndics of Cambridge University Library. Shelfmark: P. 2. 20.
Dr William Gouge, rector of St Anne's, Blackfriars, reputed to resemble the '*Effiges* of
Moses' 'towards his latter end'.

for his 'choleric disposition' and 'mighty fervor of spirit', Thomas Hooker quite
literally lifted up his voice like a trumpet to denounce incorrigible sinners, as did
William Whately, the 'roaring boy' of Banbury, and Hugh Clark, another early
Stuart Boanerges who had 'an excellent pair of lungs' which he used to strike
shame and terror into the wicked.[235] Stephen Marshall had to be towelled down
after his sermons and Richard Greenham's 'shirt would usually be as wet with
sweating, as if it had been drenched with water'.[236] Such preachers may well have

[235] The quotation about Hooker is cited in Hunt, *Puritan Moment*, 197; Clarke, *Lives of thirty two English divines*, 131.
[236] Quoted in Francis Bremer and Ellen Rydell, 'Performance Art? Puritans in the Pulpit', *History Today*, 45/9 (1995), 52; Clarke, *Lives of thirty two English divines*, 12.

IOANNES MORVS S: Theo: Prof.
Ergo age Magne mori nil tandem More morare
Hic totus viues, nescic More mori
Corpore mente Simul te More hæc tabula pingit
Ille abſens aderis non moriture More

PLATE 46 Henry Holland, *Herωologia Anglica hoc est clarissimorum et doctissimorum* (London, 1620), 209. By permission of the Syndics of Cambridge University Library. Shelfmark: SSS. 40. 19. John More, the 'Apostle of Norwich'.

made use of the histrionic antics and mannerisms reprehended in Bernard's *Faithfull shepheard*—'unseemely gestures' such as violently 'casting abroad' one's limbs, sudden 'stouping downe' and 'very unadvisedly' standing erect, intemperately smiting the pulpit, thumping one's breast and, above all, the 'vaine and phantasticall motions' employed in 'prophane pastimes' and plays. Like Andreas Gerardus, he may have feared these techniques would minister occasion to 'scoffers and jesters amonge the rude sorte . . . to procure sport and laughter in their inn-kettinges and tipling feastes' by mimicking them.[237]

As Michael McGiffert has remarked, England's Hoseas also practised the storyteller's craft of suspense.[238] They kept God's sentence of spiritual desolation constantly pending, never presuming to pin down a date, though they did make audacious claims about the inevitability of this dreadful event. 'I am not a prophet,

[237] Bernard, *Faithfull shepheard*, 89–90; [Gerardus], *Practise of preaching*, fo. 177ᵛ.
[238] McGiffert, 'God's Controversy', 1169.

nor the sonne of a prophet to set the time, either of forty or fifty, daies or yeares more or lesse,' protested John King, alluding to Amos vii. 14; 'he sitteth above to whome it is best knowne, and is comming in the cloudes to determin that question'.[239] 'Am I a Prophet?', echoed John Lawrence; 'No, nor the Sonne of a Prophet, yet this I dare boldly say, Unlesse we suddenly repent, we perish.'[240] It was axiomatic that, unlike their Hebrew predecessors, the 'Evangelicall Prophets' of early modern England did not have 'Oraculous warning by Immediate Revelation'.[241] Theophany was a thing of the past, avowed one Elizabethan Zechariah, 'nowe we are not to looke' to be instructed by visions—'therefore away with all Anabaptisticall dreames'.[242] Occasionally, however, we do find Protestant ministers intimating that they had something like a direct line to the sky. 'But how long time hast thou, England, thou England?', Hugh Latimer cried to the Edwardian court; 'I cannot tell, for God hath not revealed it unto me; if he had, so God help me, I would tell you of it . . . but I cannot tell how long time ye have, for God hath not opened it unto me.'[243] Thomas Hooker went one step further in suggesting that he had been entrusted with a special ambassadorial mission: 'What if I should tell you what God told me yesternight that he would destroy England and lay it waste? . . . What sayest thou unto it, England? I must return an answer to my Master that sent me, yea, this present night'.[244]

It is not surprising that some eminent clerics acquired a reputation for prophesying the future. John Foxe was credited with foretelling the destruction of the Spanish Armada and James Ussher, primate of Ireland, with predicting the War of the Three Kingdoms. He earnt his place in contemporary history books with a sermon preached at Great St Mary's in Cambridge on Charles I's coronation day on 1 Samuel xii. ('If you still do wickedly, you shall be consumed, both you and your king'). John Preston was another preacher esteemed as an oracle: taking up a text from Isaiah at Whitehall in 1627, he insisted that God was whetting His sword to strike England and that His anger had already begun to manifest itself in 'blasted enterprizes', bad accidents, and the 'miscarriage of . . . businesse'. When news came through no more than a few days later of the disastrous retreat of the duke of Buckingham's expeditionary forces from La Rochelle and the Isle of Rhé, Preston was heralded a prophet and called a second Micah.[245]

---

[239] King, *Lectures upon Jonas*, 456.

[240] Lawrence, *Golden trumpet*, 14. Cf. Grent, *Burthen of Tyre*, 20.

[241] Gore, *Summer sermon*, in *Ten godly and fruitfull sermons*, 29; Dyke, *Sermon preached at the publicke fast*, 9. See also Jackson, *Judah must into captivitie*, 7, 83–5; Abbot, *Exposition upon the prophet Jonah*, 10–11; Udny, *Voyce of the cryer*, 57.

[242] A. W., *Fruitfull and godly sermon*, sig. A7^{r-v}.

[243] Latimer, *A most faithfull sermon*, in *Sermons*, ed. Corrie, 246.

[244] Hooker, *The Danger of Desertion*, in *Writings in England and Holland*, ed. Williams *et al.*, 244.

[245] On Foxe, see Thomas Fuller, *Abel redivivus or the dead yet speaking* (1651), 381–2. Foxe's prayers on behalf of the nation during the crisis were credited with being 'actually instrumental to the victory'. Latimer and Jewel were also alleged to have prophetic powers: Hugh Latimer, *27 sermons preached by the right reverende . . . maister Hugh Latimer* (1562), sig. A4^r and Laurence Humphrey, *Joannis Juelli Angli, episcopi Sarisburiensis vita et mors* (1573), 252–8. (I owe these references to Thomas Freeman.)

These cases are extremely revealing, but information about how most jeremiads were received is frustratingly scant. We simply do not know whether their hearers squirmed uncomfortably in their seats as the minister dissected society's ills, trembled and went pale in their pews, or turned a deaf ear to his disagreeable discourse. In the experience of Robert Bolton and Bartimaeus Andrewes the unregenerate rabble railed against the 'Jeremies, Michaiahs, and John Baptists of the time', reviling these 'true hearted Nathanaels' as 'pestilent Fellowes', 'blacke Ravens come from hell', 'Doctors of despaire, and unmercifull dispensers of damnation'.[246] According to Zelotes, the godly pastor in George Gifford's much-plundered *Countrie divinitie*, preachers who administered the harsh 'Corrasives and Cauterizations' of the Law were 'haynously taken' and 'sayd to be murtherers, beecause they preach but the dead letter which doth kill'.[247] The reprobate multitude could 'at no hand abide' this kind of 'home-speaking': the only sermons they applauded were those which sowed 'pillowes . . . under their arme-pits'.[248] Few divines differed in thinking that their daily and hourly warnings were scoffingly dismissed as 'olde wives' and 'winters tales', 'fables', 'unpleasing newes', and 'but a skar Crow', while they themselves were abused for making 'muche ado aboute nothing' and 'accounted as the filth of the street, and of-scouring of all things'.[249] The 'painefull Sermons' of England's Noahs, said Thomas Sutton despondently, too often 'proved but like paper bullets shot against a brazen wall'.[250] These rhetorically conditioned appraisals and vociferous complaints should, of course, be regarded with a degree of healthy scepticism: clerical pessimism was at least partly a side effect of internalization of the role of Old Testament prophet itself.[251] Repeated professional failure was inbuilt in the Israelite paradigm: God's emissaries expected—and, one suspects, even pretended—to be ignored, despised, and belittled.

It would be wrong to overlook the sizeable sector of a Paul's Cross congregation which, as Francis White observed, 'presse[d] to this and such like places' 'more for fashions sake then any true devotion', all too familiar with the providential commonplaces reiterated there every week.[252] Some probably regarded this type of preaching as a pious rigmarole: relatively unperturbed, even faintly bored, gluttons for punishment, they nevertheless kept returning for more.

On Ussher, Turner, *Compleat history*, pt I, p. 66. On Preston, *Sermons preached before his Majestie*, 83–4; Ball, *Life of the Renowned Doctor Preston*, ed. Harcourt, 159.

[246] Bolton, *Discourse about the state of true happinesse*, in *Workes*, 164–87, quotations at 165, 164, 178; Andrewes, *Certaine verie worthie, godly and profitable sermons*, 169.

[247] Bolton, *Discourse about the state of true happinesse*, in *Workes*, 158; Gifford, *Countrie divinitie*, fo. 75ʳ.

[248] Bernard, *Faithfull shepheard*, 71–2; Udny, *Voyce of the cryer*, 4, 11. Cf. William Hull, *Repentance not to be repented of* (1612), fo. 13ᵛ.

[249] Hampton, *Proclamation of warre*, 17; King, *Lectures upon Jonas*, 466; Stockwood, *Sermon preached at Paules Crosse on Barthelmew day*, 48, cf. 18; Price, *Laver of the heart*, 65, 69.

[250] Sutton, *Englands summons*, in *Englands first and second summons*, 16.

[251] For some echoes in Scripture, see Lam. iii. 45; 1 Cor. iv. 13; Luke xxiv. 11.

[252] White, *Londons warning, by Jerusalem*, 60.

Robert Saxby, a clothier from Brenchley in Kent, was one individual for whom such sermons apparently became rather addictive: he regularly trooped to St Anne's, Blackfriars, and Smithfield's St Bartholomew the Great to soak up the prophetic wisdom of William Gouge and Thomas Westfield, summarizing the expositions of Scripture he heard in a voluminous notebook, most of which, he concluded rather lazily, were 'very Remarkabell'.[253] We should also consider the evidence to the effect that the jeremiad was actually a crowd-pleaser. Manningham spoke of the urban 'multitude' thronging after popular preachers, hovering in church porches where they could barely hear their heroes, but might just glimpse them in the distance; and a Laudian bishop sneeringly compared lecturers with 'ballad singers and happy horse sellers' because of the large audiences they attracted in market towns and fairs.[254] Perhaps some found their terror tactics and tongue-lashings rather invigorating, taking perverse pleasure in the recurrent threat that God was about to annihilate England—much as their modern counterparts might relish a horror film or read an enthralling cliffhanger or thriller. Those who took down sermons in their pocket diaries verbatim, engaged in 'repetition' of their substance and 'heads', were 'verie instant' with their local minister to print them, or sent their own notes to the press without obtaining permission must be adjudged true enthusiasts.[255] On children and adolescents prophetic rhetoric could have an electrifying and intoxicating effect—as the outbursts of that 11-year-old Jeremiah William Withers of Walsham-le-Willows, and the diabolical/divine speeches of Thomas Darling, the young demoniac from Staffordshire dispossessed by John Darrell in 1586, attest. An ardent disciple of Arthur Hildersham of Ashby-de-la-Zouche, the 'Boy of Burton' hoped he might live 'to thunder out the threatenings of Gods word, against sinne and all abhominations, wherewith these dayes doo abound'.[256]

Sermons, remarked the celebrated demagogue Stephen Marshall, were like 'bellowes', 'of great power to stirre up' and inflame the 'coales' of men's hearts: 'experience shewes us that zealous preaching makes zealous people'.[257] Sometimes such occasions resembled revivalist camp meetings or sessions of group psychotherapy. Like the great open-air communion services of 'holy fairs' which became such a central feature of Scottish presbyterian culture in the early seventeenth century, they too must be regarded as deeply satisfying and stimulating

[253] CUL Add. MS 3117. See e.g. fo. 15ᵛ. He usually added that the preacher had raised many good 'excamples' and 'docctrines', fos. 9ʳ⁻ᵛ, 10ʳ. Saxby's notebook also includes a transcription of most of Thomas Sutton's *Englands second summons*: fos. 119ᵛ–129ʳ.

[254] Manningham, *Diary*, ed. Bruce, 75; PRO SP 16/493/28 (Petition of the parish of St Dionis Back-Church, London, to the House of Commons, [Dec.] 1642, regarding the innovations and outrages of Dr John Warner, bishop of Rochester and rector of the church).

[255] On sermon repetition, see Collinson, 'English Conventicle', 240–4. Richard Stock claimed that his auditors were 'verie instant with mee to print it': *Sermon preached at Paules Crosse on Barthelmew day*, sig. *8ʳ. Two sets of notes of Hooker's *The Danger of Desertion* have survived: see id., *Writings in England and Holland*, ed. Williams *et al.*, 221–2.

[256] For Withers, see Ch. 4, above. For Darling, Bee, *Most wonderfull and true storie*, ed. Denison, 2.

[257] Marshall, *Divine project*, 40 [*vere* 44].

rituals which could lead to emotional outpouring and cathartic release.[258] Famous preachers like John Rogers of Dedham could reduce their congregations to a quivering mass by 'personating' God threatening to take the Bible away from the wicked English people. This heart-rending skit wrought 'so strange an impression' that 'the place was a mere Bochim, the people generally . . . deluged with their own tears'. And at least one of his hearers, when the service was over, was 'fain to hang a quarter of an hour upon the neck of his horse weeping before he had power to mount'. So many crowded into the church where his funeral was held in 1636 to pay him tribute that the gallery 'sunck and crackt' and threatened to collapse. '[H]ad yt faln as blackfryars did under the popish assembly, yt would have ben a great wound to our religion,' one contemporary noted, but 'yt pleased God to honour that good man departed with a miracle at his death' and prevent the floor from falling in.[259] These were the television evangelists of late Tudor and early Stuart England, cult figures and bearers of religious charisma.

Was providential preaching, then, intrinsically unappealing to the majority of the early modern populace? Were godly ministers as impossibly out of touch with their auditors, as stubbornly inflexible in their approach to the task of refashioning traditional mentalities, as revisionist historians have sometimes implied? This chapter has sketched a rather different scenario. Susan Brigden has spoken of preaching as 'a popular spectator sport' in the mid-sixteenth century, when Protestantism enjoyed the prestige of an irreverent protest movement.[260] A sensitive reading of the English jeremiad suggests it may have retained some of its allure even after the 'new religion' had shed its novel first skin. Prophetic discourses were not overly cerebral and they betray manifest links and continuities with their medieval predecessors and with the multifarious products of the ephemeral press. Sermons which presented the spectacle of God's terrible judgements were not inconsistent with the proclivities of those who spent their hard-earned pennies on sensational but moralistic newsprint. In short, they sit uneasily with conventional characterizations of Calvinism as coldly rational and introspectively bookish. Zealous Protestantism could, in the broadest sense of the term, be a popular religion.

[258] Schmidt, *Holy Fairs*, 87–8.
[259] *The Works of Thomas Goodwin, D.D., Sometime President of Magdalene College, Oxford*, ed. J. C. Miller, 11 vols. (Edinburgh, 1861–5), vol. ii, pp. xvii–xviii; Emmanuel Downing, writing to John Winthrop on 6 Mar. 1636: *Winthrop Papers*, ed. Ford *et al.*, iii. 369.
[260] Brigden, 'Youth and the English Reformation', 100.

Conclusion

On 15 January 1636, William Rogers, a young apothecary who had practised 'Chirurgery and Physicke' in the large and populous parish of Cranbrook in Kent, was solemnly buried. At his funeral, attended by many of his grieving patients and neighbours, the local vicar Robert Abbot preached a moving sermon on the text of Proverbs iv. 19 ('The way of the wicked is as darknesse; they know not at what they stumble'). Fulfilling the unmarried doctor's last dying wish, Abbot traced his slippery descent into licentiousness and impiety and admonished his 'wicked companions' 'to runne from the stinking dens of sinne'. Brought up in a religious household, only in his early adulthood had Rogers begun to stray from the path of righteousness: 'First, delight in vaine company crept upon him, next drunkennesse, next neglect of Prayer, Word and Sacraments; and lastly a setled obstinacy in these sinnefull and bewitching courses.' Repeatedly exhorted to amendment by his diligent pastor and threatened with excommunication for his contumacy, at length the prodigal resolved to return contritely to the fold. But on the very morning of his promised reappearance at church he fell ill with 'the fit of an Ague', which, in less than a fortnight, would convey him to his grave. Overwhelmed by remorse and guilt and frenzied with despair, Rogers's final hours were 'deeply mudded in horrour and perplexity': in them he fully internalized the wrath of the Almighty against him, experiencing the psychological torment of a self-accusing conscience. The outcome of this 'whole combate' was an unshakeable conviction that because he had cast off Christ he must be eternally damned. Just before he died he passed 'this heavie doome upon himselfe, I must bee burned in the furnace of Hell millions and millions of ages'. Despite Rogers's own certainty about his reprobate status, Abbot told his auditors that speculation about his 'finall estate' was to be firmly eschewed, judgement on this matter being reserved 'to the highest tribunall'.[1]

The deathbed paroxysms of this Wealden apothecary, as described by Robert Abbot, bear a striking resemblance to the tortuous inner struggle of that most famous of spiritual renegades, the Venetian lawyer Francis Spiera. So arresting are the similarities that it is tempting to suggest that the Cranbrook clergyman had consciously modelled his narrative on this classic cautionary tale about the

---

[1] Abbot, *Young-mans warning-peece*, quotations at 6, 2, 5, 9, 13, 18–19, 22, 23, 5, 6 respectively. William Rogers's burial on 15 Jan. 1636, together with a later note concerning Abbot's sermon, is recorded in the parish register: Centre for Kentish Studies, Maidstone, P100/1/15 (Register of Baptisms, Marriages and Burials, Cranbrook, 1559–1667). For the ecclesiastical history of Cranbrook in this period, see Collinson, 'Cranbrook and the Fletchers', esp. 427–8.

terrible consequences of religious apostasy—a tale which by the 1630s was already something of a Protestant topos.[2] Published a few months after William Rogers's funeral, by April Abbot's sermon *The young-mans warning-peece* had been crudely summarized in a ballad, a 'mournefull ditty' designed to be sung to the sombre 'preaching tune' of 'Doctor Faustus' or 'Fortune my Foe'.[3] And like Spiera himself, Rogers was destined to pass into godly mythology and become a paradigm of the psychomachy which accompanied evangelical conversion. In 1649, the story of his 'woefull death' was retold in a pamphlet entitled *The terror of a troubled spirit*.[4]

This Kentish vignette neatly encapsulates some of the central themes of this book. It highlights the degree to which preaching and cheap print were interacting spheres of discourse in early modern England. Just as there was a constant two-way flow between published texts and oral tradition,[5] so were sermons and inexpensive ephemera symbiotically linked, caught in a complex and mutually enriching equilibrium. Seepage and haemorrhage occurred in both directions. Stories of God's judgements first recorded in the devotional works of grave Calvinist divines might reappear as popular songs, shorn of theological subtlety and set to the strains of a well-known melody; moralistic journalism rustled up by unscrupulous stationers and hacks might be immortalized in clerical anthologies and reference books; 'strange newes' of apparitions, portents, and tragic accidents could travel back and forth across the frontiers between literacy and illiteracy, piety and profit. Clearly, pamphleteers and Paul's Cross prophets, red-nosed rhymsters and zealous ministers, cannot always be situated in stark opposition. Indeed sometimes they can even be found in active collusion. The world of the pulpit and edifying tract was by no means inherently at odds with the world of commercial publishing and the titillating broadside.

The episode in Caroline Cranbrook may also shed fresh light on the rough and irregular interface between clerically prescribed predestinarian piety and the mentality of sections of lay society usually jumbled into the category of the 'profane' and 'ungodly'. Like other incidents we have explored in the course of this book, it suggests that the relationship between the fervent Protestantism of 'professors of the Gospel' and the religious outlook of those they labelled 'atheists' and 'reprobates' is rather more intriguing than some recent scholarship has presumed. We need to set aside rigid dichotomies and sterile polarities and demonstrate

---

[2] See MacDonald, 'Fearefull Estate of Francis Spira'. As noted in Ch. 2 n. 80 above, there are two extant contemporary accounts by Gribaldi and Bacon. Bacon's account was circulating in MS prior to publication. Spira's story was also summarized in a ballad registered in 1587 and in Beard, *Theatre*, 73–4.

[3] *Youths warning-peice. In a true relation of the woefull death of William Rogers of Cranbroke in Kent an Apothecary, who refusing all good counsell, and following lewd company, dyed miserably* (1636). Entered *SR* 8 Apr. 1636: iv. 359.

[4] *The terror of a troubled spirit* (1649), which also included an account of the deaths of Francis Spiera and Anthony Fittes, is cited in William Tarbutt, *The Annals of Cranbrook Church . . .*, 3 vols. (Cranbrook, 1875), iii. 29. I have been unable to trace it.

[5] Watt, *Cheap Print*, esp. 323; Niccoli, *Prophecy and People*, pp. xii–xiii.

sensitivity to the 'on-going dialogue or dialectic' between the two;[6] we need to discard models which stress fierce confrontation and stubborn resistance for ones which emphasize cautious negotiation and creative compromise.[7]

Similar remarks might be made about the Calvinist doctrine of providence and those alternative systems of explanation and action which it was designed to displace and erase. Protestant providentialism, I have argued, was a flexible and permeable conceptual framework within which some older and ostensibly incompatible habits of thought could be absorbed with relative ease. In turn it was assimilated into a broader filament and tissue of beliefs about the intrusion of supernatural forces in the earthly sphere. Notwithstanding the intolerance of Reformed dogma towards rival ideologies like magic and astrology, fate, chance, and fortune, what we have uncovered in tales of God's judgements and stories of prodigies and portents is evidence of a fruitful and enduring synthesis: novel priorities interweave with inherited formulas, orthodox religious tenets blend with proverbial wisdom and indigenous folklore.[8]

This reciprocal process was facilitated by the existence of areas of ambiguity within Protestant theology itself: ambiguity about the relationship between human activity and divine will, about the actual mechanisms by which the Lord brought His purposes to pass, about the precise status and proper interpretation of occult phenomena.[9] Around the hazy edges and in the more dimly lit corners of Calvinist doctrine potential contradictions could lie undisturbed and old and new could coexist without too much friction.[10]

These regions of partial overlap and imperfect correlation are surely of considerable significance in the context of England's prolonged, patchy, and political Reformation—in the context of a national Church comprised largely of involuntary Protestants. Such continuities must have done much to smooth the turbulent passage of the mid-Tudor religious revolution. Too often the Reformation has been characterized as an aggressive effort to implant a set of alien precepts in a hostile intellectual environment, an iconoclastic campaign which swept away time-honoured attitudes and customs and replaced them with innovatory precepts and practices which inevitably offended the instincts and sensibilities of conservative laypeople. This book, however, has painted a rather different picture. Like Bob

---

[6] Lake, 'Popular Form, Puritan Content?', 333 and *passim*. See also id., 'Deeds against Nature', 258, 277, 283 and *passim*; Holmes, 'Popular Culture? Witches, Magistrates and Divines', esp. 94, 99–100, 103–4, 105.

[7] See Peter Burke, 'A Question of Acculturation?', in *Scienze credenze occulte livelli di cultura: Convegno internazionale di studi* (Florence, 1980), esp. 204, and Valerie Flint's illuminating exploration of the dialogue between the church and magic in the early Middle Ages: *Rise of Magic in Early Medieval Europe*, esp. 400, 407.

[8] Cf. Duffy's remarks on late medieval religious culture: *Stripping of the Altars*, esp. 60, 72, 184. David Hall and Raymond Gillespie paint a very similar picture for New England and Ireland in the same period: Hall, *Worlds of Wonder*, 7, 11, and ch. 2 *passim*; Gillespie, 'Religion of Irish Protestants' and *Devoted People*, chs. 6–7.

[9] See above, 14–15, 226–32, 176–80 respectively.

[10] Note the similar remarks of Godbeer, *Devil's Dominion*, 17.

Scribner's work on the cult of 'incombustible Luther' and Leigh Eric Schmidt's research on festal communions in presbyterian Scotland, it has revealed 'some interesting wrinkles' on popular Protestantism and its connection with late medieval Catholicism. It has highlighted further aspects of traditional observance and piety which were not eliminated but 'rehabilitated and maintained in Reformed guise'.[11] As we have seen, many anecdotes of providential punishment had precursors in the legends of the saints; post-Reformation prophets followed in the footsteps of the itinerant evangelists and plebeian seers of the late Middle Ages; celestial apparitions were superficially Protestantized and allowed to persist; and the patterns of activity inherent in Roman Catholic propitiary rituals were reproduced in the rites of appeasement to which afflicted individuals and communities resorted after 1559. Miracles and martyrs likewise resurfaced, albeit somewhat modified in line with the new Calvinist climate. The syncretism between pre- and post-Reformation forms which these phenomena reflect suggests that the advent of Protestantism did not effect as sharp and radical a break with the past as much of the historiography of this subject has implied.

However, it would be wrong to interpret them merely as evidence of Catholic survivalism, the resilience and dissimulation of popular belief in the face of a particularly aggressive type of cultural imperialism. Nor is it always simply a case of Protestant ministers tacitly condoning and tolerating what they could not eradicate, turning a blind eye to dubious, if relatively innocuous, tendencies.[12] Godly reformers did not set out to suppress and smother beliefs about divine interference in the natural world and human affairs; on the contrary they nourished and encouraged them.[13] Anxious to undermine devotion to the saints and false presuppositions about the power of witches, they laid fresh, indeed unprecedented, emphasis on the omnipotence of God and placed providence at the very centre of their eschatalogical thinking. Eager to uproot sin and iniquity, they promoted the notion of what Bob Scribner called 'a moralised cosmos': deformed babies, destructive tempests, dreadful calamities, and raging epidemics were all declared to be signs of divine wrath and forerunners of impending punishments.[14]

We also cannot afford to ignore the extent to which Protestant ministers actively exploited, engaged with, and sought to rechannel common assumptions. Historians are beginning to question the view that clerical evangelists made no concessions to the intellectual capacities and cultural heritage of the constituencies they sought to arouse and persuade. Michael MacDonald has shown how divines adopted medieval and demotic beliefs about suicide to win the souls of inveterate sinners; Peter Lake and Michael Questier have recently revealed how imaginatively they

---

[11] Scribner, 'Incombustible Luther'; Schmidt, *Holy Fairs*, 213 and *passim*.

[12] Cf. Scribner, 'Introduction', in id. and Trevor Johnson (eds.), *Popular Religion in Germany and Central Europe, 1400–1800* (Basingstoke, 1996), 10–11.

[13] For a somewhat similar argument, see Ann Kibbey, 'Mutations of the Supernatural: Witchcraft, Remarkable Providences, and the Power of Puritan Men', *American Quarterly*, 34 (1982), 125–48.

[14] Scribner, 'Introduction', in id. and Johnson (eds.), *Popular Religion*, 8; and id., 'Reformation, Popular Magic, and the "Disenchantment of the World"', 485.

could use the prison and scaffold as sites for converting the religiously indifferent, enlisting the emotional and ideological energies released by the spectacle of the public execution to sway uncommitted members of the crowd.[15] The dispossessions performed by puritan exorcists might likewise be seen as ingenious forms of missionary activity.[16] In the same way preachers deliberately harnessed drastic accidents, appalling disasters, and national emergencies to incite their congregations to heartfelt contrition and urge them to return to the path of righteousness. Here, as in the course of catechizing, they adjusted their language and message according to their audience and the pastoral context, avoiding thorny issues and glossing over some of the more arcane and paradoxical aspects of Protestant theology.[17] They allowed people to believe that God responded spontaneously to their prayers; that flagrant offenders came to bad ends and descended automatically to hell; that human beings could play a part in their own redemption; that there was still a place for miracles in post-Reformation cosmology.[18] In this respect they may perhaps be congratulated for 'a canny sense of priorities', even if it was sometimes at the expense of academic orthodoxy and at the risk of perpetuating older rhythms of thought.[19]

No less significant is the continuing willingness of zealous Protestant clergymen to present their message of repentance and providence in imaginative ways. Patrick Collinson and Tessa Watt have highlighted how readily the early reformers harnessed traditional media like ballads, pictures, and plays for polemical and evangelical purposes: their use of genres combining text, image, and song represented a studied attempt to exploit and reshape the culture of the sub- and semi-literate. As Protestantism made the transition from dissident sect to settled institutional Church it undoubtedly adopted a more sober and authoritarian tone, turning away from some of the techniques it had warmly embraced in its initial revolutionary phase.[20] But there are grounds for thinking that the alleged withdrawal from inherited cultural materials and commercially successful formats around 1580 was neither as abrupt nor as complete as at first glance it seems. Peter Lake's cases of puritan pirating of the murder pamphlet can be supplemented by examples of clerical conscription of 'true and wonderful newes' as a vehicle for moral exhortation, doctrinal instruction, and sectarian propaganda.[21] Nor should we forget the theatrical and revivalist qualities of prophetic preaching: they suggest that

---

[15] MacDonald and Murphy, *Sleepless Souls*, 31, 35; MacDonald, *Mystical Bedlam*, esp. 167–8, 174–5. Lake and Questier, 'Agency, Appropriation and Rhetoric under the Gallows', and eid. 'Prisons, Priests and People', in Nicholas Tyacke (ed.), *England's Long Reformation 1500–1800* (1998), 195–233.

[16] Walker, *Unclean Spirits*, 4–5 and *passim*.

[17] Green, *Christian's ABC*, 276, 298–9, 386, 569.

[18] See above, 150–6, 103–4, 305–7, 226–32 respectively.

[19] Adapting an insight of Ronald Hutton in 'English Reformation and the Evidence of Folklore', 116.

[20] Collinson, *From Iconoclasm to Iconophobia*; id., *Birthpangs*, ch. 4; Watt, *Cheap Print*, ch. 2. See also Geoffrey Parker, 'Success and Failure during the First Century of the Reformation', *P&P* 136 (1992), 63–9.

[21] Lake, 'Deeds against Nature'; 'Puritanism, Arminianism and a Shropshire Axe-Murder'; 'Popular Form, Puritan Content?'.

Protestant ministers were no less expert at invoking and manipulating the emotions of their hearers than enterprising Jesuit missionaries in England and other parts of Europe which the Society sought to reclaim to Catholicism.[22] Philip Soergel's recent study of the Counter-Reformation in Bavaria ascribes its triumph in the region to the creativity of its lay and clerical protagonists, to their skilful appropriation of older rituals, beliefs, and practices to revive enthusiasm for the resurgent Church of Rome. In their struggle for confessional hegemony, he contends, they exploited one of Protestantism's 'weakest links': its inability to foster devotions that could rival the wonder-working appeal of traditional religion.[23] The evidence presented here almost directly contradicts this view. Indeed it underlines that flexibility and adaptability to different social strata and cultural conditions which helped make Calvinism into such a successful international movement and which allowed it to penetrate areas ranging from Hungary and Prussia to tiny pockets high in the Pyrenees and remote districts of the Gaelic-speaking Scottish Highlands and Islands.[24]

Of course, the providentialism of the bulk of the populace was not a passive clone of the intense and introspective variety recommended by the clergy and practised by the 'saints'. Unlearned parishioners subtly edited, altered, and ignored the elaborate tenets propounded by their university-educated pastors and preachers. In the eyes of puritan ministers like George Gifford, the hybrid of half-digested predestinarian doctrine and half-remembered Romanist teaching engendered by this process was as much a 'mingle-mangle' as the Elizabethan Settlement itself. He and his colleagues were apt to brand the religion of the 'common sort of Christians' as residually 'popish' and 'pagan', as Catholic and heathen 'superstition' intermixed with 'a little smacke of the Gospell'.[25] But we should not take their rhetorically inflated statements too literally. We should not deny the religious culture of rural congregations the label 'Protestant' just because it betrays traces of earlier systems of thinking and living. It is probably more useful to think of it as an organic unity within which, as Scott Dixon has argued, traditional attitudes were gradually invested with different values until the original framework for understanding was shattered. Beliefs, by this means, were slowly but thoroughly transformed.[26]

[22] Cf. Duffy, 'Long Reformation', 64, whose negative comments in this regard are criticized by Collinson, 'Comment', 82. For Jesuit techniques see Gentilcore, 'Missionary Strategies'; Johnson, 'Blood, Tears and Xavier-Water'.

[23] Philip Soergel, *Wondrous in his Saints: Counter-Reformation Propaganda in Bavaria* (Berkeley and Los Angeles 1993), esp. 4, 9–10, 99–101, 159, 229.

[24] See the essays in Andrew Pettegree, Alastair Duke, and Gillian Lewis (eds.), *Calvinism in Europe 1540–1620* (Cambridge, 1994), esp. Jane Dawson, 'Calvinism and the Gaidhealtachd in Scotland', 231–53.

[25] See e.g. Gifford, *Countrie divinitie*, fos. 26ᵛ–27ʳ. This dialectic between clerical and lay religion is one of the chief themes of Gillespie, *Devoted People*.

[26] C. Scott Dixon, *The Reformation and Rural Society: The Parishes of Brandenburg-Ansbach-Kulmbach, 1528–1603* (Cambridge, 1996), 201–2. For a similar way of conceptualizing cultural change, see Carlo Ginzburg, *Ecstasies: Deciphering the Witches' Sabbath* (Harmondsworth, 1991), esp. introd. and conclusion. Note also John Van Engen's comments about the 'total synthesis' of Christian and non-

Nor should we share the conviction of the clergy that men and women who continued to make use of the services of astrologers, healers, diviners, and wizards were necessarily 'unreformed'. Protestantism could not and did not eliminate the ideological eclecticism which characterized lay mentalities at every level, it merely added another element to the repertoire of ideas and techniques contemporaries drew upon to account for the catastrophic and inexplicable and to alleviate their troubles and misfortunes. Ordinary individuals invoked varying explanations according to the situations and circumstances in which they found themselves. On the other hand, ingrained providential assumptions did not preclude a degree of practical scepticism and 'rationalism' on particular occasions: late Tudor and early Stuart commentators complained about the credulity of the 'meaner' and 'vulgar sorts of people' but they also deplored the impiety of parishioners who demanded where Adam and Eve had acquired the thread to sew their coats of fig leaves, thought biblical stories like the feeding of the five thousand on five loaves and fishes implausible, and attributed floods, storms, and fires to the vagaries of Dame Fortune and the workings of an autonomous Nature.[27] Scholars and learned gentlemen likewise moved between models of causation depending on the evidence which lay before them.

We also need to consider Keith Thomas's contention that the Reformation may actually have fostered greater recourse to 'non-religious' strategies for counteracting their tribulations and afflictions. Deprived of the ritual equipment with which late medieval Christians had combated daily adversities and informed that repentance, prayer, and patient reliance on divine will were the only legitimate staffs they could lean on, it is quite possible that early modern Protestants turned to magic and astrology in default.[28] This development, it might be suggested, does not reflect hostility to the Reformation so much as adaptation to the theological environment which was now in place. Moreover, as Richard Godbeer has argued in the context of early New England, it may in fact attest to a deep internalization of Protestant precepts: forms of divination provided a release from precisely those anxieties about one's spiritual status engendered by Calvinist soteriology itself.[29] Intent on penetrating the mystery of election and discovering the secrets of the future, people twisted keys in Bibles and prayer books and laid great store by the passages at which they were randomly opened.[30] Despairing of her own salvation, the godly

---

Christian in medieval religious culture: 'The Christian Middle Ages as an Historiographical Problem', *American Historical Review*, 91 (1986), 519–52.

[27] Parishioners demanding to know where Adam and Eve obtained thread to sew their coats of fig leaves are cited in Martin Ingram, 'From Reformation to Toleration: Popular Religious Cultures in England, 1540–1690', in Tim Harris (ed.), *Popular Culture in England, c.1500–1850* (Basingstoke, 1995), 106. For popular doubts about biblical literalism, see Topsell, *Historie of foure-footed beastes*, sig. A5ᵛ.

[28] Thomas, *Religion and the Decline of Magic*, 89, 132, and chs. 7–12; Scribner, 'Introduction', in id. and Johnson (eds.), *Popular Religion*, 9.

[29] Godbeer, *Devil's Dominion*, esp. 52.

[30] David Cressy, 'Books as Totems in Seventeenth-Century England and New England', *Journal of Library History*, 21 (1986), esp. 99–102.

matriarch Mary Honeywood violently hurled a Venetian glass to the ground declaring that she was as 'surely damn'd' as it would be shattered into fragments: when it 'rebounded again, and was taken up whole and entire', observers thought the episode 'little lesse than miraculous'.[31] And, as we have seen, puritans were no less prone than their non-puritan neighbours to decipher *digitus dei* in meteorological, botanical, and zoological oddities and to scrutinize them as oracular signposts. Despite the despondency of the parochial ministry, providentialism seems to have been no less important a part of the piety of 'cold statute Protestants' than of experimental Calvinists.

It also functioned as a cultural adhesive uniting disparate groups at moments of communal emergency and crisis—not least those junctures at which the fate of England herself seemed to be hanging precariously in the balance. When hostile Catholic powers were poised to invade her shores and the papist fifth column at home threatened to subvert her from within, belief in providence fused with anti-popery and xenophobia to create a potent brand of patriotism and to forge a powerful sense of confessional identity. When foreign navies failed and assassination plots were sabotaged, it fostered an inspiring myth of elect English nationhood. But, alternately self-congratulatory and self-castigating, providentialism had the capacity to undercut as well as promote cultural and ideological homogeneity. It was a common language and vision fraught with internal contradictions and tensions, a pliant discourse which could precipitate social, ecclesiastical, and political polarization.[32] Not only was it slowly mutating in the circles of the learned under the influence of advances in natural philosophy and embryonic epistemological shifts; it also became both a stimulus to and an index of the instability and conflict which characterized the decades leading up to 1642.

These tendencies were greatly exacerbated by the Civil War and Interregnum: the engulfment of providence in factional strife and sectarian struggle assisted in undermining its credibility and contributed to a growing disavowal of previous assumptions about the scope and legibility of divine activity on earth—at least in some sectors of society and the Church. In the face of its appropriation by radical groups and the proliferation of crudely partisan publications employing it as a polemical weapon and tool, providentialism began very gradually to retreat to the edges of the intellectual mainstream.[33] Simultaneously, cheap print about supernatural phenomena started to liberate itself from the role of mere handmaiden to the pulpit and tip the balance away from edification towards entertainment.[34] By the late seventeenth century it was becoming commonplace for Newtonian

---

[31] Fuller, *Worthies*, 2nd pagination, 86.

[32] Here I have been influenced by the comments of Kevin Sharpe and Peter Lake, 'Introduction' to eid. (eds.), *Culture and Politics in Early Stuart England* (Basingstoke, 1994), 11–12, 17–20; David Underdown, *A Freeborn People: Politics and the Nation in Seventeenth-Century England* (Oxford, 1996), 9–18, chs. 2–3, and *passim*.

[33] Much recent work has conceptualized the decline of witchcraft and supernatural beliefs in these terms. See the works cited in Ch. 4 n. 228, above.

[34] Thomas, 'From Edification to Entertainment'.

scientists and Royal Society theologians to link 'fanatical' dissenting sects and evangelical Calvinists with the gullible multitude, assailing their mutual fascination with prodigies, portents, and special providences as a contemptible form of 'enthusiasm' and 'superstition'. In dissociating themselves from the notion that the Almighty perpetually intervened in the temporal realm, Restoration exponents of 'rational religion' were effectively redrawing the boundary between official and unofficial belief, marginalizing a body of ideas which had long been part of Protestant as well as Roman Catholic orthodoxy.[35] Even so, as historians of the eighteenth century will remind us, there was a lingering incompleteness about this process of erosion: such convictions persisted, and not merely among the 'ignorant' poor but also their better educated social superiors.[36]

In the long run Protestant theology and the technology of print did perhaps contribute to the dissolution of older ways of explaining the puzzling and unpredictable, but the evidence presented in this book suggests that in the short term they operated in the opposite direction, reanimating rather than eradicating a rich seam of assumptions about the occult. The preceding chapters strongly reinforce Bob Scribner's thesis that the Reformation did not in fact lead to the demystification of Christianity and 'the disenchantment of the world'. It did react fiercely against the materialism of late medieval piety by stressing the inner, spiritual, and metaphysical aspects of worship and faith; it did seek to draw firmer boundaries between the coercion and the supplication of sacred power; it did redefine the sacrament of the mass as a symbolic re-enactment rather than an ineffable thaumaturgic act. But it cannot without serious qualification be heralded as the grandsire of the Enlightenment, a kind of halfway house on the road to 'the age of reason'. Protestantism may have presented itself as a deliberate attempt to remove the magical and miraculous elements from religion, but its overall effect was surely to leave the universe saturated with supernatural forces and moral significance.[37]

---

[35] See Richard S. Westfall, *Science and Religion in Seventeenth-Century England* (New Haven, 1958), ch. 4; John Redwood, *Reason, Ridicule and Religion: The Age of Enlightenment in England 1660–1750* (1976), esp. ch. 6; Michael Hunter, *Science and Society in Restoration England* (Cambridge, 1981), esp. ch. 7.

[36] I am grateful to Jonathan Barry for discussions on this point.

[37] See Scribner, 'Reformation, Popular Magic, and the "Disenchantment of the World"', and note the comments of Lake, 'Popular Form, Puritan Content?', 332–3. Cf. Thomas, *Religion and the Decline of Magic*, chs. 3–4, esp. 87–9; Eire, *War against the Idols*, 311–18.

BIBLIOGRAPHY OF PRIMARY SOURCES

Full bibliographical details of secondary sources will be found at their first reference in the footnotes. Anonymous items are alphabetized under the first significant word of the title. A number of the conjectural dates and authorial attributions made by the compilers of the *STC* have been rejected. *STC* and Wing numbers have been included where relevant. Place of publication is London unless otherwise stated. Where an edition other than the first has been used 'edn.' has been added after the date of publication or the number of the edition has been supplied.

MANUSCRIPT SOURCES

Bury St Edmunds, Suffolk Record Office

FL 522/11/22 (Townwardens' accounts, Bardwell).

Cambridge, University Library

Additional MS 3117 (Commonplace book of Robert Saxby, clothier of Brenchley in Kent).
Additional MS 3320 (Notebook from *c.*1614–29, including notes of sermons delivered in Cambridge between 1627 and 1629).
MS Dd. 3. 64 (Letters of Matthew Poole).
MS Dd. 11. 73 (Commonplace book of William Whiteway 1618–34).
MS Mm. 1. 29 (Notebook of Thomas Earl, minister of St Mildred, Breadstreet, 1564–1600).
MS Oo. 6. 115 (Miscellaneous notes and extracts of William Jackson, fl. 1675–95).

Cambridge, Trinity College

MS O. 7. 3 (Historical collection relating to the reign of Charles I, anonymous diary 1625–7).
MS R. 16. 22 (Painted prophecy of Paul Graebner presented to Elizabeth I, 1585).

Gloucester, Cathedral Library

MS 40 (Fragments of letters and other loose papers).

Ipswich, Suffolk Record Office

FC 62 D1/1 (Parish register of St Mary, Cratfield).

London, British Library

Additional MS 6177 (Copies of letters and documents preserved among the Burghley and Cecil Papers at Hatfield House, 1585–1609).
Additional MS 15225 (Poems and songs compiled *c.*1616, apparently by a Catholic).
Additional MS 21203 (Papers relating to the English Jesuits).
Additional MS 21935 (Nehemiah Wallington, 'Historical Notices').
Additional MS 28032 (Diary of Walter Yonge, 1604–1628).
Additional MS 35331 (Diary of Walter Yonge, 1628–April 1642).
Additional MS 38492 (Townshend Papers, vol. i. Religious Questions).

Additional MS 38599 (Commonplace book of the Shanne family of Methley, Yorkshire).

Additional MS 70062 (Memoranda of Sir Robert Harley, unbound).

Cotton MS Vespasian A. XXV (Collection of ballads, songs, and other miscellaneous transcriptions made by Henry Savile of Banke (1568–1617), probably recusant, mainly *c.*1576).

Egerton MS 784 (Diary of William Whiteway of Dorchester, 1618–34).

Egerton MS 1693 (Letters addressed to Robert Beale, clerk of the Privy Council, 1569–1593).

Harleian MS 353 (Historical Collections 1546–1559).

Harleian MSS 389–90 (Letters of Joseph Mede to Sir Martin Stutevile, 1620–5, 1626–31).

Harleian MS 416 (Papers of John Foxe).

Harleian MS 651 (Miscellaneous medieval chronicles and an account of a miracle at Ipswich, 1516).

Harleian MS 1221 (Miscellaneous tracts and papers).

Harleian MS 7019 (Miscellaneous papers of the seventeenth century, including a report on 'innovations' in Laudian Cambridge).

Lansdowne MS 6 (Burghley Papers 1562–3).

Lansdowne MS 7 (Burghley Papers 1563–4).

Lansdowne MS 15 (Burghley Papers 1572).

Lansdowne MS 19 (Burghley Papers 1574–5).

Lansdowne MS 30 (Burghley Papers 1580).

Lansdowne MS 33 (Burghley Papers 1581).

Lansdowne MS 37 (Burghley Papers 1582–3).

Lansdowne MS 99 (Burghley Papers, miscellaneous).

Lansdowne MS 101 (Burghley Papers, miscellaneous).

Lansdowne MS 207C (*Collectanea* of Gervase Holles, iii).

Lansdowne MS 819 (Papers relating to Dr Fox and his family, 1584–1654).

Royal MS A XIX (Petition from Henoch Clapham to Henry Prince of Wales 1604).

Sloane MS 397 (Nathaniel Bacon, 'A relation of the state of Francis Spira').

Sloane MS 598 (Notes of sermons delivered in Cambridge in the first half of the seventeenth century).

Sloane MS 648 (Prophecies and visions).

Sloane MS 1457 (Nehemiah Wallington, 'A Memorial of Gods Judgements upon Sabbath Breakers, Drunkards and Other Vile Livers, 1632').

Stowe MS 156 (Transcripts of state papers and political tracts, *c.*1565–1629).

London, Dr Williams's Library

MS Morrice A ('Old Loose Papers').

MS Morrice B(2) ('A Seconde Parte of a Register').

London, Guildhall Library

MS 959/1 (Vestry minutes and churchwardens' accounts, St Martin, Orgar, 1471–1615).

MS 5020 (The 'Great Book' of the parish of St Pancras, Soper Lane, 1616–1740).

London, Inner Temple Library

MS Petyt 538, vol. 47 (Original documents and transcripts); vol. 52 (Transcripts of letters, mainly on ecclesiastical matters, and largely addressed to John Whitgift, archbishop of Canterbury, 1579–85).

London, Lambeth Palace Library

MS 1485 (Inscriptions in London churches, *c*.1638).

London, Public Record Office, Chancery Lane

SP 12/17, 23, 155, 194, 283 (State Papers Domestic, Elizabeth I).
SP 14/21, 117, 152, 153, 154 (State Papers Domestic, James I).
SP 15/11, 28, 42 (State Papers Domestic, Addenda).
SP 16/32, 141, 142, 278, 303, 327, 335, 350, 354, 355, 361, 362, 493 (State Papers Domestic, Charles I).

London, University of London Library, Senate House

Carlton MSS Box 17/8 ('Certaine sermons godley & learnedley preached by Mr Nicholas Felton Doctor of Divinitie and taken from his mouth by ——').
IHR MS 979 (Anonymous notebook containing notes of sermons delivered in 1628–9).
London MS 302 (Sermons of Herbert Palmer, 1626–44).

Lowestoft, Suffolk Record Office

116/E1/1 (Churchwardens' Accounts, St Mary, Bungay).

Maidstone, Centre for Kentish Studies

P100/1/15 (Register of Baptisms, Marriages, and Burials, Cranbrook, 1559–1667).

Oxford, Bodleian Library

MS Ashmole 174 (Astrological notebooks of William Lilly).
MS Ashmole 207 (Medical and Astrological Notebooks of Richard Napier, Feb. 1603–Apr. 1605).
MS Ashmole 1491 (Simon Forman, *Adversariorum*, ii).
MS Eng. hist. e. 198 (William Wodwall, 'The Acts of Queen Elizabeth').
MS Eng. poet. e. 14 (Miscellaneous poetry).
MS Sancroft 28 (Notebook of William Sancroft).
MS Sancroft 51 (Notebook entitled 'Divination: Dreams, predictions, prophecies fullfilld').
MS Tanner 467 (Arthur Bownest–William Sancroft correspondence).

Preston, Lancashire Record Office

DP 353 ('Severall Sermons upon divers occasions by Christopher Hudson Preacher of Gods wo[rd] at Preston in Lancashire. 1641').

Shrewsbury, Shrewsbury School

MS Mus X. 31 ('Dr Taylor's Book').

Stafford, Staffordshire Record Office

D 260/M/F/1/5 (Account and commonplace book of John Persehowse).
D641/3/P/4/13/3 (Jerningham Papers).

Stonyhurst, Stonyhurst College

MS A. IV. 7 (Modern transcripts).

Washington, DC, Folger Shakespeare Library

MS V. a. 339 (Hall commonplace book).

MS V. a. 436 (Nehemiah Wallington, 'Extract of the passage of my life; a collection of my written treatises').

PRINTED SOURCES

ABBOT, GEORGE, *An exposition upon the prophet Jonah* (1600). *STC* 34.

ABBOT, ROBERT, (Bishop), *Antilogia adversus apologiam Andreae Eudaemon-Joannis Jesuitae pro Henrico Garneto Jesuita proditore* (1613). *STC* 45.

ABBOT, ROBERT, (Minister), *Bee thankfull London and her sisters; or, a sermon of thankfulnesse* (1626). *STC* 56.

—— *The young-mans warning-peece; or, a sermon preached at the buriall of William Rogers, apothecary* (1639 edn.; 1st pub. 1636). *STC* 60. 7.

Abstene fra sin or ze sal fal under, for the day of the Lord is befoir the dur ([Edinburgh, 1579?]). *STC* 17328.7.

Acts of the Privy Council of England. New Series. 1542–1631, ed. John Roche Dasent *et al.*, 46 vols. (1890–1964).

ADAMS, THOMAS, *The barren tree* (1623). *STC* 106.

—— *The workes of Thomas Adams. Being the summe of his sermons* (1630). *STC* 105.

ADY, THOMAS, *A candle in the dark* (1655). Wing A673.

ALLESTREE, RICHARD, *A new almanack and prognostication* (1630; 1640). *STC* 407.13, 407.23.

AMES, WILLIAM, *The marrow of sacred divinity* (1642). Wing A3000.

ANDERSON, ANTHONY, *A sermon preached at Paules Crosse* (1581). *STC* 570.

ANDERSON, R. C. (ed.), *The Book of Examinations and Depositions, 1622–1644*, ii. *1627–1634*, Southampton Record Soc. 31 (Southampton, 1931).

ANDREWES, BARTIMAEUS, *Certaine verie worthie, godly and profitable sermons, upon the fifth chapter of the Songs of Solomon* (1583). *STC* 585.

Anno, 1623 . . . ([*c*.1623]). BM *Satires*, 63.

Anthony Painter. The blaspheming caryar (1614). *STC* 19120.

AQUINAS, St THOMAS, *The 'Summa Theologica' of St Thomas Aquinas*, trans. the Fathers of the English Dominican Province, 27 vols. (1911–35).

The araignment, examination, confession and judgement of Arnold Cosbye: who wilfully murdered the Lord Burke, neere the towne of Wansworth (1591). *STC* 5813.

ARBER, EDWARD (ed.), *A Transcript of the Registers of the Company of Stationers of London 1554–1640 AD*, 5 vols. (1875–94).

ARSANES, *Orations, of Arsanes agaynst Philip the trecherous kyng of Macedone . . . With a notable example of Gods vengeance uppon a faithlesse kyng, quene, and her children*, [ed. T. Norton] ([1560?]). *STC* 785.

ARTHINGTON, HENRY, *The seduction of Arthington by Hacket especiallie, with some tokens of his unfained repentance and submission* ([1592]). *STC* 799.

ASHTON, JOHN (ed.), *A Century of Ballads* (1867).

ATTERSOLL, WILLIAM, *Three treatises. 1. The conversion of Nineveh. 2. Gods trumpet sounding the alarum. 3. Physicke against famine* (1632). *STC* 900.

AUBREY, JOHN, *Three Prose Works*, ed. John Buchanan-Brown (Fontwell, Sussex, 1972).

AUGUSTINE, St, *Saint Augustine, of the citie of God*, trans. J. H[ealey] (1620 edn.). *STC* 917.

AVERELL, WILLIAM, *A wonderfull and straunge newes, which happened in the countye of Suffolke, and Essex, . . . where it rayned wheat* (1583). *STC* 982.5.

—— *A dyall for dainty darlings, rockt in the cradle of securitie* (1584). *STC* 978.

—— *Foure notable histories, appyled to foure worthy examples* (1590). *STC* 979.

AWDELY, JOHN, *A godly ditty or prayer to be song unto God for the preservation of his church, our queene and realme, against all traytours, rebels, and papisticall enemies* ([1569?]). *STC* 995.

B., A., *The sabbath truly sanctified* (1645). Wing B28.

B., G., *Of a monstrous childe borne at Chichester . . . with a short and sharpe discourse, for the punishment of whoredome* ([1581?]). *STC* 1030.3.

B., H., *The true discripcion of a childe with ruffes borne in the parish of Micheham, in the countie of Surrey* (1566). *STC* 1033.

BABINGTON, GERVASE, *The workes of the right reverend father in God Gervase Babington, late bishop of Worcester* (1615). *STC* 1077.

BACON, FRANCIS, *The essayes or counsels, civill and morall* (1625). *STC* 1147.

—— *Sylva sylvarum or a naturall history in ten centuries* (1627 edn.). *STC* 1169.

—— *The Works of Francis Bacon, Baron of Verulam, Viscount St. Alban, and Lord High Chancellor of England*, ed. James Spedding *et al.*, 7 vols. (1857–9).

BACON, NATHANIEL, *A relation of the fearefull estate of Francis Spira, in the yeare, 1548* (1638). *STC* 1178.

—— *The Official Papers of Sir Nathaniel Bacon of Stiffkey, Norfolk, as Justice of the Peace, 1580–1620*, ed. H. W. Saunders, CS, 3rd ser. 26 (1915).

BADDELEY, RICHARD, *The boy of Bilson: or, a true discovery of the late notorious impostures of certaine Romish priests in their pretended exorcisme . . . [of] William Perry* (1622). *STC* 1185.

BAILEY, WALTER, *A briefe discours of certain bathes or medicinall waters in the countie of Warwicke neere unto a village called Newnam Regis* (1587). *STC* 1191.

BALDWIN, WILLIAM, *et al.*, *A memorial of suche princes, as . . . have been unfortunate in the realme of England* ([1554?]). *STC* 1247.

—— *A myrrour for magistrates* (1563 edn.; 1st pub. 1559). *STC* 1246.

BALL, THOMAS, *The Life of the Renowned Doctor Preston, Writ by his Pupil, Master Thomas Ball, D.D. Minister of Northampton, in the Year 1628*, ed. E. W. Harcourt (Oxford, 1885).

[Ballad describing natural portents, including a woman of 59 years giving birth in Prague, fragment] ([1580?]). *STC* 1325.

BALMFORD, JAMES, *A short dialogue concerning the plagues infection* (1603). *STC* 1338.

[BANCROFT, RICHARD], *Daungerous positions and proceedings* (1593). *STC* 1344.

—— *A survay of the pretended holy discipline* (1593). *STC* 1362.

BARGRAVE, ISAAC, *A sermon preached before the honorable assembly of knights, cittizens, and burgesses, of the lower house of parliament* (1624). *STC* 1415.

BARKER, JOHN, *The true description of a monsterous chylde, borne in the Ile of Wight* ([1564]). *STC* 1422.

—— *Of the horyble and woful destruccion of Jerusalem* ([1569?]). *STC* 1420.

BARLOW, JOHN, *Hierons last fare-well* (1618). *STC* 1438.

BARNES, THOMAS, *The court of conscience: or, Josephs brethrens judgement barre* (1623). *STC* 1475.

—— *The wise-mans forecast against the evill time* (1624). *STC* 1478.5.

—— *Vox belli, or an alarme to warre* (1626). *STC* 1478.

BATMAN, STEPHEN, *The doome warning all men to the judgemente* (1581). *STC* 1582.

A battell of birds most strangly fought in Ireland ([1621]). *STC* 5764. 7.

BAUGHE, THOMAS, *A summons to judgement* (1614). *STC* 1594.

BAXTER, RICHARD, *A Christian directory: or, a summ of practical theologie, and cases of conscience* (1673). Wing B1219.

—— *The certainty of the worlds of spirits* (1691). Wing B1214.

—— *Reliquiae Baxterianae*, ed. Matthew Sylvester (1696). Wing B1370.

BAYLY, LEWIS, *The practise of pietie directing a Christian how to walke that he may please God* (1613). *STC* 1602.

B[EADLE], J[OHN], *The journal or diary of a thankful Christian* (1656). Wing B1557.

BEARD, THOMAS, *The theatre of Gods judgements* (1597; 1612; 1631). *STC* 1659, 1660, 1661.

—— and TAYLOR, THOMAS, *The theatre of Gods judgements . . . The fourth edition, with additions* (1648). Wing B1565.

—— —— *The theatre of God's judgments* (Glasgow, 1786).

BECON, THOMAS, *The Early Works of Thomas Becon*, ed. John Ayre, Parker Soc. (Cambridge, 1843).

BEDE, the Venerable, *The history of the church of Englande*, trans. Thomas Stapleton (Antwerp, 1565). *STC* 1778.

B[EDFORD], TH[OMAS], *A true and certaine relation of a strange-birth . . . Together with the notes of a sermon, preached . . . at the interring of the sayd birth* (1635). *STC* 1791.

BEDINGFIELD, ROBERT, *A sermon preached at Pauls Crosse the 24. of October. 1624* (1625). *STC* 1792.

BEE, JESSE, *The most wonderfull and true storie, of a certaine witch named Alse Gooderige of Stapen hill . . . As also a true report of the strange torments of Thomas Darling*, ed. J. Denison (1597). *STC* 6170.7.

BELL, THOMAS, *Thomas Bels motives: concerning Romish faith and religion* (Cambridge, 1593). *STC* 1830.

BELLARMINE, ROBERT, *Disputationum . . . de controversiis Christianae fidei, adversus huius temporis haereticos* (Ingolstadt, 1601 edn.; 1st pub. 1586).

BENEFIELD, SEBASTIAN, *A commentary or exposition upon the three first chapters of the prophecie of Amos* (1629). *STC* 1866.

BENSON, GEORGE, *A sermon preached at Paules Crosse the seaventh of May, M.DC.IX* (1609). *STC* 1886.

BERNARD, RICHARD, *The faithfull shepheard amended and enlarged* (1609 edn.). *STC* 1940.

—— *A guide to grand-jury men, divided into two books* (1629 edn.). *STC* 1944.

BEZA, THEODORE, *A shorte learned and pithie treatize of the plague*, trans. John Stockwood (1580). *STC* 2046.

—— *Propositions and principles of divinitie*, trans. [J. Penry] (Edinburgh, 1591). *STC* 2053.

BICKNOLL, EDMUND, *A swoord agaynst swearyng* (1579). *STC* 3046.

—— *A sword against swearers and blasphemers . . . inlarged with sundry examples of Gods judgements* (1611). *STC* 3050.3.

BILSON, THOMAS, *The effect of certaine sermons touching the full redemption of mankind* (1599). *STC* 3064.

BIRCH, THOMAS (ed.), *The Court and Times of James the First*, 2 vols. (1849).

BIRCH, WILLIAM, *A warnyng to England, let London begin: to repent their iniquitie, & flie from their sin* ([1565]). *STC* 3080.

BIRD, SAMUEL, *The lectures of Samuel Bird of Ipswidge upon the 11. chapter of the epistle unto the Hebrewes, and upon the 38. Psalme* (Cambridge, 1598). *STC* 3088.

BISSE, JAMES, *Two sermons preached, the one at Paules Crosse the eight of Januarie 1580* (1581). *STC* 3099.

The bloudy booke. Or, the tragicall and desperate end of Sir John Fites (alias) Fitz (1605). *STC* 10930.

Bloudy news from Germany; or, the people's misery by famine. Being an example of God's just judgement on one Harto [sic], a nobleman in Germany ([1672–95]). Wing B3269.

BOAISTUAU, PIERRE, *Certaine secrete wonders of nature*, trans. Edward Fenton (1569). *STC* 3164.5.

BOCCACCIO, GIOVANNI, [*De casibus illustrium virorum.*] *Here beynneth the boke calledde John Bochas descrivinge the falle of princis*, trans. John Lydgate (1494). *STC* 3175.

—— *The decameron containing an hundred pleasant novels*, trans. [J. Florio?] (1620). *STC* 3172.

BOETHIUS, ANICIUS M. T. S., *De consolationae philosophiae. The boke called the comforte of philosophye* (1556 edn.). *STC* 3201.

BOLTON, ROBERT, *The workes of the reverend, truly pious, and judiciously learned Robert Bolton . . . as they were finished by himselfe in his life time* (1641). *STC* 3512.

The book of common prayer (1676; 1678; 1711). Wing B3646, B3651.

BOURNE, IMMANUEL, *The rainebow, or, a sermon preached at Pauls Crosse* (1617). *STC* 3418.

BOWND, NICHOLAS, *The doctrine of the sabbath, plainely layde forth* (1595). *STC* 3436.

—— *The holy exercise of fasting* (Cambridge, 1604). *STC* 3438.

BOYS, JOHN, *An exposition of the last psalme. Delivered in a sermon preached at Paules Crosse the fifth of November 1613* (1615). *STC* 3464.

BRATHWAIT, RICHARD, *Whimzies: or, a new cast of characters* (1631). *STC* 3591.

BRENTZ, JOHANN, *Newes from Ninive to Englande, brought by the prophete Jonas*, trans. Thomas Tymme (1570). *STC* 3601.

BRETON, NICHOLAS, *Strange newes of divers counties, never discovered till of late, by a strange pilgrime in those parts* (1622). *STC* 3702.5.

B[REWER], T[HOMAS], *The weeping lady: or, London like Ninivie in sack-cloth* (1625). *STC* 3722.

BRIDGET, St, OF SWEDEN, *The Revelations of Saint Birgitta*, ed. William Patterson Cuming, EETS, os 178 (1929).

A briefe conjecturall discourse, upon the hierographicall letters & caracters found upon fower fishes, taken neere Marstrand in the kingdome of Denmarke (1589). *STC* 17488.7.

BRIGHT, TIMOTHY, *Characterie. An arte of shorte, swifte, and secrete writing by character* (1588). *STC* 3743.

BRINCKMAIR, L., *The warnings of Germany. By wonderfull signes, and strange prodigies seene . . . betweene the yeare 1618 and 1638* (1638). *STC* 3758.

BRINTON, THOMAS, *The Sermons of Thomas Brinton, Bishop of Rochester (1373–1389)*, ed. Mary Aquinas Devlin, 2 vols., CS, 3rd ser. 85–6 (1954).

BRISTOW, RICHARD, *A briefe treatise of divers plaine and sure waies to finde out the truth in this doubtfull and dangerous time of heresie* (Antwerp, 1599). *STC* 3799.

BROKE, THOMAS, *An epitaphe declaryng the lyfe and end of D. Edmund Boner &c* ([1569?]). *STC* 3817.4.

B[ROUGHTON], H[UGH], *Moriemini. A verie profitable sermon preached before her majestie at the court* (1593). *STC* 1034.

BROWNE, THOMAS, *Pseudodoxia epidemica: or, enquiries into very many received tenets and commonly presumed truths* (1646). Wing B5159.

BUGGS, SAMUEL, *Davids strait* (1622). *STC* 4022.

BULLEIN, WILLIAM, *A dialogue bothe pleasaunt and pietifull, wherein is a godlie regiment against the fever pestilence* (1573). *STC* 4037.

BULLINGER, HENRY, *A hundred sermons upon the Apocalips of Jesu Christe* ([1561]). *STC* 4061.

—— *The Decades of Henry Bullinger Minister of the Church of Zurich*, trans. H. I., ed. Thomas Harding, 5 vols., Parker Soc. (Cambridge, 1849–51).

BUNNY, EDMUND, *A necessarie admonition out of the prophet Joël* (1588). *STC* 4090.5.

BUNYAN, JOHN, *The Works of John Bunyan*, ed. George Offor, 3 vols. (Glasgow, 1859).

—— *The Life and Death of Mr. Badman Presented to the World in a Familiar Dialogue Between Mr. Wiseman, and Mr. Attentive*, ed. James F. Forrest and Roger Sharrock (Oxford, 1988).

[BUONACCORSI, ANDREA], VALESCO, SIGNIOR (pseud.), *Newes from Rome. Of two mightie armies . . . Also certaine prophecies of a Jew serving to that armie, called Caleb Shilocke, prognosticating many strange accidents, which shall happen the following yeere, 1607*, trans. W. W. ([1606]). *STC* 4102.5.

—— *A Jewes prophesy, with newes from Rome* ([1607]). *STC* 4102.7.

BURGHALL, EDWARD, 'Providence Improved', in T. Worthington Barlow, *Cheshire: Its Historical and Literary Associations, Illustrated in a Series of Biographical Sketches* (Manchester, 1852), 150–89.

BURNET, GILBERT, *A relation of the death of the primitive persecutors* (Amsterdam, 1687). Wing B5863A.

The burnynge of Paules church in London in the yeare of oure Lord 1561 (1563). *STC* 19931.

B[URTON], H[ENRY], *Israels Fast. Or, a meditation upon the seventh chapter of Joshua; a faire precedent for these times* (La Rochel [London], 1628). *STC* 4147.

[BURTON, HENRY], *A divine tragedie lately acted, or a collection of sundry memorable examples of Gods judgements upon sabbath-breakers, and other like libertines* ([Amsterdam], 1636). *STC* 4140.7, 4140.8.

BURTON, HENRY, *For God, and the king. The summe of two sermons preached on the fifth of November last in St Matthewes Friday-Streete. 1636* ([Amsterdam], 1636). *STC* 4141.

BURTON, ROBERT, *The anatomy of melancholy* (Oxford, 1621). *STC* 4159.

B[USH], E[DWARD], *A sermon preached at Pauls Crosse on Trinity Sunday, 1571* (1576). *STC* 4183.

C., J., *A warning for swearers. By the example of God's judgements shewed upon a man born near the town of Wolverhampton* ([1677]). Wing C77.

C., W., *The fatall vesper* (1623). *STC* 6015.

CAESARIUS OF HEISTERBACH, *The Dialogue on Miracles*, trans. H. Von E. Scott and C. C. Swinton Bland, 2 vols. (1929).

CALAMY, EDMUND, *Englands looking-glasse, presented in a sermon, preached before the honourable house of commons, at their late solemne fast* (1642). Wing C236.

Calebbe Shillocke, his prophesie: or, the Jewes prediction ([1607]). *STC* 22434.

Calendar of Letters and State Papers Relating to English Affairs (of the Reign of Elizabeth, 1558–1603), Preserved Principally in the Archives of Simancas, ed. M. A. S. Hume, 4 vols. (1892–9).

Calendar of State Papers and Manuscripts, Relating to English Affairs, Existing in the Archives and Collections of Venice, and in other Libraries of Northern Italy, ed. R. Brown et al., 38 vols. (1864–1947).

Calendar of State Papers, Domestic Series, of the Reigns of Edward VI, Mary, Elizabeth and

James I, 1547–1625, ed. R. Lemon and M. A. E. Green, 12 vols. (1856–72); *Reign of Charles I, 1625–1649*, ed. J. Bruce *et al.*, 23 vols. (1858–97).

CALVIN, JOHN, *An admonicion against astrology judiciall and other curiosities, that raigne now in the world*, trans. G. G[ylby] ([1561]). *STC* 4372.

——*A Defense of the Secret Providence of God 1558*, trans. Henry Cole (1857).

——*Institutes of the Christian Religion*, trans. John Allen, 2 vols. (Philadelphia, 1936).

CAMDEN, WILLIAM, *Annales. The true and royal history of the famous empresse Elizabeth queene of Englande France and Ireland &c* (1625). *STC* 4497.

CANNON, NATHANIEL, *The cryer* (1613). *STC* 4576.

CARAMAN, PHILIP (ed.), *The Other Face: Catholic Life under Elizabeth I* (1960).

——(ed.), *The Years of Siege: Catholic Life from James I to Cromwell* (1966).

CARDWELL, EDWARD (ed.), *Synodalia: A Collection of Articles of Religion, Canons, and Proceedings of Convocations in the Province of Canterbury from the Year 1547 to the year 1717*, 2 vols. (Oxford, 1842).

CAREW, RICHARD, *The Survey of Cornwall*, ed. F. E. Halliday (1969).

CARIER, BENJAMIN, *A copy of a letter, written by M. Doctor Carier beyond seas . . . Whereunto are added certaine collections found in his closet . . . of the miserable ends of such as have impugned the Catholike church* ([Eng. secret press], 1615). *STC* 4621.

CARLETON, GEORGE, *A thankfull remembrance of Gods mercy* (1624; 1627). *STC* 4640, 4642.

CARPENTER, JOHN, *Remember Lots wife. Two godly and fruitfull sermons verie convenient for this our time* (1588). *STC* 4665.

——*A preparative to contentation* (1597). *STC* 4664.

CARR, JOHN, *A larum belle for London, with a caveat to England* (1573). *STC* 4684.

——*The ruinous fal of prodigalitie: with the notable examples of the best aprooved aucthours* (1573). *STC* 4685.

CARTER, BEZALEEL, *A sermon of Gods omnipotencie and providence* (1615). *STC* 4692a.

CARTWRIGHT, THOMAS, *Cartwrightiana*, ed. Albert Peel and Leland H. Carlson, Elizabethan Nonconformist Texts I (1951).

——*The second replie of Thomas Cartwright: agaynst Maister Doctor Whitgiftes second answer touching the churche discipline* ([Heidelberg], 1575). *STC* 4714.

——*A brief apologie . . . against all such slaunderous accusations as it pleaseth Mr Sutcliffe in severall pamphlettes most injuriously to loade him with* (Middelburg, 1596). *STC* 4706.

CARYL, JOSEPH, *An exposition with practical observations upon the book of Job*, 2 vols. (1676 edn.; 1st pub. 1645). Wing C758.

CASE, WILLIAM, *A sermon of the nature and end of repentance* (1616). *STC* 4767.

Certaine prayers collected out of a forme of godly meditations, set forth by his majesties author- itie: and most necessary to be used at this time in the present visitation of Gods heavy hand for our manifold sinnes (1603). *STC* 16532.

A certaine relation of the hog-faced gentlewoman called Mistris Tannakin Skinker (1640). *STC* 22627.

Certaine sermons appoynted by the quenes majesty, to be declared and read (1563). *STC* 13664.5.

CHADERTON, LAURENCE, *An excellent and godly sermon, most needefull for this time* (1580). *STC* 4924.

CHALLONER, RICHARD, *Memoirs of Missionary Priests*, 2 vols. (n.p. 1741–2); ed. J. H. Pollen (1924).

CHAMBER, JOHN, *A treatise against judicial astrologie* (1601). *STC* 4941.

CHAMBERLAIN, JOHN, *The Letters of John Chamberlain*, ed. Norman Egbert McClure,

2 vols., the American Philosophical Soc., Memoirs XII, parts I & II (Philadelphia, 1939).

CHAPMAN, JOHN, *A most true report of the myraculous moving and sinking of a plot of ground, about nine acres, at Westram in Kent* (1596). *STC* 4997.

CHAPPELL, WILLIAM, and EBSWORTH, J. WOODFALL (eds.), *The Roxburghe Ballads*, 9 vols. in 14 (1869–97).

CHASSANION, JEAN, *Des grands et redoutables jugemens et punitions de Dieu advenus au monde principalement* (Morges, 1581).

——*Histoires memorables des grans et merveilleux jugemens et punitions de Dieu avenues au monde* (n.p., 1586).

CHEASTE, THOMAS, *The way to life* (1609). *STC* 5106.

Christs teares over Jerusalem. Or, a caveat for England, to call to God for mercy, lest we be plagued for our contempt and wickednesse ([*c.*1640]). *STC* 14543.

CHURCHYARD, THOMAS, *A warning for the wise . . . Written of the late earthquake chanced in London and other places* (1580). *STC* 5259.

——*The mirror of man, and manners of men* (1594). *STC* 5242.

——*The wonders of the ayre, the trembling of the earth, and the warnings of the world before the judgement day* (1602). *STC* 5260.5.

CITOIS, FRANÇOIS, *A true and admirable historie of a mayden of Confolens, in the province of Poictiers: that for the space of three yeeres and more hath lived, and yet doth, without receiving either meate or drinke* (1603). *STC* 5326.

CLAPHAM, HENOCH, *An epistle discoursing upon the present pestilence* (1603); 2nd edn. *Reprinted with some additions* (1603). *STC* 5339, 5340.

——*Henoch Clapham his demaundes and answeres touching the pestilence*, ed. Pere. Re. ([Middelburg], 1604). *STC* 5343.

——*Doctor Andros [Lancelot Andrewes] his prosopeia answered* ([Middelburg], 1605). *STC* 5338.

CLARK, ANDREW (ed.), *The Shirburn Ballads 1585–1616* (Oxford, 1907).

CLARKE, SAMUEL, *The marrow of ecclesiastical history* (1654). Wing C4544.

——*A mirrour or looking-glasse both for saints, and sinners, held forth in some thousands of examples* (1657; 1671 edns.; 1st pub. 1646). Wing C4551–2.

——*Englands remembrancer, containing a true and full narrative of those two never to be forgotten deliverances* (1657). Wing C4150.

——*A collection of the lives of ten eminent divines* (1662). Wing C4506.

——*The lives of thirty two English divines* (1677 edn). Wing C4539.

CLAY, WILLIAM KEATING (ed.), *Liturgical Services: Liturgies and Occasional Forms of Prayer set forth in the Reign of Queen Elizabeth*, Parker Soc. (Cambridge, 1847).

——*Private Prayers, put forth by Authority during the Reign of Queen Elizabeth*, Parker Society (Cambridge, 1851).

COGHAN, THOMAS, *The haven of health . . . with a short censure of the late sicknes at Oxford* (1584). *STC* 5478.

The cold yeare. 1614. A deepe snow (1615). *STC* 26091.

COLLIER, JOHN PAYNE (ed.), *A Book of Roxburghe Ballads* (1847).

——(ed.) *Broadside Black-letter Ballads* (1868).

COOKE, RICHARD, *A white sheete, or a warning for whoremongers* (1629). *STC* 5676.

COOPER, THOMAS (Bishop), *Certaine sermons wherein is contained the defense of the gospell nowe preached* (1580). *STC* 5685.

COOPER, THOMAS (Preacher), *The blessing of Japheth, proving the gathering in of the gentiles, and finall conversion of the jewes* (1615). *STC* 5693.

—— *The mystery of witch-craft* (1617). *STC* 5701.

—— *The cry and revenge of blood* (1620). *STC* 5698.

CORBETT, EDWARD, *Gods providence, a sermon preached before the honourable House of Commons* (1642). Wing C6241.

CORDEROY, JEREMY, *A warning for worldlings, or a comfort to the godly, and a terror to the wicked* (1608). *STC* 5757.

CORTANO, LUDOVICO, *Good newes to Christendome . . . Discovering a wonderfull and strange apparition, visibly seene for many days togither in Arabia* (1620). *STC* 5796.

CORYATE, THOMAS, *Coryats crudities. Hastily gobled up in five moneths travells* (1611). *STC* 5808.

COSIN, RICHARD, *Conspiracie, for pretended reformation* (1592). *STC* 5823.

COTTA, JOHN, *A short discoverie of the unobserved dangers of severall sorts of ignorant and unconsiderate practisers of physicke in England* (1612). *STC* 5833.

CRADOCKE, EDWARD, *The shippe of assured safetie . . . conteyning . . . a discourse of Gods providence* (1572). *STC* 5952.

CRAKANTHORP, RICHARD, *De providentia dei tractatus* (Cambridge, 1623). *STC* 5973.

—— *A sermon of predestination, preached at Saint Maries in Oxford* (1620). *STC* 5980.

CROMER, MARTIN, *A notable example of Gods vengeance, uppon a murdering king* ([1560?]). *STC* 6046, 6047.

CROMWELL, OLIVER, *The Writings and Speeches of Oliver Cromwell*, ed. Wilbur C. Abbott, 4 vols. (Cambridge, Mass., 1937–47).

CROSFIELD, THOMAS, *The Diary of Thomas Crosfield M.A., B.D. Fellow of Queen's College, Oxford*, ed. Frederick S. Boas (1935).

[CROUCH, NATHANIEL], B[URTON], R[ICHARD/ROBERT] (pseud.), *Admirable curiosities, rarities, & wonders in England, Scotland, and Ireland* (1682). Wing C7306.

—— *Wonderful prodigies of judgment and mercy* (1682). Wing C7361.

CROWLEY, ROBERT, *An apologie, or defence, of those Englishe writers & preachers which Cereberus . . . chargeth wyth false doctrine, under the name of predestination* (1566). *STC* 6076.

CUPPER, WILLIAM, *Certaine sermons concerning Gods late visitation in the citie of London and other parts of the land* (1592). *STC* 6125.

A curb for sectaries and bold propheciers (1641). Wing C7620.

D., JOHN, *A discription of a monstrous chylde, borne at Chychester in Sussex* (1562). *STC* 6177.

DANE, JOHN, 'John Dane's Narrative, 1682', *New England Historical and Genealogical Register*, 8 (1854), 147–56.

DARRELL, JOHN, *A breife narration of the possession, dispossession, and repossession of William Sommers* ([Amsterdam?], 1598). *STC* 6281.

—— *An apologie, or defence of the possession of William Sommers* ([Amsterdam, 1599?]). *STC* 6280.5.

—— *A brief apologie proving the possession of William Somers* ([Middelburg], 1599). *STC* 6282.

D[AVIES], J[OHN], *A scourge for paper-persecutors, or papers complaint, compil'd in ruthfull rimes against the paper-spoylers of these times. With a continu'd just inquisition of the same subject, fit for this season. Against paper-persecutors. by A. H.* (1625). *STC* 6339.5.

DAWES, LANCELOT, *Gods mercies and Jerusalems miseries* (1609). *STC* 6388.

DAY, THOMAS, *Wonderfull straunge sightes seene in the element, over the citie of London and other places* ([1583]). *STC* 6433.

DAY, W. G. (ed.), *The Pepys Ballads*, 5 vols. (Cambridge, 1987).

DEACON, JOHN, and WALKER, JOHN, *Dialogicall discourses of spirits and divels* (1601). *STC* 6439.

DEE, JOHN, *The Private Diary of Dr John Dee and the Catalogue of his Library of Manuscripts*, ed. James Orchard Halliwell, CS, 1st ser. 19 (1842).

Deeds against nature, and monsters by kinde (1614). *STC* 809.

DEKKER, THOMAS, *A rod for run-awayes. Gods tokens, of his feareful judgements* (1625). *STC* 6250.

—— *The blacke rod: and the white rod* (1630). *STC* 6492.5.

D[ELONEY], T[HOMAS], *A proper newe sonet declaring the lamentation of Beckles in Suffolke, which was . . . most pittifully burned with fire* ([1586]). *STC* 6564.

—— *Canaans calamitie Jerusalems misery* (1618). *STC* 6181.2.

DELONEY, THOMAS, *The Works of Thomas Deloney*, ed. Francis Oscar Mann (Oxford, 1912).

DENISON, STEPHEN, *The white wolfe. Or, a sermon preached at Pauls Crosse* (1627). *STC* 6607.5.

DENT, ARTHUR, *A sermon of repentaunce* (1583 edn.). *STC* 6650.

—— *The plaine mans path-way to heaven* (1601). *STC* 6626.

—— *A platforme, made for the proofe of Gods providence* (1608). *STC* 6646.7.

—— *The plaine-mans path-way to heaven. The second part* (1612 edn.). *STC* 6638.

DENT, DANIEL, *A sermon against drunkennes: preached at Ware* (1628). *STC* 6673.

DERING, EDWARD, *Maister Derings workes* (1590). *STC* 6676.

The description of a monstrous pig, the which was farrowed at Hamsted besyde London ([1562]). *STC* 6768.

The devils conquest, or, a wish obtained: shewing how one lately of Barnsby-street wisht the devil fetch her . . . and her body was found as black as pitch all over ([1665]). Wing D1226.

D'EWES, SIMONDS, *The Autobiography and Correspondence of Sir Simonds D'Ewes, Bart., During the Reigns of James I and Charles I*, ed. James Orchard Halliwell, 2 vols. (1845).

—— *The Diary of Sir Simonds D'Ewes (1622–1624): Journal d'un étudiant Londonien sous le règne de Jacques 1ᵉʳ*, ed. Elisabeth Bourcier, Publications de la Sorbonne Littératures 5 (Paris, 1975).

DILLINGHAM, FRANCIS, *Laurence Chaderton, D.D. (First Master of Emmanuel)*, ed. E. S. Shuckburgh (Cambridge, 1884).

The disclosing of a late counterfeyted possession by the devyl in two maydens within the citie of London ([1574]). *STC* 3738.

Discours veritable et tres-piteux, de l'inondation et debordement de mer, survenu en six diverses provinces d'Angleterre (Paris, 1607).

The discription of a rare or rather most monstrous fishe taken on the east cost of Holland ([1566]). *STC* 6769.

'Documenta de S. Wenefreda', *Analecta Bollandiana*, 6 (Paris, 1887), 305–52.

DOD, JOHN, and CLEAVER, ROBERT, *Ten sermons tending chiefely to the fitting of men for the worthy receiving of the Lords Supper* (1610 edn.). *STC* 6945.

—————— *A plaine and familiar exposition of the ninth and tenth chapters of the Proverbs of Salomon* (1612). *STC* 6954.

[DOLETA, JOHN], *Straunge newes out of Calabria: prognosticated in the yere 1586. upon the yere 87* ([1586]). *STC* 6992.

DONNE, DANIEL, *A sub-poena from the star chamber of heaven* (1623). *STC* 7021.

DONNE, JOHN, *The Works of John Donne, Dean of Saint Paul's, 1621–1631*, ed. Henry Alford, 6 vols. (1839).

DOVE, JONATHAN, *An almanack for . . . 1639* (Cambridge, 1639). *STC* 436.11.

DOWNAME, JOHN, *Lectures upon the foure first chapters of the prophecie of Hosea* (1608). *STC* 7145.

——*Foure treatises, tending to dissuade all Christians from foure no lesse hainous then common sinnes* (1609 edn.). *STC* 7141.

——(ed.), *The summe of sacred divinitie first briefly & methodically propounded* ([1620?]). *STC* 7148.

Dreadfull newes: or a true relation of the great, violent and late earthquake. Hapned the 27. day of March, stilo Romano last, at Callabria, in the kingdome of Naples (1638). *STC* 4349.5.

DUPORT, JOHN, *A sermon preached at Pauls Crosse on the 17. day of November 1590 . . . commonly called, the queenes day* (1591). *STC* 7365.5.

DYKE, DANIEL, *Certaine comfortable sermons upon the 124. Psalme: tending to stirre up to thankefulnesse for our deliverance from the late gunpowder-treason* (1616). *STC* 7395.

DYKE, JEREMIAH, *A sermon preached at the publicke fast* (1628). *STC* 7424.

The dystruccyon of Jherusalem by Vaspazyan and Tytus ([1513?]). *STC* 14517.

EARLE, JOHN, *Micro-cosmographie. Or, a peece of the world discovered; in essayes and characters* (1628), ed. Edward Arber (1868).

EBSWORTH, JOSEPH WOODFALL (ed.), *The Bagford Ballads: Illustrating the Last Years of the Stuarts* (Hertford, 1876–80).

ELDERTON, WILLIAM, *The true fourme and shape of a monsterous chyld, whiche was borne in Stony Stratforde, in North Hamptonshire* ([1565]). *STC* 7565.

England's new bell-man ([1690]). *Wing* E3001.

Eniautos terastios. Mirabilis annus, or the year of prodigies and wonders (1661). *Wing* E3127.

ETIENNE DE BESANÇON, *An Alphabet of Tales. An English 15th Century Translation of the Alphabetum Narrationum of Etienne de Besançon*, ed. Mary MacLeod Banks, 2 vols., EETS, OS 126–7 (1904–5).

EUDAEMON-JOANNES, ANDREAS, [L'HEUREUX, ANDRÉ], *Ad actionem proditioriam Edouardi Coqui, apologia pro R. P. Henrico Garneto Anglo* (n.p., 1610).

[EVERARD, JOHN], *Somewhat: written by occasion of three sunnes seene at Tregnie in Cornewall, the 22. of December last* (1622). *STC* 10599.

EWICH, JOHANN, *Of the duetie of a faithfull and wise magistrate, in preserving and delivering of the common wealth from infection, in the time of the plague or pestilence*, trans. John Stockwood (1583). *STC* 10607.

An example of Gods judgement shew[n] upon two children borne in high Dutchlan[d] in the citie of Lutssolof ([1582?]). *STC* 10608.5.

Exemplum literarum amici cuiusdam ad omicum quendam suum, de vera origine conflagrationis pyramidis, & templi Paulini Londinensis (1561). *STC* 19930.5.

False prophets discovered (1642). *Wing* F345.

A fearefull example. Shewed upon a perjured person. Who . . . did . . . desperatly stabbe himselfe (1591). *STC* 19965.

FEATLEY, DANIEL, *Clavis mystica* (1636). *STC* 10730.

FENNER, WILLIAM, *A treatise of the affections; or, the soules pulse* (1642). *Wing* F707.

FIELD, JOHN, *A godly exhortation, by occasion of the late judgement of God, shewed at Parrisgarden* (1583). *STC* 10844.8.

FINCELIUS, JOB, *Wunderzeichen. Warhafftige beschreibung und gründlich verzeicnus schrecklicher wunderzeichen und geschichten* (Jena, 1556).

FISHER, JOHN, *T[he copy of a letter] descri[bing the wonderful] woorke of G[od in delivering a] mayden withi[n the city of Che]ster, from an [horrible kind of] torment* (1564). *STC* 10910.

FISHER, WILLIAM, *A godly sermon preached at Paules Crosse the 31. day of October 1591* (1592). *STC* 10919.

FISKE, NATHAN, *Remarkable providences to be gratefully recollected, religiously improved, and carefully transmitted to posterity* (Boston, 1776).

FITZ-GEFFREY, CHARLES, *The curse of corne-horders: with the blessing of seasonable selling. In three sermons* (1631). *STC* 10938.

FITZGEFFREY, HENRY, *Satyres and satyricall epigrams: with certaine observations at Black-Fryers?* (1617). *STC* 10945.

FITZHERBERT, THOMAS, *The second part of a treatise concerning policy, and religion* ([Douai], 1610). *STC* 11019.

FLEMING, ABRAHAM, *A straunge, and terrible wunder wrought very late in the parish church of Bongay* ([1577]). *STC* 11050.

——*A bright burning beacon . . . conteining . . . a commemoration of our late earthquake* (1580). *STC* 11037.

FLETCHER, JOHN, *Monsieur Thomas. A comedy. Acted at the private house in Blacke Fryers* (1639). *STC* 11071.

FLOYD, JOHN, *Purgatories triumph over hell* ([St Omer], 1613). *STC* 11114.

——I. R. P., (pseud.), *A word of comfort. Or a discourse concerning the late lamentable accident of the fall of a roome, at a Catholike sermon, in the Black-Friars at London* ([St Omer], 1623). *STC* 11118.

FOLEY, HENRY (ed.), *Records of the English Province of the Society of Jesus*, 7 vols. in 8 (1877–83).

The forme and shape of a monstrous child, borne at Maydstone in Kent ([1568]). *STC* 17194.

A forme of common prayer, together with an order of fasting: for the averting of Gods heavie visitation (1636). *STC* 16553.

FOSBROKE, JOHN, *Six sermons delivered in the lecture at Kettering in the countie of Northampton, and in certain other places* (Cambridge, 1633). *STC* 11199.

FOTHERBY, MARTIN, *Foure sermons, lately preached* (1608). *STC* 11206.

FOXE, JOHN, *The Acts and Monuments of John Foxe*, ed. S. R. Cattley, 8 vols. (1853–9).

FRERE, W. H. (ed.), *Visitation Articles and Injunctions of the Period of the Reformation*, 3 vols. (1910).

FULKE, WILLIAM, *Antiprognosticon . . . an invective agaynst the vayne and unprofitable predictions of the astrologians as Nostradame. &c.* (1560). *STC* 11420.

——*A godly and learned sermon, preached before an honourable auditorie the 26. day of Februarie. 1580* ([1580]). *STC* 11434.

——*A most pleasant prospect into the garden of naturall contemplation, to behold the naturall causes of all kind of meteors* (1639 edn.; 1st pub. as *A goodly gallerye* in 1563). *STC* 11440.

FULLER, THOMAS (DD), *Abel redivivus or the dead yet speaking* (1651). Wing F2400.

——*The church-history of Britain* (1655). Wing F2416.

——*The history of the worthies of England* (1662). Wing F2440.

FULLER, THOMAS, (MA), *A sermon intended for Paul's Crosse . . . upon the late decrease and withdrawing of Gods heavie visitation of the plague of pestilence from the said citie* (1626). *STC* 11467.

F[ULWOOD], W[ILLIAM], *The shape of .ii. monsters* ([1562]). *STC* 11485.

G., P., *A most strange and true report of a monsterous fish, who appeared in the forme of a woman, from her waste upwards* ([1604]). *STC* 11501.5.

GAMON, HANIBAL, *Gods smiting to amendment, or, revengement* (1629). *STC* 11547.

GARDINER, SAMUEL, *Doomes-day booke: or, an alarum for atheistes, a watchword for worldlinges, a caveat for Christians* (1606). *STC* 11576.

GAREY, SAMUEL, *Great Brittans little calendar: or, triple diarie. In remembrance of three daies* (1618). *STC* 11597.

GATAKER, THOMAS, *A sparke toward the kindling of sorrow for Sion* (1621). *STC* 11675.

—— *Two sermons: tending to direction for Christian cariage, both in afflictions incumbent, and in judgements imminent* (1623). *STC* 11681.

——*An anniversarie memoriall of Englands delivery from the Spanish invasion* (1626). *STC* 11648.

——*Of the nature and use of lots* (1627 edn.). *STC* 11671.

GEE, EDWARD, *Two sermons. One, the curse and crime of Meroz . . . The other, a sermon of patience* (1620). *STC* 11700.

GEE, JOHN, *The foot out of the snare: with a detection of sundry late practices and impostures of the priests and Jesuites in England* (1624). *STC* 11701–4.

——*Hold fast, a sermon preached at Pauls Crosse* (1624). *STC* 11705.

GERARD, JOHN, *John Gerard: The Autobiography of an Elizabethan*, ed. and trans. Philip Caraman (1951).

GERARDUS, ANDREAS (*Hyperius*), *The practise of preaching, otherwise called the pathway to the pulpit*, trans. John Ludham (1577).

—— *Two common places taken out of Andreas Hyperius . . . whereof . . . he sheweth the force that the sonne, moone and starres have over men*, trans. R. Y. (1581). *STC* 11762.

[GERARDUS, ANDREAS], *A speciall treatise of Gods providence, and of comforts against all kinde of crosses & calamities to be fetched from the same*, trans. J. L[udham] ([1588?]). *STC* 11760.

GESNER, CONRAD, *Historiæ animalium* (Zurich, 1551–8).

GEVEREN, SHELTCO À, *Of the ende of this worlde, and seconde comming of Christ*, trans. Thomas Rogers (1578 edn.). *STC* 11805.

GIBBONS, JOHN, and FEN, JOHN (eds.), *Concertatio ecclesiae Catholicae in Anglia* (n.p., 1588); ed. and augmented John Bridgewater (1589 edn.).

GIBSON, ABRAHAM, *The lands mourning, for vaine swearing: or the downe-fall of oathes* (1613). *STC* 11829.

GIFFORD, GEORGE, *Foure sermons upon the seven chiefe vertues or principall effectes of faith, and the doctrine of election* (1582 edn.). *STC* 11858.

——*A briefe discourse of certaine pointes of the religion, which is among the common sort of Christians, which may be termed the countrie divinitie* (1583 edn.). *STC* 11846.5.

——*A discourse of the subtill practises of devilles by witches and sorcerers* (1587). *STC* 11852.

——*A dialogue concerning witches and witchcraftes* (1593). *STC* 11850.

——*Certaine sermons, upon divers textes of holie scripture* (1597). *STC* 11848.5.

GIL, ALEXANDER, *Parerga* (1632). *STC* 11879.9.

[GLOVER, ROBERT], *Nobilitas politica vel civilis*, ed. Thomas Milles (1608). *STC* 11922.

To the glory of God in thankefull remembrance of our three great deliverances unto etern[al] memory (1627). *STC* 23018.

GOAD, THOMAS, *The dolefull even-song* (1623). *STC* 11923.

The godly end and wofull lamentation of one John Stevens, a youth that was hang'd . . . at Salisbury ([1633]). *STC* 23260.

Gods handy-worke in wonders. Miraculously shewen upon two women, lately delivered of two monsters: with a most strange and terrible earth-quake, by which, fields and other grounds, were quite removed to other places (1615). *STC* 11926.

Gods warning to his people of England. By the great overflowing of the waters or floudes lately happened in South-Wales and many other places (1607). *STC* 10011, 10011.2, 10011.4.

GODSKALL, JAMES, *The kings medicine for this present yeere 1604* (1604). *STC* 11936.

GOLDING, ARTHUR, *A discourse upon the earthquake that hapned throughe this realme of Englande, and other places of Christendom, the sixt of Aprill. 1580* (1580). *STC* 11987.

GOLDWURM [or GOLTWURM], CASPAR, *Wunderwerck und wunderzeichen buch* (n.p., 1557).

GOODCOLE, HENRY, *The wonderfull discoverie of Elizabeth Sawyer a witch, late of Edmonton* (1621). *STC* 12014.

——*Heavens speedie hue and cry sent after lust and murther* (1635). *STC* 12010.

GOODMAN, GODFREY, *The fall of man, or the corruption of nature* (1616). *STC* 12022.7.

GOODWIN, THOMAS, *The Works of Thomas Goodwin, D.D., Sometime President of Magdalene College, Oxford*, ed. J. C. Miller, 11 vols. (Edinburgh, 1861–5).

GORE, JOHN, *Ten godly and fruitfull sermons preached upon severall occasions* (1646). Wing G1295A.

GOSSON, STEPHEN, *The schoole of abuse, conteining a plesaunt invective against poets, pipers, plaiers* (1579). *STC* 12097.5.

——*The trumpet of warre* ([1598]). *STC* 12099.

GOUGE, WILLIAM, *Gods three arrowes: plague, famine, sword, in three treatises* (1631). *STC* 12116.

GOULART, SIMON, *Admirable and memorable histories containing the wonders of our time*, trans. Ed. Grimeston (1607). *STC* 12135.

GRAY, ROBERT, *An alarum to England, sounding the most fearefull and terrible example of Gods vengeance* (1609). *STC* 12203.

Great Brittains arlarm [sic] ([1667?]). Wing G1665.

G[REENE], J[OHN], *A refutation of the apology for actors* (1615). *STC* 12214–15.

GREENHAM, RICHARD, *The works . . . examined, corrected and published*, ed. H. H[olland] (1599). *STC* 12312.

GREENWOOD, HENRY, *Tormenting Tophet* (1615). *STC* 12336.

GREG, W. W. (ed.), *Companion to Arber. Being a Calendar of Documents* (Oxford, 1967).

GRENT, JOHN, *The burthen of Tyre* (1627). *STC* 12360.

GRIBALDI, MATTEO, *A notable and marveilous epistle . . . concernyng the terrible judgemente of God, upon hym that for feare of men, denieth Christ and the knowne veritie* (1550, [1570?]). *STC* 12365–6.

GRINDAL, EDMUND, *The Remains of Edmund Grindal, D.D.*, ed. William Nicholson, Parker Soc. (Cambridge, 1843).

GURNEY, ARTHUR, *A fruitfull dialogue touching the doctrine of Gods providence, and mans free will* ([c.1580?]). *STC* 6805.6.

——*A doleful discourse and ruthfull reporte of the great spoyle and lamentable losse, by fire, in the towne of East Dearham* (1581). *STC* 12531.3.

GURTH, ALEXANDER, *Most true and more admirable newes, expressing the miraculous preservation of a young maiden of the towne of Glabbich* (1597). *STC* 12531.5.

HAKEWILL, GEORGE, *An answere to a treatise written by Dr Carier* (1616). *STC* 12610.

——*An apologie or declaration of the power and providence of God in the government of the world* (Oxford, 1627); *The third edition much enlarged* (1635). *STC* 12611, 12613.

H[ALL], J[OSEPH], *An holy panegyrick* (1613). *STC* 12673.

HALL, JOSEPH, *The great mysterie of godliness* (1652). Wing H383.

[HAMMOND, SAMUEL], *Gods judgements upon drunkards, swearers, and sabbath-breakers* (1659). Wing H623aA.

HAMPTON, WILLIAM, *A proclamation of warre from the lord of hosts, or Englands warning by Israels ruine* (1627). *STC* 12741.

HARISON, ANTHONY, *The Registrum Vagum of Anthony Harison*, ed. Thomas F. Barton, Norfolk Record Soc. 32–3 ([Norwich], 1963–4).

The Harleian miscellany: or, a collection of scarce, curious, and entertaining pamphlets and tracts, 8 vols. (1744–53).

[HARPSFIELD, NICHOLAS] COPE, ALAN (pseud.), *Dialogi sex* (Antwerp, 1566).

HARRIS, JOHN, *The destruction of Sodome: a sermon preached at a publicke fast* ([1629]). *STC* 12806.

HARRIS, ROBERT, *Gods goodnes and mercie* (1626 edn.). *STC* 12833.

——*Davids comfort at Ziklag* (1628). *STC* 12825.

HARRISON, WILLIAM, *Deaths advantage little regarded, and the soules solace against sorrow. Preached in two funerall sermons at Childwal in Lancashire at the buriall of Mistris Katherin Brettergh . . . Whereunto is annexed, the Christian life and godly death of the said gentlewoman* (1602 edn.). *STC* 12866.

——*The difference of hearers. Or an exposition of the parable of the sower* (1614). *STC* 12870.

HARSNET, ADAM, *Gods summons unto a general repentaunce* (1640). *STC* 12875.

H[ARSNET], S[AMUEL], *A discovery of the fraudulent practises of John Darrel bacheler of artes* (1599). *STC* 12883.

——*A declaration of egregious popish impostures* (1604 edn.; 1st pub. 1603). *STC* 12881.

HARVEY, GABRIEL, *The Works of Gabriel Harvey*, ed. Alexander B. Grosart, 3 vols. (1884–5).

HARVEY, JOHN, *A discoursive problem concerning prophecies* (1588). *STC* 12908.

HARWARD, SIMON, *A discourse of the severall kinds and causes of lightnings* (1607). *STC* 12918.

HAVILAND, MATTHEW, *A monument of Gods most gracious preservation of England from Spanish invasion, Aug. 2. 1588. and popish treason, Novem. 5. 1605. To my posterity.* ([c.1635?]). *STC* 12938.5.

HAYWARD, JOHN, *Annals of the First Four Years of the Reign of Queen Elizabeth*, ed. John Bruce, CS, 1st ser. 7 (1840).

HEMING, WILLIAM, *The Jewes tragedy* (1662). Wing H1425.

HERBERT, GEORGE, *The Works of George Herbert*, ed. F. E. Hutchinson (Oxford, 1941).

HERING, THEODORE, *The triumph of the church over water and fire* (1625). *STC* 13204.

[HEROLD, JOHANN], *Exempla virtutum et vitiorum, atque etiam aliarum rerum maxime memorabilium* (Basel, [1555]).

HEROLT, JOHANNES (*Discipulus*), *Sermones discipuli de tempore [et] de sanctis: et quadragesimale eiusdem: cum promptuario* (1510). *STC* 13226.

——*Miracles of the Blessed Virgin Mary*, trans. C. C. Swinton Bland (1928).

HERRING, FRANCIS, *A modest defence of the caveat given to the wearers of impoisoned amulets, as preservatives from the plague* (1604). *STC* 13248.

——*Pietas pontificia, seu, conjurationis illius prodigiosae* (1606). *STC* 13244.

——*Popish pietie, or the first part of the historie of that horrible and barbarous conspiracie, commonly called the powder-treason*, trans. A. P. (1610). *STC* 13246.

HERRING, FRANCIS, *Mischeefes mysterie: or, treasons master-peece, the powder-plot*, trans. and dilated John Vicars (1617). *STC* 13247.

——*November the 5. 1605. The quintessence of cruelty, or master-peece of treachery, the popish powder-plot*, trans. John Vicars (1641). Wing H1602.

HERRTAGE, SIDNEY J. (ed.), *The Early English Versions of the Gesta Romanorum*, EETS, extra ser. 33 (1879).

Hevy newes of an horryble earth quake whiche was in the cytie of Scharbaria ([1542]). *STC* 21807.

HEYWOOD, OLIVER, *The Reverend Oliver Heywood, B.A. 1630–1702; His Autobiography, Diaries, Anecdote and Event Books: Illustrating the General and Family History of Yorkshire and Lancashire*, ed. J. Horsfall Turner, 4 vols. (Brighouse, 1882–5).

H[EYWOOD], T[HOMAS], *A true discourse of the two infamous upstart prophets, Richard Farnham weaver of White-Chappell, and John Bull weaver of Saint Butolphs Algate* (1636). *STC* 13369.

HIERON, SAMUEL, *Three sermons* (Cambridge, 1609). *STC* 13427.

HILDERSHAM, ARTHUR, *The doctrine of fasting and praier. In sundry sermons at the fast in 1625* (1633). *STC* 13459.

HILL, ADAM, *The crie of England* (1595). *STC* 13465.

HILL, ROBERT, *Life everlasting* (Cambridge, 1601). *STC* 13479.

HILL, THOMAS, *A contemplation of mysteries: contayning the rare effectes and significations of certayne comets* ([1574?]). *STC* 13484.

HILL, THOMAS, *The doleful daunce and song of death: intituled, dance after my pipe* ([1655–80] edn.; 1st pub. 1568–9). Wing H2014.

HILLIARD, JOHN, *Fire from heaven. Burning the body of one John Hitchell of Holne-hurst . . . with the fearefull burning of the Lowne of Dorchester upon Friday the 6. of August last 1613* (1613). *STC* 13507, 13507.3.

The historians guide: or, Englands remembrancer (1679 edn.). Wing H2094B.

Historical Manuscripts Commission, *Third Report* (1872).

——*Seventh Report. Part I. Report and Appendix* (1879).

——*Tenth Report, Appendix, Part II (Gawdy Family of Norfolk)* (1885).

——*Thirteenth Report, Appendix, Part IV (MSS of Rye and Hereford Corporations)* (1892).

——*Calendar of the Manuscripts of the Most Hon. the Marquis of Salisbury, K.G., Preserved at Hatfield House, Hertfordshire. Parts XI, XIII, XVII* (1906, 1915, 1938).

The historie of the prophet Jonas. The repentance of Ninivie that great citie ([c.1620]). *STC* 14716.

HOBY, MARGARET, *Diary of Lady Margaret Hoby 1599–1605*, ed. Dorothy M. Meads (1930).

HOLINSHED, RAPHAEL, *The first volume of chronicles . . . The laste volume of chronicles of England, Scotlande and Irelande*, 2 vols. (1577); *The first and second volumes of chronicles Newlie augmented and continued by J. Hooker alias Vowell gent and others*, 3 vols. (1587). *STC* 13568, 13569.

HOLLAND, HENRY (Bookseller), *Herωologia Anglica hoc est clarissimorum et doctissimorum aliquot Anglorum qui floruerunt ab anno Cristi*. (1620). *STC* 13582.

[HOLLAND, HENRY] (Bookseller), *Motus Medi-terraneus. Or, a true relation of a fearefull and prodigious earthquake, which lately happened in the ancient citie of Coventrie* (1626). *STC* 13585.5.

HOLLAND, HENRY (Vicar of St Bride's), *A treatise against witchcraft* (Cambridge, 1590). *STC* 13590.

——*Spirituall preservatives against the pestilence* (1593). *STC* 13588.

—— *The Christian exercise of fasting, private and publike* (1596). *STC* 13586.

The holy bible [Authorized version] (1669 octavo edn.). Wing B2278.

HONDORFF, ANDREAS, *Promptuarium exemplorum. Historienn und exempel buch* (Leipzig, 1568).

—— *Theatrum historicum illustrium exemplorum*, trans. Phillip Lonicer (Frankfurt, 1575).

HOOKER, RICHARD, *Of the lawes of ecclesiastical politie* ([1593]). *STC* 13712.

HOOKER, THOMAS, *Thomas Hooker: Writings in England and Holland, 1626–1633*, ed. George H. Williams *et al.*, Harvard Theological Studies 28 (Cambridge, Mass., 1975).

HOOPER, JOHN, *An oversight, and deliberacion upon the holy prophete Jonas* ([1550?]). *STC* 13764.

——*An homelye to be read in the tyme of pestylence, and a most presente remedye for the same* ([Worcester, 1553]). *STC* 13759.

HOPKINS, THOMAS, *Two godlie and profitable sermons earnestly enveying against the sinnes of this land in generall, and in particular, against the sinnes of this citie of London* (1611 edn.). *STC* 13771.

HORATIUS FLACCUS, QUINTUS, *Q. Horatius Flaccus: His Art of Poetry. Englished*, trans. Ben Jonson (1640). *STC* 13798.

HORD, RICHARD, *Black-Fryers* (1625). *STC* 13806.

Of the horrible and wofull destruction of, Sodome and Gomorra ([1570]). *STC* 22890.

The horrible murther of a young boy of three yeres of age, whose sister had her tongue cut out (1606). *STC* 6552.

This horryble monster is cast of a sowe in Eestlande in Pruse ([Germany, 1531]). *STC* 15346.

HOSKINS, JOHN, *Sermons preached at Pauls Crosse and elsewhere* (1615). *STC* 13841.

HOWARD, HENRY, *A defensative against the poyson of supposed prophesies* (1583). *STC* 13858.

HOWELL, JAMES, *Epistolae Ho-Elianae. Familiar letters domestic and forren* (1645). Wing H3071.

HUGHES, LEWIS, *Certaine greevances, well worthy the serious consideration of the right honorable and high court of parliament* (1640). *STC* 13917.5.

HULL, WILLIAM, *Repentance not to be repented of* (1612). *STC* 13937.

H[UME], A[LEXANDER], *Foure discourses of praise unto God* (Edinburgh, 1594). *STC* 13941.5.

HUMPHREY, LAURENCE, *Joannis Juelli Angli, episcopi Sarisburiensis vita et mors* (1573). *STC* 13963.

I., H., *An example for all those that make no conscience of swearing and forswearing* ([*c.*1625]). *STC* 14050a.

I., T., *A world of wonders. A masse of murthers. A covie of cosonages* (1595). *STC* 14068.5.

——*A miracle, of miracles* (1614). *STC* 14068, 14068.3.

INGRAM, R. W. (ed.), *Records of Early English Drama. Coventry* (Manchester, 1981).

ISIDORE, Bishop of Seville, 'The Medical Writings: An English Translation with an Introduction and Commentary', trans. William D. Sharpe, *Transactions of the American Philosophical Soc.*, NS 14 (1964).

JACKSON, THOMAS (President of Corpus Christi, Oxford and Dean of Peterborough), *Diverse sermons, with a short treatise befitting these present times* (Oxford, 1637). *STC* 14307.

JACKSON, THOMAS (Prebendary of Canterbury), *Londons new-yeeres gift. Or the uncouching of the foxe* (1609). *STC* 14303.

——*Judah must into captivitie. Six sermons on Jerem. 7. 16.* (1622). *STC* 14301.

—— *The raging tempest stilled* (1623). *STC* 14305.

JACKSON, WILLIAM, *The celestiall husbandrie: or, the tillage of the soule* (1616). *STC* 14321.

JAMES VI and I, *Daemonologie, in the forme of a dialogue* (1603 edn; 1st pub. 1597). *STC* 14365.

JAMES, THOMAS, *A manuduction, or introduction unto divinitie: containing a confutation of papists by papists* (1625). *STC* 14460.

JEFFERAY, RICHARD, *The sonne of Gods entertainment by the sonnes of men* (1605). *STC* 14481.

J[ESSEY], H[ENRY], *The Lords loud call to England. Being a true relation of some late, various and wonderful judgments, or handy-works of God* (1660). Wing J694.

The Jesuites comedie. Acted at Lyons in France (1607). *STC* 14531.

JEWEL, JOHN, *The Works of John Jewel, Bishop of Salisbury*, ed. John Ayre, 4 vols., Parker Soc. (Cambridge, 1845–50).

JOHN CHRYSOSTOM, St, *De providentia dei, ac fato, orationes sex* (1545). *STC* 14630.

JOHNSON, ROBERT, *Davids teacher, or the true teacher of the right-way to heaven* (1609). *STC* 14694.

JONES, JOHN, *Londons looking backe to Jerusalem, or Gods judgements upon others, are to be observed by us* (1633). *STC* 14722.

JONSON, BEN, *Ben Jonson*, ed. C. H. Herford and Percy Simpson, 11 vols. (Oxford, 1925–52).

—— *Three Comedies*, ed. Michael Jamieson (Harmondsworth, 1966).

JOSEPH BEN GORION (pseud.), *A compendious and most marveilous historie of the latter times of the Jewes common weale*, trans. P. Morwyng (Oxford, 1575 edn.; 1st pub. 1558). *STC* 14798.

JOSEPHUS, FLAVIUS, *The famous and memorable workes*, trans. Thomas Lodge (2nd edn. 1609). *STC* 14810.

JOSSELIN, RALPH, *The Diary of Ralph Josselin 1616–1683*, ed. Alan Macfarlane, Records of Social and Economic History, NS 3 (Oxford, 1976).

Journals of the House of Commons. From November the 8th 1547 . . . to March the 2d 1628 ([1742]).

The judgement of God shewed upon one John Faustus, Doctor in Divinity ([1658–64]). Wing J1177A.

K., F., [lacks title-page, heading A2ʳ] *Of the crinitall starre, which appeareth this October and November. 1580* ([1580]). *STC* 14894.

K., W., *Newes from Hereford. Or, a wonderful and terrible earthquake: with a wonderful thunderclap, that happened on Tuesday being the first of October, 1661* ([1661]). Wing K26A.

The Kentish miracle; or, a strange and miraculous work of Gods providence ([1684]). Wing K327.

The Kentish wonder: being a true relation how a poor distressed widow, in the wild of Kent, was, by the providence of the Almighty, miraculously preserved in her necessity ([1672–80]). Wing K329.

KENYON, J. P. (ed.), *The Stuart Constitution: Documents and Commentary* (Cambridge, 2nd edn. 1986).

KIDMAN, THOMAS, *A new almanack for the yeare of our Lord God, 1634* (Cambridge, 1634). *STC* 469.3.

KING, JOHN, *Lectures upon Jonas, delivered at Yorke in the yeare of our lorde 1594* (Oxford, 1599). *STC* 14976.

—— *A sermon of publicke thanks-giving for the happie recoverie of his maiestie from his late dangerous sicknesse* (1619). *STC* 14983.

KNOX, JOHN, *The Works of John Knox*, ed. David Laing, 6 vols. (Edinburgh, 1846–64).

KNOX, T. F. (ed.), *The First and Second Diaries of the English College, Douay, and an Appendix of Unpublished Documents* (1878).

The Knyvett Letters (1620–1644), ed. Bertram Schofield, Norfolk Record Soc. 20 (1949).

L., J., *A true and perfecte description of a straunge monstar borne in the city of Rome in Italy, in the yeare of our salvation. 1585* (1590). *STC* 15107.

Lachrymae Londinenses. Or, Londons teares and lamentations, for Gods heavie visitation of the plague of pestilence (1626). *STC* 16753.

LAKE, ARTHUR, *Sermons with some religious and divine meditations* (1629). *STC* 15134.

LAMBARDE, WILLIAM, *A perambulation of Kent: conteining the description, hystorie, and customes of that shyre* (1596 edn.). *STC* 15176.

The lamentable burning of the citty of Corke (in the province of Munster in Ireland) by lightning ([1622]). *STC* 5765.

The lamentable fall of Queene Elnor, who for her pride and wickednesse, by Gods judgment, sunke into the ground at Charing crosse, and rose up again at Queene hive ([c. 1600?]). *STC* 7565.4.

A lamentable list, of certaine hidious, frightfull, and prodigious signes ([1638]). *STC* 15706.5.

1607. Lamentable newes out of Monmouthshire in Wales ([1607]). *STC* 18021.

Lamentable newes, shewing the wonderfull deliverance of Maister Edmond Pet sayler (1613). *STC* 19792.

Lamentable n[ews] from the towne of Darnton in the bishopricke of Durham (1585). *STC* 6280.

The lamenting lady, who for the wrongs done by her to a poore woman . . . was by the hand of God most strangely punished ([1620?]). *STC* 15120.

A lanthorne for landlords ([c. 1630]). *STC* 15225.5.

LARKIN, JAMES F. (ed.), *Stuart Royal Proclamations*, ii. *Royal Proclamations of King Charles I 1625–1646* (Oxford, 1983).

——and HUGHES, P. L. (eds.), *Stuart Royal Proclamations*, i. *Royal Proclamations of James I* (Oxford, 1973).

A Larum for London or The Seige of Antwerp. Together with The Spoyle of Antwerpe by George Gascoyne, ed. R. Simpson (1872).

The last terrible tempestious windes and weather (1613). *STC* 25840.

LATIMER, HUGH, *27 sermons preached by the right reverende . . . maister Hugh Latimer* (1562). *STC* 15276.

——*Sermons and Remains of Hugh Latimer, sometime Bishop of Worcester, Martyr, 1555*, ed. George Elwes Corrie, Parker Soc. (Cambridge, 1845).

LAUD, WILLIAM, *The Works of the Most Reverend Father in God, William Laud, D.D.*, ed. W. Scott and J. Bliss, 7 vols. (Oxford, 1847–60).

LAUTERBECK, GEORG, *Regentbuch aus vielen . . . alten und newen historien . . . zusammen gezogen* (Leipzig, 1557).

LAVATER, LEWES [LUDWIG], *Of ghostes and spirites walking by nyght, and of strange noyses, crackes, and sundry forewarnynges*, trans. R. H. (1572). *STC* 15320.

LAWRENCE, JOHN, *A golden trumpet to rowse up a drowsie magistrate* (1624). *STC* 15325.

LEAKE, RICHARD, *Foure sermons, preached and publikely taught . . . immediatly after the great visitation of the pestilence in the foresayd countie [Westmorland]* (1599). *STC* 15342.

LEECH, JEREMY, *The trayne souldier* (1619). *STC* 15364.

LEIGH, WILLIAM, *Great Britaines, great deliverance, from the great danger of popish powder* (1606). *STC* 15425.

[LEIGHTON, ALEXANDER], *A shorte treatise against stage-playes* ([Amsterdam], 1625). *STC* 15431.5.

LESLIE, HENRY, *A warning for Israel* (Dublin, 1625). *STC* 15502.

LEVER, CHRISTOPHER, *The historie of the defendors of the Catholique faith* (1627). *STC* 15537.

LEVER, THOMAS, *A fruitfull sermon made in Poules churche at London in the shroudes* (1550). *STC* 15543.

——*A sermon preached the thyrd Sonday in Lent before the kynges majestie, and his honorable counsell* (1550). *STC* 15547.

LILLY, JOSEPH (ed.), *A Collection of Seventy-Nine Black-Letter Ballads and Broadsides* (1867).

LODGE, THOMAS, and GREENE, ROBERT, *A looking glasse for London and England* (1594). *STC* 16679.

LOE, WILLIAM, *Vox clamantis* (1621). *STC* 16691.

Looke up and see wonders. A miraculous apparition in the ayre, lately seene in Barke-shire at Bawklin Greene neere Hatford. April 9th. 1628 (1628). *STC* 1904.

A looking glasse for corne-hoorders, by the example of John Russell a farmer dwelling at St Peters Chassant in Buckingham shire, whose horses sunke into the ground the 4 of March 1631 ([1631?]). *STC* 21457.

A looking-glasse, for murtherers and blasphemers; wherein the[y see] Gods judgement showne upon a keeper neere Enfield C[hase] ([1626]). *STC* 16802.3.

LOOMIE, ALBERT J. (ed.), *Spain and the Jacobean Catholics*, ii. *1613–1624*, CRS 68 (1978).

LOVELL, THOMAS, *A dialogue between custom and veritie concerning the use and abuse of dauncing and minstrelsie* ([1581]). *STC* 16860.

LUPTON, THOMAS, *A thousand notable things* ([*c*.1590] edn.; 1st pub. [1579]). *STC* 16957.5.

LUTHER, MARTIN, *Luther's Works*, ed. Jaroslav Pelikan and Helmut Lehmann, 56 vols. (St Louis, 1955–75).

LYCOSTHENES, CONRAD, *Prodigiorum ac ostentorum chronicon* (Basel, 1557); trans. into German as *Wunderwerck, oder Gottes unergründtliches vorbilden* (Basel, 1557).

McCANN, J., and CONNOLLY, H. (eds.), *Memorials of Father Augustine Baker and Other Documents Relating to the English Benedictines*, CRS 33 (1933).

MacDONALD, MICHAEL (ed.), *Witchcraft and Hysteria in Elizabethan London: Edward Jorden and the Mary Glover Case* (1991).

MACHYN, HENRY, *The Diary of Henry Machyn, Citizen and Merchant Taylor of London, from A.D. 1550 to A.D. 1563*, ed. John Gough Nichols, CS, 1st ser. 42 (1848).

The manner of the cruell outragious murther of W. Storre mast. of art, at Market Raisin committed by F. Cartwright (Oxford, 1603). *STC* 23295.

MANNINGHAM, JOHN, *The Diary of John Manningham of the Middle Temple, and of Bradbourne, Kent, Barrister-at-law, 1602–1603*, ed. John Bruce. CS, 1st ser. 99 (1868).

MARBURY, FRANCIS, *Notes on the doctrine of repentance. Delivered . . . by way of catechising* (1602). *STC* 17306.

——*A sermon preached at Pauls Crosse the 13. of June, 1602* (1602). *STC* 17307.

MARLOWE, CHRISTOPHER, *The Complete Plays*, ed. J. B. Steane (Harmondsworth, 1969).

MARSHALL, STEPHEN, *Meroz cursed* (1641[1642]). Wing M762.

——*Reformation and desolation: or, a sermon tending to the discovery of the symptomes of a people to whom God will by no meanes be reconciled* (1642). Wing M770.

——*A divine project to save a kingdome* (1644). Wing M752.

MASSINGER, PHILIP, *The Plays and Poems of Philip Massinger*, ed. Philip Edwards and Colin Gibson, 5 vols. (Oxford, 1976).

MATHER, INCREASE, *An essay for the recording of illustrious providences* (Boston, 1684). Wing M1206.

MAUNSELL, ANDREW, *The first part of the catalogue of English printed bookes* (1595). *STC* 17669.

MAXWELL, JAMES, *Admirable and notable prophecies* (1615). *STC* 17698.

MAY, EDWARD, *A most certaine and true relation of a strange monster or serpent found in the left ventricle of the heart of John Pennant, gentleman* (1639). *STC* 17709.

MEDE, JOSEPH, *Clavis apocalyptica* (Cambridge, 1627). *STC* 17766.

——— *The key of the Revelation, searched and demonstrated out of the naturall and proper characters of the visions,* trans. Richard More (1650 edn.). Wing M1601.

MELANCHTHON, PHILIPP, and LUTHER, MARTIN, *Of two woonderful popish monsters,* trans. J. Brooke (1579). *STC* 17797.

MELLYS, JOHN, *The true description of two monsterous children . . . borne in the parish of Swanburne in Buckynghamshyre* ([1566]). *STC* 17803.

MERITON, GEORGE, *A sermon of repentance* (1607). *STC* 17839.

MIDDLETON, THOMAS, *A Game at Chess,* ed. J. W. Harper (1966).

——— and ROWLEY, WILLIAM, *The Changeling,* ed. Patricia Thomson (1964).

MILLES, ROBERT, *Abrahams suite for Sodome* (1612). *STC* 17924.

MILLES, THOMAS, *The catalogue of honor or tresury of true nobility peculiar to Great Britaine* (1610). *STC* 17926.

MILTON, RICHARD, *Londons miserie, the countries crueltie: with Gods mercie* (1625). *STC* 17939.

MILWARDE, JOHN, *Jacobs great day of trouble, and deliverance* (1610). *STC* 17942.

Mirabilis annus secundus, or, the second part of the second years prodigies (1662). Wing M2204.

Mirabilis annus secundus, or the second year of prodigies (1662). Wing M2205.

Miracle upon miracle. Or a true relation of the great floods which happened in Coventry, in Lynne, and other places (1607). *STC* 1658.

Miraculous newes, from the cittie of Holdt . . . where there were plainly beheld three dead bodyes rise out of their graves, trans. T. F. (1616). *STC* 13567.

MIRK, JOHN, *Mirk's Festial: A Collection of Homilies,* ed. Theodor Erbe, EETS, extra ser. 96 (1905).

The Mirror for Magistrates, ed. Lily B. Campbell (Cambridge, 1938).

The miserable estate of the citie of Paris at this present, with a true report of sundrie straunge visions, lately seene in the ayre upon the coast of Britanie (1590). *STC* 19197.

MORE, GEORGE (Sir), *A demonstration of God in his workes* (1597). *STC* 18071.

MORE, GEORGE (Preacher), *A true discourse concerning the certaine possession and dispossession of 7 persons in one familie in Lancashire* ([Middelburg], 1600). *STC* 18070.

MORE, HENRY, *Historia missionis Anglicanae societatis Jesu* (St Omer, 1660).

MORE, THOMAS, *A Dialogue concerning Heresies* (1529). repr. in *The Complete Works of St Thomas More,* ed. Thomas M. C. Lawler *et al.,* vol. vi, pt. 1 (New Haven, 1981).

More strange newes: of wonderfull accidents hapning by the late overflowings of waters, in Summerset-shire, Gloucestershire, Norfolke, and other places of England ([1607]). *STC* 22916.

MORNAY, PHILIPPE DU PLESSIS, *A woorke concerning the trewnesse of the Christian religion* (1587). *STC* 18149.

MORRIS, JOHN (ed.), *The Troubles of our Catholic Forefathers Related by Themselves,* 3 vols. (1872–7).

MOSSE, MILES, *Justifying and saving faith distinguished from the faith of the devils* (Cambridge, 1614). *STC* 18209.

A most certaine report of a monster borne at Oteringham in Holdernesse . . . Also of a most strange and huge fish, which was driven on the sand at Outhorn ([1595]). *STC* 18895.5.

The most cruell and bloody murther committed by an inkeepers wife, called Annis Dell (1606). *STC* 6553.

A most excellent new ballad, of an olde man and his wife, which in their olde age and misery sought to their owne children for succour, by whom they were disdained & scornfully sent away succourlesse, and how the vengeance of God was justly shewed upon them for the same ([c.1600]; [c.1620]). *STC* 1329, 1329.5.

A most horrible & detestable murther committed by a bloudie minded man . . . most strangely revealed by his childe that was under five yeares of age (1595). *STC* 17748.

A most notable and worthy example of an ungratious sonne, who in the pride of his hart denied his owne father: and how God for his offence turned his meate into loathsome toades ([c.1610?], [c.1625], [1638?]). *STC* 10610, 10610.13, 10610.5.

A most rare & true report, of such great tempests, straunge sightes, and wonderfull accidents, which happened by the providence of God, in Hereford shire, at a place called the Hay (1585). *STC* 20889.5.

The most rare, strange and wonderfull example of Almightie God, shewed in the citie of Telonne in Provence, on a cruell papisticall bishop (1592). *STC* 10611.

A most strange and rare example of the just judgement of God executed upon a lewde and wicked conjurer ([1577]). *STC* 19593.

A most straunge and wonderfull herring, taken on the 26. day of November 1597. neere unto Drenton sometime the old and chiefe cittie of the kingdome of Norway (1598). *STC* 13239.

A most straunge and wounderfull accident, happened at Weersburch by Franckford (1600). *STC* 25219.5.

A most true and lamentable report, of a great tempest of haile which fell upon a village in Kent, called Stockbery (1590). *STC* 23276b.

A most true relation of a very dreadfull earth-quake . . . in Munster in Germanie, trans. Charles Demetrius ([1613]). *STC* 18285.

A most wonderful and sad judgement of God upon one Dorothy Mattley late of Ashover in the County of Darby ([1661?]). Wing M2933.

A most wonderfull, and true report, the like never hearde of before, of diverse unknowne foules . . . latelie taken at Crowley in the countie of Lyncolne. 1586 ([1586]). *STC* 6074a.7.

A mournfull dittie on the death of certaine judges and justices of the peace . . . who died immediatly after the assises, holden at Lincolne last past (1590). *STC* 15645.

MUENSTER, SEBASTIAN, *A briefe collection and compendious extract of straunge and memorable thinges, gathered oute of the Cosmographye of Sebastian Muenster* (1572). *STC* 18242.

MUNDAY, ANTHONY, *The mirrour of mutabilitie . . . Describing the fall of divers famous princes* (1579). *STC* 18276.

M[UNDAY], A[NTHONY], *A view of sundry examples. Reporting many straunge murthers, sundry persons perjured, signes and tokens of Gods anger towards us* ([1580]). *STC* 18281.

Murder upon murder, committed by Thomas Sherwood, alias Countrey Tom ([1635]). *STC* 22431.

MURRAY, JOHN TUCKER (ed.), *English Dramatic Companies 1558–1642*, 2 vols. (1910).

A myraculous, and monstrous, but yet, most true, and certayne discourse of a woman . . . in the midst of whose fore-head . . . there groweth out a crooked horne (1588). *STC* 6910.7.

NASHE, THOMAS, *Nashes Lenten stuffe* (1599). *STC* 18370.

—— *The Works of Thomas Nashe Edited from the Original Texts*, ed. Ronald B. McKerrow, 5 vols. (1904–10).

[NAUSEA, FRIDERICUS], *A treatise of blazing starres in generall. As well supernaturall as naturall*, trans. Abraham Fleming (1618 edn.; 1st pub. 1577). *STC* 18413.3.

A new ballad intituled, a bell-man for England, which night and day doth stand, to ring in all mens hearing, Gods vengeance is at hand ([c.1620]). *STC* 1848.5.

A new ballad, intituled, a warning to youth, shewing the lewd life of a marchants sonne of London ([1628–9]). *STC* 1331.3.

A new prophesie: or some strange speeches declared by an old woman living now in Cheshire, in Ranna ([1657]). Wing N723.

Newes and strange newes from St Christophers (1638). *STC* 23778.5.

Newes from France. Or a relation of a marvellous and fearfull accident of a disaster, which happened at Paris . . . by meanes of a terrible fire (1618). *STC* 11281.

1624. Newes from Holland, true, strange, and wonderfull (1624). *STC* 13574.

Newes from Scotland, declaring the damnable life and death of Doctor Fian, a notable sorcerer ([1592?]). *STC* 10841a.

NICHOLS, JOHN GOUGH (ed.), *Narratives of the Days of the Reformation, Chiefly from the Manuscripts of John Foxe the Martyrologist*, CS, OS 77 (1859).

Nieuwe Tijdinghen, no. 136 (Antwerp, 1623).

No plot no powder 1623 ([c.1623]). BM *Satires*, 95.

The Norfolke gentleman, his last will and testament ([c.1635]). *STC* 18644, 18644.3, 18644.5.

NORRIS, RAFE, *A warning to London by the fall of Antwerp* ([1577?]). *STC* 18656.

NORTHBROOKE, JOHN, *Spiritus est vicarius Christi in terra. A treatise wherein dicing, dauncing, vaine playes or enterludes with other idle pastimes . . . are reproved* ([1577]). *STC* 18670.

——*Spiritus est vicarius Christi in terra. The poore mans garden* (1600 edn.). *STC* 18668.

A notable and prodigious historie of a mayden, who for sundry yeeres neither eateth, drinketh, nor sleepeth (1589). *STC* 5678.

NUMAN, PHILIPS, *Miracles lately wrought by the intercession of the glorious Virgin Marie, at Mont-aigu, nere unto Sichen in Brabant*, trans. Robert Chambers (Antwerp, 1606). *STC* 18746.

NYNDGE, EDWARD, *A true and fearefull vexation of one Alexander Nyndge: being most horribly tormented with the devill* (1615 edn.; 1st pub. [1573?]). *STC* 18753.

ODINGSELLS, CHARLES, *Two sermons lately preached at Langar in the Valley of Belvoir* (1620). *STC* 18783.

The order of prayer upon Wednesdayes and Frydayes, to avert and turne Gods wrath from us, threatened by the late terrible earthquake ([1580]). *STC* 16512–13.

Orders thought meete by her majestie, and her privie councell, to be executed throughout the counties of this realme, in such townes, villages, and other places, as are, or may be hereafter infected with the plague, for the stay of further increase of the same ([1578?]). *STC* 9187.9.

ORMEROD, OLIVER, *A picture of a papist* (1606). *STC* 18850.

OUTREMAN, PHILIPPE, D', *The true Christian Catholique or the maner how to live christianly*, trans. John Heigham (St Omer, 1622). *STC* 18902.

P. Henricus Garnetus vende societeyt Jesu Gheanghen ende ghevierendeelt voor het gheloof binnen London op der 3 Maij. 1606 ([Holland], 1606).

P., I., *A mervaylous straunge deformed swyne* ([1570?]). *STC* 19071.

The papists powder treason ([1679?]).

PARÉ, AMBROSE, *The workes of that famous chirurgion Ambrose Parey*, trans. Thomas Johnson (1634). *STC* 19189.

[PARKER, MARTIN], *The two inseparable brothers* ([*c.*1634]). *STC* 19277.

P[ARKER], M[ARTIN], *Lord have mercy upon us. This is the humble petition of England unto Almighty God* ([1636]). *STC* 19251.3.

PARKER, MARTIN, *A true and terrible narration of a horrible earthquake, which happened in the province of Calabria* (1638). *STC* 19273.

PARKHURST, JOHN, *The Letter Book of John Parkhurst Bishop of Norwich Compiled during the Years 1571–1575*, ed. R. A. Houlbrooke, Norfolk Record Soc. 43 ([Norwich], 1974–5).

PARR, ELNATHAN, *The grounds of divinitie, plainely discovering the mysteries of Christian religion* (1614). *STC* 19314.

PARR, RICHARD, *The life of the most reverend father in God, James Usher* (1686). Wing P548.

P[ARROT], H[ENRY], *The mastive or young-whelpe of the olde-dogge. Epigrams and satyrs* (1615). *STC* 19333.

A passing bell towling to call us to mind ([1625?]). *STC* 19460.

PEACHAM, HENRY, *The worth of a penny, or, a caution to keep money* (1669 edn.; 1st pub. 1641). *Wing* P953.

PELLHAM, EDWARD, *Gods power and providence: shewed, in the miraculous preservation and deliverance of eight Englishmen, left by mischance in Green-land anno 1630* (1631). *STC* 19566.

PELLING, JOHN, *A sermon of the providence of God* (1607). *STC* 19567.

PEMBLE, WILLIAM, *The workes of . . . Mr. William Pemble* (1635 edn.). *STC* 19570.

PERKINS, SAMUEL, *A new almanacke and prognostication* (1627). *STC* 495.2.

PERKINS, WILLIAM, *Foure great lyers, striving who shall win the silver whetstone. Also, a resolution to the countri-man, proving it utterly unlawfull to buye or use our yeerly prognostications* ([1585]). *STC* 19721.7.

—— *Two treatises. I. Of the nature and practise of repentance* (Cambridge, 1593). *STC* 19758.

—— *A direction for the government of the tongue according to Gods worde* (Cambridge, 1595 edn.). *STC* 19760.5.

—— *The foundation of Christian religion: gathered into sixe principles* (1595 edn.). *STC* 19711.

—— *A reformed catholike* (Cambridge, 1597). *STC* 19735.8.

—— *The whole treatise of the cases of conscience* (Cambridge, 1608 edn.). *STC* 19670.

—— *The workes of . . . M. W. Perkins*, 3 vols. (Cambridge, 1608–9 edn.). *STC* 19649.

—— *A discourse of the damned art of witchcraft* (Cambridge, 1610 edn.). *STC* 19698.

PERSONS, ROBERT, *An epistle of the persecution of Catholickes in Englande* (Douai [Rouen], [1582]). *STC* 19406.

—— *A treatise of three conversions of England from paganism to Christian religion*, 3 vols. ([St Omer], 1603–4). *STC* 19416.

—— 'The Memoirs of Father Robert Persons', ed. J. H. Pollen, *CRS Miscellanea II*, CRS 2 (1906), 2–218.

—— 'Father Persons' Memoirs', ed. J. H. Pollen, in *CRS Miscellanea IV*, CRS 4 (1907), 1–161.

PESTELL, THOMAS, *Gods visitation: in a sermon preached at Leicester, at an ordinary visitation* (1630). *STC* 19788.

PETLEY, ELIAS, *The royal receipt: or, Hezekiahs physicke* (1623). *STC* 19801.

PHILLIP, JOHN, *The wonderfull worke of God shewed upon a chylde, whose name is William Withers* (1581). *STC* 19877.

PILKINGTON, JAMES, *The Works of James Pilkington, B.D., Lord Bishop of Durham*, ed. James Scholefield, Parker Soc. (Cambridge, 1842).

PITS, JOHN, *A prayer, and also a thankesgiving unto God, for his great mercy in giving and pre-serving our noble Queene Elizabeth to live and reigne over us . . . to be sung the xvii day of November 1577* ([1577]). *STC* 19969.2.

[PLINY] PLINIUS SECUNDUS, CAIUS, *The historie of the world. Commonly called, the naturall historie*, trans. Philemon Holland (1601). *STC* 20029.

A plot with powder 1605 ([*c.*1623]).

A plot without powder ([*c.*1623]).

POLLEN, J. H. (ed.), *Unpublished Documents Relating to the English Martyrs, i. 1584–1603*, CRS 5 (1905).

POND, EDWARD, *Enchiridion: or Pond his Eutheca: 1604. A new almanacke* (1604). *STC* 501.4.

Popish plots and treasons, from the beginning of the reign of Queen Elizabeth ([1676–97]).

The pourtrayture of Eva Fliegen the miraculous mayd that lived at Muers in Cleveland without food ([*c.*1620?]). *STC* 11088.3.

A praier very comfortable and necessary to be used of all Christians . . . that it would please the Lord God to be appeased in his wrath ([*c.*1603]). *STC* 20192.5.

Prayers and thanksgiving to be used . . . for the happy deliverance of his majestie, the queene, prince, and states, of the parliament, from the most traiterous and bloody intended massacre by gun-powder, the fift of November. 1605 (1635). *STC* 16499.

[*Prayers*] *In the time of Gods visitation by sickenesse, or mortality especially, may be used by governours of families* ([1607?]). *STC* 20197.7.

PRESTON, JOHN, *Sermons preached before his Majestie; and upon other speciall occasions* (1630). *STC* 20270.

—— *The saints qualification: a treatise* (1633). *STC* 20262.

PRICE, DANIEL, *Sorrow for the sinnes of the time* (Oxford, 1613). *STC* 20303.

PRICE, GABRIEL, *The laver of the heart; or bath of sanctification* (1616). *STC* 20306.

P[RICE], L[AWRENCE], *Strange and wonderfull news of a woman which lived neer unto the famous city of London, who had her head torn off from her body by the divell* ([*c.*1630]). *STC* 20322.3.

——*A warning for all lewd livers. By the example of a disobedient child, who . . . after died most miserably on a dunghill* ([1633]). *STC* 20324.

——*A wonderfull wonder: being a most straunge and true relation of the resolute life and miserable death of Thomas Miles* ([1635]). *STC* 20325.

——*A monstrous shape. Or a shapelesse monster* ([1639]). *STC* 20317.

——*A wonderful prophecy. Declared by Christian James, a maid of twenty years of age* ([1656]). Wing J414A.

PRICE, SAMPSON, *Londons warning by Laodicea's luke-warmnesse* (1613). *STC* 20333.

—— *Ephesus warning before her woe* (1616). *STC* 20330.

P[RICKET], R[OBERT], *The Jesuits miracles, or new popish wonders* (1607). *STC* 20340.

PRIDEAUX, JOHN, *Eight sermons* (1621). *STC* 20351.

Pride's fall: or a warning for all English women: by the example of a strange monster, born of late in Germany, by a merchant's proud wife in Geneva ([1663–74]). Wing P3447.

PROCTER, WILLIAM, *The watchman warning* (1625). *STC* 20405.

A prophesie of the judgment day. Being lately found in Saint Denis church in France, and wrapped in leade in the forme of an heart ([1620?]). *STC* 20440.

The Protestant tutor. Instructing children to spel and read English, and grounding them in the true Protestant religion and discovering the errors and deceits of the papists (1679). Wing P3843.

The Protestants and Jesuites up in armes in Gulicke-land. Also, a true and wonderfull relation of a Dutch maiden . . . who . . . hath fasted for the space of 14 yeares (1611). *STC* 20449.

PRYNNE, WILLIAM, *Histrio-mastix. The players scourge, or, actors tragaedie* (1633). *STC* 20464.

—— *A quench-coale* ([Amsterdam], 1637). *STC* 20474.

—— *Canterburies doome* (1646). Wing P3917.

—— *A briefe polemicall dissertation concerning the true time of the inchoation and determination of the Lords Day-sabbath* (1655). Wing P3916.

[PRYNNE, WILLIAM], WHITE, MATTHEW (pseud.), *Newes from Ipswich* (Ipswich [Edinburgh], [1636?]). *STC* 20469.

[PRYNNE, WILLIAM], *A new discovery of the prelates tyranny* (1641). Wing P4018.

PULLEIN, THOMAS, *Jeremiahs teares* (1608). *STC* 20493.

R., A., *True and wonderfull. A discourse relating a strange and monstrous serpent (or dragon) lately discovered . . . in Sussex two miles from Horsam, in a woode called S. Leonards forrest* (1614). *STC* 20569.

R., C., *The true discripcion of this marveilous straunge fishe* ([1569]). *STC* 20570.

R., I., *A most straunge, and true discourse, of the wonderfull judgement of God* (1600). *STC* 20575.

R., T., *A confutation of the tenne great plagues, prognosticated by John Doleta from the country of Calabria* ([1587]). *STC* 20589.

RAINOLDS, JOHN, *The prophecie of Obadiah opened an applyed in sundry learned and gracious sermons preached at All-Hallowes and St Maries in Oxford*, ed. William Hinde (1613). *STC* 20619.

[RALEGH, WALTER], *The history of the world* (1614). *STC* 20637.

RAWLIDGE, RICHARD, *A monster late found out and discovered. Or the scourging of tiplers, the ruine of Bacchus, and the bane of tapsters* (Amsterdam, 1628). *STC* 20766.

RAYMOND, JOAD (ed.), *Making the News: An Anthology of the Newsbooks of Revolutionary England 1641–1660* (Moreton-in-Marsh, 1993).

REJAULE, V., *Newes from Spain. A true relation of the lamentable accidents, caused by the inundation and rising of Ebro, Lobsegat, Cinca and Segre, rivers of Spaine* (1618). *STC* 20860.5.

Relacion de un caso en que murieron muchos Catolicos oyendo la palabra de Dios (Valladolid, [1623]).

A relation of the most lamentable burning of the cittie of Corke (1622). *STC* 5766.

REYCE, ROBERT, *Suffolk in the XVIIth Century: The Breviary of Suffolk by Robert Reyce, 1618* (1902).

REYNOLDS, JOHN, *The triumphs of Gods revenge against the crying and execrable sinne of (willfull and premeditated) murther* (1621, 1622, 1623, 1635, 1640). *STC* 20942–6.

R[HODES], J[OHN], *The countrie mans comfort. Or religious recreations, fitte for all well disposed persons* (1637 edn.; 1st pub. 1588). *STC* 20961.

RHODES, MATHEW, *The dismall day, at the Black-Fryers* (1623). *STC* 20961.5.

RICH, BARNABY, *Allarme to England* (1578). *STC* 20978.

—— *The true report of a late practise enterprised by a papist, with a yong maiden in Wales* (1582). *STC* 21004.

RICHARDSON, CHARLES, *The repentance of Peter and Judas* (1612). *STC* 21016.

RIVANDER, ZACHARIUS, *Der ander theil promptuarii exemplorum* (Frankfurt, 1581).

—— *Promptuarium exemplorum: historien und new exempulbuch* (Frankfurt, 1592).

ROBERT OF BRUNNE, *Robert of Brunne's Handlyng Synne, AD 1303*, ed. Frederick J. Furnivall, EETS, OS 119 (1901).

ROBERTS, ALEXANDER, *A treatise of witchcraft* (1616). *STC* 21075.

R[OBERTS], H[UGH], *The day of hearing . . . Hereunto is adjoyned a sermon against fleshly lusts, & against certaine mischievous May-games* (Oxford, 1600). *STC* 21089.

ROBINS, THOMAS, *England's gentle admonition; or, a warning-piece to all sinners* ([1674–9]). Wing R1649.

ROBINSON, RICHARD, *The rewarde of wickednesse* (1574). *STC* 21121.7.

——*A record of auncient histories, intituled in Latin: Gesta Romanorum* (1595). *STC* 21288.

ROBOTHAM, JOHN, *Omen Romae* (1627). *STC* 21129.

ROBROUGH, HENRY, *Balme from Gilead, to cure all diseases, especially the plague* (1626). *STC* 21129.5.

ROGERS, THOMAS, *The general session, conteining an apologie concerning the ende of this world* (1581). *STC* 21233.3.

ROLLINS, HYDER E. (ed.), *Old English Ballads 1553–1625 Chiefly from Manuscripts* (Cambridge, 1920).

——(ed.), *A Pepysian Garland: Black-Letter Broadside Ballads of the Year 1595–1639* (Cambridge, 1922).

——(ed.), *The Pack of Autolycus* (Cambridge, Mass., 1927).

ROUS, JOHN, *The Diary of John Rous, Incumbent of Santon Downham, Suffolk, from 1625 to 1642*, ed. Mary Anne Everett Green, CS, 1st ser. 66 (1856).

ROWE, JOHN, *Tragi-comoedia. Being a brief relation of the strange, and wonderfull hand of God discovered at Witny* (1653). Wing R2067.

ROWLANDSON, JAMES, *Gods blessing in blasting, and his mercy in mildew* (1623). *STC* 21415.

ROWLEY, WILLIAM, DEKKER, THOMAS, FORD, JOHN, *et al.*, *The witch of Edmonton: a known true story* (1658). Wing R2097.

RUDIERD, EDMUND, *The thunderbolt of Gods wrath against hard-hearted and stiffe-necked sinners* (1618). *STC* 21437.

S., F., *Jerusalems fall, Englands warning* (1617). *STC* 21491.7.

S., P., *Fearefull newes of thunder and lightning, with the terrible effects thereof, which Almighty God sent on a place called Olvestone, in the county of Glocester* (1606). *STC* 21511.

S., R., *The Jesuites play at Lyons in France* (1607). *STC* 21513.5, 21514.

S., T., *A song or psalme of thanksgiving, in remembrance of our great deliveraunce from the gun-powder treason* (1625). *STC* 21522.

SALTER, ROBERT, *Wonderfull prophecies from the beginning of the monarchy of this land . . . Together with an essay touching the late prodigious comete* (1626). *STC* 21630.

SALVIANUS, *A second and third blast of retrait from plaies and theaters*, ed. and expanded Anthony Munday (1580). *STC* 21677.

SAMPSON, WILLIAM, *The vow breaker. Or, the faire maide of Clifton* (1636). *STC* 21688.

SAMUEL, WILLIAM, *A warnyng for the cittie of London* ([1550?]). *STC* 21690.8.

SANDER, NICHOLAS, *Nicolai Sanderi . . . De origine ac progressu schismatis anglicani*, reissued with appendix by Pedro Ribadeneira (n.p., 1610).

——*Rise and Growth of the Anglican Schism*, trans. David Lewis (1877).

SANDYS, EDWIN, *The Sermons of Edwin Sandys, D.D., successively bishop of Worcester and London, and Archbishop of York*, ed. John Ayre, Parker Soc. (Cambridge, 1841).

SANFORD, JOHN, *Gods arrowe of the pestilence* (Oxford, 1604). *STC* 21734.

SAWYER, EDMUND (ed.), *Memorials of affairs of state in the reigns of Q. Elizabeth and K. James I. Collected (chiefly) from the original papers of the Right Honourable Sir Ralph Winwood*, 3 vols. (1725).

SAXEY, SAMUEL, *A straunge and wonderfull example of the judgement of Almighty God, shewed upon two adulterous persons in London* ([1583]). *STC* 21805.

SCHLICHTENBERGER, EYRIAK, *A prophesie uttered by the daughter of an honest countrey man, called Adam Krause* (1580). *STC* 21818.

SCOT, REGINALD, *The discoverie of witchcraft* (1584). *STC* 21864.

[SCOTT, THOMAS], *Vox populi. Or newes from Spayne* (1620). *STC* 22098.

——*Exod. 8. 19. Digitus dei. Esay. 59. 1. The Lords hand is not shortned. 2 Tim. 3. 8, 9* ([Holland, 1623]). *STC* 22075.

——*Boanerges. Or the humble supplication of the ministers of Scotland, to the high court of parliament in England* (Edinburgh [London], 1624). *STC* 3171.

S[COTT], T[HOMAS], *The second part of vox populi* (Goricom [London], 1624). *STC* 22103.

SCOTT, THOMAS, *Vox populi. Vox dei. Vox regis. Digitus dei. The Belgick pismire. The tongue-combat. Symmachia. The high-wayes of God and the king. The projector* ([Holland, 1624]). *STC* 22102.

A second and most exact relation of those sad and lamentable accidents, which happened in and about the parish church of Wydecombe (1638). *STC* 25609.

SEDGWICK, JOHN, *Fury fiered: or, crueltie scourged* (1625 edn.). *STC* 22150a.

SELDEN, JOHN, *Table-talk* (1689). Wing S2437.

SENECA, LUCIUS ANNAEUS, *The workes . . . both morrall and naturall*, trans. T. Lodge (1614). *STC* 22213.

SENG, PETER J. (ed.), *Tudor Songs and Ballads from MS Cotton Vespasian A-25* (Cambridge, Mass., 1978).

SETTLE, THOMAS, *A catechisme briefly opening the misterie of our redemption by Christ* (1585). *STC* 22267.

SHAKELTON, FRANCIS, *A blazyng starre or burnyng beacon, seene the 10. of October laste* (1580). *STC* 22272.

SHAKESPEARE, WILLIAM, *The Complete Works of William Shakespeare*, ed. Peter Alexander (1978).

SHELDON, RICHARD, *A survey of the miracles of the church of Rome, proving them to be antichristian* (1616). *STC* 22399.

SIBBES, RICHARD, *The Works of Richard Sibbes*, ed. Alexander B. Grosart, 7 vols. (Edinburgh, 1862–4).

SIDNEY, PHILIP, *A Defence of Poetry*, ed. Jan Van Dorsten (Oxford, 1966).

The Siege of Jerusalem edited from MS. Laud. Misc. 656, ed. E. Kölbing and Mabel Day, EETS, OS 188 (1932).

A signe from heaven: or, a fearefull and terrible noise heard in the ayre at Alborow in the county of Suffolke . . . Wherein was heard the beating of drums, the discharging of muskets, and great ordnance (1642). Wing S3776.

SMITH, HENRY, *The sermons of Master Henry Smith, gathered into one volume* (1611). *STC* 22728.

[SMITH, RICHARD], *An Elizabethan Recusant House Comprising the Life of the Lady Magdalen Viscountess Montague (1538–1608)*, ed. A. C. Southern (1954).

SMITH, RICHARD, *The powder treason* ([c.1615]). *STC* 22824.7.

SMITH, SAMUEL, *An exposition upon the sixt chapter of the prophesie of Hosea* (1616). *STC* 22847.3.

SOME, ROBERT, *A godly sermon preached in Latin at Great S. Maries in Cambridge* (1580). *STC* 22907.

Something written by occasion of that fatall and memorable accident in the Blacke Friers on Sunday, being the 26. of October 1623 (1623). *STC* 3101.

SOUTHCOTE, JOHN, 'The Notebook of John Southcote, D.D., 1628–1636', ed. J. H. Pollen, in *CRS Miscellanea I*, CRS 1 (1905), 97–116.

SPARKE, MICHAEL, *Crumms of comfort* (1627 edn.). *STC* 23015.7.

SPARROW SIMPSON, W. (ed.), *Documents Illustrating the History of S. Paul's Cathedral*, CS, NS 26 (1880).

A spectacle for usurers and succors of poore folkes bloud (1606). *STC* 23030.3.

SPELMAN, HENRY, *De non temerandis ecclesiis* (1613). *STC* 23067, 23067.2, 23067.4.

—— *The history and fate of sacrilege* (1698). Wing S4927.

SPENSER, JOHN, *A learned and gracious sermon preached at Paules Crosse* (1615). *STC* 23096.

SQUIRE, JOHN, *A thankesgiving for the decreasing, and hope of the removing of the plague* (1637). *STC* 23119.

STERRIE, D., *A briefe sonet declaring the lamentation of Beckles, a market town in Suffolke which was . . . pitifully burned with fire* ([1586]). *STC* 23259.

STOCK, RICHARD, *A sermon preached at Paules Crosse, the second of November. 1606* (1609). *STC* 23276.

—— *The doctrine and use of repentance* (1610 edn.). *STC* 23275.

STOCKWOOD, JOHN, *A sermon preached at Paules Crosse on Barthelmew day* (1578). *STC* 23284.

—— *A very fruiteful sermon preched at Paules Crosse the tenth of May last* (1579). *STC* 23285.

—— *A very fruitfull and necessarye sermon of the most lamentable destruction of Jerusalem* (1584). *STC* 23286.

—— *A Bartholomew fairing for parents, to bestow upon their sonnes and daughters, and for one friend to give unto another* (1589). *STC* 23277.

STOW, JOHN, *The chronicles of England, from Brute unto this present yeare of Christ 1580* (1580). *STC* 23333.

—— *The annales of England* (1605); contd. by Edmund Howes (1631). *STC* 23337, 23340.

—— *A survey of London*, expanded by A. M[unday], H. D[yson], *et al.* (1633). *STC* 23345.

A strange and fearefull warning, to all sonnes and executors (1623). *STC* 1409.5.

A strange and miraculous accident happened in the cittie of Purmerent, . . . Of a yong child which was heard to cry in the mothers wombe before it was borne (1599). *STC* 20511.

Strange and true news from Westmoreland ([1642?]). Wing S5836.

Strange fearful & true newes, which hapned at Carlstadt, in the kingdome of Croatia, trans. E. Gresham ([1606]). *STC* 20589.

Strange newes from Antwarpe, trans. I. F. (1612). *STC* 693.

Strange newes of a prodigious monster, borne in the towneship of Adlington in the parish of Standish (1613). *STC* 15428.

Strange newes out of Kent, of a monstrous and misshapen child, borne in Olde Sandwitch (1609). *STC* 14934.

Strange signes seene in the aire, strange monsters behelde on the land, and wonderfull prodigies both by land and sea, over, in, and about the citie of Rosenberge (1594). *STC* 21321.

STRAUSS, WALTER (ed.), *The German Single-Leaf Woodcut 1550–1600*, 4 vols. (New York, 1975).

STUBBES, PHILLIP, *Two wunderfull and rare examples. Of the undeferred and present approching judgment, of the lord our God* ([1581]). *STC* 23399.7.

—— *A christal glasse for Christian women* (1591). *STC* 23381.

STUBBES, PHILLIP, (cont.) *Phillip Stubbes's Anatomy of Abuses in England in Shakspere's Youth. A.D. 1583*, ed. Frederick J. Furnivall, 2 pts. (1877–82).

STURGESS, KEITH (ed.), *Three Elizabethan Domestic Tragedies* (Harmondsworth, 1969).

Sundrye strange and inhumaine murthers, lately committed (1591). *STC* 18286.5.

SUTTON, THOMAS, *Englands first and second summons. Two sermons preached at Paules Crosse* (1616). *STC* 23502.

T., I., *A horrible creuel and bloudy murther, committed at Putney in Surrey* (1614). *STC* 12630.

T., W., *A casting up of accounts of certain errors* (1603). *STC* 23632.

TARLTON, RICHARD, *A very lamentable and woful discours of the fierce fluds, whiche lately flowed in Bedfordshire, in Lincoln-shire, and in many other places* (1570). *STC* 23688.

TAYLOR, JEREMY, *A sermon preached in Saint Maries Church in Oxford. Upon the anniversary of the gunpowder-treason* (Oxford, 1638). *STC* 23724.

TAYLOR, JOHN, *The fearefull summer: or, Londons calamitie, the countries discourtesie, and both their miserie* (1636 edn.). *STC* 23756.

TAYLOR, THOMAS, *Two sermons: the one a heavenly voice . . . The other an everlasting record of the utter ruine of Romish Amalek* (1624). *STC* 23853.

——*Christs victorie over the dragon: or Satans downfall*, ed. William Jemmat (1633). *STC* 23823.

TEELLINCK, WILLEM, *The resting place of the minde. That is, a propounding of the wonderfull providence of God*, trans. T. Gataker (1622). *STC* 23862.

The Terrific Register; Or, Record of Crimes, Judgments, Providences, and Calamities, 2 vols. (1825).

TEXEDA, FERDINANDO, *Miracles unmasked* (1625). *STC* 23921.

A thankfull remembrance of Gods mercie (1625). *STC* 4643.5.

The theatre of Gods judgements. Or the vialls of wrath poured out upon obstinate and resolute sinners, in 18 remarkable examples ([1680]). Wing T844B.

THEODORET, Bishop, *The mirror of divine providence, . . . Taken out of his workes De Providentia*, ed. J. C. (1602). *STC* 23939.

——*The ecclesiastical history of Theodoret bishop of Cyrus*, trans. R. Cadwaller, ed. G. E. ([St Omer], 1612). *STC* 23938.

Three bloudie murders (1613). *STC* 18287a.

Thunder haile, & lightni[ng] from heaven ([1616]). *STC* 24059.5.

Titus and Vespasian or the Destruction of Jerusalem in Rhymed Couplets edited from the London and Oxford MSS, ed. J. A. Herbert, Roxburghe Club (1905).

TOPSELL, EDWARD, *Times lamentation: or an exposition on the prophet Joel* (1599). *STC* 24131.

——*The historie of foure-footed beastes* (1607). *STC* 24123.

——*The historie of serpents* (1608). *STC* 24124.

TORSHELL, SAMUEL, *The saints humiliation* (1633). *STC* 24142.

TRAHERON, BARTHOLOMEW, *An exposition of the .4. chap. of S. Joans Revelation . . . wherein the providence of God is treated* ([Wesel?], 1557). *STC* 24170.

——*A warning to England to repente* ([Wesel?], 1558). *STC* 24174.

A treatise of daunses, wherin it is shewed, that they are as it were accessories and dependants . . . to whoredome (1581). *STC* 24242.5.

The Trevelyan Letters to 1840, ed. Mary Siraut, Somerset Record Soc. 80 (Taunton, 1990).

A true and most dreadfull discourse of a woman possessed with the devill . . . At Dichet in Sommersetshire ([1584]). *STC* 5681.

A true discourse. Declaring the damnable life and death of one Stubbe Peeter, a most wicked sorcerer ([1590]). *STC* 23375.

A true discourse of such straunge and woonderfull accidents, as hapned in the house of M. George Lee of North-Aston, in the countie of Oxford (1592). *STC* 15353.7.

The true discription of two monsterous chyldren borne at Herne in Kent. The .xxvii. daie of Auguste ([1565]). *STC* 6774.

The true lamentable discourse of the burning of Teverton in Devon-shire ([1598]). *STC* 24093.

True newes from [Mecare:] and also out of Worcestershire ([1598]). *STC* 17764.

A true relation of Gods wonderfull mercies, in preserving one alive, which hanged five dayes, who was falsely accused ([c.1613]). *STC* 14668.

A true relation of one Susan Higges, dwelling in Risborow, a towne in Buckinghamshire ([c.1640?]). *STC* 13441.

A true relation of the birth of three monsters in the city of Namen in Flanders (1609). *STC* 18347.5.

A true relation of the French kinge his good successe . . . [with] A most wonderfull and rare example . . . of a certaine mountaine in the Ile of Palme, which burned continually, for five or six weeks together (1592). *STC* 13147.

A true relation of those sad and lamentable accidents, which happened in and about the parish church of Withycombe in the Dartmoores (1638). *STC* 25607.

A true relation of two most strange and fearefull accidents, lately happening, the one at Chagford in Devonshire, by the falling of th[e] Stanary court-house (1618). *STC* 4932.

A true report and exact description of a mighty sea-monster, or whale, cast upon Langar-shore over against Harwich in Essex (1617). *STC* 20892.

1607. A true report of certaine wonderfull overflowings of waters ([1607]). *STC* 22915.

The true report of the burnyng of the steple and churche of Poules in London (1561). *STC* 19930.

A true report of the horrible murther, which was committed in the house of Sir Jerome Bowes, knight (1607). *STC* 3434.

The true reporte of the forme and shape of a monstrous childe, borne at Muche Horkesleye ([1562]). *STC* 12207.

A true reporte of three straunge and wonderful accidents, lately hapened at Pernaw, a cittie in Lifflande (1603). *STC* 19766.

Turner, William, *A compleat history of the most remarkable providences, both of judgment and mercy, which have hapned in this present age* (1697). Wing T3345.

Two horrible and inhumane murders done in Lincolneshire, by two husbands upon their wives (1607). *STC* 4768.

Two most remarkable and true histories . . . The one relating how God most miraculously restored to health Elizabeth Goossens Taets (1620). *STC* 13525.

Two most strange and notable examples, shewed at Lyshborne the 26. day of Januarie now last past (1591). *STC* 15704.

Two most unnaturall and bloodie murthers (1605). *STC* 18288.

Twyne, Thomas, *A view of certain wonderful effects . . . now newly conferred with the presignifications of the comete, or blasing star* (1578). *STC* 23629.

[Twyne, Thomas], *A shorte and pithie discourse, concerning the engendring, tokens, and effects of all earthquakes in generall* (1580). *STC* 24413.

Tynley, Robert, *Two learned sermons* (1609). *STC* 24472.

Udall, John, *The true remedie against famine and warres* (1586). *STC* 24507.

UDNY, ALEXANDER, *The voyce of the cryer* (1628). *STC* 24513.

The ungrateful son; or, an example of God's justice upon the abusefull disobedience of a false-hearted and cruel son to his aged father ([1682–95]). Wing U65.

The unnaturall wife: or, the lamentable murther of one goodman Davis, who was stabbed to death by his wife. ([1628]). *STC* 6366.

URSINUS, ZACHARIAS, *The summe of Christian religion*, trans. H. Parrie (1611 edn.). *STC* 24537.

V., B., *The run-awyaes [sic] answer, to a booke called, A rodde for runne-awayes* (1625). *STC* 24562.

VAUGHAN, WILLIAM, *The spirit of detraction, conjured and convicted in seven circles* (1611). *STC* 24622.

VERMIGLI, PETER Martyr, *The common places of . . . Peter Martyr*, trans. A. Marten ([1583]). *STC* 24669.

VERON, JEAN, *A fruteful treatise of predestination and of the divine providence of God* ([1561]). *STC* 24681.

VERSTEGAN, RICHARD, *Theatrum crudelitatum haedicorum nostri temporis* (Antwerp, 1587).

——— *The Letters and Despatches of Richard Verstegan (c.1550–1640)*, ed. Anthony G. Petti, CRS 52 (1959).

VICARS, JOHN, *Englands hallelu-jah. Or Great Brittaines gratefull retribution, for Gods gratious benediction* (1631). *STC* 24697.

———*Prodigies & apparitions or Englands warning pieces.* ([1642–3]). Wing V323.

———*A looking-glasse for malignants: or, Gods hand against God haters* (1643, 1645). Wing V317, 318.

———*Dagon demolished: or, twenty admirable examples of Gods severe justice and displeasure against the subscribers of the late engagement* (1660). Wing V298.

VITRY, JACQUES DE, *The Exempla or Illustrative Stories from the Sermones Vulgares of Jacques de Vitry*, ed. Thomas Frederick Crane, Folklore Soc. 26 (1890).

VORAGINE, JACOBUS DE, *The Golden Legend or Lives of the Saints as Englished by William Caxton*, 7 vols. (1900).

Vox infantis. Or, the propheticall child. Being a true relation of an infant that was found in a field, neere Lempster, in Herefordshire (1649). Wing V719.

Vox piscis: or, the book-fish. Contayning three treatises which were found in the belly of a cod-fish in Cambridge market, on midsummer eve last (1627). *STC* 11395.

The voyce of the Lord in the temple (1640). *STC* 24870.

Le vray purtraict d'un ver monstrueux qui a esté trouvé dans le coeur d'un cheval qui est mort en la ville de Londres le 17. de Mars. 1586 ([1586]). *STC* 20126.

VRIES, SIMON DE, [et al.?], *t'Arminiaens Testament* ([Holland], 1618).

W., A., *A fruitfull and godly sermon, preached at Paules crosse* ([1592]). *STC* 24899.

W., R., *Martin Mar-sixtus* (1591). *STC* 24913.

WAKEMAN, ROBERT, *Jonahs sermon and Ninevehs repentance* (Oxford, 1603). *STC* 24947.7.

WALKER, RALPH, *A learned and profitable treatise of Gods providence* (1608). *STC* 24963.

[WALLINGTON, NEHEMIAH], *Historical Notices of Events Occurring Chiefly in the Reign of Charles I by Nehemiah Wallington of St. Leonard's, Eastcheap, London*, ed. R. Webb, 2 vols. (1869).

WARD, SAMUEL, *Balme from Gilead to recover conscience*, ed. Thomas Gataker (1617). *STC* 25035.

———*Deo trin-uniBritanniae bis ultori In memoriam classis invincibilis subversae submersae /*

Proditionis nesandae detectae disiectae. To God, In memorye of his double deliveraunce from the invincible navie and the unmatcheable powder treason (Amsterdam, 1621). *STC* 25043.

—— *The happinesse of practice* (1621). *STC* 25044.

—— *The life of faith* (1621 edn.). *STC* 25049a.

—— *Woe to drunkards* (1622). *STC* 25055.

WARD, WILLIAM, *Gods arrowes, or, two sermons concerning the visitation of God by the pestilence* (1607). *STC* 25057.

—— *A sinners inditement* (1615 edn.). *STC* 25062.

A warning for maidens; [or, Young Bateman] ([1650?]). Wing W921.

A warning-peice for ingroossers of corne; being a true relation how the divell met with one goodman Inglebred of Bowton ([1643]). Wing W926.

WATSON, WILLIAM, *A decacordon of ten quodlibeticall questions concerning religion and state* (1602). *STC* 25123.

WEBBE, GEORGE, *Gods controversie with England. Or a description of the fearefull and lamentable estate which this land at this present is in* (1609). *STC* 25162.

WEBSTER, JOHN, *The Selected Plays of John Webster: The White Devil, The Duchess of Malfi, The Devil's Law Case*, ed. Jonathan Dollimore and Alan Sinfield (Cambridge, 1983).

WESTON, EDWARD, *A triple cure of a triple malady. That is, of vanity in apparell. Excesse in drinking. Impiety in swearing* ([St Omer, 1616]). *STC* 25290.7.

WESTON, WILLIAM, *William Weston: The Autobiography of an Elizabethan*, ed. and trans. Philip Caraman (1955).

WHALLEY, JOHN, *Gods plentie, feeding true pietie* (1616). *STC* 25294.

WHATELY, WILLIAM, *A caveat for the covetous* (1609). *STC* 25300.

—— *Charitable teares: or a sermon shewing how needfull a thing it is for every godly man to lament the common sinnes of our countrie* (1623). *STC* 25303.

—— *Sinne no more* (1628). *STC* 25322.

W[HITBIE], O[BADIAH], *Londons returne, after the decrease of the sicknes* (1637). *STC* 25371.

WHITE, FRANCIS, *Londons warning, by Jerusalem* (1619). *STC* 25386.

W[HITE], T[HOMAS], *A sermon preached at Pawles Crosse on Sunday the ninth of December. 1576* (1578). *STC* 25405.

WHITE, THOMAS, *A sermon preached at Pawles Crosse on Sunday the thirde of November 1577. in the time of the plague* (1578). *STC* 25406.

—— *A sermon preached at Paules Crosse the 17. of November an. 1589* (1589). *STC* 25407.

WHITFORD, RICHARD, *A werke for housholders* (1533 edn.). *STC* 25423.

WIGMORE, MICHAEL, *The way of flesh* (1619). *STC* 25618.

WILCOX, THOMAS, *A short, yet a true and faithfull narration of the fearefull fire that fell in the towne of Wooburne* (1595). *STC* 25629.

WILKINS, JOHN, *Ecclesiastes, or, a discourse concerning the gift of preaching as it fals under the rules of art* (1647 edn.). Wing W2189.

W[ILKINSON], R[OBERT], *Lots wife* (1607). *STC* 25656.

WILLET, ANDREW, *Hexapla in Exodum* (1608). *STC* 25686.

WILLIAMS, GRIFFITH, *The best religion* (1636). *STC* 25718.

WILLIS, EDMOND, *An abbreviation of writing by character* (1618). *STC* 25741.

WILLISON, JOHN, *The Practical Works of John Willison* (Glasgow, [1844]).

WILSON, JOHN, *A song or story, for the lasting remembrance of divers famous works, which God hath done in our time* (1626). *STC* 22922.

WILSON, THOMAS, *The arte of rhetorique, for the use of all soche as are studious of eloquence* (1563 edn.). *STC* 25802.

WILSON, THOMAS, *Christs farewell to Jerusalem, and last prophesie* (1614). *STC* 25790.

WIMBLEDON, RICHARD [THOMAS], *A sermon no lesse frutefull then famous. Made in the yeare of our Lord God. M.C. lxxxviii and founde out hyd in a wall* (1573 edn.). *STC* 25826.

—— *Wimbledon's Sermon: Redde Rationem Villicationis Tue: A Middle English Sermon of the Fourteenth Century*, ed. Ione Kemp Knight, Duquesne Studies, Philological Ser. 9 (Pittsburgh, 1967).

The windie yeare (1613). *STC* 26092.

The Winthrop Papers, ed. W. C. Ford *et al.*, 6 vols., the Massachusetts Historical Soc. (Boston, 1929–92).

WITHER, GEORGE, *The schollers purgatory, discovered in the stationers common-wealth* ([1624]). *STC* 25919.

—— *Britain's remembrancer* (1628). *STC* 25899.

The woefull and lamentable wast and spoile done by a suddaine fire in S. Edmonds-bury in Suffolke (1608). *STC* 4181.

Wofull newes from the west-parts of England. Being the lamentable burning of the towne of Teverton (1612). *STC* 10025.

A wonder beyond mans expectation, in the preservation of eight men in Greenland (1632). *STC* 12326.

A wonder woorth the reading, or a true and faithfull relation of a woman . . . who . . . was delivered of a prodigious and monstrous child (1617). *STC* 14935.

The wonderfull battell of starelings: fought at the citie of Corke in Ireland (1622). *STC* 5767.

The wonderfull example of God shewed upon Jasper Coningham, a gentleman borne in Scotland ([c.1600]). *STC* 5631.3.

The wonderfull works of God. Declared by a strange prophecie of a maid, that lately lived neere Worsop in Nottingham-shire (1641). Wing W3377.

The wonders of this windie winter (1613). *STC* 25949.

WOODHOUSE, JOHN, *An almanacke or prognostication* (1630). *STC* 531.21.

WOODHOUSE, WILLIAM, *The .xv. fearfull tokens preceding I say, the generall judgement called domesday* ([1566]). *STC* 25968.

WOODWALL, WILLIAM, *A sermon upon the xii. xiii. and xiiii. verses of the xiiii chapter of Ezechiel* (1609). *STC* 25970.

The worlds wonder: giving an account of two old men, lately known and seen in the city of Tholouze, in France, who declare themselves to be above a thousand years old a peice, and preach repentance to the world ([1675–80]). Wing W3593.

WORTHINGTON, THOMAS, *A relation of sixtene martyrs: glorified in England in twelve monethes* (Douai, 1601). STC 26000.9.

WRIGHT, ABRAHAM, *Five sermons in five several styles; or waies of preaching* (1656). Wing W3685.

WRIGHT, THOMAS, *The glory of God's revenge against the bloody and detestable sins of murther and adultery, express'd in thirty modern tragical histories* (1685, 1686, 1688, 1691). Wing W3708, 3709, 3710, 3710A.

WULFSTAN, Archbishop of York, *Sermo Lupi ad Anglos*, ed. Dorothy Whitelock (1952).

[WYATT, ADAM], *The Lost Chronicle of Barnstaple 1586–1611*, ed. Todd Gray (Exeter, 1998).

YARINGTON, ROBERT, *Two lamentable tragedies. The one, of the murther of Maister Beech a chaundler in Thames-streete, and his boye . . . The other of a young childe murthered in a wood by two ruffins, with the consent of his unckle* (1601). *STC* 26076.

YEPEZ, Bishop of Taraçona, *Historia particular de la persecucion de Inglaterra* (Madrid, 1599).

YONGE, WALTER, *The Diary of Walter Yonge, Esq. . . . from 1604 to 1628*, ed. George Roberts, CS, 1st ser. 41 (1848).

Y[ONGER], W[ILLIAM], *A sermon preached at Great Yarmouth* (1600). *STC* 26097.

Youths warning-peice. In a true relation of the woefull death of William Rogers of Cranbroke in Kent an Apothecary, who refusing all good counsell, and following lewd company, dyed miserably (1636). *STC* 21251.

The Zurich Letters A.D. 1558–1579, ed. Hastings Robinson, Parker Soc. (Cambridge, 1842).

ZWINGLI, ULRICH, *Zwingli on Providence and Other Essays*, ed. W. J. Hinke (Durham, NC, 1983).

INDEX